WHITEHALL DIARY
Volume I

THOMAS JONES, 1923

Thomas Jones

Whitehall Diary

Edited by Keith Middlemas

Volume I

1916-1925

LONDON
Oxford University Press
NEW YORK   TORONTO
1969

*Oxford University Press, Ely House, London W.*1

GLASGOW NEW YORK TORONTO MELBOURNE WELLINGTON
CAPE TOWN SALISBURY IBADAN NAIROBI LUSAKA ADDIS ABABA
BOMBAY CALCUTTA MADRAS KARACHI LAHORE DACCA
KUALA LUMPUR SINGAPORE HONG KONG

© Oxford University Press, 1969

Printed in Great Britain
by Ebenezer Baylis and Son, Ltd.
The Trinity Press, Worcester, and London

Contents

Contents

Illustrations

Acknowledgements

When Mrs. Eirene White M.P. and Mr. Tristan Jones asked me to edit the political diaries of their father, Dr. Thomas Jones, I was greatly honoured. The experience of working on this unique historical document has been one which any historian would welcome with delight and I owe them a debt which the published version can only partly express. But I should like to thank Mrs. White especially for her help during the preparation of these volumes for publication. I also acknowledge my gratitude to Mrs. Margaret Chester, of the Oxford University Press, for her patient and substantial help in the editorial work, and to Mr. John Speirs, of Sussex University, for his assistance with the biographical footnotes.

The following have kindly given permission to reproduce copyright material: Mr. David Astor (letters from Lord Astor and J. L. Garvin); Lady Spencer-Churchill (Winston Churchill); Sir Ivison Macadam (Lionel Curtis); Lord Davies of Llandinam (David Davies); Lord Esher (Lord Esher); Mr. Eric Hughes (Sir Thomas Hughes); Lord Coleraine (Bonar Law); Lord Lothian (Philip Kerr); Miss Tallents (Violet Markham); Miss H. H. Shotwell (Professor J. T. Shotwell); Mrs. Turnbull (Pembroke Wicks); the Librarian of the London School of Economics (Sidney and Beatrice Webb); and, in particular, Lord Hankey, many of whose father's letters to T.J. are quoted.

Enquiries have failed to trace the heirs of Sir Alfred Zimmern, William Tweeddale, Ralph Wright, Sir Lancelot Storr, and Sir Robert Horne, and I apologize for the inadvertent infringement of copyright.

Introduction

When Sir Maurice Powicke learned that I was to join the War Cabinet Secretariat on its formation in December 1916, and we met shortly afterwards at All Souls, he urged me to help the historians of the future by keeping a diary. I would, he stressed, have exceptional opportunities of watching at close quarters great persons taking counsel together, great policies in the making, and I would be able to observe the little things which are always mixed with the great.[1]

There is no break in Thomas Jones's original diary in 1930: the small volumes, privately printed in Switzerland, run from 1899 to 1937 and his introduction to the volume published as *Diary with Letters, 1931–1950*, fifteen years ago, is close enough to what he would have written for the volumes for 1916–30, if he had been able to publish them in his own lifetime. Indeed, the evidence suggests that this introduction, with its incisive portraits of the Prime Ministers he served while at the Cabinet Office—Lloyd George, Bonar Law, Stanley Baldwin, and Ramsay MacDonald[2]—and his discourses on the functions of private secretaries, the life at No. 10 Downing Street and at the Secretariat at No. 2 Whitehall Gardens, was intended to cover the earlier, more confidential sections which, as a former civil servant, he could not then reveal. In 1953 he said, 'the portion of the Diary dealing with 1916–30 I have put into cold storage for my lifetime'. A version was prepared, similar in design to the *Diary with Letters*, but because he would have had to leave out too much, he did not pursue it. Circumstances have changed; the latest events described are now nearly forty years old, and with the revision of the fifty-year rule there is now no justification for withholding publication.

Thomas Jones, who up to 1917 was Secretary of the Welsh National Health Insurance Commission, was influential in many sectors of academic life in Wales and had considered standing as a parliamentary candidate for a Glamorgan constituency at the urging of his friend David Davies, a wealthy coal-owner and Parliamentary Private Secretary to Lloyd George. Thomas Jones was one of the creative brains brought in to help Lloyd George in his bid for supreme power in December 1916, and when Lloyd George became Prime Minister after Asquith's resignation Jones agreed to stay on in London to serve the newly created War Cabinet Secretariat as Assistant Secretary. Colonel Sir Maurice Hankey, the Secretary of the Committee of Imperial Defence and now also head of the Cabinet Secretariat, was to be his mentor for the rest of his official life. As for the Prime Minister, 'Our common Welsh background and our mutual use of the language made intimate relations with Lloyd George easy, and I was welcomed at the famous breakfasts and used on confidential errands to and from his colleagues.'[3] Over the next fourteen years, under four Prime Ministers, his position and duties changed more

---

[1] *Diary with Letters* (Oxford University Press, 1954), p. xiii.

[2] For biographical notes on these and other main characters in the diaries, see pp. 333–5.

[3] *Diary with Letters*, p. xxix.

widely than those of any of the private secretaries whose virtues he catalogued in the introduction to *Diary with Letters*. Only for one year, under the first Labour Government of Ramsay MacDonald in 1924, was he away from the centre of power. He was misjudged on that occasion as being too heavily committed to the former leaders, Bonar Law and Baldwin.

In 1953 he described his multifarious duties:

My position was first as Assistant Secretary, one of ten, and then as Deputy Secre-to the Cabinet, with an office, not in 10 Downing Street but at 2 Whitehall Gardens, earlier the residence of Peel and Disraeli. I was liaison officer with the Departments which dealt with industrial questions and secretary to many Cabinet Committees. There were many opportunities, before and after meetings, for brief and hurried conversations with Ministers and one learned to make good use of these occasions to judge imponderables and garner impressions of value to the Prime Minister, to whom, from the beginning, I had the privilege of direct access whenever I sought it.[1]

He gave advice freely:

I had no credal difficulty in serving each Minister in turn; we were all infected with Liberalism. I had all the influence I could wield; the only limit was my own inadequacy. By tradition I was a Welsh radical nonconformist, by temperament I was a civil servant, law-abiding, a believer in ordered progress. I believed a little in each of the three Parties, more in the Left than in the Right—'a sort of Burke with a leaven of Shelley'.[2]

Baldwin teased him with being a Bolshevik, MacDonald at first mistrusted him as a Conservative. He did in fact belong all his life to the Labour Party and perhaps Churchill came nearest to describing his function: 'He is the liberal conscience of the party.'

Why was I welcomed? I can only guess that I possessed what Whitehead calls, in the language of philosophy, 'an unspecialized aptitude for eliciting generalizations from particulars and for seeing the divergent illustration of generalities in diverse circumstances'.[3] I had lived too long among the miners and steelworkers of South Wales to fail to remind my masters that politics are concerned with the lives of ordinary folk. I seem to have helped to relieve tension in the ministerial mind, was sought for as a counsellor and prompter in the wings, and much consulted in the preparation of speeches. Sometimes this last duty meant no more than interrupting Churchill as he paced up and down the Treasury Board Room dictating a speech to a typist during, say, a coal strike and bringing a pictorial phrase into closer accord with the facts. Or it might mean writing out for Baldwin a speech that was read out a few days later to a political or an academic audience.[4]

What he wrote of private secretaries was above all true of himself: he could be a listener for Lloyd George, a skilled intermediary with the Irish leaders, a devil's advocate for Baldwin; and MacDonald used him in his second Government as an organizer to bring in the academics and economists like Keynes, Hobson, Clay, Henderson, and Layton, to solve the problem of unemployment. The complexity of the relationship with his changing masters is shown in the pages that follow.

[1] Ibid., p. xxiv.
[2] Ibid., p. xxiii.
[3] A. N. Whitehead, *Adventures of Ideas*, p. 124.
[4] *Diary with Letters*, p. xxv–xxvi.

All the time, except when too tired or too pressed for time, he kept a diary and reinforced it with letters, notes, minutes, and memoranda. In the 1930s, after he had retired from the civil service, the diary developed, from hasty jottings with occasional dissertations written up in leisure hours (such as the verdict on the General Strike), and assumed a more coherent form. Then, hearing that T. E. Lawrence had lost the manuscript copy of *The Seven Pillars of Wisdom*, he decided to put his own diaries into more permanent form and sent the completed version in 1937 to his friend Dr. Ernst Zellweger, a Swiss who had been at the Berlitz School of Languages in Glasgow when Jones was an undergraduate. Zellweger, headmaster of the Talhof School at St. Gallen, was director of a printing house at Flawil, where he had the diaries set up and printed in twenty-two small unbound volumes. Twelve copies were made; one was left for security in Switzerland during the war; some others and the original were destroyed when the Pilgrim Trust offices in London were bombed. Probably seven sets survive.

Thomas Jones seems not to have edited the material in detail before sending it to Zellweger, except to put his manuscript jottings into order, and the draft was clearly never proof-read, for it survives, full of misprints, with German words sometimes put for English. The volumes before 1930 are quite different from those after, when the diary and letters from friends form almost the whole text. Half of the early part is taken up with what may be called government documents—records of Cabinet and Cabinet Committee discussions, memoranda, notes of meetings, correspondence with Hankey and other members of the Secretariat. Less than half is diary and that is more in the nature of a running commentary on events with which he was concerned, than a personal account.

Throughout he fulfils the semi-objective role of a Burnet or a Greville. At times he includes gossip, but there is very little of the witty malice and triviality of 'Chips' Channon or the introspection of Harold Nicolson. He himself wrote: 'A diary by hypothesis forbids complete self-effacement but I hope I have also steered reasonably clear of self-glorification, the vice of this sort of book.'[1] But there was also a more compelling motive for writing. 'I found another justification for keeping a record. I was sometimes involved in confidential exchanges with opposed parties during labour and other disputes, or in secret conversations with Ministers. I then felt the need of written proof that I had faithfully interpreted the instructions of my principals.'[2] The section on the Campbell Case in October 1924, when he was nearly made the scapegoat for MacDonald's errors of judgement, reveals how necessary such a record was.

It was, he records, a relief to discover that his chief, Sir Maurice Hankey, also kept a diary 'in a stoutly bound locked book, the first I have ever seen'. Neither of them afterwards made any secret of the fact that they kept notes: in the infancy of the Cabinet Secretariat there were no precedents to govern the conduct of the Secretaries, as distinct from other civil servants. To a generation accustomed to the frequent exercise of the Official Secrets Act,

[1] *Diary with Letters*, p. xv.
[2] Ibid., p. xiii.

this may seem surprising, but the rules and the practice of today are a creation of the years after 1930. Hankey himself wrote to Jones in 1945:

> Of course there was no secret about it, and on many occasions the information I was able to give promptly from it [his diary] was of decisive importance. Not only that but an immense number of public servants from Prime Ministers to bottle-washers have not only kept diaries but they were used afterwards to describe the same sort of incidents that I described. Examples which come to memory at once are Asquith, Haig, Henry Wilson, John French and Ian Hamilton.
>
> All the Prime Ministers I ever served knew of my diary and encouraged it. Bonar Law, for instance, several times gave me reminiscences which he thought would be useful for my Memoirs. Asquith returned my manuscript letters from the Dardanelles and other papers for the same reason. . . .

Tom Jones's own notes for the Cabinet minutes often provided the basic material for his diary and he too referred to them, for example, to elucidate disputed conclusions of the Cabinet. But the fact that the names which Hankey cited are those of politicians or soldiers, all active before 1918, only emphasizes the unique position of Hankey and Jones. With changing Prime Ministers and the increasing institutionalization of the Secretariat, customs altered. Bonar Law disliked the free and easy ways of Lloyd George, abolished the 'Garden Suburb', reduced the staff and activities of the Secretariat, and changed the system of very full minuting of discussion in Cabinet to one of recording bare conclusions. Already, by the end of the 1920s, some of the Cabinet officials regarded diary-keeping as wrong, and it is inconceivable now that a member of the Secretariat should keep a record of this kind. Hankey's full diary has yet to be published and should prove as fascinating a historic document as that of Thomas Jones; but their successors were not encouraged to follow their practice and it is certain that no civil servant in recent times has kept personal records of confidential ministerial discussions.

Some of the entries in these years, especially the verbatim records of discussions, are so detailed that before considering their historical importance it may be well to question their validity. Were such long conversations recorded at the time, or immediately afterwards, or reconstructed at leisure? Jones himself apparently gave no answer; but their status can be established in other ways. He was, after all, sitting in the Cabinet room taking notes from which to write the minutes for all the discussions which he recorded. He did not have shorthand, but he used a form of speed-writing and also a system of key-words—just as he remembered his hat-peg at the Athenaeum by Newman's Tract XC. Then he had a phenomenal memory; and in some kinds of discussion, such as those with the Irish leaders, he could legitimately and obviously take notes. As he recorded of his frequent talks with Baldwin, 'Sometimes I made notes of his conversation openly on a pad as he talked.' But probably the most convincing answer lies in the internal evidence and the characteristic flavour of personalities which emerges. Time and again the character of the speaker, a Lloyd George, a Churchill, or a J. H. Thomas, comes through inimitably, in his own words. No artist, no playwright could create the atmosphere of the Cabinet, the diversity of individuals, the words of Churchill in the debates on Ireland, of Birkenhead during the General Strike, of Baldwin on Cabinet-making, of Lloyd George, gossiping about his colleagues, or of Bonar Law on his manner of preparing speeches. Time and again, in argument or in subtle negotiation, Jones's reporting reveals the man, so keenly that its validity cannot be impugned.

Any documents at Cabinet level are important to the historian. Thomas Jones quoted H. A. L. Fisher on the value of listening to the Cabinet at work: 'To listen to Cabinet debates, to watch policy in the making, to be introduced to the vast miscellany of important business which comes before the supreme council of an Empire, and to enjoy the treatment of it by the best political minds in the country is an experience which ripens the judgement as the autumn sun ripens the corn.'[1] As that experience was to an administrator, so is Cabinet knowledge to the historian. But documents such as this diary are valuable at any period because they also give the obverse of the official record: they show the views of those worsted or out-voted in the argument, the backchat of the irresponsibles or the malcontents, and the wit or sense of fun which are not to be found in minutes. It is impossible and probably undesirable to try to follow Ranke's dictum and write history as it actually was, but certainly, unless Hankey's diaries prove to be of similar quality, there will be no other source for the period which will convey in so convincing a manner how things really were and how the members of the Cabinet actually behaved. At a time when political honours had become a matter of scandal, it is pleasant to find the nation's leaders giving their real opinion of the value of honours, in the interval of waiting for a Cabinet messenger, or enlivening diplomatic history by speaking frankly about the statesmen of foreign powers. 'Why', asks Churchill, of the future of a Treaty port in China, 'should we melt down the moral capital collected by our forebears to please a lot of pacifists?' To which Curzon adds, 'in the interests of a lot of decrepit mandarins'.[2]

The opening of Government archives, welcome as it is, reveals only what Government wishes to reveal. Even the full contemporary official record may be misleading in the interests of the State. A neat formula in the minutes may hide either a chaotic debate finally guillotined by an autocratic Prime Minister, or a high-minded argument never brought to decision by a vacillating chairman. And the scope of the official record is itself limited. The Cabinet minutes do not mention discussions on party political questions, so that an important debate about the reasons for, and the date of, a general election may not be minuted at all.

To its immense advantage, Thomas Jones's diary is unselective. There are degrees of secrecy: the Secret Service is held to be secret probably forever; secrets of the armed forces, defence, and some aspects of the Home Office are more confidential, for example, than the records of the Board of Education or the Ministry of Health. Some of the Government's activities in preparing for strikes in the 1920s have never been officially acknowledged. To invoke security or the national interest is to press on tender places and to involve the

---

[1] H. A. L. Fisher, *An Unfinished Autobiography*, p. 138.
[2] See below, 23 November 1921.

historian in repercussions with which he is not equipped to deal. Many categories of records are held back even when the year they fall in is ostensibly open to scrutiny. But in the diaries the picture is complete. The activities of the Supply and Transport Committee dovetail, as they should, with Ministry of Labour policy on the General Strike; and the assessments of the use of troops for pacifying Ireland or meeting the Triple Alliance are made, as they were, with responsibilities in occupied Germany and Silesia in mind. The activity of the Cabinet is revealed in its proper proportion. The minutes may mention two conclusions but the diary may show that the debate on India took two hours and that on trading with Russia ten minutes. The lengthy sections on Ireland show, if nothing else, how great was the sheer volume of Cabinet time consumed before 1923 by Irish affairs.

The diary presents also a more direct check on official records. Even after the formation of the Secretariat in 1916, it was not always easy to decipher the conclusions to which Ministers had come. An incident on 2 June 1922 (see Vol. III: Ireland) shows how, certainly in the early days, mistakes could be made: the minuting of a decision of great importance (whether or not to use military force à outrance in Ireland if the cease-fire were not signed) was rectified and toned down only by reference to Jones's own account. The contrast between the restrained tone of some Cabinet minuting and the actual debate can be seen in the account of 9 May 1918.

The study of Cabinet government itself is built up of recorded observations of how different Cabinets behaved. But of all levels of the Government machine, this is the most flexible, the most tied to the personality of the Prime Minister, the least bound by precedent. Thomas Jones was working while the forms of recording decisions were being evolved; equally important was the work in which he and Hankey were concerned, of assembling precedents for guidance not only of the Secretariat, but of future Governments. This process of evolution can be seen throughout the diary, for example, in Hankey's proposals for preparing a Peace Book to guide departments as the War Book had done before 1918. The circumstances in which Bonar Law took over in 1922 illustrate how little the Secretariat had been formalized by then, how much still each new Cabinet was created de novo, how essentially amateurish its procedures were.

Just as they constitute a detailed check on day-to-day decisions, so the diaries correct the longer run of history. Opinions change from year to year. What politician can truly say: 'In 1921 my attitude to this was so, but in 1922 it was so, and again different in 1923?' Consistency may be a virtue on the hustings but on the issues of the day it is of little consequence in that part of a statesman's career which lies between the back benches and the time he comes to write his memoirs. Yet here the diversity of opinion is revealed; the diary gives Churchill's views on Russia in 1919, Lloyd George's on Greece and Turkey in 1921, Baldwin's on the trade unions the day the General Strike ended, Churchill's again when he was negotiating with the miners in the autumn of 1926, MacDonald's when directing economic recovery in 1929; and these are not commonly accepted portraits. It is not that memoirs are falsified; but in the press and continual torment of the business of central government, unless a thing is noted down at once it is partly forgotten; and memory is a great leveller of the many irregularities of the truth.

If the diary was no more than this, it might be a document of more interest to specialist historians than to the wider public. On many controversies, however, it gives a fresh vision and illuminates obscure passages like the plots to eject Asquith in 1916, the dismissal of Arthur Henderson in 1917, the discussion on the German peace overtures of 1918, the activities of the Supply and Transport Committee, the whole settlement of Ireland and the Irish Treaty, Black Friday, 1921, Lloyd George's attempt to buy *The Times*, the Campbell Case, the formation of the Committee of Civil Research and the Economic Advisory Committee, the affair of the Irish Boundary Commission, the lead-up to the General Strike and the Strike itself, the anti-trade union legislation of 1927, the plans for economic reorganization in 1928/9, and the fate of the Mosley Memorandum.

Whatever colours are revealed in detail are heightened by the cumulative effect of the diary. Here, in essence, is the process of government seen by a keen observer close to the centre of power for over fourteen years. The vision is, of course, political. Although the sense of awe at working with great men vanished quickly, Thomas Jones's history is concerned with individual action, not the vast impersonal forces of ideology and economics. Yet the angle of the camera is set unusually wide. The process of decision-making, the efficiency of Cabinets, the knowledge set before them, the exerting of influence, the skill and experience of Ministers, the relative importance of outside pressures, even the effect of the Prime Minister's health, are taken into account. The diary shows the interaction of politicians and Whitehall, the respective influence of dedicated officials like Sir Robert Morant, Hubert Henderson, or Thomas Jones himself. They help, above all, to piece together the unwritten and largely unwritable history of the long-term influence of the Civil Service, of men like Sir Maurice Hankey and Sir Warren Fisher, in the formation of policy.

Finally, the diary reveals the period in something like its true complexity. Except for research students, history is served up in patterns which may be conventional or paradoxical, but are always at second or third hand. It is important to know the rejected arguments, the turnings not taken. It is, for example, often asserted that during the years of greatest trouble over the coal industry in 1925 and 1926, Churchill and Birkenhead were the most right-wing, enragés members of the Cabinet. Yet no one who reads the sane private advice of the latter or the records of Churchill's sensible handling of the Coal Strike in 1926 could sustain such a superficial verdict. Both men were more complex than general history has time for. Again, in 1929–30, in the far-sighted debates of the Economic Advisory Council, the diary shows the best brains of the generation struggling with intractable problems, short, not of ideas, but of the means to translate them into action. The common view, that the second Labour Government simply failed to deal with unemployment, must be modified because their Ministers are shown to have been neither stupid nor deaf; only, like the generals of both sides in the First World War, out of their depth.

The chief difficulty presented by the publication of the diary is its immense length. Thomas Jones left out virtually nothing of importance when putting together the diary material from his vast collection of papers. Of 240 bound volumes in the National Library of Wales at Aberystwyth, only a handful of papers not in the printed diary merited inclusion and their omission was probably an oversight. As he wrote in 1953, 'The extracts which are now published constitute about one-sixth of the original diary and their publication is consistent in my judgement with the rules of reticence and the lapse of years.'[1] The remainder fills over 2,000 pages of the small volumes, well over half a million words in length. It has been possible to reduce this without the loss of anything of real historical interest. Some of the material included was personal; other sections dealt with subjects extraneous to the main theme, like the Gregynog Press or Coleg Harlech, a large part of which has been omitted. Other subjects, such as the case of Miss Violet Douglas-Pennant, or fund-raising for charities, have been taken out altogether; and there were many long memoranda on subjects of specialized interest, like trade with Russia, or the state of the coal industry in South Wales, which may have their place in other books but the retention of which would have kept the diary at an inordinate length. Jones himself cut the 1931–50 diaries in about the same proportion.

Even so, the edited version for the years 1920 to 1925 included a large amount of material on Ireland that is fascinating in its own right, but frequently distracting and, without copious annotation, undeniably obscure. It was eventually decided to divide the whole work into three volumes; the first from 1916 to the end of 1925; the second from 1926 to Jones's retirement in 1930; and the third to include all the sections dealing with Ireland. Nearly all of the latter extracts come from the period covered by Volume I, and to maintain continuity as well as to show how important a part Jones played, and how largely Irish affairs bulked in the Ministers' minds, a précis of the diary is included wherever cuts have been made. The final, Irish volume will now contain more of Jones's unique account than would otherwise have been possible.

A number of other cuts have had to be made for different reasons. Occasionally matters were dealt with which still have a remote bearing on security today. The omissions on this account are few and not of historical significance. Then on the ground of propriety, several excisions have been made; some persons mentioned are still alive; the children of others who were the recipients of political honours might be hurt by gossip of no significance today; and some of the remarks made about colleagues, recorded not least by Lloyd George, are still capable of wounding. On the whole, gossip has been restricted to what is of genuine interest in throwing light on personalities or events; and again the amount removed has been small.

A much more complicated question arose when considering the propriety of a civil servant, in a position of trust, recording the unguarded confidences of Prime Ministers and Ministers, and the uninhibited conversation of the Cabinet. Both Jones and Hankey kept their diaries at a time when they were

[1] *Diary with Letters*, p. xv.

encouraged to do so; but it is more important to point out that Jones's position was peculiar, and probably unique. Beginning as a member of the Secretariat, he took on, at the request of successive Prime Ministers, functions which no career civil servant today would undertake. He wrote speeches, to be used even in election campaigns; he exercised to the full the licence which he was given as 'liberal conscience of the party'; and although MacDonald was mistrustful of him in 1924, with the three other Prime Ministers whom he served he achieved a relationship of friendship, trust, and something approaching equality which has never been repeated. His discussions with Baldwin on Cabinet-making show him as a tactful but persistent 'friend of court'. An understanding of his exact status may be found in his intervention during the General Strike, in which he was instrumental in preventing the introduction of stringent legislation against the trade unions. It is understandable that in his own lifetime Thomas Jones could not publish even an edited version of the diary for 1916–30, but the need for restriction has now passed.

In editing the diary, Thomas Jones's original plan has been followed as closely as possible. The extracts are arranged in strictly chronological order. At the beginning of each year a summary of events is given, as in the original. The published diaries stretch back only to 1930, but this volume goes back to 1916 and it seemed necessary to include a rather fuller analysis of each year: at the end of each summary is a note of Jones's own activities during the period.

In the same way short notes have been included on the characters mentioned, with rather fuller biographical notes in an appendix at the end of the book on the principal persons who appear frequently. There are also explanatory notes, either as footnotes or as insertions in the text, to make clear some obscure references, or to give the diary more the appearance of a coherent narrative. Sometimes, where an entry was of only limited interest, a brief summary has been made. All editorial entries in the text are distinguished from the text of the diary by italic type.

Work on Thomas Jones's papers only begins with this three-volume edition of the diary. Among the papers at Aberystwyth there is material for books on Cabinet government, on the Secretariat, on foreign policy, education, and half a dozen other aspects of government, and on Welsh subjects innumerable. It is to be hoped that they will provide material for the research students of the future.

The diary itself stands apart from the rest of the Jones collection. In a much wider sense it stands apart from the often unimportant historical documentation which is being revealed as the archives are opened up year by year, as mile upon mile of departmental papers becomes available, and as secret minutes, even of the Cabinet, become unsatisfying because unrevealing. The revision of the fifty-year rule will make the inter-war years a matter of a lifetime's specialized research, the benefits of which will not be available for many years. Until then, and beyond, Thomas Jones's diary, compiled by a man who was both student and master of political activity, will give an unparalleled insight into the years after the First World War.

University of Sussex, 1968   Keith Middlemas

DR. THOMAS JONES, C.H.

A Biographical Note
by Eirene White, M.P.

When my father reached Whitehall in December 1916, at the age of forty-six, as Assistant, later Deputy Secretary to the Cabinet, he had spent all his working life in Scotland, Ireland, and Wales, with only an occasional foray into England. His background was unusual for a civil servant. Some Whitehall eyebrows were raised and there were murmurings about 'the little Welsh socialist' in the clubs frequented by the mandarins of the First Division. That T.J., as he was soon to be called, is even today remembered with affection as something of a legend says much for Whitehall, as well as for his own shining qualities.

It was the range of experience, the astonishing breadth of acquaintance, as well as a quick and lively character, speed of work, and selflessness, which made him not just an efficient minder of Cabinet business, but a counsellor to four Prime Ministers and close confidant of three of them. His relations with Ramsay MacDonald were less close, particularly in the first Labour administration, than with Lloyd George, Bonar Law, and Stanley Baldwin. That was due in part to temperamental differences and to the suspicions which put the first Labour Ministers on their guard, but it was enhanced by the fact that T.J., a socialist by conviction, albeit a gradualist, hoped for more from socialist masters and was discouraged when at times he judged that they gave less.

Born in Rhymney, Monmouthshire, in 1870, eldest of the nine children of the storekeeper of the 'company shop', T.J. left the neighbouring grammar school at thirteen to work as time-keeper in the local iron works.

He read widely, with passionate eagerness, under a manager who encouraged his staff to read when there was no work to do, and he was allowed by his mother to save his earnings, in the hope that he might qualify to enter the Welsh Calvinistic Methodist ministry. He reached the University College of Wales at Aberystwyth, preaching at weekends, and then in 1895 migrated to Glasgow University, where he stayed, as student and lecturer, for fifteen years.

At Aberystwyth, T.J. had found three teachers, including C. H. Herford, Professor of English, who could 'transform knowledge into inspiration'. At the much larger university of Glasgow, Sir Richard Lodge and A. C. Bradley set an unrivalled standard in the teaching of history and English literature. Gilbert Murray at the University, T. M. Lindsay and George Adam Smith at the Free Church College were stimulating influences, while to his own particular mentors, Sir Henry Jones (moral philosophy) and Professor Smart (political economy), T.J. owed a debt which he repaid with lifelong friendship. As R. H. Tawney later wrote, they appealed because they 'made intellect the servant of moral conviction'. T.J.'s personal hero at this period was Giuseppe Mazzini, and years later, as he was leaving 10 Downing Street for the last time, David Lloyd George signed a striking photograph of the Italian patriot with the words 'from one admirer of Mazzini to another'.

An awakened social conscience and experience of the Glasgow slums gradually turned T.J.'s thoughts from the next world to this. From the Students' Settlement he worked his 'close' of forty-four families. In December 1895 he joined the Partick Branch of the I.L.P. Keir Hardie was President of the Independent Labour Party, and Tom Mann its secretary. It was here that T.J. came to know Robert Smillie, Sidney Webb, Ramsay MacDonald, Tom Johnston, H. N. Brailsford, and others who were, or were to become, leading figures in the Labour cause. He was one of the founders and secretary of the University Fabian Society. As he wrote, 'It was a thrilling time of splendid hopes, this birth and youth of the Labour movement. We were the light-bringers, music-makers, dreamers of dreams. Only slowly did I learn, with William Morris, "how men fight and lose the battle, and the thing they fought for comes about in spite of their defeat, and when it comes, it turns out not to be what they meant and other men have to fight for what they meant under another name".'

In South Wales, too, socialism was stirring and in 1899 his mother was writing from Rhymney: 'I am glad that people are beginning to open their eyes. I think the tide is turning for the best. Poor people shall have better houses, better pay, everything.' From Rhymney to Merthyr, where Keir Hardie stood for Parliament in 1900, is only a few miles. It is even closer to Tredegar, birthplace of Aneurin Bevan.

The University group in Glasgow around 1900 to 1910 was matched by a band of public-spirited citizens and some outstanding Lord Provosts with whom T.J. became involved in wrestling with the housing problem, casual labour at the docks, trade unionism, and the like. With his wife, a former student at Aberystwyth, Newnham, and the Sorbonne and, as he would proudly and fondly say, 'a better scholar' than he was, T.J. met the woman leaders in the Labour and Suffragette cause. Mrs. Pankhurst came to stay. Mary Macarthur, Mrs. Pethick Lawrence, and Mrs. Bruce Glasier were greeted as fellow workers. It was an invigorating and exhilarating mental climate in which T.J., from 1901 assistant to Professor Smart, throve and developed. Experience was sharpened by brief sojourns in London, starting with a Russell studentship in 1900 at the London School of Economics, which was then at 10 Adelphi Terrace, with Edwin Cannan, Lowes Dickinson, and Graham Wallas to inspire and instruct, and G.B.S. with Charlotte descending periodically from their flat on the floor above. In 1905 came an appointment as a special investigator to the Royal Commission on the Poor Law, the discovery of Tawney, whom T.J. brought in to help, though he was soon diverted to leader-writing on the *Glasgow Herald*, and work for Beatrice Webb, which revealed not only her great ability and charm, but also what one of her biographers has characterized as 'that higher kind of unscrupulousness which belongs to every effective driving personality'. She was determined to produce a Minority Report and she and Sidney between them saw to it that the Majority were outclassed.

The long Scottish university recess made possible another activity which was to be of outstanding significance in T.J.'s future career. As an impecunious junior lecturer, his eye was one day caught by the offer of the Barrington Trust of 200 guineas for fifty lectures on Political Economy to be delivered in the towns and villages of Ireland. He was appointed and spent two summers traversing the length and breadth of Ireland, organizing, speaking, and publicizing. His most distinguished chairman was Cardinal Logue at Armagh, with whom he had the honour of supping on oysters and champagne. T.J. was sixteen when Gladstone was defeated on Home Rule in 1886 and he had spent a brief holiday in Dublin two years later, after first paying respects at Hawarden—from a distance. As he wrote: 'I was able, as a Welshman, to assess in some measure the magnitude of Anglo-Saxon blunders in dealing with Ireland. It is a melancholy story and one from which the English not unnaturally turn their eyes.' The knowledge of Ireland which the Barrington lectureship supplied was beyond price when in later years T.J. became caught up in the Irish Treaty and all the tortuous negotiations which preceded it. With everyone concerned, he could find some point of contact, some place or person mutually known. He had read the reports, he knew the local and the nationalist newspapers, he had at least an acquaintance, through Horace Plunkett and others, with the problems of the land. In the first decade of this century, there were many who thought that at last the tide was turning and that following the Balfour and Wyndham reforms peace with honour might result. 'I can only plead', wrote T.J., 'that I was not more blind than the statesmen of the time in thinking that the economic problem was fundamental and would be decisive.' But Lord Salisbury had been more prescient in his dictum that 'there are things they like better than prosperity', as the ensuing troubles were to prove.

A more definite move to Ireland, as it seemed, came in 1909, when T.J. was appointed to the Chair of Economics in The Queen's University, Belfast, on the same day that (Sir) Maurice Powicke became Professor of History. Here again, for an exhilarating year, he plunged into a whirl of lectures, meetings, contacts with men in industry and commerce, with workers in the shipyards, visits to Lady Aberdeen at the Vice-Regal Lodge in Dublin and, at her behest, lectures there on poverty and child health. There had been suggestions of a chair at Sheffield, a post in Toronto, the Principalship of Ruskin College, Oxford, but Belfast, when it came, seemed completely satisfying.

Nevertheless, after only one session, with what might have seemed a most impetuous casting of bread upon the waters, T.J. resigned, because he felt the call of his own country and was suddenly offered the chance to return to Wales, to organize the Welsh National Memorial to King Edward VII, a great campaign against tuberculosis. It was a path which led to Whitehall within six years. The call came from David Davies, later Lord Davies, of Llandinam, who with his sisters, the ladies of Gregynog, was one of the very few Welsh coal-owners who spent his great wealth with some consciousness of the needs of those who had toiled to produce it. It was through him that T.J. met Lloyd George, then Chancellor of the Exchequer, who included 'sanatorium benefit' in his Insurance Bill, and Waldorf Astor, M.P., chairman of the Departmental Committee on Tuberculosis. T.J. became first secretary of the Welsh Insurance Commission and it was from this post that in December 1916 he was summoned to London, to David Davies's flat in St. James's Court next to that occupied by Lloyd George, and had his first taste of Cabinet-making.

In 1930, on his sixtieth birthday, he left Whitehall for the Adelphi, to become secretary, and later chairman, of the Pilgrim Trust. In 1944 the wheel came full circle and he returned to serve Aberystwyth as President of the College until shortly before his death in 1955. His proudest achievement was the foundation at Harlech in Merionethshire of a college for adult education, in a fine house built by one of his friends and given to him by another, to enable young men and women who had gone to work direct from school to have a second chance in life, as he himself had had. His deepest sorrow was the death in a car accident of his younger boy, a lad of exceptional and brilliant promise. Pride in his other children, one a Member of Parliament, the other manager of *The Observer*, never completely filled this void.

The account of work and friendships after 1930 is to be found in *A Diary with Letters*. The story of all that T.J. did in and for Wales has yet to be recorded.

1916

The fierce debates of 1916 grew out of the conduct of the war by the Coalition Government, still largely led by Asquith and the Liberals. The machinery of government and the supreme political direction of the war was increasingly attacked, by the Conservatives, by Lloyd George, and from outside the House of Commons, and there was widespread industrial discontent, especially on the Clyde. Shortage of manpower for the war brought conscription and, in turn, a crisis of conscience and unpopularity in the country for the Liberal Party. The unrest in Ireland, culminating in the Easter Rebellion and further embittered by the execution of the rebels, and the strikes at home took second place to the troubles arising from the war. The year brought the failure and evacuation of the Dardanelles, surrender in Mesopotamia, the hideous casualties of the Somme, the apparent futility of Jutland, and the rapid increase in sinkings by German submarines. In early July, after the death of Lord Kitchener, Lloyd George became Secretary of State for War. Almost at once the question of a general election was mooted. Meanwhile discontent grew with the rise in food prices, shortages, and the clear evidence of war profiteering, the effects of conscription and the 'comb-out' in factories, and was not allayed by ministerial palliatives. The Liberals within the Cabinet were incapable of putting into effect the measures of state control which alone could prevent Britain from losing the war.

The ministerial crisis began in November. Asquith's parliamentary power began to wane and between 1 and 6 December a haggling match took place. Lloyd George started with a bid for a War Cabinet of three, with himself as chairman; Asquith finally replied with defiance and resignation. Bonar Law refused to form a government unless Asquith joined the Cabinet, which he declined to do. The King then sent for Lloyd George.

Lloyd George's new War Cabinet, of five members meeting almost daily, assumed most of the powers taken automatically by the Government in the Second World War: control of shipping, coal-mining, and food, and mobilization of civilian labour. In addition it created the Ministries of National Service and Reconstruction. The old Secretariat, which had never served as a Cabinet staff, was reorganized by Colonel Maurice Hankey, secretary of the Committee of Imperial Defence, into an efficient executive instrument of the War Cabinet, and 1916 saw the emergence of the 'Garden Suburb', Lloyd George's private staff, billeted in huts in St. James's Park. Jealousies between these organizations and government departments were not slow to develop and ran parallel to the wider disagreements between politicians and generals.

T. J. was for most of this year Secretary to the Welsh National Health Insurance Commission at the City Hall, Cardiff. In November he was summoned to London by Lloyd George, and in December incorporated into the War Cabinet Secretariat. He became first an Assistant Secretary and then Deputy Secretary under Hankey. Later he resigned from the Cardiff post and settled in London, to stay there for the next twenty-five years.

28 August   David Davies[1] to T.J.   *310 St. James's Court*
                                                              Buckingham Gate
                                                              London, S.W.

There appears to be some scheming going on about the selection of the

---

[1] David Davies (1880–1944); Welsh landed proprietor, mine-owner, and Liberal M.P. P.P.S. to Lloyd George 1916–17; cr. Baron 1932.

Candidate for South Glamorgan for the next General Election. Brace has decided not to stand again for that Constituency, . . .

L.G. is very anxious that you should come into the House and, although I know you have no ambitions in this direction, I think you would be able to do more for the Country in some position of this kind than in the one you at present occupy in which your activities do not get fair play owing to your position as a civil servant. Consequently, I mentioned your name to Sir W. J. Thomas and, probably, you will hear from him about it.

30 August   E.T.J.[1] to T.J.   *The Villa*
                                                                  Sarn, Mont.

Your bombshell to hand this a.m. It's not much use discussing it on paper but I too find it difficult to bring my mind to the new suggestion. There always seems to me such a big element of uncertainty in a political career and in any case I feel a man has to start *early* in life to make a good thing of it and to get any chance of rising out of the chess-playing, time-marking rut. You'll be 46 in less than a month! It is a very wearing life if you take it seriously unless you have a private income. . . . Physically and financially the strain would be great.

These are the points that strike a mere woman. The mental strain of course would be what you yourself made it but it would be mental strain *in an atmosphere frequently charged with excitement* which is quite a different thing from the mental strain involved in a University post or even in your present post. And you are excitable enough already don't you think?

That's enough for the present of cold water. We'll talk it over quietly when we meet. . . .

28 November   T.J. to E.T.J.   *310 St. James's Court*
Had a very successful breakfast.

    Present: Lloyd George, David Davies, Tawney,[2] Mallon,[3] Zimmern,[4]
                Hichens (of Cammell Laird & Co.).[5]

His first question to Zimmern was 'Did you write the book on the Greek Commonwealth? Sir Robert Chalmers gave me a copy when I was at the Treasury!'

We are boxed up here all day writing a Memo. which L.G. asked for within 24 hours.

    Military situation very bad.

    Government virtually defeated last night and had to withdraw the Pensions Bill.

[1] Eirene Theodora, daughter of Richard Lloyd, D. Litt., T.J.'s wife. His daughter was also named Eirene, and his surviving son Tristan.

[2] R. H. Tawney (1880–1962); historian, publicist, and political theorist of the Left, a pioneer of the W.E.A., and in 1919 a member of the Coal Industry Commission.

[3] J. J. Mallon (1880–1968); a civil servant in the Board of Trade, later Warden of Toynbee Hall.

[4] (Sir) Alfred Zimmern (1879–1957); in the Foreign Office Intelligence Department during the war, then Professor of International Politics at Aberystwyth and later at Oxford.

[5] Lionel Hichens (1874–1940); a member of Milner's 'Kindergarten' in Egypt; rebuilt the firm of Cammell Laird as chairman 1910–40.

28 November   T.J. to E.T.J.   *310 St. James's Court*
Just come in after dining in the House with S. T. John and D.D. [David Davies]. . . .

Tawney, Mallon, Zimmern, and I were boxed here—except for lunch for an hour at the National Liberal Club—till 6 p.m. formulating the Memo [see below] which L.G. asked for. Hichens came over at 5.0 and we read it over and made some changes. Then I sent out and stood by till I got it out of a typist. Then at 7.30 to the House and I handed it personally to L.G. I told him we had failed to agree on 'Coloured Labour'. He asked what about Industrial Conscription and I said Yes to that, all of us up to age 60. He said he's been talking to Robert Cecil[1] about this morning's 'ideas' and he (R.C.) was very full of the same sort of thing.

I send you a first pull of the 'preamble'. I'll get more copies tomorrow and will post you one.

December   Memorandum by T.J., Tawney, Zimmern, Mallon, Hichens to Lloyd George on the need for a new spirit in government and the conduct of the war.
. . . Germany has multiplied its iniquities but it has multiplied its efforts. Our ideals have been lofty, but our service to them has not been single-minded. We shall not overcome the enemy by imitating its methods of military or industrial organisation, but by finding a form of national concentration at once consistent with our highest traditions and compatible with the ideals which led us into this struggle. And the nation must achieve the task for itself, not wait for the Government to achieve it for it. We could not, if we would, and we would not if we could, imitate the authoritative statecraft of our opponents. When freedom is arrayed against despotism, and democracy against military force, democracy and freedom must fight for themselves and fight with the weapons that they have proved.

We are convinced that we are not so fighting at the present time. We believe that when every circumstance of the War should fire us to rise to the height of our endeavour we still allow ourselves to be hampered in matters military, economic, and financial by the surviving poison of social prejudice and class interests. We still see large profit made and advances in wages beyond what may reasonably be required to meet the increased cost of necessaries and that when the weakest members of the community are not far from starvation. We still see shipping used to import luxuries and large dividends paid by ship-owners. We still see the Government hesitating to limit the consumption of rich and poor. We still see land going out of cultivation and proposals to secure land for the purposes of the State rejected by the House of Lords. We still see position in the higher direction of our armies reserved almost exclusively to regular officers, and that at a time when almost the whole youthful ability of Great Britain is bearing arms. Most astonishing and shameful of all, we still see individuals and groups taking advantage of public necessities to forward their own self-interest at a moment when—as they

---

[1] Lord Robert Cecil (cr. Viscount Cecil of Chelwood) (1864–1958); Lord Privy Seal 1923–4, Chancellor of the Duchy of Lancaster 1925–7; President of the League of Nations Union 1923–45 and a life-long believer in collective security.

3

know well—every exceptional pecuniary gain is quite literally the price of blood. It is detestable that the conduct of industry, any more than the manning of a fire-trench, should be the subject of haggling over the division of financial spoils wrung from our country in its hour of need. The soldier at the front expects from the civilian and from the Government a sense of obedience to duty and an enforcement of discipline as severe and as exacting as that to which he is himself accustomed. The call of duty should be imposed on all alike. We believe that in the present crisis the country needs a stronger lead than it has hitherto received from the Government. The cry is everywhere for concerted action and yet concerted action is impossible without leadership.

It is in this spirit that we venture to submit the proposals that follow.

I. National Obedience

That obedience to the considered decision of the Government should be rigidly enforced upon all sections of the Community.

II. The Government and the Public

That while observing due secrecy with regard to matters as to which secrecy is for military or diplomatic reasons essential, the Government should realise that it can only secure public support on the basis of public knowledge, and should regard it as a primary duty to keep the Public fully informed as to the course of military events, favourable or unfavourable.

III. The Government and the Army

That in view of the exacting intellectual tasks imposed on the nation by the character of the present war, and of the fact that the larger part of the intellect of the younger portion of the nation is now under arms the Government should be at once swift to promote those who in humble positions have given proof of competence and ruthless in dismissing those in eminent positions who have not. In particular that it should secure that the fullest opportunities of advancement to the higher commands are accessible to officers and men who have proved their efficiency in the present war, irrespective of whether they did or did not previously follow the Army as a profession.

IV. Control of Foodstuffs

(a) That the State should extend to all necessary foodstuffs the policy of state purchase and importation already adopted with regard to sugar and Australian wheat, with a view to securing adequate supplies at reasonable prices.

(b) That the distribution of foodstuffs should be controlled by a system of rationing, with the object of equality of treatment for all classes in the matter of necessaries.

(c) That the State should undertake the work of stimulating agricultural production, and should not allow itself to be impeded in so doing by existing property rights or by the interests, real or supposed, of farmers or landlords.

V. Finance

(a) That with a view to steadying the rate of exchange, the State should seriously restrict or prohibit the importation of non-essential commodities. This policy would further involve the control of the distribution of these imports (e.g. barley) for approved purpose.

(b) That in order to liberate labour and capital for more fruitful employment, the State should prohibit the manufacture of certain commodities.

(c) That the State should take all steps in its power to encourage the export trade, for example, by giving firms engaged in the export trade a preference in the supply of raw materials.

VI. Resumption and Restriction of Profits due to the War

That with a view to securing for the State profits due to a time of public necessity, e.g. in the coal-mining or shipping industries, the Government should either:—

(1) bring certain industries under national control in accordance with the example set in the case of the railways, such national control to include provision for adequate representation of the worker, as has already been done by the War Office in the case of the Woollen, Worsted and Flannel trades; or

(2) that to industries not so nationalised, the principle of the limitation of profits contained in the Munitions of War Act should be applied.

VII. Board of Ship-building Control

That with a view to securing the best possible utilisation of ship-building resources, the Government should establish a Board of Ship-building Control, to be concerned specially with determining the character and securing the speedy provision of the ships most required during the emergency.

VIII. Age of Service

That the age of liability to national service be raised to 60.

5 December   *T.J. to E.T.J.*   *The Grafton Hotel*
Am seizing a minute while waiting for J. H. Thomas M.P. with whom I am to lunch and Joseph Davies.[1]

Travelled up with J.D. last night and the Bishop of Llandaff. Met Steel-Maitland[2] at the flat this a.m. Am trying to persuade L.G. to take J.H.T. into the War Council in place of Arthur Henderson.

Expect to see Zimmern and Mallon this afternoon sometime. League of Nations in abeyance at the moment till we see how Cabinet goes.

6 December   *T.J. to E.T.J.*   *National Health Insurance Commission*
I have just torn up the beginnings of a letter which I wrote in the Bath Club at 11 o'clock last night but which I failed to get on with owing to interruptions.

---

[1] (Sir) Joseph Davies (1866–1954); Secretary Prime Minister's Secretariat 1916–20; Coalition Liberal M.P. 1918–22, representative for Wales on the Cabinet committee on unemployment.

[2] (Sir) Arthur Steel-Maitland (1876–1935); Conservative M.P., and Chairman of the Party 1911; in 1916 Under-Secretary for the Colonies; Minister of Labour 1924–9.

Yesterday began with D.D. asking L.G. if he'd see Steel-Maitland. L.G. said yes, and that he'd come to the flat at 9.5. D.D. wished me, if I had the chance, to urge on L.G. the appointment of J. H. Thomas as the Labour member of the War Council. I had suggested this to D.D. on Monday night as a dramatic and magnanimous thing to do, and as much more likely to be efficient than Henderson. . . . D.D. put his name to L.G. *early* Tuesday— before breakfast i.e.—and L.G. said that he did not want Thomas to be able to say he'd refused the post. So I was told off to find out J.H.T.'s inner mind on the political situation, and with the aid of Joseph Davies arranged a lunch of three at the Grafton in Tottenham Court Road, J.D. hired a private room and we had a straight talk. J.H.T.'s views were:

1. Retain Asquith as ornamental P.M.
2. Make L.G. Chairman of the War Council.
3. Conscript and ration the *whole* nation, if anybody.

I then went to the Bath Club and found D.D. who had then the fresh news that Asquith had backed out of his position on Monday, refused L.G.'s terms and therefore L.G. had sent in his resignation. That was the position at 3.0. (L.G.'s terms had been:

1. Small War Council with great powers.
2. All agendas of the W.C. to go beforehand to the P.M. daily.
3. All decisions to go to the P.M. who would have absolute right of veto on them.

J.D. told me this. There may have been others as to personnel. I don't know.)

Our feeling at the moment was that an effort should be made to bring the P.M. back to the acceptance of Monday's conditions, and there is no doubt that the P.M. has a big following in the House and the country, and that L.G.'s position with Labour is shaky. So I fixed up meeting with J.H.T. for 6.30 with a view to his seeing the P.M.—with whom he is friendly. However in the meantime the Unionists in the Cabinet resolved to send in their resignations. This had been doubtful in the morning. Asquith saw then that his game was up and sent in his resignation, and the King asked for Bonar Law. But for his antipathy to L.G. no doubt the King would have sent for him, and it may even come to that yet.

D.D., J.H.T., J.D., and I had dinner at the Bath Club and talked endlessly. . . .

This a.m. L.G. rang early for D.D.—before breakfast—D.D. went across and L.G., referring to Asquith, remarked 'Well, you've got another scalp!' L.G. said that Montagu and Hankey[1] (Secretary of the Army Council I think) were coming over to breakfast, probably, L.G. thought, as emissaries from the P.M., but with what proposals L.G. did not know. D.D. didn't stay but came back and we concocted a letter to L.G. and sent it across at once urging him:

1. To avoid a general election, as it would be fought on all sorts of side issues other than winning the war. To resort to it only if bound to.

---

[1] Biographical note on p. 334

2. To try and form a Government of all parties again but with as much new blood as possible and with efficiency for winning the war as sole test.

3. To remember that Labour was suspicious of him and that he ought to get into the new Government the two best men among the Labour leaders, viz. Clynes[1] and J. H. Thomas.

The situation is changing every half-hour. D.D. is very furious that the King did not send for L.G., though diplomatically it may help George as showing that he had not made the P.M.ship a condition. L.G.'s association with Northcliffe[2] of the 'Times' and Sir Hy Dalziel[3] of 'Reynolds' has un-doubtedly alienated many Liberal sympathisers. As a matter of fact the 'Times' dropped him over the 'Hands off the Military' scare some weeks ago. D.D. had been afraid of Sir William Robertson's[4] opposition to L.G. because they have had sharp divergencies, but yesterday Major Lucas came to see D.D.—very unusual occurrence—and was most eager that L.G. should suc-ceed in forcing Asquith out. On the other hand J.H.T. was most anxious that L.G. should have strong powers in order to comb out the incompetents from the Army. There are innumerable cross-currents. I saw Huws Davies yester-day who had a rumour that L.G. had made it a condition that he was not to serve in any Cabinet that included McKenna.[5] Certainly there is no love lost there.

6 December   T.J. to E.T.J.

... J. H. Thomas told us yesterday that on the recent Zepp nights the King was hidden in a tunnel in a train, much to the disgust of the railwaymen for he badly dislocated the traffic.

Had tea quietly at the flat. Then to the W.O. where I heard that:

1. The King had *not* asked B. Law to form a Govt, but only had a powwow with him.

2. The King called together at B. Palace at 3.0 today, Asquith, L.G., B. Law, and Henderson.

3. That at this unexpected conference Asquith offered to go back to terms asked for by L.G. on Monday!!

All this may be in the papers tomorrow, but I thought I'd scribble it down.

Am going to see Zimmern at 6.30 at N.L.C., then (did I tell you earlier in the day?) to dinner there with James Morton, Tawney and Mallon. . . .

7 December   T.J. to E.T.J.   *310 St. James's Court*

I met Zimmern at the N.L.C. at 6.30. About 7.0 Tawney came and later Mallon. . . . Remained there till about 11.30.

[1] J. R. Clynes (1869–1949); trade union official, Labour M.P., Chairman of the Parlia-mentary Labour Party 1921–2. Home Secretary 1929–31.
[2] Alfred Harmsworth, Lord Northcliffe (1865–1922); proprietor of the *Evening News, Daily Mail*, and *Times*; founder of the *Daily Mirror*.
[3] Sir J. H. Dalziel (1868–1935); proprietor of *Reynolds Weekly*, the *Pall Mall Gazette*, etc.; Liberal M.P. and supporter of Lloyd George.
[4] Chief of the Imperial General Staff 1915–18.
[5] Reginald McKenna (1863–1943); Liberal M.P., Chancellor of the Exchequer May 1915–December 1916, later Chairman of the Midland Bank.

The whole atmosphere was very electric. I've never seen the Club so crowded. About 7.0 Sir John Simon[1] came in rubbing his hands almost gleefully. I saw A.G.G.[2] for the first time—fine looking, might have some good aristocratic blood in him. John Burns, J. M. Robertson, Devlin, Ellis Griffiths, John Hugh, Ellis Davies I think, Towyn Jones, Pringle, Pratt, etc., etc., About 7.0 the news was that Asquith at the afternoon conference had agreed to accept Monday's terms and the prevailing feeling at the Club was strongly against L.G. and pro-Asquith. All this element—a large majority one 'felt'—held that L.G. had come a cropper over the crisis and that 'the old man' by his supreme astuteness had once more triumphed. This was still the feeling when we came back at 9.0 and found James and Craig in the Smoke Room. . . .

By 10.0 or so the news came on the tape that L.G. had been asked to form a government with the co-operation of Bonar Law. Ernest Jones brought me the news 'from the stable' as he put it, and then discussion began afresh. Tawney and Mallon had been agin Asquith continuing. And all our group were very various about the attitude of Labour. There has been much ugly trouble in Sheffield and Manchester among the engineers, and Tawney kept saying that some way of getting the Labour leaders to 'lead' must be found, and of making the working men feel how much is at stake for them. I had a word with Gulland, the Chief Whip, about 10.0. He was 'down' and nasty. Said it wasn't likely the P.M. was going to 'black the boots' of the other crew. . . .

Later

Well, about 12.30 in came D.D. and Dr. Addison,[3] and I turned to and made tea for them and served fruit and biscuits with it! They had just walked home with L.G. to the flat next door. There are two beds in my room, so D.D. and Addison proceeded to make up the second one while I got supper. Next, orders were sent out by the lift man to have breakfast this morning at 8.15 a.m. for D.D., L.G., Addison, and J. H. Thomas of the Railwaymen's Union. I told D.D. that I'd disappear as I knew the talk would be very intimate and my job of bringing L.G. and J.H.T. together had been achieved. We sat up till 2.30 constructing the new Govt. We toyed with all sorts of names for posts primary and subordinate, I urging the bringing in of as much fresh blood as possible e.g., bring in Fisher[4] to the Bd of Education as President. Shove some nincompoop into the H. of Lords to make a seat for him.

[1] Sir John Simon (1873–1954); Home Secretary 1915–16, Foreign Secretary 1931–5, Home Secretary again 1935–7.

[2] A. G. Gardiner (1865–1940); editor of the *Daily News*, supporter of Asquith's conduct of the war.

[3] Dr. Christopher Addison (1869–1951); formerly Professor of Anatomy, Sheffield and London; Liberal M.P. 1910–22, Labour M.P. 1929–31, 1934–5; Minister of Munitions 1916–17, of Reconstruction 1917–19, of Health (the first) 1919–21, without Portfolio 1921, of Agriculture 1930–1; cr. Baron 1937, Viscount 1945.

[4] H. A. L. Fisher (1865–1940); historian and politician; President of Board of Education 1916–22; later Warden of New College, Oxford.

Query Carson[1] for War Office, or possibly Curzon.[2] Query Cawley or Wedgwood Benn as Chief Whip, and D.D. as a Junior Whip! Addison of course as Minister of Munitions in Montagu's place, and Minister of Public Health when the Reconstruction comes. (Don't smile.) I urged they should shove up John Anderson[3] of the English Insurance Commission into some important administrative post, and use E. D. Jones[4] for Finance and Contracts in the War Office, where apparently someone is badly needed. . . . A lot of the weak ones will swing round to L.G. now that they see he's in the saddle.

The great difficulty is the War Office and next the Admiralty. We agreed that two or three [Labour] M.P.'s must go into the Cabinet, e.g. J.H.T., Clynes, and Henderson.

Next we agreed that L.G. had to be urged:

1. To give unmistakable evidence to the country that he was as much the democrat as ever.

2. To deal generously with Labour—the most difficult element in the situation, for their leaders don't lead but follow.

3. To deliver a speech on the high moral note of spirit of 1914—endure to the end, etc., so as to wipe out the memory of the American interview[5] and to raise things out of the level of the Clubs and the less dignified newspapers.

4. To drop Sir Hy Dalziel of 'Reynolds' and rotters of his type.

J.H.T. arrived from Palmers Green about 8 a.m. He had spent last evening in most earnest discussion with his wife and Jos Davies as to whether or not he should accept office if offered. He is very devoted to Asquith but equally recognises L.G.'s qualities for such a time as this. When I questioned him he said he wanted to be sure as to the main lines of L.G.'s policy during the war and during reconstruction; emphasised that there had to be equality of treatment if there was to be conscription or rationing and so on. About 8.25 L.G. came in. I shook hands and wished him luck. He was all energy and didn't linger a moment as Thomas was due at the Labour Conference at 9.0. I went to the restaurant below for breakfast and when I got back Thomas had gone and L.G. and Addison were closeted together, D.D. having come out. Next L.G. and D.D. went off to the War Office, and I had a few words with Addison who expressed himself thoroughly satisfied with J.H.T.'s attitude. Presently he went off, and I 'phoned to the Bath Club and asked

[1] Sir Edward Carson, Q.C. (1854–1935), a distinguished barrister, practising at both the English and the Irish Bar; an outspoken leader of Ulster's protest against Irish Home Rule before 1914; as Minister without Portfolio, was a member of the War Cabinet from 1917 to 1918. He remained bitterly opposed to any form of Home Rule but retired from politics in 1918 and became a judge.

[2] Biographical note on p. 334.

[3] (Sir) John Anderson (cr. Viscount Waverley 1952) (1882–1958); one of the few civil servants to become a successful politician.

[4] (Sir) Evan Davies Jones (1859–1949); M.P. 1918–22; became Petrol Controller in 1917 and Controller of Mines in 1919.

[5] On 28 September 1916 Lloyd George gave an interview to Roy Howard, of the United Press of America, in which he asserted the British will to fight to a decisive conclusion. This was headlined in the U.S.A. as 'The Knock-out Blow'. It gave much offence to the Liberals in the Cabinet and Grey protested to Lloyd George. To many it seemed that Lloyd George was appealing for popular support against his own Government.

Joseph Davies to come here for a talk. He thought J.H.T. ought perhaps to be asked to pick two colleagues for the Cabinet if he (J.H.T.) is to be one of the small War Executive. J. Davies is likely to be adopted as Liberal Candidate for Crewe in place of Raymond Asquith, and the senior sitting member, Sir P. Roe, will go to the Lords. At any rate this last had been arranged with Asquith. In that case J.D. and Thomas would be the members for Derby!! There was a small incident on the 'phone this a.m. when D.D. rang up Lord Edmund Talbot.[1] 'Who's speaking?' 'The P.M.'s Secretary,' replied D.D. 'Which P.M.?' said Lord E.T.!!

12.30—J.D. gone some time now and I am due at the Home Office at 12.45 to meet Tawney and Hammond for lunch.

8 December   T.J. to E.T.J.   *310 St. James's Court*
D.D. came here about 5.0 today, had a hot bath, saw the doctor and went to bed with a temp. of 103. Influenza. Awful bad luck as he is laid up in such a critical day with so many decisions pending.

I saw L.G. first thing this a.m. for about 10 minutes at his flat. L.G. was in fine fettle—said he had put a month's work into yesterday and that the King was 'amazed' at his making a Cabinet so swiftly. I had seen Sadler mentioned with Fisher in the 'Times' for the Board of Education, and I urged that Sadler was too viewy and wordy. He agreed and said he was expecting Fisher any moment to come to see him.

During the day I've had messages or talks with Joseph Davies, Pratt, Zimmern, Kerr[2] of the 'Round Table', Addison, J.H.D. and Sutherland,[3] etc., and been personally useful I hope. J.H. Thomas was offered the post of Minister of Labour but decided to refuse. He consulted his Executive. D.D. and I are very disappointed and feel it is really owing to Henderson, who being already in the Cabinet had a big 'pull' on the situation. . . .

8 December   Joseph Davies wrote congratulating J. H. Thomas on the 'finest action of your life'—his having declined Cabinet office because of his trade union duty.

9 December   T.J. to E.T.J.   *310 St. James's Court*
I must seize a moment to tell you that I had breakfast alone with the P.M. this morning here and careered over many topics. Arranged that I should be 'seconded' for a few months and have a room at the Treasury. More soon.

Met Redmond[4] here at 10.

10 December   T.J. to E.T.J.   *310 St. James's Court*
Sunday morning in London! An unusual experience for me. There is a light fog outside and one wakes up after keeping windows open with a sense of

[1] Unionist Chief Whip.

[2] Philip Kerr, 11th Marquess of Lothian (1882–1940); co-founder and first editor of the *Round Table*; private secretary to Lloyd George 1916–21.

[3] (Sir) William Sutherland (1880–1949); private secretary to Lloyd George 1915–20.

[4] John Edward Redmond (1856–1918); leader of the Irish group of M.P.s after Parnell's death and chairman of the Irish Party after 1900.

one's throat clogged with soot. After breakfast I put through a call to Dinas Powys in response to a telegram from Joseph Davies. He wanted me to try once more to have J. H. Thomas put into the Council of Four in place of Henderson, but I think it is too late. He thought I might bring pressure to bear via Carson who has a high opinion of Thomas, but I have no leverage with Carson. The difficulty has been that Henderson is Chairman of the Labour Party and was already in the last Cabinet. He has therefore a big pull on the powers.

I can't remember where I left off in my last letter. On Friday sometime D.D. dictated some 'bedside meditations on Government making' which I was to hand in person to L.G. He urged L.G. to make Sir F. Cawley Chief Whip rather than Neil Primrose or Wedgwood Benn, the former too indolent, the latter too perky, while Cawley had character and long Parliamentary experience. He backed Thomas against Henderson for the inner Cabinet and made various other suggestions. When I got to the War Office it was to find that J.T.D. had just packed L.G. into bed for an hour's rest. While I was talking to J.T.D. a trunk call came from Glasgow from Sir J. P. Maclay[1] whom L.G. wanted to talk to re Shipbuilding Control Board. Poor J.T.D. and Sutherland in a stew as to whether to wake L.G. or not as apparently they'd been trying for ever so long to get in touch with Maclay. What they decided I don't know as I came away.

When I went back to the W.O. about 6.15 L.G. was closeted with Bonar Law, Carson, and Lord Derby so I modestly withdrew with D.D.'s messages undelivered. In the meantime I had had tea at the N.L.C. with Zimmern who brought with him Philip Kerr, the editor of the 'Round Table'—my first meeting with him. He is the 'idealist' of the R.T. group. He gave me a copy of a letter which he had sent to Sir Horace Plunkett[2] with the object of its reaching President Wilson. It was aimed against peace intervention by the U.S.A., as such intervention would really be on behalf of militarism. He argued against opening any negotiations with Germany until Germany declared her readiness to restore Belgium, France and Serbia, and to indemnify them.

About 10 on Friday night Gwynne, the Editor of the 'Morning Post', rang up and wanted D.D. to urge L.G. 'not to yield to the gentleman at Printing House Square'—this I think had reference to an attempt by Northcliffe or his minions to obtain a list of the proposed Ministers in advance. I wrote the message down and took it across to 11 Downing Street where L.G. was sleeping that night.

Yesterday (Saturday) morning it had been arranged that L.G. should breakfast here with Sir J. P. Maclay. Sutherland (one of L.G.'s secretaries) was to meet Maclay who was travelling through the night from Glasgow and to bring him here. However at 9.20 Sutherland phoned to say that the

---

[1] A ship-owner who became Minister of Shipping (1916–21).

[2] Sir Horace Curzon Plunkett (1854–1932); organizer of Irish agricultural co-operation; having been a cattle-rancher in Wyoming had many American contacts. Founded the Irish Democratic League, 1919; Senator of Irish Free State 1922–3; Chairman, Conference on Empire Agricultural Co-operation 1924.

Glasgow train was $1\frac{1}{2}$ hours late, so when L.G. arrived a few minutes later there was nothing for it but for him to have breakfast alone with me as D.D. was still ill in bed. There was so much talk that if he had as little to eat as I had he hadn't much. He was in excellent spirits and finished up with a cigar. He said H. L. Fisher seemed 'frightened' at the prospect of becoming President of the Board of Education and asked for suggestions should he refuse. I urged Sir Henry Miers[1] of Manchester, but L.G. favoured Hadow[2]—having greatly enjoyed his speech at Aberystwyth at the Eisteddfod. I opposed Hadow as too purely 'intellectual', that even his interest in music seemed entirely intellectual. Of course he was versatile and quick, but not (I believed) a good democrat. Miers I knew to be a very real friend of the Workers' Educational Association and a good administrator. Tawney had urged Paton of the Manchester Grammar School but I felt this to be not a suitable name to put forward for various reasons.

Then he asked what did I think of Mond[3] for the L.G. Board. I opposed strongly, though without anti-Semitic prejudice. I suggested a minor post, in view of Mond's undoubted services and ability. L.G. suggested First Commissioner of Works with a peerage where his name would be transfigured! (In view of what has since happened[4] I feel very angry with myself at having no name to put forward for the Local Government Board.) We talked of J. H. Thomas. L.G. felt that his refusal of the post of Minister of Labour was due to T's fear of being denounced as having been 'bought' by office. T. has been a strong anti-conscriptionist and pro-civil liberties; very friendly to Asquith, yet keen on winning the war. He it was who moved that the Labour Party should join the new Coalition. One can quite understand the difficulties T. was in.

... We talked over the lines of L.G.'s first speech as P.M. on Tuesday next and he asked me to scribble there and then some of the points I was urging. He said he would leave all personalities aside absolutely and added that he felt that Asquith's speech at the Reform Club, fine as it was, might have left out the references to 'disclaimers'. The outline put down at breakfast was roughly:

1. Restatement of the aims of the War, using once more the passage quoted by Asquith from Gladstone about enthronement of public right.

2. Invitation to the Dominions and India to send representatives to London to discover how best they could co-operate in the *direction* of the War. They were fighting not *for* us but *with* us.

3. *Social* or *civil* conscription of all, not industrial conscription merely.

4. Recapture spirit of October 1914.

I developed these more fully last night and sent them by Richard Lloyd

[1] Vice-Chancellor of London University.

[2] Sir Henry Hadow, later chairman of the Consultative Committee of the Board of Education which produced the Hadow Report in 1926, recommending the 'break at eleven' for children educated in state schools.

[3] Alfred Moritz Mond (cr. Lord Melchett 1928) (1868–1930); First Commissioner of Works 1916–21, Minister of Health 1921–2; Liberal M.P., converted to Conservatism 1926.

[4] The appointment of Lord Rhondda (see below p. 14).

George[1] to Walton Heath for to-day—'Sunday being the only day I have time to think,' as he put it, and 'when I can get a little intoxication singing old Welsh hymns.'

During the talk L.G. referred to Pitt's attack on Newcastle's premiership, which has analogies with what happened last week. I posted him to Walton last night several striking passages from Pitt's speeches during the war with France, which are very apt to-day. I don't suppose he'll quote them but they'll suggest trains of thought. Talking about speeches, he said J. H. Thomas had a touch of genius about him but he failed to find any poetry or poetic images in his speeches—such as one would expect to find in a Welshman. Thomas, by the way, was born in Newport, and his English is neither English nor Welsh. Like another Monmouthshire man known to you he drops his aspirates fairly often.

* * * *

John Redmond was due at 10 but luckily it was 10.15 or so before he came and L.G. introduced us and I had a moment's chat—George telling him that I came from Belfast! I replied that Cardinal Logue was my friend and that I had supped off champagne and oysters with him at Armagh! I withdrew to the study and left them to settle the fate of Ireland. Presently Bonar Law rang up from the War Office where he was expecting L.G. at 10.30. Sutherland arrived and L.G. went off with him and Redmond came to chat while waiting for a taxi. We talked of the Munition Centres in Ireland, of Henry Ford's proposal to put up a factory in Cork, of Mr. Ennis of Wexford with whom I stayed when Barrington lecturer. Redmond said that girls in Dublin factories were making 18 lb shells at less price than in England though the Dublin girls were paid $\frac{1}{2}d.$ an hour more than English girls on the same job. He was very proud of this. I talked to him of Oldham, whom he liked, and of John McNeill[2]—now in penal servitude—whom I met more than once in the Contemporary Club. He said John McNeill owed his life to him, for on a crucial occasion when Redmond went to plead for his life with Asquith and George, Redmond said 'McNeill is our greatest Gaelic scholar' whereupon L.G. turned to Asquith swiftly and said 'Good God! We mustn't kill a Gaelic scholar'—and that settled it!!

As soon as Redmond left Joseph Davies arrived. He wanted to know why on earth I didn't ask for at least an Undersecretaryship of the Local Government Board or the Board of Education. Newsholme, later in the day, put a similar suggestion forward. I smiled appropriately. . . . Zimmern had wired to W. G. S. Adams[3] to come and talk over Ministry of Labour. He and Adams landed here about 4.30 and had tea and much discussion. . . . Coupland came along and . . . played chess with D.D. till dinner time while the rest of us 'conceived' the Ministry of Labour. . . .

It is now Sunday evening and we've had a gloomy day from about 11 a.m.

[1] L.G.'s son.

[2] Professor of Early History, National University of Ireland, later Minister of Education in Free State Government.

[3] W. G. S. Adams, founder of the *Political Quarterly*, secretary to the Prime Minister and editor of War Cabinet reports 1916–18; later Warden of All Souls.

I phoned to the War Office and discovered to my horror that last night Bonar Law had come to L.G. and had suggested Lord Rhondda[1] for the L.G.B. and that Rhondda had accepted! D.D. said he would write to his constituents resigning his seat and would go to Egypt, Salonika, any —— place. I said I was going home to my family. That has been my mood all day. We *are* sick and no mistake. D.D. let off steam by writing a most direct and plain letter to L.G. and he dispatched Ernest Jones with it to Walton Heath. But of course it is too late. I went to Westminster Cathedral to meditate and for an hour or so D.D. has been at the pianola yelling his heart out.

10 December   T.J. to Sir Henry Jones[2]

What a week since we parted! I have seen the new Prime Minister several times and yesterday had breakfast *alone* with him. He referred to your talk with him on the fateful Friday and admitted that he had not imagined events would move so fast.

You can tell Fisher that he owes his election to *you*, for it was I who first put his name forward on Tuesday midnight to Dr. Addison who pronounced it 'an inspiration'. Of course I was acting on all I had heard you say about Fisher's quality and distinction. Some are afraid that Fisher will be too timid. Anyway you can keep him right on all main issues.

I tried hard to get J. H. Thomas into the War Executive as next to Smillie[3] he is about the most forceful man in the Labour Movement. Henderson is to him what say Bonar Law is to L.G. Thomas was offered the post of Minister of Labour but refused it.

You can easily imagine L.G.'s difficulties this week and the energy he has put into overcoming them. My deepest disappointment is that an important place has been given to Lord Rhondda. This is bad and a blunder. With the new Opposition I fear a growth in the 'Peace' party. With Rhondda and Devonport[4] and Milner[5] I am sure Labour will be very restive, though Milner's intimates tell me he is a real democrat in theory—but inhuman when he has to deal with men. Some Asquithians of repute give the new government three months and then a General Election. . . .

Some people want to make me Private Secretary to L.G. in order to keep charlatans away. If I *could* do that I would be his doorporter! All I have arranged to do is to stay up 'for two or three months'. He'll find me, he said yesterday, a room in the Treasury. There is a most genuine anxiety about him in the friendliest quarters owing to the intrigues of the screaming newspapers.

[1] David Alfred Thomas (1856–1918), cr. Baron Rhondda 1916, Viscount 1918; Liberal M.P. 1888–1910; President of the Local Government Board 1916, Food Controller 1917–18, a colliery proprietor in the Rhondda.

[2] Sir Henry Jones (1852–1922); Professor of Moral Philosophy at Glasgow University, where T.J. was one of his favourite pupils.

[3] Robert Smillie, the veteran Scottish miners' leader.

[4] Lord Devonport, Chairman of the Port of London Authority, Food Controller 1916–17.

[5] First Viscount Milner (1854–1925). After distinguished colonial service in Egypt, he was Governor of the Cape and the Transvaal and High Commissioner for South Africa 1897–1905. A member of the War Cabinet (without Portfolio) 1916–18, Secretary of State for War 1918–1919, for the Colonies 1919–21.

11 December   T.J. to E.T.J.
At 1.30 I joined Bunbury[1] for lunch at the Reform Club. There I met Sir Vincent Evans, John Anderson of the English Commission, Lever and John Mann, Mond and then about 2.30 in came D.D. Then we went to 11 Downing Street. L.G. was in bed and then about 4.30, asleep. I wrote him a note and gave it to Mrs. L.G. to give him when he woke up. I had a talk with her too. The 'staff' had crowded into No. 11 today from the War Office, and Sutherland was busy answering 'phone messages. Sir Robert Finlay called when I was there, an old man of 74 having at last reached the ambition of his life and become Lord Chancellor. D.D. went off to the War Office and came back for me about 5.30 and we went off (at L.G.'s request) to see Sir Edward Holden, Chairman of the L. C. & M. Bank. When we got here to the flat D.D. dictated the memo on 'Financial Secretary to the Treasury' to L.G. and I found a message wanting me to call up Treasury 41 'very important'. I did this and was ordered to call on Sir Maurice Hankey tomorrow at 10.30 a.m. He is Secretary of the War Executive.

12 December   T.J. to E.T.J.   *National Health Insurance Commission*
                                                    (*England*)
I saw Sir Maurice Hankey and talked over the sort of work I might do. L.G. had spoken to him. I explained I didn't want to touch office machinery but rather to act as a fluid person moving about among people who mattered and keeping the P.M. on the right path so far as possible. He quite understood. He is to see L.G. again. His place is at 2 Whitehall Gardens and they will overflow on both sides into 1 and 3 I think. Curzon, Milner and Henderson will be there each with his secretary.

W. G. S. Adams then took T.J. to the Authors' Club and proposed him for membership. He was to lunch there frequently in the future.

13 December   T.J. to E.T.J.
The important event of today—next to the German offer of peace—is that I have bought a bowler hat in Dunn's, in the Strand, and left my old one there. This was extravagance but D.D. protested against my headgear. . . .

15 December   T.J. to E.T.J.   *Authors' Club*
Am certainly having a 'thrilling time' but cannot get my own personal affair forwarded as L.G. is still very much confined at home and is only dealing with urgent matters and yesterday and today is seeing nobody. I saw Col. Hankey this morning and he said L.G. will do nothing re Secretaries until he is better. I had a most useful talk with Vaughan Nash this morning on the subject. He has been Private Secretary to Campbell Bannerman, and to Asquith;[2] very different in their ways of working of course. L.G. is the 'despair' of most Private Secretaries, partly because he is so tireless and partly because he is so unsystematic. Vaughan Nash described to me the

[1] The Accountant-General.
[2] Nash was made secretary to the Minister of Reconstruction in 1917.

kinds of work done by the P.M.'s Secretaries. Must keep in close touch with the Whips, must attend punctiliously to the demands of the Court, to Patronage, to letters from every maniac in the country, to Memos. from Heads of Departments, to interviews. He is in favour of a small Secretariat being set up, with a biggish man at the head like Sir W. H. Clark who was once L.G.'s Secretary at the Treasury, then jumped to a high post in India (which he failed in) then came back here to the Board of Trade, where he is now. He is not a 'great' man but he understands L.G. and knows the ropes of all the Offices *here*, which is very important. Another idea afoot is to build up a 'civil' side to the *War Cabinet*. This is only vague at present. There is e.g., some idea of hitching the Reconstruction Committee to it with the P.M. as Chairman. I urged on Nash the importance of keeping L.G. interested in the work of the Reconstruction Committee and I promised to do what I could in that direction. The upshot of our talk was that Nash was going to ring up Hankey and discuss things with him.

15 December   T.J. to Sir Henry Jones

. . . It looks today as if there will be a sort of 'secretariat' attached to the P.M.—properly organised under a Head familiar with the Heads of Government Departments—something more formal than the group of private secretaries. Then the P.M. has some scheme for developing a 'civil side' to the War Executive, but all is very nebulous at the moment. He has seen hardly anybody yesterday and today.

16 December   T.J. to E.T.J.   *Cuddesdon*

The Bishop[1] has just come in. He had tea with Scott Holland and has gone off with his Chaplain to do work arising out of today's Committees. He is an extraordinary compound—an aristocrat in manner and origin but a democrat in conviction and practice. He is 64 and has done three positive things—as his Chaplain put it to me—founded Pusey House, the Community of the Resurrection, and the Diocese of Birmingham.

This is like a big country house, with rooms huge and high, and long passages. This room in which I write . . . has a fine Morris paper and white doors and window sashes, a small grand piano, two Chesterfields and half a dozen low armchairs, books and papers all over the place and Arundel or Medici prints.

I have just written a line to the P.M. for tomorrow Sunday and have sent with it a typed copy of Tawney's article for the next 'Outlook' on 'Democracy or Defeat', on the chance of L.G. reading it. For I think in his heart L.G. agrees with our own position, that the people themselves must realise more and more that it is democracy that is at stake.

20 December   Sir Maurice Hankey to the   *Committee of Imperial Defence*
Secretary of the Welsh Insurance Commission
Immediate

I am directed by the Prime Minister to inform you, for the information of

---

[1] R. H. Tawney had taken T. J. to stay with Charles Gore, Bishop of Oxford.

the Commissioners, that, at a Meeting held on the 18th instant, the War Cabinet decided to appoint Mr. Thomas Jones to be one of its Assistant Secretaries, and I am to request that the Commission may be willing to consent to the loan of this Officer's services for that purpose.

2. I am to add that, in the event of Mr. Thomas Jones being so transferred, it is understood that he will continue to receive his salary from the Welsh Insurance Commission.

3. It is very desirable that Mr. Thomas Jones should be spared to take up his new duties at the earliest possible date.

28 December   T.J. to E.T.J.
. . . Had a useful time last night at Brooke's despite the terrible fog. We had with us:

Brooke	War Office
Salter	Admiralty
Wise	War Office Contracts
Enfield	Ministry of Munitions and Explosives
Mallon	Trade Boards
Lloyd	War Office Contracts.

Very useful exchange of experiences. Next Tuesday we all dine at Mallon's and so on by rota weekly.[1]

29 December   T.J. to E.T.J.(after dining at the Authors' Club)
. . . At 11.30 or so D.D. came in, somewhat excited; been talking to L.G. about his (P.M.'s) secretariat. The idea last night was

Prime Minister

D.D.	*Montgomery*	*Philip Kerr*	*J. T. Davies*	*Sutherland*
Military	Foreign and	Editor	Domestic	Press
Private	Colonial	'Round Table'		
Secretary	(from F.O.)	Labour		

Today I've been making various inquiries about Montgomery and D.D. had lunch with P. Kerr whom I have met and think highly of. D.D. himself has met Adams with me and is very struck with him and wants to bring him for *Labour* and move Kerr to *Imperial*. Later in the day the name of Masterton Smith has been suggested. He has been Private Secretary to Balfour, Churchill, McKenna, and Carson at Admiralty and Hankey thinks highly of him.

---

[1] This group of civil servants, brought together by Lloyd George's reorganization of governmental machinery and by sympathy or agreement, became known as 'the Family' (see 1917, p. 36). (Sir) J. R. Brooke (1880–1937) was later Permanent Under-Secretary at the Ministry of Transport and the Central Electricity Generating Board. Arthur (later Lord) Salter (b. 1881) was Director of Ship Requisitioning 1917, Chairman, Allied Maritime Transport Executive 1918, secretary of the Reparations Commission 1920–22. Frank Wise (1885–1933), civil servant and economist, later joined the I.L.P. and was a Labour M.P. 1929–31. (Sir) Ralph Enfield (b. 1885) was at the Ministry of Munitions from 1914 to 1918. For J. J. Mallon see note on p. 2. E. M. H. Lloyd (1889–1968) was at the Ministry of Food 1917–19.

Today had lunch with Zimmern, tea with Madariaga,[1] and shall dine with Salter and Joseph Davies at the Bath Club. Am gradually getting on to the work. Hankey sent for me half an hour ago and said it was probable 'if Italians agree' that L.G. and he will go to Italy on Monday and that L.G. had ordered me to be in readiness to accompany them. I was to say nuffin to nobody as it was quite possible the P.M. would forget all about it and change his plans many times. . . .

30 December   T.J. to E.T.J.   *310 St. James's Court*
I am seizing a minute while waiting for a call through to City Hall to send you a line. Just had another exciting breakfast—

L.G.

Waldorf Astor M.P._____   Prof. J. Y. Simpson (Edinburgh)
T.J.   Winston Churchill

D.D.

Simpson[2] just back from a visit to Russia where he was the guest of the Grand Duke in the Caucasus and of Members of the Duma at Petrograd, etc., etc. *Most* interesting account of the difficult position there—the Army and the Duma for enduring to the end and the Court a nest of reactionary and pro-German intrigue. Simpson *most* anxious L.G. should go to Russia at the earliest possible moment, but the critical position here makes it very awkward for him to go with so many urgent problems unfaced. We were all urging him to force the pace—that the country would back him. He foretold three months ago *in writing* what would happen to Roumania.

1917

This was probably the worst year of the war, in spite of the entry of the United States against Germany in April. The spring brought heavy U-boat sinkings and the March revolution in Russia. Later came the horrific casualty lists of Passchendaele, the Italian defeat at Caporetto, and, in October, the Bolshevik revolution. Peace proposals and kite-flying caused friction between Lloyd George and President Wilson and underlay the virtual dismissal in August of Arthur Henderson, whose place in the Cabinet was taken by George Barnes. Henderson set to work reorganizing the Labour Party; Sidney Webb drafted its constitution and, in December, Labour declared its war aims, based largely on the views of Ramsay MacDonald and the Union of Democratic Control. Quarrels between Lloyd George, Haig, and Robertson, the C.I.G.S., over the supreme command intensified until, before the end of the year, an Allied Supreme War Council was set up at Versailles.

On the home front, unevenly and with varying success, control to a degree hitherto unthought of was enforced on imports, prices, and the production of munitions. After a protracted struggle with the Admiralty, Lloyd George forced through plans for the convoy system which cut the losses inflicted by submarines. Commissions of inquiry into industrial unrest reported justifiable economic and social grievances. In Whitehall, thoughts were already turning to the problems of peace.

[1] Salvador de Madariaga, then a journalist in London and a close friend of T.J.
[2] Professor of Natural Science at New College, Edinburgh.

T. J. remained 'on secondment' from the Welsh Insurance Commission in status (and pay), but was making himself indispensable in the Cabinet Secretariat. He was appointed by Lloyd George to be a member of the Committee on Reconstruction, where Beatrice Webb sought to make him an ally, though the Committee proved abortive. He became secretary to the Cabinet Committee on post-war economic policy. He met Nancy Astor and visited Cliveden for the first of many times. He rejected further persuasion to enter politics but agreed to be considered for the Principalship of the University College, Cardiff. E.T.J. brought the children to London for the summer (they did not finally leave South Wales till the following year), so letters to her ceased for several months.

2 January   T.J. to E.T.J.   *2 Whitehall Gardens*
I got up yesterday and had a very exciting and important day, about which I believe I scribbled a line to you, but am not sure, owing to the whirl we were in. Anyway it is settled that

Adams will be Principal Secretary to the P.M. He will deal with the 'Labour' questions of the sort I handle here with Young.

Kerr Foreign and Colonial.

D.D. War Office and Admiralty.

? *Joseph Davies* Mines, Shipping and Railways.

D.D. will drop the Parliamentary Secretaryship and Astor[1] will take it up +Drink. Kerr knows Astor well and I believe Astor helps *Round Table* with funds.

This group is, as you can see, a tremendous improvement on anything L.G. has ever had about him and is one of the things I have long yearned for. They will keep in the closest touch with us here.

7 January   A. E. Zimmern to T.J.   *Surbiton*
I had a long talk with Fisher yesterday. He is evolving big plans[2] and as soon as he can get a talk with the P.M. he is going to ask him whether he may go ahead and bring in a bill *this year*, before the reaction sets in—to come into effect, of course, mainly after the war. If he can carry the P.M. and Bonar Law we shall, I think, see great things.

Could you not arrange for the P.M. to meet him *with you* at breakfast soon after his return?

He is thinking a great deal about the training of teachers and has arrived at the broad conclusion that *teaching ought to be a University profession* like the Law and the Church. But he finds himself up against the L.E.A. training colleges. I urged him strongly to go down and see some training colleges himself, and if he felt convinced that they were stuffy places boldly to remove them to University centres, allowing the L.E.A. to use the building for something else, e.g., secondary schools. . . .

[1] Waldorf Astor (1879–1952), 2nd Viscount 1919; M.P. (Conservative) 1910–19; Parliamentary Secretary to Prime Minister 1918, to Ministry of Food 1918, to Ministry of Health 1919–21; Chairman of the *Observer*. He and his wife, Nancy, who succeeded him as M.P. for Plymouth when he went to the Lords, frequently entertained T.J.—and other well-known political figures—at Cliveden, their country house.
[2] For education.

He has also evidently been told that to ask for more than 3 hours a week compulsory continuation education will make any accommodation with employers impossible. I told him I thought 3 hours would produce so little effect that the whole scheme would be damned and the thin end of the wedge would never get any further. In the glut of labour immediately after the war half-time at any rate up to 16 ought to be practicable. I hope you can stiffen him on this point and enlist the P.M.'s imagination. We have fought this war with the very minimum of brain power and we really cannot afford to manufacture unskilled workers at the rate we are doing.

All this is of course strictly between ourselves.

I think Fisher will do very well. He is taking big views and he evidently gets on well at the Board.

10 January   Sir Thomas Hughes, Chairman, Welsh Insurance Commission, to T.J.
I had a chat with Donald Maclean[1] this morning. He spoke in a very friendly way about you and was very delighted when I told him what you had done to 'barb-wire' the P.M. against charlatans. He said that the P.M. had been surrounded too long by a poisonous crew, whom practically everyone at Westminster knew all about, but who were apparently admitted to his inner Councils. Some of these men he said—who were now licking his boots— would stab him in the back to-morrow if it suited them. He was very insistent that this had been the great danger surrounding the P.M., and offered most willingly to be of any service to you he could as a sort of friendly human 'Who's Who'. He hopes you will make whatever use of him in this—or any other—way you can, bade me tell you so, although he will himself try to see or write you this week to tell you so—I thought I would pass this on to you straight away.

12 January   T.J. to E.T.J.   *2 Whitehall Gardens*
Had a breathless day beginning with breakfast with Sir Henry Jones at 8.30 at the Thackeray, then a hunt for Hadow at two Clubs and a failure to find him; then a call with H.J. on Fisher; then to Lever at the Treasury; then half an hour's battle with L.G. himself about Adams v. a Civil Servant. This brings me to 11.30 when L.G. had a conference with Neville Chamberlain and others. Then at 1 lunch with Robert Smillie and Mallon. Then back to No. 2 by 2.45. Then 3.15 War Cabinet till 5.15. Went out at 6.15 for tea to Club and have just come in again to the office. At 8 it is my turn to 'dine' the group of Civil Servants. Am doing so at the Club—7 of us in all. I have found my knowledge of these men most helpful. They have welcomed me into their inmost circle and discussions. After today's Cabinet meeting when Hankey and Young and the P.M. were discussing an important matter I was able to 'cut in' with information which completely altered the aspect of the problem —this I was able to do thanks to talks with Salter and the others.

I am finding Young[2] a bit *difficile* as yet—very much the Fellow of All

[1] The Deputy Speaker, influential in the Parliamentary Liberal Party, of which he was Chairman 1919–22.
[2] G. M. Young, the historian and essayist.

Souls; Amery[1] I rather avoid as a politician and pressman; but the military chaps I find 'real gentlemen'. Storr[2] very helpful and kind, Clement Jones[3] very friendly and chatty.

On 14 January T.J. made his first visit to Cliveden—the beginning of a long friendship with the Astors. To his wife he wrote:
I am in what I suppose is the Library or perhaps Mrs. Astor's own writing room. There are scores of most fascinating books and papers all about, and I am alone. Mrs. A. and I had a talk quietly here after lunch—there were seventeen to lunch—and she packed me off to bed for a rest, after first putting a fire in my room—'Warrender Room' it is called, a quarter of a mile from here, so immense does this house seem. . . .

. . . Mrs. Astor has five children ranging from a boy of 18 who has been one term at Sandhurst to a baby of 9 months. She is one of the most 'vital' women I have ever met. Kerr had prepared me for a wonderful woman. I can convey no idea of her pervasive personality. She is 30 something with a lithe figure, with not a wasted ounce in it, sharp-featured, a face all light and colour; she talks at a great rate, in the cleverest way, with a 'philosophy' free from hate, full of humanity. You feel she has a golden heart and I can understand what a mothering influence she has been to the young Knights of the Round Table. . . .

I went to the church in the grounds this morning, full of soldiers and nurses. We sang with all our might, and then Mrs. Astor took me through the wards—900 beds, for cases of all sorts, put up by the Canadian people.

28 January   T.J. to Lloyd George
I have just read Montagu's Memorandum on Reconstruction, which is coming up tomorrow, and should like to offer one or two observations.

Montagu,[4] Nash, and Bonham Carter are skilled domestic diplomatists, who will do all that gentle persuasion can to extract information from secretive Departments of State; but Nash alone could do this efficiently, and he and Dale (a first-rate Civil Servant) ought to be reinforced by someone with first-hand knowledge of industrial conditions, and of the Labour world. A man of the ability and knowledge of J. J. Mallon, of the Trade Boards, would be admirable if he could be secured. He is *persona grata* with Nash, and would bring some red blood into the rather anaemic arteries of Dean's Yard. Reconstruction after Armageddon, under the guidance of the Asquithian temperament, does not seem too promising, when one recalls, say, the land campaign.

Is it not possible to put under Montagu not only Reconstruction but the

[1] Leopold Amery (1873–1955); First Lord of the Admiralty 1922–3, Colonial Secretary 1924–9, Dominions Secretary 1925–9, Secretary of State for India 1940–5; at this time working in the Cabinet Office.
[2] Lancelot Storr, Assistant Secretary to the War Cabinet and Committee of Imperial Defence.
[3] (Sir) Clement Jones, then Assistant Secretary to the War Cabinet.
[4] Edwin Montagu (1879–1924); Chancellor of the Duchy of Lancaster 1915–16, Minister of Munitions 1916, Secretary for India 1917–22.

allied problems connected with the study of foreign conditions (economic and political) and connected with peace-making? A staff could be got together from the staffs now working more or less independently at Wellington House, War Trade Intelligence Department, and Admiralty Intelligence Section (Lowther House). Some 'Unity of Control' is very necessary if the present overlapping is to be got rid of. Take, e.g., the recent report by the Reconstruction Committee on the Treatment of Exports after the War. This must obviously be brought into relation to all sorts of considerations, foreign and imperial.

? January   T.J. to E.T.J.

Luckily up here most of the people I see are Civil Servants and I am drilling myself into shutting up discussion except to the inmost circle who themselves see all I see.

For some days—since Hankey's return from Italy—I'd been feeling a bit out of things here, and wondered whether it had been due in part to my championing of Adams as against a Civil Servant. My colleague Young is very much the super-Oxonian and also very ambitious and secretive, and as our two spheres had never been sharply delimited there had been a little overlapping. I spoke to Storr who has been *very* kind to me and helpful—that I must see Hankey, not for one minute but for ten to clear things up. (Storr has been acting for Longhurst, who is away on sick leave.) As a result I have had several satisfactory talks with Hankey and tonight he said that nothing could have been better than the way I managed the Home Secretary today on Drink Traffic, etc., etc. Anyway I'm now definitely in charge of Food, Drink, Coal Mines, Disabled, Propaganda and study of enemy and neutral countries, all *most* interesting.

11 February   T.J. to E.T.J.   *Cabinet Office*

I have treated you very scurvily during the past week in the matter of letters. It was the busiest week of my experience here, partly because I am still not in my room and have many interruptions due to callers and telephonings for Clement Jones, whose room I share. Nor have I got proper places for my papers. My non-Cabinet papers and private correspondence are in heaps in various drawers, quite unsorted and mostly unanswered.

We are also rather in a flux as to methods of working the Secretariat. This last week we are on a rota, each acting as Editor for the day. This means being responsible for preparations the day before, a full day at No. 10, and a third clearing up. My day is Friday. In addition we help the Editor and attend No. 10 when our own special subjects come up. The work is greatly increased by the uncertainty of the P.M.'s demands; agenda are suddenly scrapped, a meeting called for the afternoon or evening, usually at 5 o'clock. Subjects it was hoped to discuss are not reached and have to be fitted in to a later agenda, etc., etc. Some of the changes are, of course, inevitable because caused by changes in the war position, as reflected in foreign telegrams which are always arriving. The American situation in relation to the submarine warfare has been a main upsetter of agenda during the last few days.

*   *   *   *

One of my most pleasant experiences last week was the dinner with Mrs. Waldorf Astor at 4 St. James's Square, a biggish house, with powerful, tall women domestics who take charge of you. The dining room the size of a chapel vestry, all panelled, and at the far end of it a round table laid for seven, lit with candles and silver. There were Mr. and Mrs. Astor, Mrs. Brooks, Mr. Geoffrey Robinson[1]—editor of *The Times*, the American Ambassador and Mrs. Page. Mrs. Brooks is a sister of Mrs. Astor, and one of the 'Gibson Girls' drawn by Dana Gibson, cousin of the Astors. She has a most sweet face and was about to be married to Miss Pennant's brother—killed in the war. She was already a widow. . . . Mr. Page is an old gentlemen of sixty or so, talkative, friendly, and most unneutral; his wife even more pro-Ally than he. Indeed this American group were thirsting for war. They told me many tales of young Americans fighting, sick and dying, among the Canadian regiments. His Excellency was very indignant because he had heard nothing for days from Berlin about Mr. Gerrard and they were naturally anxious about the many Americans at the Embassy or on Red Cross work. The Editor is a youngish looking man of 40 or less, with a strong fresh countenance, with a lot of firmness but no hardness in it. Mrs. Astor told me that he had done a great deal to counter the Northcliffe instincts during the war. I thanked him for inserting the articles some months ago on the South Wales coalfield.

Talking of the Press you may have seen rumours that John Buchan[2] is to take charge of propaganda. This is so, and I am looking forward to meeting him, perhaps on Tuesday, when the subject will be discussed. He was in Glasgow just before my time. Adams knows him. I met this week, with Zimmern, Arnold Toynbee.[3] They were keen on organising a peace-making section or group for purposes of studying in advance the problems likely to come up presently, and are concerting a memorandum which I have promised to circulate.

17 February   L.G. to T.J.   *10 Downing Street*
The War Cabinet has decided to appoint a new Reconstruction Committee to replace the old Reconstruction Committee to consider

1. the terms of reference and composition of the existing Sub-Committees of the Reconstruction Committee;

2. what further enquiries should be made in connection with reconstruction.

3. Reports made to the Prime Minister from the Sub-Committees;

4. Recommendations to the War Cabinet as to what immediate action should be taken in connection with the Reports of the Sub-Committees.

It is hoped that the following will consent to serve on this committee, and I should be much obliged if you would be good enough to let me know

[1] Later Geoffrey Dawson. See p. 39.

[2] The writer, later Lord Tweedsmuir, Governor-General of Canada 1935–40. He was Subordinate Director, Ministry of Information, 1917–18.

[3] At this time engaged on government work and later in the Intelligence Department of the War Office.

whether you could see your way to serve: The Prime Minister (Chairman), the Rt. Hon. E. S. Montagu (Vice-Chairman), the Marquess of Salisbury, Mr. J. W. Hills, M.P., Mr. Leslie Scott, K.C., M.P., Mr. J. H. Thomas, M.P., Mr. J. R. Clynes, M.P., Sir J. Stevenson, Sir A. M. Duckham, Mr. B. Seebohm Rowntree, Mr. Thomas Jones, Prof. W. G. S. Adams, Mr. P. H. Kerr, Mrs. Sidney Webb, Mrs. H. J. Tennant, Mr. Vaughan Nash (Secretary), Mr. J. A. Dale, Mr. Arthur Greenwood (Assistant Secretaries).

19 February   Beatrice Webb[1] wrote asking to talk to T.J. before the first meeting of this Committee.

25 February   T.J. to E.T.J.   *2 Whitehall Gardens*
I have just come in (2.45) from a quick lunch with Mr. and Mrs. Webb, and the Tawneys at Grosvenor Road. I always enjoy a talk at No. 41, each takes up the idea of the other before the other has quite finished with it—'two in one' combination. I heard today some more details of the unique occasion when Tawney, Keeling, Gillespie, and C. M. Lloyd were separately summoned from different parts of the front and different ranks to G.H.Q. at St. Omer to discuss what action the Government might take in view of the labour troubles on the Clyde.[2] The four were members of the Fabian Society and they met unexpectedly, not guessing in the least what they were wanted for. Mallon arrived from this side of the Channel and they conferred with General Geddes, now head of recruiting at the W.O. They arranged to write an appeal from the Trade Unionists at the front to the Trade Unionists at home and I have a copy of this moving document. It was 'turned down' however and never published. Did I ever shew it to you? I forget.

Mrs. Webb is full of interest in Reconstruction and eager to begin devouring reports, but the P.M. goes abroad early tomorrow so we shall not meet I imagine for some days yet. One of the big problems to be tackled is demobilisation of the army, women's employment, etc.

I am constantly being overwhelmed with letters wanting me to do things for folk and am rather in despair how to overtake them even with a clerk's help. Letters are often of little use in these personal cases, and I simply have not the time to go round and see folk. I don't know all the right people to go to.

6 March   T.J. to E.T.J.
You will have glanced at L.G.'s speech yesterday and realised that matters are in a pretty serious position though by no means desperate. But the new restrictions will do much to bring the war home to all of us and I hope the Government will stand up to the various 'interests'. I have been of course in all that led up to the speech—especially the discussion as to guaranteed prices and wages.

---

[1] Beatrice Webb (1858–1943), wife of Sidney Webb, later Lord Passfield (see p. 34, note); at this time a member of the Reconstruction Committee and the Committee on National Registration.
[2] The strikes and the shop stewards' agitation of 1915–17.

The first report as to Imports by the special Committee under Babington Smith had been based on a cutting down (a) of 250,000, (b) of 500,000 tons a month. Last week the Cabinet decided on (b). These figures were founded on a report by Sir Norman Hill of probable losses. Early this week came a further and more alarming estimate from Sir Alfred Watson, urging a restriction of a million tons a month. This meant more meetings and delays in L.G.'s statement. Watson had been borrowed (thanks to Salter) to figure things out for the Shipping Controller, with whom also is John Anderson.

The beer position is interesting. Some five or six weeks ago the Food Controller put the supply down from 36 m. barrels of 1914 to 18 m. barrels for April 1st 1917—to April 1st 1918. Now that is cut down to 10 m. and half the breweries can easily be shut down. The position will become so unsettled that the brewers will probably readily agree to purchase by the State rather than be constantly upset in this sudden fashion. This is what L.G. is working towards. Kerr and Adams worked hard on this speech. Today there was to be a secret meeting of the Cabinet on military matters and L.G. and Hankey and Sir William Robertson will probably be in Boulogne on Monday for an important conference. We are all a bit anxious about the safe return of Milner and party as the Germans will make a dead set for them.

T.J. to E.T.J.

Just another line for no special reason except the pleasure of scribbling to you in an interval. I've been to No. 10 and heard the P.M. receive a deputation of Labour Party from the Manchester Congress. Henderson, Hodge, Adams and I with him. Wardle introduced them, J. H. Thomas spoke, Dr. Marion Phillips,[1] J. R. Clynes, Hutchison. At the end P.M. asked me would not Dr. M. P. do for Reconstruction Committee. I said *Yes*, ran after her and brought her back, and she was 'appointed' then and there. Afterwards I saw the P.M. alone for ten minutes and talked about (1) Fisher's Education Bill, (2) Ministry of Health, (3) his uncle. He said his uncle was extraordinarily unselfish and always moved away from talk about himself, his sermons, to a higher level; all quite true in my occasional experience of him. I then had tea with D.D. and some talk about Russia. I read D.D.'s memo[2] which was being typed. Quite interesting.

Ramsay MacDonald was there this afternoon. I had a few words with him.

We are all nervy about the line the P.M. will take tomorrow on Ireland. His real interest seems to have gone off. He seems rather 'fed up'.

9 March   Beatrice Webb wrote to say how glad she was that Marion Phillips had been chosen.

17 March   T.J. to E.T.J.

I was on duty at No. 10 and the Cabinet meeting was followed by the

---

[1] Marion Phillips (1881–1932); an Australian; on the Poor Law Commission 1907–8, general secretary of the Women's Labour League, later chief woman officer of the Labour Party, and M.P. 1929–31.

[2] Foretelling the collapse of the Tsarist régime in Russia.

Reconstruction Committee first meeting at which L.G. spoke for about half an hour in the most impressive and inspiring way about the great task confronting the Committee, his high hopes for it, the need of painting a new picture of Britain with fewer grey colours in it; duty of being ready with schemes for demobilisation, reform of local government, land, health, trade policy, etc. Unfortunately owing to the short notice some were absent, e.g., Lord Salisbury, J. W. Hills, and Mrs. Webb and Marion Phillips.

I had tea with Silyn at 5 and dinner with D.D. at 8.30 after 'boxing' at the Office. He was excited, as we all are, about Russia. Lvov the new P.M. is one of the best men in Russia.

March (n.d.)   *T.J. to E.T.J.*

. . . Lord Rhondda is manipulating the press very effectively in favour of a Ministry of Health. I expect we shall have his proposals before the Cabinet in a few days. He has sent a summary to the P.M. (drafted by Morant[1] really). . . .

Well—I got back to the office between 3 and 4 and was busy. About 4.30 D.D. came in to read some of the military papers which are circulated to us but not to No. 10. He had tea with me which Miss Vernon had left ready. In the interstices of his talk I managed to write a short memo to the P.M. on the new Corn Production Bill—the minimum wage side of it and put it in his box for Walton. Then about 8 D.D. and I went to supper to an 'Oyster Grotto' off Shaftesbury Avenue—De Hem's, and at 9 we adjourned to the Shaftesbury Theatre where there was a revue with Harry Lauder and Ethel Levy as leading lights and a wonderful dancer—Ivy Shilling. I enjoyed this relief immensely.

The same letter refers to David Davies's plans to buy the Westminster Gazette. *He had found out the names of all the shareholders, Cowdray, Aberconway, Elibank, Mond, etc. 'There is no doubt that a man with a paper in his pocket has a big leverage in political circles here. The P.M. particularly "studies" and "humours" such people.' (Indeed L.G. tried himself to buy the* Westminster Gazette.) *Later in the same letter:*

. . . I find many here in town who are puzzled because I have never 'stood for Parliament'. Perhaps with the new electoral arrangements proposed it may be more attractive to fight elections. Tawney said the other day that he thought we all (Mallon, Greenwood, etc.) ought to stand at the end of the war and help on Reconstruction. I am certainly obtaining a great insight into the way things are or are not done; which would be of great use later on if one were in the House. But I am not thinking ahead as to myself. I have enough to go on with and all of it intensely absorbing. But I foresee profound changes on the horizon and if L.G. has the physical strength he'll be at the head of some big reconstruction party. His superiority over his colleagues is

---

[1] (Sir) Robert Morant (1863–1920); a civil servant; Chairman, National Health Insurance Commission 1911–19, First Secretary at the Ministry of Health, which he helped to create, 1919–20.

very marked—his freshness of outlook and outspokenness, and humour. They were joking this week about making Mond governor of Jerusalem!

27 March   Mrs. Sidney Webb to T.J.   *41 Grosvenor Road*
I should very much like to have a talk to you before the Wednesday meeting.[1]
. . . I think somehow or other we shall have to arrange to meet by ones and twos or threes or fours, so as to concert action. Otherwise I am afraid meeting after meeting will go by without things happening that we wish to happen. I think my Labour colleagues are coming here, but Thomas wanted to have the meeting restricted to what he calls 'the official Labour representatives'— apparently he considers me one of them! I am not sure that you are not an-other, as in your capacity as a member of the Fabian Society you are technically in the Labour Party. But no doubt your capacity as War Cabinet Secretary would over-ride the humbler membership. . . .

4 April   T.J. to Edwin Montagu
I concur in the terms of the letter which you propose addressing to the Prime Minister on the urgent need for a Ministry of Health.

The P.M. is preoccupied at the moment with 'Drink'. Hankey will suggest on Friday that a Cabinet sub-committee be put up under Milner to look into Rhondda's proposals and report. . . .

6 April   T.J. to E.T.J.   *10 Downing St.*
. . . I've just rung up Morant to tell him that the Cabinet to-day appointed a Committee to go into the question of a Ministry of Health consisting of Milner, Henderson, Rhondda, Cornwall, Fisher, Addison, Montagu, and Barnes. We've been trying to pull something like this off for some time and I've done a good deal for it—so R.L.M. was most grateful. I think I told you that Rhondda sent for me this week and I had about half an hour with him at the L.G. Board. He strikes one as extraordinarily naive. He talked to me as if I had known him for many years. He was anxious to do two things during his Presidency—Health and Housing—he had not sacrificed his business for nothing; he wanted, frankly, to have some personal credit before going back to business at the end of the war; he thought he could help the country best in business, only when the P.M. asked him to go to L.G. Board he said yes and he was determined to serve the P.M. loyally. He would not let him down with the doctors or the Approved Societies. When he was M.P. for Merthyr he always took care to keep well in with the insurance agents and so forth. I told him of my proposal to set up a Committee as the quickest way of get-ting on with his Health schemes, as the P.M. was very preoccupied with 'Drink', and he welcomed the idea heartily and the names I had sug-gested. . . .

8 April   T.J. to E.T.J.   *Moor Cottage, Esher*
. . . Tuesday was my most interesting night as I think I told you. There was

[1] Of the Reconstruction Committee.

a Cabinet at 5 o'clock which I attended. It was to have dealt with control of coal mines but Bonar Law was delayed by a deputation in the House of Commons, so we went on after waiting a while to discuss the Corn Production Bill which guarantees prices for six years to the farmers, and also provides a minimum wage for the labourers. . . . It was about 7.15 when we came out. I took the papers to the office and hurried off to dress and with the help of a taxi reached St. James's Square by about 8.15. The text of President Wilson's speech[1] had just been published in the evening papers—so you can imagine the excitement of Mrs. Astor. She hurried me off to Waldorf's room to fetch the *Westminster* so that the speech might be read aloud and she hurried a servant off to the Embassy to get an American flag to deck the table. Presently Mr. and Mrs. Page arrived, then Balfour, Dr. Herbert and Mrs. Fisher (née Lettice Ilbert), Lady Sybil Smith (I think), Mrs. Alfred Lyttelton, a Mr. Munday from Plymouth, some titled ladies whose names I missed, and Adams who had just been fitted in as the P.M. had backed out at the last moment. Oh yes, there was the Editor of the *Times* and after dinner Philip Kerr came in. . . . Mrs. Astor teased Page a good deal at the start because U.S.A. had been so long acoming in. He retaliated with saying how hurt he and Wilson and all good Americans had been by our publication of the Statutory Black List of American (and German or pro-German) merchants. That soon passed, however, but it was plain that that Black List had deeply wounded them as an unwarrantable interference on our part.

After dinner, before we joined the ladies, the talk diverged to South Africa, Balfour[2] having heard the speech Smuts[3] made at the lunch in the House of Commons which had impressed all who heard it. Balfour said Smuts and Botha[4] were two great gentlemen who would have adorned any country in any age. This was interesting because Smuts had paid a high tribute to Campbell Bannerman whose policy at the time A.J.B. had opposed. I hear on all sides that Smuts is one of the great men of the Empire, much the biggest of the Premiers now in London. He has read everything. In the South African War, to steady his nerves at night, he read Kant's *Critique of Pure Reason*! He is much more intellectual than Botha who has the following among the people.

Since Tuesday it has been decided that Mr. Balfour shall head the Mission which we are sending to the United States to scheme out ways of co-operating with them in prosecuting the war. It will leave *immediately*. Private.

I told you of my lunch at No. 10 on Friday. I had been on duty at the Cabinet from 11.30. Balfour's departure was discussed and it was intimated that the King had agreed to his going and that the King wished to send a Message to the President (it appears in to-day's papers). But Kerr had

---

[1] Announcing the United States' entry into the war.

[2] Biographical note on p. 333.

[3] Jan Christian Smuts (1870–1950); the Boer general who became a British Field-Marshal and elder statesman. Lloyd George relied on him for advice and his ideas helped to form the Air Ministry and to fashion the League of Nations.

[4] Louis Botha (1862–1919); Boer general and political leader; Prime Minister of the Transvaal 1907–10, then first Prime Minister of South Africa.

drafted one for L.G. to send to Wilson and we were (Kerr, Hankey, and I) very anxious it should go and knew very well why the King had intervened. He wanted to forestall the sort of message L.G. had sent to the Russian P.M. Hankey went off to have lunch with Balfour. Kerr and I stayed behind, and Astor joined us and (after Bonar Law cleared off) we went as a mock deputation to L.G. urging him to send his Message. After a bit he agreed to do so by way of a statement to the Press and representatives of the U.S.A. and you would read it in Saturday's papers. He then asked us up to lunch and we talked of twenty things—whether we could avoid starvation though the submarines became much more damaging, whether we should protect key industries after the war, why Cabinet refused to publish the Manifesto to the workmen of all nations from the Committee of Workmen at Petrograd, the proposed Ministry of Health etc., etc. He was in very good form and Astor and I came away about 3.30. He was leaving in the evening for Bath for a wedding and was due back last night.

Hankey is away till Tuesday morning. Clement Jones on duty today. I'll go back sometime tomorrow.

12 April   T.J. to E.T.J.
Hankey asked me yesterday if I would act as Secretary to a Cabinet Committee on Post-War Economic Policy of which Milner would be Chairman plus Henderson plus Dominion Premiers. This will take a lot of doing, with my normal work, and will be extremely interesting and important.

16 April   Today we held the first meeting of the Committee[1] to consider the Economic and Non-Territorial Desiderata in the Terms of Peace—not my wording—at Whitehall Gardens. Milner in the Chair, Arthur Henderson, Wellesley representing Eyre Crowe, Walter Long, Borden, Joseph Ward, Smuts, Meston, the Maharajah of Bikanir, and Herbert Fisher present. Also Martyn and Lambert from the Colonial Office in attendance. The Committee has a wide reference, embracing the Resolutions of the Allied Economic Conference held in Paris last June, the reports of Balfour of Burleigh's Committee on Commercial and Industrial Policy, the position in regard to the renewal of treaties, e.g., the Berlin Act, the treatment of enemy interests, indemnities, shipping, the League of Nations and the freedom of the seas. We are to meet daily. Long got Hewins invited to our next meeting.

Japan and Russia have been running away from the Paris Resolutions and of course America was not a party to them. They were aimed at the economic encirclement of Germany—which is absurd. Cambon is asking that the conditions of trade after the war shall be as before the war. To carry out the Paris Resolutions it will be necessary to denounce all treaties. The most favoured nation clause is in most of them. Shall we give M.F.N.

[1] Of the passages on the Milner Committee, these of 16 and 17 April may have been written as a continuation of a letter to E.T.J., dated 14 April or may be the first extracts of the Diary proper in this selection. Those of 19, 20, and 24 April seem to have been dictated to his secretary for the Diary (see end of letter of 18 April).

treatment to Germany? It is impossible to suppose that we would accept the conditions of the Treaty of Frankfurt imposed by Germany on France. France is also afraid of Imperial preference. What will be the shipping tonnage position at the end of the War? The lever for bargaining with Germany will be the food situation in Germany. When the war ends Germany may have three million tons of shipping. What facilities shall we give it? Access to our harbours? What about dumping? Should not Germany be made to pay value of ships sunk or give up her ships to the Allies? May have to put on a fifty per cent. duty for a year or two against German goods and subject them to licence.

These were the preliminary ideas canvassed this afternoon.

17 April Another meeting of the Committee on Economic Terms of Peace, when Milner summed up yesterday's discussion, chiefly that the Paris Resolutions were an unstable foundation on which to build a common policy towards our enemies. What meaning should we give to 'the period of economic reconstruction' in the P.R.? Would twelve months be too short and five years too long? Fear expressed that after the war the Enemy Powers would exploit the raw materials of the Empire. Much talk of treaties. When is a treaty not a treaty? Can we assume that rights of neutrals are abrogated because some of the parties are at war? Abrogated as regards belligerents but not neutrals. Is there any object in our trying to cancel our treaties with neutrals in order to free ourselves *vis à vis* Germany and the Allies? Suppose we carry out the Paris Resolutions we should be forced to differentiate against neutrals who enjoy treaties with M.F.N. clause. In the period of reconstruction you'll bump against the neutrals. Must reserve a breathing space—twelve months might do. All the world will be crying for capital. Engineering firms will have orders for 25 years ahead. Inconceivable that we or America will be able to do for Russia what Russia will need after the War. Only Germany can supply her. You cannot hope to bind Russia for five years. Which is better—to get Russia not to enter into M.F.N. clause for twelve months or to get Russia to say, 'We do not intend to come in because we cannot go on for five years'? U.S.A. will be the exporters of capital after the war. But will U.S.A. with her high tariff want to give M.F.N. treatment to Germany? Ought we to aim at effecting agreements with the Allies which would preclude their entering into most favoured nation arrangements with Germany? If Germany becomes a democratic government will not that fact modify your policy? It is very difficult to prohibit exports without the state taking them over. Cannot trust Germany to deal fairly with raw materials. She will want to bargain for them and we can accord her a share in them, e.g. by assuming state ownership.

Joseph Ward[1] put extreme imperial case, Fisher the more moderate position, Smuts in the middle. Borden[2] drafted a resolution which provided that

[1] Sir Joseph Ward, Prime Minister of New Zealand 1906–12 and 1928–30; Minister of Finance 1915–1919.
[2] Sir Robert Borden, Prime Minister of Canada 1911–20; attended the Versailles Peace Conference.

the peace terms should not prevent the Empire controlling its natural resources and their development.

18 April   T.J. to E.T.J.
. . . When I got to the flat I read a bit and D.D. came in presently from the House where there had been a debate on the *Nation*—L.G. speaking very warmly and making much capital of a phrase in an article that 'our soldiers were wanting'. He went off after his speech and as he was going out met D.D. and asked him 'Well, what do you think of it?' D.D. replied, 'A very fine speech on a very bad case.' L.G. retorted 'Oh—go to Hell!' and went off.

The P.M. was probably overwrought by his effort. Poor D.D. has been restless for days, because he feels he has no definite job and is not pulling his weight. But that is how the P.M. works. Adams, e.g., he rarely sees, Kerr much oftener, Astor sometimes. Kerr pumps things into him and he seems to agree and then he goes and does the opposite. You hate and love him in turns, as Kerr put it to me today. Of course L.G. has been 30 years in politics and now he has no *Liberal* backing in the Cabinet; the 'atmosphere' is one to develop hesitancy and shirking issues of a democratic character. Kerr walked with me to Milner's, full of plans to try and form a Fourth Party in the House, preparatory to increasing it when the General Election comes, with men like Greenwood, Mallon, and Co. . . . What angers D.D. so much is that the P.M. yields constantly to the War Office and defends their stupidities in public instead of letting them know what he thinks of them. . . .

I was at the Cabinet this morning for an hour or so. Hoover[1] was there, the American head of the Belgian Relief Commission—just about to leave to become Food Controller in U.S.A.

Too late tonight to tell you the story of the Milner Committee. I'll piece it together and dictate it to Miss Vernon. She is away so I'm extra busy but 'full of beans'.

19 April   Eyre Crowe[2] has put in a memorandum on Peace Treaties to Milner's Committee in which he favours the view that all former treaties remain abrogated except those explicitly revived or renewed in the treaty of peace.

Indemnities discussed, and distinction drawn between claims of Belgium and Serbia and those of Roumania and Poland. Former should be met at expense of Germany. Payment in kind preferable to payment in money. France has suffered most. Must distinguish between indemnifying the desolated countries and exacting indemnities for ships illegally destroyed. Brutal destruction of our mercantile marine. Indemnities in kind arising from territorial gains must be taken into the account. To put anything into terms of

[1] Herbert Hoover (1874–1964); Chairman of U.S. Belgian Relief Commission 1915–19; U.S. Food Administrator 1917–19. President of U.S.A. 1929–33. See 1918, pp. 70–71.
[2] Sir Eyre Alexander Crowe (1864–1925); Assistant Under-Secretary, Foreign Office; a plenipotentiary at Versailles, 1919, and Permanent Under-Secretary, Foreign Office, 1920–5.

peace which will have to be enforced over a long period of years a mistake. How could it be enforced? A continuing obligation would be a continuing irritant. Time limit important.

What about the Bagdad railway? General feeling that the concession should cease. If Turkey lost all but Asia Minor what would be the position? There are political and economic interests. There are many French share-holders and French want to step into German shoes.

General desire for more positive post-war economic action within the Empire, voiced by Dominion members of the Committee. Fears that Germany will be highly organised for purchasing at minimum price after pushing her products in foreign countries and will so manoeuvre transport charges as to reach markets otherwise unattainable. Anxiety was expressed about the interests of the Crown Colonies and the need for safeguarding them. We have allowed France to occupy the Cameroons and Togoland.

20 April Today Milner brought up draft summary paragraphs on Enemy Interests, Indemnities, and Shipping for discussion. The draft favoured in-demnity in kind. . . . Complete reparation was not to be expected, and it was most undesirable to attempt to exact tribute over long period of years. How equitably to allot reparations among the Allies would be a hard nut to crack. Belgium was *sui generis*, then France, then Serbia. Then came British and Allied claims for shipping destroyed. But attempt to distinguish between ships lawfully and unlawfully sunk would be an interminable job. Better secure a fixed amount of tonnage and proceed to distribute it among the Allies in proportion to their losses.

This did not go far enough for Sir Joseph Ward, the New Zealand Finance Minister. He wanted a large money indemnity from the Enemy Powers and the transfer of the German navy, and Montagu even suggested that Germans might be requested to build ships in their own yards to be transferred as part of the indemnity.

There was an interesting but not unanimous discussion, ranging between a small minority who wanted the last penny and those who did not want to fight the German people after peace was made. The terms must depend on the nature of the victory. . . . Ward did not welcome the prospect of England paying a ten shilling income tax while Germany was bounding forward with her commercial development. Henderson objected to Montagu's proposal because of the control it involved and the troubles with workmen which would follow in both countries.

Then we passed to discuss the League of Nations, guided by a paper by Lord Robert Cecil called, 'Proposals for diminishing the occasion of future wars' and a paper by Eyre Crowe commenting on Cecil's.

Here are the chief ideas expressed in a first-rate discussion. You could not enforce prohibition against Germany building submarines. If you concentrate manufacture of arms in Governments you leave the smaller Powers defence-less. But it might then be easier to get big Powers to agree not to attack the defenceless. Blockade is matter of sea power. As England is the great sea power she would have to carry out this blockade and she would become policeman of the world—an unpopular role which U.S.A. ought to share with her. If Great Britain and U.S.A. had spoken plainly together to Germany and Austria very doubtful if they would have gone to war. Prevention of future wars must depend on growth of public opinion, but less than a majority can upset the social order in modern nations. Even in a democracy you cannot have every transaction discussed in advance. . . . One plan would be to have a League as Court of Conciliation with an agreement to submit disputes to a Tribunal. But see Senator Lodge's speech. It is dangerous to attempt something too elaborate, and the worst course is for a nation to undertake to support a treaty which goes beyond the opinion of the nation. May have to put up with a 'Vigilance Committee' of a few nations. It will be a great thing to get nations into the way of consulting one another before going to war. . . .

The Treaty at the end of the war should not be permanent. It should come up for periodic revision. There is no chance of getting European nations to submit really vital issues to an arbitral court. It is too early to interfere with sovereign rights, but before you go into a war you should meet in a room, i.e., the method of conference. The hatred of war has grown a millionfold and there is a peril in abandoning preparation. May have a treaty which bears the semblance of peace and leads to supineness.

The Committee were all agreed that some machinery should be created to minimise danger of war—the difficulty is the right form. Wilson is pledged to a League to Enforce Peace. Smuts was asked to draft the views of the Committee in a resolution.

His draft will come up on the 24th for our fifth and last meeting.

24 April   Final meeting of Milner's Committee to discuss draft of report to Imperial War Cabinet. Much trouble over kind versus money. Was potash better than sovereigns? Kind economically preferable, but the Committee do not wish to exclude money and indeed think it should also be exacted— *wherever possible*, or should it be *wherever feasible*, or *as far as found beneficial*.

Then, on League of Nations, the members ranged between those who hope for much and those who hope for little. The latter fear danger of being lulled into false security by a League, and the danger of comprehensive and ambitious projects. Are you to have a general conference to interfere in the affairs of the world? Think of the agenda and what a field day the small Powers will have. Even the Hague Conferences have led to animosities. Conferences will lead to the nursing of grievances, and to instability. Who will be our next enemy? We may soon be quarrelling with our allies. You must not exclude punitive action in domestic affairs. Take U.S.A. and Mexico. U.S.A. will call Mexico domestic. (Thus Walter Long, Eyre Crowe, and Llewellyn Smith.) Must devise machinery for consultation and conciliation and possibly arbitration. The promise of the future is to get Powers to consider problems which may lead to disputes. Take exploitation of undeveloped countries like Africa. It would be valuable to delimit spheres of influence and to deal with disarmament of native races. Lord Roberts has suggested a quinquennial conference making treaty of peace for a definite period. Milner's idea was a periodic conference to review the Treaty of Peace and to review territorial settlement, and before any controversy became acute there should be a conference which could be summoned at any moment to deal with dispute; it might be the same conference as that which met periodically. Periodic and Emergency Conferences. They agreed to include a sentence of Borden's: 'The proposal which seems to promise the best results proceeds along the path of consultation and conference for composing differences which cannot otherwise be adjusted.'

On 24 April Sidney Webb,[1] whom T.J. frequently consulted about Labour opinion, sent him his views on war-time restrictions. On 1 June T.J. wrote to Webb for advice on a possible successor to Lord Devonport as Food Controller, a post which ultimately went to Lord Rhondda.

On 6 June Mrs. Webb wrote to T.J., worried about the work of the Reconstruction Committee being held up. Montagu, becoming restive, had suggested resignation.

Similar letters during July indicated a high degree of overlapping and lack of specific terms of reference among the various committees working on reconstruction, commercial policy, emergency legislation, and the future expansion of housing, education, and health. Finally, in an undated letter, probably early in August, Mrs. Webb wrote:

What is happening about the Reconstruction Committee—is it dead or will it be revived?[2] I am inclined to recommend that it should be definitely discharged with gracious thanks from the P.M. for its services. That would leave the new Minister with a free hand to choose his amateur advisers—if he wants any—and, *what is of the utmost importance, to select his own staff. . . .*

I have enjoyed my work on the Committee and liked all my colleagues, but it was clear the machinery had grit in it from the start and had to be scrapped. I shall not in the least mind being discharged from a responsibility which I could not under the circumstances fulfil. The sub-committee on Local Government is going extremely well—it is quite remarkably efficient and progressive.

When shall we see you again?

Then followed the affair of the Stockholm Peace Conference. There had been support for the Russian peace proposals, which followed the March Revolution, both in the Labour Party and in the House of Commons. When a peace conference of Socialist parties of all nations was called at Stockholm, Henderson was sent to Russia in May on behalf of the War Cabinet and given power, by Lloyd George, to replace the British Ambassador, Sir George Buchanan, if he thought fit. Henderson returned convinced that the only way to help Russia in the war was to accept the proposals and send delegates to Stockholm. The War Cabinet disliked this idea; and Henderson prejudiced his position by going to France with MacDonald (then at the height of his war-time unpopularity) to negotiate details of the conference. Up to then he had clearly done his duty as Lloyd

[1] Sidney Webb, Baron Passfield (cr. 1929) (1859–1947); social reformer, historian, and propagandist; at this time on the Labour Party Executive; drafted the Labour statement of 1918, *Labour and the New Social Order.*

[2] Dr. Addison was made Minister of Reconstruction in September 1917 and the Montagu Committee was dissolved.

George wished; but he carried the Labour Party special conference in favour of Stockholm, on 10 August, and that evening was condemned by his War Cabinet colleagues. As he left No. 10, he met T.J. . . . .

10 August Notes of conversation with Mr. Arthur Henderson
'They want to sack me. I won't resign. If they ask me to resign I'll take my resignation to the Labour Party. I saw the P.M. on Tuesday evening [7 August] in the garden. I put before him these three proposals: that nothing should be said about the legal aspect of the case: that the Government should come to no decision until after the Labour Conference on Friday: and ?'[1]

Mr. H. opened his pocket book and shewed me a folded typed letter which he implied he could use with some effect if he was going to be sacked.

'The P.M. told me I was not to bully him and I replied that it was he who was bullying me.'

Henderson resigned from the Government on 11 August, the circumstances being tantamount to dismissal.

23 August . . . [Lord Rhondda] came with me to lunch at the Authors' Club and said that he had breakfasted the previous day with the P.M., and that the P.M.'s cheerful temper was a tremendous asset to the country and infected his Ministers. He (Rhondda) had been very depressed about the Ministry of Food in the first few weeks after he took office, as there was such a want of organisation in the office; but he was now feeling more hopeful. I said that was due to his holiday—he was just back from Penithon, a country house belonging to the Haigs, on high moorland between Newtown and Llandrindod. . . . Rhondda uses it for a fortnight's holiday each year. I told him he ought to give it for the rest of the year as a guest house, to W.E.A. students from the S. Wales coal-fields. But he seemed to have some difficulty in grasping my idea.

29 August At 8, went to the Sidney Webbs' reception to the members of the Conference of the Socialist and Labour Parties of the Allied nations. Found Sidney Webb and Arthur Henderson and most of the leading delegates thoroughly exhausted with the two days' confusion and strain of trying to understand seven nations at once. All agreed that far too much had been attempted and that much better plan would have been to have had the debates for a week at a Fabian Summer School. It was clear, too, that several of the delegates were present deliberately to prevent the Conference being a success. Thomas[2] kept in the background, coaching Rénaudel. I suspect, too, that some of our Labour Ministers did what wrecking they could. Henderson introduced me to Thomas but I found he had as little English as I had French.

I found Henderson still very sore about his treatment by the P.M. He

[1] Presumably T.J. had forgotten the third proposal.
[2] Albert Thomas (1878–1932); French statesman, Director of the International Labour Office 1920, and a well-known international figure.

asserted that the P.M., had not given him any indication since May of a change of mind regarding Stockholm until after he (Henderson) had returned from Paris. When Henderson told the P.M. that the Labour Party Executive were pro-Stockholm, the P.M. urged H. to 'chuck the Labour Party'. On the famous Friday evening (10 August) after the big pro-Stockholm vote, Henderson went to see the Prime Minister at a few minutes to six and was 'ordered' by the P.M. to sit down, the P.M. pacing up and down denouncing him for 'selling' the Government. This went on for some time, H. not even trying to put a word in in self-defence. Then Sutherland interrupted by saying that the members of the Cabinet had arrived and were waiting. Henderson told the P.M., 'I don't want a repetition of this; I will wait outside and you can send for me, if wanted.' After an hour of waiting he was told he was not wanted. It was as he was then going away that he met me near Whitehall Gardens. He talked freely about the future of the Labour Party, saying he would do all he could for the war, but would try to develop some form of criticism of the Government's policy, and, after the war, attempt to re-cast Labour representation in such a way as to bring in a larger infusion of the non-trade-unionists. He mentioned no names, but was clearly referring to the younger intellectuals who are keenly sympathetic with Labour.

I had some talk with Harry May of the Co-operative Wholesale Society and J. S. Middleton, Assistant Secretary of the Labour Party. They were very bitter at the Government's treatment of the Co-operative movement in the Ministry of Food and denounced the farce of offering Smillie the Food Controllership early in the weeks of the Leeds Conference. I said why had not the C.W.S. taken on the Food Controllership? I knew Barnes had sounded May on the point, after Devonport's resignation. May replied it would be the cemetery of the C.W.S., as Devonport had filled all the important billets with private traders, all of whom would have to be dismissed if a co-operator took the helm. He added that the only way, apparently, to deal with the P.M. was to get the co-operators to 'play hell'. He was certain that before the war was over, Asquith would be back in power.

*　　*　　*　　*

I left about 10 when there were perhaps 40 present, the Frenchmen very conspicuous by their gesticulations. Professor Mantoux had spent a good deal of the evening interpreting Henderson and Thomas to one another, Henderson visibly perspiring under the ordeal.

Marion Phillips told me she had heard Jaurès at a Conference in Copenhagen where the majority of the audience probably were unable to understand him, but his oratory was so overwhelming that most of his hearers were in tears.

10 September ... Dined with 'The Family'. Mallon was back from the Trades Union Congress at Blackpool where he said Henderson had secured a tremendous personal success, uniting even the pacifists and the extreme right. Sexton actually called for three cheers for Henderson at the end of Henderson's speech. The same evening Henderson, Mallon, Mary Macarthur, J. S.

Middleton,[1] Cole,[2] and I think W. C. Anderson met and talked over the re-organization of the Labour Party on a constituency basis. There is some chance now of the trade unionists and the co-operators really joining up into a new political formation. The name suggested at this meeting was the 'People's Party'. Mallon, Cole, and Co. are to draft a programme for discussion at the next meeting of the Labour Party. Henderson thought that it should be possible to run about 200 candidates and to steal the Government's reconstruction thunder.

Mallon is seeing A. G. Gardiner to find out how far the 'Daily News' would support the new Party. 'The Family' were delighted with A.G.G.'s article last Saturday on the conscription of wealth, in which they saw traces of Sidney Webb. . . .

8 October   The question of T.J. and the Cardiff Principalship was raised again. T.J. was loath to answer and wrote to E.T.J.:
I am writing with complete honesty when I say that I do not feel adequate to the Cardiff job. I am not a distinguished scholar. I am not interested in constitutional questions or in Committee work of the sort a Principal has to be immersed in from day to day. I consider E.H.G. very able at this kind of work, whatever be his other drawbacks. I should be certain to load it on to other shoulders and as always only do what I was interested in—as at the City Hall and as also at this office. You have said that I never do the work I am paid to do and there is much truth in your observation—though this confession will I fear be used by you someday against me. The power of public speaking—which is now atrophied—I might be able to recover slowly. It is, I grant, an important asset and no doubt I would sometimes make a speech which would stir the stagnant or prejudiced minds of folk. A further and serious drawback which I feel is the lack of religion, in any ordinary and acceptable sense of the word. I have little or none of the theological creed left. All my faith is summed up in saying that the world for me is spiritual. This of course *means* a tremendous lot and has very practical application and unpopular application to the life of South Wales.

As to my personal predilections, you know them, and how they are much more closely interwoven with Aberystwyth than Cardiff. On the other hand, I quite agree that if the opportunity comes at Cardiff and not at Aber one would not (solely on the ground of liking) reject the Cardiff chance, for Cardiff is still in Wales.

Next as to the chances of being elected. My considered view is that they are not great. The electors would naturally turn to a doctor or scientist in view of the developments immediately pending at Cardiff and Swansea. No doubt this feeling which I have that I would not be elected makes me very unwilling to let my name go on. But one ought not to mind being beaten by a better man.

[1] Chief Labour Party constituency organizer and later Secretary of the Party.
[2] G. D. H. Cole (1889–1959); writer and historian; prolific Labour pamphleteer; later Professor of Social and Political Theory at Oxford.

As to other possible 'lives' I agree that the Insurance Commission does not use the best bit of me, for there is now so much routine. At this War Cabinet job of course the opportunities of good work are far greater and are only limited by one's imperfect powers. There is ample scope for far-eraching if anonymous influence on the course of legislation. As between this and insurance there is no doubt. But as between this and work in and for Wales, that's another and more difficult choice. Tawney and Joseph Davies have more than once urged me to think of standing for Parliament after the War, and with the inside knowledge I now have, one could be more useful than before this War Cabinet experience; but I'm not drawn to the M.P.'s life. I'm too old to learn quickly all the wondrous ways of the House of Commons, much as I should like to help the Labour movement, if, as seems possible, the basis is to be widened so as to embrace university men of my sort among the approved candidates at the next election. The attraction of the M.P.'s life is that M.P.s are of all sorts, and I would be one of the sorts, but all College Principals are respectable and dignified and I have a strong dislike to being either. There speaks the Celtic strain. The notion of being a 'Principal' has a certain ludicrous inappropriateness in my sight, but no doubt as you don't see it that way the truth is I am more respectable etc. than I am willing to admit to myself.

This letter is becoming analytical . . . and is a sign that I have been too much alone. I must stop—but there's a lot in my feeling against having to be on platforms with Lord Mayors and Bishops and other hollow pomposities. I think it is the *real* reason why the prospect oppresses me!

I should not only laugh at them, but I should make the students laugh at them. That is all very well for a Professor but a Principal should worship at the orthodox shrines. . . .

30 October   T.J. to E.T.J.
I dined with Brooke and Co. last night in the Temple and about 10.30 we had a raid warning. I got home all right by tube and bus, the streets were deserted and I heard nothing before falling asleep.

Last Saturday in Brooke's room there was an interesting private gathering to discuss the programme of the new Labour Party. Henderson, Sidney Webb, Mallon, Tawney, Cole, and Greenwood[1] were there. . . .

16 November Lord Morley's *Recollections* published to-day and also Lord Northcliffe's letter announcing that he had declined the P.M.'s invitation to take charge of the new Air Ministry.[2] Everybody is discussing the letter. At

[1] Arthur Greenwood (1880–1954); Assistant Secretary, Ministry of Reconstruction 1917–19; Labour M.P. (1922–31, 1932–54) and Minister; Deputy Leader of the Labour Party 1935–45.

[2] The President of the Air Board who, with Smuts, had done most to create an independent Air Ministry was Lord Cowdray. He had reasonable hope of the new post but Lloyd George needed Northcliffe's support. For reasons which his letter did not express, Northcliffe declined the 'offer' publicly, and this letter in *The Times* was the first that Cowdray heard of it. He resigned at once, and Lloyd George ultimately appointed Lord Rothermere, Northcliffe's brother.

the Cabinet, the P.M. said he first saw the letter in the newspapers. Carson called it 'monstrous and lying'; Curzon asked the P.M., 'Did you offer Northcliffe the post?' The P.M.—'I discussed it with him undoubtedly.'

7.30 p.m. Saw David Davies and found him very agitated. He read me an articles on the Paris speech which is to appear in the nest issue of the 'Sunday Times'. D.D. puzzled as always at the P.M.'s failure to do things simply and directly. Why not have dismissed Sir William Robertson three or four weeks ago and made Henry Wilson C.I.G.S.? That would have avoided complications as to Wilson's relation to the Army Council.

* * * *

8.15 p.m. To dinner with the Astors and Balfour, Mrs. Alfred Lyttelton, Sir Henry Jones, Geoffrey Dawson,[1] Editor of 'Times', and Philip Kerr there. Mrs. Astor damning Northcliffe with all the curses she could command. She said she was going to get the Labour Party up against Northcliffe. As Balfour had not read the letter, Mrs. Lyttelton read it aloud between the courses. When she finished, Balfour simply said 'Amazing'! We moved on to talk about Northcliffe, Rothermere, Hulton, Bottomley, and other irresponsible controllers of the Press. P. Kerr charged the Press with 'doctoring' the news. This roused Dawson to maintain that the 'Times', the 'Telegraph', and the 'Morning Post' and possibly the 'Chronicle' were scrupulously careful 'to give the news honestly and in due proportion which is more than—he held— can be said of the 'Daily News' which, e.g., published the P.M.'s Paris speech and completely distorted it.

H.J. said that the people who live in London make too much of the Press. They hear too much gossip in London. Outside, the country makes up its mind quietly on the big issues.

Dawson declared that a few hours earlier Leo Maxse[2] had begged him to publish a three-column attack on the P.M., in the 'Times'. Dawson refused. It will probably appear in the 'Morning Post' or the 'Globe'. Balfour suggested that just as Maxse had compiled a Potsdam Diary of the ancient and modern views about the Kaiser, someone should contrast Maxse's changes of opinion. . . . Balfour was asked if it were really true that he never read the newspapers. He pleaded guilty to having read every morning since the war the middle page of the 'Times', because it gave all the war news, but that he only looked at the titles of the leading articles. . . . Balfour, by the way, had not heard that Morley had been writing or had published his Recollections. Balfour's favourite reading seemed to be novels with a happy ending of which he finds the supply far too short.

6 December 7 p.m. Dined with H.J. only at the Sceptre, and he discussed Cardiff College . . . Haldane at lunch to-day suggested that I ought to be

---

[1] George Geoffrey Dawson (born Robinson) (1874–1944); private secretary to Lord Milner in South Africa 1901–5; editor, *Johannesburg Star*, 1905–10; joined *The Times* 1911, editor 1912–19, 1923–41.

[2] Leopold Maxse (1864–1932); journalist and political writer, editor of the *National Review*.

Secretary of the University of Wales, as that would be a stronger position than Principal of one of the Colleges, but H. J. disagreed. Morant, to whom I mentioned this, said judging by the experience of London he would prefer the Principalship. . . .

Whatever the issue, I shall be perfectly happy. Twelve months tomorrow the P.M. kissed hands at Buckingham Palace, and I have never had a more enthralling twelve months. . . .

The P.M. was not at the Cabinet this morning; I saw him at 11.20 a.m. looking very nervously tired—he was just then going off to bed. I am sure that the raid at 5 a.m. this morning had upset him—as they always do, for he has little physical courage left. Some weeks ago the Cabinet Meeting broke up at the order to 'Take Cover', and he went to shelter at the Foreign Office. H.J., who was with him, said he was all of a tremble.

7 December   Breakfasted with the Astors and H.J. Mrs. A. very angry with the P.M. over Rothermere's appointment as Air Minister. After his great speech in the House on the Supreme War Council, he could have done anything with the country; then he goes and appoints R. while he neglects men of moral worth like Astor. More than that, he used Astor and Philip Kerr as virtuous windowdressers, while in the background he works through Sutherland, Northcliffe, and Co. I replied that the P.M. could not be changed—that he was the one man possible; the load upon him was overwhelming, and we all had to carry on hoping that when the War ended there would be a reshuffle, and we might get him again at the head of the moral and progressive forces.

11.30. Went across to the Cabinet meeting and found the P.M. and Curzon were in bed, while Carson was closeted with Bonar Law and Cave, trying to settle Irish troubles which had arisen in the House last night on the new Franchise Bill, so we were reduced to Barnes[1] and Smuts, and although we had a meeting with two as quorum, Smuts was against going on with the business, and we adjourned until 5.30 this evening. I gathered that Barnes had seen some leaders of the Engineers this morning, and had told them that Government's pledges as to recruiting will have to be withdrawn owing to need for men.

19 December   T.J. to E.T.J.
. . . My day yesterday was very exciting. Went to the flat and got hold of Zimmern to help—lunched together and wrote hard till 5 and then dictated it to typist. Air raid warning about 6.30. Went at 8.15 to dine with P.M. and found him in F.O. basement with Mrs. L.G. and Megan & co. Stayed with them till the raid was over, about 10 p.m. and had a good time. I asked him his view on the suggestion that I should go to Cardiff. He said 'I am all for it.'

29 December   Left Barry for Llandinam. . . . At Taff Station met the Welsh Liberal organiser, who wanted to know if I was at the back of David Davies'

---

[1] George Nicoll Barnes (1859–1940); Labour M.P. 1906–18, leader of the Labour Party 1910–11, Minister of Pensions 1916–17, member of the War Cabinet 1917–18. Resigned from the Labour Party 1918 but stayed in the Government as Minister without Portfolio until 1920 and in the Commons until 1922, when he left public life.

movement for a new Welsh National Party, pledged to refuse all offices and titles.

* * * *

D.D. was full of the League of Nations, and demanding that the Allies should immediately call a Convention, charged with the job of framing the machinery for the League. While backing the League, I maintained his suggestion was quite impracticable, as the men competent for the job are busy running the War.

Dick Jones[1] was very critical of the P.M. and of the Cabinet generally, and said the pacifist agitation in South Wales was gaining in strength, and that there was widespread distrust of the Cabinet, owing to the presence in it of Milner, Curzon, and Carson. Why could we not try for a peace on Bolshevik lines? I did what I could to defend the Cabinet, and to explain our obligations to our Allies, and chaffed D.D. and R.J. with having arrived at the position of the Labour Party—a position I had occupied for some 20 years or more.

31 December To London via Shrewsbury, where I picked up Arnold Bennett's 'These Twain'.

8. p.m. dined with the 'Family' at Mitre Court. Present: Wise, Lloyd, and Brooke, of the Ministry of Food, Salter of the Ministry of Shipping, Enfield of the Ministry of Munitions, and Major Compton-Smith, home on leave from the Front, J. J. Mallon and myself. Everybody discussing the Bolshevik terms of peace.[2] The Major said that if we had 50 Cambrai victories, we should not be substantially nearer smashing the Germans, as they could go on withdrawing indefinitely into fresh lines. He had lived four years in Germany, and contrasted the vigorous weeding out of Generals during their manœuvres, with our habit of nursing incompetence. After more than three years of war, the old regular caste was still entrenched. I recalled the P.M.'s efforts to defeat them at the War Office, and how he had once told me that the trouble was that they did not so much oppose or quarrel with you, as paralyse you. You gave orders and you soon found that innumerable detailed obstacles arose in the way of their execution.

1918

The year opens with President Woodrow Wilson's Fourteen Points, put forward as a basis for international peace, and ends with the Armistice signed at Compiègne on 11 November, immediately followed by a General Election at which Lloyd George was returned at the head of a Coalition Government with a majority of 262 votes over his opponents.

[1] The Rev. Dr. Richard Jones, minister at Llandinam and a close friend of T.J.
[2] After the Bolshevik Revolution an armistice had been signed with Germany. The Bolshevik leaders proposed general peace negotiations and when the Allies refused they negotiated alone and from a position of weakness.

In March, Ludendorff launched his great offensive, regaining the line of the Somme and pushing back the French to within forty miles of Paris. By mid-July, his force was spent. The British counter-attacked with tanks. In the Middle East, Allenby entered Damascus and the Allies penetrated the Balkans from Salonika. On 4 October Germany appealed to President Wilson for an armistice.

At home, food rationing was finally imposed. The shortage of man-power became acute. The miners and the engineering workers, particularly on the Clyde, resisted an extension of the call-up. The Labour Party withdrew its support of the Government. Unrest in Ireland, in abeyance during the meetings of the Convention set up in 1917 by Lloyd George and Redmond, reappeared when the Convention produced no acceptable solution and when an attempt was made to extend conscription to Ireland.

T.J. was preoccupied with post-war social reforms. He allowed his name to be considered for the post of Principal of University College, Cardiff, but the appointment was deferred. Hankey had already indicated that he hoped T.J. would remain with the Cabinet Secretariat in London. As secretary to the Committee on the Irish Home Rule Bill, T.J. began to undertake responsibility for Irish affairs and met many of those with whom he was to work on the Irish settlement in 1921–2. In October, when Hankey went to Paris to prepare the ground for Versailles, T.J. took over as acting secretary of the War Cabinet. Because of the pressure of this work, the Diary for the autumn is fragmentary.

1 January   Found the War Cabinet atmosphere completely changed. Everybody talking of peace. Smuts and Kerr returned from their secret mission, where they had met Mensdorff.[1] The line now is to publish a declaration on War Aims as a counter-offensive to the offer of the Central Powers to the Bolsheviks.[2] The P.M., Smuts, and Lord Robert Cecil are preparing drafts on such a declaration. Their idea is to make it ultra-democratic, to go to the furthest points of concession, so as to produce maximum effect in Turkey and Austria, and not less to support the war spirit at home, which has seriously weakened, partly through weariness, through the atmosphere caused by soldiers returning, through the increasing difficulties in obtaining food, and through the distrust of the Cabinet's War Aims.

The Labour World is all on edge owing to the inequalities in the application of the advance of $12\frac{1}{2}\%$ to skilled time-workers. . . .

3 January   1.15 lunched with the R.S.G. Group[3] in the basement of the 'Garton Foundation' in Dean's Yard. Present: A. E. Zimmern, J. L. Hammond,[4] J. J. Mallon, Joseph Thorp, G. D. H. Cole, Arthur Greenwood, and myself. All the talk again on possible peace terms. Zimmern very insistent that Ludendorff was on top in Germany, that the Prussian mentality had not changed, that their terms of peace were spurious, that at any sign of revolution at home they would turn machine guns on their own people ruthlessly,

---

[1] Former Austro-Hungarian Ambassador in London. These negotiations resulted from the accession of the Emperor Charles in November 1916 and had dragged on without success because Austria-Hungary could not shake clear of Germany.

[2] The Brest-Litovsk treaty.

[3] A weekly luncheon group founded in 1917 by Joseph Thorp, dramatic critic of *Punch*, which met first in Romney Street and afterwards in a kitchen basement in Dean's Yard lent by Sir Richard Garton. T.J. for years attended regularly and was often its informal chairman.

[4] J. L. Hammond (1872–1949); social historian, editor of the *Speaker*.

as they had done in 1848. Others urged that industrialism and social demo-cracy were far more powerful factors in the situation to-day than in 1848. All agreed that it was essential, in order to keep our own people right, to make some more definite declaration of our minimum peace terms.

7 January Walked from War Cabinet with Hankey. He asked me about effect of P.M.'s speech. Told him it had been splendid on Labour. 'How did the change come about?' I asked. 'I think I gave it the first shove,' said Hankey. 'On the Saturday before Christmas, I woke up at 6 a.m., and had an idea how to answer the six points of the Brest-Litovsk programme. I wrote the points out in bed—came up to Town—dictated them in draft form. The very same time the P.M.'s mind was travelling along the same road. He sent for me to have lunch; told me he wished an answer written to the B.-L. pro-gramme, under the following heads—and proceeded to enumerate the various points I had been working at. A Memo. came before the War Cabinet at a hush meeting on the following Monday, but the Cabinet did not like its terms. The P.M. suggested that several members should attempt to draft a reply to B.-L. for circulation and discussion. That is how the thing started.' Important to remember that Balfour was absent. He has always been against a categorical statement of terms. The other important factors operating at this time were: 1. The secret mission to Mensdorff undertaken by Smuts and Philip Kerr. 2. The depression felt after the Cambrai reverse. 3. The Labour manifesto on War Aims, which made a most favourable impression on many sections of opinion outside the Labour Party. 4. The Lansdowne letter.[1]

9 January Dined at Authors' Club, Mallon acting as host. Present, besides M., Tawney, Zimmern, Greenwood, Reid (of the Trade Boards), and A. G. Gardiner, editor of the *Daily News*. My first meeting with A.G.G. The talk entirely about the War, and the relief we all felt at the speeches of the P.M. and Wilson. We wondered how much Wilson meant by his sentences about economic equality. Was he heading for universal Free Trade, or for some low tariff arrangement?

Towards the end of the evening I threw out a suggestion, which was warmly embraced. I argued that if the impending combing-out leads to strikes of a very serious character—as it probably will among the engineers—it may become necessary in the interests of national unity and for the prosecution of the War, to take every possible step to remove the prevailing mistrust of the War Cabinet in the ranks of Labour.

The rank and file have no faith in Milner, Curzon, Carson, as likely to work for a democratic peace, nor do they trust the P.M. But the P.M. is absolutely indispensable to the efficient running of the war. Therefore, I argued, it may become necessary to ask the other three to make the 'great sacrifice' of office, for the war's sake. Labour can stop the war, if it chooses, and knows that it can do so. The next step would be to put into the Cabinet

[1] Lord Lansdowne, after months of urging peace negotiations, finally wrote to the *Daily Telegraph* in favour of a compromise peace.

Henderson, J. H. Thomas, and Smillie, to act on behalf of the Labour Party. It would be well if they refused any salary, so that their position should not be prejudiced. This plan would have the advantage of carrying Labour along, and it would rapidly influence the P.M.'s outlook, and pave the way, not only to a democratic peace, but to a period of democratic reconstruction at home.

I put the above to Hankey, as he was going to lunch with the P.M. . . .

11 January   P.M. came to the Cabinet, very annoyed with the headlines in the *Evening News* and *Evening Standard* of the night before. One of them had in large letters 'U-Boats—Serious Situation'. For days and days the papers have been talking about the food queues—all most excellent propaganda for use against us by the enemy. The P.M. had seen Geoffrey Dawson, the editor of the *Times*, and told him to mend his ways. Derby undertook to see Hulton[1] who, with Northcliffe, as the P.M. said, were becoming a most menacing and powerful combination. Fortunately they hate each other. The P.M. was urged, and ultimately agreed, to see Northcliffe himself, though he said that the line that Northcliffe would take would be 'We must tell the people the facts'.

On top of this Robert Cecil produced a copy of the *Herald* which had come out with the full text of Trotsky's[2] appeal, and with Litvinov's[3] message to the workers of Great Britain. At once there was a desire to suppress the *Herald*. I whispered to Hankey, and he to the P.M., that it was already on sale, and, therefore, it was too late. Cecil said that he favoured either complete liberty of the Press or rigorous all-round suppression of offenders, the *Morning Post* not less than the *Herald*. The P.M. maintained that the evening papers, with their sensational headlines, did far more damage to the morale of the nation, than did the *Herald* with its limited circulation of 40,000 or 50,000; Milner said that these *Herald* articles were a direct attempt to upset the War Cabinet, and that the effect of the suppression of the *Nation* had been very good for it. This the P.M. doubted. Carson wanted to know whether some paper could not be got to go for Northcliffe. The P.M. replied 'Only the *Daily News*, and it is always girding at him.' Carson asked whether Northcliffe could not be got to defend himself in the House of Lords, and all agreed that there was not the slightest chance of that. Then Carson said that it was a very great mistake to pay so much deference to the Trade Unionists, as if they were the only people in the country that mattered. Curzon's remedy was that the P.M. should talk to the editors. . . . I passed a note to the P.M., pointing out that to squash the *Herald* just now, when the Government was about to comb out for the Army, would be a most mistaken move, and he whispered back that he quite agreed. Ultimately it was decided that Cecil should take the matter up with Cave[4] and Barnes (who was absent).

[1] Sir Edward Hulton (1869–1925), the great newspaper proprietor.

[2] At this time Trotsky was People's Commissar for Foreign Affairs, and chief negotiator of Brest-Litovsk.

[3] Maximilian Litvinov, first Bolshevik representative in London, deported 1918 (see p. 48, note 2.

[4] George Cave (1856–1928); M.P. 1906–18; Solicitor-General 1915; Home Secretary 1916–18; Lord of Appeal (cr. Viscount Cave) 1918; Lord Chancellor 1922–4, 1924–8.

I saw Cecil as we went out, for two or three moments, and told him that his line of equal treatment was the only safe line from the Labour point of view, if there was to be any suppression at all. Later in the day I urged the same on Barnes.

Lunched with Adams, who was much exercised about the results of the Irish Convention. He was finding it difficult to get the P.M. to face up to the situation, and there had been a letter to the P.M. from Redmond, waiting many days for an answer. Adams had walked out with the P.M. that morning, and urged him to go right through with the recommendations of the Convention without swerving to the right or to the left, and without getting entangled in fresh compromising negotiations. The Nationalists and Southern Unionists appeared to be united, while Ulster remains irreconcilable. The P.M. has said that the Government will not coerce Ulster, but he has also said that the Government will proceed, if there is substantial agreement in the Convention. Adams urged the P.M. to be willing to contemplate the departure of Carson from the Cabinet. The P.M. said 'It is open to Carson to show himself an imperial statesman or a mere obstructionist.' Milner and Curzon are prepared to back the findings of the Convention.

12 January At 4 p.m. took tea with the Webbs. They were just back from lunching with Haldane[1] and Hankey, where they had been discussing the reorganisation of Government Departments after the war. Mrs. Webb has drafted a proposal, which Hankey will show me, providing for, I think, some fourteen Ministries—Defence, Production, Research, Transport and Communications, etc.—and including a Prime Minister's or a Cabinet Secretariat. She is discussing her scheme with big Permanent Secretaries in turn, Hubert Llewelyn Smith, Morant, Sir Edward Troup.[2] It is a very interesting illustration of the way in which we are governed. As she said, if you ask these Permanent Secretaries to put forward schemes on their own, to a Committee, they are very slow and cautious, but if you put before them a well thought out scheme, they are most helpful in improving it. . . .

I tried my suggestion of replacing the Cabinet trinity by a Labour trinity,[3] but they were dead against it. It would be fatal for Labour to enter the Cabinet, they argued, without the backing of a majority in the House. Henderson has vowed he will not again enter the Government without such backing. They could only enter on conditions which would not be accepted, viz. the abolition of profiteering, conscription of capital—in a word the equalitarian state. Next, if they came in, and were to become really effective, Sidney Webb would have to replace Hankey. They were satisfied that Labour was not yet intellectually and administratively equal to the responsibility. They might be in five or ten years time—the task now was to rope in all

---

[1] Richard Burdon, Lord Haldane (1856–1928); Chairman of the Committee on the Machinery of Government, which reported later in the year. He had been Secretary of State for War and Lord Chancellor in the Liberal Government but was dropped when the first Coalition was formed because of his alleged pro-German sympathies. In 1924 he became Lord Chancellor in the Labour Government.

[2] Board of Trade, Ministry of Health, and Home Office respectively.

[3] That is, Henderson, J. H. Thomas, and R. Smillie.

45

the intellectual assistance possible. The Labour Conference next week would probably set up a whole series of new Committees, for the consideration of foreign affairs, industrial and commercial legislation, etc. The experience in the Cabinet had done one great service to Henderson. He was no longer unwilling or ashamed to depend partly on the help of intellectuals, having seen how dependent Cabinet Ministers were on such assistance.

12 January   The College Committee dealing with the appointment of a new Principal for Cardiff decided to put forward four names to the Council and Senate. T.J. had the strong support of the Chairman, Lord Pontypridd, and of Sir Henry Jones, Dr. (later Sir Henry) Hadow, the Hon. W. N. Bruce, and A. L. Smith, Master of Balliol. He described his position to Professor Hetherington (Professor of Philosophy at Cardiff, later Vice-Chancellor of Glasgow University).

14 January   T.J. to Professor Hetherington
I am most awfully obliged for your letter about the College job. . . . There is no doubt whatever that Barker[1] is a very good man—a far better scholar than I am, with fine democratic sympathies, and with some administrative experience. I think you will have to weigh him very carefully. I can only clearly score him on the Welsh ground, and probably I have had more rough and tumble administrative work to do. Won't you consider Sibly too? . . .

Now as to your question. . . . The position really is this; there is a very private Committee, discussing the rearrangement of the various Departments of State. Hankey has been consulted as to his views just as other permanent Secretaries have been consulted. What he told me was (a) that he was certain in his own mind that the Cabinet Secretariat would continue in peace time, (b) that he hoped to offer me the post of Chief Secretary of the Civil Departments (Board of Trade, L.G.B., Board of Education, etc.), while he would run the Defence Group (the War Office, Admiralty, Air, etc.). As I told H.J., this suggestion rather bowled me over for a minute or two, as I was bound to recognise that such a post would be one of very great power, and one in which I could do a great deal for Wales. But I turned it down because I know how attractive London is, and must be, to many of our ablest Welshmen, and how essential it is, therefore, that some of us should stay at home and face the issues there.

. . . Of men who know Barker and me sufficiently well to weigh us up, I can only think of Adams (10, Downing Street, S.W.1). He would give an honest opinion.

I am very sorry for you, and if I can help further, don't hesitate to write. I have a delightful impersonal feeling in the matter.

In the event, after some disagreeable manoeuvring by various interests, none of the four nominees was appointed and T.J. stayed in London (see 8 February, p. 52).

17 January   P.M. 55 to-day.
We had Sir Joseph Maclay, the Shipping Controller, at to-day's Cabinet

[1] Sir Ernest Barker, a distinguished classical scholar and political scientist; at this time a Fellow of New College, Oxford.

meeting. He was just back from France, very much enraged at the waste of Chinese labour. Some tens of thousands had been brought over via Vancouver and Halifax, but the War Office seems to have forgotten to bring over any foremen to handle them. Result—great congestion and waste at the ports, about which Sir Joseph waxed very eloquent. 'Six of them are not doing the work of one man. They are fed like turkey-cocks—they wear overcoats— even gloves at their work', and so on. The P.M. is always tickled by Sir Joseph, who is a typical evangelical ship-owner, terribly hard on the crews of the ships, with the reputation of screwing them down in pay and food, but tremendously concerned about their souls and their intemperance! Lord Derby[1] had the vaguest notion of what the labour situation was at the Front, so the Adjutant-General was sent for. He came in with his solemn face—the P.M. with mock solemnity recounted Sir Joseph's indictment—idleness, over-feeding, overcoats and gloves—a veritable polytechnic tour to Europe, as he phrased it. The A.-G. admitted that there was room for improvement—that there was difficulty in finding foremen who could speak Chinese, and con-cluded his defence by saying that the War Office were sending to China for some missionaries to look after the labourers! This was too much for the P.M. who rocked with laughter, and said that he had no great faith in turning parsons into gangers, and Sir Joseph's face showed that he too had little faith in missionaries for such a job.

19 January   William Tweeddale (a Glasgow employer) to T.J.
The chief causes of trouble seem to be 1) the friction and disappointment over the 12½ per cent bonus. 2) The objection to military service on the part of the younger men—those who were really skilled men at their trade (e.g. engineering) and those 'dilutees' who have gone in since the War, some of whom were attracted by the big wages, and many who rushed in to get ex-emption from the army; and the Clyde Shipyards contain an astonishing number of these last. Foremen have all along been tormented to find jobs for friends and others, with the result that one man's work is spread over two or three. The employers being paid on a percentage basis make no ob-jection to this state of things. The I.L.P., and Pacifists generally appeal to these men and make their objections appear more formidable. A favourite phrase recently has been, 'not one man for Alsace-Lorraine'.

*   *   *   *

If the Government would further restrict 'profiteering' and make some levy on capital, both these measures would have a salutary and steadying effect on Labour.

The luxury trades should be much more restricted. The other day a huge circular came addressed to my non-existent wife, advertising everything from fur coats to cups and saucers.

It is probable Clyde men may strike as they threaten, but I see that Sir Auckland Geddes is coming next week, and hope this visit may avert it. Matters are certainly serious.

[1] Then Secretary of State for War. He had been Director-General of Recruiting, 1915–16, and was later Ambassador to France, 1918–20, and again Secretary for War, 1922–4.

20 January   Sidney Webb to T.J.   *Victoria Hotel, Nottingham*
Is this[1] what is needed? If not, I would write a letter addressed *to you* (or to anyone else indicated).

We are *very* seriously alarmed (at the Labour Party Conference) by what is reported from the districts; and we are sending by express today to the Prime Minister our most serious warning against hastily pressing forward the man-power Bill. We are not, of course, in any way responsible for the industrial side of things; but the men coming from all parts say that the rank and file *do not yet understand* what is proposed, and are very angry. The secretaries and shop stewards are doing all they can to prevent an outbreak; but they all say they are in the utmost apprehension of a spontaneous and tumultuous 'down tools'. They fear that taking the Committee Stage this week will make the pot boil over, whereas another week's talking might enable the men to be got in hand. . . . I cannot believe that a few days can make much difference to the military position; and the Lords' amendments to the Reform Bill will anyhow extend the present session. I really believe it is a most serious crisis in the industrial centres.

27 January   Sidney Webb to T.J.   *41 Grosvenor Road*
It seems as if no better person than myself is likely to be found willing to stand as a Labour Candidate for London University. If this is thought advisable by any considerable number of graduates, I would not refuse. But it is important to get something of the sort under way quickly, and I have been asked to send you the enclosed preliminary requisition. Can you put it into the right hands? . . .

29 January   T.J. to Sidney Webb
I am glad there is a chance of your standing for London University. I shall at once see to the forms you have sent me being put before some London graduates. My wife is a London M.A., and she will, I am sure, 'get busy'. . . .

8 February   A very lively discussion at to-day's Cabinet on our relation to the Bolsheviks, the Poles and Ukrainians, and the other parties who are now squabbling in Russia.

The P.M. seemed very much alive, almost as fresh and fit as though he had enjoyed a long holiday. He sat in his usual place with Bonar Law on his left and Hankey and me on his right. Opposite were Lord Derby, Lord Robert Cecil, Milner, Curzon, Balfour, Harding, General Macdonogh (Director of Military Intelligence), Philip Kerr, and Ormsby-Gore. Barnes was absent attending a Trade Union Conference on man-power. The subject had been up the day before, and had been adjourned to enable Balfour to submit a draft telegram to Lockhart,[2] our intermediary at Petrograd since Sir George

[1] He enclosed a letter from the Labour Party Executive to the Prime Minister.
[2] (Sir) R. H. Bruce Lockhart, then head of the Special Mission to the Soviet Government; arrested, imprisoned, and exchanged for Litvinov in October 1918.

Buchanan returned. Lockhart wanted to have a more official status in dealing with Trotsky, and the suggestion was that he might be called Political Agent or Official Intermediary, or some such name which would commit us less than that of Ambassador.

Balfour started off. He was more precise and vigorous than usual, and he was obviously prepared. He wished to raise three questions, firstly, the enlistment of the Russian subjects in the east end of London, against which the Bolshevik Ambassador, Litvinov, was protesting, and threatening to publish the correspondence on the matter. It had been referred on the 23rd January, to the War Office, but Derby had forgotten to call a Committee.

'We have a bad case,' said A.J.B. 'I told the War Cabinet that. The position is very awkward. We have done nothing to meet the Bolsheviks. How am I to carry on a controversy with them? I sent in a memorandum about it. The War Office protested, and I think Cave also did. Now the Bolshevik representative sends me this message. It is very awkward, but relatively it is a small matter. The next is more important. One of the most important decisions which will have to be made by the War Cabinet, is the attitude to be adopted towards the Poles. On the previous evening Robert Cecil, the D.M.I., and I met Count Horodysky.[1] The Count pointed out that there were now three separate Polish armies, amounting to about 60,000 men. They were well armed, well fed and paid, and very keen. In addition there was a Roumanian army of between 300,000 and 400,000, well drilled, armed, and prepared to follow their Generals. Are we, or are we not, going to use these for the war? What was to be our relation to the Bolsheviks? There was a rumour that the Poles had captured the Bolshevik Headquarters Staff. Then thirdly there was a telegram that morning from the Bolsheviks, complaining of our refusal to allow stores to be taken from Vladivostock. If that could be settled diplomatically, it would be a great advantage to do so. But how about an agreement with the Poles? Such an agreement would not necessarily mean a break with the Bolsheviks. We would only acknowledge the Bolsheviks where they were *de facto* in power. I urge that the War Office press on the east end affair, and secondly, that the War Cabinet considers its policy towards the Poles. I asked the Director of Military Intelligence to prepare a draft telegram to Foch for our consideration.' Here A.J.B. read the draft.

P.M. 'There is a very important telegram from Lockhart, suggesting the desirability of giving a visa to the passports asked for by the Bolshevik Government for Messrs. Petrov and Chicherin to visit England, and of recognising the Bolshevik Government.'

A.J.B. read through this telegram.

P.M. 'I again repeat what I said yesterday. We are taking a great responsibility in not listening to the man on the spot. On three occasions when Buchanan gave us advice, e.g. about War Aims and Stockholm, we didn't take it, and we were wrong.'

A.J.B. 'I don't think it can properly be said that we rejected his advice.'

[1] Polish Representative in London.

Robert Cecil 'My view is that we have taken too much the view of the man on the spot. It was a mistake not to back Korniloff.'[1]

P.M. 'Both may be true. It may be that, to use a golfing term, we ought to have followed the stroke right through.'

R.C. 'I believe there was a moment when a strong telegram to Kerensky, "You must co-operate with Korniloff", might have saved the situation.'

P.M. 'The soldiers might have refused. Here you have got emphatic advice.'

A.J.B. 'On what spot is Lockhart? Can he speak for all Russia? He says nothing about the Poles. He is not the Labour man on the spot here. He knows about Petrograd, but has to get his views of other places from other men.'

B.L. 'What about the attitude of the Bolsheviks to Germany? And their effect on Germany?'

A.J.B. 'Lockhart dogmatizes about the effect the Bolsheviks are producing in Germany.'

P.M. 'My view is that Russia is our most powerful ally now in Germany, and especially in Austria.'

Milner 'I don't see it. It is marvellous how miserably feeble the effect of Socialism in Germany is.'

P.M. 'I don't doubt Lockhart's view as to the influence of the Bolsheviks in Germany. Dittmar's explanation was that the Bolsheviks' proposal of no annexations and no indemnities had been refused at Brest-Litovsk. The moment German workmen believed that peace was not to be concluded, they revolted.' *The P.M. then read Balfour's draft.*

* * * *

A.J.B. 'The reason I put that in is that the atmosphere at Petrograd makes Lockhart regard Bolsheviks as angels of light.'

P.M. 'Rather proves they are! The criticism of the Bolsheviks always comes from those 3,000 miles away from them.'

R.C. 'Read Captain Proctor's memo. about them.'

A.J.B. 'I make a modest suggestion that the Bolsheviks are not angels of light!'

P.M. 'We want the Bolsheviks to make themselves a greater nuisance to the Germans than to us.'

Here Hardinge proposed that Lockhart should be called an 'official intermediary'.

R.C. 'When Milner and I went to Paris we agreed a line of policy to pursue; one part of it was to send Lockhart as unofficial agent, and treat Bolshevik Government and Rada at Kiev as representing local authorities. Much to my regret I am not in agreement with the Prime Minister on this point, so probably I am wrong.'

A.J.B. 'That is an unnecessary display of modesty.'

[1] Appointed C.-in-C. by Kerensky but then interned when his army programme proved unpalatable. Freed after the Bolshevik Revolution, he formed a volunteer army and was killed in the Caucasus in March 1918.

R.C. 'My feeling has been that we have followed too much the worship of the rising sun.'

P.M. 'That is, in acknowledging the *de facto* Government?'

R.C. 'I say stand by your friends.'

B.L. 'That's moral but not expedient.'

R.C. 'Don't let us get into metaphysics. There is not a word about our obligations to the Poles, Roumanians, Armenians, Cossacks—that is the great vice of Lockhart's mind just now. He is looking at it from Petrograd and forgetting Russia. It is fatal to hearten Bolsheviks and dishearten Roumania. I am against any step suggesting we are going hat in hand to the Bolsheviks, as if afraid of them. It would dishearten Roumania. It is important to get the Bolsheviks to make peace with Roumania.'

P.M. 'We sent a telegram about Roumania from Paris.'

Hardinge 'It was sent to Lockhart.'

R.C. 'We must not betray the Roumanians and Poles at this moment. Count Horodysky begged us to do nothing for a week or ten days. I agree that the right thing is for the Poles to take their place on the flank of Roumania. The first thing is to look after our friends. . . . For the moment we can make no public or official approach to the Bolsheviks.'

P.M. 'I am with you. Lockhart must be told. . . .'

A.J.B. 'I don't see any difference with Robert Cecil except that he uses language which suggests that we are abandoning our friends. That's too strong. To abandon friends is treachery. To do something for your friends which they do not like is not treachery. The reason for the delay is the Poles; Horodysky implored us to do nothing for a few days.'

P.M. 'Take the analogy of Greece. We did not abandon our friends, but put ourselves in a better position to help our friends. In Greece you had two communities led by the King and by Venizelos. The King was our enemy—Venizelos our friend. The King handed over vital positions, divisions, and guns to the enemy. What did we do? We recognised both, but we utilised our position at Athens to protect Venizelos.[1] If we had not been there Venizelos would have had a worse time. Take the case of Roumania. We decided at Paris to make representations about Roumania to Trotsky. I should think after this telegram Lockhart would be in a better position to deal with Trotsky, and to protect Roumania. I don't see that we are doing more for Trotsky than for the Ukrainians—they are our worst enemies. Kaledin[2] is funking—Alexieff[3] is fighting. We must not be too sure that the Poles are our friends. They are not fighting Germans. The Poles are fighting the Bolsheviks. You have an army of Polish landowners fighting Socialists. I accept the Foreign Secretary's position.' . . .

* * * *

[1] Eleutherios Venizelos (1864–1936); Prime Minister of Greece five times between 1910 and 1933. An ardent supporter of the Allied cause in the war, while King Constantine sympathized with Germany. He represented Greece at the peace conference and was in close sympathy with Lloyd George until 1922.

[2] Alexei Kaledin kept the Cossacks loyal to the Tsar but shot himself in February 1918.

[3] General M. V. Alexieff, retired C.-in-C., helped Korniloff and Denekin to form the Volunteer Army on the Don in 1918, to fight the Red Army.

The decision was to adopt Balfour's draft, with Kerr's addition, and the closing sentences of R. Cecil's. The talk was swift and animated throughout. After the meeting I had a few minutes with the P.M. . . . 'You see the moment we get to fundamentals we are "Poles' apart" '—Extending his hands as far asunder as he could and laughing in his merry way, having thoroughly enjoyed himself and almost inviting one to tell him 'What a good boy you are.'

8 February   T.J. to E.T.J.   *2 Whitehall Gardens*
I have heard over the 'phone that the Council has invited Principal Griffiths to remain on another year. This is a victory for the 'Rhondda Press'. And so far as I can see now, it is goodbye to Cardiff College. I went to Hankey and told him the news at once. He was *most* kind—glad I was to stay, as great things would be happening in the coming year, wished me specially to be about at the Reconstruction period, said I had and was exercising much power here for the country as a whole as also for Wales.

8 February   Sir Thomas Hughes[1] to T.J.   *Cardiff*
The Donkeys! *And* they'll rue the day's work before the year is up!

For *your* sake I'm glad you have the respite because I know how you enjoy every minute of your life at the hub of the wheel. And for *ours* too because there's still a chance for us. But for *Wales'* sake I'm sorry and, I think, most of all for righteousness' sake and cleanliness' sake!

12 February   Considerable agitation this week at the Cabinet over the appearance of Colonel Repington's article in the 'Morning Post'.[2] Hankey mentioned it to me this morning shortly before going across to the Cabinet Meeting at 12.30, where a draft of the P.M.'s speech was to be discussed. Hankey said that the P.M. has a bad cold and was very difficult to manage. 'I wish,' said Hankey, 'that I had not gone away for the weekend, as Derby got at the P.M., with the result that the P.M. offered Sir William Robertson Henry Wilson's job at Versailles; Wilson[3] to come back here as the Chief of the Imperial General Staff. Robertson has refused, and the P.M. fears that he has seen Asquith. I don't think there has been an opportunity for this as he has been to Eastbourne for the weekend. The P.M. wants to mention the Robertson affair in the House, but I have been trying to dissuade him. Yesterday the Cabinet, after consultation with Sir Gordon Hewart,[4] decided to seize the machinery of the 'Morning Post', but after last night's meeting Cave saw the P.M., and put up legal and other obstacles, and the P.M. wobbled.'

I said that for a long time I had felt Derby to be a public danger, and Hankey that he himself had been wondering whether Milner might not be sent to the War Office—which seemed to me a good suggestion.

---

[1] Chairman of the Welsh Insurance Commission.
[2] Criticizing the conduct of the war.
[3] (Sir) Henry Wilson (1864–1922). He did supersede Sir William Robertson as C.I.G.S. in 1918 and became a member of the War Cabinet. He was murdered by Sinn Feiners in London in 1922.
[4] The Solicitor-General.

I left Hankey and had a few minutes with Barnes before he went across to No. 10. I urged him to force the issue of the 'Morning Post', as it was most unfair to bully the weak Labour papers, and let the rich Tory papers go scot free. Barnes agreed, but he has no fight in him. He ought to offer to resign, but he gives one the impression of being far too comfortable for anything so heroic.

In the afternoon Clement Jones told me that Milner had sent for Ormsby-Gore[1] and had discussed his resignation, because Milner thinks Robertson ought to go.

20 March There was an amusing discussion at the Cabinet to-day of the Honours question, in view of a debate in the Lords, raised by Selborne.

Curzon reminded the Cabinet that he had promised that the P.M. would satisfy himself that in giving honours no question of money was involved. Secondly, a statement of the reasons for which the Honours were given would be made in the Press. J. T. Davies, the P.M.'s Secretary, thought the promise had been met by the brief particulars published on 1st January.

'It is really very difficult,' said Curzon 'to say why anybody does get Honours. Why is F. E. Smith made a Baronet? All that one can say is that he is Attorney-General—of Lavery, that he is a painter. Then take X. . . .'

Bonar Law. 'What more can you say?'

Curzon. 'I will put that question to the House; "what more do you want?" ' . . .

*   *   *   *

Bonar Law. 'You must not pretend to say that these Honours are not to be given for Party services, but only not for corrupt services.'

Curzon. 'Why are any of us made anything? It is very difficult to say.'

*   *   *   *

Later, there was a short discussion on the League of Nations. Barnes wanted to know what line Curzon would take in reply to a discussion at the House.

Curzon to Barnes. 'If you can give me your views, I'll be glad to hear them. The men who spoke last night are pacifists, Parmoor, Loreburn, and Lansdowne. I don't intend to say anything condemnatory. The principle has been conceded. I thought of dealing with the difficulties. The speakers last night disagreed among themselves. Parmoor said all the Powers must come in at once. Parker, who is a judge and is not much of a politician, held that in the long run Germany and Austria will have to come in. 'It all depends' Curzon went on 'how the war is going to end. The League of Nations [idea] assumes we are victorious. The limitation of armaments is at the bottom of the whole thing. It is all very well to talk of sanction and economic pressure. No sanction is worth anything short of a police force. Lansdowne was against reduction of armaments. He is simply out for peace.'

After the meeting Hankey and I had a talk with Barnes, Hankey referring to a paper he had written, supporting the idea of using Versailles as a nucleus

[1] W.A.G. Ormsby-Gore (later Lord Harlech), Milner's P.P.S. and an assistant secretary to the War Cabinet.

of the League's machinery. He referred to the Foreign Office Committee, before which he had given evidence a few days ago. The Committee, he felt, was dominated by legalists and diplomatists belonging to the old gang at the Foreign Office.

The P.M. was not at this Cabinet, as he was pre-occupied with the ship-building debate which was to come on during the afternoon. He feels that the critics of the Government on this issue are genuinely concerned, and that it is not 'engineered' by the Asquithians.

*   *   *   *

At 6 o'clock I went to the Ministry of Food to see Wise. Wintour, Wise, and E. H. M. Lloyd and two or three others have, during the war, been respon-sible for developing a thorough-going control of raw materials; first at the Contracts Department of the War Office, and secondly, at the Ministry of Food. They tackled wool, jute, leather, at the War Office. Meat, butter, margarine, milk, and so forth at Palace Chambers. They were the first to recognise that control of the final product and prices could only be made effec-tive by controlling production at every stage. They have absolutely eliminated middle-men and speculators, and these disgruntled sections are combining in an attack via Derby and the P.M. For weeks there have been rumours that the control of supplies would be taken out the hands of the Food Controller, and that he would be restricted to rationing. Rhondda has repeatedly tried to secure the control of the purchase of army meat, but has failed. After much pressure on Derby and Sir John Cowans,[1] there is some likelihood of the army meat rations being substantially reduced and brought nearer to what is allowed to our manual workers at home. At the moment the Ministry of Food is not unpopular in the country and there is a rumour that Rhondda will be glad to slide over and become Minister of Health. . . .

10 *April*   At this morning's Cabinet, General Maurice[2] described the new German attack around Armentières,[3] and said he thought a new crisis was approaching, as the Germans had fresh divisions, and ours were tired, having been brought up from the Somme; further, they were reinforced by young drafts unfamiliar with the ground. This led to a discussion of the comparative rifle strength of ourselves and the enemy. The figures worked out exactly evenly at 1,450,000 on the Western Front. Maurice, who has always im-pressed me as very balanced in his appreciations, said he had spoken to Sir

[1] An administrator of great ability who carried out smoothly the expansion of army services during the war.

[2] Major-General Sir Frederick Maurice, Director of Military Operations, Imperial General Staff, 1915–18.

[3] The first German attack had been on the Somme on 21 March. By 23 March the Germans had advanced forty miles and the British army faced a major defeat. Lloyd George took over the War Office, shipped the reserves from England to France in a week, and appealed for and won President Wilson's assent to the engagement of American troops. On 26 March Milner crossed to France to restore co-operation with Foch and on 3 April Lloyd George gave Foch 'the strategic direction of military operations'.
The second German attack began on 9 April but gained less ground and left Ludendorff with a dangerous salient to protect. Haig talked of fighting 'with our backs to the wall'. Pétain continued to obstruct Foch and to proclaim a defeatist attitude.

Henry Wilson over the 'phone, suggesting the bringing up of French reserves. This led to a discussion on how far there was now, under Foch, a single battle front, and the P.M. remarked with great emphasis 'Unless the French treat this battle as as much a French as a British battle, then we are beaten', and went on 'the real trouble now is between Pétain and Foch. I told Clemenceau[1] that, and he said "Leave that to me". rather implying that it is no special concern of ours. But I told him it was my business as well as his.' It was then suggested that the P.M. should send a letter to Clemenceau, and the P.M. suggested that Milner should go over if necessary, with the letter. It was important that Clemenceau should be seen; phrases in a letter were apt to give offence; it would be better for Milner to go over and talk to Clemenceau. Maurice pointed out that Wilson was to-day seeing Clemenceau, and that it might be better to wait. It was agreed that Maurice should speak to Wilson at lunch time, and ascertain how he had got on with Clemenceau; it could then be decided whether Milner should go at once or not. Milner was willing to go to France, and to stay there for some days, on behalf of the Cabinet.

The P.M. recalled a question he had put last week to Haig: 'Which would you prefer—that we should press the French Government and Foch to make an attack south of the Somme, or that we should press them to send divisions to help you? He and Laurence replied that they would prefer us to press the French to make an attack. It doesn't look as if they were right.'

Milner. 'We may fall between two stools. Their attack which they are preparing might be a better diversion. It is very difficult for us to interefere with the Generals at every critical moment.'

P.M. 'Whether or not Pétain—who has a provincial mind—is interfering with Foch—that is the whole and the only point. Wilson can find out whether Pétain is standing in Foch's way. If Foch is Generalissimo for us, he is also for the French.'

Hankey reminded the P.M. that Haig asked that it should be put on record that he wanted a French attack. Foch and Pétain had said: 'We regret we agree.'

Maurice. 'Five days ago they (the French) said they would not be ready till the 12th.'

Milner. 'It is just as well for me or somebody to go across. You would be more reassured. We want the French to help us. If they could make an attack in the next few days it *might* be better than to divert divisions to us.'

P.M. 'So long as you are convinced that Pétain regarded it as *one* fight.'

Maurice. 'The Germans would not mind giving up ground on the south. We cannot give way one inch in the north. What I should fear most is their falling back more or less willingly in the south before the French.'

Derby then gave some estimates of the casualties in the battle from 21st March to 6th April, viz. 7,000 officers and 105,000 other ranks, definitely known. In one of the hospitals out of 5,000 cases, there had only been 8 deaths; 4 of them from gas gangrene, and not one from tetanus.

[1] Georges Clemenceau (1841–1929); Premier of France 1906–9, 1917–20; presided at the Peace Conference, 1919.

It has always been most difficult for the Cabinet to extract information about casualties from the War Office. More than once I have heard the P.M. speak very sharply to the W.O. people about our having to learn from the Germans first of all the number of casualties, and prisoners.

Admiral Hope, Deputy First Sea Lord, then, in about a minute, gave the sinkings for the previous day. Several days the Naval Report has been most favourable—hardly any losses.

(Zimmern told me at lunch today that Curtis was returning from India and his boat was torpedoed. The torpedo was seen, and the ship's gun fired at it in the water, and blew its head off, and saved the ship.)

Just as Hope finished his brief daily tale, a telegram came in from Mr. Duke to say that De Valera was counselling the Sinn Fein organisations to oppose conscription, by strikes of transport workers, and shooting of soldiers and police. The Cabinet spent about two minutes on this. The P.M. remarked: 'That is a thing the Home Forces must see to. They have tried dock strikes here also, and we must make it clear to every dock labourer that if he isn't working at the docks, he will be in the army.' Barnes and Derby were requested to see Sexton and Ben Tillet. . . .

*   *   *   *

As the Cabinet rose, Derby asked the P.M. how he had got on at the man-power debate on the previous night. I felt the P.M. was conscious that his speech had not been a success, and that he was trying to make the best of it. One rather missed the buoyant, cheerful note, so characteristic of him. He replied to Derby that the opposition was less than he had expected. 'Carson came down on the side of conscription,[1] and exasperated the Irish in the last degree. It looked as if the Irish were trying to work themselves up into a frenzy.' Bonar Law thought that Devlin[2] was bidding against Dillon[3] for the leadership of the Party. The P.M. thought that Healy[4] was the really formidable opponent, and that the first part of his speech, where he criticised our generalship, was important. 'He took the same line', said the P.M., 'as the Manchester Guardian to-day, namely, that the case for more men is not made out, but that the case for change of leadership is.' This delicate question of leadership was not pursued; the P.M.'s not infrequent references to the

[1] In response to back-bench protests at Ireland's freedom from conscription, Lloyd George offered a bargain: the Convention having failed, Ireland could have Home Rule but only at the price of conscription. Carson at first opposed this. The Irish M.P.s refused the bargain and withdrew, linking up with Sinn Fein. Conscription was denounced by the Roman Catholic hierarchy and on 23 April a twenty-four-hour general strike shut down the whole of Ireland except Belfast.

Conscription was never actually applied and Lloyd George dropped the idea of Home Rule. But as A. J. P. Taylor says, 'this was the decisive moment at which Ireland seceded from the Union'.

[2] Joseph Devlin (1871–1934), Irish journalist and nationalist politician, M.P. at Westminster (1902–22).

[3] John Dillon (1851–1927), at this time chairman of the Irish Nationalist Party. He was defeated at East Mayo later in the year and retired into private life.

[4] T. M. Healy (1855–1931), Irish nationalist leader, journalist, and elder statesman, who supported the policy of settlement by peaceful means.

Manchester Guardian always produce an uncomfortable feeling at the Cabinet. The P.M. never misses reading the M.G.'s articles by 'A Student of War' (Sidebotham). The P.M. went on to point out that the Allies required more men because we are not one, but three armies. 'Haig is just like Pétain. If Haig had English divisions down in the south defending Belfort, he would have gone to their help. We must get these Generals into a new frame of mind about the unity of the battle front.'

As we separated, Bonar Law said that the man-power Bill would be through next Tuesday night.

This meeting, which lasted just over one hour, was one of the most depressing I have attended. Both Curzon and Milner were very gloomy; Smuts and Barnes said nothing. Balfour, who was present most of the time, and sat at my side, solaced himself with half a sheet of note paper, on which he drew a sketch of a big tree in the foreground and some distant hills in the background! The P.M. was all the time working hard on his blotting paper! It was difficult to believe that in such an atmosphere the gravity of the situation on the Lys was realised. Part of this depression which one felt was, no doubt, due to the physical reaction of the P.M. after his speech of the previous day.

I saw Philip Kerr at lunch, and found him equally worried, and prepared to bet the Germans would be in Calais in three weeks. We agreed that one fundamental weakness was the P.M.'s attempt to keep his hands on every lever. Kerr thought that Derby was retained at the War Office simply because the P.M. knew he could use him as a tool, whereas if Milner went there, the P.M. would have to let go some of his power. Similarly with Auckland Geddes[1]—the P.M. knew that he could get his own way.

I found Hankey similarly depressed. He had tried, either at breakfast or lunch, to persuade the P.M. to take a more conciliatory line with Ireland; to take advantage of some indications in Devlin's speech that, given Home Rule, Devlin and Co. would do their best for recruiting, but the P.M. was quite implacable. We discussed, with Leslie Wilson,[2] a plan by which a Recruiting Committee might be set up for Ireland, containing representatives of different parties, and Hankey was to try and persuade the P.M. to adopt it.

12 April   When I entered the Cabinet room this morning, Henry Wilson was explaining to the P.M. the loss of Merville, on a big map. As the C.I.G.S. had given the military situation to the P.M. before the meeting began, we heard little about it. The P.M. asked Wilson who was keeping an eye on the Generals on the Western Front, to see that the good ones were advanced, and the bad ones degraded. The C.I.G.S. replied that Haig was, whereupon the P.M. said that Haig might be a good General himself, but that he was not good at choosing his men. The estimated casualties of the Germans up to the 8th April was 250,000 as against 150,000 for us.

---

[1] Sir Auckland (later Lord) Geddes (1879–1954); Director-General of National Service 1917–19; Ambassador to the United States 1920–4; brother of Eric Geddes.
[2] Of the Ministry of Labour.

The P.M. read a letter which he had just received from Lord Reading.[1] It said that the British retreat and German success had come as a great shock to President Wilson; that Wilson was willing to render all possible help, but that his administrative machinery was defective.[2] Reading said Wilson would be much influenced by the recommendations of the Supreme War Council, and the C.I.G.S. undertook to assemble it at once.

There was some talk of moving a formal vote of thanks to the United States in the House of Commons, but the P.M. objected to going beyond what he and Curzon had said in their speeches, because if much more were made of the coming of the American troops, the House would ask 'Why all this fuss over man-power at home?', and Milner reminded the Cabinet that the Germans were already saying that we were screaming to the Americans for help.

We passed to Ireland. The P.M. said the temperature was much cooler in the House on Thursday. Dillon had made an impassioned speech to his followers in a private meeting, in favour of good behaviour in the House. Henderson (moved I think by Barnes) had seen Dillon on Thursday, and believed that he had mollified him a bit. Derby announced that he would bring away gradually all the Irish Reserve Battalions from Ireland and put English ones in their place. Bonar Law said that Geddes did not believe it worth while keeping the priests in the Bill, because of the opposition it would arouse. Barnes objected to this concession. The P.M. pointed out that the priest meant more in Ireland than he did here. If they were taken, the women would lose their heads. Carson was against taking them. The P.M. said that a Nationalist member had been overheard to say, on the other hand, that if anything could have reconciled him to conscription in Ireland, it was that the priests would be taken. 'They are taking priests in France,' the P.M. went on, 'but the French are an infidel nation.' At which the C.I.G.S. chimed in 'The French churches are full of women.' 'Wales was rather shocked at it,' added the P.M. Bonar Law had received an impassioned letter from Hugh Cecil against it, and Bonar Law added in his cynical fashion, 'He considers religion an essential occupation.' He advised leaving it to Cave and Geddes to decide, according to the temper of the House. Cardinal Bourne had seen the P.M. and had pointed out that the Church of England was the only Church which could afford to have two or three men running a Church. The P.M., who had been for it some days ago, had shifted his ground, and said that a certain amount of feeling would be outraged by bringing ministers into the bloody business of war. Ultimately, it was agreed to leave it to Cave and Geddes; Barnes disliking this decision.

Next came the question of conscripting M.P.s. Derby said nothing in the world would give him greater pleasure, and the P.M. rattled off a list of obnoxious critics of the War Office (including David Davies), whom Derby would like to put in the firing line. Derby found no support. It was agreed to leave it to Members to decide whether to go or stop.

[1] Then Ambassador to the United States.
[2] This in fact indicated the opposition of General Pershing, commanding the U.S. forces in France, to committing his still unprepared troops.

We then got to the main subject of the meeting—the Government's policy in the East. The Cabinet's decisions of what to do in Russia are always of a most inconclusive character, because Milner and Robert Cecil utterly disbelieve in Trotsky, while the P.M. holds that there is something to hope from Trotsky and the Bolsheviks. The Government's advisers are similarly divided; General Knox being on Cecil's side, Lockhart on the P.M.'s side, and General Poole leaning to Lockhart's side.[1] The situation is complicated by the unwillingness of the Americans to co-operate with Japan at Vladivostock. All the discussion had special reference to Murmansk and Archangel. Should we send cruisers and a landing force to these ports, to protect our stores, and cut the line at Kola, should the White Guards threaten from Finland? General Poole, on whom Milner relied, was in favour of our securing a definite foothold at Murmansk, and the Americans were willing to send a cruiser there. 'At Vladivostock', Milner urged 'you were threatening to take something from Russia. At Murmansk you are saving a port for the Russians, and the local Soviet will welcome your help.'

P.M. 'I fear that we are treating the Bolshevik Government as though it were no Government. Under the old regime you would not have gone to Murmansk and Vladivostock without the Tsar's permission. You are out for the same policy as during the French Revolution—seizing Toulon, and one place after another.'

(Russia is never discussed without the French Revolution being drawn in sooner or later! Each member of the Cabinet regards himself as an authority on the French Revolution!)

Curzon. 'I am against these flirtations with Trotsky.'

R.C. 'The local Soviet was, until quite recently, anxious that we should land and protect them. The Central Soviet disagreed, and Chicherin spoke to Lockhart, and Lockhart hoped we would be tactful.'

Smuts (who very rarely speaks) referred to the Conference at Volodga, where it was urged that intervention should be Allied intervention, and with the assent of the Russian Government. 'Should we not get the consent of the Russian Government?'

R.C. 'I agree, but ought we to delay so long as to allow time for the Germans and Finns to get there?'

Milner. 'You want the force there to act if wanted.'

———

Milner. 'Can we test Trotsky? We want to hold the railway for Russia. If he says no, then we can wash our hands of him.'

P.M. 'You cannot put a proposition in that way to any country. Our first and proper attitude is that laid down by the Foreign Secretary. "Deal with the *de facto* Government, whether it is Tsarist or Bolshevik." '

Milner (with some heat, which with Milner means that his voice, instead of rising, almost vanishes!). 'I have not put it in diplomatic language as I am not a diplomatic agent to Trotsky. Is it not reasonable to tell Trotsky: there is a danger of this port being taken by his enemies and ours, and as we are

[1] These were stationed in Murmansk, Moscow, and Archangel respectively.

59

going to co-operate, would he object to our holding the port? If he says "No, I would rather you did not interfere", then I should draw my own conclusions.'

P.M. 'Why not have our ships there with troops, and in case of danger we could land our troops?'

And this, with some modifications, was the agreement reached.

Then they went on to talk of Archangel, Eric Geddes wanting to know definitely what was the Government's policy. The C.I.G.S. urged that Archangel was part of the Russian problem, and that problem was one problem: how to prevent the Germans bringing more divisions from Russia to the Western Front.

*   *   *   *

C.I.G.S. 'This place will belong to us or to the Boche. There is no more chance that Russia will have a military force that will bother the Germans in this war. I think the Japs should come to the Urals, and we should take energetic action. Unless we do that, we shall see division after division going to the West, to Hazebrouck, to Calais.'

P.M. 'What more can we do with America hostile?'

R.C. 'I fear America is hostile. Having definitely made up our minds that we cannot act without America, the only way to do is to try via Trotsky, but I am a heretic, for I don't believe in Trotsky.'

P.M. 'No, I am the only heretic in this room.'

C.I.G.S. 'I don't believe or disbelieve.'

R.C. 'I would press the questions of Murmansk, Armenia, Caucasus, Poles, and ask Trotsky, why are you always on the side of Germany? I would push Trotsky to the utmost.'

Hankey, who rarely intervenes: 'Has the problem been put *as a whole* to Trotsky and Wilson?'

Curzon. 'Lockhart is with Trotsky; We have Wardrop at Moscow; Woodhouse at Petrograd; we have other ambassadors at Volodga, on the whole taking the side of Trotsky. We ought to have our representative there. Our representation in Russia is chaotic.'

P.M. 'I am impressed that the men on the spot are all on one side.'

Milner. 'Poole thinks the Bolsheviks can be led.'

P.M. 'Could the Japs march to the Urals? Semenov has turned up with 300 "coolie brigands"—these have to go on to Lake —— where he will then have 50 more!! That is how you are going to prevent 20 German divisions going to Hazebrouck! America is sending divisions to the Western Front. I shall be surprised if we don't get 300,000 infantry. Better a certain American support than a doubtful Japanese support.' (To C.I.G.S.) 'Gather all these propositions together; draft something which can be presented as a whole to Wilson; point out how important it is that Russia should be energised to give trouble to the Germans, and why Wilson should join us in pressing Trotsky.'

This was the decision reached.

Milner. 'Lockhart does not keep our end up with Trotsky.'

R.C. 'He is a very young man where everybody is a little mad.'

P.M. 'But even Poole is not without a dram of insanity because you say he is rather pro-Bolshevik.'

R.C. 'So was Henderson.'

P.M. 'And Albert Thomas came back a Bolshevik!'

R.C. 'And has ever since been trying to explain it away!'

15 April   First meeting of Committee on Irish Bill held today with Walter Long[1] in the chair. The members present: Curzon, Duke, Addison, Cave, Hewart, Barnes, Smuts, and Herbert Fisher. Liddell, Batterbee, Adams, and T.J.

Walter Long opened by voicing feeling of House of Commons where, he said, members saw little chance of getting a Bill through which did not fit into a federal system.

Cave insisted that the Committee was free and not tied to the Convention Report. Federation was one way of avoiding controversy.

There followed a debate on the purpose of the Committee. Long thought it should produce a Bill which would pass the House of Commons. Curzon and Fisher wanted to rule out a federal solution, for which England, Scotland, and Wales were not ripe. Long thought the only chance for the Bill was to give it a federal complexion. With this, the Ulster Unionists would accept one Parliament for Ireland. The Committee decided, because of the urgency of the question, to proceed with a draft Bill, leaving the main debate open.

16 April   Cabinet had decided that best plan would be for Long as Chairman to draft a bill and submit it to his Committee for discussion. At the second meeting today he said the Committee must make up its mind on three questions.

1. Ulster Minority
2. Financial Proposals
3. Form of representation of Irish people in the Imperial Parliament.

20 April   After a long debate T.J. told Hankey that he thought the Government's Irish policy was 'a mad one' and Hankey replied that he was 'fed up with the Irish'.

30 April   League of Nations Lunch to-day at the Carlton, at David Davies' invitation. Present: Wickham Steed of the 'Times', just back from three weeks in Rome, Arthur Henderson, Garvin, Sir William Collins, J. H. Thomas, A. F. Whyte of the 'New Europe', Delisle Burns, J. A. Spender of the 'Westminster', C. A. McCurdy, M.P., Sir Willoughby Dickinson, M.P., M. Roger Mourize, Mark Sykes, D.D., and T.J.

D.D. has for some time past been trying to galvanise into greater activity the existing League of Nations Society of which Dickinson and Aneurin

---

[1] Walter (later Viscount) Long (1854–1924); Conservative M.P.; Colonial Secretary 1916–18, First Lord of the Admiralty 1918–21. He was a contender for the leadership of the Conservative Party against Austen Chamberlain in 1911 when Bonar Law emerged as a compromise choice.

Williams are the leading lights. He has been for immediate universal propaganda, while they have been afraid of weakening the country's resistance to the enemy, and of being mistaken for pacifists, because the L. of N. idea meets with ready acceptance from the latter. A week or two ago D.D. put down £5,000 for propaganda, and is by way of getting control of the Society. He has elaborated a scheme on a big international scale which will require about £20,000 a year to run. I introduced Delisle Burns[1] to him as a possible secretary of the foreign section of the scheme, and walking away from the lunch to-day D.B. said he thought he would take on the job.

*   *   *   *

J. H. Thomas said he found railwaymen much less easy to move now than in August, 1914, and feared that if a German peace offensive started, many of the men would be for coming to terms. It was, therefore, all-important to counter such tendencies by L. of N. propaganda.

Spender[2] feared that without such a fighting creed of peace we should be again at the mercy of the dynastic and diplomatic school when the Peace Congress arrived.

Garvin,[3] in a very earnest and very fluent speech, showed how the aeroplane had abolished the old squabbling over frontiers, and if multiplied indefinitely, the tyranny of the flying instrument would always menace the little nations. Hence the importance of moral demarcation rather than geographical in the future.

9 *May*   Irish Committee. Chamberlain profoundly impressed with financial difficulties of federal scheme. . . .

A draft bill had been circulated but without financial proposals. It included Ulster Committee and other features to which Barnes objected as going beyond the Convention. Chamberlain pointed out that with the Report must be read the Prime Minister's letter. Ulster could have had any terms she liked if she had given a firm offer to come in. Convention had left many difficulties unfaced.

Long insisted that the P.M. had urged him to see the Committee carried out in full the pledges made to Ulster. . . . 'We are making a great concession. You won't get a bill through which does not contain safeguards for Ulster. I would vote against it and leave the Government. The Committee must either report to Cabinet that it could not agree or. . . . All we have done is to draw up a bill which is consistent with federal system.'

Barnes thought an Ulster Committee an insult to a high-spirited nation. . . . Addison argued that the more generous the Bill was as a whole to the Irish Parliament the less the Nationalists could object to the safeguards for Ulster. Smuts agreed. . . .

[1] Cecil Delisle Burns (1879–1942), the social philosopher, at this time working in the Ministry of Reconstruction. He did not take the job, though for a few months in 1919 he went to the League of Nations Labour Office (precursor of the I.L.O.).

[2] J. A. Spender, editor of the *Westminster Gazette*.

[3] J. L. Garvin, editor of *The Observer*.

Long replied that the bill in any form would receive no support in Ireland. Ulster would oppose, led by Carson; Nationalists would not attend; the moderate Nationalists would fear the Sinn Feiners. Carson would not make up his mind till the bill was introduced. He would be asked to abstain. The Irish Attorney would resign the day the bill was introduced and he would not be re-elected. 'You will have no Irish members.'

Cave suggested two possible ways:

1. Clean cut—six counties. Ulster would put up with that.
2. Try to get near to the clean cut, but giving Ulster advantage in Parliament for a special term of fifteen years to break the fall.

* * * *

Chamberlain pointed out that the reason why it was proposed to apply conscription to Ireland was that the issue of compulsion had been raised and the Nationalists had replied with a direct challenge to the unity of the Empire. To withdraw from compulsion was to surrender unity.

Smuts replied: 'In abstract principle you are right; but facts are actuated by prudence and wisdom; these are conjoint, associate measures. We have had so many failures over Home Rule in peace time that we are not justified in raising the issue at this terrible time unless there is substantial agreement. These safeguards ought to be submitted to both parties; if both say, "To hell with your safeguards", then the Government is beating the air, and letting loose forces of civil war when we are fighting for our life. I go further: this is a big imperial question. Surely it is wise for Government to say that it will consult the Imperial War Conference next month. As to associate measures, we should hold over conscription too. I do not think you can apply conscription to Ireland without forcing civil war. You can have it in peace time.'

Long. 'You won't have civil war, [but] it is idle, criminal, to apply conscription to Ireland today. I governed Ireland with two-thirds against me and one-third for me. But today the Government of Ireland, Lord Chief Justice, are against you. The situation is a new one. The Government is in a serious position. If they abandon policy openly, only resignation is possible. There is an alternative. The new Government of Ireland has not been sworn in. It will have to restore order and stamp out intrigue. If we wait until after Whitsun we may have a different state of affairs in Ireland. Must get Ireland to think of the war. Give the Irish Government a chance of securing recruits by some arrangement. We may get a total change in six weeks' time Meanwhile the Committee could proceed to put the Bill into shape.'

9 May   T.J.'s report of the proceedings above (9 May) for the War Cabinet, showing the contrast between official and unofficial reporting.

A full meeting of the Committee on the Irish Bill was held to-day, all the Members being present. Some discussion took place upon the general character, and upon some of the provisions, of the Draft Bill, but it was pointed out by the Chairman that the Bill was by no means yet complete and that therefore the discussion could only be of a very limited character. . . .

It was however strongly urged by General Smuts that the Committee should not enter upon the consideration of the Bill until it was complete in every respect, and this view found acceptance with most of the Members, if not all. At all events, it was eventually unanimously adopted by the Committee.

Discussion then arose upon the general aspects of the Government's Irish policy. Considerable differences of opinion became manifest, but upon one point every Member of the Committee was agreed, namely, that as a preliminary to proceeding with the Government policy either in respect to conscription or of the grant of self-government to Ireland it was first necessary that the new Irish Administration should restore respect for government, enforce the law, and, above all, put down with a stern hand the Irish-German conspiracy which appears to be widespread in Ireland. The Committee were unanimously of opinion that until this has been done neither branch of the Government's policy had any chance of success. The atmosphere at this moment in Ireland is most unfavourable, but it is likely that it may be completely changed when the new Administration have succeeded in enforcing the law.

It will be apparent from these considerations, both particular and general, that the early introduction of the Home Rule Bill is an impossibility and the Committee were of one mind in deprecating any statement in Parliament, which would seem to imply that the Bill could be taken at an early date. Some apprehension was expressed as to the effect of answers already given to questions, and it was thought that the Prime Minister and the Leader of the House should have clearly in mind the fact that delay is unavoidable owing to the impossibility of completing the draft of the Bill and, further than this, that delay is in itself absolutely necessary in order that any Bill may have a reasonable chance of success.

24 May   Ralph Wright[1] to T.J.
. . . Seriously though, I repeat this war is lasting much too long. I am fed up. Everyone I know from general to private is utterly fed up with thinking about the war—still worse, as far as most of us go, we know that the only thing we must never allow ourselves to do is to think about it, for then we should really go mad. Outside our jobs there is nothing to do, nothing to think about, nothing to be interested in. Even a fine day means hard ground for this next push and a fine night, even when you're at rest, as we are now, means bombing. You go in to billets and find a couple of ripping little children to play with, and then at night you find them shivering with fright because the Boches are overhead, and all you can do is to tell them lies about their being quite safe, and to curse the war to hell. You daren't even get really fond of anyone, for if you do he gets killed. You've just got to shut yourself up, to teach yourself not to feel, to stifle completely your imagination and your sympathy.

But enough of all this, I'm not the first one to tell you this. . . .

Now look here, what you've got to do is to tell me something cheerful. Tell

---

[1] A young friend of T.J.'s serving on the western front.

me that all this beastly business in Parliament that seems only to succeed in chucking out good soldiers and keeping L.G. in power is not so base as it looks. Tell me that Northcliffe doesn't really rule England. Tell me that there's someone with enough power to see to it, at the end, that all this bloody misery is not going to lead to a beastlier England. Tell me even, though I do firmly believe it, that we're going to win. Tell me that freedom is not dead, and by freedom I mean a solid English or French thing; I mean a state of existence where anyone if he's getting too fed up can tell his superior to go to hell, and go his own wise or foolish way.

Tell me that Lord Milner is not set on my doing my duty after the war according to his lights; tell me too that within 6 months after the war I shall be free to kick the hindquarters of any general who displeases me. Tell me in fact that when at last we've beaten Germany we won't wake up to find that her spirit has beaten ours.

4 June Irish Committee. Long announced that Cave wished to be relieved of attendance as he thought the Committee was ploughing the sands.

Shortt[1] reported a great deal of sullen passive resistance in Ireland where they were preaching that they had a right to do what Ulster had done, and Lloyd George and Dr. Clifford. 'Nobody believes we ought to introduce a Home Rule Bill now. We must go on drafting and say we have not finished.'

Curzon did not see how it was possible to proceed. Conscription had been tacitly dropped. A Proclamation had been issued that day. Parliament should be asked to exonerate Government from its pledges for three or six months in view of the state of Ireland.

Smuts agreed that the position of the Government was humiliating and should be explained, otherwise it would lose prestige. . . . Could the Government not say, without committing itself to federalism, that it was appointing a Committee to examine the question. It was tomfoolery to go on drafting. With this Barnes and Chamberlain agreed. . . .

*   *   *   *

Long to draft a memorandum for Cabinet.

6 June Irish Committee. Long's memorandum for Cabinet considered and amended. Barnes wanted to omit reference to conscription. Addison wanted to proceed with the draft bill, others wanted a general examination of the federal solution.

Long reported that his up-to-date information was that any Irish Bill would be vigorously opposed by Ulster and that Midleton[2] in the South had not a single follower. Meanwhile the Nationalists were split into three or four parties. The only chance was to produce a bill applicable to the whole Kingdom of which Ireland would take its share. The draft statement was to go to the Cabinet. The finance and Ulster clauses of the bill had not been

---

[1] Edward Shortt (1862–1935); Liberal M.P. 1910–22; Chief Secretary for Ireland 1918–19; Home Secretary 1919–22.
[2] Lord Midleton, a great landowner and leader of the Unionists in Southern Ireland.

agreed. Left to Long to adjust draft in light of discussion and send it to Cabinet if Fisher and Shortt agreed to it.

Labour unrest did not die down after the Unrest Commissions of 1917 and the not ungenerous award of 12½ per cent. to munitions workers and 7½ per cent. to piece-workers in July 1917. In the summer of 1918 a new wave of strikes swept the country—by munitions workers in Coventry, by police in London, claiming official recognition for their union, by cotton workers in Lancashire. Churchill wished to draft the strikers into the army, but Lloyd George, sensing a new militant and implacable temper among the working class, met them with some concessions.

25 July   Arthur Greenwood to T.J.   *Ministry of Reconstruction*
I enclose a short minute prepared for Dr. Addison on the present discontents.

I hope the Govt. won't try the 'firm hand' touch. Either it will fail, or it will leave the situation worse than before.

Robert's speech was unfortunate and I gather that Winston is in one of his Napoleonic moods.

I believe the men will respond to decent treatment but I don't think they will get it from the [Ministry of Munitions], and it isn't any good getting the men to come to London. Somebody ought to go to the men. Moreover the M. of M. ought not to be allowed to pursue its policy of dictatorial control from London.

30 July   Imperial War Cabinet
Mr. Hughes[1] raised the question of Russia with reference to intervention of Japan and telegrams from Lord Reading pointing out that he cannot press Wilson or Wilson will not do what he has promised to do. Now only going to give us 80 divisions by next July instead of the 100 promised.

P.M. 'We are trying to press Wilson to go a little further; Japs have taken the line we expected they would take—they felt it an insult to be asked to send 7,000 men. Now the Japs are taking the bit between their teeth.'

Balfour. 'Reading will be here on Monday.'

Hughes. 'You are going to have endless trouble from Wilson in the conduct of the War and with the terms of peace.'

Chamberlain. 'Yes—in the peace—but you cannot change the President.'

17 August   J. G. Newlove, secretary of the Postal and Telegraph Clerks' Association, wrote to T.J. about the restrictions on civil servants in the matter of political activity. T.J. wrote to Hankey on 31 August: 'This should not be allowed to develop after the manner of the Police' (i.e. the police strike for union recognition).

12 September   The Diary records this comment on Lloyd George from the Manchester Guardian:
His Government is not, and even after a successful general election it could hardly be, a homogeneous Government. It is avowedly a Coalition, and it is a

---

[1] William Morris Hughes, Prime Minister of Australia 1915–23.

Coalition in which one of the two great parties in the State finds almost its only really dynamic force in the person of the Prime Minister. And there is this further to be said: that the Prime Minister himself is not exactly a simple figure. He is, so to speak, a sort of coalition in himself. There are in him diverse, even contradictory, elements striving for the mastery. . . .

He has in him at the core much of the precious metal of humanity; he has also, which in this connection is at least as material, a clear and strong sense of reality. He has imagination to realise the world as it will be when the struggle and the passion are over-past and the nations must somehow learn to live together again. . . .

28–30 September   *T.J. spent a weekend at Oxford, discussing economic policy in the reconstruction period with a group under the auspices of the Political Intelligence Department of the Foreign Office, including Lord Eustace Percy[1] and Alfred Zimmern.*

? October   *The Treasury announced that T.J. was to receive an allowance from War Cabinet funds bringing his salary up to £1,200, so long as he was required to act as Secretary of the War Cabinet in Hankey's absence in Paris.*

7 October   *There was another meeting of the group of civil servants and economists who had met at Oxford the week before, this time to discuss immediate problems following the end of hostilities.*

9 October   *The Webbs asked T.J. to meet George Russell[2] and two others who came over to represent privately to the Labour Party the grave situation in Ireland.*

14 October   *The final meeting was held of what Eustace Percy called the 'Economic Duma'; afterwards its memorandum on controls, etc. was submitted to Lord Robert Cecil and the Economic Defence and Development Committee.*

The German Government had appealed on 4 October to President Wilson, alone, for an armistice and peace negotiations, in an attempt to get easier terms than they could expect from Britain or France. Wilson replied on the basis of his Fourteen Points and for nearly three weeks negotiated directly, and with considerable inconsistency. During this period his allies were hard put to discover the policy to which they were being pledged.

15 October   At the Cabinet.
For some time there have been signs that President Wilson was losing caste in the eyes of the P.M. A month or two ago the P.M. remarked at a Cabinet discussion that the President read the 'Nation' regularly and drew inspiration from it, and also from the 'Manchester Guardian'. Today Wilson's *Second Note to Germany* arrived. There had been a preliminary 'hush' meeting at 11.0 attended by Milner, Henry Wilson, Hankey, and probably Philip Kerr and Amery. The P.M. went out for a few minutes at the close of this and when he

---

[1] Lord Eustace Percy (1887–1958); one of the more progressive young Conservative backbenchers and later a protégé of Baldwin in the Cabinet.
[2] Æ, the Irish poet, painter, economist, and journalist.

returned at 11.35 or thereabouts Ministers were in their places and his first sentence was: 'Who's got my "President Wilson"?' referring to the Foreign Office telegram. The dialogue proceeded:

A.J.B.: One of the most humorous documents ever produced.

Hankey: The end of it is an encouragement to Bolshevism.

A.J.B.: But Wilson is a great enemy of Bolshevism.

C.I.G.S. (beginning the Military Statements for the day): We took 10,000 prisoners yesterday. Very good day. . . . Only 2 fresh divisions (German) from Switzerland to the North Sea which have been rested. They are in a great hole; but we are so tired—there's the trouble and the French are still more tired.

While the C.I.G.S. was going on with his report Balfour began a conversation with the P.M. across the table:

A.J.B.: I've seen Venizelos.

P.M.: I've got to polish Pashitch[1] off. Would they go together?

A.J.B.: They'd be all right.

*   *   *   *

Chamberlain raised a point about terms of a possible armistice with Turkey.

A.J.B.: Venizelos asks that we should not lay down same rule here as we did for Macedonia where we forbade Serbs and Greeks to enter Bulgaria. That was all right there, but does not apply to Constantinople. After Venizelos left, the Italian chargé d'affaires came to see me and said there was some idea that Greek soldiers were going to be used to occupy Smyrna. He hoped it was not going to be done. It would be disastrous, and he referred to the Treaty of St. Jean de Maurienne.

P.M.: But Russia did not agree to that. Must protest against that view.

A.J.B.: Tell Allenby to keep Italians, English, French and everybody out. Leave Smyrna out. Don't occupy it.

Milner: No immediate danger of occupying it.

A.J.B.: I've written up the interview. Tell Allenby there'll be damned row if you occupy Smyrna, so don't do it if not bound to.

P.M.: I'm hoping the British Fleet will have something to say to Smyrna.

Chamberlain: Appeal for armistice may go to French and not to Allenby.

There was no decision and we passed on to hear Wemyss give the Naval Statements. These the P.M. heard impatiently as he wanted to get back to Wilson's Note.

Curzon: The Note is in the American press. It came *en clair*. Can I give it in my House this afternoon?

B. Law: I had thought it would be in the papers. I shall be asked and I can read it.

Milner: If you read it out it will be received with rapturous applause by the Commons and by the public.

Hankey (after inquiring): It is on the tape already.

B. Law: If I read it out I shall be asked supplementaries.

---

[1] Prime Minister of Poland.

Curzon: Any objection to saying, This states the terms on which President Wilson will be prepared to approach Allies.

At this point, to the obvious annoyance of the P.M., Milner and the C.I.G.S. excused themselves and withdrew to attend the wedding of General de Radcliffe, the D.M.O.

P.M.: What's to be said to this?

A.J.B.: I should consult Clemenceau.

P.M.: He (Wilson) was not at all in this temper yesterday. I had a telegram from Eric Geddes.[1] (Sends for it and reads it, as apparently some of the Ministers had not seen it. The telegram had been dictated in the presence of the President. The President did not want our armistice terms to involve enemy in undue humiliation but wanted to prevent them gaining any military advantage from the armistice; he was bent on breakup of Austria in interest of the oppressed nationalities; his views on the freedom of the seas were unformed; he agreed that America should be represented in London by someone—Col. House.)

A.J.B. (referring to freedom of sea): There's no harm in that.

Reading: He means that for League of Nations.

P.M.: I take it his theory is that all nations will be in the League. He's a curious mixture of old Bryce and Sir Arthur Yapp (General Secretary of the Y.M.C.A.).

Chamberlain (referring to part about arbitrary power): Nothing so humiliating as to tell them to alter their Government at his orders.

A.J.B.: This is a very confused document. This last par. is capable of a thousand interpretations. Destruction of arbitrary power. I'm ready to admit that democracy is less monstrously bellicose than despotism.

Chamberlain: Arbitrary power can work secretly.

Curzon: It's only a quotation from his original speech.

Reading: The German Government has accepted that.

A.J.B.: It is inconsistent with our policy in Russia of leaving Russians to settle their own affairs.

Reading: Which he has laid down.

P.M.: In future the Germans will never want to make peace with Wilson again. If they'd come to Foch, Haig, and Pétain, they'd have heard something definite.

Curzon: It's not bad for us.

Reading: Wilson is in a trap and has got to get out.

A.J.B.: I don't want to go beyond making Germany impotent to renew the war, and obtaining compensation. I don't want to trample her in the mud.

B. Law: Are we to allow Wilson to commit us more and more?

Reading: We have sent him a message (re armistice being matter for military) on which he has acted. He has acted completely as we suggested, except perhaps in regard to third point (arbitrary power).

Chamberlain: On this 3rd point, we should say we are not prepared to go

---

[1] (Sir) Eric Geddes (1875–1937); First Lord of the Admiralty 1917–18, Minister of Transport 1919–21, chairman in 1919–21 of the economy committee whose report was known as the 'Geddes Axe'.

on to fight to get rid of Hohenzollerns. Maybe Emperor will abdicate. Wilson might then accept constitutional government with a junior member of the Royal House on throne. Don't let us come out as preservers of the Hohenzollerns.

Curzon: Why say anything now on that. Leave it alone. He's not consulted us on that.

B. Law: He (W.) ought not to communicate with them—not even verbally without first consulting.

Curzon: He'll say he's only corresponding.

B. Law: Suppose he lays down conditions which we may have to reject?

P.M.: He rushes from one extreme to another. Now offers terms Germans cannot accept. We'll make peace whenever we can get the peace we want.

Reading: Need we take further notice?

B. Law: The danger of his taking a pacifist line is gone.

Reading: Position is clear to me. On 7th October, the day before his message, State Department gave out to the Press, 'No Surrender'. Then when they saw the document from Germany[1] the Representatives were troubled, because they saw Wilson caught in his own trap. What appeared in papers? 'Unconditional Surrender?'

A.J.B.: His style is most inaccurate. He's a first-rate rhetorician and a very bad draftsman.

Reading: What do you expect from a man who typewrites his message in his little room without consulting anyone?

*   *   *   *

The German Government accepted the Fourteen Points on 23 October. Meeting on 4 November, the Supreme War Council at Versailles made reservations on the freedom of the sea (in favour of Britain) and compensation from Germany (in favour of France); and in this form they accepted the President's terms.

22 October   T.J. was offered the post of Director of Social Studies at Aberystwyth. T.J. to J. H. Davies
Thanks for yours. I am absolutely tied up with most urgent Cabinet work and can only give a moment to deal with your questions. I have not seen the correspondence which I believe has passed on the matter. I have only written to Sir Henry Jones last July and I send you copies of what I told him. The conclusion I have come to is that I ought not to give up the important post I have here of Assistant Secretary to the War Cabinet and Secretary to the Home Affairs Committee to become Director of Social Studies at Aberystwyth. I should feel too restricted in that position to carry out the schemes I have in mind. . . .

On 17 November Waldorf Astor wrote to T.J. enclosing a copy of a note he had sent to the Prime Minister. In it he said that Britain's leadership in the resettlement of Europe might be threatened by Herbert Hoover's mission to Europe and Germany's appeal to President Wilson. It was, he suggested, urgently necessary that Britain's own policy

---

[1] See note in text, 4 October.

should be quickly formulated and some 'leading British personality' made responsible for its execution. His own suggestion for this role was Lord Reading. To T.J. he wrote:
. . . I am somewhat perturbed at the immediate prospect of conflict. Clemenceau summoned a meeting of the Inter-Allied Shipping and Food Organisations in Paris; L.G. practically stopped our representatives going, as apparently he did not want Clemenceau to take this lead. As the work would probably have been done subsequently in London by our mainly British organisation he may have probably lost the substance while grasping for the shadow. It is conceivable also that this action may throw the French back into Hoover's arms, where they have not infrequently reposed in the past. Just at the moment when we look like getting them into our pocket owing to their indignation at Hoover's loudly proclaimed statement that *HE* was going to feed their people in the evacuated territories. You will gather from the notes that the chances of friction with Hoover and with the great Professor[1] if he accompanies him, are real. I cannot but think it is vital and urgent that we should get someone of outstanding position, like Reading, to collar the existing Allied machinery before it breaks, so that when Hoover and Woodrow arrive they can each be more or less quietly placed into the niches which ought to be ready for them.

11 December   Ralph Wright to T.J.
Thank you immensely for your letter. My last letter . . . was I expect thoroughly undeserving of an answer. It was written at a time of real depression.
I shall certainly do exactly what you tell me, put myself entirely in your hands. . . .
Anyhow, I'm your man, hand and foot, for as long as you want me. You're one of the few men I've met who, I believe, is not playing his own hand, and if I could work under you I'd be happy. . . .[2]

1919

The protracted peace negotiations at Versailles overshadowed this year, the haggling of officials being superseded by the horse-trading of the Council of Four, President Wilson, Lloyd George, Clemenceau, and Orlando. Lloyd George exercised a moderating influence over the frontier proposals for the defeated Germany, but reparations were fixed at a level which drew strong criticism from, among others, J. M. Keynes,[3] whose *Economic Consequences of the Peace* was published late in the year. On the credit side, proposals for a League of Nations, drafted by Smuts and Robert Cecil, formed the basis of the Covenant.

Under pressure from Churchill, arms and men were sent to support the White Russian interventionists against the Bolsheviks. Gandhi began his campaign of civil disobedience in an India clouded by the Amritsar 'massacre'. Violence erupted once again in Ireland, where, in December 1918, Sinn Fein had triumphed at the general

[1] Presumably Woodrow Wilson.
[2] There is no record that he ever did so.
[3] Biographical note on p. 334.

election, overwhelming the more moderate Nationalists. In January they held the first meeting of the Dail, their 'alternative Government', bent on full independence.

Industrial violence broke out on the Clyde, the Liverpool police went on strike, while demobilization and looming unemployment caused fear of widespread civil strife. In February, the Sankey Commission was set up to examine the coal-mining industry, but in its report it divided on the issue of nationalization. Many of the hopes for social reconstruction went unfulfilled. The Ministry of Health came into being, but war-time controls were swept ruthlessly away. Lloyd George, mostly in Versailles until peace with Germany was signed on 28 June, kept his Coalition Government afloat, with help at home from Bonar Law.

T.J. remained in charge of the War Cabinet secretariat, while Hankey showed his true genius for organization in the difficult surroundings of Versailles, where his un-disputed competence soon put him in command of the official machine. In October, the small War Cabinet was replaced by a normal Cabinet of twenty. T.J., disappointed in his hopes of obtaining the one academic post he really wanted, the Principalship of the University College of Wales at Aberystwyth, for which he and David Davies had great plans, settled down to another ten years in the Cabinet Office in Whitehall.

17 January   T.J. to Sir Maurice Hankey

After the Meeting of the War Cabinet this morning Churchill told Curzon and Chamberlain[1] that he was very anxious that the Cabinet should discuss on Monday—if possible—the question of retaining an army of 1,000,000 on a compulsory basis. A Bill for the continuance of compulsory service would be necessary. The idea would be to retain about 1,700,000 who had joined within the last two years and reduce this to 1,000,000 who would be retained on very much higher rates of pay than at present. I gathered that Sir Eric Geddes, Sir Auckland Geddes, and Sir Robert Horne[2] were in favour of the proposal. Churchill wants the general principles discussed here before the matter is referred to you in Paris.

There were objections to having the subject on Monday at such short notice and it has been put down for Tuesday and a telegram has been sent to Milner asking him to attend.

Sir Douglas Haig is also being kept here for Tuesday's meeting.

Churchill's Memorandum on the subject will be circulated late tomorrow (Saturday).

This is of course a matter of first class importance and I am letting you know of it at the first opportunity.

18 January   Sir Maurice Hankey to T.J.   British War Cabinet Offices, Paris

You are simply splendid. The P.M. was much annoyed about Churchill's proposal and has written to him to stop it. He has promised not to mix your name up in it, as we don't want to make trouble between you and anyone else. You were absolutely right to let me know and the P.M. is very pleased.

I have had a most gruelling time. There have been a series of important 'hush' meetings. I had to take the first one or two alone, but subsequently had Caccia and Abraham to help me.

---

[1] Austen Chamberlain. Biographical note on p. 333.

[2] Sir Robert Horne (1871–1940); Conservative M.P. 1918–37, Minister of Labour 1919–20, President of the Board of Trade 1920, Chancellor of the Exchequer 1921–2.

After havering for some time the P.M. decided yesterday afternoon to nominate me as British Secretary of the Peace Conference. This means my taking over, more or less, part of the F.O. organisation. Lord Hardinge[1] has been extremely nice about it. Now, therefore, I have under my control three distinct departments:

Sir Maurice Hankey

British Imperial Delegation (War Cabinet staff)	British Secretariat of Peace Conference (Foreign Office staff)	British Secretariat of Cabinet of Nations (Versailles secretariat).

* * * *

You cannot imagine how I am burdened with petty questions of precedence, etc. ... I have also had incessant drafting committees where I have had single-handed to fight the French on all sorts of nice and rather novel points, particularly about the constitutional position of the Dominions and India. The whole thing gabbled in French usually at the end of a tiring day.

The building of the League of Nations is a desperately tedious business, but I see a splendid structure rising. President Wilson and L.G. are working most splendidly together. The American secretaries and I are as blood brothers. Clemenceau a big man. So look at the splendid growing young tree and not at the leaves of my troubles and difficulties.

T.J. sent regular reports to Hankey from January to March, especially on the Home Affairs Committee's discussion on Housing and Land; also on the size of the army of occupation (Churchill now proposed holding 800,000 men) and the labour unrest (strikes on Clydeside and in Belfast) at the end of January.

8 February   T.J. to the Prime Minister, on industrial unrest[2]

1. Bolshevik propaganda in this country is only dangerous in so far as it can lodge itself in the soil of genuine grievances. There is no doubt that large numbers of work-people are expecting a big and rapid improvement in their social and industrial conditions. They are disturbed by all sorts of rumours, usually exaggerated, that the surplus factories and stores of the Government are being handed over at ridiculously low prices to the profit-makers.

2. Much of the present difficulty springs from the mutiny of the rank and file against the old established leaders and there seems to be no machinery for bringing about a quick change of leaders. Working men are notoriously tender towards the man in office and most unwilling to sack him, however incompetent or out of touch. The Government's decision to stand by the accredited leaders is the only possible policy but it does not get over the fact that the leaders no longer represent the more active and agitating minds in the labour movement.

[1] Charles Hardinge (1858–1944); Viceroy of India 1910–16, Permanent Under-Secretary, Foreign Office, 1906–10, 1916–20, Ambassador in Paris 1920–2, cr. Baron 1910.

[2] Written after the violent Forty-Hour strike in Glasgow, which ended in riots in George Square.

3. A definite reiteration by yourself of the Government's determination to push forward with an advanced social programme is the best antidote, and this should be followed up by instructions from you to the Departments concerned to get on with the necessary Bills at top speed.

Sir Robert Horne yesterday suggested at the War Cabinet that a fresh series of local commissions on Industrial Unrest should be set up like those you appointed a couple of years ago. I think this device too thin. We have not carried out the recommendations of the last series. What is wanted is real, concrete proposals from the Departments and these to be pushed through the House. The Whitley Councils[1] are coming into existence and they should be appealed to and asked to meet at once and consider improvements in the conditions of their respective industries.

(a) *Hours*. Could the Government not bring in an 8 Hours bill for the main organised industries (except Agriculture) and then allow exemptions to be granted by licence?

(b) *Wages*. The miners are demanding 30% on pre-war earnings and 18/– War Bonus. The Railwaymen are putting forward fresh demands. I think you should say frankly that the Government is unwilling to commit itself to these big advances to the highest paid workers (and thereby create an industrial House of Lords) until more has been done to secure a national minimum for the lower paid in these two industries and for those in the low skilled and unskilled industries: that therefore you contemplate an immediate extension of the Trade Boards in order to secure the enforcement of this national minimum.

(c) *Housing*. It would be helpful if you gave a summary of the enormous tenders that the Minister of Supply has put out. The figures are impressive.

You should tell the big Municipalities (e.g. Glasgow) that you hope they will tackle the re-housing of their cities with something of the wartime energy that you shewed at the Ministry of Munitions. We do not want to wait 20 years for these houses. Hundreds of thousands should be put up in the next 5 years.

(d) *Land*. The Government are determined to pass a measure for the rapid acquisition of land by public bodies at reasonable and not inflated prices and that the chances of delay by lawyers and obstructionists will be reduced to the smallest possible compass.

(e) *Prices*. The Ministry of Food should give you immediately some indication of what their prices policy is to be for the next 6 months. It may be impossible to reduce prices, and greatly increase consumption. On the other hand it may be possible and wise for the Government to cut its losses on its stocks and let some of the stuff out during the cold months.

(f) *Drink*. The Cabinet has let out 25% more beer and to-day a request has come from the Ministry of Food for permission to let out 25% more spirits. This whole question should be freshly surveyed. A proposal which now finds favour with many is that a sort of referendum should be taken at once and each district be given the choice of

[1] Joint consultative councils in industry, and the lower grades of the Civil Service, which took their name from the Speaker, J. H. Whitley.

    (a) Total prohibition
    (b) Nationalisation in the district as in Carlisle
    (c) Retention of present conditions.

Another proposal is that the Balfour Act should be greatly expedited by taking far more money from the brewers for purposes of compensation of closed public houses.

10 February   T.J. to Sir Maurice Hankey

You will have read between the lines of the Minutes that we had a lively time last week. As I told the P.M. on his arrival, we kept the pot 'boiling 'for him.

The fuss about the Railway Clerks was quite unnecessary but the attitude of the Railway Executive towards Trade Union recognition was only slowly emerging from the prehistoric period. . . . Behind the scenes the Federation of British Industries and Allan Smith of the Engineers were prophesying into Bonar Law's ears the commercial downfall of the country if superior beings like stationmasters and inferior beings like booking clerks were allowed to meet on the same (Union) platform. For an hour or two Bonar Law was afraid that even the Coalition might founder on this question, but as it would be impossible to carry the country against recognition and as the Clerks refused to be manoeuvred into a conflict on any other issue there was nothing for it but to capitulate.

The threat of the electricians to put us into darkness[1] was a much simpler matter. They were so clearly in the wrong that the public would readily condone the use of the army and navy to man the power stations. Lights were to have gone out on Thursday at 6.0 and we had a Cabinet summoned for that hour, but such was our faith in the good sense of the men that we did not provide candles in No. 10.

The funniest discussion was at this same 6.0 meeting over the strike of the drivers on the Tubes. We had a large Duma present and it was announced at the very outset that the Railway Executive and the men had agreed to accept a particular formula, but, alas, this formula was unacceptable to the Cabinet and we had the spectacle which you can imagine better than anyone else, of about 25 people trying to draft an agreement of two sentences long which would at once placate the managers and men and save the face of the Government who, through Bonar Law (badly advised by Stanley and Horne), had written a published letter to Bromley.[2] If a verbatim note of this discussion had been published last week the Coalition would have collapsed and the P.M. would be free to start with a clean slate. The whole wrangle was over the ordinary, reasonable physical requirements of the men and the precise number of minutes required to satisfy them, the estimate varying from none upwards. I am very curious to know whether or not Curzon and Long have ever been in a Tube and am thinking of referring the question to the Ministry of Research.

[1] Electricians in London threatened to strike in sympathy with the Forty-Hour strike in Glasgow.

[2] John Bromley (1876–1944); member of the General Council of the T.U.C. and Secretary of A.S.L.E.F.

The P.M. arrived promptly at 6.0 at Charing Cross and about 6 minutes later was closeted with Bonar Law and Barnes. I saw him a little later and he was extraordinarily cheerful and vigorous and happy about your doings in Paris and full of schemes of dealing with the miners and the railwaymen should they come out during the next week or two. I urged him to make a big pronouncement of the Government's social policy at once so as to counter the prevailing distrust. He then gave me several versions of the King's Speech with orders to dovetail them into something new and strange. But once more, alas, this production was subjected to a Duma for one and a half hours this morning, and its fond parents will hardly recognise their offspring when they see it. Some of our Elder Statesmen were rather shocked at its democratic accents, but the P.M. very adroitly on Sunday got an advance copy submitted to the King and Stamfordham[1] wrote back suggesting that His Majesty thought the allusion to labour troubles ought to be strengthened! At this news the Duma became more democratic than the P.M. himself, with perhaps the exception of Bonar Law who appeared to be suffering great pain throughout the meeting.

But I must not gossip in this fashion. I am endeavouring to behave more or less with the serious dignity appropriate to an Acting Secretary and the whole Office Staff are playing up most cordially. . . .

I don't think I told you that we have stopped printing the Minutes for a few days until these lightning strikes are over as I got a hint from the F.O. that some of the men were Trade Unionists first and citizens afterwards. J. H. Thomas's speech on this topic in today's papers is splendid and should have a great steadying effect.

11 February   Sir Maurice Hankey to T.J.   *British Delegation, Paris*
. . . My opinion is that the time has now come when we ought to get a move on about the War Book. I do not make this suggestion because I think we are going to have another war. God forbid! But unless the Departments have something to work to they will not go into their records properly. The musical society must always have a concert in sight. Moreover, I think it is important from another point of view. I feel sure that the real Minister of Defence must always be the Prime Minister of the day, and that it is very important that the Prime Minister should keep under his own hand, and in his own Office, the co-ordination of defence matters. I doubt if we have yet come to the time when we ought to re-establish the Committee of Imperial Defence. It seems to me that while the Peace Conference is sitting no real progress can be made in the great questions of defence policy, and if the League of Nations becomes a reality, it will have a paramount influence on these questions. Nevertheless, I think we ought to keep the idea of the C.I.D. alive, and I have always felt that the Department that has the War Book has the key of the whole defence organisation in its hands.

[1] Arthur John Bigge, Lord Stamfordham (1849–1931); assistant private secretary to Queen Victoria 1880–95, private secretary 1895–1901, private secretary to Prince (later King) George 1901–31.

My feeling is that you ought to try and have a few words with the Prime Minister about it. . . .

I am afraid you have had a gruelling time with these strikes, but I congratulate you on the excellent Minutes. If ever you have time to send me a real heart to heart letter, or to dictate me so much as you can find time for, I hope you will do so. I am stuck here for a bit, but rather hope to pay you a visit one of these days. You can, of course, show this letter to the Prime Minister if you think it would be of any use.

14 February   Sir Maurice Hankey to T.J.   *British Delegation, Paris*

I was most grateful to you for your very racy letter about the strike meetings. I have been chuckling over it ever since I read it. You must have had a very hard time but I think you have done extraordinarily well.

Things here are looking a little better. I think that the results of the Armistice discussion are most beneficent. I hope that in a week or two we shall really be able to draw the teeth of Germany and demobilisation will become possible on a much larger scale. I think I can claim quite an exceptionally large share in this result. I woke up early that morning and formed an absolute determination to drive through what I knew the Prime Minister wanted. At eight o'clock I was drafting and by half past nine I had got the approval of Milner, and Balfour whom I found in bed. Before eleven the Americans were in line. I had a great stunt with shorthand writers and typists outside the room and the draft went through about seven editions, which were all labelled at the top—10.30 Edition, 12.45 Edition, etc., up to the Final Edition, and eventually we got it through. Orlando,[1] who was a spectator, came up to me afterwards and complimented me on the extraordinary efficiency of the arrangements which enabled the clean drafts to be got out so quickly. Haig, also, was extraordinarily appreciative. I do not want to take too much personal credit because the policy was nothing to do with me, but once our people had agreed to the policy I drove it like blazes.

I am not very much in love with the League of Nations constitution drafted by the Commission but it is infinitely better than the earlier draft and I think something may be made of it. At present we are quite uncommitted.

President Wilson leaves to-day and, for my part, I am genuinely sorry. I think he is really a very big man although his weaknesses are that he sees his own political difficulties very big, and other peoples' political difficulties very small. This makes him very obstinate and when he is obstinate he makes interminable high-falutin speeches. Personally he is extremely agreeable and has an enormous fund of amusing anecdotes. Without the P.M. and him the Conference will rather lack reality. Moreover, Orlando leaves to-day and, on the whole, we shall be left with a very reactionary team at the meetings of the Big Ten.

I think I see daylight in most departments of the Conference's activity but, at present, it is no more than the earliest flush of dawn.

No more now.

[1] Prime Minister of Italy.

18 February   T.J. to Sir Maurice Hankey

I had some time with the P.M. this morning and put before him your suggestion about the War Book and about the Ministry of 'Complaints'.

War Book

He was not very definite one way or the other about the War Book but I was satisfied that the letter could go out as a direction from him, and Wilson is considering your Draft today and will let me know at once. I will probably take an opportunity of mentioning the matter to B.L. and the others.

Ministry of 'Complaints'

The P.M. was very much more alive to the big question of complaints and it is quite clear that he wants it to be a section of our Secretariat. He said that he daily receives from 400 to 1,000 complaints from all parts of the country, and they are at present dealt with by rather inexperienced clerical staff. Whenever he dips into them or when they reach him circuitously at Walton Heath he generally finds some point in most of the letters well worth following up. To have this work well done requires persons able to weigh the complaints and able to set in motion appropriate action, or in serious cases, to call the P.M.'s personal attention. As he is evidently bent on getting something done, the only point I kept urging was that any action taken on such complaints would necessarily have to be in the P.M.'s own name—we could not take it as a Secretariat or a Department. He did not demur to that. I regard this morning's conversation as a preliminary skirmish and you can return to the fight when you have an opportunity.

23 February   Sir Maurice Hankey to the Prime Minister

. . . On the general questions of speeding up, Italy is the main obstruction. On the Territorial Committees, for example, Crowe tells me that the Italians are using every artifice for obstructing business. For example, the Greek Commission was delayed several days because of the alleged indisposition of Martino,[1] whereas, on that very evening, I met him in the doorway of the Edward VII Hotel going out for the evening. The Italians also at the Commission refuse to express any opinion on the questions, and allege that they are instructed not to express opinions. They refuse to say that their Government will give them any instructions. Crowe asked Martino, after one of the meetings, what it all meant, and Martino replied: 'You would not talk to us alone when we came to London in December, and you will not talk to us or make arrangements with us in Paris, and consequently we are not going to express any opinions on these questions!'

The Italians are so obstructive that I believe, in order to get on, we may either have to be blackmailed into coming to some definite agreement with them, or else be very rough with them. We cannot, however, promise them what they want in Asia Minor until we know what the American position is as regards a mandate in Turkey. . . .

*   *   *   *

[1] The Italian Representative.

So far as your own visit is concerned, I think the main task will be to settle the question of whether military and air conditions of peace are to be imposed as an advance instalment on Germany, and secondly to see the senior British Empire Delegate on the important Commissions with a view to speeding up. Finally, and perhaps most important of all, to see if any progress can be made on the subject of the frontiers of Germany. Conversations on this subject have been proceeding between our experts and the Americans, who, I understand, are in pretty close agreement. I think there is no reason to believe that the French will be in disagreement about the Eastern frontiers of Germany, and they will be sounded this week. The question of the Western frontiers, however, remains more or less where it was, except that from various quarters I hear that the French are opening their mouths wider than ever, and want now to retain the bridgeheads on the Rhine in military occupation by the Allies until such time as Germany is admitted to the League of Nations.

P.S. My idea is that, when all the Commissions report, we shall be able to draft roughly the lines of the Peace Treaty as a whole, and then we shall have some give and take over the whole scheme. The moment for this will be President Wilson's return.

27 February   T.J. to Sir Maurice Hankey
... We have had rather a gruelling time here during the last ten days between Labour troubles, on the one hand, and Conferences and Committees on the Rehabilitation of Industry, on the other. Today there has been a big Industrial Conference in the Central Hall with representatives of masters and men numbering about 1,000 and with Horne in the Chair. We had speeches from Sir Allan Smith, Clynes, Arthur Henderson, J. H. Thomas, with the P.M. winding up. It was a difficult audience, but favourable, on the whole, to the Government's desire to set up a Committee to examine Industrial Unrest.

Throughout the week the P.M. has been magnificent—full of energy himself and speeding up everybody else. Eric Geddes' new Ministry[1] has been launched and Addison's Health Bill. Early next week we shall have the Land Acquisition Bill, the Land Settlement Bill, the Housing Bill, the Electricity Supply Bill, and, perhaps, an Anti-Dumping Bill before the Cabinet. The P.M. is very anxious to deal with these before he returns. I do not think he can get back until the end of next week.

One of the most worrying features of the moment is the growing unemployment and the difficulty of getting the country's industry going. We had a full conference of Ministers on this subject on Tuesday under the P.M. and there has been another this afternoon under Auckland Geddes.

The conclusion of peace is really becoming very urgent from a trade and labour standpoint. Of course there are subterranean obstacles which hardly come to the surface in the discussions—the Tariff question and the fear of the P.M.'s social policy. On the latter he was perfectly splendid on Tuesday. Several were drawing rather long faces and piling up the financial bogey and

[1] The Ministry of Transport.

the P.M. forced the Ministers to tell him how much they could spend in the next twelve months. The bill came to £71,000,000. He then asked: 'Supposing the War had lasted another year, could we not have raised somehow or other another £2,000,000,000?' It was blank nonsense to talk of a bagatelle like £71,000,000—a cheap insurance against Bolshevism.

28 February   T.J. to Sir Maurice Hankey

We had Foch's and M. Tardieu's papers about frontiers discussed for about three quarters of an hour this morning and you will receive the hush Minute. Curzon was unprepared and the discussion was adjourned until probably Tuesday. The dominant note today was that we should do all that is possible to please France in the West in order that we should be let alone by her in the East. The P.M. explained the buffer republics that Clemenceau would like to see set up between France and Germany, but it was generally agreed that it would be impossible to prevent such from co-operating with Germany and that the small States had had such bitter experiences in the past before they were united by Bismarck that they were not likely to want to dissociate themselves from the Empire. It was urged also that Wilson was sure to be dead against any such device. . . .

5 March   Sir Maurice Hankey to T.J.   *British Delegation, Paris*

While I have immense admiration for the enormous amount of work that is being done at home by means of Conferences, I am a little anxious on one point, namely, the difficulty of getting the conference proceedings into our indexes. Throughout the war I have always regarded the War Cabinet minutes as a central index of all the activities of the first order in the Government. For this reason, as you yourself will constantly have observed, I have always tried to get Conference Reports either printed as an appendix to the Minutes or *taken note* of in *some* such way as will ensure the Conclusions appearing in the index to the minutes. I encountered this difficulty as regards Versailles, and the plan I adopted there was simply to print the Conclusions as an appendix and see that the War Cabinet took note of them.

If you can manage it, I think you should adopt some such procedure, or devise some plan of your own, for getting the Conclusions of the many important Ministerial Conferences into the index. Otherwise, when you or I are turned to, at short notice, to produce a decision we may not be able to lay our hands on it. It is one of the great disadvantages of the Conference method of doing business. Of course, by reference to the Office Index we could probably produce the decision, but that takes longer.

5 March   Sir Maurice Hankey to T.J.

. . . We shall have the Reports of all the Territorial Commissions in by Saturday and to-day will take place the first meeting of a Super-Territorial Commission, which will draft all the other Reports into the Peace Treaty map. Several of the other Commissions are also quite close to reporting, so that on the spade-work side I am quite optimistic.

There remain, however, a number of great questions of principle, such as the Western Frontier of Germany and the disposition of Turkey, which can only be settled by the highest authorities, and it is for such questions that we need the presence of the Prime Minister so badly. If things went really well, I believe we could get the Preliminary Treaty of Peace by the end of the month, but this is a good deal to hope for.

I fancy that the economic and financial conditions are going to be our bottle neck. Reparation is especially a difficulty. I am afraid that those Election pledges will be like a millstone round our neck. My impression is that the Germans may have deliberately allowed the Spartacists[1] a good deal of rope in order to frighten us into the idea that we cannot get any indemnity. It is a very horrible and dangerous spectre to raise and I doubt if Scheidemann[2] and his lot will ever be able to lay it. The question that really alarms me is as to whether, even at the end of the month, there will be a German Government with which we can deal. If not, we are going to be faced with a position of extraordinary difficulty. All the evidence we get shows that there really is an appalling state of affairs in Germany. The question is: can we get through the preliminaries of peace in sufficient time, and in such form, as to save Germany? Reparation is one of the questions that makes this extraordinarily difficult. It is outrageous and intolerable that Germany should not pay, and yet, if she is made to pay, we may raise such a danger as may overwhelm civilisation itself.

I have followed the Prime Minister's operations in England with immense admiration and enthusiasm and am delighted at his speech yesterday to the new Council.

24 March   T.J. to Sir Maurice Hankey
There was rather a heated discussion at the War Cabinet this morning on the question of equipping the Roumanian army as you will see by reading between the lines of the very full Minute.

Churchill grew very hot and prophesied vast and immediate disaster as the result of the dilatoriness of the Peace Conference. Curzon took much the same line. Bonar Law was most unwilling to come to a decision on a subject which he held was primarily one for you in Paris. Chamberlain was opposed mainly on financial grounds. At the end Curzon pressed very hard that permission should at least be given to direct to Roumania the ships which were about to go to Denikin[3] and this was agreed to subject to the P.M.'s concurrence.

Will you draw his special attention to the Minute?

26 March   T.J. to Sir Maurice Hankey
You will have been relieved to hear of the Miners' decision this morning to

---

[1] The Communist movement in Germany, led by Rosa Luxemburg and Karl Liebknecht, responsible for the Bavarian uprising in the spring of 1920, which was extinguished by the use of regular troops.

[2] The German Chancellor.

[3] General A. Denikin, founder of the Volunteer Army on the Don in 1918 and afterwards commander of the counter-revolutionary armies in South Russia.

recommend their districts to accept the Sankey Report.[1] It would have been madness for them to do otherwise but naturally yesterday we were kept in great uncertainty. Smillie preserves, even to his intimates on the Executive, the most cryptic silence as to the line he will take. I saw one of them just before the meeting of the Executive last night and he was even then uncertain what Smillie would do, though hopeful that he would stand for peace.

I think Sir Robert Horne, of whom I have seen a great deal, has done very well through the crisis and I believe he will secure the increasing confidence of the labour people. They are, of course, more likely to trust him than his predecessor [Churchill]. Bonar Law, who was extremely grave yesterday, was quite cheerful when I saw him this afternoon. He had just been warning Churchill that the country must be convinced that we are not in for a big army and navy and he half jocularly told Churchill that as soon as the P.M. returns he (B.L.) would move at the Cabinet that the expenditure on the Forces should be reduced to £20 millions per annum! B.L. added that the P.M., with his usual insight, had gone to the root of the matter in pressing for disarmament and that he must be backed on that at all costs. It is significant that at the Miners' Conference this morning a resolution was passed calling for the repeal of the Military Service Acts and threatening *industrial* action if this is not done. This is symptomatic. It is partly due of course to the big Coalition majority which B.L. now agrees is far too big to be wholesome.

10 April Dined alone with Lord Haldane at Queen Anne's Gate. After dinner sat in his study on the second floor where above the mantelpiece I think I counted five portraits of Hegel, three of Goethe, two of Schiller, and one of Voltaire. Haldane smoked and talked nearly the whole time, I doing not more than leading him along to subjects which I wanted him to talk about.

Of the Ernest Cassel gift[2], £150,000 has been earmarked for the School of Economics and Haldane projected various schemes for training the future Civil Servant at the School in view of the growing expansion of State enterprise. He thinks a special effort should be made to send the more promising officers from the Navy to the School after they have been to Dartmouth, and knocked about at sea for a little time.

This led to a talk about the Admiralty and its need of a General Staff for which Jellicoe's book and Pollen's provided ample justification. The Navy after the war would not be large and therefore the quality of the men at the top was of first importance, and he would like to preside over an Enquiry with Beatty and Haig and some of the younger Admiralty officers. I promised to tell the P.M. this. Walter Long would be against anything for the improvement of brains. Churchill had never known how to use experts. Jellicoe was

---

[1] A Royal Commission on the coal-mining industry was set up under Mr. Justice Sankey early in 1919. It reported, in conflicting senses, in June 1919, the recommendations ranging from full nationalization to a complete return to private enterprise.

[2] Sir Ernest Cassel founded an educational trust in 1919.

timid and religious. Nelson would never have allowed the German fleet to escape at Jutland.

Reverting to the School of Economics I laid stress on the importance of the teachers there and in universities generally having opportunities of working in Government departments during vacation or possibly for a sort of sabbatical year.

. . . He talked next of Ireland. Lord French[1] had served under him for six and a half years, and having some regard for his old chief, he had invited Haldane to the Vice-Regal Lodge. Haldane went there on 16 January, stayed at the Lodge for about three days, found French very worried in the midst of some thirty-six Departments, many of them hardly on speaking terms with each other. During his visit Haldane disappeared from the Lodge and got into touch with some of the Jesuits and Sinn Feiners and evolved some scheme of conciliation by which a Committee would be set up with Haldane as Chairman whose duty it would be to do for Ireland what the Machinery of Government Committee had recently done for England, i.e., work out some scheme of administration for Ireland, on the assumption that there would some day be some Home Rule Act and some good will behind it. On this Committee Haldane would have put an Ulster man and De Valera himself, and he was certain from his enquiries that their co-operation could be secured. Haldane wrote a Memorandum to French on these lines and French wrote to Walter Long, who in reply told him 'to go to Hell' or words to that effect. Then French was taken ill. (It was at this time that French tried to persuade the Cabinet to release the Irish prisoners but was blocked by the Cabinet.) Since January the position has become worse but Haldane thinks that his scheme might still be attempted and wants 20 minutes with the P.M. on the subject, preliminary to a lunch with the P.M., French, and Macpherson.

He referred to the muddle Curzon has made in Egypt and thought it dangerous to retain him at the F.O. Curzon was intelligent and could express himself with vigour but his decisions were nearly always wrong.

* * * *

Last Sunday Haldane had taken the Webbs down to see Lord Morley.[2] They had talked labour questions and the Webbs thought not very highly of Morley's observations and thought him a smaller man than Wells or Shaw, but this Haldane would not at all admit. Morley's mind had a massiveness and range to which these others could not pretend.

11 April   T.J. to Lloyd George
Horne and Geddes met a number of the coalowners yesterday. The owners are very sore about the way in which they have been publicly condemned with their case only half heard. The making of the increased wage retrospective to January will cost them about ten millions and many of them say they

[1] The Viceroy. For the only time in history both the Viceroy and the Chief Secretary for Ireland (Macpherson and then Hamar Greenwood) sat in the Cabinet from 1919 to 1922.
[2] The biographer of Gladstone; a Liberal Unionist, owning land in South Devon.

cannot find the money. They are also violently opposed to any 'participation in management' by the men. On the other hand some of the more enlightened owners like our friend D.D. [David Davies] will welcome any scheme of genuine co-operation. Some of us are working out schemes of *socialisation* as distinct from *nationalisation* with representatives of the miners, consumers, and owners on the Board. The crucial matters are (1) to preserve the initiative and responsibility of the technical experts, (2) to secure the goodwill and energy of the miners as producers. . . .

14 April   The Cabinet met at noon. Churchill had been summoned for the first item on 'Permanent Commissions in the Air Force' but did not arrive till about 12.15. Meanwhile we had started with the 'Electricity Supply Bill'. B.L. asked me what I thought about the Clause prohibiting strikes and I said it ought to stand as public opinion would support it in the case of electricity even if it might not in the case of railways. Addison was the only Minister opposed. Horne was sent for and he agreed to its insertion.

Then we passed to the Air Force. Churchill was asking for only fifteen hundred permanent commissions. Chamberlain said he was putting £100 millions in the Budget for the three Services. He had suggested £150 to the P.M. in Paris but the P.M. would not hear of such a figure. Churchill said that £100 millions equalled only £60 before the war and the result of the P.M.'s attitude would be that one of these days we should have to recall our troops from Egypt or India, or possibly Ireland, 'which would be preferable' chimed in B.L. Seely[1] then asked for Cabinet sanction to recruit up to 30,000

[1] J. E. B. Seely (1868–1947); Secretary of State for War 1912–14. Under-Secretary for Air 1919; later Lord Mottistone.

for the Air Force at present rates of pay, it being desirable to get hold of the men who had been trained during the war as they exhausted their gratuities and were in the mood to rejoin. Churchill tried to argue the case for larger Budget provision but was blocked by B.L. and we passed to the Report of the Committee on Secret Service.

*   *   *   *

Re the Rhine frontier, Clemenceau had feared great trouble with Foch but apparently he had been pacified. Wilson had been against the arrangement about the Saar coalfield and also the Indemnity scheme and L.G. had put up to him an ultimatum saying that if Wilson did not agree on indemnities then L.G. would agree to nothing. Of the indemnities some £5,100 millions were assigned to France and £2,200 millions to this country. B.L. asked: What will our lunatics at home say to this? Churchill replied that the country would be quite satisfied and that the newspapers misrepresented the country and so did the wild men in the House. B.L. went on to say that the P.M. in his speech will probably go for Northcliffe and that the Paris 'Daily Mail', which in France was regarded as the organ of the British Government, had been most mischievous during the last few days making trouble between us and France, and there was also a pernicious article in today's London 'Daily Mail'. Chamberlain said he had long been of the same opinion as Lord Robert

Cecil that the urgent need today was to feed the Germans first. B.L. said he was very doubtful whether the Germans would accept the terms they were to be offered whereupon Churchill replied that they would be traitors to their country if they did. In the event of their refusing, Foch was being asked what the military could do, said B.L. 'They could occupy Westphalia,' said Churchill, 'but what is the good of that?'

Earlier in the meeting Churchill had declared that the War Office were strongly in favour of raising the blockade[1] and he referred to Gen. Haking's[2] paper to the Cabinet which strongly supported feeding Germany. 'I am afraid Haking is a Bolshevik,' said B.L., referring to a sentence in Haking's memorandum that Bolshevism was the result of the ill-treatment of the working classes in the past. Someone said we were all apparently in favour of raising the blockade, why not? Auckland Geddes suggested it was the fault of Cecil Harmsworth[3] and the Blockade Department. Curzon did not deny this but I rather think that the opposition must come as much from the F.O. as from Harmsworth. . . .

8 May   T.J. to Sir Maurice Hankey
I heard that Churchill has got a Committee set up with Long as Chairman and Masterton Smith as secretary at which the representatives of the General Staffs of the Army, Navy, and Air Force, in addition to Long, Churchill, and Seely, attend to deal in effect with problems of co-ordination—much after the fashion of the C.I.D. This information has come to me from a private but reliable source which I cannot name in a letter. I told Bonar Law about it and he is strongly of the opinion that the Prime Minister must be chairman of any C.I.D. Committee.

One has the strong impression that Churchill is persistently pushing forward his policy in various directions, and, with the Prime Minister away, it is not easy to resist him. The discussion on Aircraft Supply this morning and on the addition of temporary officers are fresh illustration.

10 May   Sir Maurice Hankey to T.J.   *Paris*
Just a line to ask if you have modified your views as to honours. No one has deserved them more and I should love to put your name forward. If your principles stand in the way I should like to tell the P.M. so, in order, at least, that he may know what I think about you.

*   *   *   *

P.S. If there is any particular honour you have a fancy for give me a hint.
   T.J. again declined.

---

[1] Which by now was causing a grave risk of starvation in many parts of Germany, to say nothing of lasting under-nourishment. It was, of course, a better diplomatic lever to force Germany to agree to the Versailles terms than any occupation of territory.

[2] Chief British representative in the Allied Armistice Commission; headed the British military mission to Russia and the Baltic in 1919.

[3] Cecil Harmsworth (1869–1948); younger brother of Lords Northcliffe and Rothermere; a member of Lloyd George's Secretariat 1917–19, Minister of Blockade 1919, junior Minister at the Foreign Office 1919–22.

14 May . . . Churchill fiercely resisted Chamberlain's suggestion[1] as an invasion of ministerial responsibility. It was up to ministers to come to decisions and of course to consult the Treasury. This endless referring of things to committees made for delay. Then Chamberlain replied that it was impossible for him to give detailed attention necessary to proposals brought before him, sometimes suddenly and casually by ministers and that it was not possible for his Treasury advisers to be completely au fait with the reaction of proposals. Churchill went on very hotly and personally to protest against the present system of Cabinet government with its super-ministers and had a passing dig at Auckland Geddes. He referred to a definite undertaking given him by the P.M. before the last Election that there would be an end to the system of super-ministers. When Churchill was at his most provocative stage B.L. cut in very sharply that while he was in the chair he would not allow such speeches as Churchill was making and that if Churchill did not like the present system he could leave it.

Curzon proceeded to pour oil on the waters by suggesting a compromise which was ultimately adopted and later on B.L. very magnanimously apologised to Churchill and withdrew the words he had used and the incident closed.

After the meeting Curzon remarked that Churchill had succeeded in doing what no one else had done—put B.L. into a temper. B.L. mentioned the matter to me today and I told him truly that I had been surprised at his apology, the provocation having been so great. Of course I have known, as Secretary of the Home Affairs Committee, that Churchill would never attend it and on more than one occasion while Acting Secretary he has voiced his resentment at our taking notes of the discussion. I think the feeling of most of us present was strongly with B.L.

17 May Lunched with Haldane. Was shewn into the drawing room on the first floor. Haldane came in while I was admiring some water colours by a daughter of Edmund Gosse. He said they occupied places on the walls where were formerly hung some presentation pictures of the German manoeuvres given to him by the Kaiser which he had removed in deference to the plaints of his friends. I remarked that he had not dethroned Hegel and Schelling from his study—he replied 'No, nor from anywhere else'. We lunched alone and he began with the Archbishop's Enabling Bill which he regarded as raising far reaching constitutional issues. He would oppose it, so would Lord Crewe and Lord Buckmaster. I said I thought the Cabinet had probably never heard of the Bill but that I would draw Bonar Law's attention to it. . . .

. . . On the whole he thought the Government was in a bad way. I asked him about the squabble over Kitchener and the shells.[2] Haldane said that

---

[1] Made at a Cabinet meeting, that the consequences of the departmental proposals about servicemen's pay should be referred to financial experts.

[2] A reference to the shortage of munitions in 1915. Kitchener was Secretary of State for War 1914–16 and was drowned when sailing on a mission to Archangel in 1916, when H.M.S. *Hampshire* struck a mine.

Asquith based his speech on a telegram from Kitchener which Asquith had not preserved and which search at the War Office had not discovered. Kitchener's appointment was a great example of newspaper government. Kitchener was a great man but he knew nothing about modern warfare. He was all right in the East with dervishes but was not good against the scientific Germans. Lord Roberts was equally ignorant and neither knew how to use experts. On the other hand, when Kitchener took a decision, right or wrong, he pushed it through—that was his virtue. Haldane introduced Kitchener to the War Office and for the first two or three days of the war had his hand very much on the machine and then Kitchener took control. Haldane produced from his drawer a letter dated November 19, 1918, from Sir Douglas Haig, paying Haldane a very high tribute for his work in laying the foundations of the army organisation and regretting the persecution to which he had been subjected.

23 May   T.J. to J. T. Davies
Will you please suggest to the P.M. that in my view it would be advisable, if at all possible for him, to invite Herbert Fisher over for a night to Paris. Fisher, Shortt, and Addison have been exchanging views and I believe all three are very concerned about the state of Ireland and disturbed at the suggestion that Sinn Fein be 'proclaimed'. They recognise that no constructive policy can be developed in the P.M.'s absence but they don't want the pitch queered in the meantime.

I believe all three Ministers, and certainly Fisher, are deeply apprehensive about some aspects of the Peace settlement and at the growing signs of criticism in this country. I need not develop this but I strongly urge that Fisher should be sent for.

2 July Clement Jones came in and gossiped about Paris. He said that Milner, Barnes, and Smuts had not been helpful. Barnes was suffering from swelled head and he hoped the *Daily Mirror* rumour that he was going to Berlin as ambassador was true! Smuts' relations with the P.M. had been so strained that they refused to meet each other at lunch. The P.M. maintained that they ought to have been more constructive and positive in their criticisms during the debates instead of coming in at the tail end with their protests. Living all together at the same hotel and meeting at meals and conferences, on the stairs and in corridors and never being able to escape from one another had been too much for their tempers.

Had a talk with Barnes. In his view the villain of the 'Peace' was Wilson, who had proved himself to be anything but a strong man and a child in the hands of Clemenceau, who, as Barnes put it, 'could buy him at one end of the street and sell him at the other'. The French President apparently made an enormous impression on Barnes by his ability. Barnes had written several times to the P.M. protesting about the terms of the Peace Treaty especially the Reparation Clauses. The P.M.'s defence had been that Wilson had apparently committed himself in advance to Clemenceau before meeting the

P.M. and that this had repeatedly happened. I told Barnes what Bullitt[1] told me, viz., that Wilson had tried to carry out his principles and that at a certain stage, finding he was being beaten, he had threatened to leave the Conference and go back and tell the Americans that it was hopeless trying to pull up negotiations to the level of his principles, and that great pressure had been brought on Wilson, not only by the French and ourselves, but also by Hoover and House, who urged that if he broke up the Conference revolution would be precipitated in Europe and perhaps in England. Barnes doubted this and thought that Woodrow Wilson had made no effective stand for his principles. Barnes had favoured Keynes' financial scheme of an international pool but when this was defeated they were left with the plan of Lord Sumner and Lord Cunliffe, both stony hearted men.[2] Further, there was the poisonous influence of Hughes, who seemed to exercise a good deal of power over the P.M., Barnes thought. He ridiculed the suggestion that he was going to Berlin.

We passed to home politics. He was annoyed at B.L.'s pronouncement against nationalisation and said he proposed to declare himself in the opposite sense. He thought from recent conversations that the P.M. was moving to the Left. He had heard nothing about a Centre Party. I said I thought B.L.'s influence considerable owing to his quiet pertinacity.

Sent for by Bonar Law. He shewed me the draft of an answer which he proposed to give this afternoon to a Parliamentary question on drink. The answer summarised the Cabinet's decision and he was going to see the P.M. about it. I said I had come to think that it was better to have no legislation just now beyond continuing in some shape the Liquor Control Board, and that the Government ought to tackle the question next session and go strong for state purchase and local option. I appealed in a personal and very earnest way to Bonar Law to join forces with the P.M. in trying to solve this question. I told him that isolated as he was from the lives of the common people the distress caused by the abuse of strong drink was probably never present to him, whereas those of us who knew the conditions of great cities like Glasgow and the mining districts intimately felt there were few ways in which statesmen could increase the happiness of mankind so much as by taking away the profit-making motive of the sellers of strong drink. On this he said that he entirely agreed that the Government ought to face the question and that he himself for 20 years had been in favour of state purchase. This astonished me and of course I could not tell him that he had given no great evidence of his belief during the 20 years. . . .

8 July   T.J. to Sir Maurice Hankey
Owing to the prolonged discussion this morning on the coal question, your second message stating that the P.M. was in favour of putting up the price came in good time. . . . Sir Evan Jones made it quite clear to the Cabinet that to operate the present system of limiting profits in effect means that he

---

[1] W. C. Bullitt, President Wilson's emissary on a special mission to Russia in 1919, later American Ambassador in Russia and France.

[2] A judge and a director of the Bank of England respectively.

has to manage the mines of the country—owing to the studied apathy of the coal owners. The sooner, therefore, we get a decision on the Government's policy with regard to the Sankey Report the better. The Chancellor of the Exchequer drew a most lurid picture of the country's financial position.

I gather that Sir Auckland Geddes will be in Criccieth for the weekend and I hope you will force a decision on this matter.

10 July   T.J. to E. F. Wise

Thanks for your letter and memo.[1] I tried Bonar Law on the co-operative machinery in connection with clothing only this morning—before receiving your letter—but he was convinced that there would be such a howl from the private traders that it was useless for the Government to recognise Co-ops in any way. I told him that I thought the Labour Party would soon be clamouring for a Clothing Commission on the lines of the Coal Commission. He thought action was necessary much sooner than the time when a report could be expected from a commission. Further, a commission would only bring out facts without providing remedies.

A suggestion is under consideration for the setting up of Local Tribunals to investigate specific complaints of profiteering. The idea is to resuscitate the Tribunals used by National Service with the addition of some women. It does not seem very promising.

Drop in if you have a chance.

11 July   T.J. to Sir Maurice Hankey

1. Naval Estimates

You will have seen the two papers by the First Lord and the paper by Chamberlain on this most important question. I am deliberately delaying their consideration by the Cabinet until the P.M.'s return as they raise issues of the first importance. The crux of the matter—as it seems to me—is, having squashed Germany are we now going to start building against America? It is clearly in the minds of the Sea Lords. If they get their way we shall manufacture Bolsheviks faster than Hoover produced his pigs.

I know your own love for the Navy, but I think even you will hesitate to endorse the new estimates. The world's capital is now practically controlled by the U.S.A. and it is sheer madness for us to try to compete with them or to do anything to provoke building by them.

2. Coal

The root consideration here is to secure the active good-will of the miners in order to increase the output. Putting up the price to the consumers may delay nationalisation but it won't necessarily secure more coal. I earnestly hope that before the P.M. comes to a decision he will see either Sankey or Redmayne.

The miner's representatives on the Commission know that there exists a plan for unification of control worked out before the appointment of the Commission in the Coal Controller's department. It was only produced to

---

[1] On the need to check the rise in the price of clothing—a large factor in the cost of living.

the Commission a day or two before they reported. Something on the lines of that scheme short of nationalisation may be feasible.

3. Treasury

When considering the reconstruction of the Government I hope you will recall our past talks about strengthening the Treasury. Watching as I do the Cabinet discussions day by day, one grows to have a horrible feeling that no one master mind is gripping our financial position in its entirety. The Chancellor of the Exchequer, conscientious, industrious, and with much commonsense, is overwhelmed. One feels he is fighting a losing battle. Ought he not to have at his elbow someone of the calibre of Reading or Revelstoke?

You won't mind my throwing out these suggestions?

12 July   Hankey wrote to T.J. agreeing in principle with all his suggestions.

12 July   Sir Maurice Hankey to T.J.   *Criccieth*
This is very secret and strictly personal. I enclose a copy of two Memoranda which I have today evolved.

The first is a draft memo on the organisation of the Cabinet. This is based on my own ideas, which happened to be almost identical with proposals which were sent very privately to the Prime Minister by Winston. I have amalgamated them into the enclosed. The P.M. wants to cut down the Cabinet to 15 Members, but I think he will find it very difficult, and I am not sure that it matters under this scheme. P.M. is in general agreement with these ideas, though he has not yet seen the scheme.

The second Paper shows my general idea for the Secretariat. It is boiled down from a much longer Paper which I was going to send you, but which, on the whole, I think I will keep back.

I need not say how immensely I shall value your opinions on these two Papers. If they meet with your general views, we might perhaps reserve discussion on points of detail until my return, but if you have any serious criticism, I should be glad if you could find time to drop me just one line.

I am sure that, as regards Assistant Secretaries, we must sooner or later revert to the employment generally of Civil Servants. . . .

15 July   T.J. to Sir Maurice Hankey
We had a very protracted sitting this morning on the question of Army, Navy, and Air Force pay. Fisher, as Chairman of the Committee, had simply correlated the rates of pay proposed by the Services and had made little or no attempt to keep them down. Bonar Law and Chamberlain were rather aghast at the figures now proposed—e.g. basic rate in the Army 2/9 rising to 4/- in two years; second lieutenant 13/- a day, plus allowances, making about £358 a year. After some pressure, Churchill showed some willingness to allow part of the pay to be regarded as a price bonus to be varied with the course of prices; but the Admiralty refused to budge an inch and took the usual line of expecting the Cabinet simply to register without alteration the decisions already reached. Bonar Law proposed to have the matter held up

for the return of the Prime Minister, but the Admiralty would not wait and the discussion was adjourned until tomorrow. Bonar Law's main point was that if, as he believes, prices come down considerably in the next five years, the rates now offered will look absurd and will cause much agitation. . . .

15 July   T.J. to Sir Maurice Hankey
I have read the re-organisation scheme which you very kindly sent me and I think it is most admirably thought out. It seems to incorporate fully our lessons gained here during the war. I need not worry you with small points of detail at this stage. The working out of the scheme will be disturbed by the Ministers who happen to occupy certain posts at the moment. Among the nine below the eighteen, you have Eric Geddes, Addison, and Worthington-Evans.[1] The last named has more than once, I believe, pestered Bonar Law about his 'Cabinet Status'. Montagu is another very restless Minister who will probably not be satisfied if he is not on your Executive Committee—and even then he may not be satisfied!

I think it likely that, while you may be allowed to retain some or all of the present Assistant Secretaries who are not Civil Servants, the Treasury will probably press, as you hint, that the Office should normally be recuited from the Civil Service plus the floating margin of M.P.'s to which you refer.

17 July   Provisional decisions at a Conference held in Criccieth
Present: The Prime Minister
Sir Auckland Geddes
Sir Robert Horne
Sir Hubert Llewellyn Smith
Professor Chapman
Sir Maurice Hankey.
  1. No nationalisation of the coal industry on a Post Office basis.
  2. Nationalisation of mining royalties.
  3. Social amelioration in mining districts as a charge on royalties of ungotten minerals.
  4. Consultation with mining owners re possibilities of combination by districts, and, if so, what arrangements to be made: e.g. division of profits after wages, charges, and dividends on capital.

9 August   T.J. wrote to E.T.J. describing the funeral of Principal Roberts of Aberystwyth and mentioned the difficulties that would arise if he were offered the Principalship.
. . . I am quite willing to go to chapel and preferably to Sunday School, provided I can have a Sunday of *rest* in the week! I can't work at my pace without some easygoing spell and sleep. It is this and your surveillance and the bracing London air that keeps me going so well. In the truest sense, so

---

[1] Sir Laming Worthington-Evans (1868–1931); Conservative M.P. 1910–31, Minister of Blockade 1918, Minister of Pensions 1919–20, Minister without Portfolio 1920–1, Secretary of State for War 1921–2, 1924–9, Postmaster-General 1923–4.

far as I know myself, the last two and a half years, in London, have been the most religious of my life, the most emptied of all selfish thoughts, the most wholly devoted to the service of God and man. But this I cannot cry aloud and if the chapel test is applied then of course I shall go under hopelessly.

Of course I was bound to feel, in the memorial service, a great desire to run away from the whole business and go on with the work in London, which I *can* do. . . .

24 August   Winston Churchill to Sir Maurice Hankey   *War Office*
I have again looked through the proofs of the official history of the first four months of the naval war[1] and I remain of the opinion that it is impossible that such an account should be published unaccompanied by authentic documents. The work is conceived in a spirit of hiding the truth and it would grossly mislead the public in regard to some of the most notable episodes of that period. If the book were to be published it would be necessary for me to publish simultaneously a considerable series of authentic documents. I have given directions for these to be collected and printed in order that they can be submitted to the Cabinet at the same time as the question of publishing the official history is discussed. Pending such a discussion I cannot agree to any publication being made.

I have no doubt that the proper course for an official history is to publish a series of authentic documents selected so as to give a fair and truthful picture and edited in such a way as to make them interesting and intelligible as well as from the point of view of State secrets which still have a current importance. It is futile to state there are thousands of pages of such documents. The great bulk of them are not relevant to any general story of the war and are mere matters of routine. What is wanted is the important operative telegrams, orders, and minutes, and these there can be no difficulty in supplying in a moderate compass so long as the intention is to expose the truth without regard to individuals. This course should be pursued both by the War Office and the Admiralty, and I understood that it was generally in accordance with the Prime Minister's ideas. This is the course which I shall continue to press upon the Cabinet. . . .

28 August   Today Edwin Montagu circulated to the Cabinet a series of extracts from the P.M.'s speech on War Aims he made to the delegates of the Trade Unions on 5 January, 1918. Montagu rubbed them in by heading the extracts in heavy type: 'Lest We Forget'. Here are the three extracts.

'Nor are we fighting to destroy Austria-Hungary or to deprive Turkey of its capital, or of the rich and renowned lands of Asia Minor and Thrace, which are predominantly Turkish in race.'

'Outside Europe we believe that the same principles should be applied. While we do not challenge the maintenance of the Turkish Empire in the homelands of the Turkish race with its capital at Constantinople—the passage between the Mediterranean and the Black Sea being internationalised

---

[1] Written by Sir Julian Corbett.

and neutralised—Arabia, Armenia, Mesopotamia, Syria, and Palestine are in our judgment entitled to a recognition of their separate national conditions.'

'I can venture to claim that I am speaking not merely the mind of the Government, but of the nation and of the Empire as a whole.'

T.J. to Sir Maurice Hankey
This is not very 'nice' is it? We have 50 copies but I have held it up in case you should feel like sending a note to Montagu. Anyway we will await your instruction.

Sir Maurice Hankey to T.J.
I am afraid it would be useless for me to write. He was always quoting this in Paris. I think you will have to circulate. Of course the reply is that this passage of the speech on 5 Jan. was intended as an invitation to the Turks to come out of the war. They did not do so, but went on fighting, causing the death of thousands. Added to this they have shown their continued incapacity for rule since then by permitting further massacres. I daresay this will draw on Montagu a sharp reply from the P.M.

9 September   Sir Maurice Hankey to T.J.   *Normandy*
We shall be going up to Paris about Friday, and one of the subjects which I expect will be discussed is the question of Syria. One of the difficulties in regard to this question has always arisen in connection with the oasis of Tadmor. You will remember that the Sykes-Picot Agreement gave Mosul to the French and left Palestine undecided. Last December, Clemenceau agreed that we should have Mosul and Palestine. Since then, we have insisted that we must also have communication by a British railway and pipe line from the Mosul area to the Mediterranean, probably at Haifa, and we have always urged that Tadmor was necessary to the construction of the railway and pipe line.

The point on which we want to get some information is as to whether a pipe line could, in fact, ever be constructed. I should be very much obliged if you could get hold of Sir Frederick Black, who, as you know, after being in the Admiralty and the Ministry of Munitions, has gone either as Chairman or as a Government Director, in any case as a Government nominee, on the Anglo-Persian Oil, which is a company under government control which, through related companies, has a concession over the Mesopotamian oilfields. You should explain to him that the matter is very confidential. . . .

10 September   T.J. to Sir Maurice Hankey
. . . I saw a man today just back from the Trade Union Congress in Glasgow. He felt the atmosphere very 'Left' and said that Smillie had an 'enormous success'. He was much impressed by Hodges. J. H. Thomas told me that, unless the P.M. moves very definitely towards the Left even if it involves a general election, it will be impossible to check the growth of Direct Action

movement. The interview with Ironside published by the *Daily Express* had a considerable effect on the delegates who thoroughly distrust Churchill. The *Daily News*, too, has been making capital out of the Reconstruction pamphlet just issued, on the Military Mission of the British Empire, about which Clyne wrote on Saturday.

On 26 September T.J.'s father died. He wrote to E.T.J.:
I think I must owe him a lot so far as I can judge by trying to stand outside myself and look on. . . . I went to Rhymney [his birthplace] yesterday. . . . The place looked extraordinarily dilapidated, a sense of ruined houses and rough stony roads with one or two new buildings stuck in the middle of it all like a last challenge to the forces of decay all around. Only the hills looked enduring and unchanging, with a drizzle of rain falling as of old. There is an awkward uneven way from the station to the grave on the bleak hillside—all part of my very earliest memories, even to a spring by the wayside which is still running. The grave itself is a largish enclosure with two headstones in it and room for a third. Grandfather, grandmother, and their 4 children— Elizabeth 18, Thomas 10, Enoch 32, and Mamma are buried there. Dad will be the last to be put there.

10 October   Lancelot Storr to T.J.   *Offices of the War Cabinet*
My own conviction (which must be shared by every generous-minded man 'in the know') is that *you* really settled the recent railway strike. Consequently you deserve an earldom and at least £25,000! But you, as the most modest man of my acquaintance, would refuse these: and you are probably right in thinking that your acceptance would undermine and destroy your exceptional influence in the labour world.

I write with some (I hope, pardonable) feeling on the subject as I have never yet met a man who commanded such universal respect and affection as you do. . . .

The one academic post that T.J. really wanted was the Principalship of the University College of Wales at Aberystwyth, where both he and his wife had been students. In October he decided to become a candidate for it. Once again the enthusiasm of his friends, this time in particular of David Davies, who, with his sisters, was a generous patron of the college, failed against local prejudice and a particularly unpleasant campaign of innuendo in the Welsh press. The dream of a partnership between T.J.'s vision and the Davies' wealth was shattered. It was not until after the Second World War that the college was largely rebuilt, on the hill above the town, looking out over Cardigan Bay, as T.J. had always intended. Nor, in 1919, could he foresee that he would spend the last ten years of his life as the much honoured President of the college for which he cared so deeply. After the Aberystwyth post had gone to the college Registrar, T.J. was sounded for the Principalship at Swansea, and Lord Aberdare wrote asking if he might have the honour of proposing him for the deferred appointment at Cardiff. But by this time T.J. was sickened by academic politics and firmly turned down both proposals. The wounds inflicted at Aberystwyth were not easily healed.

1 December   Lord Esher[1] *to E.T.J.*

T.J. should not think ever of the 'City'. As long as he has money *enough*, nothing matters. A 'fortune' is not worth the making. If he could get *one* millionaire friend to come into the Garton Foundation[2], he should take it over. £1,500 a year for himself and then make it the centre of all propaganda for the new world. He is cut out to be St. Francis of Assisi or Ignatius Loyola and *not* William Waldorf Astor!

If I was his age, I could make the G.F. the heart of modern education. I believe in the barefoot friars and *not* in a Minister of Education. Fisher*men* not Fisher! No great thing in this world has ever been achieved by organised effort. Only by a *Man*, acting on the souls of men. You may call him Socrates or Moses, Paul of Tarsus or Napoleon. When machinery begins to work you get the Catholic Church or the British Cabinet. I should like T.J. to take over a great propaganda and send out his friars far and wide. *But* I agree (such are the exigencies of civilisation) that we require a millionaire, like Joseph of Arimathaea. No one has ever appreciated what he did for Christianity! The mere fact that T.J. thought of himself as a street minstrel, with you and Evans as his chorus, is a sign of grace. Tell him to cheer up. It is wonderful to go through the world singing.

8 December   Sir Alfred T. Davies[3] *to T.J.*   *Board of Education*

Many thanks for letting me see the enclosed papers: I congratulate you heartily upon them. Such testimony as they contain must at least be a solace when you are tempted to feel saddened, if not disheartened, by recent events.

I am beginning to despair of our fellow-countrymen when called upon to exercise patronage in their democratic assemblies. I cannot forget that the Central Welsh Board rejected both an Owen Edwards and a William Williams, preferring in each case a much inferior man. And so it goes on. If this kind of thing is done 'in the green tree' what will be done 'in the dry'? The question will have a very direct bearing on the continued efficiency of our Welsh Inspectorate for Education, for strong efforts will be made very soon (in fact are now being made) to wrest that branch of educational service from Whitehall and transfer it to a local body in Wales. In that event there will be plenty of opportunity for a repetition of what has just happened in your case. Alas for Wales and Welsh Education!

1920

The post-war boom continued, with prices and wages rising steadily and British manufacturers expanding their output to meet the expected restoration of the world market. In this buoyant atmosphere the Labour Party and trade unions rode high.

[1] Reginald Baliol Brett (1852–1930), second Viscount Esher; Liberal M.P. 1880–5, a close friend of Edward VII and George V and, like Haldane, much concerned with the machinery of government. Secretary, Office of Works 1885–1902; member of Committee of Imperial Defence. Lawrence Burgis, who was on the staff of the War Cabinet Secretariat, was his private secretary 1909–13.

[2] An educational foundation set up by Sir Richard Garton.

[3] Permanent Secretary of the Welsh Department at the Board of Education.

The Trades Union Congress was created and trade union membership rose to eight million. On the far left, the Communist Party of Great Britain was formed and, urged by Lenin, entered on a policy of parliamentary intervention, which was rebuffed by the Labour Party. Plans for a General Strike flourished and were put into political effect in August, when the threat was enough to stop the Cabinet's plan for intervention on behalf of Poland in the Polish-Russian war. Imaginative leadership was shown in many unions and Ernest Bevin won concessions for the dockers at their commission of enquiry. But the two sides in the coal industry reverted to trial by ordeal: after threats throughout the summer, the miners came out on strike in October. Lloyd George used the Emergency Powers Act against them, but also made concessions. While the euphoria of the boom lasted, Lloyd George also extended unemployment insurance to cover almost the whole working population. It was fortunate that he did so when unemployment was believed to be a temporary phenomenon, because in the winter the boom broke. The return to the pre-war economy had been a fiction; the old international market no longer existed; and the primary producers of the world faced ruin from over-production and falling prices. By the end of the year unemployment was rising fast.

The European stage was filled with the working of the League and conferences without end, to settle Germany and reparations, and to quieten French fears for future security. Lloyd George was the prime mover, both at San Remo and Spa, but the French military occupation of German towns, and Belgian plans for old-style balance of power alliances, betrayed the existence of an alternative diplomacy, opposed to that of the League. British policy towards Russia changed abruptly, from backing the Poles in their war against Bolshevism, to negotiations for a trade agreement with the Russian representatives.

The situation in Ireland grew worse, as intermittent outrages developed into guerrilla warfare. To reinforce the R.I.C. against the I.R.A. came first the Black and Tans, and then the Auxiliary Division. Brutality, arson, and murder became commonplace. The Cabinet was faced with the ancient dilemma: Home Rule or coercion. Home Rule itself was out of date. Lloyd George brought in the complicated Government of Ireland Act, giving a Home Rule parliament to Ulster as well as the South, with a single Council for all Ireland at Westminster. The setting of a date for elections in 1921 raised the question of what would happen with Sinn Fein in control of most of the administrative machinery of the South.

T.J. became steadily more involved in Irish affairs and was the acknowledged expert in the Cabinet Secretariat. He began to put his own views for a settlement direct to Lloyd George. He saw Sir Robert Morant frequently, before the latter's death in March. He was appointed to the Board set up by the Carnegie Endowment to prepare the Economic History of the War and he agreed to write the section on Wales and the war.

13 January   T.J. to Sir Maurice Hankey

The Cabinet met at 4.30 this afternoon with Mr. Chamberlain in the Chair. Sir Eric [Geddes] gave a report of this afternoon's conference at which he had met six of the N.U.R. representatives. I may be able to catch the post with the Minutes but I wanted to convey the impression left on the Cabinet by Sir Eric and the Railway Managers who were present. They feel pretty certain that there will be no immediate strike and are satisfied that Thomas and Cramp[1] are doing their utmost to preserve peace and help the Government and get the terms accepted. Geddes and Horne are drafting the reply of the Government tonight and will meet the railwaymen tomorrow at 3.

[1] J. T. Cramp, assistant secretary of the National Union of Railwaymen.

They will stand firm (1) on the average as against the maximum; (2) for the sliding scale varying with the cost of living; but (3) will not object to the application of the Great Britain settlement to Ireland and will undertake to deal with odd grades and individual cases of hardship.

15 January   T.J. to Sir Maurice Hankey
You will long ere this have heard of the happy termination of the Railway trouble. It was a very near thing: in fact, I believe, the voting was 28 to 25 and the voting to refer the matter to the Triple Alliance was equally close. There is no doubt that Thomas and Cramp have worked loyally by their bargain with Geddes and done their utmost for peace. There is a chance of some of the branches, e.g. Yorkshire and South Wales, proving rebellious buy Bromley of the other Union has issued instructions to his men not to join in any spasmodic and local outbursts. I sent you the Government reply. Geddes and Horne agreed to omit the greater part of the preamble . . . at Thomas's request because, as he rightly put it, this preachment (written by Horne) would not help the 'atmosphere'.

There has been a big meeting this afternoon of the Supply and Transport Committee[1] with Churchill, Long, and a number of other Ministers present to discuss the question of protection during a big strike. Churchill made it perfectly plain that he could not furnish troops and the general feeling was in favour of reviving the project of a Civic Guard. However, I think, in view of the railway settlement, that the power of the Triple Alliance has been greatly weakened and that we are not in immediate danger of anything on a big scale.

I hope that the P.M. has sent some congratulatory message to Geddes and Horne.

17 January   Sir Maurice Hankey to T.J.   *Claridge's Hotel, Paris*
Personal and Secret
The ministers who have come over here seem to have the 'wind-up' to the most extraordinary extent about the industrial situation. C.I.G.S. also is positively in a state of dreadful nerves on the subject. Churchill is the only one who is sane on this subject, and on the subject of Denekin *he* is a nuisance. From a meeting yesterday evening I came away with my head fairly reeling. I felt I had been in Bedlam. Red revolution and blood and war at home and abroad!

It seems to be Horne who has upset them all. What is the evidence? My own impressions are all the other way. I do not deny many disquieting features, but according to my observations they are less disquieting than they have been during the last few months. Basil Thomson[2] had certainly suggested this. The output of coal is better, and the bankers tell me that business

[1] The organization to maintain essential supplies in the event of a major or general strike, set up by Lloyd George in 1919. It existed for several years and was the platform from which the Government handled the General Strike in 1926.
[2] Sir Basil Thomson (1861–1939); former Governor of Dartmoor and Wormwood Scrubs prisons, Assistant Commissioner of Police 1913–19, Director of Intelligence, Scotland Yard 1912–21.

is beginning to move. All this indicates a better state of affairs. I am all for reasonable precautions but all against panic measures.

I have told the P.M. what I think ought to be done. I am dead against trying to create a citizen guard or increasing the army in a hurry on any pretext. That will only precipitate the very trouble we want to avoid. And the men won't come without an appeal of such a character as would make trouble inevitable. This is the proper policy:

1. Make absolutely sure of your arms and munitions.

2. Prepare the cadres of your future organisation.

3. If and when trouble arises, you have only to hold up your little finger to get as many men as you require to ensure security. That is the moment to form your permanent organisation.

Let me know what you think. I shouldn't be surprised if, as the result of the Presidential election,[1] we came bundling home next week. Clemenceau says his position in the peace conference is unaltered, and he will finish off the questions of Russia and the Adriatic, but will not go on to the Turkish question.

I shall be glad to get away as I have taken a dislike to this hotel. It is not unjustly termed the Hotel des Cocottes, and is a very unsuitable residence for the P.M. and a serious mission. I am heartily sick of continental music and the sight of painted women.

19 January   T.J. to Sir Maurice Hankey

I entirely agree with your view of the industrial outlook for the next few months and think that Horne exaggerates the danger of a social upheaval. The railway settlement is bound to weaken any united action by the Triple Alliance. One knows how furious Smillie and Bob Williams[2] are with Thomas and in today's papers Henderson is down on him for accepting the principle of the sliding scale. I do not mean that there will be peace in the railway world for long. In South Wales, at any rate, there will be no peace until there is a definite declaration on railway nationalisation. As to the miners, they are busy developing their campaign and a number of able leaflets are being written by their best men in furtherance of this. This means that, for some time at any rate, they will try constitutional methods rather than resort to direct action. What Churchill and co. forget is that there are other ways of averting discontent than with civil guards and the military. Take this last example of the delay of the President of the Board of Trade in issuing the reports on profiteering—the deliberate delay, if not attempt at suppresssion as the Labour people are saying. The 'Herald' has been clamouring for the reports and it was left to the Trade Union Secretary of the Wool Sorters (Mackinder) and Sidney Webb to force the issue on Friday at the meeting of the Central Committee. Probably the spinners (masters and men) will throw the entire blame of profiteering on to the Board of Trade, because, if I remember aright, they urged the Board of Trade to revert to the standard clothing

[1] At which the ailing President Wilson was replaced by W. G. Harding.

[2] Robert Williams, Secretary of the National Transport Workers' Federation 1912–25 and a member of the Labour Party delegation to Russia in 1920.

scheme and the Board of Trade turned it down. I remember personally at a Cabinet Meeting urging Inverforth[1] to revive the scheme with the aid of the great quantities of cloth in the hands of the Government, but he would not hear of it. This was at a discussion we had just before the P.M. returned and rushed the Profiteering Act through. I quote this as an example of the sort of thing which spreads distrust of the Government, not only through the Labour world but among the middle classes who are heavily hit by the price of clothing.

I had a long talk with the Coal Controller today and found him fairly sanguine except about Lancashire, where, he says, the trouble will continue for another fortnight. . . . In the east end of London the position is that there is just enough to meet current demands but no margin whatever. This is partly due to bad transport, but also to the fact that the east-enders are prosperous and are consuming right up to their ration. I told the Coal Controller that it was odd that I could get in Hampstead as a new settler any amount of coal, coke, and anthracite! The Coal Controller is getting out a statement of the whole situation for the P.M.

T.J.'s notes on a conference on industrial disturbances, held on 2 February, illustrate the Cabinet's fears of industrial action and revolution in 1919–20.
The Prime Minister first discovered from the Adjutant-General[2] the number of troops in Great Britain and Ireland as Churchill and the C.I.G.S. in Paris had painted a very lurid picture of the country's defenceless condition. The A.G. omitted particulars of the gunners but the P.M., who throughout played the rôle of taking the revolution very seriously, insisted on being given the number of guns, and then turned to Trenchard[3] asking—'How many airmen are there available for the revolution?' Trenchard replied that there were 20,000 mechanics and 2,000 pilots but only 100 machines which could be kept going in the air. During the war it took 46 men to keep one machine in the air. The pilots had no weapons for ground fighting. The P.M. presumed they could use machine guns and drop bombs.

The Home Secretary then outlined his proposals to raise a special temporary force of 10,000 soldiers for the national emergency. The P.M., I think, believes that the Home Office has been got at by the War Office and that this was a War Office dodge for increasing the number of army recruits, and when he pointed out that 8 battalions intended for the plebiscitory areas had been detained at home, Shortt's demand for the 10,000 collapsed.

Munro[4] pointed out that the existing police force was inadequate either for the revolution or for large industrial strikes accompanied possibly by sabotage.

[1] Andrew Weir, cr. Lord Inverforth 1919 (1865–1955); senior partner, Andrew Weir and Co., shipowners and merchants, and president, A. Weir, Shipping and Trading Co. Ltd., Surveyor-General of Supply, War Office 1917–19, Minister of Munitions 1919–21.
[2] Lieut.-Gen. Sir George Macdonogh.
[3] Air Marshal Sir Hugh Trenchard (1873–1956); Chief of Air Staff 1918–29, Commissioner, Metropolitan Police 1931–5.
[4] Robert Munro, later Lord Alness (1868–1955); Secretary of State for Scotland 1916–22.

The P.M. 'You won't get sabotage at the beginning of the strike.'

Roberts.[1] 'You will have to take sabotage at the beginning of the strike into account. There are large groups preparing for Soviet government.'

Eric Geddes. 'You have got to reckon on the electric power stations being put out of order.'

The P.M. '10,000 troops would be of little use. How long will it take the well-disposed to range themselves on the side of law?'

Eric Geddes. 'Some of the local London Councils would not help as they are in the hands of Labour. It is doubtful if the electric engineers who helped in the railway strike would help again.'

Macready[2]. 'On our information we do not run to the revolution yet. If there is an outbreak of strikes and if there is a sufficient force available, civil or military, to stop it *at once*, it will fizzle out. We were told today that 700 rifles were concealed in Liverpool. Supposing sabotage and violence get ahead it is very difficult to say how far they will go. We are taking private steps to secure the aid of a certain class of citizen. It is no good taking on trade unionists. They cannot be expected to take part against their organisation.'

Roberts. 'The extreme elements are alienated from the Labour Party.'

The P.M. 'The danger of a Labour Government is that they would not take effective action against extremists. An army of a million men would not be able to prevent the great power stations being suddenly put out of gear.'

Eric Geddes. 'You could not wreck the terminal stations on the railways with a hammer. It would need a band of men so you would get warning.'

Horne. 'The miners are not going to repeat the railwaymen's failure. They are going to be organised with the transport workers and will only allow food to go to places and co-operative stores which they approve. They mean to prevent the country running on and will have bands of people waylaying vehicles.'

Long. 'The peaceable manpower of the country is without arms. I have not a pistol less than 200 years old. A Bill is needed for licensing persons to bear arms. This has been useful in Ireland because the authorities know who were possessed of arms.'

Shortt. 'The Home Office had a Bill ready but in the past there have always been objections.'

Bonar Law. 'All weapons ought to be available for distribution to the friends of the Government.'

Inverforth. 'We have a surplus of all kinds of munitions. We have been selling them to the Baltic States.'

The P.M. 'Could you tell us where they are and how they are guarded?'

Horne. 'Considerable consignments have come from Ireland to Glasgow including hand grenades.'

Then followed an amusing cross-examination by the P.M., first of Macready and then of Macdonogh, as to the comparative value of hand

---

[1] G. H. Roberts (1869–1928); Minister of Labour 1917–18, Food Controller 1919–20.

[2] General Sir Nevil Macready (1862–1946); G.O.C. in C. Forces in Ireland 1920–2.

grenades in the war in France. They hedged until one felt that they had never seen a hand grenade and pointed to the presence of the C.I.G.S. for a reply. Long intervened and said that Lord French's car had been blown up in Dublin by a hand grenade and the C.I.G.S. settled the matter by saying that he would rather be fired at by a rifle from a window than blown to fragments by a hand grenade.

Macready said that there were a number of soldiers among the Metropolitan Police who could use rifles and Auckland Geddes pointed to the Universities as full of trained men who could co-operate with clerks and stockbrokers. (During the discussion Bonar Law so often referred to the stockbrokers as a loyal and fighting class until one felt that potential battalions of stockbrokers were to be found in every town.)

Lord Lee protested against the suggestion to disband the Industrial Unrest Committee which had been making all the preparations under Sir Eric Geddes.

A Committee was set up to arrange for a census of munitions and weapons and for making them available.

Then followed some altercation between the P.M. and the C.I.G.S. as to the figures given in Paris and the figures given this morning of the available troops and as to their distribution, the C.I.G.S. pointing out that there were no barracks, no married quarters, and no training ground in the North and that on the 1st April there would be only 3 battalions in Scotland. Eric Geddes had no motors organised to move battalions about the country.

At this stage Churchill entered, and the P.M. continued to ply the A.G. for the figures of soldiers on the Rhine, France, Flanders, the Black Sea, Palestine, and India. He professed great surprise at hearing that there were 77,000 troops in India when the pre-war figure had been 70,000 troops and Churchill replied that India was in a state of extreme ferment and Afghanistan possibly at the beginning of a war. The P.M. said that the Indian figures must be gone into as the demands he had seen from the Government of India were appalling.

Then followed some further talk about the 10,000 and the battalions detained from the plebiscitory areas.

The P.M. 'In Paris, having heard of the condition of things at home, I told Clemenceau and Nitti[1] that the eleven could go to the plebiscitory areas.'

The C.I.G.S. was afterwards prepared to part with 2, and 1 had started so 8 remain here.

Horne suggested the preparation of secret lists of reliable men by the Chief Constables and Eric Geddes suggested having the Mayors up, but in view of the number of Labour Mayors and the difficulty of keeping the matter secret, there was opposition to this suggestion.

It transpired that the police were already keeping records of motor cars and drivers. Macready protested against an application he had received from the War Office asking what protection the police were providing for

---

[1] Francesco Nitti (1868–1935); Italian Prime Minister 1919–20.

their own staff. This led to a suggestion that each office in Whitehall should organise its own protection with the aid of its own clerical staff.

Mr. Long said it was amazing how free access was to Government offices.

Auckland Geddes suggested approaching the principals of the Universities privately. This, it was felt, could not be kept secret.

Churchill urged that the time to begin preparations of that kind was when the strike started. If anything were to be done publicly then it ought to be done with complete thoroughness. The Territorial Force would be recruited from 16 February. If there was a riot, e.g., in Oxford, the police could not call on the Territorial Force, but if there was a grave national emergency then there would be a Royal Proclamation and the Territorial Force would be embodied and available.

*   *   *   *

. . . In the case of a big strike there would be after the outbreak a period of bitterness and then of violence. Things would take time to work up.

The P.M. 'Lots would depend on propaganda before the strike. The propaganda now is all on one side.'

Churchill, continuing: The second kind of trouble would be a revolutionary attempt to seize the reins of Government. It would only be started by small handfuls of men and it was for the Chief Commissioner of Police to deal with, and troops would be available quickly in the centre of London. This would be a sort of Gunpowder Plot. The third type would be sabotage at the start of a strike and it was impossible to guard against that. On the other hand any cruel case of sabotage would put the strikers in a bad position with the public, would split their forces, and would be the best sort of propaganda.

Horne pointed out that the extreme element would take advantage of an industrial strike.

Chamberlain would call out the special constables the moment there was a strike of the Triple Alliance and would not wait for any case of sabotage.

*   *   *   *

Then the Conference passed on to authorise certain grants of money to carry on the preparations, to withhold stores from sale, etc. . . . Ultimately it was agreed that the Home Office vote should bear the burden.

Then came a request from Eric Geddes to be relieved from the Chairmanship of the Strike Committee. This he pressed with great persistence despite very flattering references to his special qualities for the job from Bonar Law and the P.M. Eric Geddes did not want the Ministry of Transport branded as a strike-breaking department and he had too much to do, and only one Parliamentary Secretary. It was not a Transport matter.

The P.M. 'If the strike breaks out its first brunt will fall on you.'

Churchill. 'It is not strike-breaking, it is feeding the people.'

Chamberlain. 'It is really defence of the foundations of civilisation.'

Churchill. 'It is essentially a transport matter.'

The P.M. 'It is the pivot of the whole matter but he (Eric Geddes) must have the support of the ministers. I do not know whether this thing is coming. I am only taking the view of the Minister of Labour. If we are going to have trouble in the course of a month I hope Ministers will be able to give their personal attention to the details of organisation. The country was greatly impressed last time with the Government's preparations. It helped the stability of the State. I beg the Minister of Transport to go on until we see if this materialises in the next 4 or 6 weeks.'

At last Eric Geddes agreed to carry on for a couple of months. Throughout the discussion the P.M. did a lot of unsuspected leg-pulling as he does not believe in the imminence of the revolution and more than suspects the War Office of trying to increase the army on these lines.

Eric Geddes in trying to escape from his job said it was not a responsibility to be put on one minister whereupon Churchill at once chimed in and said it was a very proper responsibility for a minister. There was a momentary fear that Churchill would offer himself for the job and perhaps this had some influence with Geddes' holding on to it. . . .

3 February   . . . This morning received a message from Montagu's secretary to say that he would like to see me at a nursing home in Manchester Street. Spent from 6 to 7 with him. I told him that no further decisions had been taken with regard to Turkey[1] and that Nitti was now ready to come to a Conference in London but that Millerand[2] was making difficulties. The P.M. had today wired to Millerand to say that he did not mind going to Paris for the spectacular part of the Treaty making—the signing, etc.—but that the discussions must take place in London, and that if the French Ministry could not come over, then we would have to go on making our own Treaty with Turkey.

I told Montagu the decisions reached by the Cabinet last week on Russia, viz., that peace was not to be made with the Bolsheviks, but that trade was to be opened with the co-operatives, that we were to support the Georgians, etc., with munitions, that we were not to send our ships to Odessa to embark refugees to places outside Russia, that if the border Baltic States made war on the Bolsheviks we would not support them, but, on the other hand, if the Bolsheviks made war on Poland, we would go to their assistance. Montagu said our diplomacy as conducted by Balfour and Curzon had been deplorable and if he left the Government they would be the persons he would attack most vigorously for letting so many opportunities slip. Curzon had committed us to the defence of Persia whereas Persia could have had peace with the Bolsheviks and so could the other border States had we encouraged them diplomatically.

He then passed on to home affairs and recalled the situation in February 1919 when he was in Paris with the P.M. His mother died and he wrote to the P.M. asking if he might cross to England for the funeral. He received a very kind letter from the P.M. asking him to breakfast on the following day before he left for England. At this breakfast the P.M. asked to see Sankey with a view to his producing a report which left the door open for nationalisation.

[1] See p. 112 for Montagu's memorandum on the treatment of Turkey.
[2] Alexandre Millerand (1859–1943); French Foreign Minister 1920; President of the Republic 1920–4.

Montagu was convinced that the P.M. was not at that time unfavourable to nationalisation. Montagu saw Sankey in the House of Lords and took up towards him a very 'judicial' attitude. Then followed the discussions at the Cabinet and the P.M.'s House of Commons statement which in Montagu's recollection departed somewhat from the precise wording of the Cabinet Minutes. I told Montagu what had happened last week at the Deputation of the Miners and how we were expecting the report of the independent accountant for circulation to the Cabinet and the Miners Federation. He said that Haldane had recently been discussing the matter with Hodges[1] and Tawney and believed that they were anxious to move on constitutional lines in view of the by-election successes. Montagu thought that the P.M. ought to declare himself in favour of nationalisation, at the same time explaining that he did this because he now understood from the miners that they were against a suitable centralised or bureaucratic control. This would be a way for the P.M. to climb down. . . .

3 February At 7.15 to St. James's Square where I dined with Lord and Lady Astor . . . The P.M. had been to luncheon with them. They had been denouncing Churchill and the reactionaries and the need for a new political advance and the P.M. had turned to Astor and commanded him to write the sort of manifesto which he thought the P.M. could and ought to make at this juncture. Astor had phoned for me to help him with this job and we worked away till 11.0 on a programme which started with a sort of nationalisation of railways, coal, and drink. Then we went on to Health and the municipalisation of hospitals and milk, and then devolution and minor Bills. I did not tell Astor that earlier in the week the P.M. had asked H. A. L. Fisher to do precisely the same thing and we had arranged a room in the Cabinet Offices and an expert shorthand typist to whom Fisher delivered, with much eloquence, his notion of what the P.M.'s speech should be.

5 February Long's Committee[2] reserved for Cabinet decision question of inclusion of Six Counties or whole of Ulster in Northern Parliament.

9 February Saw Hankey on his return from Cliveden. He thought the house party had not been very successful owing to the large numbers. There were twenty-two guests. He had a walk with the P.M. in the morning and gave him an outline of the coal policy which I had posted to him (Hankey) on Saturday. The P.M. said that he agreed generally that we ought to move along the lines indicated in my note.

Opinion, he said, was very much divided as to the course the P.M. should take just now. Garvin urged him to resign on the ground of being tired and needing a holiday. If he went on a voyage for a few months, he would come back refreshed and would soon begin to count again. Against this it was urged

[1] Frank Hodges (1887–1947); General Secretary, Miners' Federation of Great Britain 1918–24; member of Royal Commission on Coal Mines 1919; Labour M.P. 1923–4; Civil Lord of the Admiralty 1924.
[2] On the Irish Bill.

that his successor would begin to reap where he had sown, e.g. houses; and, if he had any skill, would take to himself the credit due to the reconstruction spade work done by the P.M. Others took the line—Why worry? Why not carry on? The Government had a big majority in the House. If necessary, why not about Easter or at the beginning of next session reconstruct the Cabinet without a general election? The Prime Minister could ask all Ministers to put in their resignations. He could then bring in some fresh men.

On my way back from lunch met Tom Griffiths[1]—one of the Welsh Labour M.P.s. . . . He had seen Arthur Jenkins,[2] one of the younger leaders, who assured him that the rank and file would go on with the fight even if their leaders let them down and would resort to direct action. If only the P.M. would come out for Nationalisation and throw over his present colleagues if they did not agree, he would rally a tremendous support to himself in the country. If not, he would sink between two stools. . . .

*   *   *   *

At the Cabinet this morning the P.M. gave Winston a dressing down about Russia. Winston had been complaining that we had no policy. This the P.M. described as ridiculous. Our policy was to try to escape the results of the evil policy[3] which Winston had persuaded the Cabinet to adopt. Winston was not only backing the wrong horse but a jibbing horse, namely Denikin.

10 February   Lord Esher to T.J.
The P.M. told the King the other day that he gets no letters, and even if one by chance slips into his hand he only half reads it. So, perhaps you will tell him that there is only one way to handle Millerand: a 'franchise brutale' equal to the old boy's own. I expect I am the only Englishman who ever made friends with Millerand. We got drunk together—or rather, I did. Anyway, I got K[4] and M to understand each other.

Well, no cajolery, no compromise, no wit, or rhetoric, will have any effect. The old man wears blinkers, *a mule in blinkers*. A stick and a steady pull with the reins. Thus you can inspire him with confidence. No other way. He has an exaggerated regard for uniform on soldiers' backs. He would listen more to Henry Wilson (though he would shy at his Irish humour) than to Winston. He—being a really good lawyer—would lay out F.E. flat.

The P.M. (who can lose his temper, or pretend to) should try a gust of passion. I used to tell K, 'Always stand up when you talk to M, never sit down, nothing will annoy him more'. And it did. And it answered.

Still, I think the P.M. has been badly 'let down' over this German business. What were you all doing in Number 2 and Number 10? *You* are not addicted to large 'consommation' like some of the P.M.'s colleagues!

[1] A representative of the Miners' Federation; Labour M.P. 1918–31.
[2] Assistant Secretary of the Miners' Federation; Labour M.P. 1935–46; P.P.S. to Clement Attlee 1940–5; father of Rt. Hon. Roy Jenkins M.P.
[3] Intervention.
[4] Probably Lord Kitchener.

17 February   Report to Cabinet of Committee on Ireland by Mr. Bonar Law recommending whole province of Ulster should be included in Northern Parliament.

24 February   Cabinet decide in favour of Six County area plus Belfast and Derry.

11 March   Austen Chamberlain to T.J.   *Treasury Chambers*
I think you might adopt one of these alternatives for the Minutes of today's meeting. They are better than 'submit' which is harsh.

The C/E stated that he was unable to agree with the decision of the Cabinet, but that he would accept it.
The C/E accepted the decision of the Cabinet though he was unable to approve it.

16 March   Mrs. Sidney Webb to T.J.   *41 Grosvenor Road, S.W.*
Sidney and I are very much concerned about Sir Robert Morant's death, not only from a personal point of view—and he was one of our best friends—but also from the standpoint of the re-organisation of Local Government in relation to health. I wonder whether it would be possible to get Sir John Anderson as Permanent Head of the Ministry of Health? That is really the only chance of preventing the Ministry of Health from relapsing into a Poor Law Board, which might suit the Labour Party excellently, but would not suit the people of England! And as I do not think the Labour Party will come into power for some time, I prefer to think of the people of England.

If the P.M.'s new Party is to have any kind of success it will have to build itself up on National Health as an alternative to the more thorough policy of Socialism. We must at least get a minimum of health even for Capitalism.

18 March   Violet Markham[1] to T.J.
. . . Events in Germany have tragically fulfilled the course which I prophesied to you a month ago. When I went back about 18 February the country was in a ferment over the war criminals list which gave a tremendous impetus to the Monarchist and reactionary movement. Then came the Manifesto of the Supreme Economic Council which had a very steadying effect. The mark began to improve, and during the fortnight before the revolution some elements of hope appeared to enter into the situation. Unfortunately this wiser and more conciliatory policy came too late to check the wave of reaction against the Ebert Government, a state of affairs for which I can only feel the Allies have the most grave responsibility, in as much as common sense dictated our supporting the only Government which was of any use to us for the purposes of the peace. The counter-revolution began as I thought it would from the right but, as I also expected, has swung to the left. I have

---

[1] Violet Markham, C.H., a close friend of T.J. She had been Mayor of Chesterfield and a Liberal parliamentary candidate and was on a number of Government committees during the inter-war years. Her husband, Lt.-Col. James Carruthers, was with the British Army of the Rhine at Cologne.

been satisfied all along that the Germans mean to stand by the revolution. I am absolutely unimpressed with the fears expressed in many quarters about a revival of warlike designs. The grave peril I see ahead is internal disorder, under the stress of which the whole foundation of society in Germany may crumble. As I told you before, my view is that if Germany collapses the rest of Europe will collapse in her wake. On the other hand if she can be propped up and restored, in course of time the others will recover.

The practical suggestion I have to make at this time is that if the Fates are kind enough to give the Allies another chance by re-establishing the Ebert Government, we should try and give that Government a helping hand by dealing with it more generously than in the past, and above all by trying to re-establish the economic and industrial position in Germany. . . .

* * * *

As I am writing to you, may I speak to you about another matter? In Sir Robert Morant I have lost one of my greatest friends. . . . His death at this moment leaves the Ministry of Health in a most critical situation. If the Department Board falls again under the old reactionary Local Government Board spirit which Sir Robert killed himself trying to root up, I feel that the Ministry might as well put up the shutters as regards any constructive scheme of health. The one chance of saving the position, in the opinion of some of Sir Robert's friends, is for Sir John Anderson to be appointed the new Chief Secretary. He was trained by Sir Robert, knows his mind, and how to carry out his work. . . . I am venturing to press this point on you in view of the great task of social reconstruction which is at stake in this matter.[1]

8 April *Extract from a Cabinet Minute*
Following on the despatch of the German Government Reichswehr into the Ruhr Valley to disband 'red' troops, the French have occupied Frankfort and other German towns. The number of Reichswehr in the neutral zone is approximately 20,000 as against 17,500 permitted. The French have disregarded the unanimous views of the rest of the Allies in sending troops to the Ruhr.

The Supreme Council is due to meet at San Remo on 9 April, to conclude the Turkish Treaty and to close the Peace conference. Large questions relating to Egypt, Syria, Palestine, Cilicia, Tangier are still outstanding. France's unfriendly act has bedevilled the situation and will cloud the proceedings at San Remo. . . .

8 April Discussion of Ministers on the Occupation of the Ruhr Valley
P.M.: Compare the Ruhr Valley with South Wales. If we sent troops there J. H. Thomas and some of the Labour leaders might complain but if we did not preserve order it would be complete abdication of government. We want information on a number of matters—1. the history of the suppression of the Commune in France. The Germans were in occupation of France at the time. It has important historical bearing on the present problem and I

---

[1] The post in fact went to Sir Arthur Robinson.

should like an accurate account of what happened. 2. A resumé of facts in the Ruhr Valley case. I do not know what they are. The evidence is conflicting. Some say the 'Reds' are in command. 3. I should like to have the opinions of Kilmarnock and Robertson. An ambassador should give his opinion to his Government and not be simply a post office. 4. We should get from Robertson (Rhineland Commissioner) information as to the real facts of the Red rebellion. 5. What truth is there in the suggestion of the newspapers that the agreement entered into (Bielefeld) between the German Government and the 'Reds' has been broken by the German Government?

Gen. Radcliffe: Our information is that there are 20,000 troops in the Ruhr basin as against the 17,500 allowed.

P.M.: This is a very serious departure by the French Government from united action. The first time. My suggestion is that until this is cleared up we should instruct Derby to withdraw from the Conference of Ambassadors dealing with enforcement of the Treaty and let the Governments deal with the situation. We have given the French various positions of honour, Foch at the head of the armies, Nollet as President of the Military Mission in Berlin. We may be landed one day in war with Germany through French action. Or we may have to repudiate our allies. They have sent black troops to Frankfort. If the Germans sent niggers from German Africa to Newcastle? Frankfort is a proud city!

A.C.: Like Manchester.

P.M.: Yes, or Birmingham. People here would say we can only die once, we won't stand this insult. I am sure there will be street fighting and bombardment in Frankfort. In a couple of years the Germans will have fed themselves up with sausages and be as virile as ever and they will recall their having fought for 5 years against superior forces and held their own. The French will go on and on like this and the Germans will become more and more formidable. This is an old conflict between Foch and Clemenceau. Foch in fact defeated Clemenceau and turned him out. These new men are weak and want to appear strong. That poor creature Poincare[1] is trying to show how much stronger he is than Clemenceau. Foch gives the cue and Millerand follows.

B.L.: Even this French account in the Press puts us in a false position. It was discussed at the Ambassadors Council and our representative was there.

Curzon: The situation is really rather bigger than has been suggested. According to present arrangements the Supreme Council will meet at S. Remo on 19 April. It is supposed to meet there in a friendly spirit to finish the Turkish Treaty and to finish the Peace Conference. If things continue as they are we shall meet the French P.M. in a spirit of hostility. We shall be bound to bring home to him his unfriendly action. At S. Remo there are big issues to be discussed. I have to say from my experience over the way that the French are making difficulties at every turn. There are half a dozen questions they won't settle and towards which they take up a disagreeable attitude and

[1] Raymond Poincaré (1860–1934); French Premier 1911–13, President of Republic 1913–20, Premier and Foreign Minister 1922–4, Premier 1926–9. An obstinate defender of extreme French claims, he reduced successive British negotiators to despair.

they will have to be referred to S. Remo. If anyone thinks we are going to settle at S. Remo in two or three days it is a mistake. We shall be there for ten days. All this points to the necessity of a serious talk before S. Remo with the French P.M. There are outstanding questions about Egypt, Tangier, Palestine, Cilicia, Syria and the financial clauses of the Treaty. Upon these supervenes the Ruhr trouble. Your reply does not cover the ground. A good deal of ostentatious work was done at the Ambassadors Conference. Your demand now will become known and a public explanation will be asked for and will have to be given. We can either 1. give a statement of the history of the case and send it with a formal protest to France, or 2. in view of S. Remo, Millerand should come over here as we cannot carry on business in this fashion. At S. Remo you will find yourself hung up by half a dozen questions in which the French are showing the most disagreeable spirit. Berthelot and Cambon continually refer back questions to Millerand and Millerand is not only acting as P.M. of France but as President of the Peace Conference and regards the whole body as concentrated in himself.

P.M.: I have always been in favour of winding it up (Ambassadors Conference) because as long as it is going on the French will be doing this sort of thing in the name of Europe.

* * * *

Here is a Conference to decide upon action and the French Government on their own take steps in defiance of the whole of the Allies. The Conference is a farce. If the French take such action they must do it on their own responsibility and not count on us. This is the time to stop it. It may not be serious now but it will be very serious in a couple of years. I would accept no responsibility for French troops in the Ruhr valley. . . .

* * * *

Curzon: If you hold the view that the Ambassadors' Conference should be shut up it could be put forward but there are many small matters which it would be difficult to do without it.

Sir Eyre Crowe referred to the reports of the Military, Naval, and Air Control Missions which required Allied decisions.

P.M.: I agree with Nitti that these Military Missions ought to go. The Germans think that the coup d'état was due to us. This is probably based on the thoughtless words of some soldier on one of these Missions.

Gen. Radcliffe: The Missions are in Berlin to control disarmament.

P.M.: It would be far better to deal with that from here and to send me over to see if it is being carried out. But I am not on that now. You must somehow or other mark our protest against the action of the French.

Curzon: The whole of my statement is in the same direction. Shall we publish our views?

P.M.: Why publish now? You are dealing with an allied Government. During the war I had several passages of this kind with Clemenceau and they were not published.

Curzon: You may have to make a statement in Parliament.

P.M.: I am coming to that later. My view would be to say that we thought it undesirable to make a statement at the present stage in view of the meeting to be held at S. Remo. I think Parliament would take that.

A.C.: We should know what we want to arrange to do. Curzon says we should bring Millerand here. If he comes something must be done. My inclination would be, if I knew what we wanted, to make the strongest protest against their action in defiance of an expressed view.

P.M.: He has marched his troops in. All you can do is to ask him to withdraw his troops in 24 hours. No government would do that. We should make it clear that if the French are going to take independent action they must do it on their own responsibility and so it is idle to have conferences without this clear understanding.

Milner: A temporary withdrawal of our Ambassador would give point to our protest.

P.M.: There have been endless conferences at which it (Ruhr basin) has been discussed.

Curzon: This Conference sitting in Paris has an enormous amount of work to do and if you had to read as I have the most of its work. . . .

P.M.: I have read every line of them and that is why I remember them better than you or Eyre Crowe.

Curzon: If you mean to close the Conference, close it.

P.M.: The Hungarian Treaty is the one thing I should except. I would shut it down for all else.

Curzon: I should like to communicate with Derby as to the work of the Ambassadors Conference.

P.M.: Footling to communicate with him and lose four days. The French know that this Cabinet is sitting today. I suggest a very strong protest to the French Government stating the whole of the facts—the agreement of the Allies—in spite of it the French take action—questions will constantly arise and it is vital to preserve unity—no single power can enforce against resuscitated Germany—purely question of taking action after giving German Government 14 days to restore order—under these circumstances we wish to make it clear that if the French take action independently we can take no responsibility—idle to hold Ambassadors' Conferences in Paris to consider enforcement of the Treaty when one party takes independent action in case of disagreement—and idle to carry on until we get clear understanding. I would not go on without this clear understanding. The French think they can whistle for us and call us up if war breaks out.

*   *   *   *

B.L.: It follows that until this matter has been cleared up we cannot allow our representative to attend where his representations are disregarded —that is our line.

A.C.: I think all round this table agreed that the action of the French is intolerable and not to be tolerated.

P.M.: We may be very badly landed some day. There is a telegram in the *Manchester Guardian* about the French firing into the ground. I do not know the Germans and how they would stand it.

Hankey: The C.I.G.S. has stated that 60 per cent. of the French army of occupation is black.

P.M.: There are ugly tales going round of the behaviour of the black troops towards German women. We must make it clear that we won't spill British blood to defend that sort of thing. We must do it dramatically or it will make no impression on the French. The press here ought to be informed that the French have acted against the views of all the Allies as expressed both at the Ambassadors' Conference and the Supreme Council. . . .

12 April A message came at 11 a.m. that Bonar Law wanted a Cabinet called at 12 o'clock to discuss the French reply just received. Curzon was in bed and B.L. discussed the draft reply with him over the telephone.

The Cabinet met at 12 in the dining-room at No. 10 as advantage was being taken of the absence of the P.M. to clean the Cabinet room. Bonar Law, Chamberlain, Milner, Eric Geddes, Addison, Shortt, Munro were present. B.L. asked me to get Eyre Crowe in and I suggested bringing Philip Kerr. The meeting started by a number of Ministers complaining that they had seen none of the F.O. telegrams exchanged between us and the French. I said their distribution was the business of the F.O. and not of the Cabinet Secretariat. As a matter of fact the F.O. telegrams only reach a small inner circle of the Cabinet and from time to time protests are made by those left out. B.L. called on me to read out the French reply to our first telegram and our reply sent on Saturday 10th. He then read the French Note received this morning and the reply which he had concerted with Curzon. He told the Cabinet that the French reply did not make clear that they would withdraw the troops from the five towns occupied. It might be read to mean only Frankfort and Darmstadt. It was also not absolutely clear that they would evacuate until all the German troops had been removed from the Ruhr basin and might wish to ignore the agreement of last August to allow 17,500 troops there. A telephone message had been sent to Derby to get these points cleared up but no reply had come.

The discussion proceeded on the assumption that the replies would be satisfactory. B.L. had arranged with Chamberlain before the meeting to contradict *The Times*' allegation of a difference between Chamberlain and the rest of the Cabinet. The discussion turned on two points: 1. Should Derby resume attendance at the Ambassadors' Conference and should reference be made to this either in the reply to France or in the House of Commons. 2. Should any reference be made to the approaching conference at San Remo.

As to 1. all were in favour of Derby's returning to the Conference but felt nervous as to the P.M.'s attitude. The general opinion however was that so long as the door was explicitly kept open for the P.M. to raise the whole question at San Remo the P.M. would not object to Derby's attendance. The discussion was dominated throughout by the sense that the P.M. was determined to have the whole matter dragged out at San Remo and that the Cabinet must therefore adjust its course to that fact. No words therefore could be admitted suggesting that the matter was closed.

*   *   *   *

Further in regard to the Derby point : In order to obtain the P.M.'s view on Derby's attendance at the Conference it was suggested that I should send him a wireless. The Cabinet were told that he had no cypher with him. Then someone suggested I should send the message in Welsh and this was agreed to. Later in the day however I found the P.M. had a cypher with him and thus Welsh just failed to become the language of international diplomacy.

14 April Saw B.L. this morning about the Agenda for tomorrow's Cabinet meeting. . . .

After arranging the Agenda, Bonar Law spoke to T.J. about the treatment of Irish prisoners in Mountjoy prison. He was worried about what would happen if some of those on hunger-strike were to die.

. . . I drew B.L.'s attention to our complete lack of information about the real position in Bavaria as between the peasants backed by the Catholic aristocracy on the one hand and the industrial workers in the towns on the other. I said I had been urging the P.M. to strengthen our labour intelligence[1] as the average F.O. man was useless. He suggested I should write again to Hankey at San Remo and try to get the P.M. to raise the matter with Curzon there.

15 April The Cabinet met in the dining-room of No. 10 with a full attendance to discuss the Budget statement. Eric Geddes appealed to B.L. to allow a window to be opened, a thing B.L. vehemently objects to but today he agreed. The result however was unfortunate as the big swinging doors of the room were constantly being blown by the wind and creaked as if someone were outside trying to hear the Budget secrets. The Chancellor of the Exchequer[2] is always very fidgety about the door of the Cabinet room being kept closed and naturally this creaking annoyed him a good deal and at last I closed the window. Macnamara[3] walked in for the first time as Minister of Labour and a Cabinet Minister and was very cordially received after his victory at Camberwell, very much more cordially than Montagu on his return the other day after a long illness. *His* reception was monosyllabic. He is very much out of sympathy with the P.M. and Curzon's policy on Turkey and has put in a long memorandum of protest and this memorandum, in an expurgated form, he wanted, as the chief representative of India at the British Empire Delegation, to be sent to the Peace Conference, but the P.M. disallowed this and ruled that representations to the Supreme Conference must now go through himself. Hankey thinks that Montagu is preparing a retreat from the Government and is building up a case.

Before taking the Budget B.L. asked to be allowed to make a statement about the Irish prisoners. . . .

He was afraid that there would be trouble whatever was done with the prisoners on

---

[1] It took Ernest Bevin to achieve this.
[2] Austen Chamberlain.
[3] Thomas James Macnamara (1861–1931); Financial Secretary to the Admiralty 1916–20, Minister of Labour 1920–22.

hunger-strike and had asked Lord French to try and save the Government's face by putting them in hospital. However, French released them on parole. Law did not ask the Cabinet to share responsibility for what he had done.

A.C. 'I am ready to share responsibility. It was a very difficult position.'

There was a general murmur of agreement. At this stage Churchill and Horne entered and the Chancellor began to outline his Budget statement and went on for about an hour with slight interruptions.

4 May   Violet Markham to T.J., from Germany

... I thought the state of affairs in the Saar profoundly unsatisfactory, and I am afraid the French are making a sad muddle of their handling of the German population. The situation too in Alsace Lorraine was disquieting. Anyway, both provinces indulged in a general strike while we were there as a protest against Alsatians being replaced by Frenchmen.

San Remo has however cheered me up greatly. *The Times* may fume and rage as it will, but competent military opinion in our area is solidly with the Prime Minister both over Frankfurt and his subsequent line at San Remo.

I am feeling more hopeful at the moment than I have done since the Armistice. The situation with the French is difficult. They seem so incapable of taking a big view and the silly pin pricks in which they indulge at *our* expense is some measure of their treatment of the Boche. ...

14 May   Sir Maurice Hankey to T.J.   *Lympne, Kent*

Sylvester not being on the spot I am driven back on the extraordinary and unaccustomed exercise of my own fist.

I have not had much luck about business. The P.M. is looking old and not very fit. He has not his normal energy. His medicine man has been down and told him he is getting on top-hole, but that, if he breaks his cure by coming up to Town even for a couple of days, he may just undo most of the good, but that, if he will only be patient and stay on, he will be fit for anything after the Whitsuntide holidays. In the circumstances I could not well press him to return. Moreover Winston was here and I did not get much opportunity to raise our business. The moment I did, the P.M. said it was time for his afternoon rest! So much for my diplomatic method! ...

They talked of the Agriculture Bill and Geddes' railway policy.

Finally, I mentioned the question of inter-Allied indebtedness, and he said he was dead against any scheme of remission at present. However, we shall be better able to judge of this after Chamberlain has had a talk with the P.M. and after tomorrow's conference. ...

... Millerand arrives in a couple of hours, and after that our minds will all be moving in other directions.

This[1] is a very lovely place looking across the Romney Marshes to the sea. If I were convalescent and comfortably settled here, nothing would induce me to budge.

I have sent Maclay a note to tell him to comply with all War Office demands for sea transport to Ireland.

[1] Sir Philip Sassoon's house.

14 May   T.J. agreed to write a volume on 'Wales and the War' as part of the Economic History of the War under the auspices of the Carnegie Foundation for International Peace.

On 31 May Lloyd George and various Cabinet Ministers met the Viceroy and the Irish Government. Lloyd George opened by saying, 'I am glad to see you all back alive', and the meeting then discussed the situation in Ireland, the breakdown of civil government, and problems of crime and agrarian outrage. Communications were difficult and the Government had the problem not only of catching criminals but of getting an Irish jury to convict them. More troops, martial law, hanging were all advocated; and Ministers searched for extra powers under older legislation. Churchill was in favour of extreme coercion, while Lloyd George preferred to increase the financial burdens until public opinion repudiated the unrest. The raising of a special force, later to be known as the Black and Tans, was discussed, and a provisional target of 2,000 men fixed for recruiting purposes.

4 June   Two important and impressive discussions of the project for a Capital Levy have taken place this week. Sir William Pearce[1] has presided over a Committee on War Wealth and has rejected the proposal to raise £1,000 millions put forward by the Inland Revenue. So the Revenue put as an alternative a scheme for £500 millions to be collected over 10 years, but the bulk of it in two. The non-official witnesses believed the Levy would produce panic and disaster. But we are collecting £300 millions out of the Excess Profits Duties. The choice the Chancellor had offered was a continuous E.P.D. at a high rate beginning with 60 per cent., or a War Levy, plus 40 per cent. E.P.D., with an early termination of the E.P.D., say 40 per cent., 30 per cent., 20 per cent., over three years and then no E.P.D.

The case for the War Levy is that debt should be reduced while money values are the same as when the debt was contracted and not when it costs you more to pay them. We should also try to cut at the Floating Debt. The popular argument is that certain people have been growing richer while the country has been growing poorer. But you cannot make taxation follow the line of moral cleavage. You cannot distinguish money made during the War from money made out of the War. It is hardly worth the fuss for less than £500 millions. The banks, commerce, the Stock Exchange are unanimous in denouncing the levy. They would prefer the E.P.D. at a high rate. The Governor[2] was inclined to a forced loan but that would play havoc with loans now pending.

Chamberlain summed up admirably the pros and cons. There was for the first time a great anti-capital political party. The black-coated classes are angry with men who have waxed fat while the masses have grown poorer. A tax, despite the vast series of valuations, was the wise policy but for one thing —the panic. It was monstrous that a sum like £500 millions should produce panic, but the City had an unreasoning fear which frightened the Chancellor.

Some who favoured the Levy for moral reasons weakened when they heard that the Inland Revenue could only take dates and tax all wealth above a

[1] A manufacturer of chemicals; Conservative M.P. 1906–22.
[2] Of the Bank of England.

certain line irrespective of its origin. It was agreed that taxation was already so steep that there was difficulty in financing the soundest businesses. The moment profits began to drop so would the yield of the E.P.D. There was not a great deal of difference between the yield of E.P.D. and the yield of the War Levy over, say, three years.

The political argument for was strongly put. The Pearce Committee was in favour, so were the Treasury officials. Asquith in favour and also some sound financiers. If not faced it would be said the Government was in the hands of the profiteers and plutocrats. It will be very hard anyway to hold our immense electorate by reason and not by force and still hold the capitalist system. May bring on the City the very disaster they fear. They always get into a panic. It is expedient to do it whatever the yield.

But, it was asked, would the Levy be just? In most cases prices were fixed at which commodities were bought. One skilful firm made more than another less skilful and that is what we would now take away. People will ask what guarantee they have that this is a final cut.

As the debate proceeded one wondered at the end whether the Levy would produce any cash at all—such was the picture of the probable panic.

The P.M. summed up against, to the disgust of Winston.

29 June   Through K. Walter, director of the Reciprocal News Service, T.J. made enquiries about Irish opinion and whether it would be possible to reconcile it to a Dominion solution. Walter sent two replies, one from a colleague of Arthur Griffith,[1] and another from sources in the Republican 'administration'. T.J.'s action is interesting since it was almost certainly instigated by Lloyd George and shows the moment at which he began to sound out opinion about a Dominion settlement.

30 June   Discussion on Proposed Military Agreement with Belgium

Curzon: A year or more ago we had some correspondence with the Belgian Government who were making an effort to revive the old agreement with them. We declined except on condition of a guarantee of neutrality by them as in 1839. This they were unwilling to give and the negotiations came to nothing. Latterly there has been some correspondence about the conversations which were going on between the Belgian and French military authorities with Foch representing France. The question under discussion is not a Treaty of Alliance or a guarantee but how to meet a possible military contingency as in 1914 should the Belgian frontier be invaded by Germany. The Belgian Ambassador says that this is a case in which we should be morally if not technically involved and that we ought to participate in any agreement drawn up. . . . Turning to the political aspect I am a little alarmed at the growth of French influence in Belgium. Their Ambassador has been making concessions in the matter of Luxembourg. There was the theatrical display when they sent a battalion into Germany at the time of the Ruhr trouble. At the moment France is in the ascendant and I am anxious therefore not to disappoint Belgium at this moment. All they ask us is to take part in conversations with their Chief of Staff and Foch. They do not ask us to

[1] Biographical note on p. 335.

take part in an agreement if we do not want to. The Belgian Government have been quite frank. There is the other point of view taken by Mr. Chamberlain that our people came into the war because of the 'scrap of paper' and that this is an obligation which we would be sure to take up.

The P.M.: So long as it is a mutual one.

Curzon: We should at least pay them the compliment of taking part in the discussion. It will be rather difficult if we refuse.

B.L.: This alarms me. If we have preliminary military talks and then do not make an agreement we shall annoy them all the more. If this were raised in the House of Commons we should be charged with entering into the old agreements and with flouting the League of Nations. If there is to be an agreement it should be mutually binding as Mr. Chamberlain says. We do not know where we now stand with the Anglo-American Treaty guaranteeing France. Why involve ourselves indirectly in this? We are looking at all these questions far too much in the way we used to do before the war. There is no danger from Germany.

Mr. Chamberlain recapitulated what he had said in his memorandum—

1. The independence of the Low Countries is of first importance to us.

2. We cannot afford to see France overwhelmed. That was the view of the late Liberal Government before the war. It should be remembered that the German proposal was to take away no part of France on the continent but to take her colonies from her.

3. If we cannot afford to let 1. and 2. take place then it will be necessary to get this idea into the minds of our people. They do now realise the importance of the neighbouring coast lines as they have never done in my lifetime. To count that when the moment arrives they will act instinctively and will be united again as they were this time is impossible unless we get 1. and 2. as a sort of 'Ark of the Covenant' idea—just as the Americans would go to war for the Monroe doctrine. This vital British interest should be recognised at once and should be put publicly to the people.

B.L.: Is there not a danger of rather mistaking the situation? During the 40 years before 1914 France was the danger. Is there any real danger from Germany?

*   *   *   *

Mr. Churchill: I am against going into this now. It is not the moment but we shall have to come to it on the basis of a defensive guarantee of the frontier against Germany. That is a terrific thing to give and our one great gift and we should not give it unless we get all the conditions we require to safeguard our co-operation from misuse. We need it as part of the full settlement of policy with France of European affairs and not only European affairs. This is not the moment. If we go into it now we shall be drawn from point to point into a guarantee without a definite Treaty.

P.M.: You will get nothing in return.

Mr. Churchill: The chief return we ought to get is to make France and Belgium adopt a reasonable and enlightened policy for the revival of

Germany. I would be inclined to give France and Belgium an assurance of help in order that they may get rid of their fears on the understanding that such an agreement would not prevent our good friendship with Germany. Nothing would be impossible if we could bind France, Germany, and the U.K. together. We could then reconstruct Europe and Russia. The only great weapon we have with France is the power of this guarantee.

*   *   *   *

Mr. Balfour: I am inclined to think that we may have to come to an arrangement of this sort because the coast is our interest but why rush into it now? There is no German army. A defensive alliance is contemplated by the League of Nations. It may come on for discussion there. The military discussion of a German menace now is grotesque. There is no hurry.

*   *   *   *

The P.M.: It is really rather absurd to have these Conversations. Germany in three months will have fewer guns than Belgium. France and Belgium and the U.K. will have 50,000 to 60,000 guns and men running to 1,000,000. To enter solemnly into discussions because this miserable thing called Germany may invade Belgium is so ridiculous that I cannot imagine a man with the common sense of the Belgian King pressing it. The House of Commons and British opinion won't understand it and they will say that all our talk of disarming Germany is simply not true. It is not really a defensive idea. France is full of the idea that she is going to control, overwhelm, and keep under Germany, and she wants to enter into these discussions in order to bully Germany. That is not quite our attitude—not quite. It is only France who could give us trouble now.

Winston: America?

The P.M.: That is another matter. We heard almost the same speech here before 1914 from the lips of another Foreign Secretary (Grey). Cambon said that it would not be binding; but, when 1914 came, we knew that it *was* binding. If we had not gone to the aid of France, France would have accused us—and with some reason. You cannot enter into these military Conversations and say they do not mean anything. I think at this stage we should not enter into them. The Treaty with Belgium was a guarantee of neutrality; but there is nothing to prevent Belgium joining France to invade Germany.

*   *   *   *

Chamberlain: I am sorry about the decision taken. I think a good deal of French fretfulness would be removed if she saw us standing in with her. Our fear that the Treaty or engagement would lead France to aggressive action ought to be guarded against in the document itself.—Chamberlain then referred to what had taken place before the war under Lord Grey and the objection then was that an agreement would make France aggressive.

Churchill: You could not have got a Treaty then if you had tried. You would have lost your head.

Curzon: 'Danger not serious and discussions premature'—is that my line?

P.M.: Yes, that is the line.

On 23 July the Cabinet held an important discussion on Ireland, in which the balance of views was shown. Military opinion suggested that only the most stringent restrictions, martial law, Press control, and immigration restrictions, could now succeed in keeping Ireland quiet. But the experts and civil servants suggested that a large proportion of Sinn Fein was reasonable and that negotiation could take place.

The Cabinet was worried about the security of the army, but at this stage the greater number of those who spoke favoured the Bill then before the House of Commons. Lloyd George suggested that if the experts' view was known to the public, the Bill would have to be abandoned. Churchill wanted a trial of strength and to raise an army of 30,000 men in Ulster. Others, less extreme, pointed out that the present Bill could not pass the Lords until the autumn and that six months would be left in which trouble could spread even wider. In an important intervention, Curzon accepted the view of the experts, that 90 per cent. of Sinn Fein were prepared to negotiate, and Bonar Law agreed with him. Fisher (who said that this was 'the first real discussion in his time in the Cabinet of the Irish Question') and Walter Long favoured coercion: but by the end of the meeting, Lloyd George was seen to be moving towards a form of Home Rule not far removed from Dominion status.

On 24 July T.J. summed up the discussion in a note for the Prime Minister, emphasizing the weakness of the army and the narrowness of the choice between coercion and negotiation. He suggested that Lloyd George should soon make a major speech, appealing for peace, and making one final offer—Dominion Home Rule (except in defence matters and ports) for the South and self-determination for Ulster. Failing a settlement, the Government would then use force.

26 July The P.M. read a telegram from the Soviet Government agreeing to a conference with the Great Powers. The P.M. said that, on receipt of this on Sunday, he had phoned to B.L., Curzon, Balfour, and Churchill, and had communicated it to Millerand and suggested an immediate conference. Millerand had agreed to Boulogne at 12 o'clock tomorrow. A copy had been sent to the Italians also.

The P.M. asked Curzon and Worthington-Evans (for coal) to accompany him and he said that he was having a telegram drafted inviting the Soviet Government to equip their trade envoys with wide powers of negotiation. The reason for this was that Millerand was entangled with parliamentary pledges about debts owing by the Russians. But it was clear in Spa[1] that Millerand would join in if he got some vague undertaking from the Russians.

Churchill: The armies are still fighting.

P.M.: Not inside Poland.

Churchill suggested that the Soviet's offer might be accepted after the Armistice Commission had met.

P.M. said that the Armistice was on—he had received a telephone message from the Polish Embassy.

Churchill: Our acceptance turns on what Armistice terms the Russians offer the Poles.

[1] The Spa Conference.

The P.M. suggested that we should get Krassin[1] and Kamenev[2] here now.

Churchill: Why—until we know the Armistice terms?

The P.M.: It would be an advantage to have them here now. Trotsky had been over-ruled by Lenin. Trotsky wanted to dictate peace at Warsaw. Lenin did not want it and has had his way. Unfortunately Trotsky would be at the Armistice. But Kamenev was Lenin's man and it would be useful to have him here.

B.L. suggested that the telegram should begin on the assumption that the Armistice is being arranged 'and put that as ground for our change of mind'.

P.M., in reply to Churchill who said that the Russians were the aggressors, said that the Russians would be just as justified as we were in imposing armistice terms on the Germans in asking for a bridgehead on the Niemen. To say that the Poles were only counter-attacking was just what the Germans said. . . .

Churchill . . . went on to refer to the fact that the Soviet Government were subsidizing the *Daily Herald*, as a reason for delaying the visit of Krassin and Co.

The P.M. replied that was negotiated by Lansbury[3] himself when in Moscow.

*   *   *   *

. . . Then Curzon raised the point as to whether the proposed Conference was to be with the leading Powers of the Entente only.

The P.M. said that the passage was ambiguous and capable of either interpretation.

It was agreed that in their reply it should be made clear that we would invite the Border States to the Conference.

*   *   *   *

30 July   T.J. to Sir Maurice Hankey

I have asked Storr to send you his notes of the Boulogne Meeting so that you may get the 'atmosphere'. Krassin will be here on Monday or Tuesday. You will no doubt be hearing from Kerr on the general question. Any conversations of the P.M. with Ministers which I have heard have shown a strong desire on his part for peace, and a very active hope that nothing shall happen to prevent the Conference with Russia. He was not very pleased with an article by Winston in the *Evening News* on Wednesday which was much boomed and which has been read as an invitation to Germany to join the Allies in an offensive on Russia. There was also a heated passage at yesterday's Cabinet on Wrangel, when the P.M. discovered that we had four

[1] L. B. Krassin (1870–1926); professional engineer and revolutionary; organized the supply of munitions for the Red Army in the civil war; Commissar for Trade and Industry, leader of the trade delegation to Britain 1920; Ambassador to Britain 1925–6.

[2] L. B. R. Kamenev (1883–1936); President of the Moscow Soviet 1918–22; chairman of the Council of Labour and Defence after the death of Lenin in 1924; expelled from the Party with Zinoviev in 1927; readmitted, then expelled again and executed for alleged conspiracy in 1936.

[3] George Lansbury, the Labour leader (M.P. 1910–12, 1922–40). He was a founder, in 1912, of the *Daily Herald* and its editor from 1919 to 1923.

'Intelligence' officers (Army) in the Crimea and Long admitted to two or three Naval members. Instructions have been issued to have these reduced if possible.

The Irish situation continues to be as disturbing as ever. More murders. Crimes Bill of drastic character to be pushed through the House next week. Miners' demands refused but no labour troubles likely until October. Bread subsidy to stop in December. No discussion yet of Persia and Mesopotamia— nor of oil. All postponed. P.M. tired and refused to come up for a Finance Committee today.

He has on two occasions quoted from your letters in the Cabinet.

Good luck!

On 4 August, Lloyd George, Bonar Law, Long, and Hamar Greenwood (Chief Secretary for Ireland) met a deputation of Southern Irish businessmen to discuss the Government's Home Rule Bill. The Irish were all for abandoning the Bill and substituting a prompt, bold, and generous offer of Dominion status. Lloyd George pressed the representatives for detailed information. Who was in control in the South? Whom could he talk to? What, he asked, would be the position of Ulster? What would happen to Ireland's share of the United Kingdom war debt; and what control would the United Kingdom have over Ireland's defence, especially her harbours, vital for protection against submarines? Above all he wanted 'to see the Sinn Feiner on the bridge, or someone who can speak for Ireland. I do not care if he is a Sinn Feiner as long as he can speak for Ireland'.

25 August   Violet Markham to T.J., from Germany
. . . It has been clear to me for some time past that the Peace Treaty will break down owing to international Labour. The heavy economic penalties of the Peace rest on the shoulders of the *workers*. The workers will refuse to carry them and there will be an appeal to the workers of Allied countries to assist in their mitigation. Moderate indemnities would not have been challenged. But the cry that the workers of Central Europe are going to be kept in economic servitude for many years to the forces of international capitalism has already been started, and it's a cry which will grow in volume. . . .

About the Saar. You may remember we were there in April and found every symptom of serious trouble brewing. The trouble has come: the whole district has been on strike and the Saar basin is practically standing on its head. I feel *very strongly* about the extraordinarily false position of the League of Nations in the Saar. The League is a mere catspaw in the hands of the French who do what they like. The French have a large Army of Occupation, the mines are handed over to them absolutely: further, they control the railways and the customs. The strike arose over the effort of the French to dismiss German officials. This game was on foot in April; of course it has infuriated the Saar. There have been wholesale arrests, house searchings and machine guns in every street. Is it desirable for the League of Nations to be mixed up in these proceedings, and if they are technically responsible, why are the French allowed to dominate the situation in their own most unfortunate way? . . .

On 25 August, a group of Ministers held a discussion about the case of Terence *McSwiney, Lord Mayor of Cork, who was on hunger strike in Brixton Prison. He was suffering from tuberculosis and in danger of dying. He was not released and died later in the year, after a fast of seventy-four days.*

11 September Pybus, Managing Director of the English Electrical Co., called to suggest that the P.M. should summon a private conference of engineer employers with a view to persuading them to drop the lock-out against the electricians. I went across to see B.L. and found the P.M. with him, but instead of discussing the electricians the P.M. turned to a telegram just received from Derby saying that the French were wanting to get out of the Geneva Conference which had been agreed to by them at Spa. Just at this moment Hardinge came in and the P.M. stormed away at the bad faith of the French in trying to break one agreement after another. 'They were worse than the Bolsheviks; we must take a firm stand; we must let the French know that rather than break our word in this matter we will stand by the Germans and let the world know.' It was agreed that Curzon, L. Worthington-Evans, and Hardinge should go into the matter on Monday and draft a reply.

Hardinge then told the P.M. about the British officers on the Plebiscite Commission in Silesia who were so disgusted with the partiality of the French to the Poles that they were resigning. The French have been arming the Poles and disarming the Germans. Several Germans have been done to death by the Poles who had been supplied with bombs. It was now suggested that both French and English Missions should be recalled and new Missions appointed.

B.L. thought the French had done well in Syria by their drastic move and he wished they would take on Mespot. The P.M. thought if they got Mespot they would just look after Mosul and let the rest go hang. Hardinge interpolated that it was too soon to pass judgment on the success of the French treatment of Syria. There was probable trouble ahead.

The P.M. turned to Egypt and asked Hardinge if Curzon knew anything about Milner's proposals for reform.[1] Curzon, it appeared, had not been consulted, nor had the P.M. nor B.L. nor Balfour. No one could understand how so cautious and experienced a statesman as Milner had blurted out his proposals without consulting anyone. B.L. said it would take the P.M. all his skill to get us out of the mess. Hardinge thought the proposals would not be acceptable in Egypt and would be mischievous in the sense that they would form the basis for further demands.

The P.M.: Up to the beginning of 1918 Milner was first rate. His mind had been working admirably and his advice had been most valuable but then he suddenly took it into his head to want to go to the War Office.

B.L.: No, no, you wanted him to go there.

P.M.: No, indeed, I didn't. I was very much against his going there. I

---

[1] Lord Milner, now Secretary of State for the Colonies, had proposed plans for reform and settlement in Egypt, following a revolt in March 1919.

wanted, I forget who, I think it was Chamberlain. Well, he went there and for about 6 weeks all went well. Then he suddenly became tired and never recovered his grip.

B.L.: Well, he did one great thing to help you while he was there. He got unity of command.

P.M.: No, indeed, he didn't. He got a most futile thing called co-ordination. He went to Doullens and got it arranged that Foch should be Chief in an advisory capacity but with no power to order English or French troops about. This did not satisfy Foch who kept saying that he was still merely M. Foch and I had to go to Beauvais and make Foch generalissimo, the trouble having been that while Haig was quite loyal and willing to obey Foch, Pétain had refused.

During the P.M.'s account I had tried to interject that at any rate Milner had paved the way for unity of command at Doullens but the P.M. would have none of this from me or B.L. though I distinctly remember the P.M. at the Cabinet congratulating Milner on the great success of his mission. . . .

Lloyd George's break with Milner has been attributed to many causes. Probably it originated in Milner's actions in dismissing General Maurice in 1918 and during the political storm that followed.

22 September   Sir Maurice Hankey to T.J.
On my way to Town today I decided to write to you strongly urging you to take several weeks' leave as everything is quite quiet here, saving the Coal Strike. Your letter, therefore, in no way upsets my intentions but merely confirms my instincts, which were that you ought to have a good spell of leave. Everyone is back now except you and Storr and with Howorth and Wilson to help me you need have no fears about being away. I am very glad to hear that you are going to undertake a drastic cure for your neuritis.[1] I feel rather responsible for it having been away so much, but you know I have not been able to help it. If the Coal Strike comes off and is a serious strike, the time that we shall want you will not be for several weeks—that is to say, towards the end of the strike. As Geddes describes it, a coal strike is creeping paralysis, unlike a railway which is more like a 'stroke'. The acute stage will come when the negotiations to end the strike are reached. On the other hand, if we avoid the strike, which I still believe to be possible, I don't see any reason why you should be back before Parliament meets. We had a 'clear up' Cabinet yesterday and I don't believe that at the moment there is any outstanding question. Neither can I see any question, other than the Strike, to arise much before Parliament meets. Ireland, of course, is always with us and in a few weeks' time the Russo-Polish business may become acute. It looks to me, however, more likely that my ideas will work out and we shall, for many months, be able to wash our hands both of Russia and Poland and leave Eastern Europe to work out its own difficulties in its own way, which I am convinced is the best course. Mesopotamia and Persia are quieter and likely to quiet down. Finally, unless he is kept by the Strike, Winston is off to

[1] T.J. went to Harrogate for a 'cure', taking with him his daughter Eirene, aged ten, as a companion.

Italy tomorrow. This summary will show you that, apart from the Strike, all the elements of disturbance will be absent. Personally I have never known the Office so quiet since the War Cabinet was formed.

I am having quite an easy time. The P.M. is still going away for long week-ends and likely to do so for some time to come. When he goes away I go away, and I have really had more rest since I came home than I had during my so-called, but wholly fictitious 'holiday' at Lucerne. . . .

At a Conference on the Irish Bill, on 13 October, Lloyd George came out against making financial concessions. If the rights of customs and taxation were given away at this stage, there would be nothing left with which to negotiate if the Irish became conciliatory later. So long as the Government retained these powers, Sinn Fein was at their mercy. Later, he asked the officials if it was possible for the Government to retain control of part of the South, while allowing the Sinn Fein Parliament to govern the rest.

On 3 November, Churchill, pressed by the military authorities, circulated a memorandum on reprisals in Ireland. The situation was deteriorating and the British troops could no longer be restrained from taking action on their own account.

The Cabinet discussed Ireland again on 1 December, after an assassination near Cork, which seemed more like a military operation than an outrage. Lloyd George pointed out that there was now a case for declaring a state of siege or martial law in that part of Ireland. The debate centred on whether to apply sanctions by districts or to the whole of Ireland. Lord Milner gave his experience of martial law in South Africa.

However, Lloyd George then saw Archbishop Clune (of Perth, Australia), who went over to Ireland as an unofficial emissary to Arthur Griffith. A month's truce was suggested, and on 13 December the Cabinet discussed the conditions on which a truce would be granted. Negotiations through the Archbishop continued during December.

21 December   T.J. to Sir Maurice Powicke[1]

There is a short account in the War Book of the working of the War Cabinet in a report which was published in the years 1917 and 1918 under that title. The fullest account is in the first of these volumes. What is said there as to the working of this Secretariat still holds true with minor adjustments. This is now the Cabinet Secretariat. We record the meetings of the Cabinet on the whole more briefly than during the war, and the Minutes are no longer printed. These changes were made in the interests of greater secrecy. There is no acknowledged Inner Cabinet, but there are Cabinet Committees, two of them of a permanent character:

(a) The Finance Committee, at which the Prime Minster presides.

(b) The Committee of Home Affairs, of which Fisher is Chairman.

There are, in addition, ad hoc Committees for problems as they arise; recent examples are a Committee on Housing, on Unemployment, on Land Settlement. We provide Secretaries for all these Committees from our staff. Hankey and I alone of the Secretaries attend the Cabinet. We also have what we call Conferences of Ministers when it is not desired to bother the Cabinet as a whole. To these Conferences Ministers are invited according as they are likely to be interested or not in the subject on the Agenda. It is a convenient

[1] The historian.

device, some would suggest, for excluding Ministers! Ministers do not smoke at Cabinets, but they do at Conferences!! Minutes are kept of all these Meetings, but their distribution is, in practice, very much within the discretion of the Cabinet Secretary. There are degrees of secrecy as there are of truth. Certain Ministers always get all Minutes, and in this sense perhaps may be regarded as the Inner Cabinet. It is obviously desirable that the Leaders of the two Houses should be aware of most things under discussion.

The business of the Cabinet originates with Memoranda sent in under the name of the Ministers of the various Departments. These are usually prepared by their staffs, and we put them on the Agenda when we think they are sufficiently ripe. This means, of course, that we are constantly intercommunicating with the Departments concerned, and that we endeavour to see that decisions are not rushed.

The above is the general scheme, but the P.M. is above the law, and does not undertake either to read Memoranda, or to abide by the Agenda which we so scientifically prepare for him.

On 23 December the Government of Ireland Bill became law. The next day the Cabinet discussed whether it would be wise to postpone negotiations with Sinn Fein until the Act had come into effect. At this stage, they thought that Sinn Fein was becoming discredited, but they recognized two dangers inherent in delay—intervention from the United States, and trouble between the military forces and the police. They set great store by the chances of a bona fide *election under the new Act in Southern Ireland and realized that the character of the election would depend on the success of pacification in the early part of 1921.*

1921

This year marked the full development of the main social and economic feature of the inter-war years: mass unemployment. By March 1921 the figure was twice that of December 1920, and by June it was more than two million. The first thought was public economy and the Geddes Committee was appointed on 16 August. A disguised form of protection was introduced with the Safeguarding of Industries Act. Control of the railways was abandoned and the mines were returned to private owners, who promptly proposed a cut in wages. The coal strike, which began on 1 April, had behind it the threat of a more general strike backed by the Triple Alliance (miners, railwaymen, and transport workers) but, through divided counsels, this collapsed in ignominious confusion on 'Black Friday', 16 April. The coal strike dragged on until July. Unemployment benefit was extended for periods longer than those covered by contributions, but although this mitigated hardship, it provided no cure. Dr. Addison left the Ministry of Health and his going symbolized the end of 'reconstruction'.

Lloyd George failed to obtain any economic advantage to Britain from the Dominions Conference held in the summer, but his hand was strengthened for the naval conference which opened in Washington in November. Balfour, heading the British delegation, was able to achieve the only significant inter-war limitation of armaments, giving naval parity to Britain and the United States, with Japan some way behind. Meanwhile, in Turkey, Kemal Ataturk was forming his revolutionary state. Greece still held Smyrna and Lloyd George, almost alone in the Cabinet, supported her.

Apart from unemployment, the year was dominated by the efforts to reach a settlement in Ireland. In March, Bonar Law resigned on grounds of health, but his influence in matters affecting Ireland remained potent.

Brief summaries of the events leading up to the Irish Treaty, and references to them in the diary, are included here. The full story will appear in Volume III.

On 23 December 1920 the Government of Ireland Bill became law—unwanted by the South and welcomed with little enthusiasm even in the North, where its implications (the recognition of Ulster's separate status) were more clearly understood. The South was more preoccupied with the 'troubles', and martial law was imposed on Cork, Kerry, Limerick, and Tipperary, followed in January 1921 by Clare, Wexford, Waterford, and Killarney. After many doubts on the part of the British Government the elections were allowed to take place in May. An absolute Sinn Fein majority was returned in the South.

Tentative peace negotiations continued in the shadow of the military rule of the Chief Secretary, Sir Hamar Greenwood, involving among others Alfred Cope, Assistant Under-Secretary at the Castle. Lloyd George, in the House of Commons, professed himself ready for settlement. On 5 May Sir James Craig met De Valera,[1] but no noticeable improvement emerged in the armed relations between North and South, which were made worse when the Ulster election returned a heavy and intransigent Unionist majority. During May the terror intensified; the Customs House in Dublin was burnt, and Sinn Fein extended sabotage to England.

King George V's speech at the opening of the Northern Ireland Parliament on 22 June opened the way for a truce on 11 July. Lloyd George invited De Valera to a conference in London where he met Sir James Craig, without success. Finally Lloyd George put forward a proposal for a conference. De Valera hesitated, prolonging the correspondence with obscure replies through August until at last, in September, the Cabinet, losing patience, terminated the exchanges and offered the conference, without prior conditions, on 11 October. De Valera accepted; five Irish negotiators were chosen to meet the British ministers in London and from their prolonged deliberations emerged the Irish Treaty, signed on 6 December. Ireland received virtual Dominion status and a Governor-General, while Britain retained military facilities. The North could join but, if within one month it did not, then a Boundary Commission was to be set up to determine the final line between North and South. The settlement was disputed by half the Southern Cabinet and the split between the followers of Griffith and De Valera led directly to the Civil War in 1922.

Throughout 1921 T.J. was almost wholly preoccupied with the Irish negotiations. On 13 July he was asked to be secretary of the Irish Conference when De Valera first met Lloyd George, because Lloyd George preferred not to use Hankey, an Englishman. His work became steadily more important to the negotiations as the autumn wore on, and on at least two occasions, the weekend of 29/30 October and around 22 November, it was he who held the participants together. How much Lloyd George relied on him may be gathered from the summary of the lengthy story which is included here. During Hankey's absence in Washington, T.J. again acted as secretary to the Cabinet.

29 January   Sir Maurice Hankey to T.J.   *Hotel Crillon, Paris*
This is only a short line to remind you not to overlook the importance of calling for the departmental reports for the King's Speech well before the Opening of Parliament. Personally, I nearly always overlook it until the last moment.

I had dictated a long yarn about the position of Reparations, but the whole thing suddenly cleared up last night and this will be unnecessary. In case

[1] Biographical notes on p. 335.

Bonar Law would like to see it I enclose a Note showing the continuous negotiations that went on throughout Friday. . . .

Note on the Negotiations at Paris on 28 January 1921, by Sir Maurice Hankey

In the morning a formal Meeting was held at 10.30 a.m. of the Committee set up on the previous evening by the main Conference.

At this Meeting the French made proposals, the basis of which was—

The Annuities in the Boulogne Agreement plus 15 per cent. on the value of German exports for the year.

Sir L. Worthington-Evans stated that he had no authority to accept these proposals and that he must report the matter to the Prime Minister.

The Prime Minister rejected the proposals.

After lunch the Prime Minister and Lord Curzon had a prolonged discussion with M. Briand in the course of which Mr. Lloyd George laid down the following entirely new proposal as a basis for discussion.

'Have no fixed Annuity but propose an Annuity equal to 25 per cent. of the exports of Germany. Arrangements to be made for Germany to pay Annuity in part by the supply of such labour and material as may be required for repair of devastated regions.'

At about 4.30 p.m. M. Briand left the Prime Minister with the understanding that each should discuss the new basis with their respective experts.

*   *   *   *

The French representatives could not accept the new basis for the reason that they did not consider that it would provide suitable security on which they could raise a loan for immediate use.

As the result of this series of conversations, however, a fresh project was drawn up. . . .

*   *   *   *

At 6 p.m. [this] was laid before the Prime Minister by Sir L. Worthington-Evans and Lord D'Abernon[1] who were accompanied by M. Jaspar and Col. Theunis.

The proposal was not acceptable to the Prime Minister who pointed out that it would be absolutely impossible for the Germans to pay the amounts laid down during the first two years. The result would be that within the 12 months there would have to be further Allied Conferences to decide what was to be done, owing to the fact that Germany had not paid.

*   *   *   *

The Prime Minister authorised Sir L. Worthington-Evans and Lord D'Abernon to state that if the remainder of the proposals contained in the Brussels Report in regard to the reduction of the cost of the Armies of Occupation, etc., were adopted, the British Government would be disposed to agree.

*   *   *   *

[1] Ambassador in Berlin 1920–6.

At 7.45 p.m. M. Loucheur[1] called to see Mr. Lloyd George and stated that the French Government would accept the new scheme subject to the period during which 4 milliard gold marks and 5 milliard gold marks were to be paid be cut down each from 5 years to 3 years. The reason for this request was that under the present scheme the maximum of 6 milliards was reached later than in the case of the Boulogne Agreement. Mr. Lloyd George accepted this proposal and the scheme was approved.

28 January Luncheon with Bonar Law and his son (who is employed in the City) at No. 11. B.L. had told me yesterday that he wanted to talk over his forthcoming Rectorial Address which he has to deliver in Glasgow in early March. He was very worried about it as he would have very little time to prepare anything and was very tired. When I urged him to take a holiday he said he had lost all interest in holidays since the death of his sons.[2]

He had been reading the Addresses of several Lord Rectors and thought Disraeli's—though short—the best. He had heard Gladstone deliver his and was much impressed while listening to the G.O.M. and vowed to himself that he too would be Lord Rector some day. Rosebery's Address he thought very fair, Chamberlain's a failure. I said he would have one great advantage over most Lord Rectors as he would deliver his without notes whereas the others read laboriously. . . .

B.L. told me that he had disciplined himself severely in the preparation of speeches to such an extent that he had never written a line of any speech he had delivered in the 20 years he had been in the House of Commons. In the early days he would sit down for 2 or 3 hours and not only meditate on the ideas of a speech but would frame every sentence precisely in his mind. After 2 or 3 hours of this he would be utterly exhausted. Since he had taken on the Leadership of the House there had been no time for this meditation but he had reaped the advantage of the discipline he had undergone in the preparation of his earlier speeches. He thought the P.M. was now quite a good speaker and that he had greatly changed for the better since he had become Prime Minister. The difference between him and Asquith was that every speech of the P.M. shewed marks of original observation and reflection.

B.L.'s father had been a man of great oratorical gifts but for the last 5 years of his life he had been the victim of a despondency so great as to amount almost to insanity and he had resisted all attempts to bring him to one of the large towns. Going on to the subject of his Address, he had been thinking of some sort of appreciation of the psychology of the people immediately before, during and since the War but did not feel quite equal to the subject and he was inclined to talk of the qualities important for success in business and in public life. They were much the same. One had to give at any rate the impression of sincerity, of being reliable, of playing the game fairly. These qualities were as important as the power of speech. What told in the case of men like the P.M. and Carson was their total personality. Carson was a poor speaker.

[1] A French Treasury official, later Minister of Finance.
[2] Two of whom had been killed in the war.

He went on to discuss the so-called intuition of successful business men and statesmen. These intuitions were the result of subconscious processes of prolonged meditation, the results of which were seen when decisions had to be taken. In every Cabinet of which he had been a member there were two or three leading figures. The others were men who could easily be matched for ability in the business world. All that had happened was that some had gone into business instead of into politics. There had been a great change in the composition of the Cabinet and of the House of Commons in his time. When he entered politics the 'ruling classes' still ruled. Now there was only one hereditary Peer in the Cabinet. He did not know whether Curzon would like attention drawn to that fact. . . .

Reverting to his remark about his determination one day to be Lord Rector he said that when young he was very ambitious and he remembers during a School Board Election in Glasgow saying to himself 'Pitt at 23 was Prime Minister, and here am I 23 and I am not even a member of the Glasgow School Board'. He was sure he was much more ambitious at that time than Lloyd George at that time. On the other hand, in his case the child was not father to the man as he had ceased to be ambitious whereas the P.M.'s love of power was only comparable to Gladstone's. For that reason he was not likely readily to quit office.

I said that one heard on all sides that the country was fed up with the P.M. and that I always replied that there was no alternative on the assumption that B.L. and L.G. would continue to co-operate. B.L. said he was certain that there was a Tory reaction in full swing and that that might make the continuance of the Coalition impossible even if there was no great leader on the horizon. He thought that the Key Industries Bill[1] would be a severe test of the Coalition. The P.M. had said recently that he would stand strictly by the pledge he had given at the time of the Election and that if it were necessary for him to give up office he would do so and support B.L. from outside! B.L. added smilingly that he had no intention of going forward on those terms and I remarked that he and the P.M. were both men of resource and would no doubt find a compromise on the Key Industry trouble.

30 January Met the P.M. at 5.40 at Victoria on his return from the Paris Conference. I then saw him for about 10 minutes alone at No. 10 at 6 p.m. He complained of feeling tired and of having caught a cold owing to the over-heated rooms at the Crillon. He refused to look at business and he said he would clear off at once to Chequers as he would have three speeches to deliver on Saturday next at Birmingham where he is to receive the Freedom of the city.

I asked him his impressions of the results of the Conference. He was obviously very pleased that Briand had been forced to a conclusion. 'The trouble was that Briand had no effective backing in the country and was very nervous about his parliamentary position. He had nothing like the

---

[1] A continuation of the anti-dumping legislation, to protect what had been regarded as key industries during the war from unfair foreign competition. It was, however, a move towards protection and, as such, an uneasy matter for the Liberals in the Cabinet.

place among the French people that Clemenceau had. At the beginning of the week matters looked very black but as the week went on the tone of the French press became more favourable to us. Briand is rather like Asquith, lethargic, and wanted to postpone disagreeable duties. I had to force him to face realities. On Friday I spoke in a private interview very sharply.'

I said that B.L. was very tired and was worrying about his Rectorial Address at Glasgow.

P.M. 'B.L. ought to take to drink. Unfortunately he is a teetotaler. I ought to be a teetotaler as drink depresses me on the whole. Failing drink the only remedy for Bonar is a wife.

'I too have a Rectorial to give in the autumn at Edinburgh. I think I will talk about the House of Commons. I have never been to a University but after 30 years I ought to know something about Parliament.' I said 'You could take Mill's Representative Government and compare the situation today with what it was in Mill's day.'

The P.M. 'Parliament is being challenged on two sides—by the Soviet and by the Press. I think that might do for a theme. That has only just occurred to me.'

He then asked me to come round at 8 o'clock to have some dinner and to sing Welsh hymns.

8 p.m. Returned and met B.L. coming out from the Cabinet room where he had been talking with the P.M. Miss Stevenson joined us at dinner upstairs and the conversation somehow got quickly on to Victor Hugo! I confessed I had never read any of the novels and this set the P.M. going and with great eloquence he told us the story of *Les Miserables*—'the greatest book ever written not excepting Holy Writ. I have read it 20 times. I envy you. I read it in Dick's cheap edition of the classics. I remember Hugh Price Hughes reading a chapter aloud one Sunday afternoon soon after I came to London: the chapter about the convict stealing the spoons and the Bishop's intervention.'

I remarked that my little girl was just now reading '93'. This sent him off to give us an account of it. He remembered the names of all the chief characters. He had never read any of Hugo's poetry.

Sometime during dinner the Germany Indemnity was mentioned. The P.M. said they could pay the 100 millions a year easily enough. I suggested it was less than the capital of Lord Leverhulme's companies[1] and that he could minimise it by speaking of it in that fashion.

This led us to talk of Leverhulme's cutting out his head from Augustus John's portrait which proceeding the P.M. approved and was obviously thinking of John's portrait of himself. I said John was a man of genius who had seen the savage side of the P.M.: the square jaw I had sometimes seen in the Cabinet and which I was sure Briand had seen last week. Miss Stevenson chimed in that she was delighted to hear me say all this as there were more than enough of the 'Sunday school' portraits of the P.M. about and it was most important that posterity should see his other face.

---

[1] Lever Brothers, manufacturers of chemicals.

We adjourned to the drawing room and for an hour Miss Stevenson played Welsh music. . . .

Later Bonar Law came in and the Prime Minister told him about the by-election pending in Cardiganshire.

B.L. 'I have been saying you would rather lose 20 seats than one in Wales.'

P.M. 'I had rather lose a whole General Election. The Cardiganshire people are the cutest in the world. It would never do for me to go down there. Slim is not the word to describe them.'

Here Lloyd George produced a letter from De Valera, and although Bonar Law tried to postpone a discussion, he persisted. He wanted to meet De Valera, and was impressed at the thought of how much a quick settlement might mean—including an arrangement of the British war debt to America, a subject which was played on by Irish-American sympathizers. T.J. intervened with a plea that the idealism of Irish nationalism should be accepted. As they left, Bonar Law told T.J. that he believed coercion was the only answer; he had come to the conclusion 'that the Irish were an inferior race'.

On 14 February the Cabinet debated whether to publish the Strickland Report, on an outrage committed by the R.I.C. Lloyd George and the majority were opposed to making the full report public and the Cabinet instead adopted a formula admitting that grave acts of indiscipline had taken place.

On 15 February, T.J. lunched with Sir John Anderson and learned that De Valera had wished to meet Lloyd George. Arrangements for a meeting had been held up, partly because the Government had no certain knowledge about De Valera's intentions. The negotiations through Archbishop Clune had broken down over the surrender of arms. T.J. believed that Bonar Law was the main opponent of conciliation and that he had a strong influence on the Prime Minister.

7 March We were 10 or 15 minutes late in starting as the P.M. and B.L. had been kept at St. James's Palace bringing to an end the Conference[1] with the Germans. Immediately on his arrival the P.M. gave a hurried account in the briefest outline of the breakdown of the negotiations. Simons,[2] he said, had offered the Paris annuities plus the 12 per cent. on exports but this offer was subject to Silesia remaining in German hands and to some arrangement being made about German trade, the nature of which was not exactly explained. Beyond the 5 years he had no proposals. He was willing to have a variable annual payment but he would fix neither minimum nor maximum nor suggest a figure. The allies felt (firstly) that there was no security as to the 5 years. Simons might be back in 5 weeks because of the verdict of Upper Silesia. In the second place there was no shadow of a proposal as to the remainder of the term. 'I think it is clear he has not the authority to settle. That is what all this means. He would like to settle but he has his public opinion shrieking "Don't give in". Putting the sanctions into operation is an essential preliminary to coming to terms. The Paris proposals were not unfair

[1] On Reparations.
[2] The German Finance Minister.

in the main. Of course there could have been minor modifications of them. We have, therefore, notified the Germans that the sanctions will come into operation immediately. The armies are to march to Düsseldorf, Ruhrort, and Duisburg tomorrow or the day after.'

Mr. Chamberlain referred to Dr. Simons' appeal to history.

The P.M.: They fluctuate between abject, cringing appeals and a sort of unconsidered insolence. They do not realise it is insolence—not in the least. It is all very well for them to say that the war was not caused by them alone and that history may have a different verdict and may revise our verdict. That is silly. The verdict has been given.

Mr. Chamberlain then tried to explain what the point of the German remark was, that even from a *chose jugée* there was an appeal to history.

The P.M. said that he asked them when did history begin. Did it begin from 5 years hence?

Mr. Fisher (smiling): The war began with Dr. Livingstone's journey to Africa.

The P.M.: One of the proposals we considered and which the Germans would accept is that we should be entitled to direct purchasers of German goods here to pay a portion of the price into the Exchequer here and that the Exchequer receipt should be regarded as part payment. Supposing a man buys £1,000 worth from Germany. Then the Board of Trade or the Treasury would direct him to pay £500 to the Treasury and get a receipt; the purchaser would then send the receipt to Germany and the vendor would get German currency which would be useful to him because in it he would pay his wages, rent, etc. At present our trade with Germany is £50 millions a year and we would thus get £25 millions a year. I know this proposal has been criticised but I know of no other way to get payment.

Sir A. Mond: It suits the Germans very well. They have simply got to print more paper. They need not raise fresh taxation.

Mr. Chamberlain: The Germans put up a somewhat similar proposal at Spa. They proposed a portion of the goods, not the price of the goods.

The P.M.: That was a creation of credit in Germany for the purchase of German goods.

Mr. Chamberlain: Curzon thinks that the Germans found out that the French were not keen on this proposal and that they therefore accepted it hoping to divide us.

The P.M.: What the French want is the west bank of the Rhine.

Mr. Montagu: They had rather that than the money?

The P.M.: I think so.

In October 1920 the Government had settled the miners' strikes temporarily, on the miners' terms. This only postponed the struggle, which was fought in circumstances increasingly unfavourable to the miners. By March 1921 the post-war boom had broken; the number of unemployed in Britain was 1½ million and coal exports had fallen. Two problems appeared to be insoluble—how to deal with the small and now unprofitable pits such as those in the Forest of Dean, and how to attract, at a time of recession, the investment which alone could make the rest of the coal industry profitable for the future.

The economic crisis ended whatever hopes of reconstruction the Coalition Government still retained. The railways were handed back to the private companies and the date for the mine-owners' resumption of control was set at 31 March 1921. The owners offered new agreements—cuts in wages and district rates. The miners demanded a 'national pool' of wages. In return, the owners began a lock-out on 1 April.

The Government was now in the position of mediator, rather than a direct party to the dispute. This explains why the Cabinet did not consider it until 4 April.

4 April The first Cabinet Meeting after the Easter Recess and the reconstruction of the Ministry. The P.M. welcomed Sir Alfred Mond but made no reference to Dr. Addison who is now Minister without Portfolio. Mr. Chamberlain chaffed Sir Robert Horne on his cheerful countenance, due, as he put it, to a surplus of £230 millions. The P.M. paid some compliments to the Ministry of Food and the Ministry of Munitions, and the Cabinet settled down to discuss the coal strike which had started on 1 April.

Sir Robert Horne: For months since the last strike, the coal owners and miners have been trying to arrive at a basis of further regulation of the remuneration, and had agreed on certain principles: namely a standard wage to be a first charge on the industry and, corresponding to it, a standard profit for the owners. They did not arrive at the precise proportions of the profits to wages. Future surplus profits were to be divided in certain proportions between owners and men, the owners proposing 80—20 and the men 90—10. On both these issues a settlement could have been arrived at but the snag throughout has been the insistence of the men on wages being paid on a national basis. That involved pooling of profits; the owners would not agree to this and it would have been detrimental to the industry. Upon this the negotiations broke down. When the owners saw no satisfactory settlement possible they agreed to put up at the pit heads a scale of district wages, in some districts slightly higher than the existing wages (South West Yorks and Leicestershire) less in others (e.g. Forest of Dean where it would be 44s. as against a recent wage of 80s. and 29s. before the war). Over all, the wage average is about £2 a week better than the pre-war wage and compared favourably with other industries. These particular offers had not been discussed. The men heard them but did not negotiate with the owners in their districts. At my last meeting with them the miners complained that in Durham and Notts the wages were not up to the figures which could be afforded in those districts. I offered to intervene but Hodges objected. Hodges admits that the wages demanded cannot be afforded by the industry even if the owners forgo their profits.

The P.M.: That is a very important admission. You don't want to fight on the coal owners' profits but on subsidies.

*   *   *   *

Sir Robert Horne: . . . The demand now is for 1. a subsidy 2. a national pool. They have not discussed district wages. It is all wrong for Cramp to say that this is a blow at wages.

The P.M.: What is the attitude of the Triple Alliance?

Sir Robert Horne: The railwaymen in some districts are against joining. It depends on what view they take of the advantages gained in fighting now or in August (when the railway agreements come to an end). The dockers are said to be against fighting now. . . . They could have a pooling arrangement for wages separately. Hodges mentioned that but I have avoided it. The men want the profits from Yorkshire to pay the men in the Forest of Dean.

The P.M.: It is another way of getting at nationalisation.

Dr. Macnamara: The Ministry of Labour is anxious about the Triple Alliance and unless Thomas, Bevin,[1] and Gosling[2] can go to the miners with some constructive policy on Wednesday their men will join in.

Sir Robert Horne: Pooling is not practicable either by the men or by the masters.

Dr. Macnamara: Then it becomes an industrial dispute and the machinery of the Industrial Court Act or an Enquiry could be resorted to by the Triple Alliance.

Mr. Fisher: The men fear this is a cut at wages.

The P.M.: Who has got an Intelligence Department? What is the Home Office opinion?

Mr. Shortt: The railwaymen are inclined to come out. We don't anticipate immediate disturbance. On the Tyne and Tees the men will certainly come out.

Sir Eric Geddes: On the one railway I have direct information about (the North Eastern) I am told the men won't look at it.

The P.M.: I don't think J. H. Thomas knows where he is or he would have been along to see me. He wants no revolution. He wants to be Prime Minister. He does not want to be a commissary for Bevin.

Dr. Macnamara: We have got to fight the subsidy. If we can do nothing positive then the Triple Alliance will join in.

Mr. Fisher: There is great resentment at the division of Yorkshire into three districts (by the mine-owners).

The P.M.: We have got to fight the problem as a whole.

Mr. Chamberlain: I have given authority to spend money as required and confirmed the decision of the Secretary of the Treasury. Ought we to consider getting more armed forces?

Mr. Shortt: We must have an announcement made in the House of Commons. I am putting down two resolutions announcing the occasion of emergency; there is a message from the King signed by him and regulations will have to be issued and a resolution moved confirming these regulations.

[1] Ernest Bevin (1881–1951); national organizer of the Dockers' Union 1910–21; General Secretary of the Transport and General Workers' Union (which he helped to create) 1921–40; won a national reputation in the General Strike, 1926; member of the General Council of the T.U.C. 1925–40; Labour M.P. 1940–51; Minister of Labour and National Service 1940–5; Foreign Secretary 1945–51.
[2] Henry Gosling, Labour Party leader on the London County Council and President of the Transport and General Workers' Union.

Lord E. Talbot:[1] The Prime Minister brings the message to the Bar and the Speaker reads it to the House for consideration on the following day.

The P.M.: A statement is to be made tomorrow by the Chancellor or the President of the Board of Trade and the Dumping resolution adjourned. We have got to subordinate all to this. It may drift into a big fight with the direct actionists. Everything depends on the influence brought to bear on the railwaymen and transport workers. When can you detach them best? I should think tomorrow. The Labour Party will be for moderation. They have nothing to gain politically by it.

Sir Robert Horne: The dockers are meeting tomorrow, the railwaymen Wednesday.

The Prime Minister: The railwaymen will be decisive. A moderate statement by Horne would have a cooling effect.

Lord Curzon referred to the procedure he would follow in the House of Lords with regard to the proclamation of the King's Message.

The P.M.: Our line is to be moderate and conciliatory.

Dr. Macnamara: J. H. Thomas and the other leaders will be stampeded by their own people.

The P.M.: Is it an attempt to control the action of the State or has it come in the ordinary course?

Sir Robert Horne: The Bolshevists were turned down at the I.L.P. Conference. There has been no concerted action about this strike. The miners' conference turned down the moderates at the Executive and have taken the bit into their teeth. (Delegates Conference of 25 March refused by 723 to 321 to enter into any temporary arrangement on a district basis.)

Mr. Montagu referred to the 'dismal speeches' of the miners' leaders in that day's papers.

Mr. Fisher: Hodges' speech was miserable, the speech of a coward (F. Hodges' speech in Yorkshire).

Mr. Chamberlain suggested the line Horne's speech should take: export trade just beginning to revive, things looking up, now foreign markets will turn more and more to American coal.

Dr. Macnamara hoped that the Ministry of Labour's machinery for dealing with industrial disputes would be indicated.

Mr. Chamberlain: What does that give them?

Dr. Macnamara: A drop from 80s. to 44s. is a bit thick. Give them the hope that their case is going to be examined.

Sir Robert Horne: The miners' leaders in the Forest of Dean know that the owners cannot pay more.

The discussion then moved to the question of troops. We had 18 battalions of which 7 were Irish and we were not sure of their temper.

Sir. L. Worthington-Evans: We need 18 battalions to hold London. We had 3 battalions at Malta, 2 of which we could bring home. There were 4 battalions in Silesia. They could be brought back to the Rhine at once.

---

[1] Edmund Bernard Talbot (1855–1940); Unionist Chief Whip 1913–20; as Lord Fitzalan became Viceroy of Ireland in 1921.

There are 7 battalions in Egypt. I have wired to Allenby to ask if he can spare any. Our reinforcements would thus be 2 from Malta, 4 from Silesia via the Rhine, and one or 2 from Egypt. There are troops at Constantinople but we could not contemplate their withdrawal. The Greeks had not been very successful in their advance.[1]

The Cabinet agreed to bring 2 battalions from Malta.

Lord Curzon urged that to withdraw battalions from Silesia would produce a possibly serious disaster.

Mr. Chamberlain: We are in front of a situation here which may require all our forces. I am all for holding the British coalfields rather than Silesian. You might bring two battalions from the Rhine and fill up from Silesia.

Sir L. Worthington-Evans: Tell Briand privately that we are doing this.

The P.M.: The point is the French are partisan in Silesia and are doing their best to help one side by propaganda. The French would like us to clear out. It would end in a war between Germany and Poland.

Lord Curzon: It opens up a serious vista.

The P.M.: Is the position sufficiently serious?

Sir R. Horne: You cannot run any risk. There might be trouble by the end of this week. Withdrawing the men (by a majority of 1) is serious. They will urge extreme courses because they have no funds.

The P.M.: Then we must take troops from Silesia.

The Cabinet agreed that Curzon was to look into the Silesian situation.

The debate continued on whether to use Yeomanry troops, and how best to bring back the battalions from Malta or Silesia.

The P.M.: I have a strong feeling of the undesirability of taking troops from Silesia.

C.I.G.S.: We have got to let the French know. We can say publicly that we are bringing them back to the Rhine but privately that we are bringing them to England. I doubt whether the French will fill up the gap in Silesia. We can take troops from Ireland.

The P.M.: Yes, if bigger trouble here and let Sinn Fein go.

C.I.G.S.: I have been asked for 2 battalions for Liverpool docks. They come from Ireland. Got 1 in Glasgow.

The P.M. suggested that the Lord Chancellor should draft a Bill which could be got through in a single day.

Sir L. W.-E.: We got the Pensions Bill through in $1\frac{1}{4}$ hours.

The P.M.: That was by agreement.

C.I.G.S.: Loyal citizens could join the territorials and also put them into the reserve but our present idea is that they could join the territorials. We have 44,000 reservists. We could pick up 20,000 or 30,000 but we have to call the reservists up.

Lord Birkenhead:[2] We should decide without delay around which force loyalists can gather. We ought not to be shot without a fight anyway.

[1] In their campaign against Turkey.
[2] Biographical note on p. 333.

Lord Lee raised the question of stopping the leave of the fighting forces.

Sir E. Geddes: If the railwaymen come they will come without notice. Things are not looking well.

The P.M.: I am impressed by the Lord Chancellor's suggestion that we should consider the force around which loyal citizens should rally in the case of first class trouble. Geddes, L.W.-E. and Macnamara and the Home Secretary are rather alarmed.

Under these circumstances we must not take risks. We must have a plan in case something happened. 12 hours would make all the difference in the world in such a struggle. I suggest that Lord Birkenhead and the Supply and Transport Committee should consider with the C.I.G.S. and other advisers what steps to take to get an organisation of loyal citizens. I wish Winston were here for this. He would be useful.

C.I.G.S. referred to the defence of London again.

The P.M. agreed that the centre is the important thing in a revolutionary movement.

5 April A Conference of Ministers was called at short notice for 10.30 this morning with the P.M. in the Chair to consider the coal strike. Four or five Ministers were present at the start and others dribbled in during the morning, the Minister of Labour arriving about 5 minutes before the end. . . .

The P.M. began with what he called the usual letter which Cramp sends him on the eve of industrial trouble calling attention to the victimisation of a number of railwaymen and asking the P.M. what he was going to do about it. . . . As Cramp was likely to make great play with these cases at the N.U.R. Conference on Wednesday, the P.M. urged that a letter should go to Cramp at once referring him to Geddes and that, before the meeting, the defence of the railways companies should be communicated to J. H. Thomas.

Asked what line J. H. Thomas was likely to take in this struggle the P.M. who had seen him yesterday replied that Thomas was all for peace. 'He does not want a row to please Hodges. I have complete confidence in Thomas's selfishness.'

The P.M. then read a telegram he had received from Sir William Robertson of Dunfermline asking for the immediate help of naval ratings from Rosyth and for military protection. Twenty-four hours' delay would be dangerous. . . .

The P.M. remarked that the miners in the Scottish villages were a savage folk. Munro, who came in later, said that . . . police aid from quiet areas could not be spared, that the Chief Constable of Fife reported that only naval or military assistance would be effective.

Mr. Bridgeman added that Forgie and Nimmo, two coal-owners, told him that the miners were going about in gangs of 2,000 strong, some crowds with women, dashing towards the pits and frightening the men at the pumps. There were plenty of volunteers if they could be protected.

Horne was cross-examined about the figures of wages appearing in the newspapers and the P.M. suggested that in his speech that afternoon in the

House he should warn the public against the misleading character of average figures which included the wages of boys. Horne said the Miners' Executive had refused his assistance in settling district wage figures with the owners as they wanted to confine the issue to the principle of national control. In his speech he would stress national control and the miners' demand for a subsidy and would point out that the only alternative in districts like Cumberland was to work on the wages offered by the owners or to close the pits and go on unemployment benefit. He did not want to be drawn into the wages issue and get lost in a rabbit-warren of figures.

The P.M. 'Some of these figures are very useful' . . . but, interjected some Minister—'figures are always very pliable in your hands.'

Mr. Chamberlain. 'I ought not to say this to you, Prime Minister, in the presence of your colleagues, but I remember in some Budget discussion in the House when we were in opposition, I protested to Harcourt that the figures you were using were very inaccurate: "but", replied Harcourt, "the Chancellor uses figures as adjectives".'

The P.M. 'Very good, very good.'

Mr. Chamberlain went on to suggest that an emergency committee should be set up in Edinburgh to act for the Cabinet. . . .

The debate continued, on the arrangements for Scotland, and the use of Territorial troops. The P.M. and Chamberlain drafted a letter to be sent to local authorities and the Cabinet broke up, having arranged to meet daily during the strike.

5 April 1.30. Lunched with Hankey at his Club. He had been talking to the P.M. much on the lines of my talk with Horne yesterday that we were not in for a big row. He thought too that Horne ought to have found some way to meet the specially hard cases and avoid the very big drop in wages threatened in these areas. I reminded him of the position last November when it was only under pressure from the miners that a terminal date was fixed for an interim report of the negotiations with the masters: that at that time all the stress was on inducing the miners to produce: that the P.M. in the negotiations kept saying that the Government was taking the risk of a fall in prices and were offering a bonus to the men. Then when the miners responded and produced an increased output and prices fell the Government ran away from that bargain and suddenly introduced an Act decontrolling coal on 31 March instead of in August—the reason probably being that it had occurred to someone that to decontrol in August would coincide with the return of the railways to the companies.

Hankey thought that the Cabinet yesterday had taken such an alarmist view because Henry Wilson had travelled up from the country with Mr. Chamberlain and had infected him with his own panic, and that Mr. Chamberlain infected his colleagues, and by the end of the meeting, the P.M. himself.

6 April At a conference of Ministers on government conciliation, the Prime Minister described the conversations that he and the Chancellor of the Exchequer had had with

L

Herbert Smith[1] and Hodges. He told them that he was to announce in the House of Commons that the Government would offer to conciliate, provided that there was no subsidy to be paid and no resumption of government control.

The mine-owners' offer (some limitation of profits) and the use of Territorial forces were considered. Flooding in the pits, particularly in Fife, was a major problem.

Amongst other emergency preparations, warnings were issued to the Roads Commissioners, the R.A.C., and the A.A., and the closing of Regent's Park, to prevent public demonstrations, was considered.

7 April Conference of Ministers at 10 Downing Street
The Prime Minister stated that there was no great leadership among the miners since Smillie's resignation. Smillie had had a flair for leadership. He was a master in the art of handling men.

Mr. Chamberlain said there was a grave misunderstanding among the miners of the character of our countrymen.

Sir Robert Horne stated that the Triple Alliance were to meet that day.

*   *   *   *

Mr. Montagu suggested the Government should approach the Labour Party.

The P.M. said that Mr. Clynes and Mr. Henderson and Stephen Walsh[2] had discussed the position the night before with him. They had now to consider how this menace was to be met. According to Sir Basil Thomson the railwaymen were not altogether backing the miners warmly. The remarks made by Mr. Bromley[3] compromised them.

Sir Eric Geddes remarked that fortunately Bromley was a very obstinate man. J. H. Thomas had let him down over Ireland and had not been forgiven.

Mr. Munro reported that the three storm centres were Fife, Lanark, and Ayr. . . . Ayrshire was restive, but Mr. James Brown, M.P., a Miners' Agent, had gone north to try to maintain law and order and secure that the pits should be pumped. Brown was a good moderate man.

Sir L. Worthington-Evans said he had received a report from Sir Francis Davies, G.O.C. Edinburgh. The troops could not be used for the defence of pumps—not enough of them. No request had been received from Lanarkshire for military assistance.

Mr. Shortt stated that the unrest in Wales was increasing. . . .

*   *   *   *

The P.M. then suggested that it would be well to strengthen the Sub-Committee already appointed under the Chairmanship of the Lord Chancellor to go into the question of the rallying of loyal citizens. . . . and that they

[1] Herbert Smith (1862–1938); born in a workhouse, worked in coalmines from the age of ten; President, Yorkshire Miners' Association, 1906–38, Miners' Federation of Great Britain, 1922–9, International Miners' Federation, 1921–9; led the miners in the General Strike, 1926.

[2] Stephen Walsh (1859–1929); a Lancashire miner; Vice-President, Miners' Federation of Great Britain 1922; Labour M.P. 1906–29; Secretary of State for War 1924.

[3] Secretary of A.S.L.E.F., whose union could easily effect an embargo on the movement of coal.

should go into the question of all defence connected with the strike, including the raising of special troops and the use of the Crown forces.

Mr. Chamberlain asked if they should have power to act on behalf of the Cabinet.

The P.M. replied that main issues, such as large questions of policy, would have to come before the Cabinet for decision, e.g. calling up reserves.

*   *   *   *

. . . The P.M. then said that he would try to see J.H. Thomas and Dr. Macnamara said he would try to see Ernest Bevin and Mr. Gosling during the lunch hour.

Mr. Chamberlain asked the P.M. what he proposed to say that afternoon in the House. Did he intend to inform the country in general of the serious-ness of the situation? Would he make any appeal to loyal citizens where mines are affected, or a general appeal?

Sir Eric Geddes remarked that the P.M.'s letter of appeal to Local Authorities was in safes in the banks throughout the eleven districts ready for issue.

The P.M. said he would prefer to wait till after the meeting of the Triple Alliance before issuing the appeal. . . . 'Must be careful in saying we are "not out to break wages down"—sooner or later got to have wages down.'

Sir P. Lloyd-Greame.[1] 'The way we (Publicity Dept.) are putting it is that the claim of the miners is for a subsidy which would be a burden crippl-ing other industries.'

Sir Joseph Maclay. 'The working people only see the *Daily Herald*. There should be a million leaflets issued.'

Discussion moved on to the publicity arrangements, and Lloyd-Greame got authority to spend money (£1,000) on sending men to Scotland to work up Government case in local papers from inside—e.g., *Edinburgh Evening News, Glasgow Bulletin*, etc.

Sir E. Geddes suggested switching trouble from figures.

Mr. Chamberlain urged that argument should be put, in other than the mining districts, e.g., Birmingham, Manchester, Leeds, that the miners were pulling up all other industries.

Sir P. Lloyd-Greame (against issue of leaflets) pointed out that the art of propaganda was to conceal it. Last strike the Government was sending out matter to 900 newspapers via the Coalition and Unionist organisations, etc., and the local political organisations were paid, and the public suspected little or nothing.

During the Conference Montagu passed me a note: 'I can't help wondering what is going on in your well-stocked brain. Have you anything to contri-bute?'

T.J. 'Sorry, no, except nothing provocative should be said until Triple Alliance moves; P.M. should see J.H.T., etc., at once.'

Montagu. 'I hope you will see to both these points.'

[1] Sir Philip Lloyd-Greame, later Cunliffe-Lister, cr. Viscount Swinton 1935 (b. 1884); Conservative M.P. 1918–35; at this time Secretary of Overseas Trade Department; President of Board of Trade 1922–3, 1924–9; Secretary of State for Colonies 1931–5; for Air 1935–8.

8 April The P.M. informed the Conference of the latest developments. J. H. Thomas had suggested in the House on the previous evening, with or without the miners' authority, that both should be summoned by the Government to a joint conference with the pumping of the mines as a first condition. He had sent a letter that morning to Hodges suggesting a Joint Conference 'which should deal in the first instance with the question of the pumping and preservation of the mines and that the matter be disposed of before any other question was entered upon'.

*   *   *   *

At this point J. T. Davies came in with a letter of acceptance from Evan Williams[1] on behalf of the Mining Association.

Geddes. 'Things are getting worse, incipient disorder spreading in Scotland and beginning to get to England.'

P.M. 'We can't call up the reserves until we hear how things are going.'

Mr. Munro. 'The Sheriff of Lanark says yesterday is the quietest day.'

Geddes proceeded to read the daily bulletin giving the reports from the districts.

*   *   *   *

P.M. '. . . the probable reply of the miners will be—"we will come unconditionally"; that would put us in a fix rather.'

Chamberlain. 'If the miners accept a conference it will hardly be the moment for issuing a proclamation.'

L.W.-E. 'I am not suggesting you should issue it now but it may be a matter of hours.'

Fisher. 'Is it not vital to protect the pits? It is a primary obligation of government.'

There was then some discussion as to how much should be communicated to the House of Commons and some objection was voiced to the use of the phrase 'disposed of'[2] in the P.M.'s letter.

P.M. 'I saw the Transport Workers last night, Bevin and Robert Williams. Macnamara brought them along. They are very anxious not to come out. Bevin had put the point: supposing the men agree to pumping, will they then be allowed to discuss national wage and national pool. I said, yes, but we cannot subsidise nor resume Government control. But the miners could put forward their scheme and the owners can say we cannot accept it. I saw Evan Williams and he agrees we cannot rule out a discussion of national wage and national pool. Then Bevin said: "Supposing the mineowners refuse to accept." I said: "We are not arbitrators".'

Montagu. 'You do not gain much by making conditions in advance. If Horne is right the miners won't send the pumpers back unconditionally. The essential thing in this dispute is the central or local arrangement of wages.'

P.M. 'No, not arrangement. They want a national flat rate system.'

[1] (Sir) Evan Williams, colliery owner and President of Mining Association of Great Britain.
[2] This phrase was the nub of the argument between Lloyd George and Montagu, the Prime Minister thinking that without it the letter would be too permissive. The words were finally included (see letter, p. 142).

Horne. 'The owners say this is a barbarous method of warfare. Suppose they evicted the miners from the companies' houses? Every day that passes pits are being wrecked [by flooding] and we must get this pumping question out of the way.'

Chamberlain. 'Are we at liberty to put our case and our reasons for rejecting the men's scheme?'

Horne. 'Nothing will be ruled out of discussion but nothing will be discussed before pumping is disposed of.'

Maclay. 'This is their only weapon now.'

Mond. 'It is the only desperate thing they have got. They have got no money.'

Chamberlain. 'There has been no surrender on the part of the Government up to the present. If they come to a conference without conditions there is no surrender of substance but only of form but if you discuss national wage system before the pumping men are back then there is a surrender of substance.'

Montagu. 'The miners feel they can't come into a conference with conditions. We intend the first condition shall be the return of the pump men.'

P.M. 'It is very difficult to get a clear line in the House of Commons. If we have a discussion then something will be said about the national board and then you would go from point to point. It is much too serious for mere face-saving. The owners will not come unless this thing is out of the way first. I would take the same view if I were an owner. If we drop conditions and meet we would be putting the owners in the wrong where on merits they are right.'

Montagu. 'I quite agree.'

P.M. 'We had great difficulty with the owners last night. A joint conference would make discussion impossible. There would be 75[1] persons and no leadership. It would be a rowdy meeting.'

At 12.15 p.m. J. T. Davies brought in the miners' reply agreeing to a conference 'entirely free from any preliminary conditions as to what is to be or is not to be discussed. We desire to be free to fully discuss every aspect of the present situation with a view to arriving at a speedy and honourable conclusion.'

P.M. 'There you are. The miners say you must discuss everything.' (P.M. really against further effort for a conference.)

Montagu. 'Suppose you summon both and the chairman says "the first question on the agenda is pumping". The conference will then either stop or go on.' (At this point Montagu began the suggestion of a reply to the miners and fought for it with Curzon's support and Macnamara's until he won.)

Chamberlain. 'The mine-owners are not at your beck and call. There has been great difficulty in getting them to go so far. Horne failed alone and the P.M., Horne, and I had to do it together. We are straight up against the point that we might put the owners in the wrong.'

* * * *

[1] *Note in Diary:* Apart from Govt. representatives the numbers would be about 35 owners and 22 miners.

P.M. 'Thomas has announced that the railwaymen and transport workers will strike but he is waiting for the Triple Alliance to confirm.' (This news came on a slip handed to the P.M. by J. T. Davies, his private secretary.)

Horne. 'That means that the miners have communicated their decision not to come to the conference.'

P.M. 'We must avoid marching into a morass. It was hard yesterday to keep the issue clear in the House.'

Several attempts were then made to draft a fresh letter to carry out Montagu's suggestion.

*   *   *   *

By 12.40 there was general assent to Chamberlain's draft reply as amended and the P.M. and Horne went out to fix its terms finally and returned at 12.55 and read the following which met with a chorus of approval:

Dear Mr. Hodges,

I have to acknowledge receipt of your letter of this morning. You state that you desire to be free to discuss fully every aspect of the present situation with a view to arriving at a speedy and honourable conclusion. This is also the wish of the Government. We have never suggested that any limitation should be imposed upon discussion, but as regards the order in which matters are to be discussed the national interest in the preservation of the mines is paramount and it must take first place. Whilst the mines are hourly being flooded and ruined and one of the most valuable of national assets being destroyed it is impossible to expect other questions to be debated. Accordingly the question of the safety of the mines must first be discussed and disposed of before other matters are taken up.

I therefore invite you to a Conference in this sense and will be glad if representatives of your Federation will attend at the Board of Trade this afternoon at 3 o'clock for this purpose.

Yours faithfully

D. Lloyd George.

*   *   *   *

I went out to arrange to send a copy of the letter to Evan Williams.

There was then more discussion of troop movements.

Chamberlain. 'There is no quicker way than by depleting Ireland. You should urgently begin with the Defence Force. We are threatened now with a general strike. The Defence Force would be a demonstration of public opinion by men of good will. Until it is begun there is no chance for men of good will to shew themselves. We ought to hoist the flag in every district.'

P.M. 'Have you thought of announcing this to the House?'

Chamberlain. 'We should do this at the close of business. L.W.-E. should draft the announcement.'

P.M. 'We can keep the House going. (To Curzon) You can adjourn in the Lords. Is the sanction of Parliament necessary?'

L.W.-E. 'We have got to inform Parliament.'

P.M. 'That means a debate on Monday.'

Chamberlain at 1.5 reads a message from Basil Thomson (Scotland Yard) that the Vehicle Workers are coming out tomorrow night and the Dockers also, though probably not more than 40 per cent. of them.

Macnamara. 'Don't bank on that percentage.'

P.M. 'This railwaymen's strike will interfere with the movements of the reserve. We had better now adjourn until 3 p.m. If the miners accept you will get a notice putting off our meeting.'

*   *   *   *

P.M. then suggested a drafting Committee should meet at 2.30 to deal with the various announcements. The P.M. left. . . .

A discussion on publicity methods followed.

Chamberlain. 'Cannot we have a sort of "Save the Nation" appeal?'

Fisher. 'All these messages are too slow. We need a patriotic appeal to the miners telling them they are being misled, the Government is acting for all.'

Macnamara. 'You cannot cure at once the misrepresentation and exaggeration which has been going on for years.'

Lloyd-Greame (in charge of Publicity). 'I have seen the advance draft of the announcement of the Transport Workers for tomorrow—"Prepare—this is the beginning of a national attack on wages".'

Geddes referred to the Strike Books which had been issued to the various districts and deposited in the banks and said that by inadvertence the P.M.'s appeal had been dated 6 April.

Chamberlain. 'The Home Secretary is to encourage special constables simultaneously with War Office action.'

Curzon. 'I understand we have (a) reservists, (b) the new Defence Force, (c) Special Constables, (d) volunteers to unload trains, etc.'

Amery (Chief Civil Commissioner). 'The Civil Commissioners in the 11 Districts are trying to prevent overlapping.'

Chamberlain. 'Fisher and Lloyd-Greame should draft an appeal to the miners to save property.'

The P.M. returned at 1.20 having been in touch with some Intelligence officer. 'There is some information that Hodges has communicated with all local secretaries to the effect that a subsidy can be forced from the Government. It looks like running amuck.'

Stanley Baldwin. 'What a fool.' (His only contribution I think throughout the whole discussion.)

P.M. 'The Durham and Yorks miners are by no means in this fight. They think it a great folly and that it will last a fortnight.'

8 April   3.30 p.m. The Conference took note of the following reply by the Miners' Federation to the Prime Minister's letter sent during [the debate] the same morning:

8 April 1921   The Miners' Federation

Dear Prime Minister,

I have to inform you that your further letter has been considered by my Committee. We note your clearly stated condition that the question of the 'safety of the mines must be first discussed and disposed of before other matters are taken up'. We think the condition stands in the way of a resumption of negotiations.

As previously stated, we are willing to meet the owners and the Government in conference at once if we are allowed to meet unconditionally. We trust that the Government will raise no obstacle to ensure this end.

Yours truly,

(Sd.) Frank Hodges.

A short discussion followed as to the desirability, even at this late hour, of trying to arrange a further and nominally unconditional meeting between the two parties, but, on a full review of the circumstances, it was agreed that no useful purpose would be served by such further attempt.

It was agreed that the Prime Minister should send the following reply to the Miners' Federation:

8 April 1921   10 Downing Street

Dear Mr. Hodges,

I have received your letter, and I note with the greatest regret the decision at which your Committee has arrived.

In view of the grave consequences involved it is difficult to understand how any discussion designed to promote a settlement could usefully proceed unless we were all agreed that the first task should be to secure the preservation and safety of the mines without which there must be widespread and continued unemployment and distress, not only for those whose occupation is in the mines, but for the whole industrial population.

So far from placing any obstacle whatever in the way of negotiation, the action of the Government has been dictated solely[1] by a desire to remove the main obstacle that stood in the way of fruitful negotiation. The mines are vital to the life of the community; their destruction is as fatal to the nation as would have been defeat in war and to secure their preservation must be the paramount duty of Government.

Yours faithfully,

(Sd.) D. Lloyd George.

A discussion followed about arrangements for the Proclamation calling up the Army Reserves. This required the immediate return of the King from Windsor, as the communication to Parliament had to be under Sign Manual.

[1] *Note in Diary:* Altered by L.G. from 'solely for consideration for national interests'.

9 April   3.45 p.m. The First Sea Lord reported that the Admiralty could provide 2,500 men within twenty-four hours. There was more deployment of forces to South Wales and Scotland and telegrams, appealing to the nation, were sent to Local Authorities. It was later agreed that:

1. The Government shall summon a conference of the representatives of the Miners' Federation and the Coal-Owners to meet at the Board of Trade on Monday, 11 April, at 11 a.m. to discuss all questions in dispute between the parties.

2. The Miners' Federation shall tonight issue notices to the branches of the Federation urging their members to abstain from all action which will interfere with the measures necessary for securing the safety of the mines or will necessitate the use of force by the Government (to prevent officials or others from being interfered with while employed on these operations).

12 April   The conference met, as arranged. The miners demanded a national pool of profits and a national settlement of wages. The Government thought that the pooling arrangement was impossible without permanent state control and that a voluntary scheme could not work. They put forward instead a proposal for a standard wage in each district 'which shall be the first charge on the proceeds of the industry in each district'—no profits to be payable until the standard wage was satisfied. The principle of the standard wage would be fixed nationally but the amount by districts. This was unacceptable to the miners.

After the breakup of the joint conference with miners and owners a Conference of Ministers was urgently called for 6 p.m. in Chamberlain's room in the House. I was late and found the P.M. trying to explain to Addison, who was asking questions very clumsily on the situation, that the pooling of profits would mean a subsidy from the other districts to North and South Wales: that during control expenses went up and output went down and that neither the miners nor managers put their backs into their job. The so-called heavy reductions would still leave it possible for piece workers to earn from £4 to £5 10s. a week and non-piece workers £3 6s. 9d. 'You might as well have a pool in agriculture. The seams in South Wales are deeper and thinner, in Yorkshire they are fat. Any standard which is within the capacity of the poorer mines we are prepared to force the owners to pay, but the men want to have a contribution from the richer to help the poorer.'

Sir Robert Horne added some further explanations and Eric Geddes gave examples of pools which were in operation in other industries but Horne pointed out that these were all voluntary combinations. In reply to a question from Montagu (which I had prompted) P.M. said that no one wanted to suggest a pool of wages. Churchill called attention to the drastic character of the reductions proposed by the owners. Horne replied that the owners had offered in every case, except Durham and Notts, all that could be got out of the industry, and reminded the Conference that the miners got £12½ millions of housecoal every year. Churchill appeared to be very critical of the way the whole business had been managed (in his absence in the East). Horne resented this rather hotly and A.C. then delivered a vote of confidence in his colleagues who had been in charge of the negotiations. Addison asked if this, that, and the other had been explored. The P.M. replied hotly that they had been doing nothing else but exploring for months and that there was nothing between the men's proposal and nationalisation.

Mr. Shortt. 'This is a strike for nationalisation.'

There was then some discussion about the red revolutionary number of the *Daily Herald* which was said to be coming out that night. It was agreed on the whole that it would help recruiting if it came out. About 7.30 the P.M. said he would be glad if Ministers would remain within reach to deal with any message which might come from the miners and later on possibly from the Triple Alliance. The P.M. had his dinner sent in to his room at the House, Hankey and I dined in the Harcourt Room with O. Locker Lampson and when we got back we heard that the miners' letter breaking off negotiations had been received and that the Triple Alliance had adjourned their meeting until 10.15 p.m.

13 April 9.55 a.m. Spoke to J. H. Thomas on the telephone. He said he was desperate; that he had striven last night to get the Triple Alliance to go to Downing Street today in vain. As he put it 'Things were as black as death. Of course we shall stand by the miners. They feel we have let them down over the pumps and we must not desert them over the pool of profits.' I urged him to try to get the question of a pool of wages re-opened and that that, with what was conceded yesterday, ought to be enough to form a basis for a central organisation which might grow into what the miners are asking for.

10.55. J. H. Thomas's secretary rang up to say that the Sub-Committee of the Triple Alliance had met (Thomas, Cramp, Gosling, Williams, Smith, and Hodges) and were going now at 11 to the full meeting of the Triple Alliance. Thomas felt quite sure that they would not seek a meeting with the Government and he urged me to see the P.M. and try to move him to invite the Triple Alliance. I went across to No. 10 and saw the P.M. who was just starting out for a drive. I gave him the message. He said 'I think we had better have the strike. Let them kick their heels for a week or a fortnight. It will help the moderates against the extremists. What I most wish is that I had some Conference abroad to go to urgently and then I could come back in a fortnight and take up the negotiations again. You had better tell Chamberlain and tell him to think it over.' I then saw A.C. with Sir N. F. Warren Fisher[1] and later spoke to Sir Robert Horne. He was of the opinion that the P.M. would probably not move any further but might make a statement in the House.

12.15. Message from Thomas's secretary to say that the Triple Alliance refusal was on its way to No. 10.

---

[1] Sir Norman Fenwick Warren Fisher (1879–1948); Permanent Secretary to the Treasury and head of the Civil Service 1919–39; with Hankey, one of the two most powerful men in Whitehall during the inter-war years.

12.50. Thomas spoke to me to say that Electrical and half a dozen other Unions were joining them. 'The men think that the Government are mobilising for fight. I am afraid we are right in it now. Have you seen *The Times* this morning and the *Manchester Guardian*? *The Times* has a very good article. Is L.G. really wanting to fight?'

T.J.: I think he feels that the moderate leaders have not got the men in hand and cannot restrain them.

J.H.T.: He is making a huge mistake. I sent down the letter by hand deliberately.

T.J.: I saw him before he went out and told him it was worth making one more effort to get the Sub-Committee or the Twelve. What is the Committee of Twelve?

J.H.T.: The Transport Workers and the Railwaymen. I do not think Herbert Smith and Hodges will come back. They cannot prevent us if we are invited to come back. We might bring some miners. My letter gives him the opening.

T.J.: The P.M. will be back about 1. There will be a debate in the House this afternoon.

J.H.T.: Of course. I am feeling very worried. It is awfully serious. I cannot let the men down. I have done my best. Good luck.

3.0 p.m. J. H. Thomas rang up again to ask if the P.M. were approaching the Triple Alliance. I said no, not at this stage. We could see how things went in the House this afternoon. J. H. Thomas said tomorrow would be too late. 'We shan't be able to cancel the notices. The Associated (Bromley's) Union and the Clerks[1] are coming out.'

I said I had done my best with the P.M. both at 11 and at 1 o'clock.

Informal Conference of Ministers
Present: The Prime Minister, Mr. Chamberlain, Sir Robert Horne, Lord Curzon, Sir Eric Geddes, Hankey, and T.J.
The reply from the Railwaymen and Transport Workers had been received a short time before the meeting and it was decided to communicate it to Parliament that afternoon. There followed a discussion as to whether it was better to have a debate in the House today or tomorrow on the situation; the P.M. against a debate today as it might force the Government to take up positions, so he asked A.C. to get in touch on the telephone with Clynes or Henderson.

Sir Robert Horne. 'Are you asking the Sub-Committee of the Triple Alliance to come to see you?'

The P.M. 'If you want them to come I'd have discussion this afternoon in the House. The House would force parties to come together again.'

Mr. Chamberlain was inclined to invite them so the P.M. could say 'I

---

[1] The Associated Society of Locomotive Engineers and Firemen (A.S.L.E.F.) and the Railway Clerks' Association.

want to be quite certain that you have had the thing put to you properly—
the substance of the Government's offer.'

The P.M. 'Consider what that means. It means the beginning of negotiations. If I were left alone without newspapers and without Parliament I
would leave the miners alone.'

Sir Eric Geddes. 'They want to be coaxed.'

The P.M. 'There is nothing that we can propose that Hodges can now
accept. (To me)—don't you agree?' I said I thought the Triple Alliance could
still bring great pressure to bear on the miners if the Government offer were
advanced in the direction of a wages pool. The P.M. disagreed and said that
the wild men were already condemning Hodges for accepting a slight
reduction in wages.

Lord Curzon was for postponing parliamentary discussion to give time to
the country to realise what was taking place. 'When they realise the Triple
Alliance is coming out tomorrow night they will be flabbergasted.' There
was a reference to *The Times* leader which on the whole favoured Hodges and
I said J.H.T. was counting on *Times* support.

Lord Curzon said '*The Times* wants to harm you, Prime Minister.'

The P.M. 'It is funk, really.'

Sir Eric Geddes. 'Are you now of opinion that the best tactics is to play
for delay?'

The P.M. 'Yes, I want delay without obviously playing for it. I do not
mind their coming out. I believe you can prick the bubble. These men have
always had the idea they can strangle the community.'

Sir Eric Geddes. 'Do they mean to pull the trigger?'

The P.M. 'It will go off as happens when several boys are playing with a
loaded pistol. The chief leaders are against a strike but the majority are for.
If we have a debate in the House today we shall hear the voice of reason—
the cooing voice of Clynes, and Bob Cecil will deliver his League of Nations
speech again.'

Mr. Chamberlain. 'He is the worst type—the sentimentalist with some of
the wisdom of the serpent.'

Sir Eric Geddes. 'Are the men free to cause trouble again with the pumping?'

The P.M. 'They have issued no notice about it. They will begin to realise it
does not pay them.'

*   *   *   *

Mr. Chamberlain was then called out to speak to Henderson who said the
Labour party were meeting at 2.15 to decide their procedure. The P.M. told
Horne to get his statement ready. A.C. said that he would try and see
Asquith. The P.M. reiterated that a debate should be avoided—'it would
drive you to take positions which would handicap you in negotiations'. There
followed a long discussion as to the exact form of the statement which the P.M.
and Curzon should make in the House, particularly which tag should be
used at the end of the statement: e.g. 'hope wiser counsels may prevail during
the next 48 hours so that the disaster may be prevented' or 'let us all have a
little time to consider the serious situation which has arisen'. After 10 minutes

drafting or so the P.M. got an outline agreed.[1] I went off to Dean's Yard and lunched with Arthur Greenwood, Professor Halévy (Paris), and two or three others.

13 April   J. H. Thomas and Robert Williams wrote to the Prime Minister announcing the N.U.R. and Transport Workers' decision to strike at 10 p.m. on Friday 16 April.

14 April   Present: The Prime Minister, Horne, Eric Geddes, Macnamara, Bridgeman, Gowers, Hankey, and T.J.

Gosling, J. H. Thomas, B. Williams, Bevin, Cramp, and 8 or 9 others.

11. a.m. Deputation enters Cabinet Room, Gosling and J. H. Thomas speak.

11.40. The P.M. withdraws with colleagues to consider their statement.

11.45. The P.M. returns with his colleagues and speaks till 12.45 when he again withdrew leaving the Deputation in the Cabinet Room.

1.5. The P.M. and his colleagues return to the Deputation. Gosling and Thomas speak for about 5 minutes.

1.10. The P.M. briefly replies. The Deputation withdrew and it was agreed by the few Ministers present to put in action the Government's machinery which had been prepared for the eventuality of a strike.

1.30. The Supply and Transport Committee met hurriedly at 2 Whitehall Gardens.

Later in the day the P.M. and his colleagues met a deputation from the Federation of British Industries led by Sir Peter Rylands.

Seebohm Rowntree[2] called at 3.45. I told him the position which had arisen at the end of the Conference this morning and suggested he might see some fourth party which could come into the negotiations afresh and seek a compromise on a basis of the Government offer of August 1919 plus National Wages Board, the National Wages Board to form a *temporary* pool consisting of the miners' offer of 2*s.* a day, the contribution from the owners and a subsidy from the Government.

15 April (noon)   On the previous evening two meetings took place in the House of Commons, when first the mine-owners and afterwards Mr. Frank Hodges addressed a group of Members. The latter had made the more

---

[1] *Note in Diary:* 'The Government deeply deplore this decision. There is no doubt that the situation thus created is one of great and increasing gravity, but I hope that wiser counsels may yet prevail. Meanwhile the Government have been concerting the necessary measures to meet the emergency.'

Early in the meeting there was some fun over J. H. Thomas's description of the situation over the 'phone to one of the P.M.'s secretaries: 'It is hellish bloody buggery' and later when seeking a formula Curzon reverted to this and said he wished he could use it in the Lords. This reminded the P.M. of another 'phone conversation of J.H.T. with J. T. Davies (P.M.'s secretary) some time ago. 'Jesus Christ, J.T., them Geddeses *is* bloody duds.' Sir Eric enjoyed this immensely.

[2] Chairman of Rowntrees Ltd., a well-known social worker and publicist, responsible for some of the most illuminating studies of poverty, industry, and unemployment of the period.

favourable impression of the two. Towards 11.30 p.m. a question was shot at him asking if he was prepared to discuss wages, and he replied in the affirmative. In answer to another question he said that he was prepared to postpone the question of the pool and discuss a temporary solution of wages only. No record had been taken, and a group of Members, whom the Prime Minister had seen after midnight, had not agreed as to exactly what Mr. Hodges did say.[1] The Prime Minister had, however, felt the matter was sufficiently important to necessitate his writing to the Miners' Federation inviting them to meet representatives of the Government and Mine-owners at 11 a.m. He himself, with the Lord Privy Seal, the Chancellor of the Exchequer and the Minister of Labour, had proceeded to the Board of Trade, when they had met the owners, but the Miners' Federation had not put in an appearance. They were reported to have met together first, and afterwards to have repaired upstairs at Unity House to meet the Transport Workers and Railwaymen. A definite answer has been promised in half an hour's time.

15 *April*   *The Prime Minister to Mr. Hodges*   *10 Downing Street*
Several Members who were present at your House of Commons meeting last night have conveyed to me the purport of your concluding offer. They had not taken down the actual words you used, but the general impression made on their minds was that you were now prepared to discuss with the owners the question of wages without raising the controversial issue of the 'pool', provided the arrangements to be made were of a temporary character and without prejudice to a further discussion of proposals for a national pool when a permanent settlement comes to be dealt with.

If this is a fair representation of your suggestion I invite you and your fellow delegates to meet the owners at the Board of Trade at 11 this morning to consider the best method of examining the question of wages.

Position at 3 p.m.
The Miners' Federation declined to meet the owners on the terms suggested in the Prime Minister's letter.

It was agreed:
(a) That the House of Commons, which had adjourned until 4 p.m., should be invited to re-assemble:
(b) That the Prime Minister should read both letters to the House of Commons, preceded by a statement based on the lines of his concluding remarks at the last meeting with the Mine-owners and Miners.

Mr. Hodges to the Prime Minister   *The Miners' Federation of Great Britain*
My Executive Committee have fully considered your letter and ask me to state the only condition upon which a temporary settlement can be arrived at is one that must follow the concession of the two principles already made known to you, viz., a National Wages Board and a National Pool. In these

---

[1] This was the crux of the whole strike, and the origin of the 'betrayal' of Black Friday. Hodges' off-the-cuff answer was used with great skill by Lloyd George to widen the split between moderates and extremists which Thomas had earlier revealed.

circumstances my Committee feel that no good purpose would be served in meeting the Owners today on the basis suggested in your letter.

4.45 p.m. The Prime Minister informed his colleagues that he had heard from Mr. J. H. Thomas that the strike of the Railwaymen and Transport Workers was definitely postponed until tomorrow and that the chances were remote of its taking place.

Warnings had been received from reliable quarters to the effect that the withdrawal of the Railwaymen and Transport Workers would probably result in resentment against them among the miners, and that for the present the mining districts were the danger areas.[1] The protection of railway junctions and other objectives on the railways should, therefore, be specially considered.

Naval ratings had been moved on the previous day to Glasgow, Newcastle, and other centres in the North and in South Wales, and instructions had been issued three days ago requesting the Commanding Officers to keep in the closest touch with the Chief Constables of their districts.

Mr. Frank Hodges, the General Secretary of the Miner's Federation, has resigned his post and his resignation has been accepted.

16 April 11 a.m. Conference with Railway and Transport Unions: J. H. Thomas, Cramp, Bevin, Gosling, etc. L.G., C. of Ex., Geddes, Bridgeman, etc. The P.M. passes note to me.

P.M.: It is not enough to have good cause.

T.J.: You must also have wise leaders.

P.M.: I'm sorry for the miners—they're a patriotic lot. I'm not heartless enough for this sort of thing.

Conference (Ministerial) on the industrial dispute

The Prime Minister informed his colleagues that, after the Cabinet meeting on the previous day, he had received a letter from Mr. J. H. Thomas and Mr. Cramp.[2] Some answer had obviously been necessary, and he had therefore been obliged to depart, in the letter though not in the spirit, from the Cabinet's decision. Agreed.

*   *   *   *

The Conference agreed—

That Sir Philip Lloyd-Greame should arrange for the publication of a statement in the Sunday newspapers emphasising such facts as the tremendous break in prices, the lack of markets abroad, the extent of American competition, the importance to our financial and industrial position of coal produced at prices which enable us to compete successfully with other nations in exports both of coal and manufactured goods, the effect on this of wages

---

[1] This was an under-estimate of the bitter recrimination which followed the collapse of the Triple Alliance.

[2] On behalf of the N.U.R., A.S.L.E.F., and the National Transport Worker's Federation, cancelling the strike.

costs per ton of coal at different periods, and the fact that a temporary settlement would be of little or no value.

*18 April   A letter of thanks to volunteers was sent out in P.M.'s name. The Defence
Force had now reached a total of 70,000 men with a further 10,000 who had registered.
It was to be a useful lesson for the future, but the effect over the next four years, after so
easy a government victory, was that the Supply and Transport Committee organization
was allowed to run down. Thus the Government were caught out on 'Red Friday' (30
July 1925).*

24 April   T.J. to Bonar Law   *2 Whitehall Gardens*
I hear you are about to leave Cannes. After your resignation[1] I pictured you
exchanging the steady flow of Cabinet Papers for a flood of letters of condolence and I wanted to allow the flood to abate before venturing to send a few
lines of gossip. But clearly I must delay no longer or you'll be back before I
scribble my few lines. Your departure was most sudden but it was better than
'living at this poor dying rate', as the hymn says, like, shall we say, some
Ministers without Portfolio.[2] I am glad you got away before the strain of the
coal strike came on and I like to think how fitting it was to end a long chapter
of your life by summing up its lessons in the Rectorial address for the sake
of the youth who are to follow after.

It has been very different at No. 10 without you. The central fact in your
day was the constant consultation with the P.M., your mutual trust and
diversity of gifts. I daresay the full co-operation took a little time to grow
and time must be allowed to your successor. I like the new Lord Privy Seal[3]
for the simple reason that he is now much less overwrought than when as
C. of Ex. he had daily to oppose the demands of his profligate colleagues.
He is now almost gay and debonair with leisure for a joke and a tale—the
one I liked best being about the P.M. in his inaccurate budget days using
figures 'like adjectives'. A.C. talks more in Cabinet than you did and is less
elastic in mind than you appeared to be! Horne also has changed counte-
nances with Chamberlain and can only smile with difficulty. The coal business, the dread of a budget speech (now removed), the unfriendly sallies of
Churchill, and too few holidays have united for the moment to rob the new
Chancellor of half his buoyancy and made the miners take him for a hard-
fisted owner. Addison had ceased to build houses without bricklayers and has
joined the (newly) unemployed.[4] The Secretariat are trying to invent Committees for him. Boscawen[5] promises to talk a lot and thus makes up for the
long silences of Stanley Baldwin. Gordon Hewart[6] is within the Cabinet

[1] For reasons of health (though with no suspicion of the cancer that was to kill him two
years later) Bonar Law had resigned in March.
[2] Such as Addison—see below.
[3] Austen Chamberlain.
[4] As Minister without Portfolio.
[5] Sir Arthur Griffith-Boscawen (1865–1946); Conservative M.P.; became Minister of
Agriculture in February 1921; Minister of Health 1922–3.
[6] Sir Gordon, later Lord, Hewart (1870–1943); Attorney-General 1919–22, Lord Chief
Justice 1922–40.

prepared to oblige the P.M. with a speech on any subject on any side of it without notice. The Secretary of State for Air is outside. Montagu is obviously unhappy and Churchill sulky. But I am naughty and must turn over a new leaf.

And firstly, Coal. The opinion is general that the owners ought never to have put forward such a big cut in wages and that some scheme for graduating the fall should have been devised concurrently with de-control. This has been Churchill and Montagu's line and they are right politically however right logically Horne may be. Luckily for the Government the miners confused the issue by flooding the mines and clamouring for a subsidy. The P.M. fastened on this and rode off on the back of the poor pit pony and pulled round. But—not having you at his elbow—he deliberately stifled discussion in the House only to find that it broke out without his knowledge in a meeting with the owners (where their spokesmen did badly) and then in the meeting with Hodges which led to the midnight deputation to No. 10. On this same Thursday the F.B.I. got cold feet and . . . came hurrying to No. 10 with protests against the big wage cuts. It was a very black breakfast of kippers and *Manchester Guardian* on Friday a.m. at No. 10, the P.M. and Horne depressed because they wanted the fight to go on and had avoided the House because of the fear of being forced into 'positions', T.J. hilarious at the success of Hodges and believing that the miners now had the ball at their feet with two or three hundred M.P.'s as half-backs if not full-backs. But when during breakfast I rang up Hodges his voice was glum and I realised that he had 'slept over it' and realised that he had gone beyond his Executive. During the day we heard he had been beaten by one or two votes. Then came the collapse of the Triple Alliance and the Red Revolution was postponed once more. It was the most exciting day since the Armistice—three Cabinet meetings and endless comings and goings, the P.M. in great form as the day went on in his favour. The Strike Committee very sick. They had been waiting for two years to press the button. They had pressed it. The Strike Books had been issued from the secret banks where they had been concealed; the milk cans were rolling down to Devon and could not be stopped, the troops were steaming in ship and train from Ireland, from Malta, from Silesia to defend us from the men of Fife. The Duke of Northumberland was lecturing about Moscow and the Miners in the *Morning Post*. But Jim Thomas upset it all and despoiled Sir Hindenburg Geddes of the fruits of victory and was being damned as traitor by the miners and was hardly being thanked as Saviour by the Cabinet, so hard is it even for Welshmen to please everybody. On Saturday the Miners' leaders went home sulky and bitter and came back a week later and on Friday last the P.M. got the parties together once more and appealed in his best emotional style for a friendly effort at a settlement. Herbert Smith spoke and then Evan Williams—both miles apart. Then the P.M. began to wheedle them into a discussion 'without prejudice' and by infinite patience and good humour entangled them in a discussion of wages. From this I think we shall slide into at any rate a temporary settlement, the owners going without profits for 3 or 4 months, the men putting up with a reduction of from 2s. to 3s. a day and the C. of Ex. finding the rest. In effect we are doing now what Hodges put before the M.P.s.

Reparations I can tell you very little about. The P.M. went to Lympne without Curzon or Balfour or Chamberlain. Verb. sap.

In Ireland the decision is to let the elections go on. In Ulster there will be bloodshed, and in the south the Sinn Feiners will be returned without contests. They will refuse to take the oath and the Government will have to decide whether to try some sort of truce or Constituent Assembly or Crown Colony. Meanwhile no General will name a date when murder will cease and the Chief Secretary has dropped his optimism of six months ago and now talks of pacification in years rather than months. The P.M. appears to be as firm against any fiscal concessions as he was last autumn—saying they might be the ground for fresh demands. The tenacity of the I.R.A. is extraordinary. Where was Michael Collins[1] during the Great War? He would have been worth a dozen brass hats. Can't you get him to spend a weekend with you in France unofficially!!! I'm sure the P.M. has a secret admiration for him and his hands are no bloodier than those of the Angora butchers[2] we entertained lately and his cause is quite as good. He'll be canonised some day.

I must stop spinning this most improper screed and stop indulging in the frankness which you used to permit on the hearthrug at No. 11. But it would be rather fine if when you return rested and refreshed you found a way of peace with Ireland. Think about it.

All your old Secretaries seem rather like so many lost orphans with you away and I confess to feeling a little like that myself. Perhaps that will condone so many tiresome pages.

On 27 April the Cabinet had to decide whether or not to postpone the elections in Southern Ireland. If they were allowed to continue, 128 seats would go, uncontested, to Sinn Fein. Balfour wished to carry on, supported by Churchill, Addison, Worthington-Evans, Fisher, Mond, and Baldwin, Austen Chamberlain wanted to postpone them, and he was supported, tentatively, by Montagu, Shortt, and Munro. Montagu put in a memorandum suggesting an offer of a truce for the purpose of negotiation.

After he had heard all the views, Lloyd George announced that, although he had been in favour of postponement, he had now changed his mind. A great deal depended on the semi-official negotiations with Sinn Fein, but there seemed to be no firm leadership with which to negotiate and he opposed Montagu's proposal. He spoke again of Dominion status but was primarily concerned not to pay a price which the United Kingdom would later regret. He spoke harshly of Irish greed in bargaining; then summed up in favour of the elections going ahead.

30 April   Luncheon with Geoffrey Fry at his flat in Mayfair. Miss Watson (one of Chamberlain's secretaries, formerly Bonar Law's), and Dick Law (B.L.'s son from Oxford, about to join Inner Temple). Much gossip about Sir Robert Horne. I said he had no convictions. . . . Miss Watson added that he was much changed for the worse by his sudden rise to the Exchequer.

[1] Biographical note on p. 335.
[2] I.e. the Turks.

Miss W. worships Bonar Law and will talk endlessly about him. She described
Clemenceau walking on terrace of No. 10 with B.L. and putting his arm
round B.L.'s, saying: 'All great men are humbugs'. Mrs. Fry in for part of
the luncheon—daughter of Lord Burghclere who was made by Gladstone
President of the Board of Agriculture because he had translated the *Georgics*.
We talked of Tawney's new book, *The Acquisitive Society*, expanded from his
pamphlet, and I gave Fry a copy. Also today sent a copy to Lord Esher.

*On 30 April the Cabinet discussed the German default over reparations payments due
on 1 May 1921. The French were threatening an Allied occupation of the Ruhr. Great
Britain was not prepared to follow France in threatening mobilization.*
  The Cabinet were considering the German Einwohnenwehr (defence force).

P.M.: The Germans must dissolve this force of 300,000 men plus an army of
100,000.
  Churchill: They had a terrible fright in Bavaria at the time of the rebellion. If we get a satisfactory arrangement on money we ought not to pledge
ourselves now to go into the Ruhr for the sake of the odds and ends; we
should go in on money if Germany is contumacious, but if we get agreement on Reparations, don't let us pledge ourselves now to go in for odds and
ends.
  P.M.: I don't believe France will march seven divisions if Germany
accepts. Certainly not if Bavaria cuts her troops down to 50 or 70 thousand.
  Churchill: We owe a great debt to the P.M. and Curzon for putting so
firmly our objections to France.

                    *   *   *   *

  P.M.: If we get our cash—that's all I'm out for, as against not Germany
but France and Belgium.
  D'Abernon: A great deal depends on the U.S.A. I think the terms are very
good now.
                    *   *   *   *

*1 May, Sunday   The same debate continued. The French attitude was by now less
threatening. Churchill appeared more moderate than Lloyd George.*

Churchill: I'm entirely against the principle. 'We will concentrate armed
forces, etc.' I don't think this country wants to take aggressive action and I
don't think the French will do it, if we don't go in with them, when they
realise the consequence of going in alone. If we hold firm they'll be more
reasonable. 15 May is as good as 1 May. This is our last chance. Until we
commit ourselves we can wield enormous pressure. . . .

                    *   *   *   *

  Chamberlain: P.M. has been trying to make it easy for Germany; Germany
has never responded to our efforts; the first effort of Germany comes when
Britain and France begin to speak in real earnest. The 1st May in itself is not
important. It is a treaty date but it becomes important because Briand has

said in the Chamber, 'Wait until 1st May so that we may keep in line with the Allies.' The only chance is to make the Germans feel the axe.

D'Abernon: I think all this illegal and against the Treaty.

Curzon agreed with this. He wanted to ensure United States support for British action.

Churchill: You are asking a community to mortgage their future exertions, the exertions of their scientific men, their genius for organisation and finance to be maintained for a couple of generations; how can you delude yourself with that? They'll default again unless they resolve in their wills. I think they've done wonderful things since the Armistice, disarmament, ships, coal, money for reparations. They must believe they are getting off cheap. We are now acting against our better judgment and compromising our sound point of view to meet the French. I fear we shall be left without our policy and not completely with theirs. I fear too that in taking this step we shall be drawn into others. I beseech the P.M. to take a very firm stand now and say we wish to make a settlement with Germany by agreement.

*   *   *   *

P.M.: Consider the situation in France with its devastated area, its deficit of 15,000 m. francs attributable to the rebuilding of the devastated areas. Frenchmen have been forced to raise money; Germany can pay; she can't pay our demands and her own debt; French entitled to say, 'Our debt should come first'. The unreasonable point was that the French, without the decision of the Commission, should march to the Ruhr and *then* say, 'This is how you are going to pay'. . . . Why should we go to America? I'd communicate direct with Germany. America has got swelled head already. I'm told by Americans not to feed that. I'd go straight to Germany and say, 'If you don't accept, we'll enforce'. I've been pleading for a fair opportunity—7 or 10 days. Germany won't accept, except under duress. How can she? Every Minister would have to go except 'under duress'. To Curzon, 'That is your proposal'.

Curzon: It is mine.

P.M.: Our decision is practically Curzon's. (To Curzon) You alter draft and meet French as far as possible.

*   *   *   *

Chamberlain: I share all the horror of Churchill and Montagu of being dragged into the Ruhr, but I do not see it is in our power to avert it. It is only in the power of one nation to avert it—Germany. We can only give Germany time. To ask France at this stage to let Germany submit counter-proposals is to ask of the French what is impossible for them to grant, and it is not friendly to them to ask the Germans to do it. You've gone on and on, and you can't ask the French to prolong negotiations indefinitely.

4 May   Bonar Law to T.J.   *Hotel Loti, Paris*

Thank you very much for your long and interesting letter which gave me just the picture of Downing Street which I am so interested to have. I can't of course form any idea from what I see in the papers of how the machine is working and I should like very much if you could send me occasionally a frank account such as you have given me in this letter.

L.G. must be having just about the hardest time he has ever had and I imagine that he must be in great anxiety about the German business as well as the troubles at home.

I am better in health than I have been for years and I am sure that the physical weakness which the doctors found in me was only the result of mental causes, and that if I had stayed on something like what happened to Wilson would have happened to me also. I am sure however from my feelings already that L.G. with his temperament would be utterly miserable if he were to drop out of everything as I have done, but even his buoyancy will not last indefinitely under the terrific strain he is always undergoing. Poor Addison! He must feel pretty wretched and his Ministry without Portfolio cannot last very long I fear.

9 May   Sir Robert Horne to T.J.   *Treasury Chambers*
I am most grateful to you for sending me Tawney's book on 'Acquisitive Society'. I do not feel like an acquisitor, although you call me one. The only moss which I gather is the accretion of age, while the exuberance of youth departs from me. I have only dipped into the book, but what I have seen of it is very arresting and I have no doubt that I shall be a better man when I have read it. I know that you are anxious to save my economic soul and I am very glad to think that you believe it to be worth saving.

12 May   Meeting of the Cabinet at 4 p.m. in Chamberlain's room at the House. Geddes, Mond, Gordon Hewart, and Lord Birkenhead absent. Churchill and one or two smoking—this practically never happens at a Cabinet at No. 10, and until quite recently only rarely at the House of Commons. Balfour began with the debate which went on through the previous night on the 'Safeguarding of Industries Bill' and asked that a formal letter of protest should be sent to Asquith to mark the fact that the Liberal Party had deliberately broken faith with the Leader of the House—a thing the Irish never did. Chamberlain read passages from Hansard showing that the arrangement had been to stop at 11 p.m. . . .

The Cabinet then resumed the discussion of a 'truce' with Sinn Fein, which had been adjourned on Wednesday morning to allow the views of the Chief Secretary and his advisers to be obtained.[1]

The Prime Minister stage-managed the proceedings perfectly. During the reading of the documents from Ireland he remained quite impartial, but slowly, as Balfour spoke, he allowed his inclination to show. Most of the reports were against a truce, Greenwood basing his opinion on signs that the rebels were being worn down by repression.

Balfour made a long and well-argued plea against concessions, on the grounds that they eroded the British position. Against him were ranged Montagu, Addison, Fisher,

[1] This was also the day before nominations for the Southern Irish Parliament had to be made.

and Churchill, though for different reasons. Curzon was less sure than he had been before. Lloyd George summed up his own views in a brilliant review of the position. Unable to trust the Irish leaders, least of all De Valera, unwilling to concede too much, he was against a truce at that moment. Later, when order had been restored, as he intended it should be, he might agree. He convinced Austen Chamberlain, and at the end, T.J. jotted down the names as they had emerged:

For Truce		Against Truce
Addison	P.M.	Shortt
Churchill	Balfour	Curzon
Fisher	Chamberlain	Worthington-Evans
Munro	Horne	Denis Henry
Montagu	Fitzalan	

There followed a brief discussion of the Coal Strike and of the insurance rights of Reservists 'called-up'; the new proposals for increasing charges for letters, telegrams, etc., were approved.

19 May   T.J. to Bonar Law   *2 Whitehall Gardens*

All is quiet here and there is little to say. Ministers are away but within hail. The P.M., the papers say, is at No. 10 but he is chiefly at Chequers. Hankey is at Brighton. Philip Kerr has left and gone on a tour to the North Country to make his first acquaintance with 'the lower orders'. There is, I believe, a coal strike on, but it is forgotten under the blue skies and warm sun of London. The gardens are full of blossom and the song of the birds and no one wants to see the smoke of a chimney again. From Parliament Hill I can see 'all the city, all the temples topped with turrets, all the men' away to the heights of Sydenham. There are millions out of work, so Dr. Macnamara keeps on reiterating, but the charabancs were never fuller in the mining valleys. Either the cost of living figure is all astray or the miners are the most thrifty of men and are spending their savings or they are piling up debt or Lenin is financing them. Their law-and-orderliness is most depressing to my Bolshevik heart. Or are they ruining us by their inactivity and deceptive cheerfulness? True there are 'conversations' proceeding. Frank Hodges motored to Lympne a couple of Sundays ago and drank many liquor (or is it liqueur) brandies and played ping pong with Lady Rocksavage. Then he saw the P.M. at the house of some nouveau feudal family in Kent. Then he was motored back to town and took Mrs. Hodges to hear Melba at the Albert Hall. And on Monday he denied to the Press having seen the P.M. All which is a slippery slope which I fear will end in Respectability or worse. Then the P.M. disturbed Horne's Sabbatical Rest and brought him up to town and set more conversations going, this time with the owners who cannot so easily be corrupted with brandy and motor cars having long ago acquired immunity. And then Macnamara asks me to find out where the Minister of Labour is and I whisper to the P.M. 'please smooth Macnamara'; he snaps at me, and asks Macnamara to Chequers.

'Reparations' we regard as a triumph for the P.M. The French were going to march 'tomorrow' so the P.M. said he must see his colleagues 'tonight'. The Cabinet reject the French proposals. They are illegal; they break the sacred Treaty; they ignore the Reparations Commission. So he plays up his colleagues and gains the necessary respite while L.W.-E., Montagu, Mond—with Churchill butting in—work out a scheme of reasonable payments and time is given to Berlin to get a new Government. Mond very pro-French, Churchill pro-German, Montagu betwixt and between, L.W.-E. with both eyes on the cash, Jaspar mediating, Curzon drifting,[1] and Sforza listening. The Reparations Commission were treated rather unceremoniously and it was not easy to remember their high judicial authority. Towards the end of the Conference they were hastily ordered to get up from dinner and catch the night boat and present themselves before their Supreme Superiors—the P.M. going into J.T.D.'s room and storming his instructions to the poor private secretary so that neither Paris nor telephonist could understand what was wanted, while in the Cabinet room sat Briand and the Duma of thirty polyglot experts awaiting his return.

But all this is ancient history. Silesia[2] now fills the front window. It is a long time since you first heard the P.M. give his version of Polish history and you know his fixed ideas about their feeble leaders and poor spirit. He has proposed a weekend meeting of the Supreme Council, with the U.S.A. man in but they won't play—the new man is termed 'a bounder' (unofficially) and has offered to send back to Silesia the 4 battalions we brought to the Rhine because of the strike. Opinion here is puzzled with the levies of the French and wonders when their bellicosity will be satisfied. Briand is putting off the meeting until he has met the Chamber and meanwhile has told us that he wants nothing better than to carry out the Treaty, that it hardly befits us to talk about having withdrawn our soldiers but that he is most anxious to bring his views into accord with ours. Korfanty's insurgents—the telegrams say—are short of food and money and are sobering down.

The ghastly tale of horror from Ireland continues. Peace-makers are exploring Dominion Home Rule, others are building hopes on the meeting of De Valera and Craig. There is no change in the policy of the Government and there is to be no 'sign of weakness'. I had a Paper today written by some young Oxford dons to put up to the P.M. suggesting the Dominion Premiers as arbiters of the sort of Dominion status which might be conceded to Ireland. . . .

24 May During the recess the P.M. had seen Frank Hodges and Horne had been in touch with Sir R. Dennis Bailey, a Notts coal-owner. A great air of mystery had surrounded these conversations and with the exception of two or three Ministers, the Cabinet were in the dark about their tenour. The P.M. made a statement about them today but of so vague a character that Macnamara, Churchill, Montagu, and Addison put some leading questions to his great annoyance. The P.M. said that F. Hodges had made some proposals, had then said he must see Herbert Smith and yesterday had refused

1 'Drifting' in the printed version, but 'drafting' is perhaps a more likely reading.
2 The settlement of Germany's eastern frontier and Upper Silesia.

to meet the P.M. possibly feeling he had gone too far. He was meeting Herbert Smith and Robson that afternoon. 'They are very leisurely about it. There seems to be no leadership.'

Lord Birkenhead: Are they feeling the financial pinch?

Sir E. Geddes: The other unions are helping them a little.

P.M.: Mond and Fisher are feeding them (i.e., through the Guardians and the Local Education Authorities).

W. S. Churchill: The unemployment insurance finance is bankrupt. So far the unemployment dole has kept the country quiet and prevented a violent upheaval but at enormous expense to the state. It is plain we could have stopped the strike very much more cheaply in advance. There is a great feeling for the men in the country. He hoped the country would explore new possibilities and try to bring the boat to shore in the next 10 days.

Sir Robert Horne (replying to Macnamara): Yes, I have seen the owners. They had a stormy meeting last Friday and tomorrow are to meet again when it is hoped they will be in a better frame of mind on the question of a national settlement. That is a settlement which will involve uniform advances and reductions. The men claim that during the war wages went up uniformly and should now go down uniformly. The difficulty is that South Wales is so badly hit that any uniform reduction would leave wages so high that pits could not start.

Macnamara: Would the owners agree to arbitration?

Horne: Yes, on standard wages and on the relation of wages to profits.

Macnamara: I believe the House of Commons will take this matter out of our hands.

Addison: I am sure the country thinks with Churchill.

Chamberlain (trying to smooth things): When negotiations are at this stage there is a great danger of proposals leaking out. Therefore it will be better not to discuss them.

P.M.: It is not desirable to discuss detailed proposals.

Montagu: If proposals can be made which would secure peace by varying the Government offer of £10 millions, will you pass that?

P.M.: I am against it. It is thoroughly bad.

Churchill: That is a hard saying.

Horne: Other trades will clamour for subsidies.

Churchill: Look at the cost of your Defence Force, etc.

Horne: That is a blackmailing argument.

Chamberlain: The P.M. said in the House that while it was cheaper to buy off men with a subsidy, would it be cheaper in the long run.

P.M.: The delay is not due to us. We have indicated the lines on which we are willing to proceed and have varied our proposals.

Montagu: Is the £10 millions sacrosanct because it is a figure scientifically reached?

Macnamara: Any variation of the £10 millions upwards would be regarded by the extremists of the miners' federation as a victory for them. That would be fatal.

Addison: That is the last thing we should want to do but the House of Commons will think that we are letting matters drift.

P.M.: Frank Hodges will not be able to tell me anything until tonight. It is very odd that there is not much pressure to bring the dispute to an end.

Mond: Employers say—fight to a finish.

P.M.: That is because they have no orders. It is not altogether bad. I do not feel myself in a hurry to settle.

Churchill: That is the worst thing I have heard. I very much regret to hear that.

P.M.: There is a very big issue involved. It is the readiness or otherwise of workmen to accept an economic basis for their wages. I do not know it is far wrong to say that the whole industrial future of the country is menaced. It is essential to bring it home to the miners and they are facing the facts very differently from what they were a few weeks ago. Layton of the Iron and Steel Industries Association and John Hodge for the Trade Unionists have put in a memorandum to me on the importance for other industries of getting cheap coal.

The Cabinet debated the question of whether more troops should be sent to Upper Silesia to strengthen the British position at the next meeting of the Supreme Council. Two Irish battalions were sent although the Secretary of State for War was opposed to this and pointed out the dangers in Ireland, where a summer campaign to 'break the back of the rebellion' was planned. His memorandum (C.P. 2964) assumed that, on the War Office's definition of requirements in Britain, the Rhineland, Silesia, Turkey, Egypt, and the Middle East, there would be a surplus of three cavalry regiments and eighteen infantry battalions available for reinforcements for Ireland. The recommendations continued:

1. That the Cabinet now decide that in the event of a nominated Government being set up in Southern Ireland, martial law should be proclaimed over the whole of its area.

2. That drives and other similar intensive operations should be inaugurated.

3. That the Navy should blockade the ports and prevent gun-running and movement of Irish Republican Army troops.

4. That the additional forces available should be put under the command of the General Officer Commanding in Ireland.

2 June The Cabinet continued the discussion of the guarantee to the farmers for growing oats. The experts had advised that so far as one could forecast the course of prices, the Government might be called upon to pay nearly £12½ millions for wheat and over £17¼ millions for oats on this year's crop in next year's budget. In return we had got practically nothing by way of increased arable cultivation. Everybody except Lord Lee was aghast at the prospect of having to pay this enormous subsidy. . . . Ultimately it was agreed that Sir A. Griffith-Boscawen should try to bargain with the farmers on the basis of a subsidy of not more than £2 an acre to be paid them in cash round about October this year instead of waiting for the ascertained results at the end of March 1922. It was a gamble that the State might save a good many millions. As Churchill put it, there was always a great desire in the agrarian breast to take ready money.

At the same meeting the Cabinet debated whether to extend martial law to the whole of Ireland; but then a new chance of opening negotiations presented itself. General Smuts wrote to Lloyd George on 14 June, suggesting that the Government should use the opportunity presented by King George V's speech at the state opening of the newly elected Ulster Parliament, in order to 'foreshadow the grant of Dominion status to Ireland'. He enclosed a draft which might be used in the King's speech.

Meanwhile, the Irish Situation Committee of the Cabinet was discussing the implications of martial law in what Balfour called the 'most ensanguined hue' and T.J. sent the Prime Minister a report. The military commanders were at pains to make Ministers realize how severe the resulting coercion would be. T.J. and Hankey were both concerned in the constitutional implications of the King's Speech in Belfast. After considering drafts by Smuts and Craig, the Committee asked Balfour to make a fresh draft and this was substantially the form of the speech which was delivered on 22 June.

Two days later, T.J. was asked to summon a secret meeting of Ministers on Ireland. Lloyd George had received news that De Valera might respond to the King's appeal. He intended to invite Craig and De Valera to London, and the meeting discussed how negotiations could be conducted, and the text of the letter which was to be sent. As a guarantee of the Government's good faith, four members of the Dail—Griffith, McNeill, Staines, and Duggan—were released from Mountjoy Prison.

27 June The P.M. told his colleagues that he had spent about 7 hours yesterday (Sunday) at Chequers plus Horne arguing the coal situation with Herbert Smith, Frank Hodges, and Robson who had been brought there by Sir Denis Bailey. He had taken a very stiff line on the £10 million, suggesting the Government might give it as a loan. The leaders made out a very strong case that without the £10 millions they could not start in some of the districts. Ultimately he agreed to give the £10 million on condition that the men went back to work on Wednesday and that there would be no more balloting and wasting of time. Smith, Hodges, and Robson agreed that if this offer were now refused they would break away from their colleagues and tell the miners to go back to work. They were to consult their Executive this morning and to let him know the result. 'I have heard nothing so they are probably wrangling. I told them I could not finally promise the £10 million without consulting the Cabinet as it reversed our previous decision. In the course of the discussion Herbert Smith said that he had never been in favour of the pool.'

The Cabinet agreed to let the P.M. and Horne have unfettered discretion to give the £10 million and to make any conditions they liked.

Before the meeting started Sylvester gave me a draft of what he thought had been the final terms offered to the men at Chequers. This is what Horne and P.M. agreed to before their final talk.

*   *   *   *

We then went on to talk about the Greek refusal of the offer of mediation by the Allies,[1] during which the P.M. said that he stood alone as pro-Greek in the Cabinet but that he was willing to treat the Turks and Greeks on an absolute equality. Churchill said that was his view and that he was prepared to blockade whichever of the two proved to be the more provocative.[2]

After the letter inviting De Valera to a meeting had been sent, it was agreed that General Smuts should follow on an 'unofficial' mission to Dublin. He went on 5 July and returned the next day for a conference of Ministers in London. He had met De Valera, Griffith, and others, and found them deeply suspicious of a meeting at which Ulster would be represented. Smuts took great pains to persuade them and asked them to consider seriously the proposal of Dominion status. This, he thought, had impressed them, but they continually harped on visionary aims and believed that they could win the Republic by force of arms.

During the discussion, Lloyd George posed the questions of a truce and of a meeting without Craig, and both were agreed to. De Valera crossed to London to meet Lloyd George on 14 July. Craig attended the Conference but only for one day. He remained immovable, relying on the de facto *recognition of Ulster's separate entity under the 1920 Act.*

On 13 July T.J. was asked to be Secretary to the Irish Conference, because, as Hankey said, the Prime Minister did not want 'an Anglo-Saxon to run the show'. Lloyd George intended to have only Balfour with him at the later meetings and when T.J. objected that he was the most irreconcilable Minister, Hankey said that that was why Lloyd George wished to implicate him in the negotiations.

On 20 July, the Cabinet considered draft proposals for a settlement, in which Ireland was offered Dominion status, with financial and legal autonomy and her own police and internal services; Britain retained control of the sea and was to have military, naval, and air base facilities. Ireland should bear a proportion of the National Debt and war pensions, and should guarantee not to impose tariff barriers against Britain. This settlement was to be embodied in a treaty which was also to give full protection to Northern Ireland. De Valera returned to Ireland to consult his colleagues and the Dail was summoned for 16 August.

T.J. mentioned some of the talks in a long letter to Bonar Law:

22 July   T.J. to Bonar Law

I have not forgotten despite the cumulative evidence against me. For a long time there seemed nothing useful or interesting that I could say. I do not attend the meetings of the Imperial Conference—they are taken by Colonel Wilson. This year there is a shorthand record of the proceedings made. As a result there has been on several occasions almost a mutiny of the staff here. The Dominion Premiers—especially Mr. Hughes—when they read their utterances as faithfully recorded by the stenographers are ashamed of them and proceed to rewrite them and keep the staff waiting half through the night for copy. I can give no first-hand impressions. I have seen something of

[1] France and Russia had both concluded treaties with Turkey, leaving the Greeks to rely solely on Britain as their ally against the Turks. Nevertheless the Greeks refused to extricate themselves and began a new offensive, directed at Ankara.

[2] An interesting comment in view of his later attitude.

Smuts, whom you know, but nothing of Meighen[1] whom perhaps you do not know well. He is said to be very pro-U.S.A. on most matters, especially on the Pacific question. He is keen on the League of Nations but at the recent dinner he made the dullest speech on that topic. Canadians (with notable exceptions!) do not strike me as abnormally humorous. Churchill has taken minor topics at the Colonial Office, and at present the Premiers are meeting *alone* to talk over constitutional relations and foreign relations. So far as I have read the voluminous reports, the most brilliant pages are those devoted to Curzon's history of this wicked world during the last twelve months. You can picture him moving with majestic omniscience over the continents, rolling out one sweeping generalisation after another and suddenly revealing minute knowledge of a path over a small hill in the Caucasus.

But it is Ireland that has prompted me to write to you today. De Valera left for Dublin this morning having had four long interviews with the P.M. He was supposed to be carrying in his pocket the 'British proposals' but as a matter of fact he had left them behind yesterday at No. 10 and I recovered them this morning and am sending them to the Mansion House tonight. His visit has been most helpful to the cause of peace because he and the P.M. have met face to face and alone. The P.M.'s first idea had been to have with him Balfour, Chamberlain, and Hamar Greenwood, but luckily De Valera did not want any colleagues with him so the P.M. was able to drop his. The P.M.'s account is that De V. is not a big man but he is a sincere man, a white man, and 'an agreeable personality'. He has a limited vocabulary, talks chiefly of ideals, and constantly recurs to the same few dominating notions. He agreed to drop 'the Republic', the P.M. telling him that there was no Irish or Welsh word for it, and therefore it was alien to the spirit of the Celt! He was willing to be within the Empire, to recognize the King, to go without a Navy. What he chiefly seemed to want was *Irish unity*—that we should not *impose* partition, that there should be an All-Ireland Parliament with real financial and other powers, while leaving to Ulster the autonomy she now enjoys so long as she wishes to retain it. He was not unwilling to contribute to the War Debt. The crux of the problem as usual is the relation of Ulster to this question of unity. While the P.M. was closeted with De V. I was with Mr. Barton (Minister of Agriculture) and Art O'Brien (Ambassador) at No. 10. I found it almost impossible to make any of them admit the reality of the Ulster difficulty. They will have it that we created it and that we continue to exploit it; if we left Irishmen alone they would quickly settle their squabbles. You know the sort of stuff. As the negotiations proceeded the P.M. got a draft prepared by Sir Edward Grigg[2] of the sort of proposals we should put up to De Valera. This draft was worked over by Chamberlain, Balfour, and Smuts. It was shown in an early edition to Craig. Then on Wednesday evening the P.M. had it read out to the Cabinet, who made some verbal changes only. Then he took it to the King; then Grigg and I took it

---

[1] A. Meighen, Prime Minister of Canada 1920–1 and a member of the Imperial War Cabinet.

[2] (Sir) Edward Grigg, later Lord Altrincham (1875–1955); journalist, private secretary to Lloyd George 1921–2.

to De Valera at a private house in West Halkin Street at 11.30 p.m. Yesterday there was another interview with the P.M. during which De V., while not accepting our proposals, agreed to make counter-proposals after consulting his colleagues. I think this means that he is not unfavourable to the proposals in substance, but must try and bring his left wing along with him. Michael Collins is all right but some of the gunmen will be irreconcilable. Meanwhile the Hierarchy, the Press, and all moderate opinion in Ireland is yearning for peace, and when De V. reaches Dublin he will come under this influence, it is hoped. Barton I found a reasonable man—educated at Oxford, landowner, Protestant, joined up in the war, and lost two brothers in it. Erskine Childers I thought to be on the edge of a breakdown and very overwrought and 'logical'. O'Brien is more diplomatic as an Ambassador should be and it is less easy to read his mind. My aim has been to try and get them to trust the P.M. as the one man who could bring a peace that would be accepted by this country and be at all satisfactory to Sinn Fein. Throughout the P.M. has been superb and the 'Proposals' when they see the light will be accepted by the whole world I think as one of the most generous acts in our history. Briefly it is 'Dominion status' with all sorts of important powers, but no Navy, no hostile tariffs, and no coercion of Ulster. There is a Territorial Force for Ulster, and for the South. It is *hoped* they will contribute to the Debt, etc. An instrument 'in the form of a Treaty' is proposed. This caused a lot of heart-burning inside and was only got through by the passionate pleading of the P.M. and his references to South Africa, Scotland, Sarsfield and the Treaty of Limerick, etc. I suggested to him on our way to Buckingham Palace that if he settled Ireland he might be satisfied and 'go to Heaven', but he would not hear of such a dull destiny. 'There is still Europe', he replied.

About the rest of the world which revolves around this office there is little to add. Addison has left us and we do not miss him. Horne is making 'heavy weather' at the Treasury. I'm told he does not 'read' his papers assiduously as was the manner of his recent predecessors and he is unable to divine their contents as is the manner of others. He does not husband his physical powers. I hear remote rumours of serious attempts to get Mr. Asquith to withdraw from public life to make room for Lord Grey, but there are always rumours, and if the P.M. settles Ireland nothing matters. Hankey is LL.D. of Edinburgh and the broiling heat of London makes not the slightest difference to his amazing powers of work. He is just returning from a meeting on Japan and I must hurry off to see him before he catches a train, but not without saying that I hope you are building up lots of reserve strength and playing more golf than chess.

30 July   Bonar Law to T.J.   *Etaples*

Thank you very much for your long and interesting letter.

The real difficulty of the Irish business will prove now, as always in the past, to be Ulster. I greatly fear that De Valera will find it impossible to treat Ulster as entirely outside his sphere and on the other hand I am sure that no settlement can be carried in England which imposes anything on the new Ulster Parliament which they do not freely accept. If anyone can carry it it is the P.M. and success would be almost as big as winning the war. The longing for peace on both sides of the Channel is a strong lever but I am afraid of the partition difficulty. Personally, now that the Unionists in the South are all for agreement with Sinn Fein, I would give the South anything or almost anything, but I would not attempt to force anything on Ulster, and your letter does not enable me to judge how that difficulty is to be met.

I am now so well that I never even think of my health, and though I am delighted to have the picture of my old school, which your letter paints, before my eyes I am still enjoying doing nothing and I have the feeling that I am entitled to do what pleases me in future—including doing nothing for ever and ever if that appeals to me.

I think Northcliffe has got himself into a mess over his interview and my sympathies are all with Curzon and the P.M. I do not like the advertisement which all this is giving him, but if the P.M. is directing the reprisals I have no doubt they will be artistic.

P.S. I have just this moment got your second letter.[1] I am indeed very anxious for peace in Ireland and must do what I can to help, but I do not think there would be any use in my writing Craig. The limits within which he can move are very restricted and indeed, while, as I said earlier, I would give the South almost anything including even fiscal autonomy if they wished it, I would not quarrel with Ulster even to make peace with the South.

What you say about Barton does not surprise me, but during the political struggle before the war the thing which probably influenced me more than anything else was the conviction that Ulster, in spite of her bigotry, was right, that she had just as much right to shape her own destiny as against the South as Ireland could possibly have as against Great Britain.

The P.M. is very wise and can estimate the forces on all sides better than anyone probably, but I earnestly hope he will not make what I am sure would be the mistake of trying to put pressure on Ulster to accept any arrangement which brought them in any way under the control of a Dublin Parliament, however shadowy that control might be. That I am sure could not be carried in England. Perhaps I am still unconsciously influenced by the old party feeling, but I do not think so.

2 August Luncheon with P.M., Horne, and Hankey. Some talk of the Geddes Economy Committee. I pretended, in Churchill's manner earlier at the Cabinet, to deprecate these departures from constitutional precedent and to hint that the business of a Chancellor was to be one. P.M. chaffed me that what I really objected to was the personnel—millionaires, and that I would prefer to entrust the country's finances to a Committee of Webb, Tawney, Cole, and Arthur Greenwood. As the meal advanced, the talk degenerated, as it tends to do when Horne is about, into rather obscene story-telling. . . .

10 August   Chamberlain to the Prime Minister in Paris[2]
I assume that you will get back on Sunday at latest. Your presence during

[1] This letter is not in the Jones papers.
[2] Where he was conferring with Briand about the Silesian question.

Consolidated Fund Bill is essential for House expects statements on Ireland, Supreme Council, etc. Do you wish De Valera to be told that you must inform Parliament of proposed terms of settlement before it rises? Some Cabinets will be necessary before Ministers disperse and you will require to consult Cabinet before deciding finally about Geddes Committee. Ministers as well as House are restless on the subject and Geddes himself not very happy.

De Valera replied to the British proposals on 10 August. He criticized them sharply and put forward a long statement of Irish claims, phrased in language which seemed to make a settlement remote. But the letter ended by expressing a willingness to meet. It was handed by the Irish representatives to Austen Chamberlain, who thought it very grave. T.J. talked with the Irish and tried to point out how irreconcilable their claims appeared; later he put their views in a letter to Lloyd George (in Paris) and tried to tone down the finality of Chamberlain's reply. From this encounter, the importance of T.J. as an intermediary may already be judged.

12 August   In the evening to Victoria Station to meet P.M., Hankey and Co. returning from Supreme Council meetings at Paris. Ran into Art O'Brien on the platform. He was there to meet the Sinn Fein ambassador from Rome. Grigg and I motored with P.M. to No. 10. He was in great form describing the way he had pulled off the reference of Upper Silesia to the League of Nations—an idea which had been ventilated at a Conference of Dominion P.M.s by Hughes and also had been suggested by Hankey. The P.M. had kept it up his sleeve until the last minute. The night before, late, he had con-fided it to the Italians under pledge of secrecy. Then next morning, 'I saw Briand in this (travelling) suit—he saw at once I was leaving for home. I told him I saw no way out but the League of Nations. He took it like a man. I shouted to Hankey at half past ten to call a Supreme Council at 11.0 and I caught my train at 12.' He was immensely pleased with the dramatic charac-ter of the whole procedure. Then he questioned me on Ireland rapidly and said De Valera's answer was 'a silly answer'. When he got in to No. 10 Sylvester told him that the Whips were very disgruntled with Chamberlain's handling of the house, that Leslie Wilson[1] had almost quarrelled with him; I added that Chamberlain was much too nervous to be left to handle Ireland and he jerked out with a wave of his hand, 'He's a bloody fool', and went upstairs to dress for dinner which was to be at Chamberlain's at No. 11. Besides the P.M. and Chamberlain there were Churchill, Birkenhead, Hamar Greenwood, Fitzalan, and Grigg, and as a result of the discussion Grigg drafted a reply to De Valera which the P.M. produced at the Cabinet next day, but not until well on in the meeting.

On 13 August, the full Cabinet discussed De Valera's letter, and found it obscure. Ministers were concerned to keep the discussion clear and precise on fundamental principles; Ireland was not to be allowed to secede from the British Empire, nor could

[1] Conservative Chief Whip.

Britain abandon control of the seas. A Committee was set up to draft a reply, which was, essentially, a repetition of the proposals of 20 July; and the full correspondence was published on 15 August. No doubt of the Government's alternative policy existed in London. Martial law and a full-blooded campaign of repressions would be imposed if Sinn Fein rejected the offer.

During August T.J. was receiving letters from Alfred Cope,[1] in Dublin Castle, giving summaries of the views of the Irish leaders, which enabled him to inform Lloyd George more fully. On 24 August, the Dail rejected the terms and De Valera reiterated the nationalist arguments, claiming the right of small nations to self-determination. Once again, the purport of his letter was not clear and Lloyd George was able to find some hope in it.

13 August   Luncheon at No. 10 with P.M., Macready, and Miss Stevenson. Some talk about Ireland. Macready had read Arthur Griffith's *Resurrection of Hungary*, and had ticked off the various items which had been copied from Hungary and achieved by the Sinn Feiners. He told us how the Viceroy— the first Catholic since Tyrconnel—had been getting the Chapel at the Castle restored for services. They had asked a Dicky Quinn to do this and it had been decided that he should secure a suitable picture of the Madonna, Joseph and the infant Jesus to hang above the altar. When the Viceroy and his Lady arrived to inspect the Chapel they found a picture of Charles the Second, Lady Castlemaine and their baby!

We got talking about the Eisteddfod and the P.M. sent a Welsh maid to fetch his copy of the Prize Poems from his bedroom and for the rest of the meal he read and translated with great gusto 'Y Ffordd Fawr', repeating over and over the choicer examples of assonance and contrast.

25 August   P.M. came up from Lympne to No. 10 just before 1 o'clock and I 'phoned for Barton and Art O'Brien and McGrath to come along with De Valera's reply. They handed it to him in the Cabinet room and after a few courtesies left after a couple of minutes. He read the letter alone and then Chamberlain, H. Greenwood, Montagu, Grigg, and I were given the letter to read in turns and were asked not to consult each other as to its meaning. Then he made us stand on a black stone on the terrace and deliver our opinion. The majority, including himself, fastened on the last paragraph as the operative one—the one beginning, 'On the basis of the broad guiding principle of government by the consent of the governed, peace can be secured' and argued that the reply was not an absolute refusal. 'That was the principle of Gladstone's Home Rule campaign—we can accept that,' said the P.M. But everyone was very perplexed as to the real meaning of the letter. I had it reproduced and circulated to such ministers as were available and called a Cabinet for 5 o'clock when the P.M. again invited each minister to give his view. During the meeting he instructed me to wire for the absent ministers—Birkenhead, Eric Geddes, Baldwin, Gordon Hewart, Macnamara, Boscawen, and with the exception of the first and last they came. B'head

---

[1] (Sir) Alfred Cope (1880–1954); Assistant Under-Secretary and Clerk of the Irish Privy Council 1920–2; general secretary of the National Liberal Association 1922–4.

was on his yacht at Deauville and wired that he was 'weatherbound', but that he was prepared 'to agree with the P.M. in every particular'! Boscawen was in Scotland on his honeymoon.

About 7 o'clock the P.M. sent for me. Found him discussing draft reply with Grigg. He said he wanted some good quotations from famous Irish leaders showing their allegiance to the Crown, for inclusion in the reply. Suggested I should go to the library of the National Liberal Club to hunt for them, but first would I join him at a scratch dinner. Did so. Grigg and Sylvester there also. Dish of fried ham and some tinned fruit, claret, coffee, cigars. He wanted advice as to some really big book to read on his holiday in Gairloch. I remarked my surprise at finding from 'Makers of the Modern World' that he had been reading Mommsen. He said he had—also Ferrero, Samuel Dill, some Xenophon in the 'Loeb' series; Thucydides entangled him by the number of small towns. His favourite was Rollin's Ancient History which I used to see in many volumes in Wales when a boy. He talked again of 'Y Ffordd Fawr', and said the Crown Poem might just as well have been written in prose, 'but perhaps', he added, 'you think Masefield a poet?' He went off to see Charles Hawtrey act in 'Ambrose Applejohn's Adventure'. I went to the N.L.C. but found that the pamphlets of the Home Rule campaign were inaccessible; so I took St. Quintin Hill with me to Hampstead and we sat up until 3.0 going through my Irish books. I dug out the passage in Thomas Davis' letter to the Duke of Wellington, which was used, but we had throughout an uncomfortable feeling that a contradictory quotation could be got from each writer, especially from speeches delivered in America. On my way home I called on Chamberlain to borrow Lecky's *Leaders of Irish Opinion* but he hadn't a copy. I got from him, however, Barry O'Brien's *Life of Parnell*.

About 10 a.m. went to No. 10 and was sent upstairs with Grigg to discuss the draft which Grigg had prepared overnight. P.M. in bed in a dressing gown. His head looked bigger than ever. A large room with huge pieces of red mahogany furniture and a hotch potch of feeble pictures higgledy piggledy on the walls. Above his bed two longish rows of books—chiefly light novels but also I noticed *Letters of Luther* and Roget's *Thesaurus*. Below the bookshelves was a framed text from the Book of Job worked in silk threads: 'There is a path which no fowl knoweth and which the eye of the vulture hath not seen.'

On 27 August, Lloyd George replied to De Valera. Using T.J.'s quotations, he repeated the earlier arguments, leaving the initiative to the Irish, either to break off or to resume negotiations. De Valera's reply was as difficult to follow as the earlier letters, and although Cope wrote to T.J. to say that the Dail were prepared to negotiate, many members of the Cabinet were in doubt.

Lloyd George was on his holiday in Scotland, at Gairloch, and he summoned an unusual meeting of the Cabinet at Inverness on 7 September.

6 September To Inverness from Euston 7.30 p.m., with Chamberlain, Mond, Shortt, Macnamara, Baldwin, Boscawen, and Birkenhead. Chamberlain's first words were: 'This is outrageous, dragging us to Inverness. Why did the P.M. not have the Meeting in Edinburgh?' The P.M. had in fact sent a message to Chamberlain some days earlier asking him to come up for an informal Cabinet at Brahan on Tuesday and Chamberlain had refused categorically. I went to my berth at 9.30 leaving the Home Secretary busy with a bottle of whisky and six soda water bottles.

7 September   I got up at 7.0 at Blair Atholl and for the next 3 hours enjoyed the scenery. At Inverness Burgis had secured bedrooms at the Station Hotel, a room for Ministers and a room for the Secretariat. The P.M. was break-fasting at Moy with the King. Horne arrived at Inverness about 10.45 with the Draft Reply to De Valera drawn up by the Ministers who had been at Brahan. This was circulated in advance of the Cabinet Meeting to such Ministers who were available at the Hotel. Besides the Ministers at the Hotel we had Generals Macready and Tudor and half a dozen District Commissioners from the South and West summoned at the P.M.'s request. Sir John Anderson and Cope were also in attendance. Anderson, Cope, and I were busying ourselves before the Cabinet Meeting with various Ministers in the interests of a friendly reply to De Valera. In particular Anderson saw Chamberlain and Cope saw Montagu. Luckily the P.M. did not arrive till 11.25 which gave us some time. . . .

Lloyd George invited each Minister to give his opinion on the draft of the reply to De Valera. From the beginning, it was clear that this could be conditional or unconditional. At lunch-time, T.J. noted that the Ministers' views were as follows:

Unconditional	Conditional
Macnamara	Birkenhead
Munro	Churchill
Boscawen	Horne
Chamberlain	Worthington-Evans
Shortt	Hamar Greenwood
Montagu	Eric Geddes
Mond	
Baldwin	
Fitzalan	

The Prime Minister realized that the meeting was fairly evenly divided and before it adjourned for luncheon he summed up but did not say what he himself thought. Instead he warned the meeting that the problems of allegiance to the Crown and membership of the Empire were vital and that if a break was to come on these, it would be better then than later. In the afternoon a final draft (the ninth) was agreed and sent off. It asked for a definite reply as to whether De Valera was prepared to enter a conference, proposed for 20 September at Inverness, 'to ascertain how the association of Ireland with . . . the British Empire can best be reconciled with Irish national aspirations'.

While we were having the final copy typed we went on to discuss unemployment and Armenian refugees, the P.M. giving everybody plenty of rope on these subjects so that there should be no time to discuss the final draft again.

It was brought in, read by him alone and signed in the Cabinet Room at 3.45, handed to Barton by him in an adjoining room immediately after, and Barton hurried away to catch the 4.2 train for Dublin. Just after he had left, Cope, who had got from one of the Ministers a copy of the final reply, rushed to catch the same train to travel back with Barton. I phoned to the station master to hold the train back for Cope. Chamberlain, Mond, Baldwin, Macnamara had already left to catch the same train. The P.M. lingered about for a bit looking at the pictures in the Town Hall. Then he himself dictated a press notice which was given to Lord Riddell[1] who later read it to a crowd of pressmen. Then he went off to Brahan Castle where an informal Cabinet discussion was held on unemployment and German reparations. Churchill, Shortt, Horne, Fitzalan, Macready, Tudor, and Grigg were there and there was no doubt much talk about Ireland but nothing was put in the Minutes. At the end of the Inverness meeting, Montagu handed me a note of his views with a request that they should be recorded in the Minutes.

Next morning I took the morning train for the South travelling as far as Preston with Boscawen. The only thing I remember of his conversation which was extremely dull was a retort made by Joe Chamberlain to Lloyd George. Chamberlain was supporting the Birmingham Water Bill bringing the water from Rhayader in Radnorshire to Birmingham. Lloyd George was protesting against this injustice to Wales when Chamberlain replied 'I thought the water dropped from heaven, but in this case it drops in Wales and has to be filtered.'

9 September   T.J. to Sir Maurice Hankey   2 Whitehall Gardens
I returned last night from the pic-nic at Inverness. It was a great success.[2] The weather was perfect, the town highly flattered, the Provost important, the P.M. beaming, and even the Ministers who had scowled and growled at Euston melted into friendliness when they saw how delighted the Highlanders were to have them in their midst. Burgis had got everything into perfect order and on a scale which would have pleased the most fastidious G.H.Q. in France. What the Treasury will say presently we must not anticipate. At any rate he blocked one bill for the payment of a car to convey the Chairman of the Economy Committee to Culloden Moor and the neighbouring golf course!! The Council Chamber in which we met reminded one of a Police Court. There was a highly raised dais for the Judge or Chief Magistrate, a slightly lower dais in front for the Clerk of the Peace and then a horse shoe arrangement with a well in the middle. It had been intended to put the P.M. into the highest seat with a desk before him, a vase of flowers on his left, and an ivory hammer on his right with which to keep his colleagues in order. I was to sit below and then the Ministers round the horse shoe. However, as the P.M. is only *primus inter pares* I put him in the middle of the horse shoe with Chamberlain on his right, myself on his left, and left the exalted seats unoccupied. The first session went on till 1 when we

---

[1] Newspaper proprietor, and representative of the British Press at the Peace Conference, 1919–22.

[2] The signatures of those present, including T.J.'s, are still on view in the Town Hall.

adjourned for luncheon for 45 minutes and finished up about 10 minutes to 4 in the usual mad rush, handing Barton the fair copy of the reply with the ink wet, just in time to catch the 4.2 train for the South. The P.M. then perambulated the Town Hall with the Provost to examine the portraits and busts. After making a little speech in which he quite clearly indicated that we might want the building in a fortnight, and thus giving away to the Press something of the contents of the reply, he departed for Brahan Castle. I am sending you the Minutes which summarise the discussion. It all turned on the degree of conditionality to be put into our reply. Opinion against a break was much stronger than I anticipated and the draft with which the P.M. started the discussion was considerably toned down by the end of the Meeting. Of all the experts in attendance from Ireland—and they seemed to be legion —only Cope was called in and he was very effective in removing passages likely to be objectionable to the Sinn Feiners. Even now, as you will see from the Press, it is by no means certain that they will acept, but on the whole I think they just may do so. . . .

Lord Lee[1] was on the phone this morning from bed, much concerned about the preparations for the disarmament conference. He has been strongly advised to go off on Sunday week for a 12 days cruise to buck him up for the winter. He will be available from 1 October. I told him I doubted whether much would be done before that date and so far as possible I was sure you would meet his convenience. He is pushing on with the preparation of the case.

We have been trying to push on with Unemployment today but Mond has gone off shooting partridges and Macnamara vanished yesterday to Ramsgate but will return tomorrow. I hope we shall have a full meeting of the Committee with Horne on Tuesday.

From 12 to 19 September, telegrams and letters crossed between England and Ireland in bewildering succession. The Dail appointed five plenipotentiaries—Griffith, Collins, Barton, Duggan, and Duffy—but the Irish communications were so aggressive that Lloyd George cancelled the conference, on the grounds that they were pressing 'an impossible claim—an Irish sovereign state'. However, on 16 September, De Valera suggested a conference 'untrammelled by conditions'; and Cope from Dublin and Hankey and T.J. from London urged Lloyd George not to try and force further concessions from the Irish leaders. Even Bonar Law now intervened to suggest a compromise. At a conference at Gairloch, on 21 September, it was decided to bring the correspondence to an end and to invite the Irish to London on 11 October, on terms similar to those of three weeks earlier. This offer was dispatched on 29 September and De Valera accepted.

20 September   T.J. to Lawrence Burgis[2]
Dr. Macnamara and Sir Alfred Mond and Mr. Hilton Young have been

---

[1] Lord Lee of Fareham, who gave Chequers to the nation as a residence for the Prime Minister. He was a member of the Imperial War Cabinet, and First Lord of the Admiralty in 1921.

[2] Lawrence Franklin Burgis (b. 1892); private secretary to Lord Esher 1909–13; assistant secretary to the War Cabinet 1918, 1939–45; military assistant secretary, Committee of Imperial Defence, 1919–21, and an assistant secretary to the Cabinet Office.

summoned to Gairloch to discuss Unemployment, on account of the arrival of the Labour Mayors there. Various Ministers, including most of the Irish Committee, will also be there to discuss Ireland. I think someone ought to be there from this Office to give whatever secretarial help is needed. There are no special papers on the Irish question. I enclose relevant papers on Unemployment. The Committee had a long meeting this afternoon, rising at 5.30, for which there are no Minutes yet but Dr. Macnamara and Sir Alfred Mond were at the meeting. The question will turn on giving State grants to Poor Law or other authorities in places like the East end of London where Unemployment is very bad.[1] The Treasury strongly oppose.

22 September   Lawrence Burgis to T.J.

*   *   *   *

We started unemployment at 10.30 and I think the first decision arrived at (already sent to you) should help the immediate difficulty. The P.M. was much impressed with your telegram about Allan Smith[2] and is sending for him, I think. The P.M. is keen on getting the co-operation of business men, bankers, trade union officials, etc., in some extensive scheme to relieve unemployment, and he may send for people up here to help him in developing this idea. Allan Smith is the first but I suspect that others, representing other bodies and interests, will follow.

*   *   *   *

The P.M. is by no means well and Dawson says he must stay here at least until the end of next week. I'm not surprised he is not well in this damnable hole where it rains from morning until night. It has not stopped since I arrived.

*   *   *   *

The confusion here is indescribable. They are trying to do the work as if they were at No. 10 and with one not very efficient shorthand typist. There is one room as an office into which everyone crowds—*no* telephone and a P.O. with a single line, one mile away. Thirty miles from the nearest railway station which it takes four hours to reach, and only one car!

I hope my minutes are all right. You will of course turn them into Conferences of Ministers. It is a good thing the Cabinet Office was represented and I hope I have kept its end up.

30 September   Sir Maurice Hankey to T.J. (who was on leave)
Just a line to keep you au courant with what is going on.

Unemployment almost entirely fills the bill at present. Two or three days ago I had a telegram from Grigg suggesting that I should send you up with the party which starts tonight, to consult with the Prime Minister about

---

[1] A reference to the phenomenon known as 'Poplarism'. In areas of very high unemployment in the East End of London, notably Poplar, the local Boards of Guardians deliberately exceeded the provision made under the Poor Law for outdoor relief, and the Mayor of Poplar and several members of his Board, including Lansbury, were briefly imprisoned.

[2] (Sir) Allan Smith, chairman of the Management Board of the Engineering and Allied Employers' National Federation.

unemployment. I replied that you had just gone on leave and that I was very reluctant to recall you, and suggested sending Wicks.[1] This was approved and Wicks leaves with the party tonight. Howorth tells me that the Chancellor of the Exchequer, after giving a very gloomy review of our financial prospects, eventually came down with a proposal to spend £10,000,000 on unemployment. Macnamara and the remainder of the Committee, after the preliminary statement of the Chancellor's, which had led them to expect nothing over about £10,000, were overjoyed, so everything is all right. I hope the P.M. will not want to spend more than this, as I am convinced we cannot afford it at present.

On 6 October the Cabinet met to choose its representatives for the Irish Conference. Lloyd George, Chamberlain, Birkenhead, Worthington-Evans, Churchill, Hamar Greenwood, and Gordon Hewart were selected. T.J. was on leave, but not idle, for he secured the release of two Irish detainees, and met the two secretaries to the Sinn Fein delegation to discuss procedure for the meetings. His position was now one of trust on both sides.

The first Conference was held on 11 October and the conversations proceeded amicably for four more meetings, without really coming to grips with the problems. Subcommittees were set up on various topics, notably defence, in which the question of naval bases predominated. The report of the talks in which T.J. acted as secretary is given in great detail in the Diary and shows clearly both the subtlety of Lloyd George and the skill of Arthur Griffith and Michael Collins. However, two issues grew larger as the talks proceeded: the relationship of Ireland with the Crown and the Empire; and the position of Northern Ireland, particularly the counties of Fermanagh and Tyrone. In the latter case, Lloyd George ardently wished the South to come to terms with the North as a domestic Irish matter. The British Government would not ignore the history of the previous twenty years and coerce Ulster.

On 19 October, Collins presented what amounted to a rejection of the British conditions on naval and air defence; and then, a day later, when the Foreign Office published a telegram from the Pope to King George V praying for an end to the 'age-long dissension', De Valera replied by telegram to the Pope, claiming the independence of Ireland based on the will of the democratic electorate. At the next meeting of the Conference Lloyd George put several grave questions and the meeting was adjourned for the Irish to prepare a reply.

The Irish memorandum, which was presented on 24 October, was a reasoned plea for freedom as a free state, rather than for Dominion status as such; Ulster, they declared, was a domestic matter for Ireland, and they would negotiate direct with the North. Although this went some way to meet their requirements, the British Ministers at once raised the question of the Crown; and then Lloyd George and Churchill met Griffith and Collins in private.

Thereafter the character of the talks changed; private discussion and bargaining took the place of the formal conferences; and in this T.J. took a large part. Ireland's offer of 'external association' was not refused but ignored, and the British memorandum of

---

[1] Pembroke Wicks, private secretary to Austen Chamberlain and then to Curzon, 1919–23; a member of the Conservative Policy Secretariat 1924–9.

27 October demanded a clear assurance in the matter of allegiance. The Irish reply was not accommodating: and Lloyd George had now to face trouble with his Unionist colleagues in the House of Commons and, perhaps more difficult, to meet Craig and to deal with an Ulster-inspired revolt of the Unionist diehards at their party Conference in Liverpool on 17 November.

Over the weekend of 29 October T.J. was able to arrange a meeting between Lloyd George and Arthur Griffith in Churchill's house, which gave the Prime Minister enough assurance about the ultimate intentions of the Irish to face the vote of censure in the Commons. His speech was well received; and Griffith began to draft the letter which was to set down on paper the essence of their private agreement.

1 November, Tuesday   Saw the P.M. for a few minutes before the Cabinet and found him very pleased with the reception of his speech. I said that I thought he had engineered it very skilfully and he remarked that it was most difficult to avoid offending his supporters in the House or the Sinn Fein delegation. Cabinet 12.30 and a Committee on the Irish Truce at 4.0, at the close of which I had 10 minutes' talk with Collins alone. He said he felt rather disappointed and flat after the morning meeting which he thought was very much more difficult than he anticipated in view of what had taken place on Sunday night. I told him that unless a reasonable compromise was reached on Ulster I felt certain that the P.M. would rather resign than start a war of reconquest. The morning meeting was a short one at 11.0 between the P.M., Chamberlain, Birkenhead, Griffith, and Collins. Then another Cabinet at 5.0 on the Middle East which Col. Wilson took with Hankey.

2 November, Wednesday   To Euston. Saw Hankey and Burgis with Balfour, Cavan, and others off to Washington via Quebec.[1]

About 11.20 Griffith and Collins had an interview with Birkenhead alone in the House of Lords. At 11.30 I was present with the P.M., Curzon, Attorney-General, Stanley Baldwin, to discuss the reply the F.O. should send to the Court of Appeal as to the precise rank of Krassin[2] in this country. Curzon had drafted a reply which tried to make out that Krassin was here solely as an official trade agent. He admitted that incidentally we had discussed the question of the famine and of prisoners with him. The P.M. on the other hand, who always has been anxious to get trade going between the two countries, reminded Curzon that at meetings with Krassin at which Curzon himself had been present, we had discussed all manner of F.O. questions and that it was important all material facts should be sent to the Court of Appeal. Curzon at first denied having seen Krassin but the P.M.'s memory is uncannily accurate on such matters as I found when I went through the papers and prepared a record of the meetings for Curzon.

Later on 2 November, Lloyd George, Chamberlain, Birkenhead, Griffith, and Collins met to draft the final text of the letter of 'personal assurance' from Griffith, as chairman

---

[1] On the British delegation to the Washington Naval Conference.
[2] The Soviet trade emissary.

of the delegation. The letter gave Lloyd George enough grounds of agreement to bring in Craig and the Northern Irish representatives. But after the first meeting, on 5 November, Craig became adamant, leaving the Prime Minister with no room for manoeuvre. On 7 November, Lloyd George told T.J. that a break was imminent, and that he would resign rather than coerce the South. He had one way out—to give the South a Dominion Parliament, to set up a Boundary Commission, and to give Ulster representation at Westminster.

T.J. gave the news of the impending break to the Irish delegates on 8 November and pointed out that if Lloyd George resigned, the alternative would be Bonar Law and a return to coercion. As if it were his own, he put forward Lloyd George's suggestion of a Boundary Commission, and this was at once attractive, because it appeared to forecast the acquisition of a large part of Ulster by the South.

In the afternoon of 9 November T.J. again saw the Irish delegates and Griffith gave a guarded assurance that they would not obstruct the Boundary Commission proposal. Meanwhile, Lloyd George had secured the support of Birkenhead and Austen Chamberlain. Thoughts of resignation had vanished and by 10 November he was prepared to bring considerable financial pressure to bear on the North to force an agreement. That day, the Cabinet discussed Ireland for the first time since the Conference had opened in October; Lloyd George portrayed the Irish delegates as sincere, simple men, who intended to work within the Empire, and he was able to cite Carson's support of the Boundary Commission—for, like the South, Ulster expected to gain.

Craig had been invited to a conference in London. His reply of 12 November was a refusal to come under an all-Ireland parliament or to agree to any alteration in the area of the Six Counties. T.J. at once took a copy of the reply to Griffith. The Cabinet met and the general opinion was that Ulster had put herself fatally in the wrong. Craig was relying on the Unionist Conference at Liverpool to strengthen his position. Lloyd George was inclined to wait until the result of the vote was known; but he wished to progress further with Sinn Fein first. He obtained from Griffith an assurance that the Irish delegation would accept his proposal to the Conference—that there should be an all-Ireland Parliament, from which Ulster could secede within twelve months.

On 15 November T.J. again saw Griffith and managed to persuade him to meet Lord Midleton and the Southern Unionists the next day. Lloyd George was still hoping for a settlement on the lines of an all-Ireland parliament and a draft 'treaty' was ready on 16 November for T.J. to show to Griffith.

Meanwhile, largely thanks to Birkenhead's intervention with Sir Archibald Salvidge,[1] a man of immense influence in Conservative Lancashire, all opposition, except a mild resolution in the name of a die-hard Tory, Colonel Gretton, was withdrawn at the Liverpool Conference, and on 17 November even this was soundly beaten, to Lloyd George's unconcealed delight. Correspondence with Craig continued, but Lloyd George was prepared to make a firm arrangement with the Irish delegation before attempting to see him. Craig asked for definite assurances and stated that he wished to be able to announce them to his own Parliament on the 29th. T.J. saw Griffith to impress on him the importance of accepting the first draft of the 'Treaty' with as little alteration as possible.

[1] Sir Archibald Salvidge (1883–1928); principal organizer of the Conservative Party in Liverpool; a former chairman of the Conservative National Union and a man of great political influence in Lancashire and the North-West.

Then on 22 November the Irish, stiffened by De Valera, presented a new memorandum, reverting to some of their former demands. The only answer which Lloyd George could give, sent through T.J., was that they must withdraw it or he would break off negotiations. Griffith insisted that he was not going back on his 'letter of assurance', and held a long discussion with T.J., the upshot of which was that he feared to give Lloyd George a blank cheque which could be passed on to Craig. In the end, T.J. persuaded them to reconsider the memorandum.

On the evening of 23 November, Lloyd George and Chamberlain met Griffith, Collins, and Barton, and for this meeting T.J. had to produce Griffith's letter of personal assurance. The interview was, apparently, satisfactory. But the next day, at a constitutional discussion in the House of Lords, complete disagreement over the question of allegiance seemed inevitable. The leading delegates returned to Ireland for instructions.

Lloyd George now saw Craig and gave him a promise which he was to announce on 29 November—that by 6 December negotiations would either be broken off or new proposals would be available; in the meantime, Ulster's rights would not be sacrificed. On 28 November, Lloyd George asked T.J. to contrive to bring the Irish leaders to meet him at Chequers, and there they met the Prime Minister in the Long Room. At the first reading of their reply on allegiance, Lloyd George said 'This means war'; but after the conversation things seemed better. He was anxious not to break off over a symbol and fresh drafting of an inoffensive clause took place; this was made acceptable on 29 November, and the British Ministers agreed to the designation 'Irish Free State'.

The Articles of Agreement were ready on 1 December and the Irish crossed to Dublin. After a confused discussion, in which the majority of the Irish Cabinet was against acceptance, they returned. Late on the night of 4 December, T.J. saw Griffith, in an important interview, and found that he and Collins had been won over by Lloyd George's efforts for peace, and that their colleagues in Dublin might, with patience, be brought nearer to agreement. Griffith asked for some concession from the North, on the strength of which the South could then sign the Treaty and, even, refrain from asking for the Boundary Commission. T.J. agreed to arrange another meeting between Lloyd George and Collins, and this time, on 5 December, Lloyd George said that the break would come on the question of 'within or without' the Empire. Convinced that the North would be forced to come in because of her economic weakness, Collins agreed to the terms.

In the afternoon, Lloyd George played a masterful hand, relying on the knowledge of Griffith's mind which he had had from T.J., and steadily wearing down the Irish delegation by alternate threats and persuasion, to the position where first Griffith, then the others, agreed to sign. Some concessions were made to the Irish on the fiscal position, and the oath was made almost meaningless. At 2.10 a.m. on 6 December, the Treaty was signed.

During these weeks Ireland took up most of the space in T.J.'s Diary, but other subjects were mentioned from time to time.

9 November   11.0 Deputation of the Miners Executive asking for Government aid to meet the low wages in the pits. We adjourned for a short time after Frank Hodges had made his statement and the P.M. remarked: 'Frank Hodges presents his case like a Chancellor of the Exchequer, in a most lucid, persuasive and moderate manner.' . . .

15 November In the passage as he was going out Grigg rushed along and tried to catch the P.M. to look at a telegram from Sir Llewelyn Smith to the Board of Trade about the 10 years' naval holiday and its effect on the armament firms and on employment.[1] The P.M. was most impatient about any suggestion of building during the holiday and recalled what had happened when 'you all were children' in the rivalry between this country and Germany. 'There must be no question of considering employment nor of building slowly a small number of ships to keep the armament firms going. That will simply mean more competition in design.'

22 November [The P.M.] then turned to discuss Balfour's reply to Briand in Washington and bade me remind him of the subject at the Cabinet that evening and in the meantime to obtain the War Office view of the two speeches. He was plainly very annoyed with Balfour for failing to stand up to Briand. France was the danger to the peace of Europe. She was bent on becoming the greatest military power in Europe. Briand had grossly exaggerated the power of Germany. He had feared that Balfour might fail in such an emergency. It was nonsense to talk of the Russian invasion of Poland. The Poles were the criminals. It was plain from this and other casual observations that the Prime Minister is preparing himself for an outspoken onslaught on France when he gets to Washington.

*   *   *   *

3.15. Full meeting of the Cabinet in Curzon's room at the F.O., arranged there in order to enable Ministers to inspect the cartoons by Goetze.[2] We arranged the Ministers round the great table in the same places as at No. 10: the P.M. half down the table with Chamberlain on his left, myself on his right, Curzon immediately opposite. The room was overheated, the thermometer probably at 70° and the five great windows all closed. Curzon's head messenger began to bring messages into the room for me after the meeting started to the annoyance of Chamberlain and I had to arrange that no one less than a private secretary should come in during the meeting. Montagu announced the asphyxiation of the Moplah prisoners and then we passed to a full dress discussion on Turkey, the Franklin-Bouillon agreement, the possible evacuation of Constantinople. The upshot of Curzon's speech was a proposal that the Allies should invite Kemal[3] to an unconditional conference. No one had any better suggestion and this was accepted, Sir L. Worthington-Evans wanted to withdraw our soldiers from Constantinople as a *beau geste* but it was agreed that this had better be used during the conference than

---

[1] The 'Ten Year Rule', adopted by the Admiralty as a basis for defence planning, on the assumption that there would be no major war for ten years. Because the rule was moved forward each year (until its cancellation in 1933) it has frequently been blamed for British unpreparedness in the thirties. But in 1933 the Navy was still the best prepared of the three services.

[2] Painted to decorate the Foreign Office staircase, between 1914 and 1919. Curzon objected to them strongly.

[3] Mustapha Kemal (Atatürk), leader of the Turkish Nationalist movement and founder of the modern state of Turkey.

before. Churchill and Montagu wanted to send at once an unofficial agent to
Angora who would secure the confidence of Kemal. This was resented by
others because it was doing what we had just condemned the French for
doing. The P.M. was not hostile but wanted a suitable agent named.
Churchill or Montagu suggested the Aga Khan but it was pointed out that
he belonged to a very small and despised sect of the Moslems. Col. Lawrence
was mentioned by Montagu but he had led the Arabs against the Turks and
probably would be massacred if he went to Angora. During the discussion
Montagu passed a message to the P.M. telling him that a Treaty of Friendship with Afghanistan had been signed that day at 2.0; that there was to be
no subsidy, no Russian consulates, etc. This came most opportunely as
Churchill had been drawing a lurid picture of our fate in the East. The P.M.
had remarked with jocularity that the attack on Turkey did not begin with
the Treaty of Sèvres but with another attack which had resounded throughout the world a few years earlier.[1] Churchill replied that he was prepared to
defend the attack on Turkey at any time and that the P.M. was in the habit
of taunting him with that.

We then passed on to discuss the pictures which had been put up on the
walls of the F.O. and unveiled the day before. They had been the subject of
endless controversy. Just before the war the artist had offered the paintings
and had prepared models which had been on show for weeks at the F.O. and
afterwards at Downing Street. The offer had been accepted by Lord Beauchamp, then First Commissioner of Works, and for $5\frac{1}{2}$ years the artist had
devoted himself entirely to the work. I had been told, and no doubt the same
news had been passed round to all the Ministers, that if the pictures were
rejected the artist would probably commit suicide. Lord Crawford delivered
a most vigorous, direct, uncompromising speech on behalf of hanging the
pictures. It was a matter primarily for his department, not for Curzon's. The
works were a notable achievement—'I say that on my own responsibility'.
He then read commendations from Brangwyn, whose works are in twenty-
seven of the National Galleries of Europe, Aston Webb, Solomon Solomon,
David Murray, Goscombe John. 'I am the fourth Commissioner of Works
who has approved this scheme. It is incredible we should turn the artist
down.' Thus the Knight of the Thistle overcame the Knight of the Garter.
For about two years Curzon had fought a rear-guard action and delayed a
decision but at last the pictures were on his sacred walls and the Cabinet
were met in his stately room. The combatants today were no longer Mond,
the painter's brother-in-law, but two noble earls. 'It was a patriotic act on
the part of Mr. Goetze. The offer had been made and accepted, but there
was no obligation, legal or moral, to take them and hang them up in the
place designed for them provided that place was not suitable. I could produce testimony to rebut the art critics who have been named. I consulted
Sir Charles Holmes of the National Gallery, Mr. McColl of the Tate Gallery.
Their views are in sharp contrast with those given to the Cabinet by Lord
Crawford. It was McColl who spoke of these pictures as "meretricious". I

[1] Viz. Gallipoli, planned by Churchill.

do not venture to give an expert criticism but this is the Foreign Office, a Victorian building, gloomy and sombre. The character of the staircase has been altered by Mr. Goetze's work. It is significant that he is not an R.A. The pictures I would describe as superior scene painting, suitable for a Town Hall, a Dancing Hall, a cinema show. They remind me of Claridge's Hotel in Paris. Hitherto we have had simple and noble pictures of statesmen. Why should we expose the Ambassadors of Foreign Powers to the temptations of these lightly clad, gambolling figures? It is true, as Lord Crawford said, that I spoke to Hayes Fisher about these pictures and he said he would be glad to have them for some other building that was going up on the other side of the Thames, but Mr. Goetze turned that suggestion down. I would ask that the pictures be accepted, that they be not hung here but stored and kept for some more suitable place. There is not a single person in the Foreign Office who does not view them with absolute horror.' There were calls for Churchill, the one artist in the Cabinet, but the P.M. closed all discussions and took a vote. The most violent objection to the pictures was expressed by Fisher upon giving his vote but he, like so many others, felt we were pledged in honour to accept and hang the pictures. Macnamara proclaimed himself a barbarian and thought the pictures excellent. The P.M. similarly protested his ignorance of art and his surprise at the excellence of the cartoons. 'The sea was like water.' Churchill thought them not bad. Chamberlain thought we were in honour bound and so voting was practically unanimous against Curzon. Montagu had left before the discussion but whispered to me that he thought the pictures horrid. The Attorney-General also left and told me to vote as I liked for him but not to let the artist commit suicide.

We broke up hurriedly as the P.M. had to rush off to a Privy Council to hear the King give his consent to the betrothal of Princess Mary to Lord Lascelles.

23 November . . . I corrected the Minutes of last night's Cabinet which Howorth[1] had written and then went off with Curtis to Vincent Square to luncheon with Edward Grigg. Philip Kerr there. Grigg complaining that it was impossible to get the P.M. to pay any attention to business. Philip Kerr complaining that at a meeting of the Board of his newspaper *Daily Chronicle* that morning the directors had been bewailing the falling circulation due to the highbrow tone given to the *Chronicle* by Philip Kerr. General disquisition followed on the relation of a cheap press to democracy. 'The public is not interested in politics except when a General Election is on, is only interested in politicians as performing animals. It is impossible in a paper the size of the *Chronicle* to discuss political questions. The utmost that can be done is a short leaderette with a snap in it. An extra page of the *Chronicle* costs £500 per day. I said I took in the *Daily Mail* for the sake of the heavy Insurance Policy but did not read it. Kerr said there were 200 women canvassing for the *Mail* going up and down the country and pushing the merits of the insurance scheme. We were all agreed that the one great paper in the

---

[1] (Sir) Rupert Howorth, an Assistant Secretary in the Cabinet Office.

country was the *Manchester Guardian* and someone remarked that it was the one thing between the P.M. and depravity. Its circulation is about 60,000 and owing to the cost of paper they cannot afford a larger circulation. The *Observer* was another good paper with a circulation of 200,000. The *Westminster Gazette* was only selling 15,000 and we were getting a very inferior morning paper in place of a quite admirable evening paper. Some talk about Balfour's weakness at Washington vis-à-vis Briand, and Grigg and I noted the symptoms of the P.M.'s preparation for an attack on the military ambitions of France.

24 November 5.0 Conference of Ministers on Wei-hei-Wei.[1] A.J.B. anxious to have our views. Could he barter it away? Curzon and Churchill strongly opposed, Curzon recalling a meeting at the Admiralty when he was responsible for taking the place. (To Chamberlain): 'Your father was there, and Lord Salisbury, the Duke of Devonshire and Goschen. We had been discussing the matter for half an hour when the Duke of Devonshire, whose mind travelled about half an hour behind everyone else, asked where the place was. We took it with the connivance of China as an answer to Russia's taking Port Arthur. It was leased to us as long as Port Arthur was occupied by Russia and our possession was not disputed when Japan took the place of Russia in the agreement. No great use has been made of it except as a sanatorium for the navy because Balfour, in entire ignorance, gave a pledge that we would not construct a railway there in order to please the Germans. He had looked at a map and thought it was surrounded with mountains and that a railway would be impossible.' At this point the P.M. got up and wandered about looking for an atlas which I presently got for him. Churchill was willing to barter it away as part of a big solution of the Chinese problem but not otherwise and he was angered at the way our position was being weakened at Washington. 'We gave away Heligoland in this light-hearted fashion, we gave Corfu away and bitterly rued it. We gave Java away, a brilliant tropical garden.' The P.M.: 'We have got many of these tropical gardens and they are full of serpents.' Chamberlain said the Geddes Committee was going to attack Wei-hei-Wei because we spent money keeping troops there. We rang up the W.O. and found there was one officer and fifty other ranks there. There was a suggestion also that the Boxer indemnity should be waived as a mark of good will. 'Why', asked Churchill, 'should we melt down the moral capital collected by our forebears to please a lot of pacifists?' 'In the interests of a lot of decrepit mandarins,' chimed in Curzon. Churchill: 'I would send a telegram beginning "Nothing for nothing and precious little for twopence" ' and this became the decision. Worthington-Evans raised the question of sending drafts to India and its effect on forces available for trouble in Ireland. More than once the P.M. threw out dark hints to his colleagues as to the state of the negotiations with Sinn Fein but said nothing definite, probably because Montagu was present and in whom he does not confide on the Irish question.

[1] The British treaty port in China.

5 December   Sir Maurice Hankey wrote to T.J. from Washington, where the Naval Conference was nearing its successful conclusion.

. . . A.J.B. is the pivot of this show. If anything goes wrong with him I *must* have the P.M. Lee is not heavy enough weight to understudy Balfour. Geddes could perhaps do it, but Lee would never allow that. A.J.B. has really achieved a very great position—he is such a gentleman, so different from the crowd, and so very adroit. A really great figure. Unless we get a really bad set back—and there are traps innumerable—we can get through with A.J.B. With things so difficult at home I think it is waste to bring Ll.G. out. No one can make the Japs and Chinese go faster because of the bad telegraphic communication and the slowness of their Governments in sending replies. It would be most exasperating for him and he could not remedy it. Moreover the whole thing is so nicely blocked in now in its broad outlines that—barring accidents—it ought to go through in due course. The British Delegation, as usual, are *facile princeps* in every branch. . . .

A week later (12 December) Sir Maurice Hankey wrote to the Prime Minister:

. . . Mr. Balfour and I are feeling in the frame of mind appropriate to Christmas. The reason for this is that the quadruple treaty has now been announced to the world and we feel that one of the great tasks for which we came to Washington has now been successfully accomplished. We recall that at the Imperial Conference last summer the matter was rightly regarded as one of great difficulty. When we came to America we were faced with the fact that the Americans and Japanese were almost at daggers drawn, and the feeling between the two countries was very bad. In addition to this there was every sign of violent antipathy in America to the Alliance. If a proper feeling was to be created for a permanent and enduring treaty, this atmosphere had to be changed. All this we studied and thrashed out for days (in the intervals of sea-sickness on board the Treaty, as Mr. Balfour puts it) with the result that Mr. Balfour prepared the draft which you have seen. As a diplomatic opening, this draft proved absolutely invaluable. The clause providing for the possibility of a renewal if circumstances should change convinced the Japanese of our trust in them and that we were not throwing them over. The remainder of the draft showed the Americans that we were going to extreme limits in order to secure their friendship and co-operation. I never thought, personally, that the draft would stand in its original shape, but it served an extremely valuable purpose, which Mr. Balfour accentuated at every conversation whether with the Americans or the Japanese. The treaty which now emerges will, I hope, meet your views as a satisfactory solution. Anyhow, at the moment of writing it has made a most favourable impression here and the utmost goodwill pervades the British, American, and Japanese Delegations, which is a good augury for our further proceedings.

6 December   T.J. to Sir Maurice Hankey

A Cabinet starts in 10 minutes and this may be my last chance of a free moment in which to send you a line. I have had much the most frantic time of the last five years during the last few weeks: endless meetings and secret interviews by day and by midnight. However the climax was reached at 2.10 this morning when the P.M., Chamberlain, Birkenhead, Churchill, on our behalf, and Griffith, Collins, and Barton on behalf of Sinn Fein, signed the 'Articles of Agreement'.

It was a wonderful day—the P.M. starting at 5.0 a.m. and snatching 25 minutes sleep just after 8.0 p.m. His patience and alertness have been extraordinary, even for him. In essentials we have given nothing that was not in the July proposals, but I need not go into constitutional details as Grigg is sending a message to Balfour.

The Cabinet today will decide to summon Parliament for 14 December. It will sit for about one week and a Resolution approving the 'Articles of Agreement' will be moved. The Irish will do the same with their 'Dail'. Shakespeare went by special train and destroyer last night to deliver the document to Craig. It was left open to Ulster to come in to an All-Ireland Parliament or to stand out.

The P.M. obviously cannot join you before Christmas. He remarked this morning that if there was a question of arranging for a new Conference on the economic world outlook it might be worth his while going across.

The Staff have been splendid throughout this most strenuous time.

6 December   5.0 p.m. P.M. sees Curzon, Horne, and Montagu about visit of Loucheur and German reparations. Discussion of taxation of bets as source of revenue in this country. L.G. tells Horne to consult Cantuar.

7 December   P.M. reported his yesterday's talk with A. Griffith about internees.
   Winston hoped the Holy Land would afford shelter for the Auxiliaries.[1]
   Macready was for releasing the internees. He was sure the Army shared that view. No charges against them.
   P.M. said that convicted prisoners was a matter for later consideration. There must be amnesty on both sides.
   Winston suggested that the Irish could be informed privately that the extreme sentence will not be carried out.
   In the discussion about Ulster which followed Austen referred to Mildmay as the one remaining member who had voted against Gladstone's Bill. And L.G. chimed in: This is an infinitely better bill than Gladstone's. Young as I was, I moved against it in the Liberal Club.

T.J. received many letters congratulating him on his part in the Irish negotiations; from David Davies, James MacMahon, Lady Hankey, Sir Thomas Hughes, Miss Violet Markham, Lord Esher, Russell Jones, Lawrence Burgis, Sir Walford Davies, Cyril Longhurst. Two examples will suffice:

6 December   From Sir Robert Horne   *10 Downing Street*
The country owes you a great debt of gratitude. Next to the Prime Minister

---

[1] Recruitment from the Auxiliaries was one of the sources of manpower for peacekeeping duties in Palestine during the early troubles arising from the Balfour Declaration on the Jewish National Home.

you have done more to bring about this settlement than anybody else. Your courage and enthusiasm have been wonderful.

7 December   From Sir Maurice Hankey

. . . The Irish news seems too good to be true. I sent off a private cablegram to the P.M. last night wiring congratulations. It really is a marvellous achievement. I know what a valuable part you have played in it throughout and with what intense joy you must regard this consummation. I congratulate you with all my heart. I am again plunged into a veritable maelstrom of activity so I must dry up.

P.S. Your letters are priceless.

On 7 December, to the consternation of the Dail and the majority of his Cabinet, De Valera repudiated the Treaty. The debate on it began in the Dail, and although the anti-Treaty movement did not gather momentum until the beginning of 1922, Griffith and Collins were soon accused of weakness in dealing with Lloyd George. At the same time, Craig began to talk angrily of betrayal and addressed an inflammatory letter of complaint to Austen Chamberlain. Ulster's chief grievance arose from growing suspicion that the Boundary Commission might do exactly as Collins expected and transfer so much territory that the North would be forced to join the South out of economic weakness.

Craig and Lloyd George met on 9 December. For himself, Lloyd George was content with the result of his labours.

9 December   '. . . The National Liberal Club have been passing votes of thanks to Asquith—a man who never came to the Club. I (L.G.) lived there. This was the one topic on which the Liberals could fairly criticize our Coalition policy—our Irish policy, and here we've got rid of it.' 'My dear P.M.,' said Winston, 'the one humiliation they can't stand is their own defeat.'

13 December   T.J. to Sir Maurice Hankey

I think I last sent you a hurried line on Friday, when Sir James Craig was closeted with the P.M. When Craig came out he remarked that there was a verse in the Bible which ran 'Czecho-Slovakia and Ulster are born to trouble as the sparks fly upwards'. He then went off to his Doctor to be inoculated— I suppose against a Sinn Fein germ. Anyhow, yesterday he charged the P.M. with a breach of faith, and we are busy in the office multiplying myriads of copies of our correspondence with him to give to the press tonight. The outlook for Wednesday and Thursday in both Houses is a lively one, specially if, as is probable, Carson and Birkenhead cross swords. Carson, who I understood was in favour of the Boundary Commission, is very disgruntled at the position into which the P.M. has manoeuvred Ulster, and he did not turn up at the dinner at Sassoon's on 7 December, to celebrate the anniversary of the P.M.'s premiership; instead he wrote a nasty letter.

Grigg and I were with the P.M. on Friday evening just before dinner, and neither of us remember seeing him so utterly exhausted. Throughout the Irish negotiations he was magnificent. All his great qualities at their best;

1 THE CABINET SECRETARIAT, 1918

Back row: Col. Lancelot Storr, Paymaster Rowe, Col. Leslie Wilson M.P., Capt. Lawrence Burgis

Front row: T. J., Col. Dally Jones, Sir Maurice Hankey, Cyril Longhurst, Capt. Clement Jones

2 AT THE CANNES CONFERENCE, 1922

Sir Robert Horne, Lloyd George, T.J.

but last week-end the reaction was in full swing, and on Saturday and Sunday at Chequers, his mind seemed to be constantly revolving round 'the end'. Grigg found it very difficult to get him to face up to the speech which he is to deliver tomorrow, and he has chopped and changed a lot about it, clamouring for stacks of material from everybody. It is high time he got a complete holiday; but yesterday Horne sent for me, with the P.M.'s knowledge, and requested me to send you the cryptic telegram which I addressed to Burgis, the object of which was to discover what were the chances of an invitation from [President] Harding to the P.M. (and Briand and Loucheur) to come to Washington to discuss the economic condition of Europe, with special reference to the possible collapse of Germany. The P.M., I believe, wanted to go off immediately and spend Christmas at sea. Horne insists that he shall stay here until we are through with the report of the Geddes Committee. The Departments are sure to set up a valiant fight against the proposed 'cuts', and Horne without the P.M. fears he may be overborne. I believe the P.M.'s doctor is strongly opposed to his going to Washington at present, owing to the importance of a complete, if short, holiday.

Tomorrow will be an important day in Dublin, and you will know the news long before this gets to you. I am sending Arthur Griffith tonight a letter from the P.M. explanatory of the Treaty, which A.G. is to read to the Dail. It has not been easy to secure consent to this letter, as it will inevitably in future be read with the Treaty, but I am hoping Chamberlain will approve in the course of the next hour.

We had a Cabinet last night to discuss the King's speech and provisional arrangements in Ireland: and it was settled to send the telegram of congratulation to Balfour, the suggestion being received with great cordiality.

We shall be busy next week on the Geddes Report. After that I hear there will be a general dispersal of Ministers to Morocco and Monte Carlo. I shall not be sorry! Meanwhile I wish you all a Merry Christmas!

13 December   Sir Rupert Howorth to T.J.

In accordance with your instructions I submit the following very brief summary of the proceedings at the meeting of the House of Lords Reform Committee this afternoon.

During the last few days, Members of the Committee have circulated memoranda which indicate great and fundamental differences of opinion, and these differences were emphasised at the meeting. Lord Curzon had submitted a scheme based on the Bryce Report under which the reformed House of Lords would consist of about 350 persons, a minority of whom would be peers elected by the hereditary peerage, Law Lords, representatives of the Bishops and a small number of Crown Nominees, and a majority would be popularly chosen by indirect election. The Parliament Act under Lord Curzon's scheme would have to be modified so as to give three years as the delay period while in the last resort differences affecting contentious legislation (other than Money Bills) would have to be settled in a Joint Sitting of the House of Lords and House of Commons, each House contributing half its members to the Joint Sitting. Lord Curzon's proposals were supported by Mr. Chamberlain. They were opposed by the Lord Chancellor and Mr. Fisher, both of whom appeared to favour a House of Lords entirely composed of Peers elected by the hereditary peerage. The Lord Chancellor and Mr. Fisher did not dissent in principle from the arrangements proposed by Lord Curzon as to the powers to be given to the new House of Lords, but the latter insisted in effect that the composition of a Joint Sitting of the two Houses must be so arranged that a Government with a substantial majority in the House of Commons should be able to pass its legislation into law at the end of the delay period.

Mr. Churchill objected most strongly to any proposal which involved any substantial modification of the Parliament Act or any alteration of the present composition of the House of Lords, though he would have no objection to the House of Lords itself making arrangements for the exclusion of unworthy members. Mr. Fisher at one time, I think, held similar views but somewhat modified them in the course of the discussion.

Every effort was made to reconcile different points of view without success and ultimately it was agreed that Lord Curzon and Mr. Chamberlain should report to the Cabinet in favour of a scheme on the lines of that drawn up by the former and that the Lord Chancellor and Mr. Fisher should report to the Cabinet on the lines of the scheme favoured by them. Mr. Churchill declined to support either scheme and stated that he would reserve his criticisms and explanations for the Cabinet.

Lord Curzon, the Lord Chancellor and Mr. Chamberlain all vigorously emphasised the view that having regard to the public pledges already given by the leaders of the Coalition and the commitments of the Conservative Leaders to their political supporters, it was out of the question for them to entertain Mr. Churchill's suggestion and that in any case they would have the very greatest difficulty in persuading their supporters to accept the alternative schemes of reform which are to be brought to the Cabinet. Mr. Chamberlain stated that the adoption by the Cabinet of Mr. Churchill's views would mean the end of the Coalition.

23 December   T.J. to Sir Maurice Hankey

I was delighted to have your long budget with your vivid account of a day in the life of a Secretary-General at Washington. It would bore you if I started a similar description of what goes on here as you know it all too well. The strain here also never seems to cease. We were no sooner out of the Irish stew as we thought than Briand, Loucheur, and Berthelot arrived, and we have had every variety of Meeting from the Secret Interview to the full-blown Plenary Session, including one or two forgatherings at 25 Park Lane, where, I believe, we sometimes had on the premises at the same time, though not in the same room, Loucheur, Rathenau, Krassin, and Worthington-Evans, the four pillars requisite for the erection of the New Europe! Howorth and Wicks did the meetings and I did the door. I told Berthelot that I could not pretend to your efficiency and he replied 'He has great experience' with which sentiment I cordially agreed. Briand struck me as very limp, possibly because of his unstable political position. He was, of course, as usual very pleasant to all of us. Loucheur did most of the talking and Berthelot hardly opened his mouth. Broadly the programme is that we should sit tight on the gold we got out of the August Agreement[1] and should forgo our chance of getting anything much in 1922. We are also trying to get Belgium to let go her prior claims. Then we are to try to give Germany some sense of security that she will not be disturbed in the next twelve months if she raises her offer from two-hundred millions to five-hundred millions. This she can do by unloading some of the gold in the Reichsbank. It is proposed to make various conditions, e.g. she must balance her budget, put up the price of coal, stop subsidies, and accept some kind of Financial Commission, etc. That is the Reparation side of the business. On the other side is a scheme to form a big Central Syndicate for the reconstruction of Eastern Europe including Russia. In this Central Syndicate England, France, and Germany will be the principle shareholders but the United States will be invited to come in. Some big percentage of the profits accruing to Germany, e.g. 50 per cent., will have to be paid into the Reparation Account. The P.M. and Horne were to see some of our leading industrialists this morning and Loucheur was to do the same in Paris. The two sections are to meet presently and have ready the bones of a scheme by the time we meet at Cannes, early in January. The P.M. leaves for Cannes[2] on Monday (Boxing Day), Horne goes with him, Worthington-Evans follows. Briand is due to arrive on 4 January and the meeting of the Supreme Council is fixed for 6 January. I am arranging for Wicks and Hill to come with me leaving Howorth in charge of the Cabinet side. I fixed it up with him and Chancellor. The adjourning of the Dail eases work in the Office for the moment. The P.M. has handed over the Irish business in his absence to a Committee with Churchill as Chairman, Hamar Greenwood, Worthington-Evans, Gordon Hewart, and Lord Fitzalan.

Briand this week threw out a suggestion of an Anglo-French Alliance and he mentioned it formally to Curzon. The P.M. and Chamberlain had a talk with Briand about it. The P.M. said that we would not mind giving France a guarantee of help in case of an invasion of French soil by the Germans, but our public opinion would not stand a more extensive guarantee involving helping France in the event of squabbles in other parts of the world, e.g. on the Polish frontier. Briand said he envisaged a more comprehensive arrangement on the lines of your Quadruple Treaty with Germany inside the compact. He undertook to put something in writing so that the matter might be further explored at Cannes.

30 December   T.J. to Sir Maurice Hankey

The Fridays seem to come round very swiftly. I have just come from a Departmental Committee at the Colonial Office which is drafting recommendations to the Cabinet on the procedure to be followed on the assumption that the Dail ratifies the Treaty. Our latest information is that the Dail, which meets on 3 January, will ratify about 5 January by a majority of 20 or thereabouts. There will then be summoned a Meeting of the members of

---

[1] On reparations.

[2] For the Cannes Conference on the payment of reparations by Germany.

the Southern Ireland Parliament, including the four Unionists, for formal ratification. Immediately that is over Griffith, Collins, and Co. will come here about the 12th or 14th to discuss the setting up of the provisional Government. The idea is to give this provisional Government very full powers, but to set it going we shall probably need an Act of Parliament. We shall also need an Act of Indemnity. For these two purposes Parliament ought to meet, if only for a few weeks, in February. But across this programme has fallen the shadow of a rumour of a General Election *before* another meeting of Parliament. How much there is in this I do not know, but the idea is being toyed with. I shall point out to the Prime Minister when I see him at Cannes that if we have a General Election before Parliament meets it will involve a General Election in Southern Ireland—which is absurd.

We are all busy preparing for Cannes. . . .

Apart from Ireland and the Supreme Council we are quiet. Chamberlain is in the country and most of the Ministers are scattered. . . .

Christmas   In Eirene's autograph album:
'With the best wishes of D. Lloyd George who owes so much to your Father for the great help he gave in settling the Irish difficulty.'

1922

This was the final year of power for Lloyd George, with much of his former glory dimmed. It ended with the break-up of the Coalition and a new Conservative administration. Lloyd George was never again to hold public office, a fact which would have seemed incredible at the time.

Economic conditions at home remained depressed, with prices falling as well as wages. The lock-out in the engineering and ship-building industries marked a further stage in the erosion of differentials between skilled and unskilled workers. Characteristic of the period was the report of the Geddes Committee. Its notorious economy axe was swung most vigorously and viciously in the direction of education, cutting out major reforms provided for in the Fisher Education Act of 1918.

The Dail approved the Irish Treaty by only sixty-four to fifty-seven votes. Arthur Griffith became President of the Provisional Government and Michael Collins was installed as Commander-in-Chief at Dublin Castle, but under DeValera intransigence grew. Rory O'Connor occupied the Four Courts on 13 April. Griffith and Collins held their peace until the General Election in June gave them a 93–35 majority. They then attacked and took the Four Courts and by the autumn the I.R.A. were driven underground. But Griffith died and Collins was shot in ambush in August. The I.R.A. attempt to involve the British in the civil war failed; after so long, the matters which were now dealt with by the British Cabinet became increasingly technical and Ireland ceased to be a major issue. Nevertheless, the Irish problem contributed largely to Lloyd George's political unpopularity.

On the diplomatic front, the Washington Naval Treaty was the only real success. Britain and France became sharply estranged, after the fall of Briand and the failure at Cannes to solve the problem of German reparations. The further attempt at Genoa in April and May to settle reparations and war debts and relations with Russia brought nothing but discredit and was followed by the dangerous German-Russian pact of Rapallo. The Balfour Note, proposing all-round cancellation of war debts, made an unfavourable impact in the United States.

Finally, came the Chanak debacle. Through sympathy for 'small nations' and friendship with the Greek Prime Minister Venizelos, Lloyd George was isolated in his support of Greece against the Turks. In August Kemal attacked and drove the Greeks to the sea, reaching the Dardanelles and Chanak, held by a small British force under General Harington. Lloyd George, Churchill, and Birkenhead threatened war. The Government appealed to France and Italy and to the Dominions as their allies. At a crucial Cabinet meeting on 15 September, their answers were considered: France offered neutrality; the Dominions, save New Zealand, nothing. Britain was about to fight a war without support. Wisely, Harington disregarded his orders to deliver an ultimatum and the Turks did not pursue their attack. The convention of Mudania on 11 October allowed a peaceful settlement.

In spite of continued loyal defence of the Government by Chamberlain and Birkenhead, this last blow was too much and a general election became inevitable. At the famous Carlton Club meeting on 19 October, the assembled Conservatives turned down the plea by Chamberlain to remain in the Coalition. Bonar Law had indicated that he would lead an independent Conservative Party and a speech by Baldwin, whose distrust of Lloyd George was intense, carried the day. Lloyd George at once resigned. Bonar Law formed what Churchill called the 'government of the second eleven' and at the General Election in November the Conservatives won 345 seats, Labour 142, the Liberals (under three heads) 117. Churchill was defeated; and in the House of Commons the Labour Party became the official Opposition, swelled with the I.L.P. at the height of its power and the 'wild men' from Clydeside.

As Hankey was in Washington, T.J. had a taste of foreign affairs by serving as secretary to the British delegation at Cannes and later in the year he was frequently concerned with the remaining stages of the Irish settlement. The fall of the Coalition brought Conservative dislike of the 'Garden Suburb' to a head and at one moment it looked as if the Cabinet Secretariat itself might be swept away. T.J. felt most insecure and looked for a possible post in the Welsh department of the Board of Education. In the event, Hankey and the Secretariat triumphed and T.J. was asked by Bonar Law to undertake the same kind of work for him as he had done for Lloyd George, which he willingly did. In June T.J. had the great satisfaction of receiving the degree of LL.D., *honoris causa*, from his old University of Glasgow. He was to receive three other such distinctions from the Universities of Wales, St. Andrews, and Birmingham, but this, being the first, perhaps brought the keenest pleasure.

T.J. was in charge of the Secretariat at the Cannes Conference, Sir Maurice Hankey being still in Washington.

3 January   T.J. to E.T.J.   *Carlton Hotel, Cannes*
I am about to start off to the Cannes Golf Club to have lunch with Worthington-Evans, Grigg, and Alden, (Worthington-Evans's private secretary). The P.M. has just gone off towards Nice to some golf club for the day. Everyone in holiday mood still. Briand arrives with Loucheur and Co. tomorrow morning. I have just been to the Yacht Club over the rooms intended for the Conference. They are very gay and distracting and I'm hoping to shift the main room from the front to an interior—so as to avoid the sun and waves. . . .

6 January   T.J. to E.T.J.
The first day of the Plenary Session is over and I am greatly relieved. I think we have come through satisfactorily as Secretaries. It is a fearfully

anxious and intense experience, and my ignorance of French and Italian is a huge drawback, but I've pulled through well I think. Anyway the P.M. is most kind to me and took me off with him alone from the Conference at 1.0 o'clock to lunch at the Villa Valetta where I had also been to breakfast, so I can't have been very much in his bad books!

Wonderful weather. Am very tired because of two late nights (1.30 a.m.) so shall vanish early tonight, before 10. You'll see the reports in *The Times* of our doings.

7 January T.J. to E.T.J.
Had a meeting of a Committee at 11.30 today and two others follow today at 5 and 6. Then a plenary session at 7!

Yesterday was the crucial day. Now I *know* I can pull the job off all right. Most beautiful sunset.

Had an interesting talk with the Belgian P.M. today; and also with L.G. on his way to the golf course. He dug me out and we were snapped once more.

8 January An Italian journalist wanted an interview with Lloyd George for his Socialist paper. I refused and he pressed for a 'Message' from L.G. This I also refused on the ground that L.G. could not give it without the consent of the Italian Prime Minister who is here. Then Giannini, the Commercial Attaché, came to me and pressed me to meet the journalist as he was an interesting fellow. I agreed and tonight we dined at an Italian restaurant. Frank Wise came with me. Giannini and Attolico were there and four or five others, besides the journalist, whose name is Mussolini.[1] It was a very flat affair owing to the language difficulty. I tried to divert the conversation to Mazzini and the struggle for Italian unity—the one Italian topic about which I knew something, but it was very heavy going, the journalist being very wary and not saying much in any language.

10 January T.J. to E.T.J.
8.0 a.m. . . . Having a swift and very full time with some relaxation at meal times. Monday, e.g., breakfast with the P.M. at the Villa, lunch with him, Briand, Bonomi, Riddell, etc., at the Golf Club (most amusing when he took the Prime Ministers over the course and taught them to play);[2] tea with the P.M., Briand, Bonomi, and Loucheur and Toretta, at the Carlton; dinner 8.30 with Beaverbrook, then at 10.30 p.m. with him and his sister to the Casino where we chatted with Bonar Law! In between this many meetings of course. Sunday had lunch at the Villa with the P.M., Horne, and Lady

[1] Lloyd George never met Mussolini; but he and T.J. met Hitler at Berchtesgaden in September 1936 (see *Diary with Letters*, pp. 249–52).
[2] *Note in Diary:* The historic golf-match. At breakfast L.G. asked me to arrange it. Photographs of it appeared in the picture papers. L.G. was already hated for his pro-German policy. The levity of a golf-match, at which L.G. was seen teaching Briand how to play the game, shocked France. Briand was recalled to Paris, offered his resignation and was succeeded by Poincaré.

Markham. . . . Sunday afternoon I got off for 1½ hours alone in a car to Grasse. . . .

Had your p.c. yesterday and can see that you too are not idle. Am glad you are not here. There are wives here who are a nuisance and distraction to their husbands! Meetings today begin at 10.30. Nothing fixed as yet for our return. You'll learn sooner in the press than from me.

11 January   A. H. Kidd to T.J.   *Board of Education*
I hesitate to trouble you with this at a time when you must be working 25 hours a day on intricate international problems, but on the off chance that there may be a moment to spare for matters domestic I send you a few words to put before you the woes of education in this benighted country and the danger of its foundering on the 'Inchcape Rock'. The Geddes Committee demand a reduction of £16,000,000 on our Estimates, which in the preliminary form in which they had them stood at £50 millions and a half.

Their proposals are heroic and impracticable. . . .

*   *   *   *

It has to be remembered that already the Government, and Fisher in particular, have incurred a good deal of criticism both from educational enthusiasts and from the Local Education Authorities on account of the arrest of developments under the Education Act. Two key Sections of the Act of 1918 are not operating: the leaving age is not yet raised to 14: nor, except in a mutilated form in London, and in a few small places, are Day Continuation Schools in existence. . . .

Geddes wanted a £10 million cut in elementary education, to keep down grants to the universities, and to alter teachers' superannuation. The writer said that if this programme were enforced Fisher would resign.

12 January   Sir Rupert Howorth to T.J.   *Offices of the Cabinet, Whitehall*
I am very ashamed of not having written before but to tell the truth we have been rather overwhelmed the last few days. On Tuesday morning we began with a Cabinet to consider your telegram to Mr. Chamberlain on the subject of the proposed French Treaty and after approving the reply, Mr. Chamberlain's Committee on the Geddes Report started and has been sitting pretty well continuously ever since.

As things have turned out there is very little trouble from the Civil Departments other than the Board of Education. The Ministry of Health will bring their Estimates down to the Geddes figure, accepting in the main the Geddes proposals subject to slight immaterial variations. The Ministry of Labour also acquiesce in the recommendations of the Geddes Committee in so far, of course, as those recommendations consist in referring the various highly contentious questions to expert Committees for examination. As you can imagine, Dr. Macnamara was supremely indignant with the Geddes Committee for daring to dream even of such sacrilege as the abolition of his Department or of criticising any of his various activities!

The Board of Education problem stands on quite a different footing. In reply to the Geddes cut of £16 million for England and Wales, plus £2 millions for Scotland—£18 millions in all, Mr. Fisher offers for England and Wales a cut of about £2½ millions for 1922–3 and some comparatively insignificant further reductions in subsequent years.[1] The whole difficulty boils down to the question of teaching cost and any very large economies can only be realised either by reducing the number of teachers or reducing the pay of teachers or by a combination of these two methods. It is strongly represented that to throw a large number of teachers on to the unemployment market would be politically a blunder and morally a crime. On the other hand the teachers say that their pay should not be reduced unless the pay of other Government servants is also correspondingly reduced. As the Committee felt some difficulty in deciding precisely how the Geddes Committee intended to effect this very large cut, Mr. Chamberlain had an interview yesterday with the Geddes Committee and the latter are today considering to what extent they will furnish us with the details. They let us know this evening. . . .

1 February   Luncheon with H. A. L. Fisher at his flat in Ashley Gardens. Told him that I had seen the P.M. this morning and found him quite adamant against any reduction in teachers' salaries. I had however seen Sir James Yoxall and fixed up a deputation of the teachers to see the P.M. tomorrow afternoon. I had also told the P.M. that Fisher would refuse publicly to advocate large classes but would do his best to reduce the number of teachers in the over-staffed districts by from 4,000 to 6,000. I said how relieved I was at the P.M.'s determination in the matter of salaries as this was the biggest thing Fisher had been able to do.

Fisher said: I put before me when I took office several objects and have at any rate realised some of them.

1. Raising the level of the teaching profession.
2. Increasing the provision and availability of Secondary Schools.
3. Adolescent Education.
4. Royal Commission on Oxford and Cambridge.
5. Medical treatment for young children.

It was true that the Fisher Act was suspended but it would revive with the return of prosperity. We agreed it was a great achievement for so short a period and bearing in mind that Fisher had given a good deal of his time to the League of Nations. He repeated that he would resign rather than publicly advocate large classes. . . .

By now the British Government had begun to transfer certain powers to the Provisional Government in Southern Ireland, and also to run down the British military strength. Towards the end of February, T.J. became increasingly worried at the state of dis-

---

[1] In fairness to the Geddes Committee, it should be said that Fisher had told the Cabinet that his 1918 Education Act would involve increased expenditure of £3 million. The true figure for 1922 was likely to be £30 million. The 'education question', having ceased to be a religious debate, now became, and remained, one of finance.

order in Ireland and the outrages and raids into Ulster, which he believed were engineered by the Dail. The North was angry and, in spite of the British Government's requests to Craig to restrain his supporters, could not be expected to remain quiet for long.

23 February   Sir David S. Davies[1] to T.J.

. . . My object in trying to see you last week was to obtain your consent to allow your name to be submitted as a candidate for the Denbigh Division. I was asked by some of the most influential coalition liberals to try to get your consent. I was told by a mutual friend that you would not entertain the offer —but if you will—the seat is, I believe, quite at your disposal. . . .

5 March   While waiting for Kellaway to come up from the General Post Office, Chamberlain suspended the sitting of the Cabinet, gave permission to smoke, and then followed a free and easy talk about the charges levelled by Montagu against the P.M. for destroying the collective responsibility of the Cabinet.[2]

Churchill said it would be disastrous if a Minister's sense of responsibility for action was weakened. There were always border-line cases when a Minister had to decide whether or not to bring a matter to the Cabinet. One had to consider pressure of public business and the political situation of the moment.

Chamberlain said the line that the critics would take in the House would be 'We can't defend Montagu, but we must attack the Government'. The charge would be that the present system was autocracy tempered by disorganisation.

Fisher referred to the charge that the P.M. had instituted the method of Conferences of Ministers and that he manipulated the choice of Ministers to suit the decision he required. That was the line taken by *The Times.*

Chamberlain said it had always been the practice of the Cabinet to relegate certain matters to committees. Much more was now done by committees, some of them regular, some of them formed *ad hoc.*

Balfour. 'The whole machine is worked harder than formerly. I am very much away but when I come home I have no Department but I am summoned, every other day almost, to a Cabinet.'

Chamberlain. 'My business is to sit in the House of Commons as its Leader, but I cannot be there because of meetings of the Cabinet Committees. Yesterday when I was in charge of the debate on Egypt I had to come out for a committee on telegrams from the Viceroy of India.'

[1] Sir David Sanders Davies, Coalition Liberal M.P. for Denbigh 1918–22.
[2] On 4 March the Viceroy of India, with Montagu's authorization, published a memorandum sympathetic to Turkey, to calm Moslem unrest in India. Curzon attacked Montagu in the Cabinet and Montagu, already estranged by the pro-Greek sympathies of the Prime Minister, resigned.
For some months, probably since their quarrel over the peace terms offered to Turkey, Lloyd George had excluded Montagu from the most contentious affairs of the Government. In particular he was allowed to take no part in the Irish Treaty negotiations.

Balfour. 'All Prime Ministers in my time have been charged either with being figureheads run by abler men or tyrants. There has never been a middle position.'

Chamberlain. 'We all know the P.M. has been very careful to put members of divergent views on committees. As to the business a Minister should bring up to the Cabinet I think the right rule is one I laid down for the Civil Servants who work for me. They must decide many things without bothering me but they must not get me into a row without telling me that they are doing so.'

Then Kellaway arrived.

16 March   T.J. to Lloyd George
I met F. W. Hirst yesterday (former Editor of the *Economist*), just back from a long tour in the United States where he stayed on several occasions with Hoover. . . .

Hirst believes . . . that the best men in the United States do not want us to pay our debts: that if there were a drastic scaling down of land armaments the debts would be forgiven for a consideration, e.g., in our case the gift of some islands in the Caribbean Sea; in the meantime we should delay paying interest so long as possible and then raise the question of making payments in goods which should be allowed to enter the United States free of tariff restrictions.

On 17 March, now seriously worried about the position in Ulster, T.J. sent a letter to Lloyd George, with a memorandum, pointing out that the bargain with the South was that Britain alone would pay for and control military forces in the North. But other military authorities had sprung up, notably the special constables and Field-Marshal Sir Henry Wilson and his 'scheme' for volunteers, which had been voted £2 million by the Northern Parliament. T.J. warned Lloyd George not to be drawn in nor to appear to connive at these private armies.

What might have happened was pointed out in a letter sent to T.J., showing that after the success of the first interview between Collins and Craig in January there was a real chance of the North coming in under a united Parliament, but that this had been destroyed by the breakdown of the second interview.

On 22 March, after a good deal of trouble in Belfast, T.J. met Kevin O'Higgins, Minister for Economic Affairs in the Provisional Government, and urged him to work for an economic conference between the two sides, and to resist any idea of a boycott of the North. Meanwhile, the Irish Free State Bill was passing through the House of Lords.

23 March   . . . Saw Albert Thomas with one of his officials. I told him that there was a feeling abroad that the I.L.O. was too aggressive generally and specially in regard to Genoa. He retorted that the International Labour movement was so depressed everywhere at present that he had to fight vigorously for the very existence of the I.L.O., and he added that had the League of Nations Secretariat been equally active they would not have been passed over at Cannes. He had met Allan Smith this morning and found him airing the communist spectre as at the bottom of the engineering dispute, the first time M. Thomas had heard an English employer trot out that reason. Tomorrow there was to be a debate in the French Chamber attacking the 8 hour day and all over Europe it was the same, part of the reaction in full swing. He had seen in a report of the French experts a passage urging that pressure ought to be brought to bear on Czecho-Slovakia to tone down her industrial legislation. He had seen Dr. Benes who was determined to maintain the standard of life as far as he possibly could.

I then asked him how was Genoa to be a success, adding that I thought the P.M. had at the back of his mind as the goal a reduction in land armaments. M. Thomas said he was in full accord with the P.M.'s ideal but that Poincaré would not assist in that attempt. The recent debates in the French Chamber still shewed a most bellicose spirit and had produced a deplorable effect in Germany. In order to carry French opinion the matter would have to be most circumspectly approached at Genoa. He had seen Rathenau and Wirth[1] in Berlin a couple of days ago. Rathenau asked was the conference to take place? Was not Lloyd George's position much weakened at home? Thomas replied that it was more solid than people imagined and that the conference would go on. Rathenau replied—'Yes, with reparations ruled out. When that decision is taken from the Chair at Genoa I shall pick up my papers, walk out and return home.' Thomas replied that that was not conduct worthy of a good European. I told him of the attitude of Hoover to European armaments, pointed out how deeply we had cut into the army and navy estimates here and reminded him of the reaction already in process in the House of Commons. He said the French people knew of the American attitude but did not take it at all seriously. Summing up, he said that his line at Genoa if he were the P.M. could be put in four propositions:—

1. the necessity for reconstruction and the benefits which would accrue;
2. reconstruction is impossible without finance;
3. finance is impossible without the U.S.A.;
4. the U.S.A. is impossible without a reduction in the European armaments.

T.J. conveyed the gist of this conversation to the Prime Minister.

28 March   The P.M. had returned from his holiday at Criccieth and had seen Signor Schanzer about the Genoa Conference. There had also been a whole series of private conferences with small groups of Ministers on the policy to be followed with the Bolsheviks. So by the time the whole Cabinet met today at 12 noon the P.M. had thought out his position aloud with his selected colleagues, the Resolution had been drafted for the House of Commons debate next Monday, and in substance the P.M., as I think, again capitulated to Churchill.[2] Every Minister was present except Balfour who is on holiday at Cannes. . . . The P.M. made an elaborate statement as to the lines which the British Delegates should follow at Genoa. There could be

[1] The German representatives.
[2] On the future position of Soviet Russia.

no restoration of trade in Europe until peace was secured. Peace was menaced all along the Western Frontier of Russia where all the neighbouring countries suspected each other. Lenin was moving away from communism.[1] We ought to support the anticommunistic elements in Russia. The Russians must accept in substance the Cannes conditions, e.g., payment of debts incurred by predecessors, cessation of propaganda, etc. If they did this we could put them on probation for a period to discover whether they were making a genuine effort to observe the conditions. During this probationary period they would be given not full and ceremonial recognition but limited *de jure* recognition in the shape of a *chargé d'affaires* who would not be received at Court. (This was the compromise with Churchill.) After some cross-examination of the Lord Chancellor as to the meaning of *de jure* recognition Churchill in passionate tones full of conviction deplored our dealings with the Bolsheviks. We had concluded a trade agreement on the understanding that if its terms had been broken it could be terminated. Its terms had been flagrantly broken and now we were being asked to go another step to meet the Soviet Government. The account received from our Moscow representative shewed that these leaders had the brains of tortuous conspirators. They were called on to give up the theories to which they had devoted their lives, they would use every effort to make breaches between the Western Powers and would be absolutely cynical in all their dealings with us. They would come to Genoa for the sole purpose of enhancing their prestige at home and would be able to go back and say they had negotiated with the strongest Power of Western Europe. They would sign papers with no intention of honouring them. Meanwhile there were 3,000,000 Russians in exile who would hear of the proposal to grant *de jure* recognition with despair. He was bitterly sorry that at a time of strong Conservative majorities and deep devotion to the monarchy we were to step out to accord this supreme favour and patronage to these people. If there were any likelihood of alleviating employment it would be different. We were already largely committed because of Cannes and he did not protest at the time as he was so far involved. The Cabinet ought to have been summoned to consider the Cannes Resolutions as was done in the case of the Anglo-French Pact.

Then going on to speak of the Pact, he asked was it to be held over the heads of the French as a threat, enforcing them to come to heel on the Russian issue? That would be illegitimate. The P.M. said that had not occurred to him but he hoped to use the Anglo-French Pact to make the French behave decently towards the Germans on the question of Reparations. 'I am with you there,' replied Churchill. Churchill then summed up by suggesting that the British Delegates should go to Genoa with a limited discretion, namely that unless the Cannes conditions were accepted in substance there should be no advance in the recognition of the Soviet Government: we were not to act in isolation nor without a general consensus of opinion: in the event of the Russians accepting the conditions and our Delegates being satisfied that they were genuinely seeking to play the game we should give such recognition as

[1] *Note in Diary:* This misjudgement was based on Lenin's speech to the Congress of Metal Workers, 6 March 1922.

was required to make the agreement reach success, but not full ceremonial recognition.

This became the operative conclusion of the Cabinet, the P.M. undertaking to give the House of Commons an opportunity of ratifying the conclusions reached at Genoa.

About 10 minutes before the end of the discussion Macnamara suggested that the Resolution to be put to the House of Commons would be regarded as a piece of political trickery, and that the Government would be charged with getting round a difficult corner by its means. From the moment the Resolution was put on the paper it would be discounted at home and abroad and the Press would say that the P.M. had not got a solid Government behind him in going to Genoa. 'There has been a long discussion in the Press,' he remarked, with deceptive naivety and turning to the P.M., 'I should think you would be aware of it?' Chamberlain interrupted: 'I am glad that remark was not addressed to me. I should have been hurt.' But the P.M. took no notice of this sole direct reference to the crisis of the last fortnight[1] and allowed Baldwin to proceed with some point about the *de jure* recognition.

Grigg and I went off to luncheon at Gatti's, Grigg full of trouble both about the P.M.'s future and his own. He had written to Criccieth urging the P.M. to resign. I told him it was a month too late and that the P.M. would not be willing to appear to resign as a man defeated by Northcliffe and Rothermere. We both agreed that the P.M. seemed to be losing his punch and grip. Grigg said that three-quarters of the Cabinet were now disloyal to him and that the rot had spread ever since he had made them dance attendance on him at Inverness. Churchill had that morning received messages from Northcliffe and Rothermere urging him to come out as the leader of the Tory Party. Grigg himself had agreed to stay with the P.M. for a year or till the Election, whichever came first. He would carry on till Genoa was over but was anxious to get out. Things were chaotic in the secretariat at No. 10; there being no effective head. Sometimes one and sometimes another acted without proper co-ordination. Complaints had repeatedly reached him about the treatment of the Court under the present régime. The P.M. went off to Criccieth for three weeks as originally proposed and the King first heard of his departure in the newspapers and sent a hot message to Chamberlain on the morning of his departure to ask 'Have I a Prime Minister or not?' Grigg very much feared that the P.M. would come back from Genoa with lots of 'Resolutions' and try to run another election on false hopes like that of December 1918. What happened in December 1918 was unfortunately the substratum of truth in Zimmern's indictment in his new book *Europe in Convalescence*.

31 March   T.J. to Lloyd George
Col. Sydney James came to see me today just back from attending the European Sanitary Conference at Warsaw. He is no alarmist and was for years familiar with epidemics in India and is a high authority on the spread

---

[1] The criticisms of the Coalition by the Conservatives and in the Press.

of disease. He asks me to impress on you that economic reconstruction on the Western frontier of Russia is utterly impracticable unless the present epidemics now raging on that frontier are scotched. He regards this as the very first item in reconstruction as the flight hither and thither of swarms of people terrified by the fear of infection and a ready prey to disease because of their starving condition makes stable trade conditions impossible. Commercial travellers, for example, fear to move about in these areas.

In January this year disease and destitution increased so rapidly that the frontier sanitary cordon between Russia and Poland broke down and by today numerous villages and towns in Poland are in the grip of epidemics (typhus, relapsing fever—a disease which like typhus is carried by lice—and cholera). Cholera is now spreading rapidly in the Ukraine and is a real danger in the Black Sea ports and to Europe. James himself spent four days in various frontier stations. I won't harrow you with the photographs he has shewn me of what he himself was witness.

* * * *

I send this today as you may care to refer to it in passing in your speech on Monday *as an additional reason for meeting the Russians face to face.*

28 April   Sir Donald MacAlister to T.J.   *University of Glasgow*
The Senate I am happy to say have just resolved to offer you the honorary degree of LL.D. at the next Commemoration on 22 June, when I trust I may have the privilege of conferring it on you. You will receive an official intimation presently, but I could not forgo the pleasure of letting you know the intention of your Alma Mater by a personal communication.

On 28 April T.J. wrote to Hankey, warning him of further military preparations in Ulster. Sir Henry Wilson was attempting to buy surplus armaments, including aeroplanes and bombs, from the Disposal Board.

5 May   T.J. to Sir Maurice Hankey
I had luncheon yesterday with Professor Shotwell[1] who had just crossed from America on the *Mauretania* after a visit of some months to the States. A brief summary of his views may confirm what the P.M. hears from other sources.

1. The Washington Conference has left an abiding fund of goodwill on which this country can draw. Hughes and Harding have spoken in that sense repeatedly in private conversation. This will be found useful when we get to close quarters on the debt question.

2. The French stock was never so low. It has never recovered from the Briand speech and the P.M.'s valiant fight for a stable peace at Genoa is widely appreciated.

3. The wealthy and other Irishmen who have political influence are sick and tired of the Irish question and consider that we have put ourselves right

---

[1] Professor J. T. Shotwell, director of the Carnegie Endowment for International Peace and a well-known writer on foreign affairs.

with the world and that it will be the fault of the Irish themselves now if they fail to go ahead. Shotwell was most emphatic that if Civil War comes we ought to keep British troops out as long as ever possible. To send them to help Free Staters would cause revulsion of feeling in U.S.A.

4. The 'soldier vote' is beginning to loom large owing to the forthcoming Congressional Elections in the autumn. The soldiers generally are very bitter about the war—feel they were beguiled into it by propaganda, that they were fleeced by France, that Europe is 'degenerate', and that Britain anyway can look after herself. There will be strong political pressure put on to get the interest paid by us in order to provide a bonus 'for the veterans of the Great War'. The farmers look upon our paying up simply as a business deal.

5. Shotwell hopes that—however distasteful it may be—the P.M. will see Hearst[1] on his visit to this country. Now that the Irish issue is out of the way, some understanding with him may be possible. Better still, he urged, would be a visit by the P.M. to the States.

So much for Shotwell.

The most important item from this end is that we expect to receive the Irish 'Constitution' in about two week's time, say 22 May. Collins has described it as likely to be 'damned democratic' and he will probably want our approval to it in a very few days as the elections are fixed for mid-June. It is therefore all-important that the P.M. should be within hail after the 22nd to prevent his colleagues turning the document down at the first glance in their fear of the die-hards. Collins may appoint a charwomen as Lord-Lieutenant, to which I see no great objection if she's a good one, but others may take a different view of what is fitting.

. . . We are all amused to see that Keynes has taken to blessing the P.M. in the M.G.

The passing of the Irish Free State Bill in March gave the Provisional Government of Griffith and Collins legal authority. But the Irish Republican Army, now the military expression of those opposed to the Treaty, set out to prevent elections being held on the issue of the Treaty. In the middle of April, Rory O'Connor and units of the I.R.A. occupied the Four Courts in Dublin. Civil war threatened. The anti-Treaty Republican Party failed to agree with the Provisional Government, which continued to establish the Treaty régime. The main question at issue was whether to hold the election on the Treaty or to postpone it. A conference in Dublin ended in failure on 29 April; but early in May the two sections of the military declared a truce, and finally, in a pact between Collins and De Valera, it was laid down that the elections should be held for a Coalition Government.

However, this did not solve the military difficulties, for, as T.J. wrote to Hankey on 12 May, Collins was asking the British Government for arms with which to attack the rebel I.R.A. when the truce elapsed. Cope gave warning that Rory O'Connor planned to involve British troops and thus wean the army away from Collins. Churchill was not inclined to supply arms until he had had assurances that Collins would in fact recapture the Four Courts; and T.J., alive to the dangers, urged Cope and Austen Chamberlain to withdraw the British troops from Dublin.

[1] William Randolph Hearst, the American newspaper tycoon.

The election in Ireland was fixed for 16 June. The draft Constitution which the Provisional Government had worked out proved, when it was submitted to London, to be as unacceptable and republican as T.J. had feared. It seemed impossible to allow the election to go forward, yet the British withdrawal continued. On 16 May, the Curragh was handed over, and ten days later, in the Collins-De Valera pact, the seats of the Dail were divided between the parties. Meanwhile I.R.A. raids on the North intensified.

Between 27 May, when T.J. again became involved, and 9 June, a confused situation existed, with the British signatories, Collins, Griffith, and the Ulster representatives meeting in London. Lloyd George eventually agreed that the election should go ahead. T.J. played a large part in the negotiations of 31 May and 1 June to resolve another deadlock over the use of the Crown title in the form of public appointments, which culminated in a private meeting between Griffith, Collins, Lloyd George, and Lionel Curtis.[1] On the evening of 1 June, T.J. dined with the Prime Minister on the terrace of the House of Commons.

When Chamberlain joined us I said that Curtis had very neatly compared negotiating with Collins to writing on water and the P.M. had added 'shallow and agitated water'. Chamberlain told the story of two soldiers at the front boasting of their respective countries: the Scot was proud of Edinburgh as the Athens of Scotland to which the Irishman instantly retorted that Athens was the Cork of Greece. Chamberlain had been reading before joining us a play written by his father in which Labouchere and Dilke were characters. The talk turned a good deal on Chamberlain's father as it is apt to do when he is not talking shop. The P.M. said that Joe Chamberlain had introduced the direct method into Parliamentary oratory and Austen said his father used to sit up to all hours preparing his speeches and eliminating every irrelevant idea or phrase. . . . This led to talk about quotations. Churchill had recently referred to Astyanax 'The young Astyanax, the hope of Troy' (Pope) and Chamberlain had asked him where he had got it from. Winston replied 'From Bartlett's Familiar Quotations', a book to which Chamberlain admitted his own occasional indebtedness. The P.M. said when he got quotations like that he could not remember them for 10 minutes. The P.M. then gave an amusing account of a skit by Raymond Asquith on a Committee of both Houses under the chairmanship of Lord Fyvie appointed to redraft the Ten Commandments. . . .

On 2 June the threat of martial law and war arose again in the Irish talks on the Constitution in London. Collins returned to Dublin, leaving Griffith and the lawyers to carry on the talks. Later he returned and the Constitution which emerged, and which was not published in Ireland before the Election, was shorn of most of its republican character. The election itself was a qualified victory for the Provisional Government and the Treaty party, and with it the pact with De Valera was broken and the projected Coalition Government abandoned.

Meanwhile, incidents along the border, in particular the occupation by the I.R.A. of the Ulster fort of Belleek, showed Churchill at his most pugnacious; T.J.'s account

---

[1] Lionel George Curtis (1872–1955); Secretary to the Irish Conference, Colonial Office adviser on Irish affairs 1921–4; active later on the *Round Table*.

Lord Riddell   Lloyd George   Massigli   T. J.   Bonomi
                                                    Briand

3   THE HISTORIC GOLF MATCH AT CANNES, JANUARY 1922

4 AT ASTLEY,
25 NOVEMBER 1923
T.J., Stanley Baldwin,
Windham Baldwin

of the tense moments of 7 and 8 June, and Lloyd George's reaction, is instructive. The
minuscule bombardment of the fort came to a happy ending.

8 June . . . We were much relieved at the absence of casualties and began to
joke about the great bloodless Battle of Belleek. 'It was a famous victory.'

At 7.45 came over the telephone Churchill's bromide communiqué to
the Press which the P.M. quickly tired of and he went off in the middle. We
had dinner outside and the P.M. ordered a bottle of champagne to celebrate
the Battle of Belleek. At dinner he produced from his pocket a letter which
Henry Wilson had sent him in 1919 in which he used the most superlative
language possible about the P.M.—'how he and he almost alone of all men
living had won the war'. During dinner Grigg gave him the substance of an
interview which Repington had had with Clemenceau. This had been
passed on by Lord Burnham. In it Clemenceau had spoken of how during
the war Poincaré wrote him letters every hour which he left unopened. After
dinner we began innocently enough with Welsh hymns but the P.M.'s desire
to celebrate the victory of Belleek led him to sing 'Scots wha hae' putting in
Winston's name wherever he could. . . .

9 June   T.J. left Chequers with Lloyd George. He recorded their conversation in the
car.

. . . Someone remarked that Hamar Greenwood was not exactly a first class
statesman, whereupon the P.M. said that the Prime Minister did not want
too many first class statesmen about him but rather good counsellors: he
himself would be quite prepared to run the British Empire with the Round
Table group, Hankey, T.J., Miss Stevenson to spot the rogues, and J. T.
Davies to look after the newspapers. This led to talk about statesmen, the
P.M. quizzing Grigg and me; who was the greatest Conservative thinker?
We all agreed on Burke. The greatest Conservative statesman? Pitt. Was
Gladstone fortunate in his biographer? Grigg said Morley's Life was not a
book. The P.M. said Morley had style but no dramatic sense, otherwise he
would have made far more out of the Grand Old Man's fights in the House
and in Midlothian. The greatest biography in the P.M.'s view was Owen
Thomas' Life of John Jones, Talysarn. . . .

What place would Balfour have in history, I asked. The P.M. replied 'He
will be just like the scent on a pocket handkerchief.' 'Joseph Chamberlain
will have a greater place. There is little positive in Balfour's achievement
whereas Joe made contributions to social and Imperial policy.' We dropped
Miss Stevenson at Hyde Park Corner and she ran off to her flat and we came
along to No. 10. I got Curtis across immediately and he summarised Hogan's
Report to the P.M. Then after hearing Curtis the P.M. rapidly read the
Irish news and leader in the *Manchester Guardian*. Then came the Lord Chief
Justice to report on the constitution and soon after 12.0 the full conference
of British Signatories began.

The Free State elections took place under threat of civil war and returned a substantial majority in favour of the Treaty. But for the next three months, until the Dail met, and accepted the constitution and proclaimed the Free State, the war flamed and burnt itself out. Whether or not the North would have come in may be debated: the civil war ensured that it did not.

13 June   Sat through debate of 4 hours on the Cabinet Secretariat, in the Official Gallery with Hankey. Much of the obloquy aimed at us is due to our being mixed up with the P.M.'s personal secretaries and with Sir Edward Grigg in the Garden Suburb. Grigg does the P.M.'s Foreign Office work and the P.M.'s activities in this direction are widely resented in and out of the F.O. Curzon is away ill. Eyre Crowe's instructions from his Chief are to carry on the Curzon policy. Balfour goes to the F.O. He is in much closer accord with the P.M. than Curzon is. The letter to Poincaré about the Hague Conference was drafted not by Crowe but by Grigg at Chequers at the P.M.'s behest and one could multiply instances. Fortunately Lord Eustace Percy took some bad examples of our delinquencies, especially one in which he charged us with bungling the reference to Upper Silesia to the League of Nations. Hankey got on to the F.O. people at once and prepared a statement of the facts which shewed that we had nothing to do with it: that it was the work of Briand and our F.O. experts. We had an absolutely clear case and the P.M. laid Eustace Percy out flat. Fortunately too we have quite recently stopped circulating Cabinet Minutes to Ministers. A copy goes to the King, for the rest we send a letter of reminder transmitting the conclusions reached to the particular Ministers concerned. The Ministers concerned we interpret rather widely so as to include usually the Leader of the House and the Chancellor of the Exchequer. We were on thin ice too on the question of whether we record the opinions of individual Ministers: the practice has varied. Sometime ago, 12 months or more, we dropped naming Ministers —unless by their express wish—but our practice is not quite uniform. Lord Robert Cecil laid stress on the P.M. determining the agenda. In theory this is so, but the P.M. is an elusive person and we have to interpret his mind not infrequently. Chamberlain is given to indicating the order in which he would like subjects taken but the P.M. is above agendas and if he wants a subject taken first the fact that it is sixth on the agenda makes no difference. This morning, for example, the first subject down was the Teachers' Super-annuation Bill but the first subject taken was not on the agenda at all. . . .

After the debate in the House dinner with the P.M. in the House of Commons. Cold salmon, cold chicken and salad, strawberries, cheese and coffee: hock to drink. After dinner the P.M. gave me to read Chapter I of his story of the war, the only chapter he has written or dictated. It was a vivid impression of 4 August 1914, seen from the Cabinet room as Big Ben tolled out 11.0 (12.0 in Berlin) 'DOOM-DOOM-DOOM'. We talked about the structure of his book. I kept saying that it should be the war as *he* saw it and not an attempt at a history of the war: that he should single out the salient stages and crises and describe them as they impressed themselves upon him and how he reacted to them. He outlined what he thought would be Chapter II: the struggle he put up for dealing with Austria in the early stages of the war. 'Always go for the weakest point in your enemy's armour is a good rule in war as in debate.' He had recently read a memorandum which he wrote at that time. Had it been listened to it might have curtailed the war by three or four years. Then he talked of the Ministry of Munitions and of the vast disparity between his estimate of the munitions that would be required and Kitchener's. Kitchener's was a minimum of 2 and 4 if possible as against the P.M.'s 16 and 32 if possible. As a matter of fact the P.M.'s 32 was found inadequate. He contemplates a chapter somewhere in the book about the relations of the statesman and the soldier in war, with comparisons with Lincoln. When Lincoln found a general in Grant he had no desire to interfere. 'When I found Foch I had no desire to interfere.' . . .

On 22 June Sir Henry Wilson was murdered in London; and the British Government at once exerted pressure on Collins for a reprisal to deal with the military threat presented by the I.R.A. in the Four Courts in Dublin. The alternative was the use of British troops, which was undesirable from every point of view. Whether under pressure, or in order to disarm the Republican Party, Collins ordered the capture of the Four Courts, and on 28 June the bombardment began. A large part of the buildings was mined and destroyed and two days later O'Connor surrendered.

11 July Luncheon with the P.M. and Hankey after the Cabinet Meeting. The Cabinet had been discussing the forthcoming debate on Honours and the P.M. was obviously perplexed as to the best line to take and asked my opinion on the Cabinet discussion. I replied that I thought it most difficult to decide what course to take but on the whole I was for his making a statement in the House of Commons on Monday in which he would state that he had continued the practice of his predecessors and in which he should state frankly that the present system is based on rewarding party services and that any alternative would land us in the worst abuses of the States and the Dominions. I should refuse to stand in a white sheet and refuse to go even so far as some of his colleagues desire and appoint a couple of advisers to be interposed between the Whips and the P.M. as an admission of default in the past. He might admit that he had not given that close care to the matter which perhaps he should have done owing to the great pressure of other duties.

. . . I also referred to the tales current about the way in which Sir William Sutherland used to hawk baronetcies at the Clubs. The P.M. at once remarked that Sutherland had had nothing to do with the recent Honours. He went on to say that the root of the agitation lay in the dislike of the Tories to his (the P.M.) having a party fund of his own. The matter had been raised immediately after he became Prime Minister for that reason. . . .

We then turned to other business. I told him of my talk with Shotwell and the proposal to amend the Covenant of the League so as to associate Germany and the States in periodic conferences for limited purposes. He said that he had very much in mind the idea of going over to Canada and from there making a hurried visit to Washington to see Harding and Hughes. Hankey ran over a number of other matters but the P.M. remained quite obviously preoccupied with the Honours trouble. He was to see Bonar Law during the afternoon and then a deputation from the House of Lords on the subject. Later in the afternoon I saw the chief Unionist Whip (Leslie Wilson). He was obviously alarmed at the feeling in the House. 156 Tory Members had signed the request for a debate and he was certain that it would not be sufficient unless there was some guarantee that recent abuses would not recur. He himself had protested to McCurdy. There were two or three names which ought never to have been in the list. He doubted whether the P.M. had given any attention to it as it was sent out to him when at Genoa.

14 July   A proposal was put up by Sir Warren Fisher that T.J. should succeed Selby Bigge as Permanent Secretary to the Board of Education.
. . . Later in the day Hankey sent for me again, and said he had seen the P.M. The P.M. took the view that he had no doubt at all that I was much more valuable here: that my own sympathies being opposed to the Government, e.g., Labour, was well known to all the Ministers, it would be very regrettable that my standpoint should not be represented at the Cabinet Office and that I had the full confidence of Unionist Ministers. So that's that.

*   *   *   *

31 July   Dinner with the P.M. and Miss Megan Lloyd George on the terrace outside the Cabinet room. Miss Megan fiercely defended Augustus John and thought him a great painter. The P.M., no doubt with recollections of his own portrait, was unwilling to concede any merit to John. John was brutal, cruel, seized on the worst elements in the sitter's character, dragged it out and exaggerated it to the point of caricature. . . . Miss Stevenson joined us at 10.0. I told the P.M. that Esher was against his writing his memoirs on two grounds. 1. The P.M. was a man of action. He had lived his life through the war and ought to let his critics squabble about his part therein. He ought not to descend from his position as Prime Minister and trouble to defend himself. 2. The fact that he was being offered and would be paid an enormous sum for the book would tell against him in the popular esteem . . . Miss Stevenson was all against my line of argument. Former Prime Ministers had private means. The P.M. was quite exceptional in the history of Prime Ministers. The P.M. himself said that he was not much influenced by the money argument but that he thought there was something to be said for postponing the writing of the book until he was out of office. On the other hand Balfour, whom he had consulted, was not against the P.M. writing the book while in office.

(A few days later I noticed in the papers what were obviously inspired paragraphs intimating the P.M.'s decision to write the book and quoting the precedents of Gladstone, Disraeli, etc., in support, obviously written by Miss Stevenson.)

. . . I left about 10.30, the P.M. going down to the House to record his vote for the safeguarding of fabric gloves.

2 August   The P.M. busy with his speech on India in the forenoon. I had luncheon alone with him at 1.30. . . . The talk moved to electioneering. What did I think would be the strength of the Labour Party at the next election? I said about 200. He thought more. I said the young intellectuals did not want a Labour government yet. They would much rather be able to exert pressure on L.G. as a Prime Minister in a progressive direction provided L.G. were willing to move leftwards. He (L.G.) said that the larger the Labour Party in the next Parliament the better he would be pleased. He thought their leaders were far too narrowly trade unionist in outlook and quoted in his support Ramsay MacDonald's article in the *Socialist Review*. I said that I wished he could go out of office with dignity on some Liberal issue; that many friends of his told me that there was a distinct danger of his out-staying his welcome and that things were really drawing into rather a ragged condition. He said the same was true of Gladstone in 1868 and of other Prime Ministers: that he had offered only the previous week to go out and there had been discussions between Balfour, Chamberlain, and others, but they had come back and told him that they would prefer him to remain in office. He proposes to be round about London through September in touch with Winston and F.E. 'After all Chamberlain is as good a Liberal as many so-called Liberals, so is Balfour, in his foreign policy, and so is F.E.'

I said I did not see what sort of positive programme he could produce for a General Election, that I should prefer his going out for a spell and letting the Tories have their run, but I think his mind was already made up. He was worried about the state of Europe, does not like to leave it in its present mess, and he wants to be loyal to the colleagues who have supported him. He talked about the drink question, said the Labour Party were tepid about it and that he doubted whether there were 20 per cent. of the population wanted anything done.

12 August   At the Cabinet meeting today L.G. passed me a note: 'If you are going to Ireland will you break your journey at Criccieth on your way back.' To which I replied: 'Most gladly'. This with reference to my representing him at the funeral of Arthur Griffith.[1]

15 August   T.J. to E.T.J.   *2 Whitehall Gardens*
Yesterday we had a most hectic afternoon. I went to lunch with Masterton Smith at 2 and then a hair cut and on getting in at 3.30 found a Cabinet starting which I was to take as Hankey had gone off to a dentist to get a tooth out! Then followed an Inter-Allied Conference which I took, and then another Cabinet! I had a fierce headache, could take no dinner, and went to bed at 10.30 with two aspirins inside me. Much better today. Saw the P.M. before he went to Criccieth and promised to join him there about Friday. I go to Dublin 8.45 p.m. tonight, and shall stay with Alfred Cope at Dublin Castle.

[1] Griffith died on 12 August. He was succeeded as President of the Free State by William Cosgrave (1880–1960), until then Minister of Local Government in the Dail. He was President until 1932.

After lunch with Edward Grigg we walked round St. James's Park to enjoy ourselves. He had just received a letter from Zimmern, the first for many years, from the South of France, urging Grigg to quit No. 10! I told Grigg that it was up to both of us to stand by the P.M., it was both a privilege and a duty, and all the more when difficulties were increasing. Grigg fully agreed. We both wish we could persuade the P.M. to take a real holiday, but there is no prospect.

In a letter to E.T.J. on 17 August T.J. described his visit to Dublin for Arthur Griffith's funeral.

20 August   Lionel Curtis wrote to T.J. about
. . . an invention which is going to have far-reaching political effects . . . called the 'Amplifier'. . . . You must realise that by means of this instrument the P.M. could sit in Downing Street and address audiences of unlimited number simultaneously in Birmingham, Manchester, Liverpool, Cardiff, Edinburgh, and Glasgow. It means incredible addition to the power of the political leader who happens to be the man who most people want to hear; it will also make him much more independent of the press. Just think what it means for the P.M. to be able as often as he likes to address huge audiences in all the principal centres of population. We have heard a great deal of 'broadcasting', but the 'Amplifier' is destined to have more far reaching effects politically.

23 August   Criccieth. When I came down I heard from the telephone operator that at 20 to 5 he had tried to make some one hear and had failed. At 7.30 message from J. T. Davies announcing murder of Michael Collins.[1] At 8.20 confirmed by message from Lionel Curtis. I sent a note upstairs to the P.M. who came down to breakfast at 9.15. 'This is terrible news.' Would I find out what near relatives survived Collins and see about messages of condolence? Would Mulcahy succeed him? L.G. sent this message to the Press:

'Am inexpressibly sad at the news of the death of this gallant young Irishman. He fell to a treacherous blow when he was engaged in endeavouring to restore ordered liberty to his country which stands sadly in need of it. His engaging personality won friendship even among those who first met him as foes and to all of us who met him the news of his death comes as a personal grief and sorrow. I sincerely hope that his death will be the last episode in this dark chapter of Irish history and that a new and brighter story will henceforth be written in the life of that unfortunate land.'

The news had a depressing effect on L.G. He read off and on 'Bardd Cwsc' till about 11 and then we went by car to Rhydybenllyg Bridge and walked via Llanystumdwy. He pointed to a spot near the Dwyfor: 'Bury me here. Don't put me in a cemetery. You'll have trouble with the relatives, and there

[1] He was shot in ambush near Macroom.

would be controversy if the Abbey were suggested. Get John Morris Jones to write a simple epitaph, not a long-winded one like that on the front of John Elias o Fon. Say

"Magwyd yn y pentref.—Prif Weinidog Prydain yn y Rhyfel Mawr." '
(Bred in the village.—Prime Minister of Britain in the Great War.)

Passed to discuss an article in the *Daily Telegraph* on the political situation and to defend his action in standing by Austen, Winston, F. E. Smith, and the 130 Liberals 'who came out with me. I preferred to co-operate with Austen, Winston, and F.E. on Ireland than with Runciman and McKenna.' Hamar Greenwood had shown great courage—or insensibility—as Chief Secretary. The best Ministers would not take it on. Redmond used his influence in 1916 against seizing the leaders of Sinn Fein.

Meanwhile Lloyd George's position was becoming increasingly insecure as the crisis between Greece and Turkey grew more serious.

7 September   T.J. to Lloyd George
Breakfasted with D.D. this morning. He was just back from Vienna and Geneva.

1. He strongly urged the importance of your going out to Geneva and making a speech on disarmament. Said this was the view of John Ward and others.

2. Urged that the Turkish situation ought to be discussed at the League and that you should tell Balfour that you see no objection. Says nothing will come of the Venice Conference and that the whole question should be referred to a commission appointed by the League with a view to setting up the international control of Constantinople. I attach a short paper on the subject which he says has wide support.

3. Said the French were jealous of Italy getting control of Austria.

He would of course be most willing to see you if you wished.

8 September   T.J. to Sir Maurice Hankey
We have got suddenly busy again owing to developments in Asia Minor. We had a long Cabinet discussion yesterday, the general result of which was determination to stand by the policy of the Paris agreement—the Treasury are to do a draft reply to Poincaré's Note on Reparations and put it up to the F.O. and the F.O. to the Cabinet.

In the afternoon we had a long Irish Committee with a very lugubrious report from Macready. No one cares to prophesy what will happen, and there is some chance, it is thought, of De Valera turning up at the Dail tomorrow! However you need not trouble with these worries.

The Cabinet, having asked for the military support of the Allies and Dominions, met on 15 September to decide finally on policy towards Turkey. Poincaré of France agreed to maintain neutrality with French troops in the Straits zone. Of the Dominions only New Zealand offered help. Mackenzie King of Canada returned a flat refusal. The Empire, indeed, had come of age.

However, Lloyd George was planning his possible retreat with care. He intended to retain the sinews of political power and, in addition to his personal party fund, tried to gain control of The Times.

At the time of his death, Lord Northcliffe wholly owned The Times, *having bought out the former proprietor, John Walter. Lord Rothermere, Northcliffe's executor, put the paper up for sale, giving Walter an option to buy it back. Walter had to obtain financial backing, which he did ultimately from John Astor, to the sum of £3 million. Lloyd George's bid, supported by David Davies, appears vastly to have underestimated the price required, even to obtain the controlling interest, which was all Lloyd George wanted. Needless to say, T.J. was called in as emissary. On 19 September David Davies summoned him by telegram, from Gregynog to Blair Atholl, to discuss the proposal.*

21 September   *Blair Atholl*
D.D.'s Proposal
Suggested Heads of Agreement re *The Times*

1. That the total purchase price to be paid for the property does not exceed £900,000.

Of this total amount of £900,000, £400,000 to be found by X's other friends, and £500,000 by the D[1] interest.

2. If the property can be secured at a lesser amount the total sum required must be found in the above proportion, e.g., if the property costs £800,000 X's interest finds £350,000 and the D interest £450,000.

3. That X undertakes to become Managing Director and Editor of *The Times* within six months of his relinquishing his position as Minister of the Crown.

4. That during the period which elapses between the acquisition of the property and the date of assuming the Editorship, arrangements for editing the paper are to be made by the Board of Directors.

5. That X be willing to enter into a Contract with the Board of Directors to place his services entirely at the disposal of the Company for a period of three or five years, and that during that period he is prepared to sever his connection with the House of Commons. This arrangement to be subject to three months' notice on either side.

6. That the Board be empowered to modify this arrangement by arrangement with the Editor in any way they think fit should in their opinion the necessity for doing so arise.

7. That the main lines of policy of the paper should be agreed upon beforehand, and incorporated in a document,[2] and that subject to the provisions enumerated in this document the policy and direction of the paper should be entirely in the hands of the Editor and Managing Director.

8. That all matters relating to the administrative and business arrangements of the paper shall be controlled by the Board of Directors.

9. That the Board of Directors shall consist of five persons, two nominated

[1] A note in the Diary explains that X was Lloyd George and D Davies.
[2] The three main points on which policy was to be agreed were the League of Nations, disarmament, and peace.

by the D interest, and three by other shareholders. The first Chairman to be nominated by the D interest.

22 September   T.J. to E.T.J.   *Perth*
I was called at six, dressed with the aid of three wax candles, a hurried break-fast and a drive through the frosty air to Blair Atholl station for the 7.5 train to Perth—a very cold journey on a stopping train—Killiecrankie, Pitlochry, Dunkeld, and Birnam and other famous names. Reached Perth 8.23 and sent off some telegrams, had a plate of bread and butter, an apple and some butterscotch to keep me going till lunch after Carlisle. The sun is smiling on the fields, the corn is still in stooks and we've just come through Auchterarder with its raspberry canes, and Gleneagles with its golf. . . .

So far as D.D. and Gwen are concerned my visit has been completely successful. My business was to obtain £500,000. Gwen agrees to £200,000 and D.D. to £100,000. I am to see Daisy about £200,000 from her and then to overcome John Owens.[1] If I succeed I shall be bound to run up to town to see the P.M. personally. I doubt if I shall be ready tomorrow evening so it may be Monday. P.M. I fancy will be at Churt. I can tell you the details of the proposed arrangement which if carried out will give the Davieses a controlling interest in *The Times*. There are conditions as to P.M. becoming a Director for a term of years, if and when he relinquishes Premiership. The other shareholders on whom the P.M. proposes to rely are Pirrie, Inverforth, and Maclay.

However, financial complications intervened, and the Davies family withdrew their support.

22 September   Sir Maurice Hankey to T.J.
. . . As regards my diary, I do not think it would be any use for the purpose you suggest. It is too disjointed. Purely personal matters are mixed up higgledy piggledy with affairs of state. There are impressions written under the influence of momentary events, that I would sooner I had not written, and which I would hesitate to show to anyone. In fact, no eye but my own has seen nine-tenths of it, and I have arranged that it goes to my executors with careful dispositions that they do not show it as a whole to anyone else. Where it might be useful is to check particular incidents or dates. I would gladly make extracts bearing on particular incidents or persons for the P.M.'s use—that is, I feel, the best use that could be made of it.[2] At the moment it is inaccessible, as it is locked in a strong box and hidden away in our house, which is empty. . . .

23 September   Curzon has had a tempestuous interview in Paris with Poincaré

---

[1] Gwen and Daisy Davies were D.D.'s sisters. John Owens was their stockbroker.

[2] A later letter from Hankey to T.J. makes it clear that Lloyd George and several other members of the Cabinet not only knew but approved of his keeping a diary, and Lloyd George sometimes made use of what he wrote.

over our policy in the Near East. Curzon wanted to make reservations about a possible buffer state under the League of Nations in Eastern Thrace. Poincaré wanted to announce immediate concessions to Kemal at Maritz and Adrianople. Poincaré attacked and Curzon defended Harington. Tempers rose and Poincaré raved at the top of his voice 'like a demented schoolmaster screaming at a guilty schoolboy'. Curzon withdrew. Poincaré apologised, and after half an hour the conference was resumed, but for some time it looked as if the only way out of the *impasse* was that the invitation to Kemal should be sent in separate terms by England, France, and Italy. Sforza supports Poincaré in his desire to surrender to the Turks.

On 10 October the Cabinet decided to call a general election. It was as a result of the opposition of Baldwin and some of the junior ministers and Conservative backbenchers that Chamberlain summoned the Carlton Club meeting for 19 October.

16 October   Hankey had luncheon with the P.M. He found him looking ten years younger than when he went to Manchester and in most hilarious spirits. He says he never had such a reception in his life. People not 8 deep but 50 deep. The newspapers gave no glimmering of the warmth of his reception. Chamberlain is to meet the Unionist Party on Thursday. Birkenhead is going to stand by him, ditto Horne and L. Worthington-Evans. Beaverbrook won't be present. He is for driving Chamberlain out and putting Bonar in but there is some chance of Bonar being 'meek and mild'.

Hankey spent the whole of last week briefing the P.M. and Chamberlain on the history of the Turkish business. I said that a stretch of Chamberlain's speech sounded as if he had read Hankey's memorandum straight on. Hankey said it was a very stodgy speech as Chamberlain had taken none of the spice but only the duff prepared for him, whereas the P.M. with his brief had of course made a ripping speech. He had come up from the country intending to butcher Asquith and Grey but had changed round at the last moment partly under Balfour's influence and taken the line that Asquith and Grey of all men ought to appreciate the difficulties.

T.J. had one more service to render to Ireland. In all the flurry of the crisis of the Coalition Government, he did not forget what had been the greatest part of his work since May 1921. He wrote to Lloyd George on 17 October to point out that even if the Carlton Club meeting let him down, he should not dissolve Parliament before it had ratified the Irish Constitution, as it was pledged to do before the Free State came into being on 6 December.

On 21 October Lloyd George telegraphed to President Cosgrave to say that his resignation would not compromise the ratification and duly, on 6 December, the Irish Constitution became law.

19 October   11.00. Meeting in the Carlton Club presided over by Chamberlain. Chamberlain's effort to preserve the Coalition under the leadership of the Prime Minister defeated. Vote largely determined by Bonar Law's speech and by the victory of the Conservative candidate at the Newport by-election announced this morning, and partly by Chamberlain's clumsy, unsympathetic, and unhumorous handling of the meeting itself.

12.30. Saw Hankey. Very apprehensive about the future of this office. Thinks drastic reduction of staff inevitable. He is aiming to bring the annual expenditure down from about £34,000 to £15,000. The first thing to be shed will be our responsibility for foreign conferences. This will go to the Foreign Office. Next we shall shed our relations with the League of Nations. Next restrict as far as possible our responsibilities for committees. . . .

* * * *

In the stop-press was Pretyman's resolution[1] which on the face of it did not seem one that could not have been accepted by Chamberlain except in so far as it did not expressly provide for L.G.'s leadership.

'That Parliament should appeal to the country at once.

That there should be an understanding with the Liberal Party.

That the Conservative Party should go to the country under its own leaders.'

4.45. To see Curtis and Masterton Smith about the safeguarding of the Irish Treaty. Curtis told me that the P.M. had gone to Buckingham Palace and he suggested that a letter should be prepared to be signed by the British Signatories to the Treaty informing L.G.'s successor that the Government were pledged to put the Irish Constitution through by 6 December, and that to enable this to be done any dissolution would have to take place immediately. We agreed to wait until the following day before taking any action on these lines. Masterton Smith gave me Edward Wood's[2] account of the Carlton Club meeting (the C.O. Parliamentary Secretary). In his view Chamberlain could have saved the situation with more skilful handling. The decision was touch and go. Many voted for the resolution without realising what it involved in Chamberlain's mind. Chamberlain had no alternative resolution or amendment ready. Balfour's speech was as bad as it could be and Bonar Law's very astute. Wood had understood that on Wednesday Chamberlain had been prepared to make it clear that he did not ask the meeting to be committed to the Prime Minister's leadership after the election, and that Chamberlain had gone back on this. We all deplored the unkind fate that had kept Churchill out of all this.[3] From the window I saw Hartshorn and the Labour leaders go to No. 10 to be told by L.G. that he was no longer Prime Minister.

When I reached No. 10 about 5.15 the P.M. was closeted with his Liberal colleagues in the Cabinet room. I went back to Whitehall Gardens and when I returned to No. 10 sometime after 6.00 the Liberal members were coming away with very gloomy faces. Macnamara spoke to me remarking 'This is a very sad business and with a bad winter in front of us the power of the

---

[1] On which the Carlton Club vote took place.

[2] Edward Lindley Wood, later Lord Halifax (1881–1959); at this time Parliamentary Under-Secretary for the Colonies; became President of the Board of Education after the fall of the Coalition.

[3] He was debarred from the Carlton Club meeting because he was still a Liberal, although a member of the Coalition Cabinet.

communists will grow rapidly'. Sir William Sutherland came along and said: 'The P.M. would never believe that there were Ministers who sat at the same table with him who went to secret cabals to conspire at his downfall. He has been told so repeatedly. Perhaps he will now believe it.' Lord Riddell was in the Private Secretary's room. He said the fatal day had been the day at San Remo when, against the advice of Foch and Henry Wilson, Lloyd George had listened to Venizelos with his promise of Greek troops for Smyrna. As for Bonar Law he was probably in the position described in an old *Punch* cartoon in which Lord Russell having been knocking at the door of the Cabinet room suddenly finds it open and runs round the corner to hide saying to himself 'Must I really go in?' Presently the P.M. came out of the Cabinet room and saw me and said in Welsh 'Rhyddid', i.e. 'Freedom', adding 'Don't go away, I want a yarn with you'. So I stayed on and later on went into the Cabinet room and found him in excellent spirits. I told him we had been misled about the Newport election. He said that the dispute in Ebbw Vale and the speeches of Evan Davies M.P. had a good deal to do with the Labour policy and that the moment he had learned the result of the Newport election and heard definitely this morning that Bonar was going to the meeting he had told Stamfordham that he would be resigning in the course of the day. J. T. Davies came in and the P.M. chaffed him about being out of a job. I remarked that I should probably be sent to the Mint or the Record Office out of the way. He said 'You ought to come with me and rouse the country.' I quickly changed the subject and talked about the probable effect of the change on the fortunes of Labour. We were interrupted by L. Worthington-Evans coming in and I withdrew to Miss Stevenson's room. The P.M. joined us there and Grigg came in when he chaffed us both for being delighted at his downfall and for having done our best to bring it about. I said we had held many prayer meetings in the basement but the Lord had been very long in answering our prayers. . . . At this stage Birkenhead came into the Cabinet room and read to the P.M. the draft of the manifesto which the Unionist leaders had prepared in Chamberlain's house for publication tomorrow.[1] It pleased the P.M. immensely. He reeled off the names of the signatories and was especially glad to see Mitchell Thompson's name among them. Sometime during this conversation a message came from Stamfordham that Bonar Law wanted a day or two to consider his position and that therefore L.G. must remain technically Prime Minister. A telephone message came from Leslie Wilson on behalf of B.L. asking by what date the Irish Constitution must be ratified by Parliament. Later on came a message that B.L. was going to consult the Party. I warned the P.M. that B.L. would almost certainly make a great effort to detach some of L.G.'s leading supporters. B.L. could be very persuasive and would ask L.G. to absolve the Unionist Ministers from their undertaking not to take office under B.L. At L.G.'s conference with his Unionist colleagues before he went to the Palace he had offered to so absolve them but they had determined to stand by him. I asked what about Curzon? Curzon wants to be Foreign Secretary whatever happens but that

[1] That is, the Unionists who had undertaken to stand by Lloyd George and the Coalition.

is the one post that Derby wants so it will be a case of 'Pull Devil, pull baker'. I said perhaps they would make Curzon Lord President of the Council. Who would be Lord Chancellor? Cave, thought the P.M., rather than Sumner or Carson.

At about 8.00 we went upstairs to dinner. On the table was the highly gilded casket given to L.G. at Blackpool when receiving the freedom. He has received the freedom of 16 towns up to date and there are 33 towns still waiting to confer the freedom upon him. I remarked what a pity it was that our best craftsmen were not employed to make these caskets. They were all thoroughly commercial in type. He said the Inverness one with its cairngorm stones was an exception and that Sheffield had given him a chest of cutlery. Mrs. Lloyd George had gone off to East Ham to a meeting and the dinner party consisted simply of L.G., J. T. Davies, and myself. J.T.D. hardly spoke a word throughout the meal except when directly questioned. The two feelings dominant in the P.M.'s mind through dinner were, I think, his reception at Manchester and the way in which Chamberlain, Balfour, Birkenhead, Horne, and L. Worthington-Evans had stood by him. He repeatedly referred to these two topics. Three weeks ago and before Manchester he did not think it would have been possible to have carried them with him. Much less would it have been possible had he taken my advice and resigned after Cannes. It was very difficult to know how and when to resign. He had read recently the account of how Gladstone in 1874 was perplexed in his search for a soft place on which to alight. His doctor would not agree to blame his health and finally he had to dissolve. He did not think B.L. had been quite straight with him in their talk on the previous day, but likely enough, added the P.M., he was not free to tell me. (I afterwards learned that it was only at a midnight meeting on Wednesday at the house of Sir Samuel Hoare[1] that Bonar Law was finally won over to definite severance from the Coalition.) As to Manchester and the reception given him by the crowds of common folk, he put it down to their belief that he was still their friend and had not betrayed them. 'You know', he went on, 'that I have not concealed my own Liberal views in the least from my colleagues in the Cabinet and that I have thrown my emphasis on that side. Dizzy finished up as a sycophant of Mayfair. The language of Mayfair is not my language. Joe Chamberlain in the end went right over. I have not done so and will not do so. The difficulty in a Coalition is to adjust your policy to the contradictory temperatures of the two parties.' Had I seen the Esquimo film at Churt? The Esquimo lived in an ice house and if the temperature was too high they melted and if too low they froze. 'What was he going to say at Leeds?' I asked. 'I am going to review the work of the Government. I am going to point out that the people who stand by me are Balfour, who put through the Washington agreement, Balfour and Fisher who are our League of Nations champions, Chamberlain and Horne who have safeguarded the nation's credit, Horne, Mond, and Macnamara who have toiled for the relief of the unemployed.' He would have very little time

---

[1] Sir Samuel Hoare, later Lord Templewood (1880–1959); became Secretary of State for Air after the fall of the Coalition. Bonar Law's decision was probably made even later in the day than that rumour suggested.

to prepare his Leeds speech because he had the Prince of Wales function at the Guildhall and then had to leave for Leeds at 4.00 and have his journey constantly interrupted for presentations and speeches. But he often did better with a speech when he had not too much time for preparation. His reference at Manchester to the old actor touring the provinces was impromptu. There was some talk about Labour. Henderson had been claimed as the coming Labour Prime Minister at Newport in J. H. Thomas's own town. The P.M.'s view was that Clynes gave least offence and would be the probable solution but that in the next House of Commons, if returned, Ramsay Mac-Donald would be the most effective Parliamentarian on the Labour benches.

Did he feel leaving No. 10? Not at all. He had no attachment to a house and its furniture. Churt was somewhat different. It was there one was creating something of one's own. He was attached to people like a dog not to a hearth like a cat. Therein he differed from his wife. There was some talk of his taking C. P. Trevelyan's house in Great College Street for a few months. I left soon after 9.00 and he went off laden with sheaves of notes for the Guildhall and Leeds which had been prepared for him by Grigg and Shakespeare and as I went home the placards had on them—'Bonar Law Premier'.

21 October   No work at the office. All concerned with its fate in view of the persistent attacks upon it in the press[1] and the confounding of it with the 'Garden Suburb'. At 12.00 Hankey went to see B.L. at Onslow Gardens and soon after 1.00 sent for me, Longhurst,[2] and Burgis. B.L.'s first question to him was: Was he (Hankey) prepared to serve him with the same loyalty as L.G., to which Hankey of course replied in the affirmative. Then Hankey outlined his proposed reductions which were warmly welcomed by B.L. B.L. spoke in very kind terms about me and until the last moment of the interview Hankey thought there was no question about my retention here, but he said that B.L.'s last words were 'I will retain him if I can' which left me in much uncertainty. Then Longhurst and Burgis withdrew and Hankey told me that B.L. had discussed my going over to take on the work for him which Philip Kerr and Grigg did for L.G. I told Hankey at once that I was not anything like such a swift draughtsman as Kerr and Grigg and that if I could remain here I would prefer to do so. . . .

22 October, Sunday   Decided to go and see Geoffrey Fry,[3] one of B.L.'s secretaries, at Onslow Gardens. Got there about 12.00. After a few words with Fry, B.L. was told I was there and I was shewn into his room where also was Miss Law. I said at once how splendid it was that the dream of his Glasgow youth was coming true. He said it was his children who at the last moment had prevailed on him and that his sister had opposed. I remarked that I could

---

[1] Especially the *Evening Standard*, which castigated it for its size and extravagance. The Garden Suburb was of course the main target of attack.

[2] Cyril Longhurst, Assistant Secretary to the Committee of Imperial Defence.

[3] (Sir) Geoffrey Storrs Fry (1888–1960); unpaid private secretary to Bonar Law; M.P. 1919–21, 1922–3; private secretary to Baldwin 1923–39.

speak with complete loyalty to himself and to L.G. as I had begged L.G. to resign long ago and I had always wanted him to be Prime Minister for at least 5 minutes. At which Miss Law interjected that she had no objection on these conditions. I added 'Well perhaps we may extend the term to 6 months as Labour is not ready to come in', and so on we chaffed and bantered for 20 minutes. I put as earnestly as I could the claims of Wicks and Sylvester. He then said that he understood from Hankey that it would be possible to borrow me from the Secretariat temporarily to help him at No. 10, especially during the great pressure which there would be during the next few weeks. He did not imply that there had been any doubt about retaining me, and I wondered whether this suggestion of temporary help was in order to discover whether I could really do the drafting well enough for him, about which I have very grave doubts. He was flushed and rather excited and as always when he is in that condition his jaw fell. He pretended to be worried about his own constituency and re-election.[1] I said unhappy and miserable as he then seemed, his misery was as nothing to that of his opponent, Sir George Paish (a most melancholy statistician). He could therefore take courage. He thought L.G. needed a rest, that his judgement was less good than it was two years ago, otherwise he could never have made the attack on the Turks in the Manchester speech on the eve of a conference with them. Had L.G. delivered the Leeds speech at Manchester there would have been no split at this moment. On the other hand the Tories had been restive even before B.L.'s own breakdown and had he (B.L.) remained with L.G. this sort of crisis would have come sooner or later. For Chamberlain he expressed several times his sorrow, for he had had the worst luck in the whole business. L.G. at Leeds had spoken very nicely of himself but of course 'George can't go on being always as nice to me though I do not think things can ever go so far wrong as to break our friendship. It is a pity George had not gone out quietly. He was starting on his campaign at a great pace and he will have a lot of fun out of the Lords who are supporting me. Indeed I could make lots of fun of them. George will always be his own party. I shall be weak in the Commons and I am wondering what to say about tariffs. If I do not safeguard myself now by some pronouncement and reserve the right to impose certain tariffs for the sake of revenue and keep down taxation I shall have to have another election to do so because it would be said I had no mandate.' I advised him that to raise that issue now would have a most disturbing effect on parties and that I understood business men wanted quiet and stability. He did not want himself to raise the issue but he was afraid he might be forced to do so. I left him with the feeling that he would be unable to stand the physical strain of the Premiership for more than 6 months but I may have been misled by the anxieties of the moment.

*   *   *   *

6.00. I saw the P.M. in the Cabinet room. . . . Captain Guest came in and I

[1] He had cause, but not on account of Paish. The Labour (I.L.P.) candidate, Rosslyn Mitchell, drafted at the last moment, reduced Law's majority to 2,514, winning 12,923 votes himself.

withdrew to Miss Stevenson's room and found her burning masses of papers in the fireplace, and looking sadder than I have ever seen her.

23 October   12.00. Met Graham-Harrison and Schuster and J. C. C. Davidson[1] to discuss the timetable of the dissolution, election, and opening of Parliament. To hold the election on Saturday 18 November and get the Irish Constitution through by 6 December would give the Commons and Lords very little time for debate. Labour wanted an election on Saturday, but it was decided to fix Wednesday, 15 November.

*   *   *   *

12.40. Saw Lionel Curtis. He told me that some one had made available a sum of money which would enable a group of Round Table men, e.g., Grigg, Philip Kerr, Lionel Hichens, and Brand, to stand for Parliament without having to rely on the party chest. Their idea was to hold together in support of L.G. and try to surround him with the 'right atmosphere'.

Curtis had come quite independently to the view on the previous day that Cope ought to be roped in the group somehow.

L.G. went to the Palace to say goodbye to the King. I had luncheon with Sir Horace Hamilton, Chairman of the Customs Board, at the Reform Club. He was Private Secretary to L.G. when he was Chancellor of the Exchequer. Naturally the talk turned on L.G. Hamilton recalled how he arrived at the Treasury at 10.00 on the morning of the news of the Sarajevo murder in July 1914: found L.G. impatiently waiting for him—'Ring up the F.O. at once and find out what they are thinking about this news. It is most serious'. Hamilton replied that it was no use to ring up the F.O. at 10, but L.G. insisted that he should go over to the F.O. and find out some responsible person if Sir Edward Grey was not already there. When Hamilton protested L.G. retorted with great earnestness:—'Don't you realise what it means? It is war. Serbia, Austria will bring in Russia, Russia will bring in France, then Germany, then ourselves.' Hamilton went off. There was no one at the F.O. but he was afraid to return and face L.G. so he loitered there until sometime before 11.00 L.G. himself, now with Churchill, came over to the F.O. to wait for Grey. We walked back from the Reform Club to No. 10 as Hamilton wanted to say goodbye to his old chief.

It was now about 3.15. Lord St. Davids was in with L.G., probably discussing the electoral fate of Gwilym Lloyd George in Pembrokeshire. As there seemed some chance that the P.M. might not really say goodbye until tomorrow I came over to see Hankey when a message came to say the P.M. was definitely leaving, so Hankey and I rushed over and went into the Cabinet room where we found Grigg and Miss Stevenson and Shakespeare. Outside were Sassoon and Sir John Anderson and Sylvester. The P.M. was full of fun, chaffing Grigg and me as the two Die-Hards who had compassed

[1] J. C. C. Davidson (b. 1889); private secretary to Bonar Law 1915–20; Conservative M.P. 1920–3, 1924–37; P.P.S. to Bonar Law and Baldwin; Chancellor of the Duchy of Lancaster in 1923; a close friend of Baldwin and later Chairman of the Conservative Party; cr. Viscount 1937. His wife, Frances Joan Davidson, was M.P. for Hemel Hempstead from 1937 to 1959 and became a life peeress, Baroness Northchurch, in 1965.

his downfall. He marched up and down on the far side of the long table, declaring this was the last time he would ever be in the Cabinet room, unless, he said, stopping suddenly, I come back as the leader of a deputation to ask some favour of the new Prime Minister. He then began a mock speech to B.L. 'Mr. Prime Minister,' he began, 'I have come here with my fellow members from Wales to ask—' Mr. Bonar Law 'Pray be seated.' Mr. Lloyd George—'I could hardly sit in the presence of Lord Curzon.' At this point I sat in what would be Bonar Law's chair and buried my face in my hands in as miserable a posture as I could command. Mr. Lloyd George, continuing 'We have come to ask for a grant for Welsh education and we also wish to approach you on behalf of the refugees from Smyrna'—and so on until we were all in roars of laughter except Miss Stevenson who could hardly conceal her sadness at parting with No. 10. Then Shakespeare asked him some advice as to his own career. I think it was whether he should go into chambers to devil for a year. L.G. said 'Yes, as Bismarck said when someone was going to be King of Bulgaria (? Roumania) "It will be an interesting reminiscence".' Then Grigg discussed which of some alternative seats he should contest, I think in Leeds, and which of certain candidates the P.M. would prefer to have beaten. Then Grigg and I tackled him on the importance of securing Cope to run his party machine at Queen Street. I said that Curtis, Grigg, and I were unanimous in our opinion of Cope's great powers of push and go. 'Very well,' he said, 'I am for it. Tell J. T. Davies to tell McCurdy.'[1] I then put before him a photograph of Mazzini which he had given me and he wrote on it 'From one admirer of Mazzini to another'. We came out of the Cabinet room. The P.M. said goodbye to Sir John Anderson and to Cope, to whom he said 'You have done great things'.[2] Then Newman, his factotum, presented him with an ornamental golf club. Hankey and I walked down the passage with him, and stood on the doorstep to be photographed, and at 4.00 he motored away with his son Gwilym to Churt, smiling to the last. On the way over with Hankey he told me that he had seen Warren Fisher about the future of the office and about my own prospects. Warren Fisher told him he could have the staff he required and gave him an assurance that I would not be 'left' but would properly be safeguarded. He had mentioned to Fisher the post of secretary to the Welsh Department at the Board of Education as one for which I had special qualifications and I understood that Fisher was going to find out how soon its present holder was due to resign.

26 October   Luncheon with Hankey and the Bishop of St. Davids. He told him about the post at the Board of Education and the Bishop expressed his delight and promised every help. On the way back Hankey told me that Rothermere had been a few days ago to see B.L., that B.L. had expressed the hope that he would lend his support to the new Government, and that Rothermere had replied that he was prepared to do so on two conditions. . . .

*   *   *   *

[1] The chief Liberal Party organizer.
[2] Referring to his part in the Irish negotiations.

Bonar Law in Glasgow pronounced the doom of the secretariat, not in the formula which Hankey had read to us as having been agreed between him and Warren Fisher, but in the following:—

NO CABINET SECRETARIAT.
BUT A RECORD OF DECISIONS TO BE KEPT.

I will speak to you first on our own foreign policy, but, of course, that fills almost the whole field, for on it hinges so much the possibility of tranquillity and stability. I have already, with the approval of my colleagues, made one change in the central machinery of Government. This was a subject on which from my knowledge I felt competent. We have decided to bring the Cabinet Secretariat in its present form to an end (cheers). That does not mean that everything connected with it has got to go. I have been a member of the Cabinet under both systems. When I joined the first Cabinet of which I was a member I remember saying to the Prime Minister, 'This is awful. There is no agenda.' I had never seen any business conducted in this way. His reply was, 'Every new member of a Cabinet says the same thing; but he gets used to it.' We have no right to get used to it. We must have an agenda at our meetings, and we must have a definite record of decisions. In the old days nothing was taken down. Members and the Cabinet get away with different views as to what the decision was. That was fatal.

But there is no need of the big body which was necessary during the war and immediately after it, but which can come to an end now. I am convinced that the work can be done quite as efficiently and far more economically by having the Cabinet secretary, who is also the secretary of the Committee of Imperial Defence, and whatever help he needs treated as part of the Treasury, which is the central department of the Government. We have already given instructions that the machinery of the League of Nations, which has hitherto been done by the Cabinet Secretariat, shall be transferred to its proper place in the Foreign Office. We have given instructions also that as regards conferences, even where it is necessary that the Prime Minister should be present, the machinery for them and the Parliamentary working in connection with them should be done by the Foreign Office, which is the proper vehicle for the purpose.

Feverish activity in the secretariat followed. Hankey drafted a letter to Bonar Law, to ask for an enquiry into the way in which the office had discharged its functions. If it was refused, he told T.J., he would resign. Hankey then saw Warren Fisher and the idea of an enquiry was dropped as impracticable.

. . . Fisher pointed out that it was not in fact possible to describe with truth the character of the work done here. Had Hankey never advised on foreign policy? What happened when the conclusions of the Cabinet were indefinite? Hankey described what happened on 15 September when the Turkish policy was settled by the Cabinet. He and I sat here drafting conclusions which were of a most comprehensive character but some of which certainly had to be given a greater precision than was warranted by any explicit conclusion enunciated in the Cabinet, and innumerable instances could be given of the delicate duty of interpreting and recording the rather vague and ragged Cabinet discussions. Hankey went on and on in this strain and then he told us that Fisher had offered as a way out a declaration by B.L. in Parliament absolving the office from the newspaper charges and this would give L.G. an opportunity of confirming B.L.'s defence of us. I said that I did not think we could as Civil Servants now expect any more than this and this was the view of Howorth, Longhurst, and Burgis. Then with a smile Hankey announced that Warren Fisher had proposed that Hankey should become Clerk to the Privy Council in place of Sir Almeric Fitzroy: that he had had this idea in his mind for some time.

At this news I relapsed into a painful silence. I was speechless and remained so to the end. I came back to my room and informed Hill and Wicks that the result of Hankey's resignation was likely to be his appointment as Clerk to the Privy Council in addition to the Secretaryship to the Cabinet and the C.I.D. Howorth remarked: 'Only Dumas could do justice to the events of this day.'

However, Hankey strongly recommended T.J. for the Board of Education post in a letter to Warren Fisher written the same day.

30 October, Monday   10.45. The new P.M. sent for me. I found him in the Cabinet room, sitting smoking in the armchair. After referring to my prospective post at the B. of E. he went on to ask me would I help him with his speeches and to begin with the speech he was due to deliver to an audience of women on Thursday? L.G. had spoken at Glasgow of promotions from the kitchen, referring to the new Under Secretaries. Would I find out what had happened under previous Liberal Governments? ...

*   *   *   *

... Birkenhead had talked about the number of peers in B.L.'s Cabinet. How many had L.G. and his predecessors? Would I go through the newspapers and call his attention to points which he ought to deal with? Had not Dizzy in 1874 taken up a negative attitude? Would I find out? Later came a message: would I read Barrie's Rectorial on Courage. Was there not something in it he could use? What had he said on women's suffrage? Had he opposed the extension of the franchise to women on the same terms as men? He was in fact favourable to so doing and was prepared to say so. But as for equal pay for equal work, well he would point out fundamental differences due to nature which could not be overcome. Could I give him this sort of help conscientiously? I said I was a Civil Servant and would serve him as I had served L.G. and as I would serve J. H. Thomas if he became Prime Minister. He went on in his naive way:—'I think my secretaries when I was in office had an affection for me which L.G.'s secretaries had not for him.' I said that was so, that L.G. was almost inhuman in his detachment.

31 October   B.L. sent for me and I took over stuff. He works quite differently from L.G. He writes nothing down, not even a peg. He had not a word written of his Glasgow speech. He finds it now much easier to work in this way. I asked did he not even arrange the order on paper of the points? He said no. 'I arrange the order in my mind.' He was pleased with the stuff I gave him in which I compared him to Barrie and L.G. to Maconachie. He developed L.G.'s metaphor of the placid stream as one making for a cataract but for B.L.'s intervention. L.G. was all right as a drummer in a cavalry charge in war but we did not want a drummer in a hospital. Then he told me the story of the Highlander who begged to hear the pipes once more. He recovered but all the other patients died. Friendly as his relations with L.G. had been and were he feared a strain on their relations for a time was inevitable owing to L.G.'s speeches. He would be bound to reply rather sharply but he hoped that when all was over they would be able to resume their old friendship. I said and he agreed that L.G.'s moral stature had grown greatly during the war and the tenure of his office as Prime Minister: that in his most intimate conversations there was only one man of whom he spoke with something akin to hate. B.L. asked me was that Curzon. I said no, he laughs at Curzon. . . . What about Churchill he asked. He distrusts him I replied. 'Well, I remember during the Irish business', said B.L., 'spending a weekend with Sir Edward Goulding. F.E. and Winston were there and both went to great lengths in denouncing L.G. while I declared that I had found him throughout a most honourable colleague. Whereupon F.E. remarked, "Of course he would not pick your pocket if he knew there was nothing in it" and more in that strain.'

I sent the P.M. a copy of the Chanak telegram from Paris which was before the Cabinet on Friday, 15 September in which Poincaré agreed to maintain neutrality of zone now occupied by allies around Constantinople straits. The prevailing view of Ministers was that the presence of French troops with ours would restrain Kemal from attacking the small inter-allied force.

1 November   Warren Fisher spoke to T.J. about the Board of Education post.
. . . When he mentioned this to B.L., B.L. said that whatever post I went to he would like me to be available whenever he wished to see me. Fisher told him that the Prime Minister had a right to send for any Civil Servant at any time. He assured me that no Minister had ever spoken to him about me except in the friendliest terms. He knew perfectly well the character of the work I had to do for L.G. and agreed that it was a strength of the Service to have men available of very diverse qualifications for the varied work of modern government. He told me the story of his negotiations with Hankey and that he had gone to great lengths to meet him but that the ultimate decision would have to rest with B.L. (Hankey is still talking of resigning to Sir John Chancellor today.) Fisher made no bones about his views that the Secretariat should be within the Treasury as the great co-ordinating Department. I did not enter into a discussion of the pros and cons of the controversy. . . .

10.00. Saw B.L. In trouble about the Pensions Ministry. I told him the man in the street would at once conclude that he had gone back on his intention of abolishing the post. He bade me draft a letter to the British Legion on the subject.

8 November Curzon talks in the City of the 'too powerful and too numerous Cabinet Secretariat'. Hankey protested and Curzon writes 'regretting his unpremeditated and hasty words' but marks his apology for private circulation in the office after attacking us in public.

10 November Saw B.L. at the close of the Cabinet. He looked done to the world and it seemed cruel to put up papers to him. Several of us were buzzing round with drafts in reply to the British Legion, ex-Service Civil Servants and others who were trying to blackmail him. We begged him to cancel Manchester and Sheffield where he was to speak on the following day. He said he was then going off to see Sir Milsom Rees who had doctored his throat for him for the Guildhall speech the night before. Later I heard that he had agreed to rest until Sunday night when he would leave London to speak in Glasgow.

11 November Various messages from Onslow Gardens where B.L. is resting. He had read Wells's speech and wants to reply to it in Glasgow. Would I also find out what his opponent Sir George Paish had said during the war and his visit to America? Could B.L. tackle him without being offensive?

12 November Saw B.L. at 3.00 and he rehearsed the main lines of the Glasgow speech. He was better and smoking in a dressing gown. In my draft I had taken the line that Wells, Paish, and Co. were utterly divorced from realities. What was the good of asking for a World Council when it was as much as B.L. could do to keep France and Italy united to us? I listened to a long exposition of the virtues of individualism and the motives which moved mankind on the usual lines proper to a Glasgow business man. I begged him to shew some real sympathy with the Glasgow unemployed, described the groups of half starved men I had seen at the street corners when there in June and how I had been told that the birds were nesting in the cranes on the banks of the Clyde. He asked for a quotation about the Capital Levy which I had given him from the *New Statesman*. I doubt if he had ever seen a copy of the paper and I had to explain to him that it was the organ of the Labour intelligentsia. This business over we had tea and gossip. He did not think he had lost any friends on either of the two previous occasions when he had upset Governments. In December 1916 at the Conference in Buckingham Palace he found that Asquith had no idea what he was up against. B.L. had spoken to him somewhat as follows:

B.L. 'There is a suggestion that there should be a sort of neutral P.M.'

Asquith. 'Who will he be?'

B.L. 'They suggest that I should be P.M.'

To this Asquith would not agree.

B.L. 'In that case L.G. will become P.M.'

Asquith. 'But apart from you, yourself, surely no one of your side will serve under L.G.?'

B.L. 'Oh yes, everyone will.'

This came as a great surprise to Asquith who had been kept in a false paradise by Mrs. Asquith despite Reading's attempts to make him understand that his term as P.M. was at an end. B.L. thought that something of the same failure to see realities had beset L.G. now during the recent crisis.

'On every occasion when I have seen L.G. since my return from Cannes I have warned him that this collapse was coming.'

There was some talk about L.G. 'He has not replied to my attack at Camberwell the other night, indeed he has been very nice and of course in his position he cannot hit out. There is a French proverb which says that some men are eclipsed when they take second place, L.G. was supreme in the first place. I wonder will he be eclipsed in the second? I was good as a second. Shall I fail in the first place?' 'Balfour told Balcarres who told me that it was an advantage to have a leader who was not intellectually much superior to the rest of the party he led.' I said rather hesitatingly that Bagehot's definition of a constitutional statesman seemed to me to fit him (B.L.) 'A man of common opinions and uncommon abilities'. I went on to quote a remark in this week's *Nation* about the victory having been won already by B.L. voicing the conservative sense of the electorate.

16 November Election results pouring in all day. Cabinet at 11.00 and Ministers very gloomy as they believe that their majority would be not more than 20. Matters rapidly improved during the day and when I saw the P.M. alone in the afternoon the figure was over 70, and I was able to cheer him up. He admitted he had felt great dismay the previous evening when the Labour results from Scotland arrived and that he was in doubt about his own seat. His Labour opponent (Rosslyn-Mitchell—who went through college with me) had put up a very skilful fight. He is a lawyer and had led the attack connected with the Rent Restriction Act. He had shewed some very effective posters contrasting delightful rural bungalows with city slums and the comfort of the children of the rich and the squalor of the children of the poor. His address, so the P.M. said, was a direct appeal to selfishness. Sir George Paish had done him no harm and he had not mentioned him in his speech at the City Hall. He was very pleased with that speech. It marked a departure from his former speeches. I told him that I thought it was a great triumph to have got him to quote five lines of poetry from Wordsworth and he was very proud of having made a quotation on his own—

'Sings each song twice over,
Lest you should think he never could recapture
The first fine careless rapture.'

There was some talk of L.G. and his future. I said I had kept away from him during the contest but would now go to see him. B.L. hoped that L.G. would take a holiday abroad. He would have a tremendous personal triumph if he visited the Dominions which would react on his position here at home.

Then we talked of Ireland. The Duke of Devonshire,[1] I said, was doing very well with the Irish Ministers. Curtis and I strongly hoped that the Government would swallow Tim Healy as the Governor-General. It was useless having a Viceroy like Fitzalan who did nothing and no Lord from the South would do. B.L. had two objections to T.H. He was impulsive and he drank too much whisky at night. I said there were precedents for the latter defect and that now he was old and less impulsive and his appointment would have a great effect on moderate opinion in Ireland. I went on to say that Cave and Salisbury were proving somewhat obstinate about the Treaty and did not seem willing to realise that it had to be swallowed without change and the Constitution ditto. B.L. thought that Cave would prove reasonable and he agreed that if the Treaty and Constitution must be put through it was better to do it handsomely than in any niggardly spirit. Returning to the Governor-Generalship he thought it ought to be possible to find someone in the Diplomatic Service for the post, someone with no political past.

1923

In May of this year, Bonar Law was overcome by cancer of the throat and, after two days of dramatic suspense, the King asked Stanley Baldwin to form a government, to the bitter disappointment of Lord Curzon. It is clear from T.J.'s account that this was what Bonar Law wished, though he did not tender formal advice. During the summer, Baldwin became convinced that protection was the only remedy for unemployment, a policy which he announced at Plymouth on 25 October. The public was not prepared for this and in the ensuing General Election, instead of the majority of ninety over all others predicted by his political staff, the Conservatives were returned with ninety-two fewer seats than Labour and Liberals combined. The Liberals formed a united front under Asquith to fight protection. The final results, declared in December, were Conservatives 258, Labour 191, Liberals 159. Baldwin decided to face Parliament before resigning, so that the first Labour Government did not take office until 22 January 1924.

The question of reparations continued to bedevil European relations but late in 1923 some hope of a settlement was heralded by an Anglo-French détente which led to the setting up of the Dawes committee of experts to determine Germany's capacity to pay. The French occupation of the Ruhr, begun in January, however, continued. In the face of German passive resistance, the French, in Lloyd George's phrase, were 'digging out coal with bayonets'. Inflation followed and the collapse of the mark. In the Ruhr itself there was chaos and by the end of the year actual famine. By contrast, Curzon, at the Lausanne Conference, settled the Turkish question single-handed, returning with not only diplomatic credit but the oilfields of Mosul. As Chancellor of the Exchequer, Baldwin negotiated the repayment of the British war debt to the United States on terms more onerous than those subsequently offered to Italy and France. Bonar Law and some of his colleagues were far from convinced but felt obliged to ratify.

T.J. worked closely with Bonar Law and was much distressed by his illness and death. Baldwin asked him to carry on and came to rely heavily on him for speech-writing. In the autumn election, T.J. helped with speeches to an extent which

[1] The 9th Duke; Civil Lord of the Admiralty 1915, Governor-General of Canada 1918–21, Secretary of State for the Colonies 1922–3.

nowadays would be regarded as unacceptable. But he was not and was never regarded as an orthodox Civil Servant. Towards the end of the year, however, he was in the running for the senior post in the Board of Education. He decided to postpone a decision until he knew whether his services would be required by the incoming Government. In the event, he remained as Deputy Secretary to the Cabinet until he left the public service in 1930.

During the year T.J. inspired the founding at Gregynog, the Montgomeryshire home of the Misses Davies, of a private printing press which took its place with the Ashendene, Golden Cockerel, and other fine presses of the period.

1 *January   T.J. to E.T.J.*   *Hôtel de Crillon*
. . . Now about my trip to Paris. . . . Besides Bonar Law and Lloyd-Greame, Sylvester, Davidson, Hankey, and the faithful Berry, we had Sir John and Lady Bradbury, Eyre Crowe of the Foreign Office, Niemeyer of the Treasury, Wigram of the Foreign Office, Cazalet just back from Oxford and acting as 'unpaid' secretary to Lloyd-Greame, Phillips and Wilkinson from the Treasury, typists and detectives. Bradbury[1] had prepared a new scheme for a final settlement, which had been approved but probably not understood by all the Cabinet on Friday. It was very technical and I was given it to read on the train. We then (Hankey, Davidson, and I) made Niemeyer[2] expound it to us until we pretended to understand it. . . .

. . . We arrived in Paris about 6.45 and Hankey, Eyre Crowe, Niemeyer, and I drove here. Crewe[3] met Bonar Law at the station. Hankey and I have neighbouring rooms with a sitting room between us and the offices of the Cabinet section are near. B.L. has a stately suite. I had a long talk with him before dinner. I told him that the country at home would agree to any terms provided they were final and that the view on the train was that he was too pessimistic about the outlook. He replied that the Bradbury scheme gave the French £1,000 millions whereas their debt *since* the armistice was £2,700 millions and therefore it meant bankruptcy. No one would have the courage to tell the French people that, though it might come after the fall of one ministry and its replacement. We had Niemeyer in. He thought perhaps the best way left to the French was to let the franc fall to 90 or so then deal with the internal debt. Of course this would mean great hardship to the French peasant and it might not be possible to stop at 90.

2 *January   T.J. to E.T.J.*
. . . After 10 I joined Niemeyer and Leith-Ross[4] (of the Reparations Commission) and Niemeyer read to me the draft of a speech for B.L. which Leith-Ross had prepared. There have been

[1] John Swanwick Bradbury (1872–1950); Joint Permanent Secretary, Treasury, 1913–19; mainly responsible for the introduction of war savings certificates; delegate, Reparations Commission 1919–25; cr. baron 1925.

[2] (Sir) Otto Ernst Niemeyer (b. 1883); Controller of Finance at the Treasury 1922–7; Director of the Bank of England 1938–52.

[3] The 1st Marquess (1858–1945), Ambassador in Paris 1922–8.

[4] Sir Frederick Leith-Ross (1887–1968); private secretary to Asquith 1911–13; British representative on Reparations Commission Financial Board 1920–5; chief economic adviser to the British Government 1932–46; principal financial expert at the European economic conferences of the inter-war years.

1. Bradbury's undiluted scheme for scaling down German payments.

2. A Child's Guide to a Knowledge of it partly Bradbury I think and partly Leith-Ross.

3. A (Grand) child or infant's guide to 2.

3 January   T.J. to E.T.J.   *Hôtel de Crillon*
Busy. Yesterday luncheon with Bonar and dinner at the Quai d'Orsay. Today Conferences in B.L.'s room all morning; luncheon with Salvador here. Now Conference No. 2 begins (3 p.m.). Outlook is black and we may return to London tomorrow!

The real meaning of the Anglo-French dispute lay in the state of the French economy, which was far more depressed than the British. The money to be extracted from Germany was vital to the maintenance of the franc.

In January Baldwin, with Montagu Norman and Auckland Geddes, negotiated a settlement in Washington. The British debt to America, with interest, then stood at $4,686,000,000. The Americans asked for payment at 3½ per cent. plus a sinking fund of ½ per cent., that is $187 million a year for sixty-one years. Baldwin could offer no more than $140 million for fifty years and he knew that there would be opposition within the Cabinet (some members of which still believed in the Balfour Note) even to this. Americans, accustomed to rates of 4 or 5½ per cent., pressed the British hard.

11 January   Draft Cabinet instructions to Baldwin
The Cabinet are unanimously of opinion that this is an offer which we cannot accept. It is equivalent to funding the loan at 3·42 per cent. and as it is highly improbable that the rate of interest would be so high as this over so long a period there would be in this absolutely no concession if the debt were an ordinary business obligation and in view of all the circumstances it would be in the opinion of the Cabinet intolerably unjust. We can hardly believe that American public opinion could permanently regard this as a fair proposal but if we once signed the bond we could not hope for any redress. The Cabinet fully realise the seriousness of their decision but we think you must say to the American Government that you are not empowered to accept these terms which are far above anything contemplated by you when you left and that you must return to discuss the matter in person with the British Government. In making this statement, if the negotiations end and become public, I think you should state that for the sake of securing agreement you agreed to recommend 3 per cent. to your Government but that you considered even that rate too high in the circumstances. Do not forget that if the American proposal were to be accepted and presented to Parliament there would certainly be much hostility and at the best there would be attacks upon America which would be very bad for the relations between the countries.

14 January   Telegram from Baldwin to the Prime Minister
Immediately on receipt of your telegram I had confidential conversation

with chairman of commission whom I am persuaded is not only anxious for immediate settlement but is genuinely friendly to Great Britain but whose position is such as to preclude separate negotiations with me.

As a result I offered at this afternoon's meeting that if commission would agree to recommend to President and to present Congress a settlement on basis of 3 per cent. interest plus half per cent. sinking fund I would ask that matter should be considered at a full Cabinet. I indicated that if commission agree to make such a recommendation I should have proposals to make on certain minor points on which, however, I did not doubt that it would be possible to reach satisfactory agreement.

We then withdrew from the meeting in order that commission might discuss this suggestion. We met again at 10 o'clock tonight and were informed that after consultation president of commission would recommend unanimity and president would endorse settlement on basis of 3 per cent. interest for first 10 years and $3\frac{1}{2}$ per cent. thereafter. Sinking fund would be at rate of $\frac{1}{2}$ per cent. throughout payable yearly or every 3 or 5 years. This would be sufficient to amortise debt in about 62 years. They offered moreover to recalculate back interest at $4\frac{1}{4}$ instead of 5 per cent. This proposal means 161 million dollars yearly for first 10 years and 184 million dollars for remaining 52 years. I believe we should obtain [agreement] to pay principal and interest in United States government bonds and date at par, and an option to pre-pay principal at any time upon due notice. These options would make bonds practically unmarketable. We are all three convinced that these are best terms we can [obtain]. They represent a tremendous advance in American opinion. Moreover it must not be forgotten that we are tied hand and foot by terms of our existing obligations and I beg you to consider the only alternative to immediate acceptance of present offer.

Report to Congress will be made by commission detailing firstly, original terms of H.M. Government's obligations and secondly, offer of commission which would have been refused. This will be followed by request to H.M. Government to pay regularly under original terms.

What then will be position of H.M. Government?

I referred above to 'immediate' acceptance because failing acceptance within next few days it will be too late to get any alteration of Funding Act through present Congress which will be adjourned on 4 March, and next Congress will probably not meet again till December. In the meantime public opinion which has moved in our favour partly because of recent action of France, partly because American public has come to believe we mean to pay, will have swung back and in new and evenly balanced Congress it is [likely] that question of our debt would be debated in bitterly partisan spirit. No reasonable settlement could then be expected until after next presidential election and how that will go no one can say except that it will not mark return to politics of Mr. Wilson. In absence of settlement British debt would inevitably become undesirably prominent issue in election.

We feel very strongly that a settlement is well nigh essential and that without it we cannot expect improvement in general financial conditions. Any such improvement will presumably be preceded by a general economic conference and at this it is vital that we should not have to take a place amongst the ranks of defaulters.

Issue then is whether settlement now proposed is so burdensome as to outweigh all these disadvantages. In my opinion it is not. I have little doubt that Great Britain would not regard 33 million sterling yearly as being too high a price to pay to escape appearing as a defaulter. This is annual payment for first ten years and it ought to be within our powers. The increase of 5 millions sterling in ten years time is comparatively small and we have time to provide against it. Further much may happen in ten years. What is quite certain is that if we fail to settle now not only American opinion but world opinion will question our willingness to pay with serious damage to our prestige.

All of us who are working here are convinced of necessity of settlement and I urge Cabinet to accept.

It appears to me in all circumstances that honesty and expedience for once go hand in hand and I gravely fear lest by trying for shadow we lose the bone.

15 January   Bonar Law to Baldwin
I have discussed the matter confidentially with McKenna who in spite of all the risks is quite definitely of opinion that we ought not to accept. In the whole proposal the suggestion that the arrears of interest should be calculated not at the rate agreed upon for the whole period but at $4\frac{1}{4}$ seems to me from the point of view of the spirit of the negotiations the worst feature. Is it not possible that you are too much under the influence of Washington which is not even the New York atmosphere. What would you have thought of such proposals before you left?

Baldwin returned to London, convinced that the last American offer was the best which could be obtained. He knew he would meet opposition in the Cabinet and from the Prime Minister, advised by McKenna and Keynes. When Baldwin returned on 29 January on the Olympic *and was interviewed by the press, he made an injudicious statement blaming the ignorance of mid-West American opinion for the hardness of the terms. Bonar Law did not disguise his opinion, either to the American Ambassador or to Baldwin, but he found himself alone in the Cabinet in wishing to reject the terms. Having said that they would reduce the standard of living in the country for a generation, he published an anonymous attack on his own Cabinet's policy in* The Times *and allowed the settlement to go through.*

5 February   Gossiped with Hankey about the events of last week. He thinks on the whole that Baldwin's interview on his arrival[1] from the U.S.A. on the Debt was inadvertence rather than premeditation. The P.M. on Tuesday at the Cabinet meeting was adamant against accepting the terms and while

---

[1] *Note in Diary, dated 2 October 1932:*

G. Fry told me that J. C. C. Davidson had thought of going to meet S. B. at Southampton and had then decided against going. Had he gone it is most probable that he would have seen the Press for S. B. and almost certainly would have been much more cautious in any statement put into S. B.'s mouth. Had he gone the history of the Debt 'might have been' quite different.

not saying the word 'resignation' went very near doing so. Only Lloyd-Greame and Novar[1] sided with him. All the others were for acceptance. On Wednesday (I think) there was a group meeting who deputed Cave and Devonshire to see the P.M. They told B.L. that they were prepared to take his view but that immediately afterwards they would resign. On the same day McKenna who throughout had been in close touch with B.L. 'ratted' and concurred in acceptance of the U.S.A. terms, so when the Cabinet met on Wednesday for a few minutes B.L. gave in.

Matters have been very unpleasant with Poincaré over the communications of the French Government to Angora.[2] Poincaré sent a note to H.M.G. saying that the French regarded themselves as free to act independently—that the Treaty of September 1914 was at an end, etc., etc. Lord Curzon telegraphed insisting that we should protest and Crewe has done this. Hankey thought that having got 80 per cent out of the Turks L.G. would have pulled off a settlement, but that Curzon lacked ingenuity and resource, and Crewe was too like Curzon.

Eric Drummond has written to Hankey a note indicating that Balfour would not be unwilling to join the Government. Chamberlain on the other hand is going to his garden till Easter: 'with complete peace of mind which is more than some people enjoy', as he seems to have remarked at Grigg's wedding, meaning chiefly Curzon, who at some dinner at Churchill's before the political crisis had told his colleagues that they could rely on him to play the game.

The news from D'Abernon[3] is that the German Government are absolutely determined to stand out against the French[4] and are making all sorts of provisions to deal with the coal problem. . . .

Luncheon with the P.M., Davidson, and Fry. First time in the big dining room, the meal even simpler than L.G.'s, B.L. taking two courses and getting as quickly as possible to a big cigar. He had come up from a couple of days at Brighton with Lady Sykes.[5] I have never seen him so depressed. I never saw L.G. even at the blackest time of the war in such a gloomy frame of mind. He started talking about Lausanne at once. Why had there been a breakdown in view of the great margin of agreement? He could not understand a break on the capitulations. (This I see is the line the press is taking—that Curzon boggled over trifles at the last moment.) I tried to get him to outline what he thought would now be the course of events in the next few weeks but he said little as he was to see Curzon later in the day. I suggested —assume the worst: had we not better get out of Constantinople at once rather than suffer the humiliation of being forced out later. Davidson said this would be interpreted as great weakness but agreed it would be less weak than being driven out later.

B.L. 'If we withdraw to the Straits in order to defend the graves that will

[1] Lord Novar, Secretary of State for Scotland.

[2] Referring to French demands at the Lausanne Conference.

[3] Ambassador in Berlin.

[4] I.e. the French occupation of the Ruhr.

[5] His daughter, who had married Sir Frederick Sykes, the first Controller General of Civil Aviation.

be regarded as an act of war.' I said I meant not simply withdrawal from Constantinople but from the Straits too and that I could not imagine the Turks would be so mad as to desecrate the graves. He then turned to the King's Speech. We should have to say something about the American Debt: as little as possible. He was still very sore about it. I remarked that L.G. was behaving admirably.

B.L. 'He is waiting his time.'

T.J. 'Well, at least he is waiting.'

9 February   10.15. With Davidson to see Sir Arthur Robinson at the Ministry of Health. Davidson had dined earlier in the week with Lord Weir.[1] Weir had recently met Henry Ford and been infected with 'standardisation'. 'I have done one thing in my life,' said Ford to Weir, 'the Ford car. I have two more things I wish to do—the reform of the hospitals of the world, and to revolutionise British agriculture.' Weir had been talking with Sir John Stirling Maxwell and Sir John Hunter about a scheme for putting up tens of thousands of houses in blocks of 200 at £150 apiece, to consist of a couple of rooms with central heating, hot water, electric light, central laundry, and a piece of land. Everything would be standardised. The building trade, employers and employed, would be ignored and the erection done by unskilled labour. At the P.M.'s request we saw Robinson who is in the middle of negotiations with the municipalities. The Government wants to get out of the Addison bog.[2] At the moment they are committed to bear the burden above a 1*d.* rate (by the way the real criminal was not Addison but Auckland Geddes and it was amusing to read the censure of Sir Eric Geddes of the Government's housing scheme directed against poor Addison when it ought to have been directed against his own brother). The local authorities want a subsidy of £6 a house for 60 years. The Government are offering £4 for 20 years—the house to be built either by the local authorities or by private enterprise. If Weir registers himself as a Public Utility Company he should be able to come within the ambit of the Government's offer. I suggested the creation of a National Housing Trust with regional branches, and if Weir is sufficiently determined there is no reason why we should not get tens of thousands of houses—ugly though they will be. . . .

At 10 Downing Street, T.J. met Cosgrave, the Irish President, and two of his Cabinet, and, realizing how impoverished the Free State was, he urged Bonar Law to persuade the British Treasury to be generous with guarantees for their loans.

Luncheon with P. J. Grigg,[3] the Private Secretary of the Chancellor of the

---

[1] William Weir (1877–1959), cr. Baron 1918; managing director of G. and J. Weir and Co., Glasgow shipbuilders; member of the Air Board 1917–18, Director-General of Air Production 1918, Chairman of the Advisory Council on Civil Aviation 1919–22; an expert in industrial production who was frequently consulted by Governments of the inter-war years.

[2] The failure of Addison's Housing Act.

[3] Percy James Grigg (1890–1966); principal private secretary to successive Chancellors of the Exchequer 1921–30; Permanent Under Secretary, War Office, 1939–42; Secretary of State for War 1942–5. Knighted 1932.

Exchequer. Grigg and his wife were full of reminiscences of their recent visit to settle the debt at Washington. What had struck them most was the vulgar display of luxury. Mellon, the Secretary to the Treasury, is worth tens of millions sterling. He and his daughter gave a dinner to the Mission at his flat. . . . There were vast bowls of solid silver filled with the most exotic flowers which come daily from Pittsburg of all places, where Mellon laid the basis of his fortune. There were great bowls of strawberries out of season, and all the rest in keeping. Mrs. Marshall Field and the other ladies were covered with ropes of pearls. The remains of the dinner would be enough to feed scores of hungry people. Mrs. Grigg discussed this 'conspicuous waste' with Lady Geddes at the Embassy afterwards and Lady Geddes informed her that at the Embassy dinner to the Mission the entrée for each person had cost 4 dollars and that 'the crumbs' left over filled two large packing cases. She had been so shocked at the waste that she had arranged to send to some negro children's orphanage the remains of Embassy dinners. I could not but recall Sir Samuel Dill on 'the Decline and Fall'. Hughes struck Grigg as just an able lawyer, Hoover as anti-British but the ablest man on the Commission. Norman, the Governor of the Bank, they positively loved. Baldwin is obsessed with Lloyd George. He distrusts all orators as dishonest.

10 February   10.30. Gillies from the Labour Party Headquarters brought Dr. Breitscheid here. Breitscheid is a German Socialist M.P. of the intellectual type. He was very pessimistic. The workmen in the Ruhr might maintain their resistance for a few more weeks but they could not stand up much longer to the French pressure. He feared that the Nationalists might start Irish guerilla tactics in the Ruhr or that the Empire might break up. Was it not possible for England and America to mediate? I said I thought America was not ripe and that we were still technically France's ally though our Prime Minister had pointed out that their present policy would prove disastrous. I asked why does not the German Government appeal to America or to the League of Nations or to the neutrals? He had seen the Finance Minister before coming across and was of opinion that if mediation came about Germany would submit to outside control of her finances, outside control of her coal supplies, guarantee of a loan based on German industry and agriculture in the shape of shares held by some international authority. The thing that was most likely to appease the French was immediate cash. I said these terms did not greatly differ from the British proposals in Paris which were sincerely meant by us as reasonable. Detachment, I added, perhaps best described our attitude and the P.M.'s letter before he became Prime Minister that we could not be the policemen of the world was a good index of his mind. Gillies said that the Labour Party would press for more positive intervention. Labour believed our Paris proposals to have been fair but would have been glad to see British reparations wiped out. It was unfortunate, he went on, that Ramsay MacDonald was at the moment Leader owing to his war record. I suggested that Breitscheid ought to see Lord Grey[1]

---

[1] Who as Sir Edward Grey had been Foreign Secretary, 1905–16, and was President of the League of Nations from 1918.

who had the confidence of France. In leaving Breitscheid urged with great earnestness the importance of retaining British troops in Cologne. I crossed over to No. 10 and reported this pessimistic interview to the P.M. who was getting ready to go to Brighton for the weekend. He said that it confirmed the information which was reaching him from other sources but he was surprised to hear the view of the Finance Minister which went beyond what they were saying in public. He gave me back Laurence Housman's *Angels and Ministers* which he said he had read but could not see the point of the last piece *Possessions*. I tried to help him.

21 February Dinner at the Cecil with the German Ambassador (Dr. Sthamer), Dufour (Labour expert at the Embassy), Count Kessler, Sir George Paish, and William Rothenstein. I had been sitting to Rothenstein[1] on the previous day at S. Kensington and he had arranged that I should meet Kessler who was an old friend of his. . . . They all wanted us to intervene with America in the Ruhr business. I quoted the P.M.'s speeches and reiterated that we were still technically the ally of France and that the P.M. had done his utmost to secure a reasonable settlement in Paris. Why did the German Government not work through the neutrals? Kessler replied that the neutrals were too timid. Why then not through America? Why should Germany not appeal to the conscience of mankind and especially to the U.S.A.? They could urge that they had surrendered virtually the 14 points and that America had been a party to the Treaty and then 'ratted'. . . . Kessler said that he had recently been in the Ruhr where he had met a large number of trade union leaders. They were determined to hold out against the French but the habit of the French officers of using the whip on civilians might madden the Germans and bring about some untoward incident. Not a day passed, he said, in which some French intermediary did not approach the German magnates with a view to concluding a gigantic trust, the basic condition of which should be 60 per cent. control by France.

22 February 10.0 a.m. Saw the P.M. and repeated the above to him. He saw nothing of value in the suggestions. If the conclusion of a business agreement between the German and French magnates will produce peace, then why not? He did not seem to mind our exclusion at this stage. I said that I gathered that in Kessler's view if peace were not concluded and the pressure continued for some time the result might be the dissolution of Germany, at which the P.M. remarked that he feared that was what the French really wanted. We then discussed the speech he was to make at the luncheon and he had started rehearsing when we were interrupted by Hankey and Davidson. However after they left he resumed. I urged that he should go pretty far in his reference to the States. What he did in fact say was:

'It is incalculable—incalculable. In my belief, if circumstances had so arranged it that America could have played her part in the peace settlement, as she played it in the war, the world would be in a much better

---

[1] For the result, see the frontispiece to this volume.

position today. I think that truth has entered or is entering, into the minds of the great American people. I hope, I believe, that it has entered the minds of the great American Government, and that when the opportunity offers, that Government will no longer stand aloof from the troubles of the Old World.'

I read him a number of striking and quotable passages from the first volume of R. Stannard Baker's *Life of Woodrow Wilson* but he did not use them. Instead he took a sentence from a speech made by Mr. Page at Plymouth: 'Our standards of character, and of honour and of duty are your standards, and life and freedom have the same meaning to us that they have to you. These are the essential things, and in this we have always been one.'

7 March   Prof. James T. Shotwell to T.J.   Carnegie Endowment for
International Peace, New York City

I was talking today with Mr. Irving T. Bush, who has erected that magnificent building at the end of King's Way on the Strand. I think you know the purpose of the building which is unique. Across the portal above the great pillars of the entrance, it will bear the inscription, 'Dedicated to the friendship of the English speaking peoples.' It is in this spirit that Mr. Bush has undertaken this great enterprise. It is more an institution than a mere business house. Toward the latter part of July it will be ready for the formal opening. Do you suppose that Mr. Bonar Law could speak upon that occasion? . . .

*   *   *   *

. . . I find America much changed from last year. The one topic of interest is foreign affairs. The Government is far behind public opinion. The attitude towards Britain is much more favourable and there is a tendency to regard British policies as having more common sense in them than those of Continental Governments. When will the time come for putting the German question into the hands of business men? I should think it could be done even yet if the objection raised to the Treasury plan that evening in Paris—namely, that the Socialist element would be suspicious of it—were safeguarded against on the one hand; and on the other hand the nationalist feeling and the sense of insecurity in France were met by a promise of non-aggression from Germany such as Cuno intended to offer but spoiled by making his speech appeal to Germans rather than Frenchmen. These are fundamentals and I am inclined to think the more I study the situation that they are the three great fundamentals. Surely it is still possible to realise the plan.

8 March . . . Saw B.L. in the House in the afternoon. Told him I was going to spend the week-end with L.G. His remark was 'He is in a fix and so am I.' He thought it rather looked as if L.G.'s effort at reunion had been rather coldly received by Asquith in his Cambridge speech. L.G. was too impatient. . . .

9 March 6.0. Motored to Churt to spend the week-end. . . . So far from

finding L.G. bored with his book, he was keener than ever on defending himself and on presenting the tremendous effort which Britain put forth in the
war. I think these are his two main motives, and a third no doubt is an
attack on the military for wasting lives in fruitless battles in France. He
always speaks much more tenderly of the Navy and its resourcefulness. I
found there was little in the inner movement of Cabinet politics which he did
not know. He is certainly as much in touch as the Prime Minister with pressmen and important visitors who come to this country. He had heard via
Churchill of the Cabinet Committee on the publication of secret documents.
He knew pretty well how the Cabinet was divided on Irak and that Curzon's
speech recently against universal skedaddle had been as much to his colleagues as to the country. We had ceaseless talk from Friday night till Sunday
night on three or four main topics which recurred again and again. He went
to bed as usual about 10, appeared next morning about 9.0, and rested from
about 3.30 till 5.30. When not at meals we were all out walking.

*　　*　　*　　*

He was very severe on B.L.'s handling of the Paris Conference and thought
it one of the most grave failures of recent years. Every effort ought to have
been made to keep Theunis on our side. The moment Poincaré saw that he
could separate us from the Belgians and Italians the occupation of the Ruhr
was inevitable. I put up the case for B.L. but made little or no impression.
No French statesman now wanted Poincaré's place, he went on, and success
for France now would be far worse for her than failure. The leadership of
Europe for the time had passed to France and we had not only lost our
prestige but also a certain incipient goodwill in Germany. Why had we not
seized on Hughes'[1] Newhaven speech and cabled out to him and prolonged
the discussions thereby? It was a disastrous failure. I asked what could we do
now? He replied that he could think of nothing unless a private interview
between Theunis and B.L. could be arranged so as to endeavour to weaken
Theunis's allegiance to France and obtain his mediation. The furnaces were
shutting down in Belgium for lack of coal and ore and there was therefore a
certain pressure on Theunis. (This suggestion too I passed on to B.L. on my
return but he did not think it was of any value.) 'B.L.', L.G. went on, 'is not
a good leader. He is always waiting for a course which was inevitable. He
could not speak to the country. His words do not travel. He had not the gift
of wireless speech. He has always rested on a more energetic personality.
Carson pushed him through the Ulster rebellion. He rested on me through
the war. Beaverbrook[2] pushed him into the Premiership. Now he has nobody.
Hogg is the only man of quality on his front bench. Bridgeman,[3] his Home

---

[1] C. E. Hughes, U.S. Secretary of State 1921–5, Chief Justice 1930–41.
[2] William Maxwell Aitken (1879–1965), cr. Baron 1917; Conservative M.P. 1910–17;
Minister of Information 1918; newspaper proprietor, owner of the *Daily Express*; a close
friend of Bonar Law.
[3] William Clive Bridgeman (1864–1935); Conservative M.P. 1906–29; Home Secretary
1922–4; First Lord of the Admiralty 1924–9; cr. Viscount 1929.

Secretary, was a positive joke in the coal strike. Salisbury would make a respectable booking clerk.'

. . . I remarked on his dig at the 'strong silent men' in his Rectorial Address and suggested Lord Inverforth was an exception. He agreed and added Birkenhead's name. He was always very silent in Cabinet. Nearly all the big business men he had known were just 'bletherers'—Schwabe, Pirrie, Leverhulme. What, he asked, did I think were politics going to be like in the near future? I replied by asking him what was his programme. I told him of my talk with Philip Kerr and went on to ask was he prepared to attack the rights of property, to subordinate capital to personality, etc., etc. 'But that was my Limehouse speech,' he went on as if Limehouse had been yesterday. 'The Centre Party is dead.' Chamberlain, Birkenhead, Horne, and himself had discharged their mutual obligations. He was all out for Liberal reunion, and he was not given to looking backwards. The land policy and the housing policy were the urgent things. He would not mind a little inflation in order to carry them out. Simon was against reunion because it challenged his chance of leadership. Simon could never make a leader. Some years ago he made a brilliant speech on Income Tax abatements, and a few days after an ineffectual speech on Home Rule. When the contrast was pointed out to Asquith he remarked—'Simon can make a masterly speech on a small topic and only a poor speech on a great one.' 'The rank and file is for reunion. Addison oddly enough, when the subject was debated sometime ago, was for a Centre Party.' I went on to urge that his future lay in leading the Left Wing of Liberalism and coalescing as much as possible with the Right Wing of Labour.

L.G. is finding Hilton Young[1] lacking in initiative as Chief Whip. During our visit it was Beaverbrook who came in for most criticism. I remember he described him at Cannes as a buccaneer. 'He and I are quits, but his treatment of Bonar, to whom he owes every obligation of friendship, is abominable. He dines with you tonight in the most cordial fashion and next morning publishes in his paper a bitter cartoon of you. Burnham would not do that or anything approaching it but that is what Beaverbrook has done with Bonar since his access to power.'

*   *   *   *

The question of drink when staying with L.G. is a diverting one. L.G., who is the most charming host, is always eager to please his guests be they T.T. or the opposite, but he has to respect the very pronounced views of Dame Margaret. Just before dinner on Friday evening cocktails were sent up to Swinton and myself. I have drunk a cocktail on two occasions in my life. . . . The habit is an utterly artificial one, and I returned my cocktail on this occasion undrunk. . . . On Saturday night with only Megan present, the men had champagne. On Sunday night with Dame Margaret present we returned to cider and lemonade, but L.G. took care that a very special cocktail was sent up to Swinton in his bedroom.

[1] Edward Hilton Young (cr. Lord Kennet 1935); Liberal M.P. 1915–29, Conservative M.P. 1929–35; Financial Secretary to the Treasury 1921–2.

19 May Reading between the lines of a leaderette in the *Daily Express* I concluded that B.L.'s resignation was approaching. Rang up the Treasury about 10.40 a.m. Geoffrey Fry replied. He was cryptic. Could not tell me anything on the 'phone. If I wanted to be in town when B.L. returned then I'd better lose no time. Decided to catch the 12.35 from Bristol, due Paddington 4.5. As I was starting for station letter from Sylvester reached me advising me to return.

Saw Waterhouse[1] about 6 p.m. at No. 10. He had met B.L. at Victoria and gone with him to Onslow Gardens, B.L.'s private house. B.L. had told him definitely that he could not go on. Waterhouse had tried to pooh-pooh this (to B.L.'s annoyance as I learnt on Sunday from B.L.). Three doctors were at the moment seeing B.L. Presently Davidson and Fry came in and we got some news of B.L. from D. who had been with him from the landing in Genoa, at Aix and in Paris. B.L.'s depression had in turn defeated Dick Law, Davidson, and Beaverbrook. In Paris they struck Amery en route for Grindelwald and brought him to dinner at the Crillon. Mrs. Davidson also had crossed the Channel, and she and Amery kept the dinner going on Friday evening, B.L. as usual eating nothing or next to nothing. Amery for delaying his resignation until the session ended, so as to give Baldwin time to grow in the esteem of the House and the country. Meanwhile Curzon would only 'expand'. This was the general feeling of us secretaries. We wanted B.L. to hang on to the end of the session. Waterhouse worried at Beaverbrook being so mixed up in affairs. He would be loyal to B.L. to the last, but he and Baldwin were poles asunder. When they found themselves in the same room Baldwin turned his back to him. If Baldwin becomes P.M. Beaverbrook will rend him—unless B.L. restrains him. Baldwin came up from Chequers this evening and dined at the Argentine Club with Davidson.

20 May Baldwin sees B.L. at 10.30 at Onslow Gardens.

Sylvester rings me about 10 to say that an important letter is being sent to the King from B.L., and is being taken to Aldershot by Sykes and Waterhouse.[2]

3.45. Fry asks me to come along and see B.L. Downstairs Lady Sykes, Dick, Kitty, and Fry—all very gloomy. 'The end has come,' said Lady Sykes, 'the doctors say he can't go on.' I felt a lump in my throat and could hardly keep the tears back. I was shown upstairs—Miss Law and Miss Watson left the room. 'Come in, my friend.' 'I hoped you would last out the session,' I said. 'With this constant pain I can't do the work so there's no choice. Read these letters.' He handed me typewritten carbon copies of 1. the doctor's report, 2. his letter to the King, 3. a letter to Curzon ending with a paragraph to the effect that he was not indicating any successor to His Majesty.

He was sitting in the room upstairs where I had congratulated him on

---

[1] Lieut.-Col. (Sir) Ronald Waterhouse, principal private secretary to successive Prime Ministers 1922–8.

[2] This evidence suggests that there is more to the 'Davidson Memorandum' than has been suggested before. The letter set out the claims of Baldwin as against those of Curzon; it was supposed to be only an aide-memoire, but its reception seems to have been well prepared.

his appointment seven months ago. The floor was littered with Sunday news-papers, and at his elbow was a tiny chessboard. A couple of novels were lying about.

His voice was a loud whisper. 'If the King asked for his advice as to a successor he would put Baldwin first.' I said I was sorry for Chamberlain who had been so near the Premiership and who was missing it again. He said that Chamberlain could make a good speech but had not first-rate political ability. Neville was better liked in the House than Austen. I agreed that A.C. was irritable and unable to make friends easily of Members, was impatient even to rudeness when they sought interviews with him. On the other hand, once out of harness he could be very delightful.

We had some talk about his private secretaries. . . .

During tea the baby[1] was the central figure and B.L. fondled and nursed it in (for him) quite a lively fashion. Later he relapsed into a long silence while we chattered. He had taken a dose of veronal the night before and I suggested he should not be entrusted with the bottle but only with the dose. Miss Law agreed that we wanted no inquests on him. Sometime during the afternoon he told me that before going abroad Beaverbrook had contrived a luncheon for B.L. with Rothermere and R. had agreed to call off opposition to B.L. during his absence. Hence the change in the *Daily Mail*.

*   *   *   *

About 9.30 Sylvester came along to a belated supper, bringing with him the rough draft of a Memorandum[2] which Waterhouse had taken this afternoon to Stamfordham for the King's guidance in choosing a successor. This docu-ment was heavily loaded in favour of Baldwin and left no doubt whatever as to the choice favoured by the writer. It pictured Curzon endeavouring to deal with a deputation from the Triple Alliance and similar labour organisa-tions; declared that Lord Derby would not serve under Curzon; Baldwin could form a Government without Curzon, but Curzon could not without Baldwin. The memorandum was drawn up last night at No. 10 by Amery and Davidson, and no doubt was seen by B.L. It was 'unofficial' and to be treated by Stamfordham with the utmost secrecy and used for the King's guidance. B.L. made no reference to it in talking with me. Baldwin returned to Chequers at noon today. How far he had been privy to the contents of the document I don't know.[3] Some six or eight weeks ago, when B.L. was at Torquay, Curzon had written to B.L. setting forth his claims to the succession. B.L. had replied briefly that there was no truth in the rumour that he was resigning. This was probably just after the *Observer* article.

At 7 p.m. I 'phoned to Criccieth and told Dame Margaret Lloyd George of B.L.'s resignation.

[1] Lady Sykes's baby.

[1] See p. 235 and note.

[3] It is unlikely that Bonar Law knew about this memorandum, which was only intended to set out his views as his staff understood them. Baldwin was almost certainly in complete ignorance of it, having been told personally by Law to expect Curzon as his successor and agreed to serve under him.

21 May Wrote a short tribute to B.L. this morning and sent it by train from Paddington to the *Western Mail*, Cardiff.

B.L. undergoes a 'minor operation' on the glands. This was to find out if there were any malignant disease about.

*   *   *   *

Stamfordham busy canvassing opinion. *Morning Post* is for Baldwin, *Daily Telegraph* for Curzon, *Observer* yesterday for Balfour.

22 May Press tending to put Curzon's chances higher than Baldwin's.

At 11.0 saw Davidson who said it was 100 to 1 in favour of Baldwin. If right then Baldwin would want me to carry on. I said B. did not know me, nor did I know Baldwin. 'Baldwin knew of me from B.L. and others.' I said I would gladly serve him as well as I knew how. Ran into Bridgeman, full of worries about the Irish deportees and the Indemnity Bill. I said I was glad Art O'Brien had been rearrested as he was a treacherous villain. 'Did I think L.G. would attack the Bill?' I said L.G. would do nothing to hurt the Free State. . . .

At 3.30 to No. 10 and discovered that Stanley Baldwin had been summoned to the Palace and had gone off in a top hat and frock coat and was to be the new P.M. All of us astonished at the swiftness of his ascent. Six years in office. Very nearly becoming Speaker when Whitley was appointed. A plain man, domesticated like B.L., fond of books and music and walks in the country. Nothing like B.L.'s brain—much slower and always eager to consult one or two others before coming to a decision; but stands by his decision once taken. Who were his political intimates? I asked Fry. He thought Bridgeman and Johnny Baird!!

At 4.25 Berry, the chief messenger, came in, very pale and agitated, and said, 'Mr. Baldwin wishes you to inform Mr. Bonar Law that he has accepted the Premiership and is forming a Government.' Gower 'phoned this to Onslow Gardens and we trooped along to No. 11 to offer our congratulations. On the way we ran into Warren Fisher and Boyd Carpenter on the same errand. . . . We found the new P.M. very self-conscious in his frock coat, surrounded by his wife and daughters. 'Thank God,' shouted Warren Fisher with the fervour of an Archdeacon. I shook hands and the P.M. said: 'I shall want you to hold my hand, Tom.' 'I'll be a cabin boy with pleasure,' I replied and we all trooped out again. I crossed to tell Hankey the news and to arrange to ring up private secretaries and ask them to send in the resignations of their respective chiefs.

I hear tonight that a great effort is to be made to get Chamberlain and Horne back to office, Chamberlain as Foreign Secretary if Curzon does not continue and Horne at the Treasury.

28 May My first proper interview with S.B. alone in the Cabinet Room. After a very friendly greeting, his face started twitching, he rolled his tongue about, and looking away into space he began: 'There are three things I want to do. We've got to settle Europe. We can't wait for Emigration and Empire

Development. We live by our export trade and can't afford to let Europe go to pieces with all the serious economic consequences.' 'And the social reactions?' I interpolated. 'We must remember Disraeli's third canon—the welfare of the people,' he went on, 'and we must try to avoid a break with Russia. Curzon will see Krassin and try to arrange the withdrawal by the Soviet Government of their Afghan propagandist agents.' I said this country would regard it as very stupid to break with Russia because of the doings of some Bolshevik in Teheran. He agreed. Then he turned to the agitation among the miners for the break up of their wages agreement. They were asking for facilities to bring in a Minimum Wage Bill—as a flank movement. Would I find out did they mean this seriously?

I then told him of the method I followed with B.L.—that I did not *write* speeches but talked over their substance with him and that just before their delivery he rehearsed them to me; that I watched and marked the foreign press for him, etc.

29 May 10.30 a.m. Saw Mines Dept. who were against giving facilities for discussion of the Minimum Wage Bill. Held that the straight thing was to tell the Miners that the Government were absolutely against the Bill. I took the opposite view: the pacific leaders were anxious to preserve the agreement, avoid a strike, and proceed by constitutional methods. We should back them and force the Whips to find a day to ventilate the position in the coalfield. During the day the Mines Dept. came round to this view.

11.15 a.m. Put the two views to the P.M. He said there must be no 'finessing' with the deputation (a dig at L.G.'s methods); his chief asset with Labour was his reputation for plain dealing. I said that if he gave the miners a day for their Bill, he could at the same time tell them that the Govt. would oppose it. That would be frank.

6.0 p.m. P.M. meets Lloyd-Greame, Lane-Fox, and officials of Mines Dept. Lloyd-Greame against facilities; I for and Gowers[1] ditto. Lloyd-G. then suggested we might ask miners to surrender one of their Supply Days. This agreed.

7.0 p.m. Deputation introduced by Ramsay MacDonald—very friendly. Hartshorn[2] out for mischief and pressed P.M. Would the Whips be taken off? P.M. hedged and Ramsay MacDonald helped him out on that point. S.B. handled deputation admirably, smoked his pipe and put everyone at ease.

1 June P.M. tells me that he wants to make a 'powerful oration' on the Miners' question when it comes up. I tell him of the pressure which will come from Labour for an Air Conference to limit war building of the countries against each other. He said that as soon as peace was signed in Europe that would be the first question he would raise. P.M. sees Philippe Millet, and Wickham Steed sent a letter to cover one from Marcel Ray

[1] (Sir) Ernest Gowers (1880–1967), civil servant and writer, who was Permanent Under-Secretary for Mines 1920–7.

[2] Vernon Hartshorn (1872–1932); miners' leader; Labour M.P. 1918–31; Postmaster-General 1924; Lord Privy Seal 1930–1.

(Loucheur's journalist) who was eager to see S.B. and other leading politicians.[1]

3 June   To 28 Queen Anne's Gate to dine alone with Haldane. . . . He knew Baldwin as a member of the Grillions, the oldest dining club in London. A man of sense, put in like B.L. by the machine (and might keep in power for several years) as Asquith was, and B.L. L.G. had no message to deliver. The country did not know Grey, and Simon was an 'able lawyer'. Curzon was bitterly disappointed at missing the Premiership. When Stamfordham came to him on the Tuesday, C. and Lady C. were expecting that he came to tell C. to proceed to the Palace. When S. broke the news C. said, 'And this is the reward of 44 years' service.' C. did not know what forces were against him. He neglected the House of Lords and took no interest in home affairs. He had ability, experience, industry, but no judgment.

Haldane said he was giving much time to Air Defence, especially to the creation of a General Staff. We hadn't one. He had put in a paper to the C.I.D. and was to dine this week with Sam Hoare and Trenchard and pump ideas into them. This led to talk of the Expeditionary Force and the War Office Staff. Winston's account of his appointment to the Admiralty in *The World Crisis* was not very close to the facts.[2] Asquith had arranged that Haldane should go to the Admiralty to build up a Naval General Staff, as he had done at the War Office. When he got there he found Winston had arrived before him. 'He is an importunate widow,' said Asquith, 'begging to be given the Admiralty.' Asquith shut both of them up in a room together to fight it out. Haldane gave in on condition that Winston would undertake to create a General Staff. This he did and H. spent three days later on at the Admiralty showing how it should be done.

H. wants us to set about building up an Air Force big enough to meet and defeat anything France can send against us, and when that is on the way we can talk with effect about limitation of aircraft. France will pay no heed to us unless she is so confronted.

4 June   Pembroke Wicks dropped in to tea. He is one of Curzon's private secretaries, but is given hardly anything to do. C. wanted a secretary with a knowledge of shorthand but he has not dictated more than two letters in six months to Wicks. For the last two months Wicks has been charged with the keeping of C.'s domestic accounts for his various houses, paying servants' wages, etc., all of which C. goes through minutely with Wicks. The other day C. enlisted his aid in packing up cushions, cretonne covers and draperies in tissue paper and boxes—though there were sixteen servants in the house —so difficult does C. find it to delegate any work to others. He keeps a duplicate set of Cabinet papers and other official documents at Carlton House Terrace, handling and sorting them himself and not using his secretaries.

[1] Loucheur came later, bearing a French proposal for a reparation settlement.
[2] In *The World Crisis*, pp. 67–68, Churchill stated that Asquith invited him to Scotland early in October and offered him the Admiralty. After he had accepted, Asquith said he could talk it over with Haldane the next day. Haldane's biography gives a third version.

Wicks confirmed C.'s intense disappointment at not being summoned to the Palace. After making up his mind to co-operate with the new Government he disappeared to Kedleston for a few days and returned to do the magnanimous thing by proposing Baldwin as leader of the party.

8 June . . . Lionel Curtis came to see me about Ireland. The Die-Hards are making one more effort to wreck the Treaty Settlement. They are working up the grievances of the Loyalists in the columns of *The Morning Post*. Carson has a letter in today headed: 'The Betrayal of Irish Loyalists: Government Inaction', and Salisbury has written a letter to the Duke of Devonshire[1] clamouring for a die-hard policy which would not only wreck the Treaty but would smash this Government. Fortunately the Duke has too much sense and honesty. The Irish Land Bill, which Carson calls confiscation, is more generous than the Loyalists expected and the landowners on the Irish Senate know and admit it. Cosgrave has done better than any of us imagined possible. If we destroy him what is the alternative? Arthur Griffith's case against Dominion Status was that with Ireland so near we'd always be wanting to meddle. Is Baldwin prepared to stand up to Salisbury? I shall put all this to him. The Cabinet Committee on Irish Affairs has, beside the Duke (in the chair), Cave (die-hard in this context), Amery (no judgment), Ormsby-Gore (defers to his papa-in-law)[2], and Joynson-Hicks[3] who has die-hard antecedents but has only just gone to the Treasury.

The new German Note appears in the Press today, briefer and more pointed than usual, and with an appeal for a conference. Possibly Keynes who has been to Berlin had something to do with its manner. Baldwin has today seen Norman[4] (the Governor of the Bank), McKenna, and Lord Grey —all friends of a reasonable attitude to Germany. Eyre Crowe and Norman have discussed extent of French financial borrowings from U.K., and degree to which we could depress value of franc with a view to bringing France to her senses. Not much to be hoped in this direction. Opinion at No. 10 is that we shall get back to something very like B.L.'s January offer in Paris.

9 June . . . Talked with Davidson about a possible scheme of universal old age pensions, and suggest that S.B. instruct Watson, the [Government] Actuary, to explore the ground. Davidson says truly it is a subject which Worthington-Evans could make his own, and incidentally it should be given him so as to keep him off reparations.

Baldwin last night guest of the Canning and Chatham Clubs at Oxford. He burnt some incense at the bust of Disraeli, and had a dig at L.G. 'One

[1] Who, as Colonial Secretary, was also responsible for Irish affairs.
[2] Lord Salisbury.
[3] William Joynson-Hicks (1865–1932); Conservative M.P. 1908–29; Postmaster General and Paymaster General 1923; Financial Secretary to the Treasury, with Cabinet seat 1923; Minister of Health 1923–4; Home Secretary 1924–9; cr. Viscount Brentford 1929; usually known as Jix.
[4] Montagu Collet Norman (1871–1950); Governor of the Bank of England 1920–44; cr. Baron 1944.

morning they opened their newspapers and read that Mr. L.G. said that Mr. Bonar Law is honest to the verge of simplicity. The British people said: "By God, that is what we have been looking for." Although I cannot hope to emulate my late leader, Mr. Bonar Law, if those six words can be uttered of me when the General Election takes place, I shall be a proud man as an individual and I shall have every confidence in the success of the party I am leading.'

10 June, Sunday   4.15 p.m. To Onslow Gardens. Before going upstairs saw Lady Sykes, who gave me the latest news of Bonar. The X ray treatment was very exhausting. She went with him to Harley Street. The expedition and treatment took about two hours and a half. He had two more visits to make after which B.L. hoped he might go out of town. She was certain that he did not know what was wrong with him and that he thought it was only 'enlarged glands'. He was taking drugs every four hours to deaden the pain. I told her that if that were so and if the doses were at all considerable, he would not last long. She went upstairs and I followed a little later so that B.L. might not guess we had been discussing him in advance. Miss Law and Sir F. Sykes there—a subdued tea party and it took me some time to raise the temperature to a mild cheerfulness. Seeing the *Observer* on the floor I remarked that I was sorry that he still bothered to read newspapers, that I found the headlines of the middle page of the *Observer* ample for my needs, and that Asquith had declared that Garvin's *Life of Joseph Chamberlain* was to run to eight volumes at least. We quickly got on to more serious stuff. He thought it had been a mistake to hurry the Germans with their Reply, that the French were still impossible. He thought Baldwin had begun well. I mentioned Salisbury and Ireland as a snag. B.L. replied that the real trouble would be over the Boundary Commission—it was a very dangerous topic. I agreed that we ought to play for its indefinite postponement but that doubtless Cosgrave would have to raise it in view of the autumn elections. The family moved out and left us alone but only for a moment. McKenna and Beaverbrook came in. Beaverbrook began at once to attack Baldwin's Oxford speech and the unfortunate 'By God'. I agreed that the British public preferred a statesmen who asked (as S.B. had done) for their prayers to one who descended to such blasphemy. McKenna gave a gloomy account of trade prospects—cotton bad, wool, iron and steel sagging, coal good. Then to the Coal Agreement. I said we could not accept the Minimum Wage Bill, but we might have to raise the present minimum somewhat. B.L. joined in all this with a perfectly clear mind, and to me his voice seemed better than a fortnight ago, but his face was much more lined, worn, and sad. Beaverbrook and I motored off to Putney and had tea again in his garden, while McKenna played chess with B.L. B.L. won two out of three games, McKenna announced when he joined us later in Beaverbrook's garden.

Political gossip is the breath of life to Beaverbrook, and we had an hour of it while waiting for McKenna. I had not talked with B. since I dined with him at Cannes. I knew from Miss Watson of his utter devotion to B.L. during these last months. Our talk was of B.L., L.G., and Baldwin. I said that I had realised on B.L.'s return from Torquay that he was done. B. said the blow came over the Washington Debt. B.L. was against Baldwin's proposals and understood that S.B. was returning to discuss them with the Cabinet. In the meantime B.L. had seen the editors of *The Times* and *Morning Post*, and Beaverbrook, with a view to securing their opposition to the American demands. Then came Baldwin's press interview at Southampton on landing, which upset the applecart. B.L. found himself almost alone in the Cabinet and realised for the first time and with a shock that he was not its master as L.G. had been. Thenceforward his grip slackened and his depression increased, and when he returned from Torquay he had thrown up the sponge. But B. did not then any more than the doctors or the rest of us imagine that cancer was at work. I thought it was worry over the Ruhr, as B.L. more than once admitted.

From Aix, B.L. had sent a 'de profundis' letter to B. begging him to come out or he would throw himself under a train. When B. got there he found B.L. taking about 10 doses of anti-carnia daily to keep down the pain he was suffering. They hurried to Paris where Sir Thomas Horder met them and ordered B.L. to London. The plan then had been to avoid resignation until the end of the session so as to give Baldwin time to prove his quality as Leader of the House.

Early in June it became clear that a decision on the question of the Irish Boundary Commission could no longer be postponed, and that both sides had prepared totally irreconcilable cases to present to the Commission.

T.J.'s papers contain many letters about Irish affairs from various correspondents, including Lionel Curtis, and his interest in them remained as keen as ever. The Civil War had ended, after nearly a year, in May 1923, leaving the Free State Government so impoverished that it only survived through a £3 million loan from the Irish banks. To make its position more secure, the Government called for another election in August and Cosgrave warned the British Government that he would have to demand the appointment of the Boundary Commission. In London, arrangements were made to invite Cosgrave and Craig to a conference at which this difficult question, with the threat of further violence when the Commission's award was known, might be avoided.

29 September, Saturday   To Chequers, arriving in time for dinner, with S.B. and Mrs. B. only in residence. We had grouse, the gift of 'Jack' Pierpont Morgan. P.M. drank whisky and remarked that he had drunk more champagne in the last few months than in many years and that he found it 'bucked him up', for the speechmaking which consumed so much nervous energy. Mrs. B.'s talk chiefly domestical—the Office of Works should appoint a woman to look after the linen and blankets in the ministerial residences; she had to use the same curtains as Mrs. Gladstone, and as they had been repeatedly washed instead of being cleaned, they had shrunk and were too short for the long windows of Downing Street; the bath at No. 10 had been put in for Disraeli, it had a lid on, was deep and narrow and dangerous. . . . She and S.B. were devoted to Chequers. . . .

After dinner we sat in the Long Gallery. I recalled the visit of Arthur

Griffith and the other Irishmen. S.B. said the library was that of an old-fashioned country house, with the usual standard editions of eighteenth century writers, but without a Life of Johnson, so far as he could find out. Bonar had been to Chequers for one night in L.G.'s time, S.B. thought.[1] . . .

30 September, Sunday   Breakfast at 9.0 with P.M. only, and then a promenade in the rose garden until 10.0, chiefly gossip about leading figures in politics. I have found that he likes to draw me to talk about L.G.—who is something of an obsession. 'I don't really know him,' he said. 'I had made up my mind for reasons which seemed good to my conscience, when at Aix—years ago—that I could not carry on and I had not the faintest notion that I should land here.[2] . . . The English people will never stand a Dictator.' I said one could say fifty things of L.G. that might appear contradictory and all would be true. I talked of his vitality, his power of sleeping in crises, his swiftness, his magnanimity, his use of the 'Sutherland' type, his debt to his old uncle and to Wales, his cheerfulness, humour, oratorical gifts. 'Could he speak well in Welsh?' I described L.G.'s speech in perfect Welsh, at the Mold Eisteddfod, on the best type of nationalism, a matter of 'culture' not of tariffs and boundaries and warfare.

Then to other names. Austen Chamberlain's woodenness, Neville's greater promise. Sir Laming Worthington-Evans—now P.M.G., very disgruntled. 'I have seen him twice and told him I'll do what is possible for him.' But the City would never stand him at the Treasury owing to his professional antecedents. 'Curzon is difficult—very bad-tempered in the forenoon but better as the day advances. He gets on Eyre Crowe's nerves, but Sir William Tyrrell[3] has humour and can handle him better. If anything happened to Curzon I should try to bring Grey back as Foreign Secretary.' Then some talk of unemployment, the grievances of farmers, the fruit growing around Evesham, of Bewdley where S.B. was born with its Welsh gate, the road to Ludlow, the poems of A. E. Housman, all very superficially, but all revealing a deep attachment to the English countryside.

At 10.0 went down in the study to work on the draft of his speech at the opening of the Imperial Conference. I had given it to him on Friday to take with him. He had read it. It was inevitably patchwork stitched together from the contributions of various departments—Treasury on Reparations and American debt, F.O. on the Ruhr, Turkey, and Corfu, India Office on India, Ministry of Labour on Unemployment. The real trouble was over the Ruhr pages, which under Tyrrell's influence made us grovel to the French to the annoyance of Niemeyer of the Treasury. I weakened the F.O. draft in various ways, by rejection and expansion. Tyrrell wanted the reference to our

[1] Law never used Chequers when he was Prime Minister, and Baldwin had occupied it instead, as Chancellor of the Exchequer.

[2] This decision was actually taken in September 1922 and led directly to the Carlton Club meeting and the fall of the Coalition.

[3] William George Tyrrell (1866–1947): Assistant Under-Secretary, Foreign Office, 1918–25; principal adviser to Lord Curzon at Lausanne 1922–3; Permanent Under-Secretary 1925–8; Ambassador in Paris 1928–34; a lifelong advocate of friendship with France; cr. Baron 1929.

'generous offer' in Paris in January to go out, but S.B. kept it in. A passage where I had said that history would condemn the Ruhr occupation went out. He was pleased with my phrase from Disraeli describing Great Britain as 'a moderating and mediatorial power' in the councils of Europe, and said it would please his party. The reference to the interview with Poincaré[1] was held up for discussion with Tyrrell in the evening. We agreed the whole of the remainder. He wrote himself, in a shy way, the passage beginning, 'The economic condition of Europe makes it essential that we should turn our eyes elsewhere . . . material condition of the people.' This was the only paragraph he actually wrote. In the midst of our talk the Sunday papers arrived and he scrutinised them swiftly and rather anxiously, beginning with the *Observer*. 'What madness is Garvin up to today?' He ran quickly through the Political Notes and was fairly satisfied. Then to Beaverbrook's *Sunday Express*, Berry's *Sunday Times*, and the Rothermere papers. His normal pose is one of indifference to the Press—a recoil from L.G.'s known interest in it —but his eagerness today gave him away.

Soon after eleven we joined Mrs. Baldwin and walked to the beacon and had a good view of the far stretching wooded plain below towards Oxford in the west and Aylesbury in the north. Some of the landscape can be seen both from Chequers and from their Worcestershire home. More talk about L.G.—not my doing. I stressed his tremendous services during the War, his firm hold of the central importance of national unity, his willingness to compromise for its sake, his buoyancy in the darkest hours. Perhaps his tolerance of rather crooked characters was due to his 'good nature'; he had most catholic sympathies. More domesticities: no bribe would persuade Mrs. B. to keep a cat; once when a guest at a dinner party, a cat jumped on to her lap and she screamed. We returned at one and I read alone Bury's *Idea of Progress* until the gong sounded. The talk turned chiefly on what the Baldwins would do when out of office—the founding of a Maternity Home was one project; S.B. would start reading again. He found he had no energy available for serious reading now. No, he would not write any memoirs; he could not live up to the literary standard set his in family circle—Kipling, Burne Jones, etc. A P.M. was bothered all day with someone or other reporting discontent here, there, and everywhere. Colonel Gretton wanted to call Parliament a fortnight before the appointed day in order to pass a tariff!! Horne was doing well as a commercial traveller. I suggested that his good stories was the secret probably, as also of his political ascent. Much talk by me of importance of Bonar's co-operation with L.G. during the War and of its elusive character when the story comes to be written.

Signed the Visitor's Book and left at 2.30 to catch my train at Wendover. Very hard to realise that I was leaving the Prime Minister of this country in that 'Temple of Peace', and that on the morrow he would address the whole wide world as the chief representative of the greatest empire the world has ever seen. Is honesty enough? As I picked up my office pouch in the study I noticed on the desk a pocket edition of the Parables of Jesus.

[1] Baldwin's personal interview with Poincaré, on 19 September, which began the détente over the problem of the Ruhr.

At six to the Cabinet Office to have the draft typed as so far approved, with the last paragraph on the Ruhr to follow in the morning. At eight to dine with Lionel Curtis. At 10.0 with him to the Hotel Victoria to see President Cosgrave and Desmond Fitzgerald. . . .

1 October, Monday 10.30 a.m. Saw P.M. at No. 10. He handed me draft paragraph on Ruhr concocted by himself and Tyrrell the night before at Chequers. He added, 'I don't think much of the result.' I said at once that it would not do, and that it made no reference to the Poincaré interview for news of which the country was clamouring. As ministers were trooping in Davidson and I went into the next room and scribbled: 'At this moment . . . difficulties.' The P.M. approved and I had it typed at once and inserted in his copy. Then Curzon approved and added, 'A fuller . . . affairs.' By this time it was nearly 11.0 and time for the Conference to begin. Baldwin, Salisbury, Curzon, Devonshire, and Lloyd-Greame (Board of Trade) were the British representatives, seated right and left of the P.M. with backs to the fire. Opposite the P.M. sat Mackenzie King.[1] The big bowl of red roses from Chequers had been removed, at my suggestion, to a side table. On Mackenzie King's right came Smuts, Burton,[2] and de Wet, the South African Minister of Justice. Next to him Cosgrave and Desmond Fitzgerald, and the stenographers. At the opposite end was the distinguished figure of the Maharajah of Alwar[3] in a native dress of figured fabric, with buttons of precious stones, bracelets, white gloves, and a dark green headgear fronted with a large and dazzling wheelshaped jewel. At his side was Sir Tej Bahadur Sapru[4]—both shepherded by Lord Peel.[5] Massey of New Zealand and Warren of Newfoundland completed the delegation. There were half a dozen secretaries seated behind their chiefs. The P.M. read his speech, every word with considerable animation. It took half an hour. He had rehearsed it to Mrs. Baldwin on Sunday, he told me. Then followed the other Prime Ministers—Smuts making the only important speech and there could be no mistaking the joy with which he welcomed the Irishmen. He spoke with great ease and rapidity, often dropping into very confidential tones. Ever since Smuts' telegram of 7 July,[6] the P.M. had been nervous of the attitude Smuts will take on the Ruhr business and I had him in mind in drafting parts of the P.M.'s speech. The British Empire, 'this greatest machine on earth', ought to pull its weight in settling the affairs of Europe—was the burden of his speech. We should strengthen the League of Nations. We cannot disinterest ourselves in Europe where there is a rapid worsening of conditions. Cosgrave followed, looking pale and speaking in a 'soft' voice, then Warren for a moment, followed by

[1] Prime Minister of Canada.
[2] Henry Burton, South African Finance Minister and a former member of the Imperial War Cabinet.
[3] One of the smaller Indian princely states.
[4] Representative of the Government of India. Later a delegate at the Round Table Conferences 1930–2.
[5] Secretary of State for India.
[6] Approving Curzon's warning to France and Belgium over the occupation of the Ruhr, and suggesting Britain should renounce the Entente.

the Maharajah. He had some sheets of foolscap in front of him with his speech written out, but he had learnt it, and kept twirling a long pencil above the sheets to show his independence of them. He spoke right out with an almost unctuous pride, on behalf not only of the Princes of India but 'in the name of the 300 millions of people of my country', 'the oldest civilisations within the Empire', 'the youngest in self-government', 'with toleration the world [could] be made the playground for God's children'; 'beyond the Empire was Humanity and the great Divinity of which after all each one of us are but active sparks'. Then came the Message to the King and of sympathy to Japan and the first meeting of the Imperial Conference was at an end.

2 October, Tuesday Press disappointed with the meagreness of Baldwin's statement about the Poincaré interview.

First meeting of the Economic Conference, under Lloyd-Greame's chairmanship. I introduced McGrath, Irish Free State, to him, but did not stay for the meeting—a crowd of about seventy, meeting in Peel's old drawing room.[1]

3 October, Wednesday Second meeting of the Imperial Conference. The Duke of Devonshire, looking more than ever like a pedigree bull in an agricultural show, read for forty minutes a review of the history of the Crown Colonies and Protectorates during the last two years—very impressive in its cumulative effect: West Indies, Africa, Ceylon, Malaya, Hong Kong, Fiji, the Falklands, and the use of Scott's 'Discovery' for research into whaling, Iraq, Palestine, and Trans-Jordania. Smuts urged the importance of keeping through communications by an all-British route from the extreme north to the extreme south of Africa and of not allowing Belgium to interrupt this. We should hold on to Palestine. 'There is no more subtle influence working in the world, I hope for good, than the influence of that international people (the Jews), full of brains and character, and dominating much bigger nations in many parts of the world through the filtration of their ideas and policies.'

Curzon replied. He and Montagu had been against the Balfour Declaration on the 'National Home'—an ambiguous phrase, but the engagement was given and incorporated in an agreement before the world at San Remo and repeated in the original Treaty of Versailles. We cannot now recede. If we did the French would step in and then be on the threshold of Egypt and on the outskirts of the canal. Besides Palestine needed ports, electricity, and the Jews of America were rich and would subsidise such development. We must be fair and firm with the Arabs showing no invidious preference to the Zionists.

5 October 10.45 a.m. Third meeting of the Imperial Conference. This was to be Curzon's day and will he rise to the occasion? He arrived a little late. Baldwin welcomed Mr. Graham, Minister of Railways from Canada, and Kevin O'Higgins, the ablest of Cosgrave's Cabinet, who was present for the

[1] In Whitehall Gardens, since demolished.

first time, Cosgrave being detained in Dublin with labour troubles. Then we all stood to hear the King's message of acknowledgment of the greetings of his Imperial Ministers. We were 27 present not including the stenographers, who changed in rotation every quarter of an hour. Curzon sat on Baldwin's left, Hankey and Devonshire on his right, and I sat immediately behind them. Maps had been pinned around the room, especially a big one of Asia Minor. The Maharajah had a new robe and precious buttons on, with a blue satin English-made overcoat, and the white gloves as before. Neither his secretary nor the Irish McGilligan were allowed in today owing to the confidential character of the speech to which we were to listen.

Curzon began at four minutes to eleven and finished at twenty to two —seated throughout. There was a good fire burning and all windows were closed. By 12 o'clock the bulky form of Massey showed signs of falling asleep; at 12.30 one or two others including S.B. were suppressing yawns; Curzon himself alternated from moments of tremendous vigour when he read to moments of lassitude when he improvised. He opened in fine style, shining away at his spectacles and appealing for secrecy, pronouncing the first *e* short. They wanted the truth and he would conceal nothing. He had a bundle of typed notes before him prepared in the various departments of the Foreign Office, but these he had read, cut up with scissors, and scrawled all over with characteristic phrases, by way of alteration or additions to the official memoranda. He had to deal with two years packed with incidents, crises, alarms and excursions, even with tragedies. Although it was now nearly 5 years since the Armistice was signed in a railway carriage in France, the tramp of armed men was still heard upon the Continent, and you had only to pick up your daily paper to hear the rumbles of almost chronic revolution in your ears. So he began his survey of the five continents. We were in the centre of a great world whirlpool and we were affected by every movement of its waters. There were flickers of light in Turkey, Egypt, and the Washington Treaty; Poland, the League of Nations. The real base of British moral authority was our loyalty to our word and to our colleagues and Allies. We have no further conquests that we desire to make. At home we had disbanded our forces with almost undue alacrity. The world knew this. We were weary of war and the very idea of war was repugnant to our people. Certain elements in our Press, powerful, wealthy, wholly unscrupulous, a source of weakness. Then dropping into a serious and confidential whisper he proceeded to refer to France in a passage for which all had been waiting:

Our real difficulty during the past two years has been the difficulty of working in absolute sincerity and friendship with our great neighbours across the Channel, the frequent desertions and the almost chronic lack of loyalty in great emergencies of the Government of France. I will give you concrete illustrations. She has broken away from us over and over again. In M. Millerand's day you will remember her unauthorised excursion into Frankfurt and the neighbouring towns. In M. Briand's day she concluded without our knowledge and behind our backs a secret Treaty with the Turks at Angora, the whole source of my difficulties at Lausanne. In the war between Greece and Turkey, although we bound ourselves to neither party and faithfully adhered to pledges, she steadily provided arms for Mustapha Kemal with which he succeeded in defeating the Greeks. At Lausanne I found her a faithless ally, deserting me at the pinch everywhere and carrying this attitude and these proceedings to a point at which the leading French delegate, M. Barrière, left the Conference and threw up his post sooner than carry out the instructions for surrender over the whole field and the abandonment of our cause which he had received from M. Poincaré in Paris. In January of the present year, as you know, in the face of our opposition she persisted in rushing into the Ruhr. Now these are facts; nobody can dispute them, and we have to realise that there is no altruism in the policy of our great neighbour. She is out for definite objects. The war gave her the opportunity, and with a defeated enemy and a distracted Europe, she aspires to attain, and she has already attained to some extent, the domination of the European continent. Her government is presided over by a minister of great ability and untiring zeal but of a stiff and rigid nature. She has a Parliament which is absolutely subservient to his decrees. She has a public opinion that would support him in any measures taken against a defeated enemy. She is pursuing a policy that in our view at any rate is far from being favourable to the recovery of the world. Now, do not imagine that when I use these words I use them lightly or that I am inspired by the smallest animus against our great neighbour and ally. No one is a more profound believer than myself in the policy of the Entente, and I do not rest that belief merely on the memories of the war, on principles of self-interest; my conviction is based on the widest considerations of world peace and world progress. If France and ourselves permanently fall out, I see no prospect of the recovery of Europe or the pacification of the world. To maintain that unity we have made innumerable sacrifices. During the last two years I have preached no other doctrine and I have pursued no other practice. During the last year alone I spent nearly as much time on the continent as I did in this country, endeavouring at every stage with laborious hands to build up that unity. I cannot say truthfully that this loyalty has received any encouragement, still less any imitation. These are things which I cannot possibly say in public but of which I shall give proofs as I go along. Some I have given you already. They make the task of conducting British foreign policy extremely difficult, and the qualities which a British foreign minister should now cultivate seem to be those not of cleverness or astuteness, still less of enterprise or daring, but those of endless patience and an equanimity that never falters. When I was in India I used to sit weekly in the Viceroy's chair under the picture of Warren Hastings, and on that picture was written the motto—his motto—'Mens aequa in arduis'. I have often thought since that a better motto could not possibly be taken for the work that a Foreign Minister has now to discharge.

18 October, Thursday 10.40. Saw P.M. at No. 10 and had some talk about forthcoming speech at Plymouth. He had had a 'brainwave' on unemployment, and thought it possible to expedite the building of cruisers, overhauling of dockyard equipment and stores, and he had asked the Admiralty to look into the matter. Then saw Hankey who was wrath with the two Indian delegates because of the rumour that they might walk out of the Conference if they got nothing. Hankey thought it a mistake to have allowed them in at all—he would let them walk out or he would not give an answer to their demands until the very last day when it would be too late to walk out. Prompted by Curtis I've been trying to fix up an interview between the P.M. and Sir Tej Bahadur Sapru. Latter and Peel do not like each other. Sapru wants at least the promise of an enquiry into how best to give effect to the resolution of the last Imperial Conference on equal citizenship for Indians in the Empire.

22 October, Monday   To No. 10. Temperature abnormal. Davidson who had been to Chequers was almost shouting, 'C.M.G.' (Curzon must go). There had been trouble over meeting Masaryk yesterday. The P.M. had gone to Chequers to entertain some of the Dominion Premiers. Curzon had gone to Kedleston. It had therefore been arranged that two private secretaries should go to the station. When the King heard of this he was wroth and said P.M. and Curzon ought to be there. Gower[1] tried to bring the P.M. but he refused as he wanted to talk with the Premiers. Gower tried Curzon. He protested he would have to get up at 5.0 to catch a suitable Sunday train. Gower pointed out that there was a train at 11 a.m. but Curzon replied that he did not travel by that line! Ultimately it was arranged that Derby and Amery should meet the visitors. Davidson thinks Edward Wood would do for the Foreign Office.

There was a marked feeling among the Private Secretaries that Baldwin's position had rapidly worsened in the last few days. The Premiers were disgruntled at telegrams being sent in their names to Washington and Paris without any consultation.[2] Curzon, it was said, was resisting discussion at the Imperial Conference as the subject of the telegrams was a routine F.O. matter.

I went in and saw the P.M. and . . . urged him to take the Premiers into fuller confidence. It was no use trying to fob them off and then table a lot of resolutions at the last moment. He appeared to agree. I then asked had he taken advantage of their visit to Chequers to talk over the French and Ruhr situation. He said, 'No!' but it was plain that his attitude to Poincaré was hardening. I said, 'It is not enough to have one honest man at an interview.' 'Poincaré has lied,' said S.B., 'I was led to believe that when passive resistance ceased he'd negotiate with the Germans.'[3] A few minutes later ministers began to troop in for the meeting of the Cabinet where arrangements for Armistice Day and the relief of unemployment were discussed.

23 October   Luncheon with Sir Edward Grigg at 9 Little College Street. Much gossip of L.G.'s visit to the States, of S.B., and the future of Parties. I hinted that there would be a 'return to Protection' campaign and a general election very quickly or next autumn—the Budget would make it difficult to have an election in the spring. We agreed that this was happening too soon for L.G. and that there would be wild confusion. There was no champion in the Government ranks comparable to Joseph Chamberlain. I saw no one with the ability and drive required to make the case. He told me that Smuts was to make a big speech on European affairs this evening, and that he had been very anxious to meet L.G. but feared he would just miss him. We agreed

---

[1] (Sir) Patrick Gower, private secretary to successive Prime Ministers 1922–8.

[2] A reference to the sending of telegrams about reparations by Curzon, in the name of the Dominion Prime Ministers, without prior consultation. The Imperial Conference of 1923 was notable for the new claims to participation in matters of Imperial Defence made by the Dominions, as well as their strong pressure for the imposition of a tariff.

[3] The Germans' passive resistance in the Ruhr collapsed at the end of September. The currency was stabilized, but the French did not withdraw their troops.

that L.G. had not (so far as we could judge) made any blunder in his tour in the States.

The Cabinet sat for over three hours this afternoon. How far the P.M. had prepared some of his colleagues for what was coming I don't know. Probably Lloyd-Greame, S. Hoare, and Amery were 'in the know'. But to most his speech came as a bolt from the blue.[1] He outlined what he proposed to put forward in Plymouth as the policy of H.M.G. After analysing the unemployed problem and stressing the new situation as compared with the days of the old Tariff Reform campaign he went on to suggest protectionist remedies, imperial development, and help to agriculture, etc. Salisbury, Derby, Devonshire, Bob Cecil, were all taken aback. Curzon was studiously non-committal. It was at Cave's suggestion (Hankey told me) that the formula recorded in the Minutes was reached:

(a) That in announcing his policy the P.M. should endeavour to avoid committing the Cabinet as a whole and embarrassing those of his colleagues who, owing to election pledges or other reasons, required time to consider their attitude.

(b) That this might be effected by the P.M. announcing at Plymouth that the Government realised that the steps already decided on in relief of unemployment were only palliatives, that owing to Bonar Law's pledge they were prevented from going further in the present Parliament, but that speaking for himself, he thought they might have to go further and apply a tariff. . . .

At the close the House of Commons members remained behind to continue the discussion, but the P.M. gave Hankey a clear indication that he was not wanted. Hankey wrote two copies of the Minutes of the Cabinet in his own handwriting and sent one to the King after the P.M. had approved the other copy—which, by the way, the P.M. signed.

This evening Smuts delivered his speech on Reparations and the P.M. went to the Pilgrims Dinner to say goodbye to George Harvey, the retiring American ambassador. Harvey read every word in an inaudible mumble. The P.M. spoke of our payment of the American Debt as a *hapax legomenon*.

24 October, Wednesday   The Press full of Smuts' speech. 'Vision at last,' said the *Manchester Guardian*, 'the most eloquent, moving and statesmanlike speech which we remember on the troubles which overshadow Europe.' The first leader in the *Morning Post* was entitled 'An English Statesman'. This was Baldwin and Smuts was relegated to the third leader. 'There has been no statesman of Mr. Baldwin's calibre since Mr. Joseph Chamberlain departed. . . . The old Free Trade controversial arguments are wholly sterile. The first essential is to secure the home market. The problem is how to reconcile agriculture and manufacture in the common interests of both. . . . In any case the Prime Minister is a man of resolution, deliberate in thought, decisive in action, shrewd yet candid, kindly yet of an unbending rectitude.' A couple of columns away there was a report of Lloyd George at Indianopolis

[1] This was not so. Salisbury, Derby, Lloyd-Greame, Hoare, Amery, Bridgeman, Chamberlain had all been consulted earlier.

appealing for 'the Lincoln touch' in the affairs of Europe, 'conciliation not vengeance'.

Everyone was discussing Smuts and heaving a sigh of relief. If only S.B. had spoken in that key five months ago and stood firm.

The Imperial Conference met at 10.45 and were photographed. The great men had come in their best black, with shiny collars and cuffs and white slips in their vests. Smuts was in this as in so much else an exception and was in his ordinary garb. But he looked serious and self-conscious when the discussion started and he and Burton had much rapid consultation. I tried to catch his eye and several times to smile my thanks for his speech but he was looking at nobody. It was only later that the P.M. told me that he knew nothing in advance of the speech that Smuts had decided to make. Today's subject was the civic rights of Indians in the Dominions. Peel opened and developed an eloquent tribute to the civilisation, religion, loyalty of India, rolling out his periods with much gravity until one felt as if in Church and as usual the Duke of Devonshire who sat next to Peel was soothed to sleep. Then came a very clever deliverance from Sir Tej Bahadur Sapru, very animated, partly read, partly improvised, infinitely polite yet unmistakable in his demands and with many a shrewd thrust at Smuts, to whom he appealed as a humanitarian, imperial statesman, and Union Prime Minister. It was unfortunate for Smuts that this subject was on the agenda on the very morning when we had all been reading his powerful speech on the Ruhr. No wonder he looked so uncomfortable, almost sad at the irony of his position. He had circulated a memorandum asking that the resolution of the last Imperial Conference should be rescinded and the right of each portion of the Empire to regulate citizenship as well as immigration as a domestic question should be affirmed. 'There is no common equal citizenship in the Empire, and it is quite wrong for a British subject to claim equality of rights in any part of the Empire to which he has migrated or where he happens to be living. . . . The newer conception of the British Empire as a smaller League of Nations, as a partnership of free and equal nations under a common hereditary sovereign, involves an even further departure from the single conception of a unitary citizenship. . . . The common Kingship is the binding link between the parts of the Empire, it is not a source from which private citizens will derive their rights. They will derive their rights simply and solely from the authority of the state in which they live.' (18 October 1923.) The Irish Free State may quote this document some day.

At the close the P.M. told me to see him during the afternoon about his Plymouth speech but it was nearly six when I got to him. He had been closeted with Hoare and with Lloyd-Greame. I gave him notes for a reply to questions by Asquith on unemployment, a note on inflation prepared in the Treasury and agreed with the Governor of the Bank. On his table he had a memorandum on Unemployment and Foreign Trade, and as we talked Curzon's section on the Ruhr arrived and a note from the Admiralty on the cruisers to be built in order to help unemployment in some of the blackest spots. He read swiftly Curzon's draft and handed it to me. We agreed it was good so far as it went. 'I am going to appeal to Poincaré to think thrice before he turns down the offer of the U.S.A. to join in an enquiry.'[1] 'I hope it will be your last appeal,' said I. 'I am the leader of the Tory Party not of the Labour Party,' said S.B. 'The Labour Party would welcome you with open arms,' I retorted, and went on: 'I tried to persuade them to take L.G. but they would not have him. Cannot a Prime Minister be sometimes guilty of going ahead of his Party and making an indiscretion?'

S.B. 'I am inexperienced and new to this job.' I could press the matter no further. 'It was all very well for Smuts to make his speech. He has no responsibility and his analogy with the Boer War was fallacious.' In his heart, he said, he agreed with me—but there was the Party. This reminded him of a talk on the previous evening with the Maharajah. 'The Maharajah told me to go straight on and do the right, trusting in God. When I said it was not always easy to know what was right, the Maharajah put his hand on his heart and said: "You always know here—in your conscience".' S.B. told me nothing of the Cabinet talk on protection—not a hint of what was coming at Plymouth, and I refrained from any reference to it. His 'coach' on this subject is Hewins,[2] whom he sees from time to time and who provides him with memoranda, which are handled very secretly. I once attended his lectures on German Economists when a student at the London School of Economics where he was given to vast and vague generalisations in sharp contrast to the clear cutting sentences of his colleague, Edwin Cannan.

At 8.0 dined at Bellomo's with E. M. H. Lloyd as guest of Mr. Causey, an American investment banker who is devoting himself to relief work in the Ruhr. With him was Mr. Manley (an American banker also) and his wife. After dinner we returned to a private sitting room at the Carlton and were joined later by Mallon of Toynbee Hall, Arnold and Seebohm Rowntree, and some others. Causey is raising 500,000 dollars as a loan to the Ruhr towns to purchase food. Schroeder, Beit, Seligman, the Rowntrees, and the Cadburys are helping. I wrote to Otto Kahn on his behalf. J. D. Rockefeller, Paul Warburg, and Hoover have blessed the plan. Manley thought the only way to bring in America was along the humanitarian road of an appeal for suffering women and children.

26 October Baldwin's Plymouth speech in the papers. Attention divided between the Ruhr and the Protection passages, and some with 'leaders' on the former only. *Times* apparently with P.M. on tariffs, *Daily Mail* wobbling, *Morning Post* ecstatic and with what may be a beginning of a campaign against Curzon. ... I was told at the Treasury today ... that the tariff policy has been pushed on by Waterhouse, Davidson, Reginald Hall, and Jackson,[3] the Whips, Lloyd-Greame and Amery. Neville Chamberlain

---

[1] That is, an enquiry by a committee of experts into how much reparations Germany was actually able to pay. The committee was eventually set up under the chairmanship of the American General Dawes and reported in 1924, providing the basis for the first economically sensible settlement.

[2] W. A. S. Hewins (1865–1931); Conservative M.P. and modern economic historian; Principal of the London School of Economics.

[3] Sir Stanley Jackson (1870–1947); Conservative M.P. 1915–26, Chairman of the Conservative Party 1923–6

when cross-examined by the head of the Customs as to detailed proposals could give no answers. Nothing settled. Opinion divided as to S.B.'s chances of pulling off a victory. Depression and unemployment his chief card, but a tax on manufactured goods won't satisfy the Die-hards, or the farmers, or the Dominions. Will R. Cecil, who has a conscience, resign? Novar is a free trader but does not count. Will Austen Chamberlain come back? Will L.G. and Asquith draw closer together or will Sir John Simon and Margot [Asquith] block any approach?

At one o'clock Miss Watson rang up from No. 10. I went across and found her in tears. She had been talking on the 'phone to Lady Sykes who had said that Bonar's end seemed not far off. He was choking. He had been to the dentist yesterday. He had been reading the papers. But the throat trouble was increasing. Miss Watson had been with him on Monday. He was very 'just', she remarked, defending Mackenzie King against some aspersion. He was surprised at S.B.'s nonchalance in the midst of 'a sea of troubles', and had told him that he thought he *ought* to be worried. I could not comfort Miss Watson and left her abruptly lest I too should weep.

Crossed to St. Stephen's Club to lunch with Pembroke Wicks, one of Curzon's private secretaries. The Marquess had not got over his jealousy of Baldwin. Wicks, who is a barrister and with plenty of intelligence, is used by Curzon to ring up telephone numbers and similar duties. Curzon has a book in preparation on the great houses and palaces of India, and has given Wicks stacks of mss to type—a good example of the Marquess's meanness. Wicks has them typed in the F.O. C.'s industry is amazing. A couple of days ago Wicks gave him 59 foolscap pages typed of the book and got them back today all done to the humblest comma. Withal he finds time to harangue his maids, choose frames for pictures, wind the household clocks, and indite notes to M. Poincaré.

As T.J. indicates at the end of the Diary for this year (see page 261), from 29 October until after the General Election he had no time to do more than jot down notes—'all too few, made on odd scraps of paper at the moment'. When at last he had some leisure, on 22 December, he put these notes into chronological order and also wrote a fuller account of the election and the events leading up to it.

29 October   Edward Wood to T.J.   *Board of Education*
You will have seen in the Press that Sir A. T. Davies is to retire on 31 March next. At Mr. Bonar Law's request, I made an informal arrangement with Sir Warren Fisher at the beginning of the year that you should be available to succeed him as Permanent Secretary of the Welsh Department and Chief Inspector on that date. I shall, of course, have to write to the Prime Minister to ask him to release you from your obligations to him, and also to obtain his formal concurrence in the appointment; but before doing so I should like to make sure that you are still of the same mind, and prepared, if he agrees, to take up the combined appointment. I need hardly say that I am most anxious that you should do so; indeed, to speak frankly, I should be hard put to it if you were to fail me.

But T.J. postponed his decision until after the General Election.

29 October   Dined with P.M. and Mrs. Baldwin at No. 10.

5 November   Rene and I at St. Columba's and then at the Abbey at Bonar Law's funeral.[1] At the Abbey we sat immediately behind members of the Cabinet. All these prayers and hymn singing very alien to the B.L. known to me. He once remarked to me that L.G. still had some sort of belief in a future life and clearly implied that he, B.L., had none whatever.

6 November   Rene and I dine with Professor and Mrs. Shotwell, newly back from Berlin, with ghastly tales of what they had seen among the middle class folk. I tell them it is useless relying on our P.M. for any positive action.

8 November   Dined with P.M. alone at No. 10.

9 November   Lord Mayor's Day. L.G. returns from America and is besieged on board by fifty journalists. Denounces Baldwin's unutterable fiscal folly—mildewed straw, etc., etc.

12 November   Saw P.M. re dissolution and King's Speech and Edward Wood (Board of Education) about my taking up post of Chief Inspector and Permanent Secretary of the Welsh Department in place of Sir Alfred Davies.

16 November   Cope, the Welsh Unionist Whip, has reported prospects in Wales to P.M., and J. C. Gould has seen P.M. as he is not 'sound' on fiscal question. P.M. tells me Mond's position at Swansea doubtful, and in Cardigan Lord Lisburne may get in between the rival Liberals, Ernest Evans (L.G'ite) and Hopkin Morris (Asquithian). . . .

17 November   P.M. tells me that whatever else the last few days have done they have revealed to him the tortuous mentality of the Cecils. Lord R. Cecil is to go to the Lords. He had also seen F. E. Smith and found the 'ego' greatly developed. Much suspicion in the mind of J. C. Davidson that L.G. is busy in secret plotting for Centre Party.

19 November   10.30 a.m. See P.M. Davidson comes in and reports great hostility among his women constituents to Lord Birkenhead. The churches have had sermons denouncing his Glasgow Rectorial address with its talk about the glittering prizes of war. D. then refers to *The Times* leader today and begs S.B. to 'lead' more vigorously in his speeches, that he is in danger of being thought not only honest but also a 'b— fool'. S.B. says he is leaving foreign affairs to be dealt with by Curzon who will make a speech in the City and show how he and Harington averted war with Turkey.
P.M. speaks at Queens Hall.

[1] Bonar Law died on 30 October.

20 November P.M. recalls remark of Richard Bell, railway leader, when shunting truck of foreign steel bars: 'Why could we not make these bars in England?' Thinks he'll use this at Reading where there are many railway-men. Thinks of going for L.G. again in his next speech. I advise against. S.B. 'The little man has been so surrounded for years with adulation that he thinks he is the only man fit to be Prime Minister. You don't agree?' T.J. 'I don't agree. L.G. has far too much humour to suffer from swelled head. He knows quite well at the time what he's up to.' P.M. 'Perhaps "swelled head" is not the word I want. That fits Winston better. . . .'

24 November Train to Worcester, then motored to Astley Hall, P.M.'s Worcestershire home. He was away speaking at two or three villages and did not come in until about 10 o'clock. Dined with Mrs. Baldwin, a daughter and her friend, Miss Trowbridge, and the younger son, Arthur, who had motored from Porthcawl. . . . Certainly better bread and meat were never served to a guest than at the Baldwin table. S.B. very pleased with his meeting and spoke with much familiarity of old friendly faces he had seen in the several villages. We retired soon after ten—I to a small cold bedroom at the end of a passage. These rambling old houses should have central heating or at least hotwater bottles.

25 November Breakfast 9.15. Then a walk through the gardens and on to a rest cottage for guests to which the Baldwins invite tired mothers and exhausted typists. Bigger than a cottage, with plain miscellaneous furniture, and a housekeeper and daughter whom we surprised at this early hour on Sunday. The P.M. marched me through the place showing me every room up and down and telling me he hoped some day I'd come and rest there. It has a fine open situation looking towards Malvern Hills but this morning they were hidden in mist. On our way back we encountered two photographers from London to whom permission to come had been given the previous day. The P.M. stood or walked for them as directed. After they had finished we strolled to a meadow in front of the house and were joined by the son and his dog. This was too great a temptation to the Londoners and we were all four taken. I bade them let me have this particular photograph as a private souvenir not for publication. They agreed but added, 'unless it makes a very nice picture'. (It appeared next day in *The Times* and later in the *Sphere*.)

Soon after 10.0 we made for the Library. . . . S.B. showed me his copy of the *Odyssey* in Greek used by him at Harrow with neat pencilled notes in the margins, his copy of Keynes's *Economic Consequences of the Peace* with a sentence (Baldwin's own) about the hardfaced men who had made money out of the war and been returned to Parliament. This recalled a remark with which he once startled Bonar Law: 'A man who made a million quick ought to be not in the Lords but in gaol.' . . .

. . . Even here one does not escape the L.G. obsession. . . . He went on to say that L.G. had been too long without rest—that his judgment was weakened. His failure in the House in the last year was conspicuous. I agreed and said that Grigg and I had tried again and again to persuade him to go away for a long holiday and change but he would not and in any case he was not like other men. His vitality was amazing. Then S.B. 'I was never with him alone for five minutes. I don't really know him [but] I was in the Cabinet and as I never said anything there I had leisure to study him under a microscope.'

He told me to look at his marked copy of Morley's Cobden and Fisher's Lecture on 'Orthodoxy', and said that if he were returned to power he would see Poincaré again and try to persuade him to behave decently to the Germans. He said this quite simply, no doubt believing he might succeed. He did not remain very long in the Library and I refused a suggestion to go walking as I thought he might wish to see something of his family. At luncheon L.G. cropped up again, Mrs. Baldwin recalling and fetching for my admiration an album of photographs in which were some of S.B. wrestling with a goat[1] twenty five years ago! . . . I came across a picture of Lloyd George as Chancellor of the Exchequer defaced. How they do hate him. . . . S.B. showed me an illuminated address from a body of miners in the family mines whose wages S.B. had paid for the six weeks during which they were idle at the time of the national coal strike. . . . Back to tea and a rapid glance at some Sunday newspapers. I saw no one else read them. S.B. early in the campaign told me to read the newspapers as he found them 'so bewildering'. He preferred to read them as little as possible because they confused him. He reads the *Morning Post*, I know, and I am pretty sure he reads *The Times* regularly. How much else I know not. He left me early after dinner, in the Library, going upstairs to Mrs. Baldwin's room, telling me he tried to spend Sunday evening with her. I said goodbye, as I was leaving early for town, while he was staying on and going to Bristol for the Colston Hall meeting. During the day his agent had called to get some polling papers signed, and I had been called to the telephone once only—from Bristol by Geoffrey Fry suggesting that S.B. should make clear that our entrepot trade would be safeguarded and that due regard would be given to Bristol's interest in using partly manufactured articles as raw materials in some branch or other of the boot trade. It was an extraordinarily quiet Sunday. I had brought two batches of Foreign Office telegrams with me on Saturday evening and had directed his attention to them, but it was late on Sunday before he looked at them. Bonar Law would do as much work in an hour as S.B. in four or five. I am never sure whether the P.M. is thinking at all or simply woolgathering. Here in his rural home one feels the old England of the villages is getting a bit of its own back for once in the person of Stanley Baldwin.

26 November, Monday   Motored in a frosty morning to Hartlebury via Stourport and over the Severn. The car decorated with red ribbons.[2] Noticed the hoardings inviting the citizens to 'Vote for Baldwin and No More Food Taxes', which I thought pretty misleading for the 'Honest' Party. Lord Beauchamp came in to my compartment at Worcester, and read the Liberal

[1] 'The Treasury nickname for Lloyd George was "the Goat" and it is almost always S.B.'s name for him in private conversation.' (*Diary, 25 November.*)

[2] The Conservative Party colours in Worcestershire were red.

papers and then a lot of Liberal electioneering pamphlets. In *The Times* I found myself walking in the field with the P.M., Arthur, and the dog. Pleased but also rather vexed because I have a first-rate record for anonymity during the seven years of work for the three Prime Ministers. Then so many, especially in Wales, will not understand how a Civil Servant does his best for his Chief, whatever the politics of the said Chief. This very morning there was waiting me at the office an invitation to go down and speak for a Liberal candidate at Ebbw Vale in Monmouthshire!

28 November, Wednesday   Motored to Euston with P.M., Mrs. Baldwin, and Waterhouse, and saw them off for Glasgow. On our way passed placards of the *Daily Herald*. 'Baldwin's Son on Premier's Policy', or some such legend. No one referred to it or to the son—they have never mentioned him in my presence.[1] At Euston I bought a *Daily News* and showed them a cartoon by Low of the *Star* depicting S.B. as an honest man, not a clever man, an ordinary man, and finally a tadpole. He enjoyed it all right but I am afraid Mrs. Baldwin did not. I told S.B. not to be unduly discouraged if he found the Glasgow audience not much given to loud and prolonged cheering. 'I too will be dour' he replied.

29 November   P.M. at Bradford. I take things easy.

1 December, Saturday   Dined at the Savage Club, guest of Marcus Paterson, the tuberculosis expert. He showed me a full-page photograph of the four of us (including the dog) in the *Sphere* with an unfortunate description of me as helping the P.M. in his campaign. Felt wretched and blamed myself for not having foreseen this and gone to the editors. I could have found out which was the likely paper but it had not occurred to me to think about it at all after Monday. . . .

4 December, Tuesday   P.M. returns from Liverpool and goes to Malvern in his own county. Mr. McLachlan, a chief official of the Unionist Central Office, was with the P.M. when I saw latter at No. 10 just before 4 o'clock. McLachlan's official estimate of the result of the forthcoming poll is:

Conservatives	.	.	.	351
Liberals	.	.	.	114 ⎫
Labour	.	.	.	145 ⎬ 264
Independent	.	.	.	5 ⎭
Unionist majority	.	.		87

   P.M. very cheerful at this prospect and almost his last words to us before going to his train were: 'I don't want any bands here when I come back!' Ronald Waterhouse very much impressed by the warmth of P.M.'s reception at Glasgow, Bradford, and Liverpool and en route. P.M. himself most affected by the Glasgow meeting. Told me that the thought of Bonar was

---

[1] Oliver Baldwin, the eldest son, having become a Socialist, lost no opportunity of attacking his father's policy and personality.

with him throughout. After the Liverpool meeting he had gone to Knowsley and had received very favourable reports of the progress of the campaign in the North from Derby and Birkenhead.

6 December   Polling Day. Rene and I for Fletcher, the Liberal candidate, against George Balfour, the Protectionist, in Hampstead. No Labour candidate. At eight o'clock I dine at the Travellers' Club as one of several guest of Geoffrey Fry. Fry has done the Church patronage for Baldwin and done it admirably, I believe. He has much money, a beautiful manor house at Oare in Wiltshire, where he had built 'cottages' for a couple of friends, a frail wife who is often ailing, and one daughter. At dinner were Waterhouse, Duff —all secretaries of the P.M., Colonel Storr (Davidson's secretary), two city friends, and myself. At 5 to 10 we got the first result in our private sitting-room. Sir Edwin Stockton was knocked out in Manchester—a Unionist Free Trader. Then Wakefield, also a loss to the Government. We pooh-poohed these. They were in the infected North. We made for No. 10 through a thick fog and I remained there until 1.30 a.m., Rene joining at 10.30. Miss Watson and half a dozen typists there too, and about midnight Davidson and Mrs. Davidson arrived from their fight at Hemel Hempstead. The faithful Berry had provided for us much liquid and solid refreshment in the Cabinet room. We were not very despondent for the first hour or so, as we were reminded of what took place a year ago when Bonar sat there in misery doubtful even about his own election. But as the Liberal and Labour gains continued in an unbroken stream, except for Middleton where Ryland Atkins, a Liberal, was defeated by a Government nominee, our faces grew longer, we saw less and less chance of the home counties putting things right. Bath and Nottingham were a great shock. If Nottingham would not vote for a tariff after all the trouble about foreign competition in the lace trade, who was going to support Baldwin? Bath we put down to folk with fixed incomes who feared soaring prices. As the night wore on Waterhouse and Gower sustained themselves with more and more liquid. Mrs. Davidson was almost beside herself with panic for the fate of a country so blind to its best interests as to vote against the one policy which could save it. I watched the growing tale of Labour victories with undisguised joy amid cries of 'You Bolshevist!'

7 December   . . . Seven years today L.G. became Prime Minister—1916.

This afternoon Baldwin returns from Worcestershire where he had been elected by about 6,000 majority and not by the 10,000 for which he had asked. He arrived at No. 10 with Mrs. Baldwin. She went upstairs and he came straight in to the Cabinet Room. There were no Ministers about to welcome him, only a couple of private secretaries and the usual messengers. It was all very depressing. He took out his pipe and tried to put a cheerful face on the situation. We ordered tea and I was then left alone with him. We went through the staggering results recorded in the afternoon papers. He scanned eagerly the fate of men personally known to him. Amazed at Chichester. The offer of a £1 an acre to the farmers had plainly 'cut no ice'. The South West had gone Liberal. 'Birmingham was splendid—steadfast

—remarkable.' 'The people of this country can't be shaken out of their fear of high prices.' I tried to comfort him with the thought that he had fought an honourable fight, free from exaggeration and abuse. He referred to Mrs. Baldwin's disappointment, 'after having just settled in here. We must go and live in a small flat. Our town house is too expensive for us. I am much poorer than I was before the war.' Then his talk took a religious hue. 'Every-one who tries in politics to do the thing he believes in simply and honestly is sure to come a smeller. The martyrs did. Christ did.' The expression was new to me and I suppose is the equivalent of the colloquial 'cropper'. When I left him to make way for Lord Robert Cecil there was no doubt that his intention was to resign right away. I rang up Davidson who was in the country smarting under a most unexpected defeat, and suggested he should come in to town on Saturday to cheer up the P.M., adding that the P.M. was hoping to get hold of Neville Chamberlain for consultation at Chequers over the weekend. The P.M. told me that on Thursday morning he had received the final estimate from his official advisers at the Unionist Central Offices and that they put his majority at 95. He was in fact almost exactly in a minority of 95. The forecasts of the other Parties were much closer.

I wanted very much to ask the P.M. how he came to make the initial error which has led to this debacle, but I felt it would be too cruel. Eyres Monsell, the Chief Whip, was not consulted! Jackson, the cricketer, and Admiral Reginald Hall are the heads of the Central Office. Much jubilation over defeat of latter in the more wholesome political circles.

8 December   9.30 a.m. To 3 Buckingham Gate to confer with the Misses Davies and Maynard and Fleure on plans for Gregynog Printing Press. Maynard had brought with him the first book issued from the Press—a short selection made by Sir Walford Davies of Poems by George Herbert. . . .

Luncheon with Sylvester and my first account of L.G.'s American trip. 'I've been through hell,' was Sylvester's summing up. It had been an im-mense public success but those in L.G.'s immediate entourage had a gruelling time. Dame Margaret had been 'fine'. Of course she would be. L.G. had got across Cope from the start. He had filled up every minute of every day, had booked L.G. to cut a sod for some chapel in Montreal on a Sunday, had billed him in some vast and impossible hall or market place elsewhere, and so forth. L.G. fumed and raged and swore he would not do this nor would he do that —but he did everything and more. On the boat going out he was like a prima donna in a green room. . . . in a fever about his first impact on the American people on landing and its effect on Canada. I told Sylvester to urge him now to move to the left, to have no commerce with the Unionists for they would only use him while it suited them, and would then again kick him out. Mond, Hamar Greenwood, and McCurdy are to be with him at Churt tomorrow.

9 December   Tea with Lord Esher at Tilney Street. He . . . had seen Stam-fordham this morning and both were much concerned about the precise position of the King in the political crisis and eager that Stamfordham should not have to go scouting from one person to another in secret trying to find out who should be sent for to succeed Baldwin. That is what happened when Bonar Law resigned. The King should be guided either by a Party Meeting or by the meeting of Parliament. I promised to put this strongly to the P.M. tomorrow morning before he goes to the Palace.[1]

20 December   T.J. to Sir John Chancellor[2]

I have been a long time acknowledging your letter of the 26 October. You can understand something of the turmoil I have passed through in the last few weeks. I had to work very closely in with the P.M. who had naturally a great many important speeches to make. The whole thing started very suddenly and its precise origin is still wrapped in mystery. Davidson gets most of the blame for the fundamental error of judgment which led to the election and the atmosphere engendered by the Protectionist Premiers is also regarded as a contributory cause. I do not know what the truth is but the plan was suddenly launched without notice at a Cabinet and within 48 hours it was announced at Plymouth. From that moment the election was inevitable. The P.M. managed to keep his team together mainly by announcing the tariff policy as one to meet an emergency. It was then felt that a rapid election was the only chance of victory for the tariff programme, for the more the country understood the policy the less it was thought they would like it. So events moved swiftly but this speed had the unfortunate result that many of the Unionist candidates were entirely ignorant of the case they had to put forward and many amusing stories are current of their attempts to explain the differences between the rival proposals. Up to the very last minute we, that is to say No. 10, were quite confident of victory and expected the Unionists to come back with anything from 70 to 90 of a majority to be followed by 5 years of strong Tory Government. You can imagine our dismay when the results rolled in.

Yesterday Asquith declared war on the Government in the National Liberal Club with the united blessing of L.G. and Sir John Simon. It is therefore practically certain that we shall have a Labour Government before the end of January. It is equally certain, I think, that the heavens will not fall and that the Capital Levy will not appear in the next budget. I believe the idea is to give the Labour Party a fair chance for some months at any rate and then possibly bring the Liberals into power without a dissolution. All sorts of gossip is current about the composition of the forthcoming Cabinet. The chief difficulty is the Foreign Office and there is some idea of Ramsay doing it and the Premiership. Haldane will probably be Lord Chancellor and Chairman of the C.I.D. There is talk of either Webb or Wedgwood for the Colonial Office; but these are idle speculations and you will know the facts before this reaches you.

[1] The Prime Minister decided to wait and face the House of Commons. The Government was defeated on the King's Speech on 21 January and Baldwin resigned the next day.
[2] Assistant Secretary to the Colonial Defence Committee 1906–11 and first Governor of Southern Rhodesia, 1923–30.

22 December, Saturday   Rest Harrow, Sandwich. About a week ago Lady Astor rang up and offered us first a cottage at Cliveden, and later, this house, as more bracing, for the Christmas holidays. We came down on Thursday bringing May, the cook. The Astors provide and feed a housekeeper and maid who are in charge. The children were unwilling to leave Hampstead, fearing to miss Christmas presents, but were quickly reconciled on arriving here and finding much to excite and delight their glancing minds. In the roof of the lounge there is a compass showing the direction of the wind, moving noiselessly in obedience to some vane outside. There is a fine large model of a sailing ship in the drawing room, a complete set of Everyman's Library, a gramophone with fox trots with which they were soon surfeited. Upstairs are hot and cold seawater baths laid on; outside a miniature golf course and some sandpits for all sorts of adventures.

Relaxing at Rest Harrow, T.J. took up his Diary again (see p. 253).

I don't know when I last wrote a line of this record, as Volume II is at Hampstead. It was, I think, about the time of the P.M.'s speech at Plymouth. I remember talking over that speech with him the day before he went to Plymouth. He never breathed a word to me of his tariff proposals. All was kept most secret, but of course I knew all about them, as I had read the manuscript minutes of the previous day's Cabinet meeting. How the P.M. came to put forward his proposals in the sudden way he did, at the time he did, is still wrapped in mystery. Davidson is chiefly blamed and it is believed that Bruce and Massey may have been in the plot. Hankey and I were given no opportunity of putting out red lights. We could have told the P.M. with what careful preparation L.G. paved the way for the Safeguarding of Industries Bill. One factor in the swift decision, in my strong belief, was the success of L.G.'s American tour. L.G.'s stock was visibly rising at home, and S.B. and Davidson were sure to fear that unless they took some dramatic and decisive step the stock might go much higher. They thought the cleavage in the Liberal ranks too deep to be bridged. They thought it inconceivable that Simon and L.G. or Runciman and L.G. would ever stand together again on the same platform. And yet all this has come to pass, thanks to S.B. This week L.G. has moved and Simon seconded a vote of thanks to Asquith in the National Liberal Club where L.G.'s name has been damned daily for the last two years by dozens of the members.

The abruptness of S.B.'s decision is plain, not only from his having invited a Free Trader like McKenna to take office, but he had discussed with me at Chequers asking Lord Grey to go the Foreign Office if Curzon could be got rid of. This was late in September or early in October.

The General Election has come and gone in a way which S.B. never fore-saw or imagined. At first he probably thought that he would be allowed to carry on until the Budget and incorporate in it his tariff scheme, but once his Plymouth speech was made, he was at the mercy of events, and was urged to push the Election on as fast as possible. Sir Laming Worthington-Evans, a political cynic if ever there was one, advised this, remarking: 'Shut your eyes and open your mouth and see what Baldwin will give you.' Was the only chance with Protection. I told S.B. that if the country had more than three weeks in which to think they would see through his policy. As it turned out they saw through it within three weeks.

Throughout the campaign I was in the closest touch with the P.M., saw him almost daily—every day when he was in town. . . . I would see him each morning soon after 10.0, tell him the main features in the speeches of the previous day and any gossip I had heard. I would indicate the sort of line to take, the points to combat or avoid. He never attempted to explain to me how protection would cure unemployment. I told him several times that all my instincts and training were dead against his policy and that I thought he would corrupt our politics still more. I had undertaken at the start to do my utmost to help him, as he had asked me to help, and this I did. . . . How far S.B.'s knowledge of the fiscal controversy went I could never make out as he would never discuss a problem with any thoroughness, never argue. I think he had been influenced at Cambridge by Cunningham[1] and he has a deep dislike of the manufacturer who has made money very quickly, and especially disliked Cardiff and other war millionaires. His view no doubt is that money should be made slowly and steadily over generations as in his own family. I am sure he had read Morley's Life of Cobden twenty or more years ago as he showed me his copy with some passages marked. These passages chiefly showed how the Anti-Corn Law agitation was financed by manufacturers and how the misery of the time played into Cobden's hands. He himself made several happy hits, e.g., about the crinolines and the mildewed straw, in reply to L.G., at Liverpool; and in other ways showed he had much humorous insight and wit. I quoted from Randolph Churchill, as adaptable to Winston's case, Milton's line, 'Down . . . [?blank in original]. S.B. replied: 'I wish I could say that Winston had left cotton (Manchester) for marmalade (Dundee) and had now gone to ladies' underclothing (Leicester).'

1924

The first Labour Government, under Ramsay MacDonald, was in a weak position from the outset, dependent as it was on Liberal votes for its survival. The most successful administrator was undoubtedly Wheatley, whose grasp of the housing problem influenced policy well beyond his own span in office. There were significant advances in education, inspired in part by the Hadow Report. But for unemployment no solution was forthcoming.

MacDonald, who took over the Foreign Office as well as the Premiership, showed zeal and initiative in foreign affairs. He worked for understanding first with Poincaré and then with his successor, Herriot. On the basis of the Dawes Report, he renegotiated the reparations settlement with Germany, so that it ceased to be the bitter and contentious issue around which all else in Europe revolved. The ambitious Geneva Protocol, a pact of mutual assistance which might have given substance to the League of Nations, was lost when the Labour Government fell. Meanwhile, the

[1] William Cunningham, economist and academic, Fellow of Trinity when Baldwin was at Cambridge and later Professor of Economics at Kings College, London.

Soviet Government received formal recognition and negotiations were concluded on the pre-revolutionary debts. It was vehement Liberal and Conservative opposition to this settlement which, in October, brought the Government down, though the point of collapse was the comparatively trivial Campbell case, in the handling of which MacDonald's behaviour was equivocal, to say the least. During the election, the notorious Zinoviev letter, believed by some even then to be a forgery, contributed to Labour's downfall. They lost forty seats, but the large Conservative majority derived from the Liberal débâcle. They were reduced from 159 to 40, as against 419 Conservatives and 151 Labour. Baldwin came in as Prime Minister with a Cabinet to which the Coalition Conservatives, Churchill, Austen Chamberlain, and Birkenhead, now returned.

T.J. remained at the Cabinet Office, but he did not work closely with MacDonald, as he had with his predecessors and, at the end, he was nearly made a scapegoat in the Campbell case. At the instance of J. H. Thomas, he became involved again in the tortuous proceedings over the Irish Boundary Commission. He was also appointed secretary to a Cabinet Committee of Economic Enquiry. On Baldwin's return, he reverted to his former position and was immediately brought into the discussions on Cabinet making.

16 January   T.J. to Sir John Chancellor

. . . We had the King's speech yesterday and within a week from now I have no doubt we shall have a Labour Prime Minister. All sorts of rumours are floating about as to the personnel of his Cabinet. I think it is pretty certain that J. H. Thomas will go to the Colonial Office. There are rumours that MacDonald is angling for the support of certain members of the House of Lords in order to avoid creating any. Lord Robert Cecil, Bledisloe, Chelmsford,[1] and Meston are privately mentioned for Foreign Office, Agriculture, Admiralty, and India Office but I believe the second and fourth have already refused. It is probable that S.B. will be leader of the Opposition and that Austen and F.E. will agree to co-operate. We are of course curious about our own fate and that of No. 10 but my information is that this office is not likely to have its glory diminished.

19 January   Dined at E. M. H. Lloyd's, with Lloyd and his wife and Clifford Allen.[2] Sir Arthur Salter and Wise joined us after dinner. This was my first meeting with Clifford Allen. He is a Cambridge man who in former days lived with Bertrand Russell, wore long hair and sandals. These he has now discarded. During the War he took up an extreme pacifist position and went to prison. I believe he was one of the founders of the Union of Democratic Control. He is Treasurer of the I.L.P., is said to be in close confidential touch with Ramsay MacDonald, and we talked on that assumption, first about Beveridge's suggestion of a General Economic Staff, to be located possibly in the Cabinet Office and to do the thinking ahead of the Labour Government. I opposed, and said that such a Staff would be suspended in mid-air and would be blanketed by the Departments. Cabinets did not err from lack

---

[1] Who became First Lord of the Admiralty.

[2] Reginald Clifford Allen (1889–1939); Chairman of the Independent Labour Party, 1924-6; later Lord Allen of Hurtwood.

of information and good advice. Baldwin notoriously blundered into the Election without seeking in advance information or advice from those best able to supply it. Ministers had far more memoranda put up to them than they ever read or digested. To the various Cabinet Committees experts from Departments accompanied Ministers. The right way was to use the experts of the various Departments and bring them together to concert policy.

C.A. did not much like this point of view. He wanted to be speculating in a much more airy way about the future Socialist State, wanted economists to draw up the order in which various industries should be nationalised, wanted an economic Doomsday Book which should show precisely how the great industries are in fact now being run, their finances, markets, etc. I warned him that any such roving enquiry would rouse the opposition of Liberal employers, and that the British mind loathed such enquiries. 'If they do, we can go to the Electorate on that issue and tell people that we are refused the information which is essential to the advancement of Labour policy.' I ventured to suggest there were more powerful battle-cries, but he seemed set on staging a public enquiry which could be used definitely as Socialist propaganda rather than for the acquisition of knowledge. His favourite phrase throughout the evening was 'The psychology of the Electorate', and he referred with pride to the fact that Ramsay MacDonald had kept flying the banner of the Capital Levy.

Talk then turned to Foreign Affairs. J.R.M. is to take the double office of P.M. and Foreign Secretary, with Clynes as Leader of the House. This last he saw was a great risk, as Clynes is so negligible a personality. It would make J.R.M.'s absence at Conferences abroad dangerous. I said J. H. Thomas would be a much better Leader of the House. He replied that Clynes was only five votes behind Ramsay for the leadership of the Party, and had therefore the higher claim. He went on to ask should Ramsay call a Conference of the Allies before the French elections? Salter pointed out that this would be a snub to America, who had just joined in the Committee of Experts. The better plan would be to await their Report, some time in March, unless they broke up from internal squabbles before then. Ramsay, Salter urged, ought to make a speech at the opening of Parliament on the lines of Smuts, and follow it with a friendlier speech to France. Allen said he was to see Longuet and the French Socialist leaders next week and that there were signs that the Socialists would co-operate more and more with the Left, with a view to bringing Poincaré down. In his view, the root problem was not reparations, but security, and he asked did we think that the Germans would allow an effective Commission to be placed in Berlin to control all German military development for a period of years, analogous to the Financial Commissioner for Reparations, which was part of Salter's scheme? I said the French would probably insist on having a French President of such a Commission and would not swallow a neutral Chairman appointed by the League.

20 *January*   Delisle Burns[1] in to tea. He wanted suggestions for the

---

[1] Now assistant secretary to the joint T.U.C.-Labour Party Research Department.

reorganisation of the Board of Trade. Could the seamen be transferred to the Ministry of Labour? Should not the Mines Department have its own Cabinet Minister? Did the Department of Overseas Trade serve any useful purpose? I told him it was better for the mines to be under an important Minister like the President of the Board of Trade, in the Cabinet, rather than have a Minister of its own outside. In any case, the future of the mines was bound to come up within the next three months. He, like Clifford Allen, was clear that one of the chief tasks of the new Labour Government would be to obtain a maximum amount of information from the Departments; but Burns, of course, wanted it for scientific purposes.

21 January   I found S.B. in great spirits: 'I have not felt so well for a long time, and I shall be tempted to be very vulgar in my speech.' I saw him later in his room at the House alone just before 6 o'clock, and he then went through the notes of his speech, chuckling in great glee over his jokes, especially his quotation from Dryden:

'I wonder that he (MacDonald) can ride into power on the old historic Parties in the State. Would he not rather say, in the words of Dryden,

"Oh! rather let me perish in the strife

Than have my crown the price of David's life." '

I had never seen him so merry before a speech. All nervousness seemed to have fled. I took objection to his entering, as he proposed to do, into an explanation why he had invited McKenna to be his Chancellor, and he dropped this. The speech went very well in the House, especially the earlier part. The weakest portion was the close, which he could have expanded into another quarter of an hour and in that way made the speech more appropriate to the greatness of the occasion. When I chided him on his brevity afterwards, he said it was a good rule to stop when people were wanting more, and that he always remembered how little chance the private Member got to speak when the leaders took up all the time.

I went off to dine at the Travellers' Club, with Geoffrey Fry, Gower, Duff, and Fergusson, the Chancellor's Private Secretary—all of us rather gloomy because of our own uncertain fate.

Back to the House, and then, soon after 11, the Division took place and Labour defeated the Government by 72.

22 January   There was a short Cabinet at 10.30. Baldwin went off to see the King and was back with Waterhouse soon after 12. I had placed a little gift on his table in the Cabinet Room—some eighteenth-century Parodies of the Poets called *A Pipe of Tobacco*.

At 1 o'clock, luncheon in Dean's Yard with Lord Esher, Arthur Greenwood, and others. Tawney in for a moment, and he, Esher, and I discussed the future of the Garton Foundation. . . . I had a word outside with Tawney about the Board of Education post,[1] and I walked with Greenwood to the House. He told me he was to be Parliamentary Secretary at the Ministry of

[1] The Permanent Secretaryship.

Health, with Wheatley,[1] of Glasgow, as Minister. Mrs. Webb had told him that I was being considered for the B. of E. post. I expressed my disappointment that A.G. was not to be Minister of Education, as together we could have made things hum, but he had stood down from a Cabinet post in order to smooth matters for MacDonald.[2]

In the House Baldwin announced the resignation of the Government, when someone on the Labour Bench shouted 'Thank God for that!' . . .

About 7.30 saw Hankey for a moment. He had been with the new Premier and his colleagues at the House of Commons and had invited Ramsay MacDonald to dine with him at the United Services Club that evening. He told me of a conversation he had had with the King earlier in the day. The King had said that Ramsay MacDonald had mentioned my name for B. of E. post and the King had asked who I was and why he had never met me. I laid no reliance on this interview, as the King seemed to suggest to Hankey that I ought to take Cabinet office. I find it impossible to know what is the true position. I believe the heads of the Treasury are dead against my going to the B. of E. and want to create some *ad hoc* position by which I shall be attached to successive Prime Ministers, but they might not want me.

On my way home saw the evening placards, 'Lenin dead (official) Ramsay MacDonald Premier'.

23 January   Hankey expanded a little about the talk with the King. He had pointed out to the King that I was older than he was and that this might be my last chance of being appointed to one of the big Permanent Secretaryships. I asked Hankey if he had broached the matter with the P.M. at dinner last night at the Club. He replied that my name had been mentioned by him more than once, but that Ramsay MacDonald did not 'rise'.

I crossed to No. 10 and found that no-one knew what his fate was to be. I saw Davidson and told him what Hankey had told me about the talk with the King, and that it ought not to be impossible to arrange that I should be appointed to the B. of E. post, but continue for a time to give the new P.M. any help I could in these initial months. He said he would talk the matter over again with S.B.

I then went to Queen Anne's Gate and had a quarter of an hour with Haldane. He is all for my going to Education, has himself spoken to Ramsay MacDonald on the matter, pooh-poohed the opposition of the Treasury, and said the new President of the Board (Trevelyan)—who was a timid person— was to dine with him this evening. Sidney Webb wanted me to go to Education. The whole system needed unification, as Tawney had pointed out; there must be a great development of adult education and more money for the Universities, to all of which I said 'Amen'. Did I know Morgan Jones, the Parliamentary Secretary? I said I did, and had lent him 'Sanderson of Oundle' for the improvement of his mind some time ago. He himself was

[1] John Wheatley (1869–1930); a miner, who founded a successful publishing business in Glasgow, 1912; joined the I.L.P. 1908; Labour M.P. 1922–30; Minister of Health 1924; the most talented of the 'Clydesiders'.

[2] Who was considerably pledged to the left wing in the matter of Wheatley's appointment.

going to shed the judicial duties of the Lord Chancellorship in order to be free to lead the Lords, preside over the C.I.D. and generally deputise for the P.M. It was by his good offices that Parmoor and Chelmsford had been secured. Indeed, he had been most closely consulted as to the making of the Cabinet. (J. H. Thomas told me, at the Astors' the other day, that it was he alone who was in the secret. Someone else told me that Henderson claimed the privileged position, while Ramsay told Hankey at dinner last night that it was not until you came to make a Cabinet that you plumbed the depths of human nature.) Haldane was very amusing about the new War Minister —Stephen Walsh, the miners' agent. Mr. and Mrs. Walsh dined with him last night, and Haldane tried to fit on him one of his frock coats, but as Walsh is only 5 ft. 1, Haldane's coat reached to near his boots. This same coat, I gathered, was being tried on Adamson, the Secretary for Scotland, this morning, probably with more satisfactory results. 'I lent Walsh a little book on War and the War Office, and told him that when he meets the Generals he is to say 'We are out for efficiency!' '

Back to the office, where Davidson rang up to say he had heard it confirmed that Ramsay had mentioned my name to the King. The No. 10 staff is to remain on. . . .

4 p.m. first Labour Cabinet.

7.30 dined at the Reform Club with Sir Arthur Salter, A. G. Gardiner, J. R. Brooke, E. F. Wise, E. M. H. Lloyd, and J. J. Mallon. Salter described the steps taken to straighten out Austria's finances, and especially the great game of bluff played in the last months of 1922 before the arrival of the representative of the League of Nations. Rumoured that Massingham was going to be our Ambassador at Berlin, and O'Grady at Moscow—both extraordinary suggestions.

24 January   I went to No. 10 hoping to see the new Prime Minister, but he was engaged all morning at the Foreign Office, and was to see Warren Fisher immediately on his return. This afternoon Hankey saw me and said that he had discussed my future with the Prime Minister. Hankey told me the story while busily engaged in signing a lot of letters. The P.M. had said that there were no signs of Selby-Bigge[1] retiring and that I had better continue at the Cabinet Office. He asked what salary I was receiving, and was amazed that it was so high; that, as for himself, he was satisfied to have a roof over his head. Hankey, instead of saying that I was worth my salary, which is half his, told me that he moved quickly away from this subject lest the P.M. should ask what he (Hankey) was receiving. I told Hankey that this was rather a depressing result of seven years' work here. He tried to put a cheerful face on things, but I refrained from telling him all I thought about it. Hankey has seen MacDonald at Hampstead, has dined with him alone, and has had ample opportunities as my Chief of discussing my future with the P.M. before Warren Fisher got into the matter at all, but he has not lifted a finger to help. I felt very sick about the whole business. The result is that I revert

---

[1] The Permanent Secretary to the Board of Education.

to the post I had when I came here, of being Secretary to Cabinet Committees, and, as I understand, have nothing to do with the new Prime Minister.

At 8 p.m. dined at Tilney Street with Lord and Lady Esher and Burgis.

All were out to put a cheerful face on matters, Esher reminding me that his father had been buffeted about and disappointed but ultimately had reached the goal of Master of the Rolls.

Esher told me that Beaverbrook prophesied that the new P.M. would fail as a man of action, and, as always, there was much speculation as to L.G.'s *rôle*. Esher was very much in favour of putting in a General Economic Staff into the Cabinet Office, somewhat on the lines of Beveridge's proposal.

On the same day J. L. Garvin, editor of The Observer, *wrote in a letter to T.J.*
. . . I wonder what your own life will be like under the new régime? If you kept a diary, and you ought to do it, you would be the Greville of our age.

Later, Warren Fisher agreed, under some pressure, to propose to the Prime Minister that T.J. should remain Principal Assistant Secretary of the Cabinet Office at an increased salary.

26 January   Sir Charles Trevelyan[1] to T.J.   *Board of Education*
I don't think we have met yet. But I have heard a good deal about you and that you have ideas about the job I have taken in hand. Will you come and lunch with me some day next week—not Monday—at my house, 14 Great College Street, and have a talk?

31 January 1.15 lunched with Trevelyan at 14 Great College Street, where I found his wife, the daughter of Sir Hugh Bell, the ironmaster, and some children. I expressed my delight at finding a President of the Board of Education who had children of his own to educate, that I thought childless social reformers like the Webbs, the Bosanquets, the Hammonds laboured under serious disqualifications. The Trevelyan children are all going through the Quakers' School at Sidcot. . . .

We started 'shop' at once: Would I say what could be done by the Minister for Education in the present Parliament? I trotted out the usual proposals—development of Secondary Education by taking off the embargo on free places; permission to local authorities to raise the school age to 15; removal of the embargo on adult education; re-organisation of the Board's finances; much closer contact with the local authorities and teachers' representatives; great development of the Intelligence Section of the Board. All through the meal I had rather the feeling of being under inspection myself, and therefore did far less than justice to my zeal for Education.

I had been told that Trevelyan was 'a sentimental ass', always under the dominion of one obsession or another; at one time a single tax; at another, co-education; but I think he must have improved greatly, thanks to the trials

[1] Charles Philips Trevelyan (1870–1958); son of Sir G. O. Trevelyan, Bt.; Liberal M.P. 1899–1918, Labour M.P. 1922–31; Parliamentary Secretary, Board of Education 1908–14, President, Board of Education 1924, 1929–31.

and adversities of the last few years. As he himself remarked, 'Though I come of a governing family, and though I was against the War, I, like others, suffered a sort of shell-shock.' My only doubt about him is whether he can impose his excellent intentions on his Department. . . .

1 February, Friday Breakfasted with Lionel Curtis in Herbert Baker's house in Smith Square, which Curtis has borrowed during Baker's absence erecting Government buildings in Delhi.

Curtis finds that J. H. Thomas is exercising a quite positive influence at the Colonial Office, and has no intention of being a passive instrument in the hands of the officials. Yesterday they had a Conference on the Irish Question, preliminary to meeting Craig and Cosgrave today. Loughnane,[1] our man in Dublin, put the case for the South with such conviction that Thomas rounded on him as an Irish Free Stater! Curtis pointed out that our representatives abroad did always tend to take the view of the State in which they were located, and that was their great value. Thomas will be the Chairman of the Conference on the Boundary Question, as the P.M. is too busy in his double job. At the moment the problem looks quite insoluble. Curtis was very anxious to bring me somehow into the negotiations, but I was quite adamant that I must stand outside.

At 11.30 I saw Sidney Webb in his room at the Board of Trade and 'put him wise' about the proposed agreement between the British Dyes Corporation and the German combine.[2] Just before the last Cabinet went out, Lloyd-Greame had tried to rush the Cabinet into a decision to ratify an agreement which, in effect, would paralyse not only the dye industry in this country but also the great scientific development of the chemical industry which has already begun. I had seen James Morton[3] yesterday, and he assured me that more progress had been made with inventions in the dye industry in the last five years than in the last fifty years in the cotton industry, and he knows both industries intimately. In his view, given another five years of the protection afforded by the Dyestuffs Act, our colour makers would be able to stand on their own feet. But, of course, the colour users and the *Manchester Guardian* want the Act repealed. . . . I advised Webb to send for Sir Frank Heath[4] and also to ask Sir Llewellyn Smith[5] to turn his critical eye on the Agreement.

We then talked of Unemployment, and it was rather disappointing to find Sidney Webb, the author of pamphlets innumerable on the cure of unemployment regardless of cost, now, as Chairman of the Unemployment Committee, reduced to prescribing a revival of trade as the one remedy left to us.

On Housing, the same watering down of great expectations is taking place.

[1] N. G. Loughnane (1883–1954); a civil servant at the Colonial Office; British representative in the Irish Free State 1923-4.

[2] Lord Haldane was chairman and T.J. secretary of a Cabinet Committee dealing with the affair. The German combine was I. G. Farben.

[3] President of the British Dyes Corporation.

[4] Secretary of the Department of Scientific and Industrial Research.

[5] Permanent Under-Secretary at the Board of Trade.

Wheatley, the Minister of Health, is Chairman of the Cabinet Committee. He is from the Clyde, but 'Pale Pink' rather than 'Turkey Red'. He harangued the Standing Committee a couple of days ago, advocating a ten years' programme of 200,000 houses per annum, each to cost exactly £500 and to be let at exactly 7s. per week. How this stupendous sum is to be raised, and how prices and rents are to be kept static regardless of all market changes, he had no idea, and it had to be pointed out to him that his scheme implied the stabilisation of wages for ten years. The officials, with the aid of Arthur Greenwood, are busily engaged in watering down this scheme also.[1]

*   *   *   *

At 1 o'clock, to the Grill Room of the Grand to lunch with Buxton,[2] the Minister for Agriculture. He cross-examined me on the Secret Service funds employed by the Government through the Foreign Office, the fighting Services, and Scotland Yard, and wondered whether now, under a Labour Government, there could not be substantial economies and an end put to spying on Trade Unions. He is very anxious I should continue to be interested in the development of an agricultural policy, and asked me to find someone who could come and help to think out in a creative way such a policy in the Ministry. The idea which is growing up is to drop the Agricultural Organisation Society and to try and work through the Farmers' Union. I said it was necessary to discover a Horace Plunkett, prepared to address fifty-two meetings before making a single convert. We went across together to No. 10 at 2.30 where the P.M. was to receive the Agricultural Advisory Committee —the first meeting of the kind since his advent to office. It was also my first visit to No. 10 under the new *régime*. As we went in, the P.M. was hurrying across to the Irish Conference. He returned at a quarter to three and spoke for about ten minutes. It was all very like old times—the same old books on the shelves, the same blotting pads, Walpole looking down upon us from the mantelpiece. I noticed three or four new books on the P.M.'s table, one of them his own, in a new wrapper, *Socialism, Critical and Constructive* . . . . On a side table there was an enormous stuffed black cat, with a red ribbon round its neck—no doubt the symbol of good luck from some fond admirer.

The P.M. wears his grey hair almost as long as L.G. His speech, too, had a strong likeness to the sort of speech that L.G. would deliver in similar circumstances. He speaks with greater fluency and greater emphasis, but, closely examined, you had the same assurance of a fervent desire to help the great national industry of Agriculture, to reconcile all conflicting interests, etc., etc., and when at the end George Edwards, the veteran leader of the farm servants, voiced his deep disappointment, the P.M. pointed out that you could not subsidise the wages of farm labourers without at once being assailed with demands from the miners, the textile workers—all of which was

[1] They failed, and Wheatley's Housing Act of 1924 became the Government's only lasting legislative success, as well as the foundation of local authority house-building between the wars.

[2] Noel Edward Noel-Buxton (1869–1948); son of a Governor of South Australia; Liberal M.P. 1905–6, 1910–18; Labour M.P. 1922–30; Minister of Agriculture and Fisheries 1924, 1929–30. Cr. peer 1930.

true to precedent. I whispered to Sir Daniel Hall, at my elbow, that we were not going to see just yet the New Jerusalem set up in England's green and pleasant land! The P.M. had to go off to deal with the state of Europe, at the Foreign Office, and excused himself from remaining. He closed with asking the blessing of God on the industry in accents more like those of Baldwin than of L.G. or of Bonar Law!

The first Conference on the question of the Irish Boundary Commission took place in London on 1 February and was almost at once adjourned for a month. The attempt to get round the Boundary trouble failed, partly because of the insistence of Ulster on adequate representation on the All-Ireland Council which was proposed as an alternative. T.J. did not attend the Conference but he kept in close touch with Cope, Curtis, and Loughnane.

2 February . . . I came away with Cope,[1] whom I had not seen since his return from the States. He had preceded L.G. and had staged the tour. L.G. had been most anxious about his arrival at New York being a success, and Cope had gone to endless trouble to secure this—a representative of the President, a gunboat which took L.G. off the steamer at breakfast-time and kept him cruising about for several hours so that he should arrive just as everybody was finishing lunch, deputations of Jews and Greeks, boxes in the theatre, bouquets of flowers at the appropriate moment to Dame Margaret—all was planned to the minutest detail. Imagine Cope's feelings when there stepped off the boat Sir William Sutherland, whose first sentence to Cope was, 'I am Lloyd George's friend, I am in charge of all his American business, you must not see the Press', etc., etc. From this point on Cope's life was hell, as Sutherland kept poisoning L.G.'s mind until at last the situation got so bad that L.G. ordered Cope to return home and gave him a couple of hours in which to pack up! Cope returned, and staged L.G.'s arrival at Southampton, and though the tension between them has been acute, there have since been some pleasant interludes at Churt among the roses. At the moment Cope is smashing up the organisation of the National Liberals as the two Parties are being merged, and L.G. is relapsing very much into the position of a Private Member. . . . [Cope] thinks that very little would turn L.G. into a country gentleman, living quietly in retirement at Churt, but I think this must be a misjudgment and that L.G. is just loafing after the terrific outburst of energy in America and in the General Election. He is always re-creating Churt, and his Rolls-Royce has been re-painted in black and gold, and, as Cope told him, 'You have made it so conspicuous that you cannot possibly go to see Lord Beaverbrook in it!' That is the sort of remark which I can imagine makes it difficult for L.G. to work with Cope.

19 March, Wednesday Curtis lunched with me. Much concerned about Ireland. . . .

*   *   *   *

[1] Who, after the conclusion of the Irish Treaty, had been given the post of secretary of the National Liberal Federation, by Lloyd George.

We talked of India. Curtis thinks we ought to send out someone like Hilton Young to report on the working of the Montagu-Chelmsford reforms[1] up to date rather than have a lot of extremists brought over here for a Conference, as Wedgwood[2] has persuaded the Cabinet to suggest to Reading.[3] I learned later from Hankey that this proposal had been considered and Lord Arnold[4] suggested it, but it was rejected by the Cabinet in favour of a round-table conference.

Dined alone with Haldane at Queen Anne's Gate. He came in at 8.15 straight from the Woolsack, where he had been defending Cope's character against a scandalous attack by Lord Muskerry, who a few days ago had charged Cope with betraying this country to the Sinn Feiners and sending some of our men to their death. This charge he had been asked by Cope to repeat outside, but he had refused, and continued to refuse despite the appeal of Lord Fitzalan and of Lord Haldane. However, Curzon came to the rescue, and very grudgingly Muskerry withdrew. The trouble about this sort of attack is that some people will say there is no smoke without a fire, but no-one who knew and worked with Cope could doubt his essential loyalty throughout all the infinitely difficult and dangerous negotiations which he put through. What would Lord Muskerry say if he knew that I helped to draft some of Arthur Griffith's replies to our own letters! And no doubt in Dublin Cope did the same. But it was our job to keep the negotiations from breaking down and to help our Chiefs to pull off the Treaty for which they were so patiently striving.

*   *   *   *

I drew him on to talk about the Treaty of Mutual Guarantee, which Bob Cecil is pressing, and I told him that Hanotaux had simply made rings round Parmoor[5] at Geneva and that it was imperative that Parmoor should be reinforced at future meetings. The French want to abolish the Temporary Mixed Commission, really because there are civilians on it, and they want disarmament dealt with by the Permanent Commission, on which there are no civilians. Haldane said he had talked the matter over generally with the P.M., and their view is that we should not bother overmuch at the moment with these problems, but should put all our money on a Conference with France in June, a settlement of Reparations, and then an attempt to bring Germany and Russia into the League. With the Council of the League thus strengthened we could tackle problems of security and mutual guarantee

---

[1] The reforms followed the Montagu-Chelmsford Report of 1918, embodied in the Government of India Act, 1919. Essentially they meant 'dyarchy', giving some power to elected legislative councils but reserving the chief powers to Governors and to the Viceroy and his Executive.

[2] Josiah Clement Wedgwood (1872–1943); Liberal, then Labour M.P. 1906–42; Chancellor of the Duchy of Lancaster 1924; vice-chairman of the Labour Party 1921–4; cr. Baron 1942.

[3] Secretary of State for India.

[4] Under-Secretary of State for the Colonies.

[5] Charles Alfred Cripps (1852–1941), cr. Lord Parmoor 1914; Conservative M.P. 1895–1914; Lord President in Labour Governments 1924, 1929–31. Brother-in-law of Beatrice Webb, father of Stafford Cripps.

much more effectively. I told him that some scientists like Professor Soddy[1] and others were eager to raise the question of chemical warfare and try to bring about some international convention, possibly to develop among scientists a professional attitude against offensive chemical warfare, comparable to that of the attitude of doctors. Haldane was familiar, as Chairman of the C.I.D., with the activities of America, France, and Germany, and said, as Balfour in effect said at Washington, that while loathing the whole poison gas business we could not agree to stop research so long as other countries engaged in it. With a strengthened League of Nations we might later on raise the matter, but it was most unlikely that Germany, in particular, who excelled in this sort of scientific preparation, would let go such a potent weapon.

20 March Luncheon at Bellomo's with Lord Astor and Garvin. Garvin told us that Churchill was in for Westminster,[2] but between Astor's house and the restaurant a messenger caught us with the figures of the recount, which put Churchill out by 43 votes. We were all sorry. The Dardanelles pursues Churchill most unfairly, for it was one of the big conceptions of the War, and if put through with vigour might have shortened the War by a couple of years. Garvin is one of the most brilliant conversationalists I meet. He talked most of the time, and when he did not I did, and Astor put in a monosyllable now and again. They were dining with [Frank] Hodges that night: what did I think of him? Was he a great man or only clever? I said that on growing acquaintance I thought he was less great than I once thought, but that, perhaps, was true of all of us when we became better known. Everything should be done to prevent a Coal Strike now, as it would mean a disastrous setback to trade. The owners' offer was much better than I expected, and it had been done in good time, and not, as with the dock employers, at the last moment. If the main issue could not be avoided, then we ought to try to move on Sir Arthur Duckham's plan of regional unification.

What did I think of the way things were going with the new Government? I replied that the P.M.'s position in the country was distinctly high, the position of business in the House almost hopeless, owing to the incompetence of Clynes and the inexperience of the Labour Whips; that J. H. Thomas was the ablest politician in the Government; he has a cold brain, like Lloyd George, is very conservative, a bit vain, and likes the comforts of this world. His colleagues were jealous of him, [because] he saw more of the P.M. than any of them. Hodges, by the way, and perhaps for similar reasons, is not popular with his colleagues. Hartshorn was a disappointment, his range was most limited, and even knowledge of his own Department seemed too great a burden for him to carry. Shaw, the Minister of Labour, had made a deplorable speech on unemployment the other day, but the fault lay partly in the fact that neither he nor the Cabinet as a whole had been able to

---

[1] The originator in part of the theory of atomic disintegration and the displacement law of radio-activity; discoverer of isotopes.

[2] Churchill had been defeated at Dundee in the General Election of 1923, and had fought this by-election at Westminster as an Independent. He now believed in the virtues of a centre party, but was in fact well on the way to his Conservative position of late 1924.

prescribe a panacea for unemployment. All Sidney Webb, as Chairman of the Committee, after 30 or 40 years of reflection on the problem, has been able to prescribe as a remedy is 'a revival of trade'. This, Garvin said, was entirely in harmony with his experience of Webb in olden days at the Coefficient Club, when Webb's mountainous brain always succeeded in producing an infinitesimal mouse. Astor said that he gathered at the Ministry of Health that Wheatley was growing in favour day by day. Their ideal Minister had hitherto been Neville Chamberlain, but they were now beginning to regard Wheatley as even an improvement on him.

But it was about India that Garvin talked most, and with great gravity. He thought it quite possible that within five years we might lose India, and with it, Goodbye to the British Empire. We took the wrong road when we took the road of dyarchy. Lloyd George was much to blame, because at that time he would back Greece instead of Turkey and the Moslems. The only solution was a federal one. . . .

Then he moved on to the sinister figure of Japan, governed by a sort of Roman Senate, shaping steadfastly a far-seeing policy, heedless of the gusts of popular favour or disfavour. From this he jumped to Ancient Rome and drew in brilliant fashion parallels between our Imperial position and that of Rome.

On 27 March, during the prolonged Boundary Commission negotiations, at the insistence of the Colonial Secretary, J. H. Thomas, Curtis asked T.J. to cross to Ireland to meet President Cosgrave and to spy out the land for him. T.J. was unwilling to become directly involved but he at length agreed and was transferred temporarily to the Colonial Office.

T.J. duly crossed to Ireland, where he met President Cosgrave and several of the Irish Cabinet Ministers. He did his best to persuade them to resume negotiations and to find a way to prevent the Boundary dispute from coming into the open. At the end of March he was acting as intermediary, through Curtis, between Thomas and Cosgrave. The Free State Government finally agreed to come back to the Conference on condition that if it broke down again the Boundary Commission would be set up at once.

28 March   Home Affairs Committee. Noel Buxton was trying to rush through an Agricultural Wages Bill which he had not laid before the Cabinet Committee on Agricultural Policy. The Minister of Labour was taking exception to clauses in the Bill which failed to give ministerial responsibility for actual wages fixed by the County Committees. Before the meeting I warned Haldane of the controversy and said it was clearly a matter for the Cabinet Committee. So when the proceedings began Haldane just steam-rolled Buxton, and the Agricultural Committee will have to meet again. On an average I should think Haldane gets through an Agenda item in about three minutes!

1.30 Discussed Irish Boundary Commission with Curtis, Whiskard, and John Dove, the Editor of the 'Round Table' who had just returned from Ireland. I had lunch with Dove, and he gave me copies of letters from Ireland which he had written to the 'Round Table' group. I also got from him a balance-sheet of the 'Round Table', as Tawney and I are scheming to set going a 'Round Table' for Home Affairs.[1]

8 April   Dined at Portman Square with Mr. and Mrs. Yates Thompson. There were also Miss Moberley Bell, Hagberg Wright, of the London Library, and St. John Hornby—a delightful group of book lovers. Mrs. Thompson had planned the dinner so that I might again meet Mr. Hornby. He was in the Sixth Form at Harrow with S.B., and Yates Thompson is an old Harrovian, now 84 years of age, and though failing, able to recall much of interest.[2] Hornby, soon after leaving College, entered W. H. Smith's, and . . he set up a private printing press as far back as 1894. I asked if he were influenced by William Morris. He had met Morris once. It was his love of doing something with his hands and his training at W. H. Smith's that had really led him to set up a press. Mrs. Thompson had laid out a number of the Ashendene books for my enjoyment, including the *Lucretius* and the *Inferno*. The *Inferno* was the last book which Hornby set up with his own hand. The type he uses was cut by Prince, who died some months ago. Prince cut the type for the Doves' Press and the Kelmscott, and it is doubtful if he has left any successor. Hornby is now thinking of doing a folio edition of Shelford's translation of *Don Quixote* and of having a new type cut for it if he can find someone competent. He much admired the Gregynog *George Herbert*, but warned me that the woodcuts, if placed on the same page as the type, would be too black. . . . . I told Hornby that I could not print a book, nor could I afford, like Thompson, an illuminated manuscript, but that last week a great honour was done me by the man who many consider our finest living Welsh poet.[3] He has asked that he may dedicate the collected edition of his poems to me. When I told them that there was some danger of Augustus John illustrating the Mabinogion they were alarmed, for, as one of them remarked, 'John was certain to put bowler hats on the heads of all the princes!'

9 April   I was in the middle of papers dealing with ex-rankers' pensions when Mr. Stanley Baldwin was announced at the door. I was startled for a moment, as one does not have ex-Prime Ministers calling on one every day, but this was very like S.B., who began 'You will never come to see me, so I thought I would come to see you.' We gossiped for half an hour in the Office and then walked up to the United Universities Club and had lunch. After asking how I was getting on, he told me something of the worries of a Party Leader in days when there are no deep political convictions to divide men of good will. He had some troublesome followers who were clamouring for a positive policy without being able to suggest one. The one he had offered had been rejected. There was nothing for it but to await events, and he imagined that that was what L.G. was doing. Austen's view was that the

---

[1] *Note by T.J.:* This came into being seven years later as the 'Political Science Quarterly'.

[2] He had been head boy when Palmerston was Prime Minister. Mrs. Yates Thompson was the daughter of George Smith, publisher of the Brontë novels.

[3] T. Gwynn Jones.

Liberal Party was done for, and they made a pitiable spectacle a couple of
days ago on the Rent Restrictions Bill, when some Liberals voted with the
the Tories, some voted with Labour, and another group, including Asquith,
L.G., and Simon, abstained. S.B. thought that Asquith was too far gone to
be even Master of Balliol. For L.G., Winston had remarked to him, there
were only three courses open: to become Prime Minister, to smash a Party,
or to settle down as an Elder Statesman. For L.G. to become leader of the
Tory Party was impossible. 'I got to the top two years too soon; I had not
had enough experience; I did not know my men well enough; if I came back
again I should have to take Curzon as Foreign Secretary, because, at any
rate, he has the knowledge.' I said 'Curzon has no positive policy; he just lives
from one foreign telegram to the next.' S.B. agreed. He reverted more than
once to L.G. and speculations as to his future. We both agreed that no-one
at the moment could make any useful guess as to how matters would go
either with L.G. or S.B. The Westminster Election had been a great worry.
He had seen Balfour, who had apparently agreed to withhold his letter about
Winston—leaving the letter, however, with S.B. to be published if the situation changed. Then Amery plunged in and published a letter which left
S.B. no option but to release Balfour's letter. He joked about having to go on
making speeches without my help, and said that they had at any rate brought
him one vote, but that the vote of a very distinguished man—Thomas Hardy.
This led us to talk about literature. S.B. has to join with Clynes on the 29th
in toasting the memory of Byron, with special reference to his European fame.
I told him of Mazzini's essay, and promised to send it along. Herbert Fisher
had asked S.B. the other day what test he would set up to discover whether
a man had literary taste or not. Both agreed on Keats' *Ode on a Grecian
Urn*.

Reverting to politics, I told him something of my visit to Ireland and the
coming trouble on the Boundary Commission, and hinted that he should
keep in touch with Carson and Craig and try to bring Ulster into a more
reasonable mood. Clement Jones joined us at coffee, and I then walked down
nearly to Palace Chambers, where S.B. has now a room and a staff of secretaries—Geoffrey Fry, Lancelot Storr, and Pembroke Wicks.

9 April   Lord Esher to T.J.
It is no business of mine, but I think all this talk about the P.M. being *unable*
to combine the F.O. with the P.M.-ship is twaddle. I have, ever since I can
remember, known something of the inner working of Governments here and
in France. The secret of efficiency is organisation. Poincaré's office is *perfectly*
run: the P.M.'s is rottenly run. L.G., of course, had a glimmering of how to
manage 10 Downing Street, *but*, the men around him were a thoroughly bad
lot, bar Philip Kerr, Grigg, and yourself. Hence the attacks on the Kindergarten. But for the P.M. to have a Chef de Cabinet is essential. Hankey
ought to fulfil this function, but he does not. He does not, because he has
never shaken off the old C.I.D. atmosphere and because he funks Warren
Fisher.

What the P.M. should do, is to make the *Under* Secretary to the Cabinet the head of *his* office, and the liaison officer between 2 Whitehall Gardens and Downing Street. He should reorganise the Home Affairs Committee on the lines of what Haldane proposed in his Reconstruction of Government Report,[1] and which he has very lamely tried to repudiate in recent correspondence with me. Ask Lawrence to get hold of these letters and you show them to the P.M.

There simply *is* no Foreign Secretary available except the P.M. himself. So it is futile to look for one.

You should rub all this in.

By 24 April, when Cosgrave met Craig in London, it was clear that agreement on the Boundary Commission was unlikely. T.J. suggested to Thomas that MacDonald should be brought in, but Thomas preferred to conduct the negotiations himself. T.J.'s papers contain an interesting memorandum which he drafted with Curtis concerning the setting up of the Commission. During the discussion at Thomas's house in Dulwich . . .
Cope ventured to suggest that Craig might be placated with a peerage. Thomas replied, 'He can have a b . . . . y Dukedom if it will do the trick; I made a Peer and two Knights yesterday. . . .' He went on to say that he would make a strictly impartial statement in the House, but that in the meantime he would bring every possible pressure privately on Craig. He would go to see 'Ned Carson', as he called him, and the King. He passed on from Ireland to talk of home politics, and he discussed with Cope the idea of a very secret dinner at his own house, at which L.G. and the P.M. should meet. J.H.T. is all for a close co-operation between the two men. I said I was doubtful whether the P.M. would attend.

Home shortly after midnight.

Lloyd George invited T.J. to Churt for a weekend.

27 April, Sunday   A car met me at Guildford and took me to Churt by about 10.30. Mrs. Carey Evans there, Miss Sophie Rees (Private Secretary to Dame Margaret), and L.G. L.G. and I talked from 11 till 1, it being too wet to walk out. He began by telling me of his visit to his constituents in Carnarvonshire. Excellent meetings, lots of young people, and a growing opposition to Labour among the Liberals. Throughout our talk he was plainly preoccupied with the relations of the Liberal Party in the House and in the country to the Labour Party, and clearly willing to be on good terms with Labour. He did not want office—he had had his fling—but he was out to help. The Labour programme was more timid and prudent than his own pre-War campaign. They were doing nothing about the land, and they would muddle Housing. I suggested they would get lots of 'kudos' from the Budget which is to be introduced on Tuesday. He replied 'Only if it is a bold Budget and if it leads to a first-class controversy.' Otherwise he did not think there would be many votes in it. He was much impressed with Wheatley's emotional eloquence: 'I had a lump in my throat when he spoke the other day on evictions.' I suggested that what the Liberal Party needed was a

[1] Of 1918.

coherent constructive policy which could be distinguished from Socialism and Toryism. He said that a number of Committees were at work shaping out such a policy, and after lunch he gave me a Memorandum by Philip Kerr, written for one of these Committees, in which P.K. urged nationalisation of minerals and a substantial increase in the workers' participation in the control of the industry. There is a Committee on Electrification also. 'But', he went on, 'the trouble is that when you have got a policy ready and Asquith launches it, it will freeze on his lips; all kindling warmth and hope will die out of it; he will present it accurately, but without sympathy.' He liked Asquith, worked cordially with him, but as a leader he was too coldly intellectual. I mentioned Cope's conversation with J. H. Thomas. He was all for meeting the P.M., either in J. H. Thomas's house, in Cheyne Row, or in Churt. It was absurd that the two Parties should not understand and help each other in the present circumstances. The two Whips, Vivian Phillips and Ben Spoor,[1] were largely to blame for the present estrangement.

* * * *

After lunch, it being still very wet, he went upstairs to sleep. We met again at tea. He said he was reading Shaw's *Heartbreak House*. In his opinion Shaw was our greatest writer, greater than Hardy, in his opinion, and certainly greater than Wells.

I caught a train back at Farnham at 6 o'clock, and before I left Philip Snowden[2] rang up from his nearby cottage to ask L.G. to go round there for supper and talk.

On 26 April the Free State Government formally requested the setting up of the Boundary Commission. The British Government asked the Northern Irish Government to appoint its representative, but Craig 'respectfully declined'. For a while it was hoped that the Governor-General might be able to do so instead, and on 30 April Sir Robert Borden, former Prime Minister of Canada, was invited to be the Chairman. He later, however, declined.

2 May   Dined at the Reform Club with Sir Arthur Salter, J. R. Brook, Ted Lloyd, Ralph Enfield; Frank Wise coming in later. Salter had been in Paris for some weeks before the appearance of the Report of the Experts on Reparations, and had met all the principal actors. Dawes was a figurehead, Owen Young was the effective person from the U.S.A., but Sir Josiah Stamp[3] had done more for the Report than all the other experts put together. But Stamp cannot write attractive English, and right at the very end Owen Young came secretly to Salter, showed him Stamp's draft; Salter criticised its style and method of presentation, and at Young's bidding re-wrote Part I. Salter insisted that Stamp should be told, and Young, Stamp, and Salter then met.

[1] Liberal and Labour respectively.

[2] Philip Snowden (1864–1937), cr. Viscount 1931; Labour M.P. 1906–18, 1922–31; Chairman of the I.L.P. 1903–6, 1917–20; Chancellor of the Exchequer 1924, and 1929–31; Lord Privy Seal 1931–2.

[3] Sir Josiah Charles Stamp (cr. Baron 1938) (1880–1941); British representative on the Dawes (1924) and Young (1929) Committees on reparations; Director of the Bank of England 1928–41.

Stamp behaved most handsomely, took his own and Salter's draft home, got up at 4 the next morning, worked on the two drafts, substantially accepting Salter's version of Part I. It was Salter who drafted the Report of the Bankers at the Brussels Conference, and he has been behind the scenes in most of these gatherings. He has a strictly logical mind, entirely concentrated on the business in hand, unmarried, and with no interest that I can discover outside the League of Nations and Reparations. His people make and run boats at Oxford.

8 May   *   *   *   *

... Met Arthur Henderson after lunch. Abercorn has gone back to Belfast to consider his action in regard to the Boundary Commission. Impressed on Henderson—as I also have on Hankey—the importance of the P.M., J. H. Thomas, and Henderson seeing Asquith, L.G., and Baldwin, with a view to their advancing together on this question. Once Craig can be made to realise that he could not split the Parties on the issue here, it would make an immense difference. Henderson said it was very unlikely that J.H.T. would be willing to join in any step which took away from his own importance in the matter.

9 May, Friday 11.30 Home Affairs Committee, with Haldane in the Chair. Members are now taking this Committee more seriously since their absentee- ism was commented on at the Cabinet. We had before us a Factories Bill with about 150 Clauses, which Haldane confessed he had sat up late and got up early to read; but the chief wrangle was about the Guardianship of Infants Bill. Haldane, Parmoor, and the Lord Advocate (Hugh Macmillan) disliked it intensely, but Slesser (the Solicitor-General), Schuster, and John Anderson, acting as they thought under the instructions of the Committee, had made a bargain with Mrs. Wintringham and her backers. The squabble was referred to the Cabinet for decision. Including the various experts there were 25 present at this meeting.

4.30 to a tea party at the Webbs', where I heard from my host of the scene in the House over the Scottish Home Rule Bill.[1] The Clydesmen had resented Sir Robert Horne getting up to oppose the Bill, he having been absent dur- ing most of the preceding speeches. They felt the Opposition was having too good a show. The understanding had been that the Speaker would grant the Closure, but as the Debate developed he changed his mind and the big Bill was talked out in a scene of great disorder.

11 May, Sunday Went this morning to Hatch End, to lunch with Sir George[2] and Lady Newman. ... He thinks Sir Thomas Horder ought never to have allowed Bonar Law to take on the Premiership. Newman recalled a famous occasion when L.G. and B.L. sent for him and begged him to use every effort to keep Terence McSwiney (the Lord Mayor of Cork) alive. His death at that moment would have been most troublesome. He had already been

---

[1] The Bill was introduced by George Buchanan, one of the Clydeside group, and its apparent 'suppression' after a parliamentary arrangement caused considerable heat.
[2] Chief Medical Officer at the Board of Education and the Ministry of Health.

hunger-striking for thirty days. Newman kept him alive for another forty-two! Newman is an old friend of the present P.M., but he, like others, finds him much given to acting and posing.

During the early part of May T.J. did his best to ease the Irish Boundary deadlock, because if the North did not appoint a Commissioner, the Commission could not legally be constituted. On 21 May the Cabinet decided to refer the points in dispute to the judgement of the judicial Committee of the Privy Council. Reluctantly, the South acquiesced.

23 May, Friday   3 p.m. motored to Oare with Geoffrey Fry, Stanley Baldwin's Private Secretary. With us was Charles Baillie-Hamilton, one of the young hopefuls of the Tory Party, fresh from Eton and Oxford. . . . Fry lives in a perfect Georgian house built about 1740 for a wine merchant, and enlarged for Fry three or four years ago by Clough Williams-Ellis.

25 May, Sunday   Fry and Hamilton got fearfully excited over the second article in *The People* recounting the interview of its Political Correspondent with Stanley Baldwin.[1] This article purports to tell in great detail the story of the preparations for the interview, and also—even more fully than in the original account—what Mr. Baldwin said. Fry had hoped up to the last minute that *The People*, as a Conservative journal, was going to let the matter drop, but here were half a dozen columns, most damaging to S.B. and the Party, if true. There was no one present at the interview besides S.B. and Wilson the journalist, no proof of the interview was submitted, Wilson made no notes during the interview, Baldwin says he never made the statement attributed to him that Beaverbrook had misused private information given him by Bonar Law. Anyone who knows S.B. intimately cannot but feel that the interview reflects substantially his general attitude to politics and to his colleagues. Wilson, on the other hand, has a bad record. He is said to have been guilty of other journalistic indiscretions when dealing with Ministers. He ought clearly never to have been allowed to see a man of Baldwin's type, or the Secretaries should have insisted on a proof. Fry is terrified lest Beaverbrook should bring an action for slander against *The People*. Its proprietor is Grant Morden, a Canadian with a reputation similar to that of Beaverbrook. Whether the two men are now on friendly terms with each other I could not discover. Some thought it unlikely that Beaverbrook would risk going into the witness-box because of his own lurid past. Fry and Hamilton decided at 11 o'c. to motor up at once to town to see their Chief, and they landed at Baldwin's house almost at the same moment as he himself arrived from Wilfrid Ashley's place in the country. They motored back to Oare and joined us at dinner at 8.30, with the news that S.B. had decided to make no public reference to the matter.

[1] This came in the middle of Baldwin's campaign of speeches between May and June, which revived the Conservative party and provided the platform of policy which was to dominate the 1925–9 Government. Party officials were worried that the article might prejudice the success of the campaign.

At the end of May Mr. Justice Feetham, of the South African Supreme Court, was invited to be the Chairman of the Boundary Commission.

27 May . . . Lunch in Dean's Yard. Halévy there, the French historian of our Nineteenth Century Economic History. He is at present working on the Boer War period. There was also present Isaac Marcosson, the well-known American journalist, who once published a book called *Adventures in Interviewing*. As I preside on these occasions, and as I was rather full of the Baldwin interview, I warned Marcosson jocularly that he would have to submit a proof to me of anything he intended to publish as the result of today's lunch! However, I took care that he did most of the talking. His favourite candidate for the Presidency for years past has been Leonard Wood. Coolidge he described as a 'cold fish', who, if he drank pints of hot toddy, would sweat it all out in iced water. This led to someone to say of Beaverbrook that if he swallowed nails he would emit them as corkscrews—he was such a twister! Curtis quoted someone as saying that the War of Independence had given us a series of Presidents on the throne and had given the United States a series of George III's. . . .

This afternoon Hankey told me that Esher's scheme for developing a Co-ordinating Committee on Civil Affairs had been approved on the previous day and that I was to be its Secretary. He was rather gloomy and sceptical about it all, and I rather shared his mood, pointing out that in the preparation of a War Book it is so much easier to exclude politics than it would be in preparing a Peace Book. I gathered that the sort of questions which it is proposed to study would deal with taxation, the Whitehall machinery for dealing with the Dominions and the Crown Colonies, whether, e.g., the Dominions should be taken out of the Colonial Office and put into the Privy Council; the position of the sheltered trades, i.e., railways, building trades, and others which do not suffer from foreign competition. I suggested Devolution as a possible topic. Warren Fisher is to put up a Treasury Minute and the matter will then probably go to the Cabinet. What I fear is that I shall not be given anything like an adequate staff to do the job properly. Hankey's success is in no small part due to the abundant assistance which he always secures. On the C.I.D. side there is a man seconded from the Army, the Navy, the Air, and India, in addition to his personal Staff.

The Secretary of the British Drama League called to ask my advice as to how best to approach the Prime Minister with a view to securing the land between this Office and the Thames as a site for the National Theatre. Found him very vague, and suggested he should call his Committee and the Committee of the Shakespeare Memorial Theatre, clear their own minds as to what they wanted, and then ask the P.M. to receive a Deputation.

6–9 June To Gregynog for Whitsun. On Saturday Ernest Rhys travelled up from Exmoor to join us. . . . Some weeks ago E.R. picked up in the London Library a copy of the *George Herbert* and he wrote praising it to Sir Walford Davies, who made the selection, and in his letter showed such appreciation of the Press idea that we decided to invite him to co-operate. His experience as Editor of the 700 or 800 volumes of 'Everyman' should be of great help to us. His 'Celtic Notes' a few days ago in the *Manchester Guardian* contained the first review of the Press that has appeared. . . . We decided that E.R. should edit a selection of Henry Vaughan's poems, and that he and Maynard should go down to Breconshire to visit spots associated with Vaughan, for the purpose of woodcuts. . . . The ladies[1] are rather keen to have a new type cut for the Press, and there was some talk of asking Edward Johnson, of Little Ditchling, to advise on this, but finally we agreed to await the publication of Stanley Morison's *Four Centuries of Fine Printing*. I think our only difference was on what price should be charged for the Ceiriog. I suggested off-hand half a guinea as the maximum that Welsh subscribers would be likely to be able to pay. This alarmed Maynard, as the book will probably cost about three or four times as much to produce. I urged that we might make our money out of the rich English Philistines when publishing the English books. After all, the Press is not out to fill the shelves of collectors,[2] but primarily to raise the taste of the Welsh people. I proposed that we should arrange to supply the County Schools with Gregynog Books, to take the place of the ordinary school prizes. What usually happens is that a quite poor text is bought and an expensive binding put round it.

On Monday evening, after the others had retired, I discussed business with E.R. in a quite frank fashion. . . . We agreed that he should be paid thirty guineas for editing and writing an Introduction to the 'Henry Vaughan'. He has obviously been badly hit by the War, and the high cost of publishing has slowed down—indeed, almost stopped—the issue of the 'Everyman' volumes. Some time ago he was driven to sell £60 worth of his first editions. Luckily the bookseller who bought these, inferring that he was hard up, disclosed the fact that he had been entrusted by Sir John Ellerman (who had made tons of money in the War) to distribute a sum of money to impecunious literary men. Subsequently E.R. inherited a legacy of £700. Now comes the Gregynog Press, and so he told me it had always been—a door opened when all seemed lost.

11 June Hankey wrote today to Sir Warren Fisher a note about the proposal to set up some sort of Cabinet Committee to deal with what Haldane calls 'Economic and Statistical Policy'. There has been much discussion of this project recently. Esher has had a letter in *The Times* about it, and on 27 May Haldane wrote to the P.M. saying he had discussed the matter informally and privately with Warren Fisher, Sir Josiah Stamp, Sir Richard Hopkins, and Hankey. On Hankey's instructions I drew up a short Memorandum and a draft Minute based very closely on the Minute which set up the present Committee of Imperial Defence. Another Memorandum is in circulation drafted by Sir Richard Hopkins. It is practically confined to statistics, and is much narrower, therefore, than the scheme which Haldane

---

[1] The Misses Davies, who financed the Gregynog Press.
[2] This is in fact what happened.

and Esher have in mind. What precisely the P.M. wants I am not sure.[1] He sent Lees-Smith[2] to see me the other day. Lees-Smith was not very clear. The P.M. was especially concerned about Unemployment, and wanted to be in a position in the middle of July to make a statement of the Government's policy which would meet the criticism that they had none. I was to give all the papers of the Shaw Unemployment Committee and the new 'ginger' Committee under Snowden to Lees-Smith, and generally Lees-Smith was to act as a sort of liaison between me and the P.M., while I would of course obtain all the information available. The truth is, so I gathered from Lees-Smith, that the P.M. is now feeling the need of someone to do for him the sort of work I used to do for his predecessors.

12 June Luncheon at the Villa Villa with Lees-Smith and E. M. H. Lloyd, of the Overseas Trade Department. Talked about the Trade Facilities Act and how far it could be stretched to help the unemployment problem. It is now worked by bankers, whose first concern is not to lose money. Lees-Smith wanted it to take greater risks.

18 June Luncheon at the Villa Villa with Lees-Smith and J. R. Brooke, of the Ministry of Transport. Discussed a possible electrical programme of the Government.

24 June R.S.G. lunch. Schaffner there. He is a member of a big Chicago clothing firm who have for some years past maintained first-rate relations with their workpeople. The success of their policy, he told me, was largely due to the personality of their first Arbitrator, a Welshman called John Williams, the wisest man he had ever known. He is staying at the Cavendish Hotel, Jermyn Street, which is kept by a Mrs. Lewis, of whom much scandal was retailed at lunch. . . . Schaffner told a good statistical story. A Roman Catholic in New York, asked by his priest why he had only three children, replied that he had stopped at three because he had read in a newspaper that every fourth child born in New York was a Jew!

This afternoon I went to the National Physical Laboratory at Teddington, and was received by Sir Charles Sherrington, Professor Schuster, and other lights of the Royal Society. I went through endless laboratories, but there was hardly an exhibit within my unscientific comprehension. . . .

[1] Later, on 27 June, MacDonald described his aim thus: '. . . a Standing Committee, analogous to the Committee of Imperial Defence, whose function will be to examine, from the point of view of ascertained and ascertainable economic data, proposals of policy, potential as well as actual. The formulation and decision of policy is a matter for the Cabinet; the business of this Committee (as is the case with the Defence Committee) would be to ensure that all the material facts and information at the disposal of the Government Service are made available in practical form for use by the Cabinet in reaching its conclusions. I am sure that my colleagues will agree with me in my view that there is room in spheres other than that of national defence for a body similar to the Committee of Imperial Defence and that the precedent of the latter Committee provides an assurance that the labours of such a body will be invaluable to the Government.' *(Quoted from a memorandum by the Prime Minister, in T.J.'s papers.)*

[2] Hastings Bertrand Lees-Smith (1878–1941); Liberal M.P. 1910–18, Labour M.P. 1922–3, 1924–31, 1935–41; Postmaster-General 1929–31; President, Board of Education 1931.

Dined at the House of Commons with Frank Murrell, Robert Richards (India Office), Hope Simpson, M.P., and Dr. Mann, who for many years has been a Director of Agriculture in India. All of us much perplexed about the Indian situation, Dr. Mann denouncing the Montagu-Chelmsford Reforms as conceived in England and quite unsuitable. The burden of his advice was that whatever we do next should originate in India and not be imposed from England. He thought Gandhi's power was not on the wane. I asked how many of the 310 millions had heard of Gandhi? He replied '309 millions'; there had never been anything like such a popular figure.

Luncheon at Claridges as guest of Otto Kahn.[1] On his right, Lord Balfour; on his left, Forbes-Robertson. T. P. O'Connor, Lord Denman, Sir Philip Gibbs, John Drinkwater, Major Beith ('Ian Hay'), Sydney Brookes and one or two others. . . . I was standing with Drinkwater when Balfour arrived, and the talk turned to the Wimbledon tennis at once. Drinkwater claimed Brooks' victory the day before as being due to some Dr. Johnson's Tablets—some cure for indigestion—which Drinkwater had administered to Brooks some hours before the game. Balfour, in his usual polite way, pretended to be deeply interested in 'Dr. Johnson's Tablets', whereupon Drinkwater produced from his vest pocket a small box and Balfour helped himself to one. Could politeness go further?

3 July Stanley Baldwin sends for me. He has been asked to preside at an Eisteddfod, was obviously pleased, thinking it to be the 'National'. Asked what sort of speech he should make and for how long. As I was sceptical he rang for Secretary who did not know which Eisteddfod. There had been a 'phone message from somewhere in Wales. They would wire to ask, etc., etc. I explained that Eisteddfods differed one from the other in glory. Later heard it was Llandrindod, not National at Pontypool, so I advised refusal.

7 July Dined alone with Haldane in order to talk of the Committee of Economic Enquiry,[2] of which he expects to be Chairman and I am proposed as Secretary. He has been defeated on the Unemployment Committee in the matter of Forestry policy and wants to bring it up on the C.E.E. . . . Much talk of the Cabinet. Ramsay keeps aloof from his Ministers and has made many bad blunders recently:—Chequers interview with Herriot, the ambiguity of his utterances, etc. He has courage but no passion, no deep sympathy with the poor.

Gladstone—'Mr. G.'—was the greatest man he had ever known and in some ways he would put Parnell next. Clemenceau and Foch—yes. L.G.— no, not since the War. Asquith, in the days of the first Mrs. Asquith, he used

[1] Banker and well-known philanthropist, who was of great service to the British Government during the 1914–18 war.

[2] This body, referred to by Haldane as the Committee on Economic and Statistical Policy (see MacDonald's minute above, p. 283, note 1), was never actually set up by the Labour Government; but in a modified form, under the auspices of Balfour, Baldwin, and Cunliffe-Lister, it became the Committee of Civil Research in 1925.

to dine with at Hampstead twice or thrice a week, and he showed me a photograph of the Asquith of those days, very like Sir Edward Grey.

8 July   Dined 8 Hill Street with Geoffrey Fry. Met for the first time Clough Williams-Ellis and his wife. . . . She is St. Loe Strachey's daughter, and does dramatic criticism, etc., for the *Spectator*. They are befriending Richard Hughes, a playwright just beginning, who has a Welsh ancestry and has settled near Portmadoc to imbibe the legendary lore of Snowdonia, I suppose. Graves, the poet, is there close by.

10 July   . . . At 9.0 to Church Street, Chelsea, to the Herbert Hughes's with Rene. John MacCormack, the tenor, and his wife there, Beatrice Harrison, the cellist, and her mother, John Ireland, the song writer, Joe Devlin, Robert Lynd and Sylvia, Harriet Cohen, the pianist, J. B. Fagan and his wife, and I know not what other brilliant Irish folk. We left with the Lynds about 1 a.m., after much delightful music-making and talk.

After Herriot's visit to Chequers, MacDonald had summoned a reparations conference in London; his main objects were to quiet French fears of German resurgence, and to win the acceptance of the report on reparations prepared by the committee of experts under the American, General Dawes. This report put forward a proposal based on what Germany could actually pay, and its acceptance, and the loan to Germany which followed it, effectively solved the problem for the next five years—until the world economic crisis.

16 July   Reparation Conference begins. First meeting at Foreign Office. Ramsay MacDonald presiding. Snowden and J. H. Thomas and Eyre Crowe for us. Proceedings delayed for some minutes because the chief Italian delegates had got themselves lost, though they had left Claridges with their staff. I suggested they had gone for a drive in the Park in order to try and agree what they would say at the Conference. I was 'in attendance' with Howorth, as it was not settled in advance whether we should summarise the proceedings or shorthand writers should take a verbatim note. We sat outside with Otto Niemeyer, Leith-Ross, and Josiah Stamp for a couple of hours and then learnt we should not be required. They broke up into three Committees, presided over by Snowden, J. H. Thomas, and Kindersley. Much trouble over Dominion representation at this Conference—Canada especially refractory.

21 July   At 8.0 to the Pilgrims Dinner to hear Charles Evans Hughes. I sat between two New Yorkers who were immensely gratified to see the Prince of Wales sitting between two Washington Ministers—Hughes and Mellon. Hughes spoke with great ease and distinction and with much more warmth of manner than I expected from the description of him as a cold legalist. He completely conquered his audience. He appeared to have notes and must have prepared and memorised carefully. Balfour sounded halting and less dexterous than usual. I shook hands with Hughes at the end and he asked about his cousin, Howell Harris Hughes, the Welsh Calvinistic preacher of Princes Road, Liverpool.

22 July   Proposed Committee of Economic Enquiry
Approved the Treasury Memorandum omitting 'public confidence', to read, 'to ensure that national problems were actually

(a) being faced and thought out in advance on a basis of fact.

(b) P.M. to take such action as he might think fit to set up the new Committee.

(c) The Secretary of the Committee should be Mr. T.J. of the Cabinet Office.'

Cabinet meet. They agree to the Committee of Economic Enquiry. The P.M. made no reference to Haldane as probable Chairman, to Haldane's disappointment.

The Prime Minister intended to be Chairman himself, in spite of objections that this would make the Committee too important in relation to the Cabinet. He wanted it to be equal to the Committee of Imperial Defence.

24 July   Dined at Geoffrey Fry's, 8 Hill Street, with G.F. and Dick Law only. All the talk about the Life of Bonar Law which Dick Law has undertaken to write with Beaverbrook's help. Dick very nervous about the job. Wondered had he not better wait 20 years. I counselled against this. He has leisure now. He has not embarked on a career. He reviews books for the *Evening Standard*. I urged him to write a full frank Life as a first draft, and he could then 'edit' for publication now, and leave his first draft in the British Museum for posterity if too frank for today. He thinks of taking Winston's Life of Lord Randolph as model. I said I thought he should lose no time in seeing Carson, Craig, and Fitzalan, who may not live long. Miss Law, B.L.'s sister, who knows the early period is, I gathered, not very communicative, and she is wrath with Baldwin over his references to B.L. and the General Election.

As the Session drew to a close three major problems presented themselves to the Government—the Boundary Commission, the Russian Treaty, and then the Campbell Case.

On 31 July the Judicial Committee of the Privy Council reported on the Irish Boundary dispute. Three days before, T.J. was told of the probable result—that legislation would be needed to appoint a third Commissioner, and that thereafter a majority decision would be enough to bind the Commission. But he found it hard to persuade Baldwin to agree to immediate legislation on an all-party basis, which was what the Government wished for. Great difficulty arose from the interpretation of the Irish Treaty of 1921, which had not been drafted with the same care as an Act of Parliament; and it became clear that, as he held the casting vote, the impartiality of Judge Feetham was going to be severely tested in any case of transference of territory.

Legislation was introduced before the House of Commons rose for the summer recess.

Meanwhile the Cabinet were deep in the final stages of the Russian negotiations. The Russians had, all along, demanded a loan as part of the treaty settling payment of

Russia's pre-revolutionary debts. On 5 August negotiations broke down, but were patched up after the intervention of several left-wing, mainly I.L.P. M.P.s. Their compromise provided for two treaties: the first to settle the debt, the second to guarantee the loan. The Conservatives immediately attacked it, not only because of the offer of the loan but because the agreement appeared to have been dictated to the Cabinet by the extremists of the Labour Party. Before the attack was mounted, however, the affair of the Campbell case came to light, as a result of an I.L.P. intervention at Question Time on 6 August. Sir Patrick Hastings, Attorney-General, was seen by James Maxton, who pleaded for Campbell, and that evening the Cabinet considered the case for the first time.

6 August   (Cabinet Minute)
The *Workers' Weekly*—Prosecution of Editor.
6 p.m. 5. The attention of the Cabinet was called to a prosecution which had been instituted against John Ross Campbell, Editor of the *Worker's Weekly*, the official organ of the Communist Party of Great Britain, under the Incitement to Mutiny Act, for attempting to seduce from loyalty to the King members of the Navy, Army, and Air Force who might read the articles in the *Workers' Weekly* entitled 'The Army and Industrial Disputes'.

The Home Secretary stated that a letter of apology had been received from the printers, who are giving notice to terminate their printing contract, and he understood the Attorney-General had given instructions that the printers should not be proceeded against.

The Attorney-General said he took full responsibility for proceeding with the case, which disclosed a bad criminal offence, but inasmuch as it transpired that the person charged was only acting temporarily as Editor[1] and was prepared to write a letter to that effect steps could be taken not to press the prosecution in the circumstances against this particular offender, if the Cabinet so desired.[2]

After considerable discussion of the procedure which had led to action being taken in the Courts without the knowledge of the Cabinet or the Prime Minister, the Cabinet agreed—

(a) That no public prosecution of a political character should be undertaken without the prior sanction of the Cabinet being obtained:

(b) That in the particular case under review the course indicated by the Attorney-General[3] should be adopted.

T.J.'s notes of this meeting (see 15 October).
6 p.m. Telegram from *Workers' Weekly* demanding resignation of Henderson.
    Webb: Director of Public Prosecution had applied to Hastings.
    Prime Minister: First I heard in House of Commons, Ammon said he'd had a Minute from Admiralty.[4] War Office agreed. Air agreed and

---

[1] He was actually assistant editor, under R. Palme Dutt; but he was one of the ablest journalists and propagandists in the British Communist Party.

[2] Campbell, although a Communist, had an excellent war record and had been very severely wounded. As Hastings later told the House of Commons, he was not a very suitable Communist to prosecute for sedition.

[3] I.e. withdrawal of the prosecution.

[4] Asking for a prosecution.

Admiralty asked for views. He minuted against it. But I said 'It will not be begun until I know'. You add 'P.M. must be informed before action taken'. In papers I read it—done.

Snowdon: Had been done then.

P.M.: I sent for Assistant Director Public Prosecution. I asked him to take files on which he acted. Hastings[1] said he did not authorise action. He was asked and said article criminal. Gave legal view. Assistant Director saw me—he produced Minute: S. of S. agrees to go on with prosecution.

Henderson: No. We agreed to transfer letters we'd received to the Director of Public Prosecutions—two documents—printer and one from Creedy. Nothing about prosecution. I asked A.-G. if he'd authorised proceedings. He agreed with you. He is under A.-G. not under me.

P.M.: I misread Minute also.

Henderson: My Secretary has known for a week that I was opposed to prosecution.

P.M.: No one agreed?

Henderson: I said it was criminal. I said get letter apology from printer who are cancelling contract. . . . Hastings said I'll write telling Director not to proceed against printer.

Chelmsford: I had papers this a.m. with Ammon's note. I noted; I think we may agree with two Secretaries because Home Office will watch matter.

Walsh: Papers brought to me by Adjutant-General and Creedy a few days ago. I went over Articles. Certain words were calculated to sow sedition. I minuted in my opinion a prosecution ought to lie. We've no power to prosecute.

Parmoor: Entire responsibility with Attorney-General.

P.M.: In case political should come to me.

(Haldane: Royal Commission to give assent to Bill at 11.30. Exit Haldane.)

J. H. Thomas: Nothing of this sort should happen without P.M. and Cabinet knowing of it.

Parmoor: Attorney-General is responsible officer and ought not to act without consulting.

P.M.: Not enough to give *legal*. . . .[2]

Wheatley: I think Attorney-General feels he has more responsibility than legal.

J.H.T.: Answer he gave in House was. . . .

Thomson: Yes.

P.M.: Nothing except against Editor. He'll do nothing more.

(Enter Attorney-General.)

Attorney-General: Temporarily taken on post of Editor—someone on holiday—if desire not to press prosecution that might be opening for Prosecuting Counsel. It would drop then. I have informally had word with one

---

[1] Sir Patrick Hastings (1880–1952); Labour M.P. 1922–6, Attorney-General 1924; one of the best-known barristers of the day, especially famous for his criminal cases.

[2] The omissions here are T.J.'s, not the editor's.

concerned with Debate tonight.[1] Make it difficult for criminal. So may get word debate won't go. . . .

J.H.T.: Create lively situation. Think they'd got us on run. Under whose authority. . . .

Attorney-General gave an account of origin of case.

(Exit Henderson.)

Bad criminal offence disclosed. Responsibility rests on me and I take it.

Parmoor: Ought you not to have consulted Prime Minister.

Attorney-General: Unfortunately there were two documents which rather looked as if there had been agreement. In case of great importance should go to Prime Minister.

Wedgwood: Like Crowsley case—railway fireman. Used 1797 incitement to mutiny. He got two years.

Attorney-General: Exceptionally bad article.

Walsh: Communication I signed did not direct prosecution. Rested with others.

Attorney-General: I should again advise prosecution, but there is a possible way out if you desire it as against this man.

Thomson: I don't remember the case at all.

Prime Minister: Settled that no one else will be arrested—I'd rather go through once started than show white feather. If you stop prosecution you will be asked all round what going to do. Editor is known—why not arrest him.

Walsh: Worst article I've ever read. One paragraph atrocious. I thought it would come before Cabinet. It would be peculiarly weak action if we abandoned prosecution having regard to all the circumstances.

J. H. Thomas: I move that it be an instruction that no prosecution of a political character take place without prior sanction of Cabinet.

(All agreed.)

Prime Minister: If put to me I should not have sanctioned it. I know the men and the game. Now in press and House of Commons. Answer given.

J. H. Thomas: Don't withdraw now in view of House of Commons.

Wedgwood: Can you shift Public Prosecutor.

Snowdon: Both hands up for that.

Prime Minister: I'd like to see that Minute again. Initial Secretary P.S.

Henderson: My initials not on. When my Secretary sent letter over proceedings were taken.

Attorney-General: Director Public Prosecution got documents signed by Army Council to Home Office and back.

Wedgwood: Who started it?

Prime Minister reads paragraph *Flesh of our Flesh*, etc., from *Workers' Weekly*.

J. H. Thomas: Tripe.

Attorney-General: No debate tonight or tomorrow. Man arrested prepared to write letter to say he was only few days.

J. H. Thomas: Real fight will start two months hence.

[1] James Maxton, one of the I.L.P. leaders.

Attorney-General: I'll accept his letter—reply being we had to take cognisance reluctantly.

Henderson: More questions tomorrow.

Attorney-General: Steps have been taken. Nothing to add.

(Attorney-General authorised.)

At a discussion among British Ministers, during a conference with the Southern Irish on 8 August, the legislative time-table for the Boundary Commission Bill in October was discussed.

P.M.: Very necessary for all of you to give me your addresses.

Clynes: Motion for whole time of House. Opposition of our people to it.

P.M.: We need the time for Govt. business. Our members won't give it. Say we'll regard it as censure of us. I'm getting sick of it. Over 60 went to lobby against our official amendment.

Webb: They don't understand necessity to move adjournment.

?: Not 60 can? us out.

P.M.: How often are we to swallow this?

Trevelyan: Whipping weak.

Shaw: We can have divisions against us with Labour members as tellers against us.

8 August   Last night P.M., Herriot, Theunis, Hyman, at No. 10.

Messenger let in General Nollet who rushed in and began a squabble with H. about evacuation of Ruhr and Rhineland territory, and wd not be ruled by L. of N., etc. P.M. tried to produce tranquillity and ultimately had to bring meeting to end by pointing to pile of despatch boxes he had to deal with before bedtime. Later remembering that he wanted to know whether his daughter had accomplished the first stage of her journey he went downstairs to ask messenger to phone, and was told that Frenchmen were wrangling in the Cabinet Room and that he was about to take them in some sustenance. When the P.M. went to bed at midnight they were still in the Cabinet Room.

MacDonald was uneasy about the minuting of the Cabinet discussion of the Campbell affair. The prosecution of Campbell was officially abandoned on 13 August and although the matter seemed to have been forgotten during the parliamentary recess, it was revived by both opposition parties when the House was recalled for the Irish Boundary legislation on 30 September. MacDonald denied that he had been consulted or implicated in the decision to withdraw the prosecution. This, in the light of the Cabinet discussion of 6 August, was not true; and as the debate, on the Liberal motion for a Select Committee to investigate, drew nearer, the Prime Minister had cause for alarm.

2 October   Sir Maurice Hankey to the Prime Minister   Secret

In the course of my conversation with you and the Lord Advocate today, you said that you could not recollect my having shown you the Minute of the Cabinet Meeting on 6 August in regard to the *Workers' Weekly*, and you repeated an observation of a general character which I have often heard you make (and with which I most deeply sympathise), that you objected to having documents pushed into your hands for approval at a time when your mind was full of other matters.

I have been able to reconstruct to some extent the circumstances in which, inevitably, I had to show you the draft Minute when you were under the greatest pressure.

You will recall that the meeting on 6 August took place at the House of Commons at 6 p.m. As Secretary-General of the London Conference on Reparations, I was unable, owing to the tremendous pressure, to attend this Meeting, and with your permission my place was taken by the Principal Assistant Secretary, Mr. Tom Jones.

Mr. T. Jones seems to have completed his draft Minutes, on the basis of his rough notes, on the following morning, 7 August. That was the last day of Parliament. Ministers were about to disperse. We felt it was important to issue the draft Minutes in order that they might be checked by members, if possible, before their final dispersal. Mr. Jones, however, was rather anxious about the particular Minute relating to the *Workers' Weekly*, and he handed me a note, timed 11.40 a.m., in the following terms:—

'Secretary.

For Prime Minister's approval. If he cannot look at all perhaps he would look at No. 5 (*Workers' Weekly*).[1]

T.J. 11.40 a.m.'

You may judge of my difficulty of getting access to you in a moment of leisure on that particular day from the following timetable of events, which I take from the records of this Office, for Thursday, 7 August:

10 a.m.	Heads of Allied Delegations.
11 a.m.	Heads of all Delegations.
2.30 p.m.	British Empire Delegation.
3.30 p.m.	Cabinet.
5.0 p.m.	Heads of all Delegations.

In order to illustrate the pressure there was on you, I daresay you remember that you were called out of the 11 a.m. Meeting to address the House of Commons, which was discussing the Adjournment, on the Russian Treaty. You took the Chair at all these meetings. I was present at most of them. We both had many preoccupations: yours over matters of high policy, mine over matters of supervising, organising, foreseeing the Secretarial needs of the Conference in all its activities.

I have no precise note of the moment at which I obtained your approval. My strong recollection is that this occurred at the House of Commons immediately on the conclusion of the Meeting of Heads of Delegations at 11 a.m.; that is to say, just before lunch. In fact, it must have been so, for Mr. T. Jones' note with the draft Minutes reached me at 11.40 a.m., that is to say, during the meeting that had begun at 11 a.m., and there is a note in the Office that the draft Minutes actually left this Office for circulation to the

[1] See above, p. 287.

Cabinet at 3.20 p.m. Allowing over an hour for the final clerical and mani-
pulative stages of the reproduction and circulation of the rather long Minutes
of this Meeting, the Office must have had authority to circulate somewhere
about lunch-time. I do not think there is the smallest doubt that I did show
you the Minute.* It is true that on some occasions, especially when I think
there is no matter of a doubtful or controversial character in the Minutes
and you are very pre-occupied, I issue them on my own authority. But in
this case a special form of notice is attached to the draft, which indicates
that they have not yet been submitted for your approval. In the present
instance, however, I have on the file a duplicate of the notice which accompanied the Minutes. It is the normal notice for an occasion on which the
Prime Minister has seen the draft, and is couched in the following terms:

'The attached draft Conclusions are circulated by direction of the
Prime Minister. It is requested that any corrections may be communicated to the Secretary not later than 12 Noon on Friday, 8 August 1924.'

No corrections were received. The fact that this form of notice was
issued is a proof that I was satisfied that you had read and approved the
draft Minutes.

I would draw your attention to the form of the above notice. It invites
every member of the Cabinet to send corrections. The Distribution List
shows that it was sent, together with the Minute on the *Workers' Weekly*, to
the Attorney-General and the Solicitor-General. Neither of them criticised
the Minute, nor did any member of the Cabinet.

From the above you will see that, if you were to see the Minutes at all
in the first draft on such an overcrowded day, I had to catch you when I
could.

* Mr. Tom Jones tells me that this entirely confirms his recollection, which is that at
the time I definitely informed him that the Prime Minister approved this particular
Minute.

2 October Statement by Sir Maurice Hankey. *Workers' Weekly* Case
On 22 September 1924, the Prime Minister in the presence of a number of
his Cabinet colleagues asked me to show him the Cabinet conclusion in
regard to the Prosecution of the Editor of the *Workers' Weekly* (Cabinet 48
[24], Conclusion 5 of 6 August 1924, 6 p.m.).

On reading the Minute the Prime Minister at once challenged its accuracy, more particularly in regard to Conclusion (b).

I made no record of this at the time, nor of the reasons given by the
Prime Minister for this challenge, but on returning to my office I mentioned
to my private Secretary, Captain Burgis, that the Prime Minister had
questioned the accuracy of the Minute, and I am asking Captain Burgis to
initial this to bear out my statement.

6 October The *Workers' Weekly*
To take note of the Prime Minister's intention to make a personal statement
in Parliament immediately before the Debate, in order to remove any

ambiguity which might have been occasioned by the terms of his answer on 30 September to a private notice question by Sir Kingsley Wood,[1] in regard to the extent of his cognisance of the Attorney-General's decision to withdraw the proceedings against the *Workers' Weekly*.

The Debate was arranged for 8 October. MacDonald had originally decided to make the statement on the preceding Friday (3 October) to explain away his answer that he had been neither consulted nor implicated in the withdrawal of the prosecution. But he was too late; and did not do so until the day of the Debate, when his prevaricating answer gravely weakened the Government's case.

6 October   This morning I wrote a draft of a speech for J. H. Thomas for Wednesday's debate. He is to reply for the Government. This afternoon a Cabinet Meeting to decide the action to be taken on Wednesday in regard to the Conservative Vote of Censure and the Liberal demand for a Committee of Enquiry. Very hush meeting. Hankey on his return told me that the Government decided to go through on Wednesday to an election if defeated. I tried to get some guidance for my brief for the Colonial Secretary but in vain. The Cabinet had spent most of the time on tactics and a lot of time on the custody of Cabinet Conclusions. They have been greatly worried not only about my Minute and my rough notes on which the Minute was based but also on the fact that the Minute has become widely known in some Departments. Apparently in the Admiralty it was 'Roneoed', i.e. multiplied. One Civil Servant who had seen it and seen the P.M.'s reply in the House of Commons to Kingsley Wood had gone to the 1st Lord and said the P.M. was lying. This has naturally caused much fear and trembling. Hankey pointed out that the present system of record keeping is the result of much experimenting. Once upon a time we wrote speeches of Ministers very fully and under their own names. Objection was taken to this as it was possible to confront individual Ministers today with what they said last week or last month. Under Baldwin and MacDonald the Minutes have been limited to a rather brief summary of the discussion and to the conclusion. The conclusion is not stated as a 'decision'—the formula is: 'The Cabinet agreed to, etc.' In future I gather even the summary of the discussion is to be dropped and only the conclusion entered, and this conclusion is not to be circulated but is to be paraphrased by the Minister to the officials of his Department concerned. That was the view yesterday, but Henderson prompted by Hankey urged the Cabinet not to scrap the present system [because] they had got into trouble over a Minute and not to do so anyway on almost their last day. He moved the discussion be postponed for a month, and J.H.T. ejaculated 'six months'. After the Cabinet Meeting I saw J.H.T. at the Colonial Office and gave him some material for his speech. His chief desire seems to be to show that he, Jimmy Thomas, has always been on the side of law and order and has stood up to the forces of anarchy every time. I have drafted on those lines and dug out for him his speeches in 1914 and 1919

---

[1] Sir Kingsley Wood (1881–1948); Conservative M.P. 1918–43; Parliamentary Secretary, Ministry of Health, 1924–9; Paymaster-General 1931–5.

which bear him out. But as he speaks last he will have to make a debating and largely impromptu speech.

7 October   P.M. at Queen's Hall. 'We shall surrender nothing. If there be an election the responsibility is not ours. The Conservatives had a straight-forward motion of censure down but the [Liberal] amendment was conceived in the spirit of mediaeval crookedness and torture.'

*   *   *   *

. . . Hankey sent for me about 4 o'clock. J. H. Thomas had said at yester-day's Cabinet Meeting *apropos* of leakages that during the railway strike of 1919 the Cabinet were daily considering his arrest and that he knew this at the time. Neither Hankey nor I could recall this nor discover any reference to it in Cabinet Minutes. Most improbable. L.G. had a high opinion of J.H.T. and would be too sagacious to take any such step. P.M. wanted to know the facts—he is full of suspicion.

About 6 o'clock Patrick Hastings' secretary rang up. Could we find the Minutes of the Ministry of Munitions for May 1920 as it was believed they would reveal material incriminating F. E. Smith. We tried Sir Graham Greene as we have not the Minutes here, but he is away on a long weekend.

Hankey went over this evening with the MS copy of yesterday's Cabinet Minutes for approval. They are not being duplicated owing to their great secrecy and the fear of leakage. On his return he rang up Stamfordham to ascertain if a messenger were going to the King tonight, so that a copy might be written out for His Majesty. No box going tonight. I showed Hankey passages in Dicey's *Law of the Constitution* bearing on the relation of the Government and the Law.

The *Manchester Guardian* today thinks a way will be found tomorrow of avoiding resignation and dissolution. The *Daily Mail* declares the Govern-ment fear to face an enquiry. *The Times* recalls the case of Sir Frederick Maurice who attacked Ministers. Bonar Law refused a Commons Committee as not impartial and offered two Judges.

8 October   *MacDonald's explanation that he had been consulted but had not inter-fered was poorly received by the House of Commons. The Conservatives withdrew their censure motion and voted for the Liberal Committee of Enquiry. Almost at the last moment, Asquith made a generous offer to forgo Liberal representation if the Committee were accepted; but the Cabinet rejected the compromise and the Government was defeated by 364 to 191.*

The Irish Boundary Commission Bill was passed and received the Royal Assent on 9 October.

9 October   When I came in this morning Hankey told me the King's Speech on the prorogation would be required. I warned several of the Departments to let me have suggestions by midday tomorrow, Friday. The Cabinet met at 11 a.m. and about 11.30 a.m. Sidney Webb suddenly entered my room and announced that Parliament would be dissolved at 6 o'clock today and that he wanted a draft of the King's Speech in 20 minutes to take back to the Cabinet or failing that to the Prime Minister. This was a bit startling but of course the attempt had to be made. I pointed out that the Department which would curse most would be the Foreign Office. He seemed to think all that was necessary was that I should write some paragraphs of hot air about Geneva, the Reparations Conference, Egypt, Russia, and so forth. He began writing at once a paragraph on unemployment while I rang up Sir Eyre Crowe and after some difficulty persuaded him to come to my room. I then got Sir Otto Niemeyer from the Treasury and Sir John Shuck-burgh,[1] one to do Reparations and the other Iraq. Meanwhile Howorth telephoned to the Ministry of Labour, Health, Education, and Agriculture for suggestions over the 'phone of what they wanted. Presently Crowe arrived with three experts who dealt respectively with Russia, Geneva, and Egypt. Sir Claude Schuster[2] blew in to say that he would like a reference made to the immediacy of the dissolution in the Lord Chancellor's remarks which follow the reading of the King's Speech. Everyone began to scribble paragraphs which I edited and shuffled about. The greatest change was in Webb's paragraph on Agriculture. . . . At 1 o'clock Webb went across to the P.M. with most of the paragraphs. I waited until Crowe and his Egyptian expert finished a squabble about the inclusion of a reference to the Sudan. Ultimately it was left for the P.M.'s decision who struck out the Sudan. The Egyptian expert had suggested that an asterisk could be put after Sudan in the text with an explanatory footnote! We proceeded to type a fair copy for the King at No. 10 which Hankey took up page by page to the P.M. for final approval. I think he saw about half the speech in this way. He made no change of any kind and left the rest to us to finish off as we liked as he had to go to a Party meeting at 1.45. At 2.10 I gave the Foreign Office printer—who had been warned to be ready by Rawlins—the final copy for printing. Meanwhile Waterhouse sent to Stamfordham a draft copy so that the King could see it before he met his Council at 3 p.m. At about twenty minutes to three Hankey was given a typed copy to put up to the King in Council in the event of my failing to deliver the printed copy. I crossed to the F.O. and stood over the printers there while they were making up. I told off Rawlins to get a taxi on the Foreign Office steps leading to the Horse Guards Parade and at four minutes to three I handed in two printed copies for the Council meeting at three. At 3.35 I heard from Waterhouse that he had received the copy signed by the King. I had shortly after three taken down to the House of Commons advance copies for the Prime Minister and Sidney Webb. The King made no alteration whatsoever in the text submitted to him.

15 October, Wednesday   I want to put down some notes on the now famous case of the *Workers' Weekly*. This matter first came before me on Wednesday, 6 August, when I took the Cabinet Meeting for Hankey in the P.M.'s Room at the House of Commons at 6 o'clock. I gave no particular thought to it again until Thursday morning, 2 October, when Howorth told me that he

[1] Of the Colonial Office.
[2] From the Lord Chancellor's Office.

understood that the Prime Minister was challenging the accuracy of the Minute I had written on the subject. I dug out my rough notes on which the Minute was based, had them typed, and went with them to see Hankey. He then told me that on 22 September the P.M. had said to him that the Minute was inaccurate. I asked in what respect, but Hankey could not tell me. He and Howorth read my rough notes and agreed that, on the evidence before them, the Minute was, if anything, an under-statement. In particular I had down 'A.G. authorised', whereas in the Minute I had used our usual formula 'The Cabinet agreed'. Throughout Thursday and Friday (2 and 3 October) Hankey was in frequent contact with the P.M. on this subject. The P.M. had no recollection of having approved the Minute, but fortunately we had ample proof that he had done so on the day following the Cabinet Meeting. All this perturbation had its origin in answers given by the Attorney-General (Sir Patrick Hastings) and by the P.M. to questions put to them in the House of Commons on 30 September—answers which, to put it mildly, were lacking in complete candour. The question put by Sir Kingsley Wood to the Prime Minister was, 'Whether any directions were given by him, or with his sanction, to the Director of Public Prosecutions to withdraw the proceedings against Mr. Campbell, the Editor of the *Workers' Weekly*, and whether he received any intimation that he would be personally required to give evidence on behalf of the Defendant at the hearing?' The Prime Minister replied, 'I was not consulted regarding either the institution or the subsequent withdrawal of these proceedings. The first notice of the prosecution which came to my knowledge was in the Press. I never advised its withdrawal, but left the whole matter to the discretion of the Law Officers, where that discretion properly rests. I never received any intimation, nor even a hint, that I should be asked to give evidence. That also came to my attention when the falsehood appeared in the Press.' That, in Hankey's words, was 'a bloody lie'. When I heard it, as I did, in the House, a shiver went down my spine. I did not know then that the P.M. had been reminded by Hankey and, as I learned later, by Sir Ronald Waterhouse, of what had taken place at the Cabinet on 6 August and had been shown the Cabinet Minute. During Thursday and Friday (2 and 3 October) Hankey tried to prevail on the P.M. to anticipate the Vote of Censure Debate in the House by making a personal statement. This suggestion he resisted, but ultimately agreed. However, the attempt to get a Question down for a statement to be made on Friday was too late. On Friday the P.M. and Macmillan, the Scottish Lord Advocate, and Spoor, the Chief Whip, met and drew up a statement which I think was then sent to Sir Robert Horne and Sir Douglas Hogg, who were to move the Vote of Censure for the Unionists on the following Wednesday. Meanwhile, at the P.M.'s request, Hankey had drafted a statement to the effect that on 22 September the P.M. had challenged the accuracy of the Cabinet Minute. This was to be put on the Cabinet Office file, presumably in view of a possible public inquiry. I pointed out to Hankey how damaging a procedure this was—to correct a Minute on the 22 September which had been approved on 7 August. and to do so after a public agitation had begun. Further, I pressed Hankey that if such a statement was to be put on our records the Prime Minister should indicate precisely in what respect the Minute was inaccurate. These considerations must have had some effect, because later the draft was torn up and never reached the office file. On the other hand, there is on the file a record by Hankey of what did take place on 6 and 7 August.

I did not myself see the Prime Minister at all during the crisis. On 8 October, after Questions, the Prime Minister made his statement to the House, and was closely (but in vain) pressed by Mr. Austen Chamberlain to reveal the whole truth. He fenced with infinite skill, and, I have reason to think, in the process still further departed from the truth when he said 'If I had not made a slip in using a word in the heat of temper—I think if temper is ever justified it was justified on an occasion like that—if I had not made that slip, none of these explanations would have been made, and all that my personal explanation asks me to do is to leave the House in precisely the position it would have been in, so far as this Debate is concerned, if I had not made that slip.' The impression left upon the House by these words was that the Prime Minister's answer to Sir Kingsley Wood was made in the 'heat of temper' and not carefully prepared in advance. My information, derived directly from Miss Watson, who arranges in Downing Street the Questions and Answers for the Prime Minister and the Leader of the House, is that the answer to Sir Kingsley Wood's Question was drafted by and reached her in the Prime Minister's own handwriting, that when she read it she recalled the Cabinet discussion, and proceeded with her own copy (i.e. Mr. Clynes's) of the Cabinet Minute, underlined by herself, to Ronald Waterhouse, who took the Minute upstairs to the Prime Minister at No. 10. Later the Prime Minister's reply was returned unaltered!

On 3 October, J. H. Thomas sent for me and told me that the arrangement for the *Workers' Weekly* Debate was that the Attorney-General and the Prime Minister would speak early in the Debate, and he would wind up for the Government. Would I prepare a brief for him, and make special reference in it to the Curragh case, and to his own record as a strict Constitutionalist? I took advantage of the opportunity to show him the rough notes of the Cabinet Meeting of 6 August. He and Marsh read them together. He told me that the Opposition had somehow got hold of the Cabinet Minute. Presently he hinted to Marsh to leave us alone together. He then turned to me, and, with the aid of the lurid language of which he is such a master, declared that unfortunately 'Mac' had gone beyond the truth and we had all got to try and pull things together. He himself did not want an Election.

On 7 October I dined with Sir Edward Grigg. I was most careful to avoid giving any hint of what was to take place on the following day, but Grigg himself made no concealment of the fact that the P.M. was increasingly distrusted. 'He always begins by lying' was his phrase, and he grew very hot about some hocus-pocus over the Lausanne Treaty. The Liberals had been silent then, as the Dominions were implicated. Grigg himself was much troubled about his position at Oldham, and will probably come to some arrangement with Duff Cooper, the Conservative candidate. He would like to see a new Coalition under Balfour, and told me that at the recent meeting

W

in Edinburgh Balfour completely eclipsed Horne and Winston in the public esteem. He said that it was L.G. who had precipitated the crisis on the Russian Treaty and had persuaded Asquith to take a strong line on it.

On 8 October, while waiting my turn to go into the Official Gallery, I gossiped with Fergusson, one of Snowden's Secretaries at the Treasury. For Snowden he had the utmost respect, for Ramsay the utmost contempt. Snowden was straight, very capable, but impatient of detail, and would only work on subjects in which he was interested. His way of preparing a speech was to scribble notes on odd slips of paper for days before the speech was to be delivered. It was an exciting job finding these odd slips and piecing them together. In official relations he was the most gentle of men, and showed none of the acidity of his speeches. . . .

28 October Today the Romney Street Group had its last luncheon in the cellar of the Garton Foundation at Dean's Yard. Sir Richard Garton, who has provided this luncheon (omelette, bread and cheese, cake and coffee) for the last seven years, is dying of cancer and is winding up his worldly affairs. Today we were:—T.J. (as usual, in the Chair); on my right John Hilton, head of the Statistical Branch of the Ministry of Labour; on my left, Vaughan Nash, head of the Development Commission; then down the table, Maurice Brett (Lord Esher's son); Schuster (Finance Officer in the Sudan); C. M. Lloyd (Sub-Editor of the *New Statesman*); E. M. H. Lloyd (of the Overseas Trade Department, formerly a Professor of Economics at Sheffield); Harold Wright (of *The Nation*); Butler (Commercial Attaché at the American Embassy); S. K. Ratcliffe (journalist and frequent lecturer in the United States); H. D. Henderson (Editor of *The Nation*); and Joseph Thorpe (the originator of the Group). When I first joined it we met in Romney Street, in the house of Edyth Goodall, the actress. We shall probably migrate to a room in the Abbey House (the old Westminster Palace Hotel) where the Plunkett Foundation is taking offices.

The General Election took place on 29 October, complicated and embellished by the publication of the Zinoviev Letter. But this lurid (and certainly forged) communication from the Comintern to the British Communist Party probably made little difference to the result of the election. Labour's successes, with the exception of housing, had been in foreign affairs; at home the Government had failed to deal with unemployment and recession. Labour won 151 seats, Conservatives 419, Liberals 40.

31 October The Labour Government met at 10.30. Hankey had not returned from Venice, so I took it. There was pretty widespread expectation outside that the Cabinet might decide to resign at this Meeting, and I believe that was the intention of the Prime Minister. There was a slight difficulty owing to the King being at Sandringham, but we knew that the King would readily come up to town if required, and there was no reason why the P.M. should not go down and resign at Sandringham. All the members were present except Webb and Wheatley, who were detained in their constituencies, and Jowett (Office of Works) who had been defeated. I entered the Cabinet

Room a few minutes before 10.30, and a minute or two later the Prime Minister came in. There was no demonstration of any kind. He was dressed in a dark suit, with a dark tie, looked pale and serious, and entered as if not certain what his reception was going to be. One gathered a general impression of everyone trying to maintain a cheerful countenance and determined to say nothing unpleasant about anybody or anything. We sat down, and the P.M. began with a reference to Jowett, 'the one defeated member of our little company'. The Cabinet then plunged into a discussion of the Election. One had expected an increase of twenty Labour Members, another had expected more. J. H. Thomas said he was 'frankly disappointed'. All agreed that up to Friday night all was going well with the Party prospects; but with the publication on Saturday morning of the Zinoviev letter there was a slump, 'the people lost confidence in us; the women were frightened; speakers felt paralysed'.[1] After some ten minutes' talk, all turning on electioneering tactics, the question of the Zinoviev letter gradually emerged as the main topic, and there were demands that the P.M. should tell his colleagues all about it. The P.M. bade me get from the Foreign Office the dossier dealing with the subject. There was an interminable delay in obtaining this, as it had been sent to Crowe, and Crowe was somewhere on his way between his house and the F.O. I had to cover the F.O. Secretaries, and could not tell the P.M. this, so for some time he gave his own narrative of what had taken place. While doing this he was subjected to constant interruptions; some friendly, some unfriendly. It was impossible to give a coherent narrative. The essence of the P.M.'s case was that when he had re-written the F.O. draft he had not initialled it, and fully expected to see it again for signature before despatch. Haldane and Snowden, who were the least sympathetic to the P.M., defended the F.O. officials throughout the discussion, and said it was not unnatural that, as he had in his first Minute favoured publication, they should have assumed they were free to go ahead when they received back a complete re-draft in the P.M.'s handwriting.[2] Other Ministers said that the custom of the Departments varied in the matter of initialling. Lord Thomson[3] who seemed to be in the P.M.'s confidence, kept interjecting that Crowe was under the impression, when assenting to publication, that the draft was in fact initialled, and subsequently telegraphed to say that he had found he

[1] The Zinoviev Letter, purporting to be signed by Zinoviev, President of the Soviet Praesidium, and Arthur McManus, leader of the British Communists, contained subversive instructions to the British Party. On 10 October a copy of it came into the hands of the Foreign Office. They sent it to the Prime Minister but he was on his election campaign and it either did not reach him or lay idle for a week. Then, on 17 October, he asked the Foreign Office to produce proofs of its authenticity. The draft of a protest to be sent to Russia was sent to him, which he returned, largely rewritten in his own hand, but unsigned, on 24 October. Meanwhile, another copy reached the *Daily Mail*, who threatened to publish it. Spurred on by the threat (according to Sir Eyre Crowe), the Foreign Office published the protest immediately. MacDonald said that he had expected to see the draft again before publication. If nothing else, the affair revealed a lamentable lack of co-ordination between the Prime Minister and the departments.

[2] It is a curious reflection on the contemporary system of keeping records that this original document was destroyed in favour of a typewritten copy made by the Foreign Office.

[3] Secretary of State for Air.

had made a mistake. The P.M. made no reference to the menace of publication on Friday by the *Daily Mail*. Haldane and Snowden pointed out the effect of this menace on the F.O., but the P.M. pointed out—and this was much the weakest part of the F.O. case—that the first news of publication reached him in South Wales on Friday night, from a *Daily News* representative. Nobody in the F.O. had 'phoned or wired, or in any way communicated the fact of publication to him. This certainly was an amazing omission. 'I felt like a man sewn in a sack and thrown into the sea.' Apparently throughout Saturday and Sunday he was without adequate data on which to base a public explanation. On Monday he saw Gregory,[1] the head of the F.O. Russian Department, in Cardiff before making his speech there. Why there should be all this delay, with the P.M. under four hours away from town, is inexplicable to one who has worked with other Prime Ministers. I believe MacDonald had no Private Secretary with him.

A group of the Cabinet, led by Parmoor, were entirely out of sympathy with Haldane and Snowden, and were all the while demanding an enquiry which would table all the available evidence and expose our Secret Service. Trevelyan was the most vocal of this group after Parmoor. Thomson belonged to it, and Wedgwood. Haldane insisted that if Parmoor had his way the result would be the assassination of some of the instruments of the F.O. It was plain that Trevelyan believed that Crowe and Gregory had stooped to a mean political trick in order to damage the Labour Party, but the Prime Minister rebutted any such suggestion with energy. He was certain that there had been no bad faith. Crowe had written to him a very moving letter of regret. Parmoor was certain that the Zinoviev letter was a forgery. Beaverbrook had assured him that it was the work of a well-known forger called Williams,[2] but Beaverbrook as a witness did not rank very high in the mind of the Cabinet.

About 11 o'clock the dossier from the F.O. arrived. The P.M. summarised it. Henderson suggested that it was now a matter for the P.M., as head of the F.O., to make such enquiries as he thought fit into the whole business. Parmoor clamoured for a public enquiry. Snowden objected and said it must be secret. J. H. Thomas suggested the appointment of three or four members of the Cabinet to go into all the documents. Snowden named Haldane, plus one or two others. Haldane replied that the P.M. could give his opinion on the document without giving his grounds for it. The Prime Minister urged the importance of distinguishing two questions:

(a) The conduct of the Civil Servants:
(b) The authenticity of the letter.

He urged dropping the first question. Parmoor resented this. J. H. Thomas suggested that they were sitting on a volcano, but Parmoor and Trevelyan were quite prepared to blow up the F.O. if they could get rid of the spy system. Once or twice the Prime Minister had to appeal to his colleagues

---

[1] Who had actually signed the Foreign Office Note of protest.

[2] It was, so far as is likely to be known, the work of the ubiquitous spy Sidney Reilly, foisted on the *Daily Mail* and the Foreign Office by an emigré Polish group, and Donald im Thurn, whose business interests were involved in the rupture of the Russian treaties.

to keep their tempers. Trevelyan is most hysterical on these occasions. Buxton says nothing. Hartshorn ventured to remind the Prime Minister that he ought to remember what he had already said at Cardiff when he said anything else. The P.M. finally suggested that there should be a Committee of the three gentlemen opposite me. These were Henderson, Thomas, and Haldane, on which there were loud shouts for 'Parmoor' from Wedgwood and Trevelyan. At last it was agreed that there should be a Committee of Haldane, Parmoor, Henderson, and the P.M. to go into the question of the authenticity of the Zinoviev letter, and I was bidden to make no reference to the Civil Service aspect of the business in the Minutes. It was agreed also to say nothing about resignation until the Committee had reported, but I was to put in the Press Communiqué a reference to the appointment of the Committee of Enquiry.

3 November   Note by Sir Maurice Hankey.   *Workers' Weekly*
The Prime Minister (Mr. Ramsay MacDonald) asked me today to be sure that, if ever the Cabinet Minute 48 (24) of 6 August, 1924, 6 p.m. should be called for, I should also bring to notice the attached transcript of the notes made at the meeting by Mr. T. Jones.

I replied that I would file a copy of the notes with the standard copy of the Cabinet Conclusions.

4 November, Tuesday   At 3.30 this afternoon Sidney Herbert[1] rang up and asked would I come to his house at 7 Carlton House Terrace, to see Stanley Baldwin. I saw S.B. at 4 o'clock for fifty minutes. He gave me a most cordial, almost affectionate, welcome. He was obviously excited. I said the wheel had come full circle much more swiftly than I had expected. He replied: 'For some time I felt things were shaping themselves towards the disappearance of the Liberal Party, but I did not think it would come so quickly. The next step must be the elimination of the Communists by Labour. Then we shall have two Parties, the Party of the Right and the Party of the Left.' Then he plunged into Cabinet-making, produced a foolscap list from his pocket, which looked as if it had on it all the possible Offices which have to be filled. He said, 'What I want from you is a Minister of Education: have we any man in the Party who takes any interest in Education? What about Cyril Cobb?[2] I said, 'He has had a lot of experience on the London County Council, but so has Eustace Percy; he has been Parliamentary Secretary to the B. of E., he is really interested in Education and has written about it.'[3]

S.B.: Now what about Labour? I mean to put Wood in Agriculture.

T.J.: Is Horne available? Wood is certainly interested in Agriculture, but if Horne is not available and if Neville Chamberlain goes to the Treasury, I would put Wood in Labour, for the same reason as I would put you Prime Minister. The Labour Members will respect Wood for his character, his frankness in dealing with them, while they will hate his ideas.

1 Baldwin's P.P.S.
2 Sir Cyril Cobb, former chairman of the L.C.C.
3 Lord Eustace Percy was made President of the Board of Education.

S.B.: But what about Agriculture?

T.J.: I would put Linlithgow there.

S.B.: I want him to carry on our Unionist organisation.

T.J.: I think you ought to have him in your Cabinet. You can put Walter Elliot as Secretary for Scotland.

S.B.: I thought of putting Gilmour, with the Duchess of Atholl as Under-Secretary.

At this point S.B. wrote down on his list, 'Percy for Education, Wood for Labour, Linlithgow for Agriculture.'[1] Then he began again: 'What would you do with Winston?'

T.J.: I would certainly have him inside, not out. I would put him in the Board of Trade or Colonial Office.

S.B.: I thought of putting him in India.

T.J.: For heaven's sake do not do that. I have seen him lose his head at critical moments in the Irish business, and but for L.G.'s intervention we would have had bloodshed on the Border more than once. If you have to take drastic action in India through Winston, everyone would blame Winston, whereas he might be quite guiltless and his action entirely justified by the situation in India. I would put Birkenhead in India.[2] He has a better judgment than Winston, and it will keep him pretty well occupied.

All of which Sidney Herbert strongly confirmed.

S.B.: But where shall I put Winston?

T.J.: Shove him in the Army or Navy; it does not matter which. Give him the one with most work.

S.B.: That means Derby must go, and I could give 'Worthy', say, the War Office, as he will want to be a Secretary of State. I am sending Amery to the Colonial Office. He is a hard worker, keen on the Colonies and on Empire Settlement. I am not sure that the Dominions have forgiven Winston the Chanak incident, and I do not want him to go the Colonial Office[3]. . . . We could put Balfour still on the C.I.D.; and I think of sending Bob Cecil to Geneva under the F.O., with Austen as Secretary of State, though I am not very happy about that. What do you think about Auckland Geddes?[4]

T.J.: I think he is rather over-rated. I think poor Addison[5] was blamed a good deal for Housing blunders inherited from Auckland Geddes. What about George Lloyd?[6]

[1] Edward Wood (later Lord Halifax)—who, as Lord Irwin, became Viceroy of India in 1925—was appointed Minister of Agriculture, Neville Chamberlain Minister of Health, Sir A. Steel-Maitland Minister of Labour. Sir John Gilmour went to the Scottish Office, with Walter Elliot as Parliamentary Secretary of Health for Scotland. The Duchess of Atholl became Parliamentary Secretary to the Board of Education. Lord Linlithgow was not given a post.

[2] Lord Birkenhead did go to the India Office.

[3] Winston Churchill was made Chancellor of the Exchequer. Lord Derby went, 'Worthy' (Sir Laming Worthington-Evans) became Secretary for War, and L. S. Amery Secretary for the Colonies.

[4] Austen Chamberlain was made Foreign Secretary and Lord Cecil Chancellor of the Duchy of Lancaster. Sir Auckland Geddes was not given a post.

[5] See page 229.

[6] Sir G. A. Lloyd became High Commissioner for Egypt—and a Baron—in 1925.

S.B.: Oh, you remember we talked about him long ago. I mean to send him to Allenby's job. He wants an administrative post. I had a very nice letter in a schoolgirl's handwriting signed 'Nancy Addison', saying that their uncle, Dr. Addison, and all his family congratulated me, adding that they came from the soil of Lincolnshire. Asquith, too, sent me a very nice letter. I think of putting Joynson-Hicks in Health—he knows all about it.

T.J.: Hankey says he would make a first-rate man at the Air Ministry—he once wrote a classic memorandum on the Air.

S.B.: Trenchard wants Hoare to go there.

T.J.: What are you going to do about the Home Office?

S.B.: I will make no change there. I will keep on Willy Bridgeman.[1]

8 November   Hankey thinks that the reason why S.B. does not put Balfour into the Cabinet is a certain sense of *gaucherie* and inferiority which he feels in the presence of A.J.B., especially since the meeting at the Carlton Club.

I worked today on a draft of a speech for the P.M. for the Guildhall Banquet on Monday evening. I drew material from the Foreign Office, India Office, and Ministry of Health, and stitched it together, adding an introduction and a conclusion. During the day I got a characteristic Minute from Austen Chamberlain—S.B. was to take care to emphasize that the Germans must scrupulously carry out their obligations—'scrupulously' underlined. S.B. has more than once expressed to me his nervousness about A.C. at the F.O., on the ground of the rigidity of his mind.

I caught the 5.4 to Wendover, and was most warmly welcomed to Chequers again by S.B., Mrs. Baldwin, and Miss Betty. They were quite obviously delighted to be back. S.B. took me into the study, and we plunged at once into business. I handed him a letter, and, putting it into his pocket, he observed 'I suppose one cannot help if Birkenhead and Winston will dine with Beaverbrook. There is no accounting for taste'.

Then he took up the story of his Cabinet-making. 'Austen told me he thought Neville would be willing to go to Housing. I saw him and offered him the Treasury. He said he would rather go to Housing, which he knew all about, and try and make a good job of it. I asked him who was I to put into the Treasury? Neville said "Why not Winston?" Ten minutes after Neville had gone, Winston came in, and I offered him the Chancellorship. He was greatly surprised, and showed it by his emotion. He pledged his loyalty and added "You have done more for me than Lloyd George ever did". My feeling was that the Treasury officials in the old days used to tell me that they believed Winston would make a good Chancellor. Then it would be a good thing to keep him fully occupied with finance, which should not bring him very much into direct contact with Labour. Had he been at Housing he would constantly be in danger of getting at loggerheads with them. Lastly, having decided to bring him into the Cabinet, to give him the Chancellorship would be bound to remove every possible personal grievance. It would be up to him to be loyal, if he is capable of loyalty.'

[1] Joynson-Hicks went to the Home Office, Sir Samuel Hoare to the Air Ministry, and Bridgeman—who was made a peer in 1929—to the Admiralty.

Then he went on to speak of the India Office. 'Birkenhead, too, was pleased. He said he had a sharp tongue and had said bitter things about me. He hoped that was past. He would help all he could, and if any action of his hurt me in future he hoped I would tell him so, have it out, and be done with it.' He went on, 'I am a bit nervous about Austen. He has written me an irritable sort of letter begging me to give Oliver Locker-Lampson office. I cannot do that. I suppose he will have to take him as his Parliamentary Secretary.'[1] I remarked that the chief criticism I had heard was over the appointment of Steel-Maitland to Labour. 'Yes, I know. I have been thinking of that post for eighteen months. At the end I had about ten minutes in which to decide, as Horne had refused. Neville recommended S.-M. He is able enough—got all those Firsts at Oxford—but is he human enough? He would have done better at the Board of Trade. He will do well administering the Office, but I am frankly afraid of him in the House.'

T.J.: Why did you not put Walter Elliot there?

S.B.: Well, I had him in mind, but my courage failed me. Eustace Percy is very pleased to go to Education. What a chance he has got! He is only 37.

T.J.: I gather that Crowe is gloomy at the prospect of having to confront Curzon at the C.I.D.

S.B.: He ought to be very grateful that he is not at the F.O.

T.J.: What about Bob Cecil?

S.B.: Well, I shall not hear until Monday. I do not want to do anything to handicap Austen right at the beginning—and that is what would happen if Bob Cecil went under him at the F.O.

T.J.: Have you had any luck with Lord Weir for the Ministry of Transport?

S.B.: No. He is too full of Housing experiments, and sugar beet, and as he is a big Admiralty contractor he does not think he ought to take it up. He told me, by the way, that he had gone to Rothermere and Beaverbrook and asked them for £100,000 apiece to help with sugar beet experiments, but could not get a cent from these patriots.

T.J.: Your acid test will be Esmond Harmsworth.[2] If you put him in it will be said you have succumbed to Rothermere.

I told him that so far as I could see in the Press the Cabinet had, on the whole, been very well received, and I read him aloud the whole of Strachey's first article in *The Spectator*, the burden of which was to reiterate over and over doubt whether S.B. would resist the soporific influences of the Conservative Party. I read him, too, the *New Statesman*'s approval of the appointment of Austen Chamberlain, Churchill, and Steel-Maitland.

We fixed some subjects for next Wednesday's Cabinet, his first. Then he said he had very much on his mind the question of introducing himself, in a three minutes' speech, a Bill to provide Prime Ministers with pensions. He would, of course, exclude himself from the operation of the Bill, but he was

---

[1] Locker-Lampson, an associate of Austen Chamberlain, had been Under-Secretary at the Home Office in the 1922–4 Government and was given the same post again, but was transferred to the Foreign Office, under Chamberlain, in December 1925.

[2] Eldest son of Lord Rothermere. He was not given a post.

very anxious to prevent in future what had happened to Asquith, L.G., and MacDonald—Mrs. Asquith having to go on a lecturing tour to the States, L.G. writing for the Hearst Press, and MacDonald taking £30,000 from Sir Alexander Grant. He also said he proposed to put up Labour, Education, Air, Agriculture, and the Scottish Office, on to the same salary level as the other Ministries.

By this time it was quarter to eight, and we hastened upstairs to dress. At the top of the stairs S.B. slipped on a rug on the polished oak floor, and came an awful cropper.

We were just four to dinner. The photographers had been to Chequers that afternoon, and Mrs. Baldwin recalled the photograph of S.B., the son, and myself, taken on a frosty Sunday morning a year ago at Astley Hall. She said it was a favourite photograph. I said that the less said about it the better, and explained that the appearance of that photograph had convinced MacDonald that I had gone over completely to the Capitalists, and during the Labour *régime* I had been 'sent to Coventry'.

The talk then turned to the election campaign and the spectacle of thousands waiting in the rain for a quarter of an hour's speech.

S.B.: I am sure Ramsay is very sore at having to give up Chequers; I must write to him. I was very curious to find out what parties had been down with him here, and it is very interesting to find from the Visitors Book that he has not had a single colleague here.

Later I had a look at the Visitors Book myself, and found MacDonald's first entry was on 1 February 1924, when he had his family with him. There followed some eight pages of signatures, and I remember among them Theunis and Hymans, Herriot, President Cosgrave, Colonel House, Sir Eyre Crowe, MacNeil Weir (his parliamentary Secretary), Margaret Bondfield, Mary Agnes Hamilton (the novelist and writer on *The New Leader*). Oswald Mosley and his lady had been there. There had been a big party to celebrate Ishbel's 21st birthday. Then on 2 November he had written, if I remember aright, 'Farewell to this house of comforting and regenerating rest'. I was very curious, in turning over the pages of the Visitors Book, to discover who had been with S.B. on the famous week-end during which it was often alleged S.B. took the decision to embark on a General Election under the banner of Protection. I found that on the week-end 13/15 October there had been at Chequers, among others, Amery and Lloyd-Greame, Neville Chamberlain and Ormsby-Gore, Mackenzie King (of Canada) and Bruce (of Australia). One can readily believe that such a gathering precipitated the disaster which followed.

But to go back to our dinner. S.B. had been reading the history of the Clan MacDonald, and was amused to think that MacDonald had been brought down by a Campbell. He told me that from Massey he had received this telegram of congratulation: 'Thank God, the Empire is safe'; from the cautious Mackenzie King 'My personal congratulations', and nothing from Smuts.

Later he joined Mrs. Baldwin in the Long Gallery and played patience, while I browsed in the Library. 'And so to bed.'

14 November, Friday The P.M. sent for me. He wants a speech done for a dinner of the London School Teachers next week. 'So many of the teachers are tinged with Bolshevism—so many cranks about; perhaps you could say something about that, and I will talk about my old school days.' That was the sum total of my instructions. We then fell to talking about the Cabinet Meeting and how glad I was to learn that he was showing so much more confidence in himself as its Chairman. He read me a letter from a banker not in politics—?Montagu Norman—congratulating S.B. on putting Winston in the Treasury and denouncing Horne for allowing personal interests to come between him and service of the State.

22 November, Saturday Today I wrote the draft of a speech to the Teachers for the P.M. and was just going home about 5 o'clock when the F.O. rang up wanting a Cabinet summoned immediately to discuss an important telegram from Allenby about the action to be taken following the murder of Sir Lee Stack, the Sirdar[1]. We telephoned furiously all over the town, and were able in an hour to get together, besides the Foreign Secretary, Birkenhead, Winston, Amery, Steel-Maitland, and Douglas Hogg. Hankey came back specially from Limpsfield and arrived about a quarter to seven. Allenby, fearing Zaghlul's resignation, had decided to **act** on his own before our final instructions (of which he had been warned) had reached him. This had greatly upset the Foreign Secretary, who proceeded to read to the meeting the terms of a severe reprimand of Allenby which he proposed to telegraph out. The telegram would not only castigate Allenby but would request that he should substitute a fresh series of demands in place of those which he had submitted to the Egyptian Government. Birkenhead at once pointed out the gravity of this procedure. Allenby would be certain to resign, which would be very awkward in the midst of the crisis, and, though we might ask him to stay on, it would become known and would greatly weaken our prestige with the natives. Amery took the opposite view and was all for strong action, whatever the consequences. The others were hesitant until Winston arrived. He put Birkenhead's points with great eloquence, and swung everybody round to support the man on the spot—except Amery. Austen himself confessed that he had been persuaded, and he got on the telephone to the P.M. at Chequers and put the position reached by the meeting. The P.M., of course, agreed, and I think we have turned a very nasty corner.

23 November, Sunday This evening Frank Wise came to supper and fought over again his election campaign in North Bradford. He was very sick—and so, I gather, is Clifford Allen—at the way in which the late Prime Minister handled the Zinoviev business. Wise is the representative in this country of some Union of Russian Co-operative Societies and has been one of the most active intermediaries between the country and Moscow, but he was

---

[1] Sir Lee Stack, the Sirdar of the Egyptian Army and Governor-General of the Sudan, was assassinated in a Cairo street on 19 November. Lord Allenby, the High Commissioner, presented an immediate ultimatum, demanding an apology and indemnities, to forestall further trouble from the Wafd party, headed by Saad Zaghlul.

completely in the dark when the Zinoviev letter appeared. All the Labour candidates turned to him, but he could give them no guidance. Stephen Graham turned up at his election meetings to bait him with questions, but Wise did a smart thing by publicly inviting the business men of Bradford to a public meeting at which they could subject him to any questions they liked on Russia.[1]

24 November, Monday   At 3.15 p.m. I saw the Prime Minister. I had some talk with him about Wise, and asked if he minded my seeing him, as from some remark S.B. had dropped some days ago I rather thought he might object. However, he did not. I told him Wise was an optimist and not a Government actuary, and that he had some of the qualities likely to carry him very far in politics—great physical vitality, great self-confidence, and great faith in the possibilities of helping mankind by political action: he might even become a Labour Prime Minister—certainly a Cabinet Minister.

*   *   *   *

Then we talked of Beaverbrook, whose spectre is never very far from S.B.'s mind. Beaverbrook had come back from Edwin Montagu's funeral in the same coach as Winston. Winston was much moved at the loss of an old friend and colleague, but Beaverbrook was utterly callous and could only retail sordid gossip of old intrigues.

28 November, Friday   The Chancellor of the Exchequer [Churchill] sent for me about 6 o'clock. I saw him alone. He was drinking some whisky-and-soda, and he got some tea for me. He was very confidential. 'I understand you talk a lot with the P.M. and that you give him advice—good advice, I have no doubt. Well, I want this Government not to fritter away its energies on all sorts of small schemes; I want them to concentrate on one or two things which will be big landmarks in the history of this Parliament, and if you are doing anything for a speech at the Albert Hall I would like you to fix on two things and make them stand out—Housing and Pensions. I think I see my way to help both of these if I can stop the Departments spending in other directions. I was all for the Liberal measures of social reform in the old days, and I want to push the same sort of measures now. Of course I shall have to give some relief to the taxpayers to balance these measures of reform. If trade improves I can do that, but we cannot have a lot of silly little cruisers, which would be of no use anyway.[2] I had some talk with the P.M. and Neville Chamberlain along these lines, and in order to avoid any mistake I put down my impressions of the talk in a letter to the P.M. Here is a copy; you had better read it.' This I did, and told him I was very grateful for his guidance, but I was sure the Prime Minister's heart was in the right place on all these matters.

[1] Frank Wise (see note on p. 17), now a member of the I.L.P., had, in 1923, become one of the economic advisers to Centrosoyus (the Russian Union of Consumer Co-operative Societies) and was regarded as being extremely left-wing.

[2] An interesting comment, foreshadowing the 'cruiser crisis' of 1925 which for five months rocked the Conservative Cabinet and which was almost entirely of Churchill's making.

Tonight the P.M. and Eustace Percy spoke to the Teachers.

29 November, Saturday   I see the P.M. used all I gave him last night except a
passage in which I dealt very delicately with the religious question. To my
surprise he quoted a passage I had given him from D'Arcy Thompson's
Daydreams of a Schoolmaster. The Chapter is called 'The Pressure of Gentle-
ness'. I read it when I was a student in Glasgow and suddenly remembered
it again after 25 years.

3 December   This evening dined with the Yates-Thompsons at Portman
Square—Herbert Fisher the only other guest. He was newly back from a
lecturing tour in the U.S.A. and was enormously impressed with their vast
wealth and gifts to Universities. One family has given £8,000,000 to one of
their Colleges—Ann Arbour, I think. They run up noble college buildings in
a few months and reproduce in their halls and libraries the roof of Westminster Hall or Christchurch, but the level of their education is considerably
beneath ours. There is some post-graduate work, but nothing corresponding
to our Honours Schools, and the women students flock to the Colleges frankly
in search of husbands. Their athletics are much more brutal than ours, the
teams playing in secret, having their own doctors, organising their applause,
and in every way running their sport as they run their factories. Fisher had
not been to the States for fifteen years. He found the Americans much
friendlier to us, and he put this down to the War, the settlement of the Irish
Question and the payment of the debt. He seemed doubtful about Prohibition. He had not been further West than Chicago, but in the Eastern States
had heard a great deal of the bootlegging that goes on, and of how the New
York Clubs go to Quebec for their Annual Dinners. The bringing of the law
into disrepute in this fashion is causing a great deal of anxiety to the best
citizens. He had hoped to make lots of money out of the tour as he is hard
up, and had put himself in touch with Lord Birkenhead's agent, but when
the draft contract reached him from New York he found one of the conditions
was that he should not lecture at any of the Universities. He could not
swallow that, so the contract fell through. . . . Wherever he went Fisher was
besieged with two questions: What did he think of Lady Astor, and when
was Lord Curzon to be made a Duke? Lady Curzon is an American, and
all the ladies there want to know when she is to be a Duchess. I promised
Fisher that, in order to promote international amity, I would represent to
S.B. the importance of elevating Curzon at an early date! Fisher found the
lectures he had prepared much above the heads of his audiences, and he was
certain that what the Americans wanted and were prepared to pay for was
gossip about our prominent men, stories of Lloyd George, the cut of Baldwin's clothes, and so forth.

Yates-Thompson showed me one of his treasures which I had not seen
before, a Greek lexicon printed in 1499 and bound by Grolier, with two
plaquettes on the cover. It had come from the library of a Yorkshire friend,
Sir T. A. Moore. It was in perfect condition, and the old collector was very
proud of it, as it came just into the fifteenth century.

8 December   Note by Sir Maurice Hankey.   *Workers' Weekly*
11.45 a.m. The Cabinet conclusion of 6 August 1924, on the subject of the *Workers' Weekly* prosecution (Cabinet 48 [24] conclusion 5) were referred to at the Cabinet Meeting on Wednesday, 3 December 1924. I at once reported to the Prime Minister that I had instructions to show him certain papers in this connection. Mr. Baldwin read the attached papers on the morning of 8 December 1924.

12 December   10.30 a.m. Talk with S.B. about his Edinburgh Rectorial Address. Gave me a series of 'notions' to work up for it.

Classics. Chief thing one learns from Classics is meaning and value of the word. No man who can do Latin Prose has any excuse for equivocation and misleading and humbug.

Mathematics. $2 \times 2 = 4$ and nothing else. Can't sail a ship into any part of the world on any other basis. If you try to make them add up otherwise you wreck the constitution.

Science. If you do not take care Science will be through the roof and leave us with no foot on the earth.

Little vulgar perhaps but wish I could say there were two things which every man who goes to sea does learn which it would be useful for us on land to remember:

1. Not to spit on the deck—in political life too much of it.
2. Not to speak to the man at the wheel. We make his task too difficult.

Move from this to the bigger world by shewing that what we stand for in this country is truth and honesty.

19 December   *From the* Manchester Guardian
LABOUR AND POLITICAL PROSECUTIONS
PREMIER'S REPLY SATISFIES MR. MACDONALD
In the House of Commons yesterday,

Mr. Ramsay MacDonald (Leader of the Labour Party) asked the Prime Minister whether it was the opinion of the Government that in instituting proceedings of a political character in the interests of the State it was or was not the duty of the Attorney-General to obtain the views of the particular Ministers concerned or of the Cabinet on points of public policy, whether past practice clearly showed that without in any way binding the Constitution or diminishing the rights of the Attorney-General this consultation had taken place and the advice of the Cabinet followed, and what precisely was the reason why instructions to the above effect issued by the late Government were rescinded.

Mr. Baldwin: The office of Director of Public Prosecutions was established by the Prosecution of Offences Act, 1879, which enacts that the Director shall discharge his duties under the superintendence of the Attorney-General, and the regulations made pursuant to that Act provide that he shall in all matters be subject to the direction of the Attorney-General. In the view of his Majesty's Government it is the duty of the Attorney-General in the discharge of the responsibility so entrusted to him to inform himself of all relevant circumstances which might properly affect his decision. When the proposed prosecution is of such a character that matters of public policy are or may be involved it is the duty of the Attorney-General to inform himself of the views of the Government or of the proper Minister before coming to a decision. (Labour cheers.) It is because in the view of the Government the instructions referred to in the question went beyond this that those instructions were rescinded. (Ministerial cheers.)

Mr. MacDonald: As the answer that has been given contained the intention of the late Government I shall not require to take the time of the House by raising the subject on the adjournment tomorrow. (Ironic Ministerial cheers.)

1925

Baldwin's Government from 1925 to 1929 set the tone for the middle years between the wars: stability, peace, and a particularly British form of isolationism. Some of MacDonald's work was undone—the Russian Treaties were rejected, the Protocol was allowed to lapse—but there was little fundamental difference between them and the Locarno pact of non-aggression, signed in London on 1 December, between France, Germany, and Belgium, with Britain and Italy acting as guarantors. The pact appeared to seal acceptance of the League of Nations and, with a clear conscience, Britain began to relax from her European preoccupations which had survived from the days of the Coalition. Isolationism was reflected in the defence budgets; with no conceivable enemy to fight, the Services were run down. It was entirely in keeping with tradition that the army suffered most, the navy least, but this was mainly because of the stout resistance by the Admiralty to Churchill's search for economies. At the Exchequer, Churchill brought tradition full circle with the return to the Gold Standard at pre-war parity. Few voices were raised in protest; even Keynes objected chiefly to the level of parity, claiming it was 10 per cent. too high. Other estimates since have put the error as low as 2 per cent.

At home, Baldwin inaugurated the new Conservatism by endorsing Neville Chamberlain's plans for reform of health, housing, and local government; and tried to sweeten industrial relations by turning down a Conservative Bill attacking the trade union political levy. Financially 1925 was a good year. For the first time the index of industrial production rose above the 1913 figures. But a million unemployed belied prosperity, the older industries continued to decline, and exports withered steadily, facing narrowing markets as the terms of world trade turned against customers in primary producing countries. So, in the heavy industries, the choice was seen as between cutting wages (to make exports competitive) and developing the home market. The latter alternative (in accordance with the fashionable under-consumption theory) was too unorthodox for most industrialists. The trade unions had, since the early 'twenties, turned to bargaining rather than strikes, but the T.U.C. stood by the miners when wage cuts resulted in a lock-out in July. The threat of a total embargo on the movement of coal caught the Government unprepared, and on 'Red Friday' a subsidy was given to the coal industry—a temporary expedient, opening the way for the General Strike. In September the Samuel Commission was set up to report on methods of reorganizing the industry, but short of nationalization or a massive outlay of capital by the owners, its recommendations were not easy to implement. The Government, using the Supply and Transport Committee directed by Sir John Anderson, prepared for an emergency; the trade unions, though spurred on by the I.L.P. and a number of communist trade unionists, did not.

THE TRADE UNION POLITICAL LEVY 1925

T.J. was appointed secretary of the Committee of Civil Research under the chairmanship of Lord Balfour; and the two men worked together at Balfour's house in Carlton Gardens. T.J. also worked with the group headed by J.J. Astor which shaped the pamphlet *Britain's Industrial Future*, and he broadened his knowledge as secretary of the Cabinet Committee on Iron and Steel. For the last time he was involved with Ireland, in the negotiations leading up to the December agreement between North and South to preserve the existing boundary rather than risk the danger of civil war.

The tone of the 1925–9 Government was to be set by the Prime Minister himself, by Neville Chamberlain, and frequently, though erratically, by Churchill. One of the first tests of the Government's philosophy came on 6 March when a Conservative back-bencher, Macquisten, brought for second reading a Bill to reverse the procedure for contracting-out of the trade union political levy.

22 February   Winston Churchill to Stanley Baldwin   Treasury Chambers
You have several times asked me my opinion about the Trade Union Political Levy,[1] and I feel I have given you only uncertain, or even contradictory, replies. This is because the question is itself both uncertain and contradictory in character, and also because we were still in the period when weighing and balancing was not only possible but right. Now, however, we are at the point when decision is imperative, and I am glad to tell you that it finds me with an absolutely clear conviction.

If we recur to main principles, we see that we have before us two worthy objects:

First, to liberate working men from the unfair and humiliating position of being compelled under threat of ruin and starvation to subscribe to the propagation of political principles which they detest.

Secondly, not to hinder by want of funds the less wealthy classes in the nation from using to the full their Constitutional rights and so being continually assimilated into the British Parliamentary system.

Pages can be written in favour of these objects, and they are both of them right and true to the national interest. The difficulty of our problem resides in the fact that they seem to be opposed to each other. Can they be reconciled?

Surely they can be reconciled by a very simple course which proceeds at every step along the path of sound conviction. Let us pass the Bill to liberate workmen from the thraldom of the Levy, and let us at the same time reduce the cost of Parliamentary elections to all classes and all Parties by substantial grants from the Exchequer. I would suggest that in supporting the Bill we

---

[1] That part of a trade union member's subscription allotted to political purposes (viz. the support of the Labour Party). By the Osborne judgement in 1909 political payments were declared illegal, but in 1913 the Trade Union Amendment Act permitted unions to raise a 'political levy'. Members could, if they wished, contract out. This meant that many paid, by default or lack of energy, or occasionally as the result of threats, who were not supporters of the Labour Party. The strength of the opposition to the Levy may be gauged from the fact that 25 per cent. of union members in the early 1920s contracted out. The position was often attacked by Conservatives, who used the defeat of the General Strike to reverse the rule, and make it necessary to contract in, by the Trades Disputes Act, 1927. This was in turn reversed by the Act of 1947.

announce that a sum of, say, £300 will be paid by the Exchequer to the expenses of any candidate who polls an adequate number of votes. If there were, say, fifteen hundred candidates, this would cost £450,000. The burden to the Exchequer could be accepted. Such a boon would take the edge off every *bona fide* candidature in the country. It would make men of all Parties more free from unwholesome excesses in Party Discipline. It would pay the greater part of the expenses of many Labour candidatures. It would gratify every Member. It would free the charge that we are anxious to obstruct the entry of Labour men to Parliament from its sting. It would supply the new fact and makeweight which we must recognise is necessary to enable us to give effect to our convictions on the main issues. The Exchequer contribution can of course be considered both in respect to method and amount.

I believe that such a combined policy would gain overwhelming support in the House and would largely cut the ground from under the feet of the Socialists in the country. The policy would be one of 'fair play to the workman whatever his opinions, cheaper elections for all parties, freedom of Members and candidates from undue reliance on Party funds'.

Such a policy must be contrasted with its alternative. When we last talked, I had not read the passage on page 7 of *Looking Ahead*[1] which Jackson showed me only on Thursday; nor did I know that you and your principal colleagues had all voted for such a Bill as this in the last Parliament. It seems to me in the light of these facts that it will be very difficult to found a successful Parliamentary argument for opposing the Bill. If there are any enemies lurking among our supporters, or disappointed elements, it would be easy for them to accuse those who were in the last Parliament of not acting up to their convictions. Such information as I have been able to gather seems to show a very strong feeling in the rank and file of the Conservative Party. Surely we cannot be surprised at this, in view of the declaration in *Looking Ahead*. Might it not be very harmful to the Government to disappoint the whole of this strong and natural feeling which has been encouraged by their Leaders before the Election and is, moreover, logically and on its merits entirely sound?

If you thought well of this plan I would propose it when the matter comes before the Cabinet, and you could bring it safely into port. I think it might command practically the united support of Liberals, though this is the first time I have ever spoken of it. Perhaps you will let me know tomorrow morning what you think.

23 February   S.B. gave me two or three general notions for speech. Many demanding peace and disarmament at home, e.g. Trade Unions. We need stable united front at home. Democracy difficult form of Government. We can do little things for Agriculture. Land changes slowly but it does change. Present is result of slow and long evolution. In last 20 years lot of people have been squeezed out by death duties. Fewer living in the country all the year round. Seeking pleasure with aid of motor car.

[1] The Conservative Party's election manifesto.

In a major speech at Birmingham on 3 March, Baldwin coupled a warning that the Government could not attempt to control industry with a plea for peace and tolerance. He persuaded the Cabinet to drop Macquisten's Bill and in the House of Commons made one of the great speeches of the inter-war years, ending with a plea for 'peace in our time O Lord'.

9 March   David Davies, M.P. to T.J.   *Broneirion, Llandinam*

*   *   *   *

There is another interesting book *The Riddle of the Rhine* which describes the phases of Chemical Warfare during the War, and demonstrates how easily Germany can re-arm herself if she makes up her mind to do so—at any rate so far as Chemical Warfare weapons are concerned. It appears to me that as the proceedings of the politicians are so futile, we might try and mobilise all the producers of chemical materials into some big international syndicate who would be prepared to place their productions at the disposal of the League for International Police purposes, and so arrange their business that no one country in the world could secure an absolute monopoly in the raw material required for chemical warfare.

I have written to Morton who understands this business from A to Z asking his opinion as to whether some scheme of this kind could be put through. There are certain clauses in the Treaty of Versailles which, if carried out according to their literal interpretation, would hit very hard the I.G. which controls the German Dye industry, the production of nitrogen and other chemical industries in Germany. If political pressure could also be brought to bear upon these huge industrial organisations, they might be induced to join in some International Syndicate such as I have mentioned. I am afraid I have no very clear ideas at present, but it seems to me that if the Gas weapon could be placed at the disposal of the League and became inaccessible to any particular Nation or group of Nations, it would be a great step in advance.

30 March   T.J. to David Davies

I was very much interested to hear from you the other day and about your ideas on Chemical Warfare. I saw James Morton a few days after and he told me he had written to you. Have you read Haldane's Callinicus? It is the work of a young Cambridge Professor, a nephew of Lord Haldane. It struck me as an extraordinarily brilliant book and it quite upset many of my pre-conceived ideas. You should not miss it.

I send a very useful summary on the [Geneva] Protocol which reached me this morning from Shotwell.

I had a long talk last week after Curzon's funeral with Waldorf Astor. We were discussing the industrial situation with special reference to some of Baldwin's recent speeches. He pointed out, quite properly, that nothing was ever said about the handicap of drink. Nothing heroic, of course, is to be expected from this Government, or indeed from Labour or Liberals until there is a much more convinced public opinion on the question. On the other hand everyone who comes from U.S.A. stresses the tremendous pull they have over there owing to their improved industrial efficiency, savings, etc., etc.

I gathered from Astor that L.G. has been contemplating some sort of enquiry by business men with a view to a political campaign later.[1] I told Astor that a completely independent enquiry by men whose impartiality could not be questioned would be much better—an enquiry not only into the industrial and other results of prohibition in U.S.A. but also into the political power of the trade in this country. I had a note from Astor this morning saying that he was prepared to guarantee up to £10,000 towards the expense of such an enquiry and adding 'If I knew I could count upon a similar amount from someone else I should feel justified in going ahead with the idea.' He asks me to sound you on the subject to find out if you would be willing to be interested and helpful. As I am not likely to see you soon I thought it better to dictate this—I ought to apologise for breaking in on your rural peace.

16 May　I wrote this morning a draft of an Address for the P.M. for the unveiling of the Bird Sanctuary[2] on Tuesday in memory of W. H. Hudson. This will be an occasion after the P.M.'s own heart. He took a big bundle of Hudson's books with him to Chequers at Easter, and this morning I dug out from the cellars of the Treasury the correspondence dealing with the grant of a Civil List pension to Hudson in 1901 and its surrender by him twenty years later when his books were at last bringing him in a satisfactory income. Earl Grey moved Edward Grey to move Balfour. At the time Hudson was not making £2 a week and was living at 40 St. Luke's Road.

17 May　Began to think of something the P.M. might say at a meeting he is to address on Wednesday evening. It is to be a gathering of Conservative students at the London School of Economics, but it is to be presided over by the Chairman of the Students' Union. I think of writing something about the study of economics, in a purely scientific way, and its relations to politics and ethics.

This afternoon I went with Eirene and Elphin to tea with Reynolds Stephens, the President of the Sculptors' Society. I met there a chemist, Dr. Scott, who talked learnedly about the glazes on ancient Chinese pottery. Lady Morant and her daughter were there, and our host showed us many of his treasures—a lacquer vase dating about 1600, which he had picked up in a barber's shop in Grantham for £5. Strange, of the British Museum, is having it photographed for a new book on the subject. Stephens thinks it a great pity that Epstein is doing the Memorial to Hudson, and said he was run by a cult backed by some influential Press men. He was enthusiastic about the little speech the P.M. made at the end of the Artists' Benevolent Fund meeting. This was an impromptu, after the reporters had left. The P.M. had told me about it. He urged the young art students not to attempt brilliancy and

---

[1] This is presumably an early reference to the Liberal series of enquiries into land, industry, and unemployment, which culminated in the campaign of 1928-9.

[2] In Hyde Park.

cleverness, which would last but for a moment, and then quoted from Keats' 'Ode on a Grecian Urn', and the last lines of 'The Pilgrim's Progress', as examples of immortal passages which would be remembered when all the politicians of today were dust.

I only heard this morning of the death of the P.M.'s mother[1] on Saturday, at Wilden. This will postpone the speech at the School of Economics. I saw the P.M. at 10.30 and told him there was nothing here for tears. I mentioned the leaderette in the *Manchester Guardian* and fetched it for him to read. He told me that the account of his mother in *The Times* had been written on his own (the P.M.'s) suggestion by J. W. Mackail. He will not cancel the Hudson engagement, and remarked on the contrast between the letters exchanged over the Civil List Pension in his case with those received nowadays. He thanked me for the notes for the Oxford speech on Milner, and said he thought it had been very well received by the students and by the Press. I asked him was he coming to preside at a meeting on Unemployment this afternoon—a very unusual thing for him to do. Outside the Committee of Imperial Defence I do not recall his presiding at a Cabinet Committee since he has become P.M. He told me that there might be a sharp conflict between the Chancellor and the Minister of Labour as to whether the Inquiry into the 'dole' should be held immediately or in the autumn. He thought, therefore, he had better be present.

12.30. To the Wayfarers' Travel Agency, to enquire about tickets to Florence. Gwen Davies wants Ernest Rhys[2] and me to go to the International Book Fair at Florence—Maynard[3] is already there—to seek out ideas for the Gregynog Press. . . . I have arranged with the Prime Minister and Hankey to be away for about three weeks from 3 June. On that day the P.M. receives the Freedom of Dundee, and has no speaking engagement until 1 July.

*   *   *   *

1.30. To lunch with P. J. Grigg, Winston's Private Secretary at the Treasury. He had arranged earlier in the morning that I was to see the Chancellor this afternoon before the meeting of the Unemployment Committee. Grigg has not found Winston so malleable as Horne or Snowden. The situation is complicated by the presence of Eddie Marsh,[4] and in the early days when Winston's bell went, both Grigg and Marsh responded, but I gather that Grigg has now succeeded in dislodging Marsh to the extent that he sees the Chancellor alone. Grigg thinks that within a year Winston will have committed some irretrievable blunder which, if it does not imperil the

---

[1] Baldwin's mother, Louisa, was one of the five Macdonald sisters. Of the others, one married Sir Edward Burne-Jones, one Sir Edward Poynter, one John Lockwood Kipling, and one remained single. J. W. Mackail, the classical scholar, married Baldwin's cousin, Margaret Burne-Jones. Louisa Baldwin had lived in solitary widowhood since Alfred Baldwin's death in 1908.

[2] Editor of the Everyman Library and adviser to the Gregynog Press.

[3] R. A. Maynard, wood engraver and typographer in charge of the Press.

[4] Edward Howard Marsh (1872–1953); private secretary to Churchill 1905–15, 1917–22, 1924–9, to Asquith when Prime Minister, 1915–16; to J. H. Thomas 1924, 1929–36; to Malcolm MacDonald 1936–7; knighted 1937. Also a writer and patron of the arts.

Government, will bring Winston down. Grigg was very despondent about Snowden, who had been one of his political idols. On the return to the Gold Standard and on making Widows' Pensions contributory, Snowden had said in public, for Party polemics, the exact opposite of what he had led Grigg to believe were his real views.

At 3.45 saw Churchill alone, in his room at the House. He was very affable, and began talking in a most general way; nor did he on this occasion ask me in terms to try and influence the P.M. in a particular direction. Instead, he unfolded his own policy on Unemployment:—There should be an immediate stiffening of the administration, and the position should be made much more difficult for young unmarried men living with relatives, wives with husbands at work, aliens, etc. In this way the drain on the Fund could be reduced. If this were done he (Winston) could then afford to reduce the contributions of masters and men to the Unemployment Fund. This would make more palatable the new burden thrown upon them by the contributory pension scheme.[1] It would make an immense impression if it could be announced that the 11,000,000 trade unionists were to pay 3d. a week less. He dresses up a project of this kind with great pictorial and rhetorical power, and it requires considerable calmness and decision to resist him. I pointed out that to make all these drastic changes in administration before the Committee of Enquiry (announced by the Minister of Labour last week) had examined the position would look odd and would be stoutly resisted. He said the Minister of Labour ought to have indicated that this stiffening policy was in the mind of the Government. Winston is really gambling on the chance of a steady revival of trade in the next twelve months, and he is the only one in the Cabinet who seems to have, what L.G. had, a sense of the dramatic in making proposals to the nation. He moved on to speak about Ireland. He had dictated some 'thoughts' on the subject over the week-end. He foresaw that Ulster could not do for itself what we were proposing to do in the way of social reform; it was too small an area; and unless we came to their financial assistance they would be reduced to a negligible status. The contrast between Belfast and Glasgow would be such as to lead to a considerable migration and to put Ulster at the mercy of the Free State. He did not pretend to see very clearly what was the best course to pursue. Off and on he talked about Beaverbrook and Rothermere and their attempts to destroy the P.M. He was all for standing up to them on the Widows' Pensions issue, so that they might realise that there was a limit to their power of shaping the policy of the Cabinet.

At 4.15 the P.M. presided over the Unemployment Committee, and did it in such a good-tempered fashion that the conflict between the Chancellor and the Minister of Labour never emerged. For the first five or ten minutes the P.M. did nothing but work away at his pipe; scouring it out and filling it, lighting it and relighting it, meanwhile telling some quite amusing stories. We also had tea served, and by the time we came to business we were

[1] Churchill's contributary old age pension scheme, introduced in his 1925 Budget, nearly doubled the income of the oldest and poorest. It was paid for, not by tightening up the unemployment fund, but by restoring the McKenna duties.

all in the friendliest mood. The upshot was to agree to a draft Bill being prepared, which Bill will go about half-way Winston wants to go.

27 May Lord Balfour circulated today to the Cabinet a note on what up to the present has been called 'The Committee of Economic Enquiry' but which he suggests should be called 'The Committee of Civil Development'. This afternoon we met in his room at the Privy Council: Warren Fisher, Frank Heath, Morley Fletcher, Hankey, and I. Lascelles was there too. Balfour opened by reading his Memorandum and he proceeded to cross-examine Hankey and the others as to how the new C.C.D. should be run. He has, as he said, *brusqué* the situation by his announcement in the Lords on the Kenya Debate. He asked what would Hankey do supposing the question of sleeping sickness were referred to the C.C.D. Hankey replied that the Secretary would see Fletcher informally in advance, the right man at the Colonial Office and the right man in the Foreign Office (because of the Sudan), and would then put up a Proposed Procedure to the Chairman of the C.C.D. The C.C.D. would meet and would refer the problem to a Sub-Committee on which outside members would be co-opted. Similar procedure has been followed in the C.I.D. with questions like Insurance of Aircraft.

Warren Fisher laid stress on the correlating duties of the new body and mentioned Afforestation and Small Holdings as an example which needed to be handled.

Heath rather wanted Balfour to issue some written suggestion that the Secretariat should meet regularly with the Heads of the Industrial Research Committee, the Medical Research Committee and the Development Commission.

Warren Fisher pointed out that the Secretary would, most certainly, keep in close touch not only with these but with others like the Statistical Head of the Board of Trade and of the Inland Revenue and from their conversations various problems needing treatment would emerge.

Hankey reminded Balfour that the C.I.D. was set up by formal Minute of the Treasury and it was agreed that this should be done in the case of the C.C.D.[1]

1 June   Lord Haldane to T.J.   *Cloan, Auchterarder*
It is very satisfactory that the Cabinet have set up the Committee of Civil Research and that you are Secretary.

We have now to push things quietly forward. I have my doubts as to the scope of the new organisation being yet grasped.

Sir Richard Hopkinson, Sir Josiah Stamp, and I worked out some pressing possible problems while I was Lord Chancellor, and about these I should like to have a private word with you when you return from your well-earned holiday.

19 June   Sir Maurice Hankey to T.J.   *Offices of the Cabinet*
Since you have been away we have made a start with the Committee of Civil

[1] Later called the Committee of Civil Research.

Research. I hope I shall see you on Monday morning first thing, but I shall be coming back from Rugby and I have a tremendously full day—C.I.D. at 11.30, Air Raids Precautions at 3, and a Cabinet at 5 p.m., and there will be a lot to read. I think, therefore, I had better just put down a few salient points before I leave for Oxford this afternoon.

The principal subject tackled at yesterday's meeting was the Tsetse Fly. It is true we also had a somewhat academic address on the subject of the Agricultural College at Trinidad, but there is no action required in that matter at present. As regards the Tsetse Fly, you will see that we have set up a Committee with Ormsby-Gore in the Chair. . . .

You will also see from the Minutes that we have set up a Committee on a financial question.[1] As to the origin of this you must look to the Cabinet Minutes. I have taken no action as yet to get the Finance Committee going. I think the best plan will be to get Niemeyer, of the Treasury, to tackle the Governor of the Bank in the first instance before you write him a formal letter inviting him to serve. In fact, Niemeyer may prefer to do this himself. The same may apply to Josiah Stamp. Get in touch with Niemeyer about it. Anyhow, the Treasury are not enthusiastic about this inquiry, and my impression is that they do not want to push it very fast. At first Niemeyer tried to resist it.

There are all sorts of developments in sight for this new Committee. Yesterday afternoon, Wilson,[2] of the Ministry of Labour, came to see me, as he is inclined to think the new Committee ought to take up certain questions dealing with Unemployment as a more or less permanent problem for the next ten years. The same idea had been thrown up at the Cabinet, but no decision had been taken. Lord Balfour was with me when Wilson came, and we had a very long talk about it. The difficulty is that the Arthur Balfour Committee[3] has to cover most of the ground. We discussed absorbing the Arthur Balfour Committee as a Sub-Committee, but I pointed out that they were a Public Committee taking public evidence, and I thought it would be a mistake to bring them into the C.C.R., and the others then agreed. The Balfour Committee are about to publish some statistical information, but are suffering from a kind of surfeit indigestion owing to the vastness of their reference, and are unlikely to report for years.

Nevertheless, we all felt that there were certain questions relating to the fundamentals of Unemployment that ought to be further explored on careful terms of reference, and Wilson went away to think the matter over. We should, of course, have to avoid clashing with the Unemployment Committee, but we could do this by bringing in its Chairman and some of its members into a new inquiry. I can tell you more of this when we meet.

Meanwhile, a great song-and-dance has arisen about low temperature

[1] The question of overseas loans.

[2] Sir Horace Wilson (b. 1882); Permanent Secretary, Ministry of Labour, 1921–30; chief industrial adviser to the Government 1931–9; seconded for special services to the Prime Minister 1935; Permanent Secretary at the Treasury and head of the Civil Service 1939–42; one of the most influential men in Whitehall between the wars.

[3] Under the chairmanship of Sir Arthur Balfour (later Lord Riverdale), a Sheffield steel magnate and no relation of Lord Balfour.

carbonisation of coal. Lane-Fox,[1] Gowers, and Heath have got themselves at loggerheads with Barstow and Niemeyer. After the C.I.D. had considered the question a few weeks ago and had blessed the idea of pushing research on a commercial scale, Heath and Gowers got in touch with the Treasury, and through them obtained (with some reluctance) permission from the Treasury to get a grant from the Trade Facilities Committee. Meanwhile, Lane-Fox had answered a Question in the House to the effect that the Government would not spare finance in order to push on this line of development. Lane-Fox has subsequently been pressed to say exactly what the Government are going to do. The Trade Facilities Committee, however, refused to allow him to make an announcement that their machinery is to be used. Consequently, I gather (though I have not quite got to the bottom of the facts) that Lane-Fox, Gowers, and Heath saw Lord Balfour, who proposed that the question should come up at the C.C.R. Barstow and Niemeyer got violently angry at this, and said that they would hold up the Trade Facilities guarantee. I have fixed up a conference on the subject at Balfour's house this morning, at which they will all be present, when I hope we shall clear it up, probably without the necessity of bringing it to the C.C.R. at all. (We tied it up and I have dictated a note on the subject.)

As regards the future of the new Committee, we shall have to go warily. There is a tendency in some Departments to fire at our heads longstanding difficulties between the Treasury and themselves, and I have already had to 'boom off' a certain amount of business on the ground that it must be discussed by the Treasury first. The Cabinet and most of the Departments appear very favourable to the new organisation. Warren Fisher is not only favourable but very enthusiastic and anxious to push it all he can. Below him, among the Controllers of the Treasury, however, there is exactly the same sort of suspicion and hostility that there was at the beginning of the C.I.D. and the Cabinet Secretariat. Above all, we must keep in with Warren Fisher and try, by means of such conferences as I have arranged this morning, gradually to educate the Treasury to know that the new organisation is their friend and not their enemy.

24 June   Pembroke Wicks to T.J.
. . . I enclose for your information a copy of a memo I sent to Waterhouse on 15 May—in case you should be discussing the matter with the P.M. at any time. I am also sending Fry a copy.

Waterhouse told me at the time that he had expanded it and put it with the P.M.'s papers. It is important as the basis of an appointment.

Although I originally made the suggestion Waterhouse was attracted by it on merits—but whether the P.M. ever had time to read it—or whether the proposal ever reached Jackson in any form I cannot say. . . .

Memo sent to Ronald Waterhouse by Pembroke Wicks
The almost complete lack of touch between the Unionist Central Office and

[1] George Richard Lane-Fox (1870–1947); Conservative M.P. 1906–31; Secretary for Mines 1922–4, 1924–8; cr. Baron Bingley 1933.

10 Downing St., and indeed with Government Departments generally, is a matter of serious concern.

The only direct contact between the two offices is that between the Prime Minister and the Chairman of the Party. It is obvious that they ought not to be expected to trouble themselves with anything but major questions of high policy, but there is no machinery for disposing quickly of questions of detail that arise between the Government and the Party machine.

What is wanted is a liaison officer who is familiar both with the Central Office Staff and with Government officials in order to secure harmonious co-operation and the quick dispatch of business. To be of any use he must be a man in a responsible position with both political and official experience— able to understand the difficulties of both sides, and accustomed to handle confidential matters—whether secrets of the Government or of the party, and one in whom both sides have confidence. He should be subordinate to the Chairman of the Party and act on his direction.

1 July 1.45 p.m. Luncheon with Lord Haldane. I thanked him for his generous reference to myself in the House of Lords yesterday in the public tête-à-tête which he and Balfour had about the Committee of Civil Research.[1] I told him how far we had got and how I proposed to keep him fully informed as to the doings of the new Committee. Their Lordships, it seems, had been quite bewildered as to the purpose of the new Committee and they were so impressed by the close of Balfour's statement that they remained dumb. 'I am not pessimistic', said the grand old boy, 'about the future of British industry; what we need is knowledge. I looked upon the faces of Inchcape and Devonport and it was plainer than ever what we want is know-ledge.' He went on to tell me of a recent pronouncement by his brother at a meeting of the Institute of Mining Engineers at Cardiff on the future of coal and steam as motive agents. 80 years ago a man called Waterston put up a paper to the Royal Society, of which he was not a Member, challenging some of Kelvin's views on thermo-dynamics, and Waterston's paper was rejected and forgotten until Rayleigh unearthed it 50 years later, but Rayleigh did not recognise its significance. J. S. Haldane came across the papers and has been working on them for years and is about to publish his results. He takes Waterston's side against Kelvin, and the practical result he sums up by saying 'I do not think that the Diesel Engine will have even a dog's chance against the future steam engine for ship propulsion'. I must tell the P.M. this as he has more than once shown his steam bias. This, I think, was the first occasion when Haldane admitted to me that he was confronted with a subject which he did not understand. He had read his brother's paper five times and was unable to guarantee its reasoning; all he could say was that his brother was a most careful student and not likely to put forward such challenging views without good grounds.

From coal we turned somehow to beer: 'So long ago as 1901 I told the brewers in a lecture in Liverpool that they must regard beer scientifically—

---

[1] The C.C.R. had grown considerably in importance when the question of safeguarding iron and steel was referred to it at the end of June.

that Moltke, when in England, had declared beer to be our greatest product, that he had gone back and told the Germans so—they had studied our beer and had beaten us, but now Barclay's have a chemist, Worthington's and Gretton's have chemists. What we need is more know-ledge. Had I seen Winston's speech last Saturday to the girls at a school in Essex? Even Winston was convinced, though he was Chancellor of the Exchequer, that there must be no stinting of funds for education. I told this to the Duchess of Atholl last night at dinner and she was going to circulate Winston's speech to the Chiefs of the Board of Education.'

*   *   *   *

3.15 p.m. Sir Frank Heath called and told me of his vain efforts to persuade the Steel Industry to unite for purposes of research. His Committee had offered to send round the steel works some competent person to study the general position and report but he was met on all sides with the cry 'We have nothing to learn'. The head of the Sheffield ring told him that 'if you were to send an inspector to us I should call my managers together before he arrived and agree with them how much and what to tell him'. He thinks that we might make united research a condition of any State subsidy.

3.45 p.m. Saw Ormsby-Gore and agreed tomorrow's Agenda of the Tsetse Fly Committee.

Wrote this evening to Bunbury resigning from the Institute of Public Administration. Owing to pressure of work I cannot possibly attend.

7 July   Philip Kerr to T.J.
... What I suggested was that it would be worth your while to send a first class man for six months on an informal roving commission to get a thorough grip of what Washington is doing in the matter of research.

From my experience there I am quite certain that Hoover and other Departments have given the closest attention, not only to the internal economic problems of the United States, but to the world economic problem. I am sure that an intelligent man could both pick up an enormous lot of practical and useful statistical information produced by their research departments, and also some very valuable general ideas as to the best way of developing the resources of the world, and as to the possible modes of co-operation between American capital and British experience in developing the Empire.

The coal industry was again to the fore in industrial disputes in 1925. After 1921, and especially since the French occupation of the Ruhr, it did well in comparison with European competitors, and in 1924 miners' wages rose. Then, successively, the French withdrew from the Ruhr, Polish production returned to pre-war capacity; and Britain's return to the Gold Standard over-valued the pound just enough to destroy all profit in the export trade. The mine-owners demanded longer hours and lower wages. Herbert Smith and A. J. Cook, the miners' leaders, bluntly refused. The Government would not consider a subsidy to encourage the reorganization without which, each year, the industry became less viable.

On 30 June the owners offered new agreements, with reduced wages, to operate from 31 July. The miners refused them and were threatened with a lock-out. The T.U.C. General Council had offered to support the miners and to handle their case with the Government.

9 July Saw P.M. alone 10 a.m. and talked first about coal. Bridgeman is to see both sides to the dispute today and endeavour to get them to meet one another. Cunliffe-Lister[1] is keeping out of the negotiations as he has considerable colliery interests. If Bridgeman fails, the Government will then announce an Enquiry with Hugh Macmillan[2] as Chairman, Sir Josiah Stamp, and Sherwood of the Shipbuilders' Union. The original idea was to ask Buckmaster to preside but he is in America. This court will report on the facts. I urged that there were two main issues, the first an immediate settlement which would keep the men at work after August 1, the second the future of the industry. To attempt the first without tackling the second would only be to postpone the root trouble to another day. To announce that the Government would enquire into reorganisation would go some way to make an immediate settlement possible. The Owners have begun badly by suggesting that profits must be a fixed portion of the proceeds and the wages fluctuating. There is not among the coal-owners a first-rate negotiator. The P.M. seemed inclined to face up to the question of unification by areas and suggested that the question of royalties might also be reviewed. He recalled how, when the steel trade was bad, he used to feel angry with the royalty owners drawing their income and doing nothing for it. We should have to buy out the royalty owners but we should remove a serious irritation.

We then talked of iron and steel. He told told me that his firm (Baldwin's) had passed their preference dividend and that the Chairman, Sir Charles Wright, had suggested to him that, for the present emergency, the Government might give a subsidy of 10s. a ton on every ton of coal used in the steel industry. I said all subsidies were most difficult to work fairly and would involve complicated supervision; that Mond's scheme[3] would not increase employment and that a far better plan would be the following. There are about 55 berths in the country capable of building tramp ships and only 5 of these were at work. There were more ships in being than the world could use at the moment but their average age was high and it was certain that with reviving trade we should see a boom in shipbuilding. Why not anticipate this? Why should not the Government give orders for 20 or 30 tramp ships which they could dispose of later on when the boom came? Why should not he and the Chancellor of the Exchequer and some third person whom they could employ, meet and settle on a secret programme of this kind and place the orders and make every effort to conceal the fact that the orders

[1] Formerly Lloyd-Greame (later Lord Swinton).

[2] Hugh Pattison Macmillan (1873–1952); cr. life peer 1930.

[3] A scheme put forward by Sir Alfred Mond, in April 1925, for using the unemployment benefit to provide work for the unemployed. The intention was that employers should undertake to employ unemployed men in their own trades, at full pay; these men would surrender their benefit, and this would be paid direct to the employer, instead, as an incentive.

emanated from Whitehall? There were, of course, objections to such a course, there were serious objections to every course, but this plan would provide genuine work which would be carried on in the normal way without the difficulties of a subsidy. He seemed impressed and indeed said it was the most valuable suggestion which had been put up to him lately.

I then ran through the draft questions which I had prepared for him for tomorrow's meeting of the Iron and Steel Committee,[1] when we are to have before us Sir Arthur Balfour and Sir William Larke.

10 July   Iron and Steel Committee
T.J. to S.B.: You are free Tuesday morning. Could we have next meeting of Committee then, so as to push on? Could ask Glynn, West and Pugh.

S.B. to T.J.: Anyone with the slightest regard for me would say: 'Thank God the P.M. has a free morning; I hope he will enjoy it. No one deserves it more.'

The mine-owners replied to the Miners' Federation, pointing out that the mining industry was making, in mid-1925, losses of £750,000 to £1,000,000 a month. To this the Miners' Federation replied on 29 July, accusing the owners of choosing selective periods to show losses and quoting the industry's profits from mid-1921 to March 1925 as £58,454,609, while the average earnings per shift for colliery workers varied between 9s. 4d. and 12s. 8d. over the same period.

. . . Further the Owners having refused to permit any investigation by the Joint Committee appointed for the purpose into the financial, commercial, or managerial control of the industry, we are not prepared to accept the dictum that the industry cannot be operated otherwise than by the payment of a rate of wages insufficient to supply the workmen with the bare necessaries of life.

2. We are compelled to express our astonishment at the statement by the Owners:

'That they have never dissented from the principle that wages at some agreed minimum rate must be a charge on the proceeds of industry before profits are taken.'

The proposals of the Owners are now exhibited at the Collieries as the terms upon which they are prepared to work the Collieries after the 31 July contain no provision for the payment of a minimum rate while the profit of 13 per cent. is guaranteed irrespective of the rate of wages payable.

Their proposal made to the Prime Minister at the proceedings today is for a 'very low national minimum rate' or district minimum rates which must make it possible for serious reductions in wages.

3. It is idle to offer an inducement that no profits shall be taken for the period of one month in the hope that the miners will accept terms and conditions thereafter still further depressing their present impoverished condition.

[1] Of the Cabinet, with Baldwin as Chairman.

4. We are not prepared to discuss the relaxation of the Seven Hours Act, the workmen we represent having intimated their determination to offer strenuous opposition to any attempt to do this, with which we are in agreement, being assured that the hours the workmen are at present compelled to be underground are as long as physical fitness for their arduous occupation can be maintained.

(Signed) A. J. Cook.[1]

Submit that to you and hope you'll have regarded wages too low. We can accept no reduction or extension of hours.

29 July   7 a.m. The papers today have the Report of the Coal Inquiry signed by Macmillan, Stamp, and Sherwood, and *The Times* has come out with a leader headed 'A Decisive Report', very much on the men's side. This will put up the backs of the owners and will not make any easier our negotiations with the men.

10 a.m. P.M. met the miners.

12.30 p.m. met the owners.

P.M., Bridgeman, Steel-Maitland, Duff, and T.J. had cold luncheon in the Minister of Labour's Room. About 3 p.m. we met the miners, about 5 p.m. the owners. 6.30 the P.M. handed the miners the considered reply of the owners and adjourned until 8 o'clock, calling the owners for 8.30 and the Trade Union Congress Committee for 9.

The spokesmen for the men being Herbert Smith, Cook, Tom Richards, with one or two interjections from Varley. The men have made no concessions of any kind throughout the day. They have refused to modify in any degree their attitude on hours and wages.

In the main prosperous federated area (Yorkshire, etc.) the notices posted in the district provided for a decent minimum but no minimum was offered in the other districts.

The owners agreed to accept the principle of a minimum in the other districts and as the day went on they agreed to state this principle in a more attractive form, namely that they were prepared for August to contemplate their 13 per cent. of profits being wiped out and any proceeds assignable to profits used to sustain wages. They repeated their statement that if the 8 hours could be restored they would be enabled to offer better terms. This was the point we had reached when we adjourned at 6.30. It has been desperately heavy going all day, and such little progress as has been made has been mainly due to Gowers and H. J. Wilson operating privately on the owners' group. I think they actually drafted the owners' proposal put to the men at 6.30.

Steel-Maitland has got up the case but he is not Birkenhead or John

---

[1] Arthur James Cook (1883–1931); a Rhondda miner for twenty-one years; joined the Communist Party soon after its foundation in 1920, resigned in 1921 over the settlement of the national miners' strike, which he advised; by 1924 again closely associated with the Party. Secretary of the Miners' Federation 1924–31. A leading militant figure and something of a bogey-man in the General Strike, 1926. Moved away from the extreme left during that year and out of sympathy with the C.P.G.B. national leadership; lined up with the I.L.P. in the Cook-Maxton Manifesto.

Simon—very far from it—and gives the impression of being more concerned to display his suddenly acquired knowledge than of solving our difficulties. That, of course, is not the case, it is only the impression his halting, apologetic method of speech conveys.

Bridgeman has said nothing and Lane-Fox has been silent. The P.M. has got to look more and more worried and helpless as the day has gone drearily on.

On 30 July, the T.U.G.C. issued instructions for a nation-wide embargo on the movement of coal.

30 July   3.30 p.m. Arrived at No. 10 at 9.45. The P.M. came in five minutes later having spent three quarters of an hour with the Chancellor. I said I felt more kindly towards a subsidy of some sort than I did last night. He said he had been discussing one with the Chancellor to be spread over 9 months and to be used to fill such gap as would remain between the terms offered by the owners and the terms which the men were willing to accept.

31 July   On this basis, of a subsidy (calculated at £10 million, but actually £23 million) to be spread over nine months, to support existing wages and an average profit, the Government gave way and, in the trade union calendar, the day became Red Friday. A Royal Commission was to be set up to examine reorganization and Sir Herbert Samuel duly took the chair. One reason for the volte face *was, as Cunliffe-Lister said, that 'We were not ready'. The Supply and Transport Committee and the organization of supplies during strikes had lapsed under the Labour Government and needed the nine months to revive. However, the subsidy and the apparently easy victory of the T.U.C. caused a deep disturbance in the Conservative Party.*

5 August   Reached Downing Street shortly after 10 a.m. and found the P.M. alone and eager to talk about his speech tomorrow on the coal crisis. He professed not to mind the unfavourable Press but was more concerned about the attitude of many of his followers in the House. There had been a meeting on the previous night to which the Chief Whip had been summoned. He had mollified the malcontents but it would be necessary for the P.M. to speak firmly about the growing menace of aggregations of labour like the Industrial Alliance. He must make it plain that the Government were prepared to fight the extremists. The nine months' respite secured by last week's agreement will give the country time to realise the attitude taken by Labour leaders last week [and] to make up their minds what to do should the time again come when the Trade Union Congress takes the step of challenging the Government. The present agreement affords one more chance to secure industrial peace; if the community is driven to arrange for the supply of its own needs it will do so with a thoroughness which will astonish the Communists. Would I draft something for him on these lines and come back late in the afternoon for a further talk? He showed me a Memorandum from Lord Salisbury to the Cabinet on the Coal Dispute and read me the last few sentences: 'Who will believe us, after the experience of the last few days, when we say we will die in some ill-defined ditch, rather than accept the national-isation of the coal industry, and inferentially, the nationalisation of every other distressed industry? I shall be only too glad if my confidence can be restored, but the moral basis of the Government seems to me to have dropped out.' 'That', said S.B. rather pathetically, 'is not very helpful, is it, after we have all been working like beavers.'

1.30. Lunch with Lord Astor in Lauriers. He thought the Government had received a very bad knock from which it would hardly recover. Philip Kerr had seen L.G. who was in great glee and determined to make the most of his opportunity.

* * * *

About 6 o'clock I went to the House with a draft of the latter half of the P.M.'s speech. The Mines Department were supplying him with a brief on the history of the negotiations. Cope had been to see me and had warned me that the prosperous companies would do extremely well out of the subsidy as a maximum profit of 1s. 3d. a ton is to apply not to individual firms but to the average of the district. In the case of the United Anthracite Company (Mond's) who are making 2s. 6d. profit, they will get about £11,000 a month from the subsidy. Sir John Mann was on the phone earlier in the day and he sent one of his accountants to see me. Mann's firm represent the Miners in the Eastern Area, and I was told that on balance about 60,000 adjustments are made every month in the accounts in favour of the Miners and against the Owners. This is owing to the Owners attempting to charge items to revenue instead of to capital, exaggerated estimates, etc., etc. It was most important that the Government should continue in its own interest to secure an independent check on the accounts put forward by the Owners. I passed on what Cope and Mann told me to the P.M. and to the Chancellor of the Exchequer. The P.M. did not pretend to understand the financial implications of the subsidy. Winston defended it as being less generous to the Owners than L.G.'s subsidy, and obviously did not care whether it cost the country £10 millions or £20 millions.

At ten to seven I walked up from the House with the P.M. to the Travel-lers' Club, Astley, the Welsh detective from Dolgelly, walking two or three yards to the right of us. There were not half a dozen dining at the Club at this early hour. We had sole, cutlet and cheese. The P.M. drank a pint of claret and I a bottle of cider. It was a rather melancholy meal. The P.M. was obsessed with the speech he has to make tomorrow. I told him I was sorry I could not spin amusing tales to divert his mind. He said nothing bored him more and the test of friendship was that you could lapse into silence with your friends. After dinner he had a smoke and I had some coffee and I again ventured to indicate pretty fully the sort of speech he should make, urging him not to think of his 'briefs' at all but to trust to the moment for the words and phrases. He was obviously tired with anxiety and remarked how weeks differed in the life of a Prime Minister—one with hardly anything to do and the next with everything to do. 'How long could one go on like this without cracking?' He wakes up two or three times in the night and although he quickly falls asleep again it is not refreshing sleep. In all this, of course, he is a complete contrast to L.G.

6 August 1.30. Luncheon with Lord Haldane, alone as usual. He was stiff with sciatica and had some difficulty in coming downstairs from his study in the roof. Our main talk was about the Coal Enquiry. He gave me a Note which Redmayne[1] had prepared for him in 1916, summarising a projected coal trust originated in 1893 by Sir George Elliot.[2] I shall have some copies made of this for the new Commission. Haldane was mainly interested in its personnel and canvassed various names. Labour were angry at the suggestion of Lord Sumner as Chairman. Haldane would not trust a single Judge on the Bench; the Philippses (Kylsant, etc., shipowners) he would not trust around the corner; there was hardly anyone in the House of Lords of any use; Sir Herbert Lawrence might do, better still would be Earl Grey if he will take it. I said I wanted someone who would go into the colliery districts and work with great energy for six months. Looking back he thought Sankey's Report was a great achievement as we had never been able to get away from it. He told me again to read Laski's *Grammar of Politics*. . . . We ought to make use of Redmayne. I outlined the P.M.'s speech to him. He said the Labour leaders were friendly but powerless.

3.30 p.m. Went down to the Official Gallery. Questions were on; House full. Churchill came up and asked what was the P.M.'s speech going to be like? I told him. At 4 p.m. the P.M. started off. He was very white but for some minutes concealed his fatigue; he spoke better than usual because of his nervousness but without the abandon of the Trade Union speech. He was, I am sure, acutely and absurdly conscious of L.G.'s presence a few benches away. It was hard to read L.G.'s face as the speech proceeded, the only movement he made was to take a slip of paper out of his pocket in order to note a point. The first half of the P.M.'s speech was cold narration of the history of the coal trade and the Government's dealings with it in the early days of the war. It was almost entirely read and was entirely without bias or emotion. The result was admirable, it lowered the temperature of the audience, some of the front bench seemed to be dozing. The second half got closer to grips with the situation on Thursday last but this also was obviously candid and Winston's Private Secretary whispered to me 'He is holding them fairly well'. Presently he reached the closing passages dealing with the menace of the Minority Movement[3] where he was certain of the cheers of his own supporters. When he sat down after 50 minutes it was abundantly plain that the Government was in no sort of danger and that the Prime Minister's frankness had once more triumphed. Ramsay followed and began badly by a gibe at the P.M.'s inexperience in dealing with great

[1] Sir Richard Redmayne, Chief Inspector of Mines 1908–20. A member of most of the committees and commissions on the coal industry.

[2] One of the more enlightened solutions suggested for an almost insoluble problem, somewhat on the lines of a national holding company, retaining some of the advantages of private companies and adding several of the virtues of nationalization.

[3] An extremist group within the trade union movement, including A. J. Cook and the Communists.

industrial crises. Ramsay was suffering in the eyes of the House from the ambiguous position he had taken up at the end of the dispute. On the one hand he had denounced the Government for surrendering to the Communists while on the other he had congratulated the Trade Union Movement on its magnificent solidarity. Then came L.G. with a mind much more concrete and he delivered a damaging attack on the looseness of the arrangements for paying the subsidy. All this was excellent. Then he proceeded to play the demagogue, talked about cold steel, and gave Cook a free advertisement at the expense of the Labour Party—all very mischievous I felt. Of course he had some amusing passages—'It was useless Joynson-Hicks barking at the Red Flag every time it flapped while his Chief was engaged in humbly gilding over the staff, and with standard gold.' The back benches of the Labour Party did everything possible to rattle L.G. during the delivery of his speech and it was rather pathetic to witness his solitariness in the House, for one knew that even the few Liberals who sat around him would throw him over if they dared. I went out and spent half an hour with Steel-Maitland discussing the personnel and procedure of the Coal Enquiry; then to dinner at the 'Ship' with Percy Watkins and back to the Official Gallery at 9.30. J. H. Thomas came up to me and said he was going to 'have it out' with the Railwaymen at a mass meeting on the Chester Race Course in about 10 days' time. 22 special trains would be run. Tomorrow morning he was going down to Pwllheli to preside at the Eistedfodd, what ought he to say? Unfortunately, I made some suggestions, whereupon he asked 'Would I draft a speech for him?' I went into the Ministers' Conference Room, turned on the lights and wrote a few pages for 20 minutes and sent them in to him in the House and hurried to hear Winston wind up in a very deft and, of course, well phrased speech delivered in admirable temper and thoroughly enjoyed in all parts of the House. By this time there was practically nobody left to condemn the Government. I had seen the P.M. for a moment earlier in the evening. I told him 'if his Trade Union speech was A plus his speech tonight was a good A. Would he have some tea?' 'No thanks, I have just had a drink.' He had not yet recovered from the strain. 'L.G.'s speech was poisonous and Winston will deal with it. Fortunately no one listens to him.' I agreed about the poison but said that there were many in the country who would be influenced by the speech. I find Winston's two Secretaries think L.G.'s line was perfectly right and that it is no use pretending that there is not a Minority Movement and that there is not a powerful Mr. Cook.

7 August Went down to the House at 11 and about 11.30 a group of us discussed the Coal Enquiry. The P.M., Steel-Maitland, Lane-Fox, Gowers (Mines Dept.), and T.J. I had already passed Haldane's suggestion of Earl Grey to the P.M. and Steel-Maitland. All agreed that he would be splendid if he would accept. I rang up Haldane to find where Grey was and was told that he was at Falloden. I suggested we should ask Haldane, who is due to travel to Cloan tomorrow, to stop at Berwick and see Grey on the P.M.'s behalf in order to bring all possible pressure on him to accept. Grey's name will be put to the Cabinet this afternoon. Steel-Maitland wants to put on a man Peacock who is in Baring's. I opposed because I thought Peacock had been mixed up in a terrific strike at Barcelona. His past would be raked up by the Miners and we should have headlines in the *Daily Herald* about importing a strike breaker from Spain, etc. The P.M. asked Steel-Maitland to satisfy himself on this point. Other names we talked about were Herbert Samuel, Sir William Plender, and Sir Hardman Lever. I suggested that it might be useful to follow the precedent of the Poor Law Commission and appoint Assistant Commissioners to go into the districts; this should expedite matters.

Herbert Samuel was eventually chosen.

9 September   A. W. Holland to T.J.   The Encyclopaedia Britannica,
                                                      125 High Holborn

As I think you know, we are revising the three volumes of the Encyclopaedia Britannica which appeared in 1921. You have already helped us in this task and I am now writing to ask you if you will do so on a larger scale.

One of the most important, perhaps the most important Biography in this work, is that of Lloyd George, and it has been decided that you should be asked to write this. The only one which will compare with it in point of length is on Woodrow Wilson. We are prepared to give something like 4,000 words to this, and we want it to deal as fully as possible with his manifold activities during the period 1911 to 1925.

I shall be glad to know if you will undertake this commission, as I am very reluctant to go to anyone else for Lloyd George's Biography.

14 September   T.J. to the Managing Editor of the 'Encyclopaedia Britannica'
I have received your letter of the 9th. Before giving the matter further consideration or seeking the Prime Minister's consent to my undertaking the task, I should like to learn:

1. The maximum time allowed for writing. Your request comes unfortunately at the end of the summer leave and not at its beginning.

2. Your terms. The condensation to scale of these crowded momentous years into 4,000 words is an appalling proposition and will involve an enormous mass of references. I could not undertake it under a fee of a hundred guineas.

The authorship of the article would have to remain anonymous in view of my special position.

15 September   A. W. Holland to T.J.   The Encyclopaedia Britannica
Many thanks for your letter. I am sorry to say that I cannot agree to your terms, much as I should like to do so. Your final condition makes it quite impossible. This article, in view of its importance, must be signed.

Thanking you for having considered this matter.

18 September   T.J. to A. W. Holland
I am not surprised to have your decision. I am very sorry to miss the chance but it is unavoidable. As you must have a signed article the best man outside

the Service I should suggest is Philip Kerr, now Secretary to the Rhodes Trustees, Waterloo Place.

Harold Spender wrote the article on Lloyd George for the Encyclopaedia. Eventually T.J. wrote a biography of Lloyd George, published by the Harvard University Press, and in the United Kingdom by the Oxford University Press, in 1951.

17 September   10 a.m. Saw the P.M. on his return from Aix. After a very warm welcome he said 'I know now what Roosevelt meant when, after a holiday, he felt like a "bull moose". This is the best holiday I have had since the beginning of the War. I have read no papers beyond glancing at the headlines in the middle page of *The Times*. What is Labour like? Are they quarrelling amongst themselves at all?' I summed up, as well as I could. . . . I moved on to the Edinburgh Rectorial address. I told him I had taken his draft and expanded it on the lines which he had indicated in his brief out-line. He was very grateful and apologetic and said he would work on it over the weekend at Chequers. I gave him Figgis's *From Gerson to Grotius* to take with him. Then he talked again of his holiday and produced from a piece of blotting paper in his pocket a lovely little blue Gentian flower which he had picked. He ranked among the most memorable incidents of his holiday a handsome youth coming down the mountain side followed by a herd of cattle and goats with tinkling bells. If only he could keep his physical vigour right through the Session he might get something done.

25 September   *A slight difference occurred between T.J. and Pembroke Wicks over the preparation of the P.M.'s speech for the Party Conference at Brighton. T.J. had drafted the part dealing with Government Departments only to find that Central Office had prepared another draft. Wicks smoothed the matter over, explaining that:*
The speech at Brighton will be a very special occasion when the Prime Minister will be speaking to his own people who will expect a distinct Party lead on the questions in which they are most interested, and for that reason the speech is one in which this Office is more concerned than perhaps any other speech of the year. . . .

After the passing of the Boundary Commission legislation in 1924, the British Government had nominated an Ulster Unionist, J. R. Fisher, as representative of the North. The Commission deliberated for a year; and the publication of its Report, imminent at the end of October, raised the threat of serious border troubles, if not of civil war.

T.J. suggested to Baldwin, on 28 October, that Craig might be prepared to accept the verdict if he was not told of it in advance, but had it imposed by the British Government. Above all, he said, Baldwin should not open negotiations on the boundary line.

30 October   I saw the P.M. at 10.15. The appointment of Wood as Viceroy[1] is in this morning's papers. The P.M. thinks he has the character for the job and that he will attract once more the best type of young Englishman to India. He went on 'I could not do right off what you wanted about Ireland.

---

[1] Of India, as Lord Irwin (later Lord Halifax).

The moment the subject was mentioned at the Cabinet they all got excited; Salisbury and Jix were bursting their buttons with eagerness to talk so I am going to see Feetham.[1] I think I will see him at the Travellers and I will tell him that while I do not want to know the details of the Boundary Report what I want is his opinion on the chances of bloodshed on the border when the Report comes out. If I can be assured on that then I can come back to the Cabinet and tell them that I think the Report ought to go through automatically, after any proper precautions have been taken.' I said I was satisfied; that for the moment it was essential to keep a strong control over Jix and Amery. Jix was Home Secretary and was prosecuting Communists for breaking the law[2] and if he wants the law kept here he must keep it in Ulster also.

We then talked about his Aberdeen speech. He thought he had better say something about economy in a general way. There had been a meeting of the Economy Committee yesterday. All that Committee could do was to save a million here and a million there on Education, Health, and so forth, all of which could be represented as an attack on the working man. It was a most one-sided policy; some way must be found for making the other classes contribute and the straight-forward way would be to put a shilling on the Income Tax. Rothermere and Beaverbrook with their millions safe did not care what was cut off the Social Services, that was a fine way of combating Socialism, but we should not be able to talk like that for two or three months yet. At this point Winston came in and he agreed that anything said at Aberdeen would have to be quite general.

10 November   An extract from a memorandum by Lord Balfour, in favour of Rosyth as a naval base, as against dockyards in the Thames estuary.
That a war with France is a most improbable eventuality I am, of course, ready to admit; but the consideration is not wholly irrelevant. Personally I do not believe there will be any first-class war in the lifetime of the youngest member of the Cabinet, least of all with France. But we do not frame our naval and air policy on prophecies of this character, nor ought we to do so. Were another Poincaré to become responsible for French diplomacy, he would be perfectly intolerable if he thought that we were not in a position to defend ourselves. It must be admitted that whatever we do the metropolitan area will always be dangerously vulnerable. But we now have a chance of at least diminishing this grave strategic weakness. Ought we to allow ourselves to be deflected from taking advantage of it by any minor considerations? . . .

On 7 November, the Morning Post *published a forecast of the contents of the Boundary Commission Report, indicating that very little territory would be transferred from North to South. A crisis followed at once in Southern Ireland, and on 21 November the Free*

---

[1] The Chairman of the Commission.
[2] In one of the rare political witch-hunts in modern British history, Joynson-Hicks instigated the prosecution of twelve leading Communists under the same Act of 1797 which had threatened Campbell the year before. All were found guilty and imprisoned.

State representative, Eoin McNeill, resigned. This gave credence to the newspaper reports. The two remaining members issued a declaration that their report had been prepared by 17 October and that McNeill had assented to it. They would proceed, since a majority decision was sufficient.

On 25 November, President Cosgrave crossed to London to meet Baldwin and other Ministers. Kevin O'Higgins and Sir James Craig followed. T.J. took part in the conferences which then took place between Baldwin and the Irish leaders at Chequers on 28 and 29 November, during which time the publication of the Report was held up.

Two alternatives were put forward by Baldwin—that the Report should be accepted and imposed impartially, in the hope of thereby minimizing trouble; or that the existing boundary should be accepted. Neither side, nor the British Ministers, knew the contents of the Report in detail, but according to Baldwin's summary the South was to gain substantially more than the Morning Post *had suggested.*

Churchill took charge of the discussions on 1 December, conducting them with considerable skill; and a day later, in a scene of remarkable warmth between the leaders of North and South, it was agreed that the Boundary Commission should be buried and the existing line should stand. The Commissioners were placated; and twenty copies of the Report, with maps, were delivered to the Cabinet Office. All others, with the plates from which the maps were made, were destroyed.

Ireland thus ceased to be an immediate problem for the British Government and on 17 December T.J. drafted a letter for Baldwin to send to President Cosgrave and Sir James Craig:

I should like to take this opportunity of conveying to you my warm congratulations now that the Agreement of the 3 December has been given the force of law.

I confidently believe that the hopes which inspired the authors of that Agreement will be realised and that it will be found to mark a new stage in the growth of neighbourly feelings throughout Ireland.

I am sure that history will attach high value to the contributions which you and Sir James Craig brought to the negotiations. The patience and determination with which you sought peace in circumstances of grave difficulty are the surest promise of the future welfare of Ireland.

BIOGRAPHICAL NOTES ON PRINCIPAL CHARACTERS

Herbert Henry Asquith (1852–1928); called to Bar 1876, Q.C. 1890; M.P. (Liberal) 1886–1918, 1920–4; defeated by Labour 1924; Home Secretary 1892–5; Chancellor of Exchequer 1905–8; Prime Minister of Liberal Government 1908–15, of Coalition 1915–16; introduced Home Rule Bill 1912; Secretary for War March-August 1914; resigned and became Leader of Opposition 1916; cr. Earl of Oxford and Asquith 1925; resigned leadership of Liberal Party 1926.

Stanley Baldwin (1867–1947); son of Worcestershire ironmaster; M.P. (Conservative) 1908–37; P.P.S. to Bonar Law 1916–17; Financial Secretary to Treasury 1917–21; President of Board of Trade 1921–2; Chancellor of Exchequer 1922–3; Leader of Conservative Party 1923–37; Prime Minister 1923–4, 1924–9, 1935–7; Lord President of Council 1931–5; Lord Privy Seal 1932–4; cr. Earl 1937.

Arthur James Balfour (1848–1930); M.P. (Conservative) 1874–1922; P.P.S. to Lord Salisbury (his uncle) 1878–80; President of Local Government Board 1885; Secretary for Scotland 1886; Chief Secretary for Ireland 1887–91; Leader of Commons and First Lord of Treasury 1891–2, 1895–1902; Prime Minister 1902–5; Leader of Conservative Party 1902–11; member of Committee of Imperial Defence 1914; attended War Cabinet meetings 1914–15; First Lord of Admiralty 1915–16; Foreign Secretary and in War Cabinet 1916–19; Lord President of Council 1919–22, 1925–9; issued Balfour Declaration in favour of a Jewish national home in Palestine 1917; cr. Earl 1922.

Frederick Edwin Smith, Lord Birkenhead (cr. 1919) (1872–1930); called to Bar 1899; M.P. (Conservative) 1906–18; Solicitor-General 1915; Attorney-General 1915–19; Lord Chancellor 1919–22; Secretary for India 1924–8; cr. Viscount 1921, Earl 1922.

(Joseph) Austen Chamberlain (1863–1937); son of Joseph Chamberlain; M.P. (Conservative) 1892–1937; Chancellor of Exchequer 1903–6, 1919–21; Secretary for India 1915–17; resigned 1917; Minister without Portfolio in War Cabinet 1918–19; Lord Privy Seal and Leader of Commons 1921–2; Foreign Secretary 1924–9; First Lord of Admiralty 1931; cr. K.G. 1925.

(Arthur) Neville Chamberlain (1869–1940); younger half-brother of Austen Chamberlain; Lord Mayor of Birmingham 1915–16; Director-General of National Service and in War Cabinet, though not an M.P., 1916–17; M.P. (Conservative) 1918–40; Postmaster-General 1922–3; Paymaster-General 1923; Minister of Health 1923, 1924–9, 1931; Chancellor of Exchequer 1923–4, 1931–7; Prime Minister 1937–40; Lord President of Council 1940; resigned 1940; responsible for Munich agreement with Hitler 1938.

Winston Spencer Churchill (1874–1965); in Boer War 1898–1900; M.P. (Conservative) 1900–6, 1924–64, (Liberal) 1906–22; President of Board of Trade 1908–10; Home Secretary 1910–11; First Lord of Admiralty 1911–15; Chancellor of Duchy of Lancaster 1915; Minister of Munitions 1917–19; Secretary for War and Air 1919–21; Colonial Secretary 1921–2; Chancellor of Exchequer 1924–9; First Lord of Admiralty 1939–40; Prime Minister and Minister of Defence 1940–5; Leader of Opposition 1945–51; Minister of Defence 1951–2; Prime Minister 1951–5; cr. K.G. 1956.

George Nathaniel Curzon (1859–1925); inherited Irish barony 1898; M.P. (Conservative) 1886–98; Under-Secretary, India Office, 1891–2, Foreign Office, 1895–8; Viceroy of India 1899–1905; entered House of Lords as Irish representative peer 1908; Lord Privy Seal 1915–16; President of Air Board 1916; Lord President of Council and in War Cabinet 1916–19; Leader of Lords 1916–24; Foreign Secretary 1919–24; Lord President of Council 1924–5; cr. Earl 1911, Marquess 1921.

David Lloyd George (1863–1945); M.P. (Liberal) 1890–45; President of Board of Trade 1905–8; Chancellor of Exchequer 1908–15; Minister of Munitions 1915–16; Secretary for War 1916; resigned 1916; Prime Minister 1916–22; Leader of Liberal Party 1926–31; cr. Earl 1945.

Maurice Hankey (1877–1963); colonel in Marines; Secretary to Committee of Imperial Defence 1912–38, to War Cabinet 1916–18, to Cabinet 1919–38; Clerk to Privy Council 1923–38; Minister without Portfolio in War Cabinet 1939–40; Chancellor of Duchy of Lancaster 1940–1; Paymaster-General 1941–2; cr. Baron 1938.

Arthur Henderson (1863–1935); son of Glasgow cotton-spinner; M.P. (Labour) 1903–18, 1919–22, 1923, 1924–31, 1933–5; Secretary of Labour Party 1911–34, Treasurer 1930–5; Leader of Party in Commons 1908–10, 1914–17; Chief Whip 1914; President of Board of Education 1915–16; Paymaster-General 1916; Minister without Portfolio in War Cabinet 1916–17; resigned from Cabinet 1917; Labour Chief Whip 1920–4, 1925–7; Home Secretary 1924; Foreign Secretary 1929–31; lost seat 1931; President of World Disarmament Conference 1932–5; won Nobel Peace Prize 1934.

John Maynard Keynes (1883–1946); economist; member of 'Bloomsbury' group; economics lecturer, Cambridge, 1908–15; in Treasury 1915–19; principal economic representative at Peace Conference 1919; disagreed with Lloyd George and resigned; published *The Economic Consequences of the Peace* 1919; close associate of Liberal Party, collaborated in Liberal Enquiries 1925–9; opposed return to gold standard 1925; member of Macmillan Committee on Finance and Industry, and Economic Advisory Committee 1929–31; principal treasury adviser 1940–6; cr. Baron 1942.

Andrew Bonar Law (1858–1923); born in Canada; iron merchant in Glasgow; M.P. (Conservative) 1900–10, 1911–23; Leader of Party 1911–21, 1922–3; opposed Irish Home Rule; asked to form Government December 1916 but advised the King to call on Lloyd George; Colonial Secretary 1915–16; Chancellor of Exchequer, in War Cabinet, 1916–18; Lord Privy Seal and Leader of Commons 1919–21; resigned 1921; Prime Minister for seven months 1922–3.

James Ramsay MacDonald (1866–1937); M.P. (Labour) 1906–18, 1922–31, (National Labour) 1931–7; Secretary of Labour Representative Committee (later the Labour Party) 1900–12, Treasurer 1912–24; Chairman of I.L.P. 1906–9; Chairman of Labour Party 1911–14; resigned 1914; Chairman of Parliamentary Labour Party and Leader of Opposition 1922; Leader of Labour Party 1922–31 (expelled from Party on formation of National Government); first Labour Prime Minister and Foreign Secretary 1924; Prime Minister 1929–31; Prime Minister of National Government 1931–5; Lord President of Council 1935–7.

James Henry Thomas (1874–1949); railway worker 1889–1904; President of Amalgamated Society of Railway Servants 1910; General Secretary of National Union of Railwaymen 1918–24, 1925–31 (expelled on formation of National Government); Vice-Chairman of Parliamentary Labour Party 1921; President of International

Federation of Trade Unions 1920–4; President and Chairman of Parliamentary Committee of T.U.C. 1920–1; M.P. (Labour) 1910–31, (National Labour) 1931–6; Colonial Secretary 1924; Lord Privy Seal 1929–30; Dominions Secretary 1930–5; Colonial Secretary 1935–6; resigned after disclosing budget secrets 1936.

IRISH LEADERS

Michael Collins (1890–1922); born in County Cork; a clerk in London 1906–16; took part in Easter Rebellion, Dublin, 1916; organizing genius behind Volunteer and Sinn Fein movement; Minister for Home Affairs after declaration of independence and institution of provisional constitution by Sinn Fein M.P.s; member of Supreme Council of Irish Republican Brotherhood; one of five Irish delegates who negotiated Treaty with British Government 1921; Chairman and Minister of Finance of Provisional Government January 1922; faced organized opposition to Treaty and on outbreak of civil war, June 1922, commanded Free State army; reduced opposition in Dublin; ambushed and killed by irregulars.

James Craig, cr. Viscount Craigavon 1927 (1871–1940); born in Belfast; in South African and First World Wars; stockbroker and Unionist (Ulster) M.P. 1906–40; Carson's lieutenant in pre-1914 struggle against Irish Home Rule and organized resistance in North; Parliamentary Secretary, Ministry of Pensions, 1919–20, Admiralty, 1920–1; first Prime Minister of Northern Ireland, under Government of Ireland Act, 1921–40.

Arthur Griffith (1872–1922); born in Dublin; follower of Parnell; journalist, playing big part in Irish Nationalist movement; founder of *United Irishman* and editor 1899–1906; editor of *Sinn Fein* 1906–14, of *Nationality* 1915–22; a Volunteer; took part in Howth gun-running 1914; imprisoned in Wandsworth 1916, Gloucester 1918, Mountjoy 1920–1; resigned presidency of Sinn Fein in favour of De Valera 1917; M.P. 1918–22; Minister for Home Affairs and acting President of Dail Eireann 1919; chairman of Irish plenipotentiaries who signed Treaty December 1921; President of Dail when De Valera rejected Treaty; the most devoted of the makers of the Free State.

Eamon de Valera (b. 1882); born in New York (a fact that saved him from execution in 1916); a teacher; joined Volunteers at foundation 1913; leading figure in Easter Rebellion 1916; sentenced to death, commuted to life penal servitude; released under general amnesty June 1917; elected Sinn Fein M.P. 1917; President of Sinn Fein 1917–26, of Irish Volunteers 1917–22; reimprisoned May 1918; escaped from Lincoln gaol February 1919; President of Irish Republic 1919–22; rejected Treaty 1921/2; fought with I.R.A. against Free State army 1922–3; founded Fianna Fail 1926; President of Fianna Fail 1926–59; M.P. 1918–21, 1921–9, 1933–8; Leader of Opposition in Free State Parliament 1927–32; President of Free State Executive Council and Minister for External Affairs 1932–7; introduced Constitution of Ireland in Dail Eireann 1937; Taoiseach (Head of Government) and Minister for External Affairs 1937–48; Minister for Education 1939–40; Leader of Opposition 1948–51, 1954–7; Taoiseach again 1951–4, 1957–9; President of Eire 1959 to present day; President of Assembly of League of Nations 1938.

MINISTRIES, 1915–1929

COALITION GOVERNMENT 1915–1916

MINISTERS IN CABINET

Prime Minister:
H. Asquith (Lib.)   25 May 15–5 Dec. 16
Lord President:
Marquess of Crewe (Lib.)   25 May 15
Lord Chancellor:
Lord Buckmaster (Lib.)   25 May 15
Privy Seal:
Earl Curzon (C.)   25 May 15
Exchequer:
R. McKenna (Lib.)   25 May 15
Foreign Office:
Sir E. Grey (Lib.) cr. Viscount 1916
25 May 15
Home Office:
Sir J. Simon (Lib.)   25 May 15
Sir H. Samuel (Lib.)   10 Jan. 16
Admiralty:
A. Balfour (C.)   25 May 15
Board of Agriculture:
Earl of Selborne (C.)   25 May 15
Earl of Crawford (C.)   11 Jul. 16
Attorney-General:
Sir E. Carson (C.)   25 May 15
Sir F. Smith (C.)   3 Nov. 15
Colonial Office:
A. Bonar Law (C.)   25 May 15
Board of Education:
A. Henderson (Lab.)   25 May 15
Marquess of Crewe (Lib.)   18 Aug. 16
Health and Local Government:
W. Long (C.)   25 May 15
India Office:
A. Chamberlain (C.)   25 May 15
Chief Secretary for Ireland:
A. Birrell (Lib.)   25 May 15
H. Duke (C.)   31 Jul. 16
Duchy of Lancaster:
W. Churchill (Lib.)   25 May 15
H. Samuel (Lib.)   25 Nov. 15
E. Montagu (Lib.)   11 Jan. 16
T. M'Kinnon Wood (Lib.)   9 Jul. 16

Munitions:
D. Lloyd George (Lib.)   25 May 15
E. Montagu (Lib.)   9 Jul. 16
Paymaster-General:
(*office not in cabinet*)
A. Henderson (Lab.)   18 Aug. 16
Minister without Portfolio:
Marquess of Lansdowne (C.)   25 May 15
Scotland:
T. M'Kinnon Wood (Lib.)   25 May 15
H. Tennant (Lib.)   9 Jul. 16
Board of Trade:
W. Runciman (Lib.)   25 May 15
War Office:
Earl Kitchener   25 May 15
D. Lloyd George (Lib.)   6 Jul. 16
First Commissioner of Works:
Lord Harcourt (Vt.) (Lib.)   25 May 15

MINISTERS NOT IN CABINET

Paymaster-General:
Lord Newton (C.)   9 Jun. 15
(*A. Henderson 18 Aug. 16 &*
office in cabinet)
Postmaster-General:
H. Samuel (Lib.)   26 May 15
J. Pease (Lib.)   18 Jan. 16
Law Officers:
Attorney-General (*office in cabinet*)
Solicitor-General:
Sir F. Smith (C.)   2 Jun. 15
(Sir) G. Cave (C.)   8 Nov. 15
Lord Advocate:
R. Munro (Lib.)   8 Jun. 15
Solicitor-General for Scotland:
T. Morison (Lib.)   8 Jun. 15
Attorney-General for Ireland:
J. Gordon (C.)   8 Jun. 15
J. Campbell (C.)   9 Apr. 16
Solicitor-General for Ireland:
J. O'Connor (Nat.)   8 Jun. 15

COALITION GOVERNMENT 1916–1922

MINISTERS IN WAR CABINET
(6 Dec. 1916 to 10 Jan. 1919)

Prime Minister:
D. Lloyd George (Lib.)
6 Dec. 16–19 Oct. 22

Lord President:
Earl Curzon (C.)   10 Dec. 16
A. Balfour (C.)   23 Oct. 19
Exchequer:
A. Bonar Law (C.)   10 Dec. 16
A. Chamberlain (C.)   10 Jan. 16
Sir R. Horne (C.)   1 Apr. 21

National Service:
N. Chamberlain (C.)[1]   19 Dec. 16
   (*Sir A. Geddes* 17 *Aug.* 17 & *office*
         not in war cabinet)
Minister without Portfolio:
A. Henderson (Lab.)
                   10 Dec. 16–12 Aug. 17
Vt. Milner (C.)   10 Dec. 16–18 Apr. 18
Sir E. Carson (C.) 17 Jul. 17–21 Jan. 18
G. Barnes (Lab.)   29 May 17–27 Jan. 20
J. Smuts[1]   22 Jun. 17–10 Jan. 19
A. Chamberlain (C.)
                   18 Apr. 18–10 Jan. 19
Sir L. Worthington-Evans (C.)
                    2 Apr. 20–13 Feb. 21
C. Addison (Lib.)   1 Apr. 21–14 Jul. 21

MINISTERS OF CABINET RANK
1916–1919
& MINISTERS IN CABINET 1919–1922

Lord Chancellor:
Lord Finlay (C.)   10 Dec. 16
Lord Birkenhead (Vt.) (C.)   10 Jan. 19
Privy Seal:
Earl of Crawford (C.)   15 Dec. 16
A. Bonar Law (C.)   10 Jan. 19
A. Chamberlain (C.)   23 Mar. 21
Foreign Office:
A. Balfour (C.)   10 Dec. 16
Earl Curzon (C.) (*Marquess*)   23 Oct. 19
Home Office:
Sir G. Cave (Vt.) (C.)   10 Dec. 16
E. Shortt (Lib.)   10 Jan. 19
Admiralty:
Sir E. Carson (C.)   10 Dec. 16
Sir E. Geddes (C.)   17 Jul. 17
W. Long (C.)   10 Jan. 19
Lord Lee (C.)   13 Feb. 21
Board of Agriculture:
R. Prothero (C.) (*Ld. Ernle*)   10 Dec. 16
Lord Lee (C.)   15 Aug. 19
Sir A. Griffith-Boscawen (C.)   13 Feb. 21
Attorney-General:
      (*office not in cabinet*)
Sir G. Hewart (Lib.)   7 Nov. 21
   (*Sir E. Pollock* (C.) 6 *Mar.* 22 &
         office not in cabinet)
Colonial Office:
W. Long (C.)   10 Dec. 16
Viscount Milner (C.)   10 Jan. 19
W. Churchill (Lib.)   13 Feb. 21
Board of Education:
H. Fisher (Lib.)   10 Dec. 16
Health:
   (*Dept. under Loc. Govt. Bd: see below*)
C. Addison (Lib.)   24 Jun. 19
Sir A. Mond (Lib.)   1 Apr. 21

India Office:
A. Chamberlain (C.)   10 Dec. 16
E. Montagu (Lib.)   17 Jul. 17
Viscount Peel (C.)   19 Mar. 22
Chief Secretary for Ireland:
(Sir) H. Duke (C.)   10 Dec. 16
E. Shortt (Lib.)   5 May 18
I. Macpherson (Lib.)   10 Jan. 19
Sir H. Greenwood (Lib.)   2 Apr. 20
Lord-Lieutenant for Ireland:
Lord Wimborne (Lib.)   10 Dec. 16
Viscount French (*E. of Ypres*)   5 May 18
Viscount Fitzalan (C.)   1 Apr. 21
Labour:
J. Hodge (Lab.)   10 Dec. 16
G. Roberts (Lab.)   17 Aug. 17
Sir R. Horne (C.)   10 Jan. 19
T. Macnamara (Lib.)   19 Mar. 20
Duchy of Lancaster:
Sir F. Cawley (Lib.)   10 Dec. 16
Lord Beaverbrook (C.)   10 Feb. 18
   (& *Min. of Propaganda/Information*)
Lord Downham (C.)   4 Nov. 18
   (*E. of Crawford* (C.) 10 *Jan.* 19 &
         office not in cabinet)
Local Government Board:
Lord Rhondda (Lib.)   10 Dec. 16
W. Hayes Fisher (C.)   28 Jun. 17
   (*Lord Downham*)
Sir A. Geddes (C.)   4 Nov. 18
C. Addison (Lib.)   10 Jan. 19
   (24 *Jun.* 19 *became Min. of Health: see above*)
Munitions (Supply):
C. Addison (Lib.)   10 Dec. 16
W. Churchill (Lib.)   17 Jul. 17
   (10 *Jan.* 19 *became Min. of Supply*)
Lord Inverforth (Con.)   10 Jan. 19
   (*office abolished* 21 *Mar.* 21)
Scotland:
R. Munro (Lib.)   10 Dec. 16
Board of Trade:
Sir A. Stanley (Lib.)   10 Dec. 16
Sir A. Geddes (C.)   26 May 19
Sir R. Horne (C.)   19 Mar. 20
S. Baldwin (C.)   1 Apr. 21
Transport:
      (*office not established*)
Sir E. Geddes (C.)   17 Aug. 19
   (*Vt. Peel* 7 *Nov.* 21 & *office not in cabinet*)
War Office:
Earl of Derby (C.)   10 Dec. 16
Viscount Milner (C.)   18 Apr. 18
   (10 *Jan.* 19 *War Office* & *Air Ministry*
         combined)
W. Churchill (Lib.)   10 Jan. 19
   (13 *Feb.* 21 *War Office only*)
Sir L. Worthington-Evans (C.)
                                  13 Feb. 21

[1] Not a member of the House of Commons

First Commissioner of Works:
    (office not in cabinet)
  Earl of Crawford (C.)   7 Apr. 22

MINISTERS NOT IN CABINET
Air:
  Lord Rothermere (Lib.)   26 Nov. 17
  Lord Weir (Lib.)   26 Apr. 18
  (War Office & Air Ministry combined
    10 Jan. 19, see above)
  W. Churchill (Lib.)   10 Jan. 19
  F. Guest (Lib.)   1 Apr. 21
Blockade:
  Lord R. Cecil[1] (C.)   10 Dec. 16
  Sir L. Worthington-Evans (C.)
        18 Jul. 18
    (office abolished 10 Jan. 1919)
Food Control:
  Viscount Devonport (Lib.)   10 Dec. 16
  Lord Rhondda (Vt.) (Lib.)   19 Jun. 17
  J. Clynes (Lab.)   9 Jul. 18
  G. Roberts (Lab.)   10 Jan. 19
  C. McCurdy (Lib.)   19 Mar. 20
    (office abolished 31 Mar. 21)
Lord Chancellor for Ireland:
  Sir I. O'Brien (Lib.)   10 Dec. 16
  Sir J. Campbell (C.)   4 Jun. 18
  Sir J. Ross (C.)   27 Jun. 21
Duchy of Lancaster:
  (office of cabinet rank, see above)
  Earl of Crawford (C.)   10 Jan. 19
  Viscount Peel (C.)   1 Apr. 21
  Sir W. Sutherland (Lib.)   7 Apr. 22
National Service:
  (office in cabinet)
  Sir A. Geddes (C.)   17 Aug. 17
  (Jan. 1919 & Ministry of Reconstruction)
Paymaster-General:
  Sir J. Compton-Rickett (Lib.) 15 Dec. 16
  Sir T. Walters (Lib.)   26 Oct. 19
Pensions:
  G. Barnes (Lab.)   10 Dec. 16
  J. Hodge (Lab.)   17 Aug. 17
  Sir L. Worthington-Evans (C.) 10 Jan. 19
  I. Macpherson (Lib.)   2 Apr. 20
Minister without Portfolio:
  Sir E. Geddes (C.) 10 Jan 19–19 May 19
Postmaster-General:
  A. Illingworth (Lib.)   10 Dec. 16
  F. Kellaway (Lib.)   1 Apr. 21

Reconstruction:
  C. Addison (Lib.)   17 Jul. 17
    (office abolished 10 Jan. 1919)
Shipping:
  Sir J. Maclay (Ld.) (Lib.)   10 Dec. 16
    (office abolished 31 Mar. 21)
Transport:
  (office in cabinet from 17 Aug. 19)
  Viscount Peel (C.)   7 Nov. 21
  Earl of Crawford (C.)   12 Apr. 22
First Commissioner of Works:
  Sir A. Mond (Lib.)   10 Dec. 16
  Earl of Crawford (C.)   1 Apr. 21
    (office in cabinet 7 Apr. 22)
Law Officers:
Attorney-General:
  Sir F. Smith (C.) (*Ld. Birkenhead*)
        10 Dec. 16
  Sir G. Hewart (Lib.)   10 Jan. 19
    (office in cabinet 7 Nov. 21)
  Sir E. Pollock (C.)   6 Mar. 22
Solicitor-General:
  Sir G. Hewart (Lib.)   10 Dec. 16
  Sir E. Pollock (C.)   10 Jan. 19
  (Sir) L. Scott (C.)   6 Mar. 22
Lord Advocate:
  J. Clyde (C.)   10 Dec. 16
  T. Morison (Lib.)   25 Mar. 20
  C. Murray (C.)   5 Mar. 22
Solicitor-General for Scotland:
  T. Morison (Lib.)   10 Dec. 16
  C. Murray (C.)   25 Mar. 20
  A. Briggs Constable (C.)   16 Mar. 22
  W. Watson (C.)   Jun. 22
Attorney-General for Ireland:
  J. Campbell   20 Dec. 16
  J. O'Connor (Nat.)   8 Jan. 17
  A. Samuels (C.)   7 Apr. 18
  D. Henry (C.)   6 Jul. 19
  T. Brown (C.)   5 Aug. 21
    (post vacant from 16 Nov. 21)
Solicitor-General for Ireland:
  J. Chambers (C.)   19 Mar. 17
  A. Samuels (C.)   12 Sep. 17
  J. Powell (C.)   7 Apr. 18
  D. Henry (C.)   27 Nov. 18
  D. Wilson (C.)   6 Jul. 19
  T. Brown (C.)   12 Jun. 21

CONSERVATIVE GOVERNMENT 1922–1924

MINISTERS IN CABINET
Prime Minister:
  A. Bonar Law   23 Oct. 22–20 May 23
  S. Baldwin   22 May 23–22 Jan. 24

Lord President:
  Marquess of Salisbury   24 Oct. 22
Lord Chancellor:
  Viscount Cave   24 Oct. 22

[1] Not a member of the House of Commons

Privy Seal:
 (*office vacant*)
 Lord R. Cecil   25 May 23
Exchequer:
 S. Baldwin   24 Oct. 22
  (*& P.M. from 22 May 23*)
 N. Chamberlain   27 Aug. 23
Financial Secretary to the Treasury:
 (*office not in cabinet*)
 Sir W. Joynson-Hicks   25 May 23
  (*W. Guinness 5 Oct 23 & office
    not in cabinet*)
Foreign Office:
 Marquess Curzon   24 Oct. 22
Home Office:
 W. Bridgeman   24 Oct. 22
Admiralty:
 L. Amery   24 Oct. 22
Agriculture:
 Sir R. Sanders   24 Oct. 22
Air:
 (*office not in cabinet*)
 Sir S. Hoare   25 May 23
Colonial Office:
 Duke of Devonshire   24 Oct. 22
Board of Education:
 E. Wood   24 Oct. 22
Health:
 Sir A. Griffith-Boscawen   24 Oct. 22
 N. Chamberlain   7 Mar. 23
 Sir W. Joynson-Hicks   27 Aug. 23
India Office:
 Viscount Peel   24 Oct. 22
Labour:
 Sir A. Montague-Barlow   31 Oct. 22
Duchy of Lancaster:
 Marquess of Salisbury   24 Oct. 22
  (*J. Davidson & office not in cabinet
    25 May 23*)
Postmaster-General:
 (*office not in cabinet*)
 Sir L. Worthington-Evans   28 May 23

Scotland:
 Viscount Novar   24 Oct. 22
Board of Trade:
 Sir P. Lloyd-Greame   24 Oct. 22
War Office:
 Earl of Derby   24 Oct. 22

MINISTERS NOT IN CABINET
Air:
 (*office in cabinet 25 May 23*)
 Sir S. Hoare   31 Oct. 22
Duchy of Lancaster
 (*office in cabinet*)
 J. Davidson   25 May 23
Paymaster-General:
 (*office vacant*)
 N. Chamberlain   5 Feb. 23
 Sir W. Joynson-Hicks   15 Mar. 23
 A. Boyd-Carpenter   25 May 23
Pensions:
 G. Tryon   31 Oct. 22
Postmaster-General:
 N. Chamberlain   31 Oct. 22
 Sir W. Joynson-Hicks   7 Mar. 23
  (*Sir L. Worthington-Evans & office in
    cabinet 28 May 23*)
Transport:
 Sir J. Baird   31 Oct. 22
First Commissioner of Works:
 Sir J. Baird   31 Oct. 22
Law Officers:
Attorney-General:
 Sir D. Hogg   24 Oct 22
Solicitor-General:
 Sir T. Inskip   31 Oct. 22
Lord Advocate:
 W. Watson   24 Oct. 22
Solicitor-General for Scotland:
 D. Fleming   6 Nov. 22
 F. Thomson   5 Apr. 23

LABOUR GOVERNMENT 1924

MINISTERS IN CABINET

Prime Minister:
 J. R. MacDonald   22 Jan. 24–3 Nov. 24
Lord President:
 Lord Parmoor   22 Jan. 24
Lord Chancellor:
 Viscount Haldane   22 Jan. 24
Privy Seal:
 J. Clynes   22 Jan. 24
Exchequer:
 P. Snowden   22 Jan. 24
Foreign Office:
 J. R. MacDonald (P.M.)   22 Jan. 24
Home Office:
 A. Henderson   22 Jan. 24

Admiralty:
 Viscount Chelmsford   22 Jan. 24
Agriculture:
 N. Buxton   22 Jan. 24
Air:
 Lord Thomson   22 Jan. 24
Colonial Office:
 J. Thomas   22 Jan. 24
Board of Education:
 C. Trevelyan   22 Jan. 24
Health:
 J. Wheatley   22 Jan. 24
India Office:
 Lord Olivier   22 Jan. 24

Labour:		MINISTERS NOT IN CABINET	
T. Shaw	22 Jan. 24	*Paymaster-General:*	
Duchy of Lancaster:		H. Gosling	6 May 24
J. Wedgwood	22 Jan. 24	*Pensions:*	
Postmaster-General:		F. Roberts	23 Jan. 24
V. Hartshorn	22 Jan. 24	*Transport:*	
Scotland:		H. Gosling	24 Jan. 24
W. Adamson	22 Jan. 24	*Law Officers:*	
Board of Trade:		*Attorney-General:*	
S. Webb	22 Jan. 24	Sir P. Hastings	23 Jan. 24
War Office:		*Solicitor-General:*	
S. Walsh	22 Jan. 24	Sir H. Slesser	23 Jan. 24
First Commissoner of Works:		*Lord Advocate:*	
F. Jowett	22 Jan. 24	H. Macmillan[1]	8 Feb. 24
		Solicitor-General for Scotland:	
		J. Fenton[1]	18 Feb. 24

CONSERVATIVE GOVERNMENT 1924–1929

MINISTERS IN CABINET			
		Health:	
Prime Minister:		N. Chamberlain	6 Nov. 24
S. Baldwin	4 Nov. 24–4 Jun. 29	*India Office:*	
Lord President:		Earl of Birkenhead	6 Nov. 24
Marquess Curzon	6 Nov. 24	Viscount Peel	18 Oct. 28
Earl of Balfour	27 Apr. 25	*Labour:*	
Lord Chancellor:		Sir A. Steel-Maitland	6 Nov. 24
Viscount Cave	6 Nov. 24	*Duchy of Lancaster:*	
Lord Hailsham (Viscount)	28 Mar. 28	Viscount Cecil	10 Nov. 24
Privy Seal:		Lord Cushendun	19 Oct. 27
Marquess of Salisbury	6 Nov. 24	*Scottish Office:*	
Exchequer:		Sir J. Gilmour	6 Nov. 24
W. Churchill	6 Nov. 24	(*became Secretary of State for Scotland*	
Foreign Office:		*15 Jul. 26*)	
(Sir) A. Chamberlain	6 Nov. 24	*Board of Trade:*	24
Home Office:		Sir P. Lloyd-Greame	6 Nov.
Sir W. Joynson-Hicks	6 Nov. 24	(*changed name to Sir P. Cunliffe-Lister*	
Admiralty:		*27 Nov. 24*)	
W. Bridgeman	6 Nov. 24	*War Office:*	
Agriculture:		Sir L. Worthington-Evans	6 Nov. 24
E. Wood	6 Nov. 24	*First Commissioner of Works:*	
W. Guinness	4 Nov. 25	Viscount Peel	10 Nov. 24
Air:		Marquess of Londonderry	18 Oct. 28
Sir S. Hoare	6 Nov. 24		
Attorney-General:		MINISTERS NOT IN CABINET	
Sir D. Hogg (*Ld. Hailsham*)	6 Nov. 24	*Paymaster-General:*	
(28 *Mar.* 28 *Sir T. Inskip &*	*office not*	(*office vacant*)	
in cabinet)		Duke of Sutherland	28 Jun. 25
Colonial Office:		Earl of Onslow	2 Dec. 28
L. Amery	6 Nov. 24	*Pensions:*	
Dominions Office:		G. Tryon	11 Nov. 24
L. Amery	11 Jun. 25	*Postmaster-General:*	
Board of Education:		Sir W. Mitchell-Thomson	11 Nov. 24
Lord E. Percy[1]	6 Nov. 24	*Transport:*	
		W. Ashley	11 Nov. 24

[1] Not a member of the House of Commons

Law Officers:
Attorney-General:

(*office in cabinet*)

Sir T. Inskip	28 Mar. 28

Solicitor-General:

Sir T. Inskip	11 Nov. 24
Sir F. Merriman	28 Mar. 28

Lord Advocate:

W. Watson	11 Nov. 24
A. MacRobert	23 Apr. 29

Solicitor-General for Scotland:

D. Fleming	11 Nov. 24
A. MacRobert	30 Dec. 25
W. Normand	23 Apr. 29

Index[1]

---

[1] For summaries of events at the beginning of each year see pp. 1 (1916); 18-19 (1917); 41-2 (1918); 71-2 (1919); 95-6 (1920); 124-5 (1921); 188-9 (1921); 223-4 (1922); 262-3 (1924); 310-11 (1925).